16

Ancient Titicaca

The publisher gratefully acknowledges

the generous contribution to this book

provided by the General Endowment Fund

of the University of California Press Associates.

Ancient Titicaca

The Evolution of Complex Society
in Southern Peru and Northern Bolivia

CHARLES STANISH

UNIVERSITY OF CALIFORNIA PRESS

Berkeley   Los Angeles   London

Frontispiece: Inca pottery. Courtesy of the Field Museum, Chicago, catalog no. 2687.

University of California Press
Berkeley and Los Angeles, California

University of California Press, Ltd.
London, England

Library of Congress Cataloging-in-Publication Data

Stanish, Charles, 1956–
    Ancient Titicaca : the evolution of complex society
in southern Peru and northern Bolivia / Charles Stanish.
        p.   cm.
    Includes bibliographical references and index.
    ISBN 0-520-23245-3 (alk. paper)
        1. Indians of South America—Titicaca Lake Region
(Peru and Bolivia)—Antiquities.   2. Tiwanaku culture.
3. Titicaca Lake Region (Peru and Bolivia)—Antiquities.
I. Title.
F3319.1.T57 S73   2003
984'.1201—dc21   2002016563

Manufactured in the United States of America
12   11   10   09   08   07   06   05   04   03
10   9   8   7   6   5   4   3   2   1

This book is dedicated to Robert McCormick Adams,

an inspiration to two generations of students at the

University of Chicago and beyond.

Contents

Figures

Maps

Tables

Foreword

Joyce Marcus, University of Michigan

The unfortunate peculiarity of the history of man is, that although its separate parts have been examined with considerable ability, hardly anyone has attempted to combine them into a whole, and ascertain the way in which they are connected with each other.

Henry T. Buckle, *The History of Civilization in England*, 1857

Henry T. Buckle would have applauded this book. Many of the world's great civilizations—Egyptian, Mesopotamian, Greek, Roman—have been the subject of books, but few of those books connect the parts into a whole as this one does. Charles Stanish combines empirical archaeological data with a wide range of models, showing us how society could be transformed from autonomous village to expansionist empire over the course of three millennia. The fact that this book covers Andean civilization, a culture far less known than the four mentioned above, makes it rarer still.

The events presented here took place in the region the Inca called "the Land of the Four Quarters"—specifically, in the largest and southernmost quarter, Collasuyu. This quarter includes Lake Titicaca, at 3,812 meters one of the highest major bodies of water in the world. This high-altitude environment looks superficially inhospitable and harsh but in fact is replete with resources. From the lake the ancient inhabitants could collect waterfowl, fish, snails, aquatic plants, and reeds for boat making. In the surrounding highlands they could hunt *vicuña, guanaco,* and both *huemal* and white-tailed deer. They managed extensive herds of domestic alpaca and llama and raised guinea pigs. On slopes and flat areas around the lake, they cultivated a wide range of crops, including the chenopods quinoa and *kañiwa*, potatoes, and tubers such as *mashwa, oca,* and *ullucu.* The water in the lake created a warming effect, ameliorating the cold in such a way that this region could become a breadbasket for farmers.

European and American explorers were fascinated by the fact that the Titicaca Basin not only supported farming but also had impressive cities such as Tiwanaku. Popular interest was aroused in the nineteenth century when the region was visited by Alexander von Humboldt, who published a book of his discoveries in 1814. He was followed by Ephraim George Squier, whose *Peru: Incidents of Travel and Exploration in the Land of the Incas* (1877) included early drawings of Tiwanaku's buildings, monuments, and carved stones. Later work by Max Uhle, Wendell C. Bennett, Arthur Posnansky, Alfred Kidder II, Carlos Ponce Sanginés, Gregorio Cordero, and Luis Lumbreras formed a solid foundation for the scholars who followed them to the Titicaca Basin—Juan Albarracin-Jordan, Brian Bauer, Marc Bermann, David Browman, Karen Mohr Chávez, Sergio Chávez, Clark Erickson, Alan Kolata, Elias Mujica, and Oswaldo Rivera, among others.

Gradually a picture of Tiwanaku's subsistence base began to emerge. In addition to being supported by extensive herds of alpaca and llamas, the region's inhabitants relied in part on an ingenious agricultural strategy in which wetlands were transformed into raised fields. Canals were excavated at intervals of five to ten meters, and the excavated soil was then piled between the canals to create large planting surfaces. Fish were installed in the canals to be used not only as food but also as fertilizer for the raised fields. Experiments by Clark Erickson of the University of Pennsylvania have demonstrated that the raised fields and associated canals created a localized warmer environment, protecting crops from frost; the canals retained heat, raising the temperature of the adjacent fields by ten to twenty degrees Fahrenheit during daylight hours. This daytime gain in temperature also helped to throw off the effect of nighttime frost. The harvest from these raised fields could be several times that of a dry-farmed field, and Alan Kolata of the University of Chicago has estimated that the 190-square-kilometer heartland of Tiwanaku could have supported hundreds of thousands of people.

In sum, a happy conjunction of lacustrine resources, raised-field farming, and extensive herding made the Titicaca Basin one of the many arenas where complex society could potentially develop. But how did that development take place, and why did it happen when it did? In this book, Stanish provides a broad framework for evaluating several explanatory models period by period and convincingly answers many key questions. Using Titicaca Basin data, Stanish evaluates the appropriateness and inappropriateness of many models, including that of competitive feasting, peer polities, persuasion and coercive models, world systems, expansionist state models, segmentary states, action theory, *ayllu* and lineage models, nonmarket versus market imperialism, and hegemonic versus territorial empire models.

Stanish himself began field research in the Andes in 1983, working first in Peru and then moving to Bolivia in 1986. His fieldwork took him first to the Moquegua Valley of Peru with Michael Moseley and Don Rice; then to Lukurmata in Bolivia with Alan Kolata and Marc Bermann; next to the Island of the Sun in Bolivia with Brian Bauer; and for the last dozen years to the Juli-Pomata region on the Peruvian side of Lake Titicaca, where he has conducted both excavation and field survey. In this book, Stanish draws on all of this fieldwork to produce a well-crafted exposition that is in the best tradition of processual archaeology.

Many bits and pieces of Titicaca Basin research are scattered through the literature; others remain unpublished, although they are sometimes presented orally at national meetings. It has been difficult for scholars and students to recognize and isolate the broad trends and significant patterns in this wealth of detail. In addition to presenting his own original data, Stanish sets himself the task of making sense of the giant, previously unsynthesized corpus of information. He shows us how the separate parts are connected; he succeeds in combining them into an intelligible whole. He explains the developmental sequence, the rises and falls of chiefdoms, states, and empires.

This book not only succeeds in making us think about the Titicaca Basin's developmental trajectory but also makes us think about the rise and fall of other civilizations. It prepares us to consider the ways in which the political and economic evolution of the Titicaca Basin is similar to, and different from, the trajectories of other culture sequences. Along the way, the book underscores how important truly in-depth knowledge of a geographic region is and how sterile our theoretical frameworks would be without such concrete examples. Combining hard-won data with great insight, this book should challenge scholars working in other regions to attempt works as broad, ambitious, and explanatory.

Preface

My first trip to the Titicaca Basin was in 1982, as the guest of the late Victor Barua and his wife, Lucy Barua. I was fascinated by the people and archaeology of this region and have returned every year since 1985 to conduct or plan research. At the time of those early trips, I realized that archaeologists and naturalists had worked in the region for more than a hundred years, uncovering a rich and deep prehistory. Beginning in 1988 and continuing every year since, I have conducted my own excavation and survey projects. This book synthesizes this accumulated research and places these data in a contemporary theoretical context.

There is much debate these days about the nature of archaeological explanation and its practice in constructing or reconstructing the past. I consider myself a processual archaeologist in the broadest sense of the term. As I hope to illustrate in this work, processual archaeology is much more holistic than its detractors maintain. I believe that many of our colleagues too quickly abandoned comparative analysis and scientific logic. The fact is that the deeper we look at regional sequences, with better and better chronologies, the more we see striking parallels between different areas of the world. There simply are a limited number of effective ways to organize complex societies, and people independently arrived at these solutions in many areas of the world. At the same time, I believe that we must produce "thick archaeologies" of the cultures of the world that celebrate the unique contributions of peoples, both present and past. In short, I seek to provide a scientific narrative that models the prehistory of the region from the first settled villages around 2000 B.C. to the Spanish Conquest in the 1530s.

Following this processual tradition, all of the

models and ideas presented in this book are testable with existing and future data as we refine our concepts of Lake Titicaca Basin prehistory. Likewise, I hope that some of the data in this book will be useful to scholars outside the Andes for comparative analyses of other areas of the world where ranked societies and states independently developed.

Because much of my research has been published, data are not reproduced here in great detail, but readers who wish to critically assess my ideas may want to consult these earlier publications, which are listed in the references section of this book. The Juli-Pomata survey is available in Stanish et al. 1997. A Spanish translation of this book and an expanded appendix on the survey sites are available on the website of the Cotsen Institute of Archaeology at the University of California, Los Angeles, under the Andean Lab homepage. A discussion of raised-field agriculture is available in Stanish 1994. Excavation data from the site of Tumatumani are available in Stanish and Steadman 1994, and a discussion of the Inca occupation is found in Stanish 1997 and 2000. Results of my work with Brian Bauer on the Island of the Sun can be found in Bauer and Stanish 2001. Additional articles listed in the bibliography may serve as a useful companion to this book. Unpublished data are also available on the UCLA website and shortly will be forthcoming in monographs. This is particularly important for the survey of the Huancané and Putina valleys in the north. Most of these data have not been incorporated in this book. However, I have written the interpretative sections in such a way that none of the ideas presented here contradict the preliminary results of that survey.

The first chapter provides an overview of the prehistory of the region and the broad theoretical conclusions of this work. Subsequent chapters introduce my theoretical framework, the history of archaeological research, and the geography, ecology, and ethnography of the Titicaca Basin. Chapters 6 through 10 synthesize the data from six archaeological periods in the Titicaca region. I have attempted to separate, as much as possible, the empirical data from my own hypotheses and theoretical speculations. Chapter 11, the conclusion, summarizes the prehistory of the region within the theoretical framework presented in chapter 2.

Some notes on terminology and orthography are necessary. I use *archaeology* to refer to the science; that is, the method and theory of studying the past. I use *prehistory* in a specific sense to refer to the actual past studied by archaeologists. *History* is used in two senses: a broad one to refer to constructs of the past, and a narrow one to refer to the study of people in the post-European contact periods. In this sense, archaeology is a method of studying history. The meaning of this term should be understandable from the context in which it is used.

I do not prefer any particular orthography for Aymara, Quechua, or Hispanicized indigenous words. I try to conform to the most common usage while respecting, where possible, historical precedent. I use the term *Pucara* to refer to the Upper Formative–period culture in the region, as well as the huge type site and corresponding ceramic style designations. I use the term *pukara* to refer to the fortified hilltops characteristic of the Late Intermediate or Altiplano period in the region. In general, I prefer a *w* to *hu*, as in *Tiwanaku*, but use the *hu* when it is the most common spelling or if it is entrenched in the literature. *Inca* is spelled with a *c* instead of a *k* because Pat Lyon insists. I use the original orthography in all quotes and maintain original orthography when used as a period designation. For most proper nouns and other terms that may be confusing, I have included a backnote with alternate spellings. Translations are my own unless otherwise noted.

Acknowledgments

This book is based on many seasons of research in Moquegua, Puno, and Bolivia. There are many people and institutions who have provided invaluable help. I wish to thank the Programa Contisuyu and, in particular, Michael Moseley, Don Rice, the late Victor Barua, Lucy Barua, Nelson Molina, and Luis Watanabe for their help with my research from 1983 to 1985 in Moquegua and for their friendship. The Moquegua research was funded by the National Science Foundation, the Doherty Foundation, the Mellon Foundation of the University of Chicago, and Patricia Dodson. The research was supervised by Michael Moseley and Don S. Rice and authorized by the Instituto Nacional de Cultura. I gratefully thank the students and faculty of the Universidad Católica "Santa María" of Arequipa for their assistance, particularly Edmundo de la Vega. I also remain grateful to the broad intellectual direction provided by my faculty mentors at the University of Chicago.

I wish to acknowledge Alan Kolata for offering me the position of field director in the Proyecto Wila Jawira in Lukurmata, Bolivia, in 1986–1987. In 1988, I began formal research near the town of Juli on the Peruvian side of Lake Titicaca, at the suggestion of the late John Hyslop. This season was funded by the Wenner-Gren Foundation for Anthropological Research, Patricia Dodson, and the Montgomery Fund of the Field Museum. The field research was conducted under the direction of the National Institute of Culture in Lima and Puno (RS ED 170–88). By 1990, the Juli Project had evolved into the Lupaqa Project, a larger survey and excavation program in the Lupaqa area of the southwestern Titicaca Basin. The Lupaqa Project was funded by the National Science Foundation (BNS-9008181) and the H. John Heinz III Trust for

Archaeological Research in South America. In 1993–1994, we excavated two sites near the town of Juli and extended our survey. This research was funded by the National Science Foundation (DBS-9307784), the Wenner-Gren Foundation for Anthropological Research, the H. John Heinz III Trust for Archaeological Research in South America, Patricia Dodson, Beverly Malen, and Robert Donnelly. Various forms of assistance from the former Vice-President for Academic Affairs at the Field Museum of Natural History, Peter Crane, are gratefully acknowledged.

For my work in the Juli area, I offer a special thanks to officials of the National Institute of Culture and fellow archaeologists in Lima and Puno, including Elias Mujica, Oscar Castillo, Oscar Ayca, Luis Lumbreras, and Luis Watanabe M. The Lupaqa Project was assisted by the anthropological faculty of the Universidad Nacional del Altiplano, including its director, Felix Palacios, Juan Bautista Carpio Torres, and Abel Torres Cornejo. Percy Che-Piu Salazar, Julio César Gómez Gamona, and Luis Salas Aronés were very supportive of our project as well. I also gratefully acknowledge the support of Fernando Cabieses and Walter G. Tapia Bueno. For their kindness and hospitality, I thank Percy Calizaya Ch. and family, Fresia Gandarillas S., Moises Sardon P., and the people of Juli, Yacari-Tuntachawi, Sillucani, Inca Pucara, Huaquina, Chatuma, Pomata, and Checca Checca.

In 1994, Brian Bauer, Oswaldo Rivera, and I began the Proyecto Tiksi Kjarka on the Island of the Sun, Bolivia. This three-year research program was funded by the Wenner-Gren Foundation for Anthropological Research, the Field Museum of Natural History, the University of Illinois at Chicago, Patricia Dodson, Barbara Weinbaum, Beverly Malen, and Robert Donnelly. Johan Reinhard graciously assisted our project on the islands, and I thank him for his collegiality. I also acknowledge the help of the Instituto Nacional de Arqueología and the Secretaría Nacional de Cultura, including Javier Escalante, Carlos Ostermann, Alberto Bailey, and Oswaldo Rivera S. I returned to survey on the Peruvian side after our work on the Island of the Sun was finished in 1997. The 1997 season was funded by the College of Letters and Sciences at the University of California, Los Angeles. Together with Mark Aldenderfer, Edmundo de la Vega, and Cecília Chávez, we created a new research entity named Programa Collasuyu, a group of scholars who continue to work in the circum-Titicaca region. In 1997, de la Vega and Chávez excavated on Esteves Island outside Puno. I thank them for allowing me access to their data. Luis Vásquez and Mary Vásquez of MILA Tours, Gurnee, Illinois, are gratefully acknowledged for their contributions to our work over the years. The 1998–2001 seasons were supported by UCLA Faculty Senate Grants, the Cotsen Institute of Archaeology Amhanson Grants, and the National Science Foundation.

There are dozens of people whom I wish to acknowledge for their professional assistance, advice, friendship, and collaboration over the last decade. I thank Elizabeth Arkush, Christopher Cackett Keller, Jay Carver, Lic. Edwin Castillo, Amanda Cohen, Kirk Lawrence Frye, Christopher Donnan, Laura Gilliam, Fernando Núñez, Mario Núñez, Aimée Plourde, Lee Hyde Steadman, Javier Ticona, Esteban Quelima, Carol Schultze, and Luperio David Onofre Mamani. I thank the former staff of the Maryknoll mission in Juli, particularly Brigid Meagher and Cati Williams, for their hospitality and friendship. I also gratefully acknowledge the input from several anonymous readers of this manuscript, and from many others who read previously published papers. This input has greatly refined my arguments.

I express my deep gratitude to the University of California Press for the superb work on this project. In particular, I thank Doris Kretschmer for initially seeing the manuscript through to contract. I offer my warmest thanks to Laura Harger, senior project editor, and Alexis Mills, freelance editor, for their professionalism and care in seeing this manuscript through to publication.

I thank Joyce Marcus for her critical commentary, her friendship, and advice. She was a great friend during a semester that I spent in Ann Arbor in 1983, and she has continued to be a source of unwavering encouragement and support. Joyce meticulously read drafts of this book and graciously agreed to write its foreword. Her advice has greatly improved the clarity and quality of my work. Rolando Paredes has been a great friend and colleague, and his contribution to the archaeology of Puno is gratefully acknowledged. Other colleagues who have provided very valuable comments over the years include Mark Aldenderfer, Brian Bauer, Bennet Bronson, Lisa Cipolla, Larry Coben, Edmundo de la Vega, Timothy Earle, Clark Erickson, Javier Escalante, Paul Goldstein, Jonathan Haas, Christine Hastorf, William Isbell, John Janusek, Larry Keeley, Chapuruku Kusimba, Michael Moseley, Mario Núñez, Johan Reinhard, Don S. Rice, Katharina Schreiber, Helaine Silverman, Adan Umire, Alaka Wali, Karen Wise, and colleagues at both the Field Museum of Natural History and UCLA. I thank Craig Morris of the American Museum of Natural History for authorizing access to the Bandelier collection and thank Sumru Aricanli for her assistance with that collection. I wish to acknowledge the gracious professional help offered to our Esteves Island project by Mario Núñez of the Universidad Nacional del Altiplano. Mario provided us with unpublished data and generously gave us information that was invaluable in setting up our excavation methodology. I offer a thanks to my friend and colleague Brian Bauer, who provided unpublished materials, obscure historical documents, and critical advice. I offer a personal thanks to Ken and Ligia Keller and their family for their gracious help and support over the years. I also thank Lupe Andrade and her family for their support during my work in Bolivia. Our crew in Puno gratefully thanks Rolando and Chela Paredes for their help over the years. Finally, a heartfelt thanks to Edmundo de la Vega, codirector of Programa Collasuyu, my colleague and close friend of many years. Errors in fact and interpretation are purely my responsibility.

Ancient Collasuyu

The first Europeans to see Lake Titicaca arrived as part of an advance force of Francisco Pizarro's conquering army in the 1530s. These soldiers had marched into Collasuyu, the great southeastern quarter of the Inca empire. Collasuyu was one of the oldest provinces of the Inca state, and probably the richest. Inca presence in the basin was correspondingly intense and vast. One of the largest Inca administrative centers was established in the northwest region of the lake at the town of Hatuncolla. Scores of Inca settlements were built along the western and eastern roads that ringed the lake, and a great pilgrimage center was constructed on the Island of the Sun, evoking the heroic memory of the earlier Tiwanaku state. Vast expanses of the Collasuyu grasslands supported millions of llamas and alpacas. On the edge of Lake Titicaca, which also produced fish, was a rich agri-cultural area where the Incas grew potatoes, quinoa, and other crops. Gold was collected a day or two to the east, and silver was mined in the highlands. From the perspective of Prehispanic economies, the Titicaca Basin was one of the richest areas in the ancient American world. Despite periodic rebellions by the Aymara-speaking peoples, Collasuyu was converted into a sprawling and productive province of Tawantinsuyu, the original name of the Inca empire. (See maps 1.1 and 1.2.)

Collasuyu was part of the Inca empire for just a few generations, but people had lived in the high plains, or altiplano, and lake area for several millennia prior to the Inca conquest in the fifteenth century A.D. The first peoples entered the Titicaca region by at least 8000 B.C. After thousands of years of hunting, gathering, and foraging economies and

MAP I.I. Political map of western South America. Shading indicates mountains.

mobile lifeways, people began to settle in permanent villages near the lake shore around 2000 B.C. This Early Formative period (circa 2000 B.C.–1300 B.C.) was characterized by small communities located to optimize use of agricultural, lacustrine, riverine, and wild resources. Settlements were spaced more or less evenly apart, probably to maximize resource catchment zones. Exchange in raw stone materials was brisk but not formalized. Production of pottery for domestic storage, cooking, and some serving was common, but there is no evidence that it was produced for exchange, political ritual, or any other use.

Sometime in the second millennium B.C., a few people in the Titicaca region began constructing small structures that were noticeably different from the surrounding houses. Built with uncut stone, they had plastered floors and walls, and were sometimes built low into the ground. These buildings are the first evidence of corporate architecture in the region. Over time, this architectural style became more elaborate: the plastered area became larger, rooms were added to the exteriors, the floors were sunk deeper into the ground, and walled terraces were built around the entire architectural complex.

This period, referred to here as the Middle Formative, represents the development of the region's first ranked societies. It is likely that these early Middle Formative buildings housed small, uncarved stone stelae known as *huancas,* symbols of a new shared elite ideology. Data suggest that by the late Middle

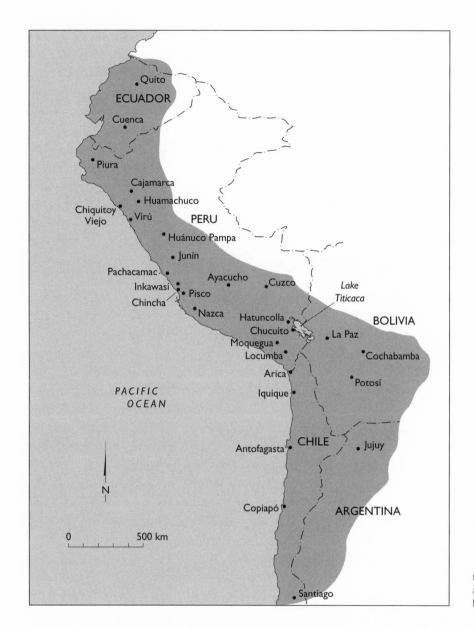

MAP 1.2. Extent (shaded area) of Inca empire at its height, circa A.D. 1530.

Formative, sites such as Canchacancha-Asiruni and Qaluyu in the north and Tiwanaku, Chiripa, and Pajchiri in the south typified the basin's primary regional centers. By this time, the special buildings on these centers were full-fledged sunken courts. These courts were partially sunk into the ground and were surrounded by other buildings.

Primary regional centers are settlements where local elite established ceremonial centers and where nonelite aggregated for social, political, and economic reasons. I hypothesize that the smaller courts associated with single sites in the early Middle Formative were abandoned and reestablished in the larger centers. Each court complex was the ceremonial architectural focus of an elite lineage that organized economic production and exchange. These late Middle Formative centers represent the successful competition of a few leaders who came together to create larger settlements.

A new art style, first discovered and described by Sergio Chávez and Karen Mohr Chávez (1975) and named the Yaya-Mama religious tradition, represents the material manifestation of the first pan-Titicaca Basin elite ideology that developed in the late Middle Formative. These stone stelae, flat-bottomed bowls, trumpets, and other high-status artifacts—which would have required some degree of craft specialization at the local level—have been found at several sites throughout the region. In sum, the first production of specialized craft objects during the Middle Formative was associated with the initial development of elite groups. Objects were produced at regional centers under the auspices of these elite, either as attached specialists or as unattached workers who moved from site to site.

Regional centers are hypothesized as being the primary residences of the emergent elite. I argue that the primary mechanism of elite development in the Titicaca Basin centered on the ability of nascent leaders to maintain complex labor organizations through competitive feasting and other ceremonies. In short, the courts and their associated ritual paraphernalia represented the material means by which these complex labor organizations remained viable.

The regional political landscape of the early Middle Formative is therefore hypothesized to be one in which several score of sites had small courts that were the focus of politico-religious ceremony that served to maintain complex labor organizations. In time, a few of these centers grew in size and drew their neighbors into intervillage political units. Unfortunately, our chronology is still too coarse to define this process with any precision. What we can say is that by the late Middle Formative (circa 500 B.C.), two political traditions—one referred to as Qaluyu in the north

and one called Chiripa in the south—dominated the region. Existing alongside these two polities were several autonomous ones, such as Sillumocco, Ckackachipata, Escoma, and others. Map 1.3 illustrates the hypothesized late Middle Formative–period political landscape.

Over the centuries, a few Middle Formative sites increased in size and complexity. These larger centers continued to be the residence of elite groups and attached populations as well as the residence of specialists who worked under the direction of, or at the behest of, these elite. By the end of the Upper Formative, Pucara and Tiwanaku had become an order of magnitude larger than their contemporaries. These two sites are referred to as "primate" regional centers, but even at their height (around the second or third century A.D.) their political power and geographical range were limited to an area of about two or three days' travel from their respective centers. Throughout the Titicaca Basin, numerous groups continued to exist either as autonomous or semiautonomous polities (see map 1.4). It is likely that the processes of state formation began in this late Upper Formative period, and that some polities were incorporated forcibly into the orbit of Pucara and Tiwanaku. But overall, the empirical evidence is quite compelling that these two polities did not have the organizational capacity to control large territories for substantial periods of time.

The patterns of complex chiefdom organization emerged from elite strategies that were first developed in the Middle Formative and then elaborated during the Upper Formative on a scale previously unwitnessed in the region. The origin of these complex chiefly societies, I believe, is best understood as the result of elite groups' efforts to attract commoner laborers and attached specialists to their centers. Evidence from throughout the Titicaca Basin indicates an elite capable of mobilizing labor for agricultural intensification, architectural embellishment, commodity production, and the organization of indi-

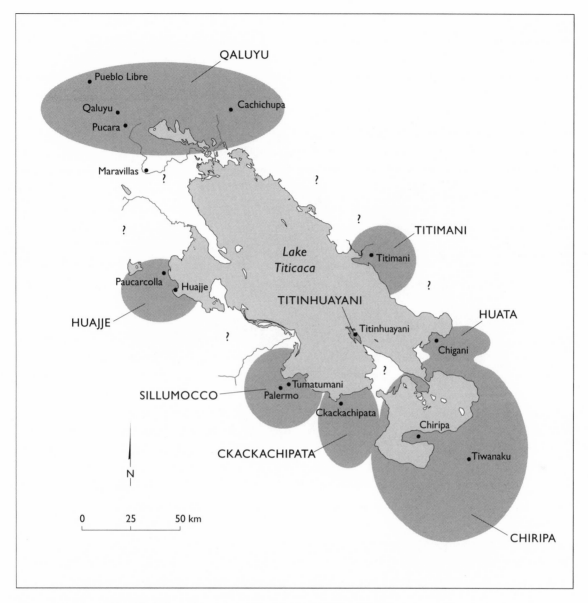

MAP 1.3. Hypothesized late Middle Formative–period polities, with selected regional centers.

viduals for conflict and trade during this period. Curiously, during most of the Upper Formative, there is little evidence of conflict *within* these societies but much evidence for conflict *between* them, which suggests that persuasive measures by the emergent elite to attract retainers took place primarily within their own communities. Force, in contrast, was used against other elites and other communities, and appears to have been restricted to intermittent raiding for booty and not used for major territorial expansion.

The Upper Formative political landscape corresponds to models of complex, competing chiefly so-

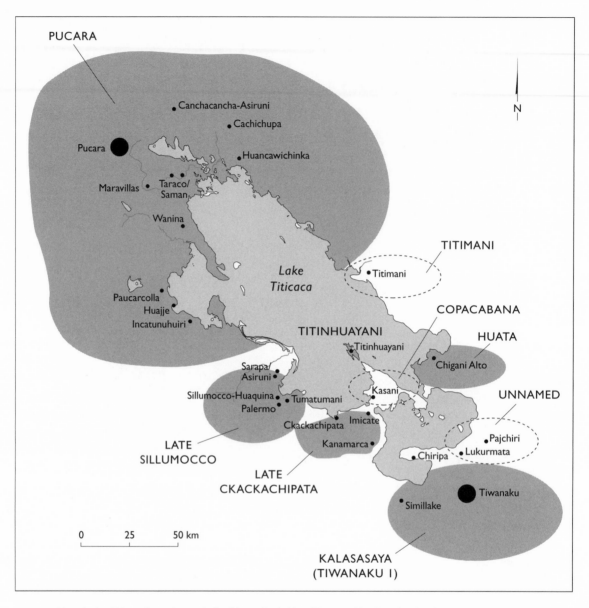

MAP 1.4. Hypothesized Upper Formative–period polities at the height of Pucara, with selected regional centers.

cieties. The hallmark of this process is the development of a regional polity beyond that of the village (Johnson and Earle 1987: 207), characterized by an organized control of labor by elites using strategies to overcome the limitations of agricultural econ-omies. Among those strategies were intensification of agricultural production to create a usable surplus, the establishment of long-distance exchange to secure objects or commodities to bolster elite status, the hosting of feasts, the assumption of ideological power, and creation of strategic alliances with neighboring elite.

There is little evidence that people in the Titicaca Basin were forced to accept these new political and economic relationships. On the contrary, the process is best understood as one generated by intense competition between aspiring elites once the exogenous factors conducive to this competition developed. These exogenous factors included the establishment of settled village life, the intensive use of agriculture and lake resources, less reliance on *puna* area hunting, and an increase in population densities that promoted intervillage exchange and other types of interaction.

Elites also created alliances with other elites through elaborate social ties, marriage, fictive kinship, and other types of intervillage interaction. The evidence for these social ties includes common motifs on pottery and stelae, and the widespread distribution of these artifacts throughout the region. These alliances provided a means by which aspiring elites could obtain exotic goods to maintain their factions. Long-distance exchange networks provided another source of exotic wealth that fed the political economy of these early ranked societies. Perhaps most important, the peoples of the region began to conduct intensive raiding against their neighbors. Trophy heads appear in Pucara and Early Tiwanaku iconography, and the remains of human victims have been found in ostensibly ceremonial contexts at several sites. By the end of the millennium, raiding organized by village leaders was a widespread phenomenon in the region.

Pucara collapsed as a regional polity around A.D. 200–300; the reasons are obscure. Around A.D. 600, a new political and economic phenomenon spread across the Titicaca Basin. The Tiwanaku peoples created the region's first archaic state, drawing on two millennia of political experimentation. Curiously, Tiwanaku did not expand immediately in the wake of Pucara's collapse. In fact, carbon dates from the Island of the Sun and other areas indicate that Tiwanaku expansion did not occur until the seventh century A.D. This means that the period from A.D. 300 to 600 was characterized by the retraction of Pucara as a regional power, with Tiwanaku still consolidating its power to the south. Map 1.5 illustrates the hypothesized political landscape in this late Upper Formative period.

By at least A.D. 650, Tiwanaku had expanded beyond its core area, absorbing the Island of the Sun and numerous basin territories to the east, west, and north, and extending outside the basin to the east and west. The small sunken court complex that first developed in the late second millennium B.C. was transformed into a vast sprawl of stately architecture at the Tiwanaku capital. The Akapana pyramid at Tiwanaku was built next to the massive Kalasasaya enclosure area, and the largest sunken court in the ancient Titicaca Basin was constructed. Palaces for the nobility flanked large temples, a great moat, and sprawling areas occupied by craftspeople and farmers. The first planned city in the Titicaca Basin, with several square kilometers of formal architecture and many dozens more in "suburban" settlements, Tiwanaku was one of the largest cities in the ancient Americas.

In the process of expansion, the Tiwanaku peoples conquered or annexed a large territory in the southern Titicaca region. By the seventh century A.D. they had established a shrine on the Island of the Sun and absorbed areas as far north as Juliaca. Colonies were established hundreds of kilometers away in Cochabamba to the southeast, in the Omasuyu region to the east, northwest into Arequipa, and west to Moquegua. The development of the region's first and only archaic state marked the crossing of a great threshold: coercive powers were now the means by which state political organizations were maintained. By the Tiwanaku period, perhaps at only one site—

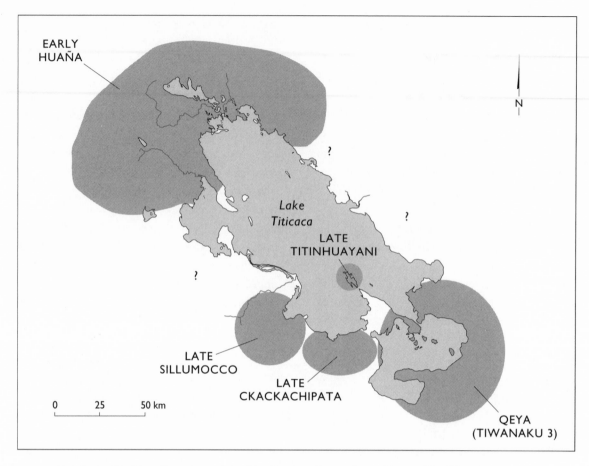

MAP 1.5. Hypothesized late Upper Formative–period polities after the collapse of Pucara (circa A.D. 200–300) and prior to Tiwanaku state expansion.

Tiwanaku itself—were people still carving and erecting the large anthropomorphic statues that were first carved over a millennium earlier. The first urban center in the Titicaca Basin was built on the remains of earlier villages at the capital of Tiwanaku, but it drew from two millennia of cultural developments in the region as a whole.

Although I view Tiwanaku as an expansive archaic state, I do not consider it structurally similar to the Inca empire. It was not a miniature version of the Inca empire, as is often assumed in the literature. Tiwanaku expansion was selective, and huge areas near the core territory and between provinces do not

appear to have been part of the system. In fact, Tiwanaku expanded in a manner notably different than that of the Inca.

Tiwanaku was the first and only expansionist state to develop in the south-central Andes. Archaeological evidence suggests that it developed in its core territory around A.D. 200 and began its expansion around A.D. 600. By the end of the seventh century, it had reached the Puno Bay, and by A.D. 800 it had peaked as a regional power (see map 1.6). By A.D. 900 Tiwanaku was in decline.

The data support the view of Tiwanaku as an expansive system with the capacity to incorporate

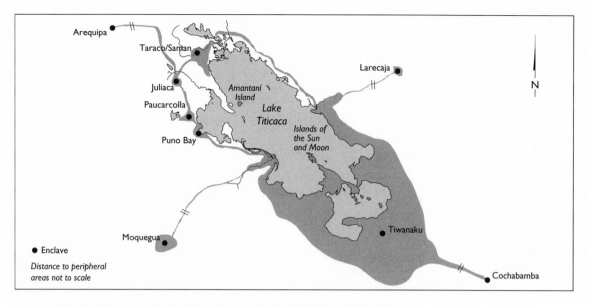

MAP 1.6. Hypothesized areas under direct Tiwanaku control at its height, circa A.D. 800–900.

other polities and to mobilize labor on a fairly impressive scale, at least in its core territory and selected enclaves. The political economy was based on local, or endogenous, production—raised-field agriculture, rain-fed agriculture, camelid raising, commodity production, lake exploitation—and external mechanisms, including the creation of extensive exchange and colonial relationships throughout the south-central Andes.

Unlike the Inca empire's tax-paying provinces, which incorporated and reorganized entire territories, Tiwanaku's subject lands were heterogeneous and noncontiguous, as were its strategies of control (see map 1.7). Tiwanaku was an archaic state that maintained a core and heartland territory, with enclaves of provincial territories around the south-central Andes. The Inca state, in contrast, was powerful enough to incorporate most of the political groups that it encountered in the highlands and in many coastal areas. The growth of the Inca was systematic, with political incorporation of subject territories increasing and expanding over time. Tiwa-

naku, however, appears to have been limited in its capacity to mobilize sufficient resources to control territories beyond the core and heartland. Tiwanaku therefore selected certain areas or enclaves using fairly specific settlement criteria. To the north, for instance, almost all of the major Tiwanaku sites (greater than five hectares) are on the road system. The rest of the smaller sites are either on the road or near permanent sources of water. There is also a strong correlation with Tiwanaku site location and proximity to extinct raised-field agricultural systems.

Areas that were not well watered and that were not on the road system in the north do *not* appear to have been incorporated into the Tiwanaku political and economic orbit. These local settlements that coexisted with but were not part of the Tiwanaku state are referred to as the Late Huaña cultures. Although we know little about the Late Huaña cultures, the available evidence suggests that a Cerro Baúl model on a grand scale operated. In this model, a state establishes enclaves in distant areas among autonomous polities. Lacking the ability to create formal territo-

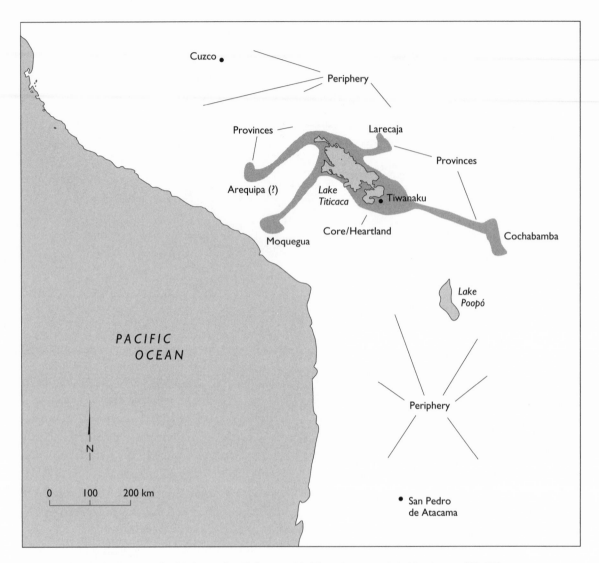

MAP 1.7. Hypothesized pattern of political control and influence of the Tiwanaku state at its height, circa A.D. 800–900.

rial organizations on the scale of an Inca province in territories more than two days' walk from the capital, Tiwanaku had a political geography outside its core territory that was a mosaic of colonies, poorly controlled territories, roads, and other strategically located state institutions.

The specific means by which Tiwanaku incorpo-rated individual polities remains obscure. Certainly, raw military force was not inconsequential, as sug-gested by trophy head iconography, the "capture" of stelae, some burning episodes, and so forth. In fact, I would argue that much of the architecture in Tiwa-naku's core is dedicated to the glorification of con-quest, particularly the semi-subterranean sunken court and the base of the Akapana pyramid, with dedicatory offerings of young humans, probably at the time of massive temple reconstruction (Manzanilla and Woodward 1990).

Substantial quantities of Tiwanaku pottery found outside the core territory provide additional insight into the expansion process. At the risk of oversimplification, it appears that two classes of Tiwanaku pottery predominated outside the core: drinking vessels and ceremonial offering vessels. Decorated *ollas,* bowls, and *tinajas* (large jars) are quite rare. In particular, *keros, tazones, sahumadores,* and incense burners represent a very large percentage of surface finds and excavated materials in the heartland as well as in provincial and peripheral territories. *Keros* were used for drinking, and the smaller, flat-bottomed *tazones* (or *cuencos-escudillas* [Alconini 1993: 91]) were most likely used for serving foods or liquids. *Sahumadores,* according to Alconini (1993: 93), were used for burning organic offerings, and incense burners were used in decidedly ritual contexts.

The eclectic nature of the ceramic assemblage in Tiwanaku-contemporary sites outside the core illustrates the complex nature of the state's expansion. The Tiwanaku materials outside the core territory are "limited, specific, and consistent," unlike the richer assemblage at the capital site (e.g., see Dietler 1990 for an analogy in Mediterranean culture). However, unlike the assemblages from Middle Formative sites, in which drinking/serving vessels made up the vast majority of the fancy ceramic vessels, assemblages from Tiwanaku sites outside the core also contained ritual burning vessels. In other words, the emulation of Tiwanaku culture went beyond the competitive feasting of emergent elites in Middle and Upper Formative society. Local elites produced a limited range of Tiwanaku-style pottery for feasting and ritual, imported Tiwanaku textiles, and allied themselves culturally to the Tiwanaku core in a manner not seen in the region up to that time.

The core and heartland territories of Tiwanaku, essentially south of the Ilave and Suches Rivers, were well integrated in the political economy of an expansionist state. Although much additional work needs to be completed, we can hypothesize some strong coercive and persuasive measures that the Tiwanaku elite may have used to align their counterparts in this part of the basin. Outside this area, in contrast, the Tiwanaku state was much more selective, choosing to control the road system and key areas of prime agricultural land. Expansion into the potentially dangerous area north of the Ilave and Suches Rivers thus proceeded in a narrow, dendritic-like pattern based on some key strategic and economic principles.

As mentioned, Tiwanaku had collapsed as a regional power by A.D. 900–1000. Although data are limited, for some areas we can define with some precision the gradual collapse of Tiwanaku influence. In Moquegua, the beginning of the post-Tiwanaku middle and lower valley Chiribaya culture is no later than A.D. 1000 (Bermann et al. 1989), and probably earlier. The contemporary Tumilaca culture of the Upper Moquegua drainage begins around the same time. In Moquegua at least, Tiwanaku influence had disappeared by the end of the millennium, fully a century or more earlier than in the core territory. In Azapa, Tiwanaku influence appears to have faded at about the same time, or even earlier, than in the Upper Moquegua drainage.

In sum, there appears to be a gradual, centuries-long retraction of Tiwanaku influence as a function of distance from the core territory. Goldstein argues that the collapse of Tiwanaku influence in Moquegua, as represented by the primary regional center of Omo, was associated with a violent episode: "The downfall of the system came from within. All indications suggest that the sudden and deliberate destruction of the Omo site in the tenth century came at the hands of rebellious Tiwanaku provincials, rather than any outside agent" (Goldstein 1993a: 42).

Although I cannot necessarily agree that the agents of this destruction were "provincials," the intentional destruction of the site is certainly instructive and suggests that the end of Tiwanaku was accompanied by some violence.

Ortloff and Kolata (1993) have argued that the proximate cause of Tiwanaku collapse was a drought that destroyed the core territory's raised-field systems. Paleoclimatic research by Binford and associates (Binford and Brenner 1989; Binford, Brenner, and Engstrom 1992; Binford, Brenner, and Leyden 1996) and earlier data from the Quelccaya ice core support this model. These combined data indicate a period of severe drought in the post–A.D. 1000 period.

So why did Tiwanaku collapse? The short answer is that we still do not know. The long answer begins with the observation that we know much more than we did a generation ago, and we can eliminate a number of possibilities. First, the collapse of Tiwanaku was slow and not accompanied by a demographic collapse: survey data suggest that roughly the same number of people lived in the Tiwanaku Valley and surrounding areas before and after A.D. 1100. Albarracin-Jordan and Mathews, for instance, located 964 post-Tiwanaku sites in the valley; during the previous Tiwanaku period, there were 339. Of course, Tiwanaku sites were considerably larger and possibly more densely nucleated. Tiwanaku itself counts as only one site, but it contained tens of thousands of people. Nevertheless, an increase in the number of sites by a factor of three is significant and suggests a minor population dispersal around the Tiwanaku capital, not an out-migration of people to other ecological zones outside the valley.

Data from the Juli-Pomata region in the western Titicaca region support this proposition. Here the number of sites in both time periods was a whole order of magnitude smaller. However, in this region we were able to calculate total site size per period in the study area. The results suggest that the population in the immediate post-Tiwanaku period either stayed the same or slightly increased. In other words, in two areas with good survey data, we can show that there was no demographic collapse coincident with Tiwanaku decline. Rather, in the immediate region the population dispersed from large, nucleated centers to smaller villages and hamlets.

It thus appears that the collapse of Tiwanaku was a political and social organizational phenomenon, not a demographic one. Although drought was certainly a factor, it cannot explain the collapse in full. Furthermore, the collapse was long, occurring over at least three generations and probably even more (assuming one generation is thirty years). Tiwanaku's collapse was not caused by an immediate crisis, such as an invasion of foreigners or a sudden climate change, but resulted from a gradual process over several generations.

The A.D. 1000–1100 drought undoubtedly would have affected the Tiwanaku populations' ability to maintain raised-field agriculture. Throughout the southern Titicaca Basin there are numerous examples of attempts to ameliorate the drought conditions by building canals, aqueducts, and reservoirs. By A.D. 1100, the technological limits of these engineering responses had been reached.

Raised fields are significant not just for the amount of food that they can produce as opposed to rain-fed agriculture; they are also an economic activity that concentrates populations. An intensive form of agriculture that produces consistent yields, raised fields permitted the concentration of large populations in relatively small areas. The drought conditions that made large-scale raised-field agriculture unfeasible would have also promoted the dispersal of populations.

This process is evident in the reemphasis on terrace agriculture and lakeside settlement in the post-Tiwanaku periods. Other evidence indicates that the post-Tiwanaku populations met the drought conditions with a classic response: the intensification of animal keeping. As mentioned above, the pasturing of animals, particularly the highly resilient camelids of the altiplano, was a very effective response to drought. The Juli-Pomata settlement data indicate at the very least a major increase in the use of the puna grazing areas in the post-Tiwanaku periods, and probably a dispersal of the population. Like rain-fed terrace agriculture, however, grazing economies can work against population nucleation.

One argument against the drought at the turn of the millennium as a major factor in the collapse of Tiwanaku relies on Quelccaya ice core data. If the data are correct, there was also a drought around A.D. 650–730, a period of Tiwanaku expansion, when the state would have been a political and economic powerhouse. One cannot use the drought at A.D. 1100 to explain collapse, and the drought at A.D. 650 to explain the rise of the state. Had the political and economic organization of Tiwanaku been as strong in A.D. 1000/1100 as it was in the mid-seventh and eighth centuries, the elite would have been able to find alternative means of bringing surplus into the capital. Instead, it appears that the turn-of-the-millennium drought helped to decentralize an already weak state. It is telling, for instance, that the Tiwanaku colonial enclave in Moquegua, perhaps the most important in the west, had fallen out of the state orbit *before* the drought. There is compelling evidence that Tiwanaku's political and economic organization was already weakened before the drought set in, as its provincial enclaves were falling apart. The changing climate on the altiplano was a final straw that broke the state.

If drought was a factor but not the direct cause of Tiwanaku collapse, what was? That is a question we still cannot answer, and which may in fact be the wrong question. A more productive focus of future research would focus on the access routes to the provincial territories that supplied the state with exotic commodities. Likewise, it will be fruitful to look at elite activities in the heartland and provinces, and see to what degree the centrifugal political and economic forces that operate on most premodern expansive systems were at work in Tiwanaku.

In the wake of Tiwanaku collapse, a new set of political and economic entities developed in the region. The evidence in the Diez de San Miguel Visita of 1567 and other documents suggests a state-level society among the Lupaqa in the sixteenth century, albeit one incorporated into the Spanish and Inca imperial systems.

Current data suggest that the rise of the post-Tiwanaku agro-pastoral polities, or *señoríos,* was partially a result of the drought that peaked around A.D. 1100 and which was simultaneously weakening the Tiwanaku state. Combined with potential enemies around the lake region, a weakened Tiwanaku military capacity would have left the provincial territories and peripheries difficult to control and inaccessible to Tiwanaku trading caravans. The early collapse of colonial areas such as Moquegua suggests that the severing of exchange routes was also a major factor in what would have been a multicausal process of decentralization in the Titicaca Basin.

In Pedro de Cieza de León's *Crónica* (1959 [1553]: chapter 100) we get a hint that immediately prior to, or during, the reign of Viracocha Inca, the Lupaqa and Colla were engaged in intense conflict. Fearing an Inca-Lupaqa alliance, the Colla initiated an attack against the Lupaqa. In the plains of Paucarcolla, between Puno and Juliaca, 150,000 troops were assembled for a large battle between the two great Aymara kingdoms.[1] According to Cieza, thirty thousand died in this battle, including the Colla king, and it was a decisive victory for the Lupaqa. Viracocha Inca was very disappointed in being unable to take advantage of the conflict, and the battle permitted the Lupaqa to become a major political power in the basin (Cieza 1976: 219).

Following the battle between the Lupaqa and the Colla, the Cari of the Lupaqa returned to Chucuito, the capital of his kingdom. (Cari was the title of the Colla chief as well as his name.) Cieza's account of what followed next is most intriguing. He says that Cari graciously received the Viracocha Inca at Chucuito, where they both drank from a golden goblet. The Inca offered a daughter to Cari, and an alliance was sealed. Significantly, this passage represents an extremely rare occasion in the documents, suggesting an equal power relationship between the Inca and a major rival. In fact, in one reading of Cieza's account, the Inca lost the battle, and Viracocha Inca had to settle for an equitable alliance between his young empire and the Lupaqa. In this account, we get a sense that the Lupaqa were as great as the Inca in power and authority in this early period of Inca expansion. The Lupaqa were a power that the Inca had to reckon with, and one that may have stopped the Inca empire's advance until the ascension of Viracocha's son, Pachacuti.

In these histories, the Lupaqa and Colla are presented as polities with hereditary kingship and the ability to mobilize substantial numbers of people. This latter observation, the ability to mobilize labor, is substantiated by archaeological reconnaissance. Sites such as Pukara Juli and Tanka Tanka represent an enormous amount of labor organization and labor expenditure. At present, there are two models of pre-Inca political organization. The first, proposed by Murra, Pease, and others, argues that the Lupaqa, the Colla, and possibly the Pacajes were state-level societies prior to Inca incursions, as suggested by information in the Diez de San Miguel Visita and other documents (Murra 1968; Pease 1973). In the second model the pre-Inca señoríos were not integrated as a state-level society, and the political structure suggested in the Diez de San Miguel Visita is seen as largely the creation of the Inca state.

The archaeological data are contradictory. Apart from the large fortresses that would have required massive labor, there is no additional evidence for complex polities. Unlike the earlier Tiwanaku and the later Inca, the Lupaqa produced no fine-ware ceramics of any substance, and no stelae. Evidence also indicates that the formal organization of the raised fields typical of the Tiwanaku period essentially collapsed, replaced by a much less complex, informal use of the fields. Lupaqa area sites have no civic-ceremonial or elite architecture such as that found in either the Tiwanaku or Inca periods and few residential structure differences that might suggest an elite/commoner distinction. Settlement pattern analysis indicates no substantial site size hierarchy with the exception of the large forts known as *pukaras,* which were not permanently occupied. There is little archaeological differentiation between the permanent, domestic villages and hamlets. The lack of elite ceramics and typical nucleated settlement patterns seen in the Late Sillumocco and Tiwanaku periods further suggests that the Late Intermediate– or Altiplano-period Lupaqa was not a state-level society. *Chulpa* tombs, traditionally interpreted to be indications of elite organization, are in fact quite common and are best interpreted as the common funerary mode for *ayllu* and/or other social groups.[2] Almost all of the large, truly rare elite chulpa tombs date to the post-Altiplano period.

The archaeological data therefore support the argument that the sixteenth-century Lupaqa state organization was a result of Inca reorganization, and not a pre-Inca, autochthonous development. Recent work by Kirk Frye near the Lupaqa capital of Chucuito also supports this argument:

The available data concerning settlement patterns, architectural features and decorated ceramics do not support the model that populations associated with Altiplano period major fortified sites were politically integrated complex societies. Instead, these data support the interpretation that the Altiplano period Lupaqa represent several small-scale political groups most likely organized at the level of what evolutionary anthropologists have referred to as simple chiefdoms. (Frye 1997: 137)

The conclusions for the pre-Inca Lupaqa also appear to hold for the Colla, the other powerful polity in the basin. Reconnaissance in the southern Pacajes area also reinforces this model of Altiplano-period political organization. In other words, the prevailing model of pre-Inca, post-Tiwanaku political economic complexity is one of smaller, autonomous societies organized around major pukaras and/or other fortified settlement clusters (see figure 1.1). They were not state-level societies by any definition; rather, they were only moderately ranked societies with little evidence of elite groups or socioeconomic differentiation.

The Altiplano period was characterized by an almost complete cessation of the political strategies used by the people of the Titicaca Basin over the previous two millennia. The sunken court tradition disappeared completely, flat-bottomed drinking vessels ceased to be manufactured, and pyramids and other earthen-filled platform structures were no longer built. Populations dispersed across the landscape and concentrated in the hilltop, fortified pukaras. The nature of conflict shifted as well. The pukaras were designed to withstand sieges or prolonged attacks, with the total area encircled by the walls of the major pukaras likely designed to include farmland, grazing land, and springs. Raiding occurred on a massive scale not formerly seen in the region.

How, then, do we explain the apparent ability of the pre-Inca Aymara señoríos to build such massive sites as Tanka Tanka and Pukara Juli, and to amass armies sufficiently large to confront the Inca? How do we explain these apparent contradictions in the archaeological and historical data?

The key to understanding the Aymara señoríos of the twelfth to sixteenth centuries lies with a segmentary political organization. It was in this context that the Inca empire occupied the Titicaca Basin. The

lake was the heartland of Collasuyu, quite probably the most lucrative quarter of the powerful Inca state, which consolidated its control in the region by a number of methods. The archaeological evidence indicates the importance of six strategies: (1) the founding of new towns, (2) the formalization of the road and *tambos* (or way stations), (3) the establishment of specialized production areas, (4) the manipulation of ideologies of power, (5) the relocation of population, and (6) the outright exercise of military power in the initial conquest and during subsequent periods of political rebellion.

In assessing the nature of Inca control in Collasuyu, it is important to emphasize that control was not monolithic and homogeneous throughout the empire, and not even within a particular region or province. Inca strategies took advantage of local conditions and represent in many ways a balance between the needs and opportunities afforded by local elites, where they existed, and the needs of the imperial apparatus. In the case of the Titicaca Basin, these six strategies were employed in a general fashion around the region, but it is necessary to reemphasize that even within the Titicaca area, the strategies varied from region to region.

Systematic survey, nonsystematic reconnaissance, and analysis of historical documents indicate that a vast number of new towns were established during the Inca period. Virtually every major Early Colonial town studied to date (with a few exceptions such as Guaqui) has an Inca component but not an Altiplano-period one. This pattern fits with the general Inca strategy of moving people from defensive locations to nondefensive ones. It is also understandable in that the Pax Incaica, or the peace imposed by Inca conquest, would have substantially controlled the internecine conflict evident in the Altiplano period. The elimination of defense as a settlement determinant would have been an additional impetus for populations to resettle in the lower areas. That is, even ignoring Inca imperial demands, with-

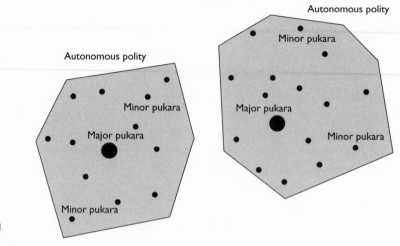

FIGURE I.I. Ideal settlement pattern for Altiplano-period pukaras and related settlements.

out the threat of raiding by neighbors, agro-pastoral populations would have been able to relocate to optimize their economic activities. Given that Altiplano-period populations were already composed of hamlets and defensive sites, the main shift would have been from the edges and walls of the pukaras down to the towns in the pampas and along the lake edges.

The Juli-Pomata survey data illustrate this process. A significant number of sites larger than 2.5 hectares were built under control by the Inca state. These sites, including such very large ones such as Juli and Pomata, represent new elite and/or administrative centers. The site size distribution data suggest that the nonelite settlement patterns (sites smaller than 2.5 hectares) remained unchanged from the Altiplano period, but an administrative level was injected or imposed on the population during the Inca occupation, as represented by the large centers.

The distribution of the newly founded Inca towns is clearly linked to formalization of the road system. The main Early Colonial and Inca centers line up along the Urqusuyu and Umasuyu road, with only a few exceptions. Of course, our knowledge of the so-called Inca roads is biased because the authors of

historical documents assumed that all roads were Inca in construction and referred to them as such. As seen above, there were linear distributions of sites in the Tiwanaku period along the later Urqusuyu road, and it is therefore reasonable to assume that such roads existed in pre-Inca times.

Nevertheless, the Inca did far more than repair and maintain an existing road system. They built a complete administrative apparatus around this transport system. Tambos were constructed and maintained by *mit'a* (or corvée) labor. Causeways were built over swampy terrain, and bridges were constructed over rivers. Populations were settled within the immediate road area, with a large percentage living within a few minutes' walk from the roads. In fact, the existence of the road became a primary settlement determinant, replacing defense as a consideration.

There is overwhelming historical and archaeological evidence of massive *mitima* resettlement in the Titicaca region during the Inca period. The growth spike in the Late Horizon in the Juli-Pomata region is partially a result of new migrations under the control of the Inca state, and such migrations are consistent with ethnohistoric reports of economic specialists such as potters, metalworkers, weavers, and others. Data from the Late Horizon demonstrate that the Inca moved in large numbers of mitima and probably moved local populations to regional centers.

Many of the mitima colonists appear to have been moved in as economic specialists, and evidence for craft specialization is substantial. Spurling's (1992) work identified enclaves of weavers and potters on the eastern side of the lake. At least one site in the Juli-Pomata survey (Stanish et al. 1997) had a significantly high number of spindle whorls on the surface, suggesting a specialized production site. Additional research has identified groups of miners, metalworkers, and other craft specialists. The Inca state also spent considerable resources to create a series of temples and shrines in the region. These efforts can be understood as an attempt to create a state religion that co-opted legitimacy for the state. The Island of the Sun, the Island of the Moon, and the Copacabana region were transformed from local shrines of the pre-Inca past to those of pan-Andean importance. The shrine complex on the Island of the Sun and Island of the Moon was part of the Inca expansion process as it incorporated the heartland Collasuyu (Bauer and Stanish 2001).

After the Inca removed the existing population of the islands and the surrounding mainland, they replaced them with perhaps as many as two thousand colonists from across the empire. They also established a set of elite women on the islands whose singular role was to serve the sanctuaries. They also built a number of state facilities on the mainland and on the islands, including temples, storehouses, special-ized housing for the attendants, and lodging for the pilgrims who would travel there through a sacred landscape filled with symbols of the state. The powers of the state and those of the sacred locations, points of intense religious devotion, became intermixed and inseparable.

The historical documents make it quite clear that when these strategies broke down, the Inca used raw military power to control the province. Entire towns were decimated, young males executed, and rebels transferred to other parts of the empire. The Inca state thus represents an entirely new phenomenon in the Titicaca Basin: a foreign conquest of a people who spoke a different language and who had occupied the area for several generations. Virtually all of the Incas' imperial strategies were based upon pre-Inca Andean patterns, but virtually all of their actions were modified by the cultural and historical context that they encountered in Collasuyu.

By 1532 the region had been carved up into a series of provinces, and in spite of the periodic rebellions by the Aymara-speaking peoples, it produced a huge bounty of wealth for the Inca state. But the European invasion brought an end to the largest native empire in the Americas. Collasuyu was one of the great provinces of that empire. Over the centuries, the physical remains of the ancient peoples of the Titicaca Basin have slowly disappeared. Still, our archaeological and historical research over the past 150 years has yielded an ever-increasing store of knowledge that celebrates the great achievements of these extraordinary people.

The Evolution of Political Economies

For centuries, social philosophers and anthropologists have tried to systematically and rationally explain the emergence of complex society in the great centers of world civilization. Since at least the late nineteenth century, anthropologists have realized that the shift from Neolithic or Formative village societies to ranked and class-based societies was somehow linked to the weakening of kinship relations and the strengthening of political and economic ones.[1] Anthropologists have long dealt with the basic problem of how the apparently strong bonds of kinship gave way to the emergence of a political class that was exempt from some of the traditional rules constraining the accumulation of wealth and power by a few. Over the generations, scientific archaeologists have conceived of this process as an evolutionary one that featured a shift from small village-level societies to more complex ones characterized by larger

populations, greater concentrations of wealth, large settlements, and hierarchical political and economic organizations.

At the same time, cultural anthropologists have grown increasingly uncomfortable with the concept of complex society. To have one, as the reasoning justifiably goes, you have to have simple or primitive societies as well. These words evoke pejorative characterizations of the vast bulk of peoples around the world in space and time. Cultural anthropologists counter with examples of extraordinary complexity of supposedly simple peoples. For instance, they have described intricate systems of kin reckoning, in many cases more complicated than those of most western groups. Complex oral histories demonstrate rich indigenous traditions that are distinct from western ones. Complex systems of exchange—like that of the famous Kula, described by Bronislaw Malinowski (1961 [1922])—represent profound cultural achievements that cannot be described by any term other than *complex*. The list of complex social organizations seemingly impenetrable or too complicated for western minds to grasp continues, all of them occurring in so-called simple societies.

Processual archaeologists, on the other hand, faced with the empirical facts of the archaeological record, recognize the obvious distinction between a huge, complex state such as that administered by the urban center of Teotihuacán circa A.D. 500 and the much smaller, rural Formative village of San José Mogote.[2] The archaeological record demonstrates that the shift from village-level societies to the dominance of Teotihuacán occurred rather quickly, in less than two millennia. Likewise, in the Nile Delta, people lived in villages of a few hundred in the fourth millennium B.C., and less than fifty generations later were building massive pyramids, conquering foreign lands, erecting monuments of unparalleled size, and feeding tens of thousands of people where previously only a fraction of that number could survive. In at least a half dozen areas around the world, and independently at least twice, people shifted from a village organization of a few hundred inhabitants to state organizations of several hundred thousand. This process occurred in a brief moment in the history of fully modern humans, and it occurred rapidly. This process is central to understanding the development of civilization as understood by both modern and premodern peoples, and it deserves our most dedicated scholarly investigation as one of the hallmarks of what it is to be a social human being.

Cultural anthropologists are correct on one important issue: the peoples of the world, today and in the past, who live and lived in village societies were as intellectually sophisticated as those who lived in the first-generation or "pristine" states, or those that live today in modern industrial states. Intellectual factors are not necessary or sufficient to explain the development of complexity in the archaeological record. In fact, an analysis of societies around the world indicates that only two areas of human organization separate the most complex state from the smallest village: the means by which people structure their political life and their economic life.[3] Polity and economy are the means by which people create subsistence and surplus wealth, and the organizations within which this wealth is created.

Polity and economy, broadly defined, constitute the core of most processual archaeological models. Kent Flannery, for instance, distinguishes between social evolution, a "reorganization of society at a different level of complexity, and cultural evolution, characterized by those features that give a group its particular ethnic identity" (Flannery 1995: 3–4). Flannery's stages of social evolution are defined largely by demographic size and the kinds, levels, and complexity of sociopolitical hierarchies, all of which have economic ramifications. This model avoids the errors of many evolutionary typologies that are constructed on the basis of certain core features—economic organization, political organization, technology—but are then used to imply the existence of an entire constellation of other features (Feinman and Neitzel 1984: 44). Most features of culture—such as language, kin terminology, writing systems, religion, and so forth—reflect a divergent evolution and cannot be understood as the products of a directed evolutionary process. It is only the political economy that becomes more complex through time, and it is only here that the cultural evolutionary process can be analyzed.

The central concept of political economy is wealth, defined in its broadest sense as any material or nonmaterial asset for which people are willing to exchange some of their labor. It is a framework for analyzing the creation and movement of wealth in societies and is an approach that views wealth as a core element of analysis. In short, political economy theory focuses on the control of wealth production and exchange, and the manipulation of ideologies of power that undergird that organization.

Production and Exchange

The manipulation and outright control of the production and exchange of wealth are central to the development of complex political economies. The production of wealth is affected by many factors, including the ecological context in which it is created, the technology available, the labor available, the size and complexity of labor organization, and so forth. This definition of wealth—what people will work for—is culturally contingent, a necessary feature of any definition that is useful for anthropological analysis.

Since no individual, household, or other economic unit is completely self-sufficient, some kind of exchange between corporate entities is essential to any economy. Wealth produced by one economic unit can either be consumed by that entity or exchanged for other wealth. Economic exchange is defined as the transfer of wealth from one individual to another, either as individuals or in groups. The exchange process has been divided into four mechanisms by Karl Polanyi and other economic anthropologists: reciprocity, redistribution, market exchange, and nonmarket exchange. To his four types I add two more: competitive feasting and tribute.

Reciprocity is defined as the exchange of an equal amount of wealth, or "like value for like value." It involves a series of symmetrical obligations between individuals or groups. It may be socially mediated—a sack of potatoes to my brother-in-law for a pound of meat—or it may be an exchange between nonrelated partners, as in the famous case of the Kula as first described by Bronislaw Malinowski (1961 [1922]). Reciprocity may be immediate, such as a direct exchange in a periodic fair or in commensal feasts (Dietler 1990; Hayden 1996), or it can be deferred for days, weeks, years, or even decades. Deferred reciprocity, in fact, is a fundamental feature of the Kula (Leach 1983: 3) and is the most prominent of many ranked political economies in the ethnographic literature. Reciprocity can occur as an indirect "down-the-line" trade where individuals conduct a series of reciprocal trades that link large distances through exchange partners. Throughout virtually all types of political economies, the mechanism of reciprocity, either deferred or immediate, makes up the bulk of exchange.

Redistribution is best conceived of as "asymmetrical reciprocity"; that is, there is an exchange of wealth that ideologically may be presented as equal, but the actual values exchanged are not equal. Redistribution implies the existence of some kind of social or political authority that can accumulate surplus for redistribution. Most cases of redistribution in the ethnographic record are recorded as voluntary, with a larger group willing to give up some surplus wealth to an authority to maintain a mechanism of distribution that avoids social conflict. Likewise, most cases of redistribution involve nonsubsistence surplus (Earle 1977, 1997).

Reciprocity and redistribution are forms of barter in which values are established by custom. Exchange for profit is not a motive. In premodern political economies dominated by these mechanisms, neutral intermediaries who move goods between exchange partners are rare. Nonmarket exchange that meets these criteria is defined by Polanyi as "administered trade." In administered trade systems, exchange values for commodities or services are determined by a political authority and not through competitive negotiation, although as in all economies, supply and demand ultimately affect exchange values. Trade is extensive in such systems, but it is not conducted in a competitive market environment. Rather than involving merchants who operate for profit, as in market systems, administered trade systems rely upon middlemen who act as agents for political authorities (Hodges 1988: 39). Middlemen make a profit in such a system by manipulating competing political elites for rights to access to exchange partners.

Market exchange is a system in which prices are

determined by negotiations between independent buyers and sellers. Some kind of money or media of exchange are central to the operation of price-fixing markets. Middlemen exist and make a profit off price differences. The distribution of wealth is determined not by political or social factors but by largely economic ones; that is, those who bid up prices the highest receive the goods and services. In nonmarket barter economies, one is socially obligated to trade with a pre-established partner, usually a kinsman. In market systems, this obligation is substantially weaker.

Competitive feasting is a type of commensal feasting that, in strictly economic terms, is a form of deferred reciprocity. One person offers wealth to another with the expectation of a supposedly equal exchange in the future. However, unlike most forms of reciprocity, the motive in competitive feasting is not the receipt of a future equal return of wealth but rather future political gain. Perhaps more so than in any other exchange mechanism, the political and the economic merge in competitive feasting. Wealth is provided strategically to obligate the receiver to such an extent that he or she must promise future labor or wealth. The successful host or giver may actually lose total wealth in the short term but gains political power and prestige. Most important, successful hosts increase the size of their following or faction and can command even greater numbers of nonelite laborers for future production.

Competitive feasting must be viewed as a major form of economic exchange in many premodern societies, not as some kind of aberrant social behavior. It is a major mechanism of political economic evolution (Hayden 1996: 127). Competitive feasting is not fully understandable as a form of redistribution, reciprocity, or trade (although cf. Polanyi 1968: 13–14). It is a distinct kind of exchange that occurs under certain conditions and is central to the evolution of moderately ranked political economies.

The final mechanism of wealth transfer is tribute.

This was not a mechanism for Polanyi, given that he was focused on the nature of internal political and economic organization. However, tribute—which is an exploitative economic relationship where one party materially benefits by extracting wealth from another through some kind of force—is a mechanism of wealth exchange and was an integral component of archaic states and imperial political economies. Although it takes many forms in a variety of historical and cultural contexts, the principal defining characteristic of tribute is that there is no expectation of any kind of material reciprocity.

In earlier theories, reciprocity, redistribution, and market exchange were viewed as complete economic systems in the sense used by Polanyi (1957), Dalton (1968), and others (see Sahlins 1972: 301). In fact, there was an implied evolutionary sequence that ran from reciprocal economies through redistributive ones to market or trade-based ones (e.g., Service 1972). This fact of intellectual history may partially explain why competitive feasting and tribute were ignored by Polanyi and Dalton as exchange mechanisms: they did not fit neatly into an evolutionary sequence. We now know that this implied evolutionary framework is empirically false. *All of these mechanisms, as well as competitive feasting and market exchange, can co-occur in societies.* Redistribution, reciprocity, administered trade, price-fixing markets, competitive feasting, and tribute represent a number of exchange *mechanisms* that can co-occur in any economy. It is the *dominance* of a particular form that gives a political economy its particular character, its evolutionary potential, and its productive capacity.

The Evolution of Ranked Political Economies

Ranked political economies are defined here as ones in which some individuals consistently acquire access to, and some kind of control over, more wealth relative to others in their group. Ethnographically, these kinds of ranked societies are not characterized by inherited status. As in the case of "Big Men" societies in the classic ethnographic literature, individuals of rank may not even necessarily be wealthy individuals—even so-called elites must produce their own subsistence. However, by virtue of their generosity and organizational efforts, they can accumulate followers through the creation of deferred reciprocities and thereby acquire social power and prestige. Individuals of rank control not only wealth but groups ranging from their extended family to whole villages and beyond. The key structural feature of ranked political economies (hereafter generally referred to as *ranked society*) is that some individuals direct the voluntary and cooperative labor of people outside their household.[4]

The central question is: How can we model the evolution of ranked society from nonranked society? If the assumption is that individuals will make strategic decisions in their own perceived self-interest, then the following observation by Robert Bettinger must be part of any evolutionary model: "however beneficial cooperative behavior might be for collective bodies and their constituents, it should not occur except when it is in the self-interest of individuals as individuals" (Bettinger 1991: 157). In other words, people will not work in cooperative groups that are directed by an emergent elite unless it is to their benefit.

The task, therefore, is to develop a model of the origin of ranked from nonranked societies that can deal with strategic decision making, the development of aggrandizing groups and individuals, the tendencies for the preservation of individual autonomy, and the existence of strong kinship relations in nonranked society that were co-opted by other kinds of aggrandizing organizations.

From a political economic perspective, the key process is one in which control of some wealth shifts from domestic groups to larger and stronger organizations. In economic and political terms, this process

is characterized as one in which control of domestic labor by incipient elites develops. The development of complex political economies rests on the ability of elites to induce individuals to give up some political autonomy along with some of their labor for what should be, for theoretical consistency, in the individual interest of almost all adult members of that society.

The Political Economy of the Domestic Group

The autonomous village society is the basis from which complex political economic evolution takes place. It is and was the basic organization of the vast bulk of the world's populations throughout history, both premodern and modern. What, therefore, is the nature of economic production, exchange, and consumption in the domestic household in agrarian society? Can we, in fact, define an archetypal organization that is applicable worldwide in space and time and therefore is universally valid for comparative purposes? I believe that the answer is yes. Given that, such a concept can be used to model the origins of complex political economies from this baseline economic unit. If so, a further definition of that kind of political economy is required.

The basic unit of economic organization in autonomous village society is defined as the average minimum number of individuals who comprise an economically distinct group that cooperates in the acquisition of wealth and that shares in the consumption of that wealth. It is the minimal unit of resource pooling and minimal unit of any division of labor. Using comparative data from nonwestern societies, anthropologists, economic historians, and others have studied the nature and composition of the minimal domestic unit around the world. In a very important article, Jack Goody surveyed the existing literature from African and Asian peasant societies and concluded that the mean agricultural work units ranged between 1.8 and 11.9 (Goody 1972). These work units were almost always composed of related individuals, hereafter referred to as *households*.[5] In fact, generations of modern research consistently point to the household, composed of between five and fifteen consanguineously related members, as the demographic range of the minimal cooperative economic unit in agrarian society.

The household is also the basic economic unit of virtually all complex societies in the premodern world. It is an autonomous economic unit that produces and shares its own subsistence. Ethnography is replete with references to the household as the basic unit, even if it is referred to in individual terms or supra-household terms.

Surplus Production and the Household

A significant advance in understanding the functioning of the domestic household began with the observations of the early-twentieth-century Russian agricultural economist Aleksandr Vasilevich Chayanov. Chayanov (1966) analyzed data on Russian peasantry, with specific reference to their economic decision-making behavior. The significance of Chayanov's observations was first extensively developed in modern anthropology by Marshall Sahlins (Sahlins 1972: 87–92) and subsequently elaborated by economic anthropologists and economic historians (e.g., Harrison 1975).

Succinctly stated, in the absence of pressures or inducements to the contrary, agrarian households substantially underproduce and underconsume relative to their economic capacity. As Sahlins describes in *Stone Age Economics,* "'primitive' agrarian economies . . . seem not to realize their own economic capacities. Labor power is underused, technological means are not fully engaged, natural resources are left untapped" (Sahlins 1972: 41). Population densities in such societies also are consistently below carrying capacities. Sahlins goes on to argue that underproduction is inherent in economies organized by domestic groups and kinship relations; thus, in essence, he defined the nature of the domestic household across

the world as a universal type. Sahlins (1972: 87) aptly named this concept "Chayanov's rule."

What is most significant about this feature of domestic economies is that it appears to be cross-culturally valid in most historical settings, ranging from peasant households in modern nation-states to village households peripheral to, or outside, state control. In other words, economies organized at the household level (that is, by domestic groups and kinship) are characterized by a considerable reserve of potential labor and wealth production.

The question of why households conform to this rule is a major issue in anthropology. It is possible that successful household organization over the generations developed as a means to avoid risk. That is, by systematically underutilizing their labor potential, households can increase their labor power in times of stress. Another factor suggested by Chayanov and Sahlins is a cultural bias against "drudgery." In the absence of market systems and the ability to store wealth, individuals do not find it in their interest to work beyond a certain limit. The reason why Chayanov's rule holds cross-culturally is less important for this discussion than the empirical fact that it does indeed exist. The existence of systemic underproduction is a significant factor in the evolution of more complex political economies.

Chayanov's Rule, Division of Labor, and the Evolution of Ranked Political Economies

The evolution of the political economy from a household-based, economically egalitarian village type to a ranked one is the first step in the development of complex society. It is a process characterized by the political manipulation of economic production and exchange by a group of people who acquire some degree of social power over the labor of others. The means by which labor is mobilized by an emergent elite to create exchange surplus has been explained by two broad types of theories that may be called *coercive* and *persuasive.* Coercive theories are characterized by unintentional surrender of autonomy by commoner populations due to exogenous factors such as resource stress from environmental degradation, population pressures, threats from other people, and so forth (e.g., see Earle 1997). Coercive theories can also involve intentional elite strategies that range from the use of sheer force to subtler means of control.

Classic cultural ecological and other selectionist models of cultural evolution rely on such assumptions. That is, the driving forces of cultural evolution are the adaptive responses by societies—in this case, higher levels of sociopolitical integration—to deal with such exogenous stresses. In selectionist models, the individual members of any society are faced with choosing the lesser of several unattractive alternatives. They must give up autonomy for protection against outsiders. Or they have to increase their production to make up for some kind of environmental stress that lowered the productivity of the land. New levels of information integration permit greater efficiencies that, in turn, provide for more wealth production under these stressed circumstances. It is justifiably assumed that people do not want to give up their economic and political autonomy or work harder but that some kinds of active or passive coercive forces compel them to do so.

Persuasive theories of labor control, in contrast, focus on the proactive role of nascent elites who use a variety of strategies such as the assumption of ideological power, co-option of separate divine descent, the control and strategic redistribution of exotic goods, the creation of economies of scale, and so forth. These strategies permit an elite to persuade others to relinquish some of their labor for access to material and/or nonmaterial benefits within their particular system of values. Persuasive theories by necessity focus on the competitive nature of leadership in early state and complex chiefly societies.

Persuasive and coercive strategies can succeed only if they result in the intensification of the do-

mestic economy and creation of surplus. The key to understanding economic intensification and appropriation of surplus is Chayanov's rule, which provides both a challenge and an opportunity for aspiring elites. The opportunity is that in any group of households there exists an untapped source of labor that can be mobilized. The challenge for elites is to induce, coerce, and/or persuade nonelites (also referred to as *primary producers*) to intensify their production above the limit inherent in Chayanov's rule. These limits are rigidly protected by kin organization, typical of societies in which the household is the most complex form of economic organization. Elites must either create or exploit a cultural context in which this rule can be overcome. Once this threshold is broken, agrarian populations can produce far more than their subsistence needs in a household level of organization, and this surplus can be used to finance the means for increasing elite power.

Overcoming the inherent limits of Chayanov's rule, therefore, is central to the process of political and economic evolution and the institutionalization of social power. It is the primary means by which elites extract surplus from nonelite populations. It is generally agreed that in both coercive and persuasive types of models there are just two ways to increase production and hence surplus from such economies. Spencer, citing Sahlins, outlines this assumption:

> There are essentially two ways to bring about an increase in surplus production as Sahlins (1972: 82) has pointed out: "getting people to work more or more people to work." Because the first strategy requires the leadership to intervene directly in the daily work schedules of individual households and villages, it is the second that is usually more compatible with chiefly decision-making. (Spencer 1998: 6–7)

It is generally assumed that in order to increase surplus production and thereby create the economic organizations and material conditions for rank and hierarchy to develop in premodern states, there must be an increase in the total amount of per capita labor from the vast majority of the population. The assumption that surplus must be derived from getting more people to work or getting them to work harder is central to models of political and economic evolution, both persuasive and coercive, but there are empirical and theoretical problems with this assumption. In the first instance, history and ethnography suggest that agrarian populations vigorously resist such demands on their labor, as outlined above. If people do resist such centralizing efforts of elites, then it logically follows that people are forced to work more by exogenous factors such as resource stress, by internal factors such as an elite that assumes some form of coercive power against the wishes of the nonelite population, or by the ability of nascent elites to persuade people to increase their per capita work seemingly against their self-interest.

Given Chayanov's rule of underproduction in household economies, there is room for individual aggrandizers to increase their own wealth production within their domestic group. Such household production has severe limits, however. Members of an individual household can double their efforts, and this will provide an exchange surplus that can be used to acquire a following. But the simple economic fact is that strictly internal household labor intensification is, in and of itself, insufficient to provide enough surplus wealth to maintain the political economy of any complexity beyond that of a very moderately ranked kind. This problem is, of course, a major weakness of persuasive models of cultural evolution. Why would people work more for others, and why would people voluntarily give up their political autonomy to members of their own society?

The assumption that people have to work more, or that more people have to work, to achieve surplus production must be challenged. The key to this apparent paradox is quite simple in economic terms and is of profound importance to understanding the

evolution of complex societies. *In short, an increase in surplus can be achieved not only by getting more people to work, or by getting people to work more, but by getting those people to work **differently** in a more **efficient** labor organization.*

As early as the late eighteenth century, the political economist Adam Smith had outlined the now classic argument that economic specialization (division of labor) by workers who are properly organized will produce far more in the same amount of time than individual laborers could produce on their own (Smith 1937 [1776]: 5). Increasing the number of individual, nonspecialized workers will increase production arithmetically; increasing the number of specialized workers will increase production at a much greater rate. That is, a more complex organization will result in greater productivity at the same level of labor input and without a concomitant change in technology. This phenomenon, in which a specialized work organization will produce more than the sum of the individuals working alone, is what Smith called "the productive powers of labor" and represents gains through efficiency of specialization.[6]

In modern economics, an economic efficiency through specialization occurs when the cost of one unit decreases as the capacity to produce the unit increases. In premodern economies, the same general phenomenon also holds. In household economies, for instance, economic efficiencies can be achieved when individuals specialize and take advantage of situations in which a marginal increase in labor cost produces a disproportionately large increase in output. This phenomenon works for any economic activity involving a number of distinct tasks, including the preparation of special food stuffs, alcoholic beverages, artisan goods, and the like. In short, surplus can be increased in an economy of this nature not by getting people to work more but by getting them to work differently, as specialized producers. What is new is the organization of the labor, not the nature or intensity of that labor.

The ability to get people to work differently and to maintain that new labor organization is the key to the evolution of ranked political economies. The intense competition between emergent elites seen in the ethnographic literature is inherent to this process. Elites compete for nonelites to join their factions. They fight against the centrifugal forces of household-level resistance to political authority. In short, when aggrandizers are able to overcome the inherent limits of Chayanov's rule, they are able to create more complex political economies. If successful, the result is the evolution of moderately ranked political economies, traditionally referred to as *simple chiefdoms* or *Big Man societies.*

Ethnography is replete with examples of the persuasive authority of chiefs in moderately ranked societies. In virtually all cases, the material cornerstone of chiefly authority is heightened economic production, and the means to increase that production is through more-specialized tasks using labor in different ways. The real question is: *How do you keep these people working together in societies in which authority is vested in kinship and economic autonomy is preserved in individual households?* If they work together, they all benefit as individuals, households, and as a group due to increased surplus production. But there is a cost: the loss of control over the products of their labor.

An autonomous household may produce less than a larger group, but it absolutely controls what it produces. A group of households working in a more specialized labor organization can produce far more, but each individual and household does not have any absolute guarantee that the increased wealth will be redistributed back to them. There is, therefore, a strong tendency to revert to household economic organization to protect autonomy. As ethnography and history teach us, people are willing to give up material wealth to maintain ideological norms of egalitarian society.

Emergent elite of ranked societies must find a way to keep a number of households working together to maintain these specialized economic units. I suggest here that these more complex labor organizations are maintained through complex ceremonies, specifically feasting hosted by chiefs or aspiring chiefs. The archaeological and ethnographic examples of fancy corporate architecture—temples, ballcourts, plazas, sunken courts, and the like—are the material remains of emergent elites' attempts to maintain the specialized labor organizations. Likewise, the production of elaborate art objects, the appearance of exotic materials, and the production of monuments all serve to enhance the cohesion of these organized corporate groups and prevent them from reverting to a household economic organization.

The Evolution of Rank and the Intensification of the Domestic Economy through Ceremonies and Competitive Feasting

Only one thing enrages me, when people eat slowly and a little only of the food given by the great double chief.

Neqa'penk.em, Kwakiutl war and potlatch chief, in Franz Boas, *Kwakiutl Ethnography*

Ritual is one of the primary assets used by emergent elites to persuade people to change the way in which they work to create effective specialized economies. Competitive feasting and other ceremonies, imbued with religious and ritual significance, constitute the principal means of organizing people to work differently in specialized labor organizations. The logic is straightforward: by working in a new kind of labor organization, more surplus is produced without affecting household subsistence activities and without requiring more time from the nonelite. That surplus, in turn, can be used by aspiring elites to host ceremonies and feasts that provide goods and social occasions otherwise unavailable. The creation of elaborate ritual, and its material manifestations in corporate architecture, serves to maintain the labor organization. The creation of elaborate rules of ritual behavior provides a means by which elites can guarantee that the surplus wealth will be redistributed at a later date. In short, ritual serves to sanctify the deferred reciprocal relationships between producing households and the elite who manage the more complex labor organization. From an economic perspective, everybody wins because there is greater surplus generated and available for the same effort by the nonelite, and the organizational work of the elite is rewarded by prestige, bigger factions, and the possibility of becoming even more powerful.

All societies have feasts. The feast is one of the most common features of collective human behavior. Competitive feasting, however, is different. Competitive feasting is a form of elite-directed gifting conducted with the explicit goal of obligating people's future labor. In most cases in the ethnographic record, the value reciprocated is their labor. Michael Dietler argues persuasively that one of the most important roles of drinking feasts in small-scale, premodern societies centers on the mobilization of labor through "work-party feasts." The hosted feast reinforces reciprocal obligations and other socially prescribed exchanges, particularly of labor (Dietler 1990: 366–370).

Successful feasting and ceremony serve to build up several reciprocal obligations. As these obligations add up, entire households can directly or indirectly be drawn into larger work units. The existence of such a process explains why Neqa'penk.em, quoted above, was angry at people who would not accept his gifts with alacrity: they were resisting his attempts to make them obligate themselves to him in the future.

Competitive feasting has been documented throughout the world in various historical and cultural contexts. Dietler refers to this kind of feasting as "entrepreneurial feasts" and notes that political and social power is "continually being renegotiated and contested through competitive commensal politics" (Dietler 1996: 93). In the ethnographic literature, competitive feasting and elite-directed ceremony are found in ranked, prestate societies throughout the world. They are ubiquitous.

The acquisition of exotic goods through long-distance trade is of particular value in competitive feasting. A large body of literature exists on the role of exotic and valuable items in the development of chiefly and early state societies in the Americas (Helms 1994; Marcus 1989: 192). The mechanisms whereby the acquisition of exotic goods promotes complexity are varied. These prestige good economy models focus on highly valued goods, of which exotic ones are particularly useful to elites to establish and maintain their status. As noted by Laura Junker, "Control over the distribution of prestige goods, whether obtained through foreign trade or produced locally by attached specialists, is one of the various means whereby a sociopolitical elite is able to maintain and expand its political power in chiefdoms" (Junker 1994: 230). The work of Mary Helms (especially 1979, 1994) stands as a classic modern formulation of prestige good theory in which exotic commodities are central to chiefly power in sixteenth-century Panama: "The most influential and powerful . . . [high chiefs] were those who were able to control access to such trade and travel routes [that permitted] . . . the acquisition of valued rank and status symbols" (Helms 1994: 58). Charles Spencer, describing moderately ranked societies in Amazonia, notes that gift giving is a "central strategy" (Spencer 1993). Likewise, Brumfiel and Earle (1987a), Earle (1987), and many others have used data from Mesoamerica, Polynesia, and the Andes to outline the means by which aspiring elites enhance their economic base with high-valued commodities.

In sum, ethnography and history provide many examples of elite strategies for using high-valued goods to strengthen the elites' factions and to lock nonelites into a series of obligatory reciprocities through competitive feasting that increases elite wealth and power. The model proposed here is that both potential aggrandizers and the population at large benefit from regular competitive feasting and the hosting of other ceremonies that promote and maintain specialized labor organization. The surplus derived from the more productive labor and from long-distance trade can be put back into the general population via the giving of politically significant goods in these feasts. In turn, the population at large does not have to work more, just differently, and they receive goods that they could not get otherwise. The successful elites garner larger factions, give larger feasts and ceremonies, maintain larger and more complex labor organizations, and eventually eliminate their competitors.

The Origin of State Political Economies

The basic political economic distinction between nonstate ranked and state societies is development of a coercive political control of domestic labor by an elite. In nonstate ranked societies, chiefs must persuade households to join their factions, primarily through competitive feasting, other competitive ceremonies, gifts, and other means of maintaining complex labor organizations. In state political economies, in contrast, institutionalized coercion develops. Such coercive powers of a state elite permit the elite not only to control surplus production but to reorganize domestic production at the household level. A concomitant of this new organization is the intensification of surplus production, because these coercive powers are capable of permanently overcoming the inherent limits of Chayanov's rule.

Competitive feasting in nonstate contexts is ritualized economic reciprocity orchestrated, but not necessarily controlled, by emergent elites in moderately ranked political economies. In competitive feasts, the labor of the organized is reciprocated by a redistribution of surplus wealth on special occasions. Control of domestic production is out of the bounds of the elite. In state political economies, in contrast, elites also gain control over domestic labor.

The evolution of a more complex political economy from moderately ranked societies to complex chiefdoms and states therefore requires at least four conditions: institutionalized hereditary leaders in offices with power to control household labor, a greater total surplus wealth to maintain that elite, a routine or institutionalized means of circulating that wealth, and a political economy in which elites break free of obligations to redistribute surplus wealth to nonelite. In other words, there must be sufficient surplus to support a nonsubsistence-laboring elite, and members of that elite must have a means of systematically appropriating a portion of that surplus without having to redistribute to the community as a whole. The persuasive elite strategies inherent in competitive feasting are replaced with some forms of hereditary power that can control domestic labor. Institutionalized and hereditary rank and office are among the hallmarks of state societies.[7]

The empirical record indicates that complex chiefdoms and archaic states are characterized by formal conflict between polities on a virtually constant basis. Raiding and other kinds of intergroup conflict are common in almost all agrarian societies. Once elites with coercive powers develop, conflict becomes formal and endemic. Patrick Kirch (1984) notes that warfare was ubiquitous in Polynesia in the prehistoric periods. Elsa Redmond (1994) argues the same for tribal and chiefly societies of northern South America. Numerous other archaeological studies from around the world in organizationally similar contexts have noted the widespread presence of war immediately prior to, and contemporary with, the development of complex chiefdoms and archaic states (see especially Keeley 1996 and Le Blanc 1999).

Marcus and Flannery have even argued that a necessary condition of the development of state-level societies is the successful conquest of neighboring polities by a dominant one: "We believe that states arise *when one member of a group of chiefdoms begins to take over its neighbors,* eventually turning them into subject provinces of a much larger polity" (Marcus and

Flannery 1996: 157, emphasis in original; see also Marcus 1992a, 1993). It is in a context of "chiefly cycling," or the rapid rise and fall of regional alliances from fierce competition, that states develop.

The evolution from an economy dominated by competitive ceremonialism to one in which coercive powers are successfully created by elites is, I believe, necessarily accompanied by interethnic conflict. The primary difference is a shift from war for capture of booty and prisoners to war for the acquisition of land and settled people. Territorial aggrandizing is a necessary condition for the development of state political economies.

This book examines the development of complex political economies in the Titicaca Basin as a process of the strategic decisions of individuals. As social power becomes institutionalized, some individuals persuade and coerce some of their fellows to increase domestic production above the limits inherent in Chayanov's rule. Some were successful; most were not. In this sense, the evolution of complex society in the Titicaca Basin is not viewed as the unfolding of universal processes. It is the successive renegotiating and reworking of the political and economic relationships between individuals and groups attempting to acquire power, wealth, and prestige in a particular historical, cultural, and physical environment. The degree to which the patterns of complex social development parallel those elsewhere in the world represents the degree to which the strategic decision-making behavior of individuals and groups is constrained and shaped in all premodern contexts.

The Geography and Paleoecology of the Titicaca Basin

When the Europeans first began their explorations and conquest of the vast South American continent in the early sixteenth century, they encountered the Inca empire, by far the largest state in Andean history and one of the largest preindustrial empires in world history. Tawantinsuyu, or Land of the Four Quarters, as the empire was then known, covered an area that stretched from central Ecuador to central Chile.[1] Its four imperial *suyus,* or quarters, included the vast and populous northwestern quarter of Chinchasuyu, the poorer but strategically important southeastern Continsuyu, the sparsely populated eastern forests called Andesuyu, and to the south, Collasuyu, by many accounts the jewel in the crown of the Inca empire.

Tawantinsuyu was a complex, powerful empire that conquered most of its known world in the fifteenth and sixteenth centuries, and then resisted Spanish aggression for a generation. But Inca power did not develop in a historical instant; the roots of Inca political and economic organization are found in the three thousand years of complex societies that preceded the formation of Tawantinsuyu.

In 1532, the Europeans conquered Tawantinsuyu but adopted many of their views of the Andean world from Inca intellectuals. This "Cuzco-centric" view of western South America dominated (and in some cases continues to dominate) our view of the prehistoric Andes. As Spanish intellectuals began to record the histories and lifeways of the Inca empire, the artificial image of what has been termed "the Andean culture area" crystallized in the western mind (e.g., see Wissler 1922; Bennett 1946a). This area essentially corresponded to the boundaries of the Inca state, a territory populated by hundreds of distinct ethnic groups and polities. Political control was tenuous in many areas, and like all premodern empires, the Inca continually fought against centrifugal forces, particularly among the various *naciones* and smaller political groups within its boundaries.

As in most expansive states, the Inca historians and intellectuals promoted the myth of an underlying unity of their empire as part of the ideological component of their imperial strategy. It was in the interest of the Inca state, as well as that of its successor, the Spanish state in the Americas, to promote the ideal of a cultural area integrated by inherent qualities that transcended ethnicity, polity, and other cultural boundaries. It was in this context that the view of a monolithic cultural area known as the Andes originated. Up to the present day, the old boundaries of the Inca state have profoundly affected the way in which we conceptualize the culture and prehistory of western South America.

Had the European conquest of the Americas taken place seven hundred or so years earlier, we would have been left with a very different concept of western South American prehistory and culture. Around A.D. 700–900, the two great states of Wari and Tiwanaku dominated the political landscape of the central Andes. With few exceptions, each of these controlled distinct populations, most likely speaking different languages and having very different cultural histories. Wari was centered in the Ayacucho Valley of the Andean central highlands.[2] The dominant language of the central highlands today is Quechua, with its related dialects. Quechua was also the largest of the *lenguas generales* of the central highlands in the immediate Prehispanic and early Colonial past (Mannheim 1991: 37). It is probable that the Wari peoples spoke a form of proto-Quechua (Bird, Browman, and Durbin 1988: 187) (see map 3.1).[3]

The great counterpart of Wari in the south was known as Tiwanaku.[4] Flourishing during the great period of imperial growth known as the Middle Horizon (circa A.D. 500–1100), Tiwanaku was cen-

tered in the Lake Titicaca basin, the demographic and cultural center of the area that we refer to as the south-central Andes. The south-central Andes is culturally distinct from the central Andes to the north and the extreme southern Andes. This typology was developed in the late 1970s and formalized by Luis Lumbreras in his 1981 book *Arqueología de la América Andina.* The basic principle is that the peoples of the south-central Andes shared political, historical, artistic, and economic traditions that, in their totality, distinguished the region from the others in prehistoric western South America (e.g., Stanish 2001b; but see Burger, Chávez, and Chávez 2000: 269–270 for a different perspective).

Today, and in the Early Colonial and protohistoric periods, the dominant indigenous language of the Titicaca region is Aymara, another great *lengua general* of Peru. Along with Aymara, two other important languages were spoken in this region, including the general language known as Pukina (Browman 1994; La Barre 1946, 1948; Mannheim 1991: 34, 48), now virtually extinct, and a less extensive language called Uruquilla. Both were certainly much more widely distributed in the past and concentrated in the circum-Titicaca region. It is probable that the Tiwanaku peoples spoke proto-Aymara and/or some ancestral form of Pukina or Uruquilla.[5]

The two states of Wari and Tiwanaku shared some artistic motifs, as evidenced in their ceramic and textile arts (e.g., see Cook 1994). These similarities have led some to conclude that the two states were expressions of the same cultural and/or political phenomenon. Apart from a general sharing of some Andean iconography, however, Wari and Tiwanaku were very different. In political terms, they were independent states that controlled distinct territories with people speaking different languages (e.g., see Matos M. 1990: 530–532; Schreiber 1987, 1992). They also created very distinctive political economies in their successful efforts to expand out of their core territories.

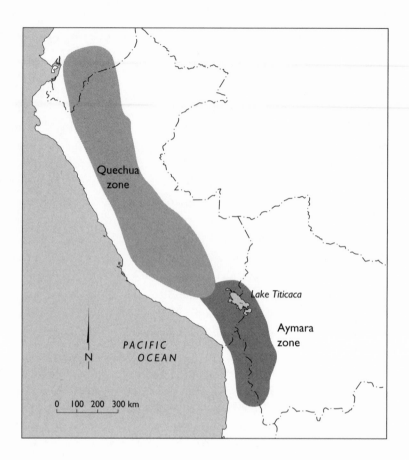

MAP 3.1. Quechua and Aymara cultural areas in the Andes.

In short, the concept of the Andes as a single or uniform culture area with an inherent unity is the product of a particular historical moment, a politically astute strategy promoted by the Inca and Spanish states. Failure to accurately perceive the relative historical and cultural autonomy of the two regions has marginalized the achievements of the people of the Titicaca area, particularly the ancestors of the Aymara speakers.

It is much more accurate to view Prehispanic Andean South America as three distinct cultural geographical areas: (1) the Quechua-dominated central and northern highlands, (2) the Aymara/Pukina-dominated south-central Andes and southern coast, and (3) the north and north-central coast dominated by Mochic and related speakers. From this perspective, it is inappropriate to force an interpretation of the Titicaca Basin into a framework developed for the central Andes as a whole. This book assesses the archaeology of the region as a distinct culture area in its own right, albeit one with occasional cultural exchanges to the north.

The Titicaca Basin Environment

The cold, windy, and stark environment of the Titicaca Basin strikes even the casual observer as an inhospitable environment for the development of complex agrarian societies. This image of the region was deeply entrenched in the academic literature and popular

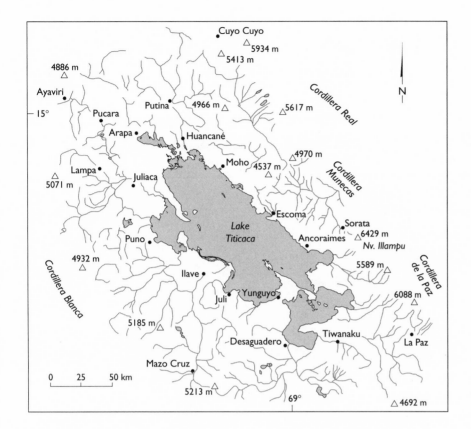

mind by the end of the nineteenth century and continues to the present day: "A bleak, frigid land . . . it seemingly was the last place from which one might expect a culture to develop" (von Hagen 1959: 272). Or, as Hewett put it even more bluntly: "It [Lake Titicaca] is clearly above the climatic zone in which the human species can attain to a physical, mental, or cultural average" (Hewett 1969 [1939]: 94).[6]

In reality, the Titicaca Basin (see map 3.2) is highly productive, particularly in regard to those commodities most valued by Prehispanic peoples. Furthermore, paleoecological studies indicate that prehistoric climates were different than modern ones, and that climate changes have had substantial effects on the region's cultures. In this chapter, I will review the modern and prehistoric ecology of the Titicaca

region, isolating the environmental factors that are central in modeling the development of the region's complex societies.

The Titicaca Basin is classified as an intertropical climatic zone, based on its geographical location and high solar radiation (Dejoux and Iltis 1991: 11). However, its high altitude and concomitant montane qualities, such as low ambient temperatures and low humidity, alter its tropical character toward typical alpine conditions. Mean annual precipitation in the Titicaca Basin varies from approximately 500 to 1,500 millimeters per year (Roche et al. 1991: 87). Map 3.3 (adapted from Roche et al. 1991) shows the distribution of isohyets in the basin based on modern climate data. In general, total rainfall is higher in the north basin than it is in the south. Three areas in the

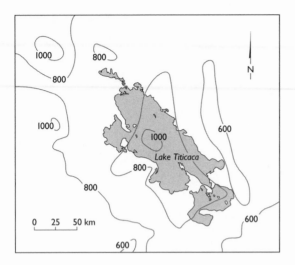

MAP 3.3. Rainfall isohyets in the Titicaca Basin. Adapted from Roche et al. 1991.

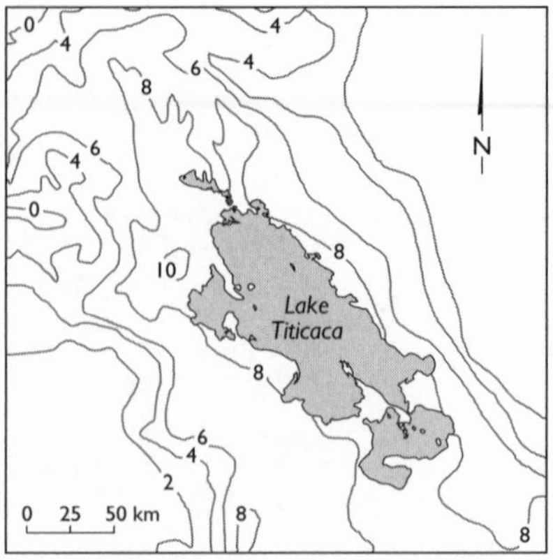

MAP 3.4. Mean temperature gradients in the Titicaca Basin, in degrees Centigrade. Adapted from Roche et al. 1991.

region have annual rainfall of at least 1,000 millimeters per year, all north of 16° latitude.

Relative monthly rainfall patterns, in contrast, are fairly consistent across the region (Roche et al. 1991: 89). The wettest months are December through March, inclusive, with precipitation of more than one hundred millimeters per month common during the rainy season. The driest months are June through September, inclusive, with some months virtually rainless. According to Roche et al. (1991: 86), median annual temperatures vary between 7 and 10 degrees Celsius. The lake itself has a mediating effect on the cold, and median temperatures are often higher than 8 degrees Celsius at the lake edge, higher than would be expected if the mass of water was not present (Boulange and Aquize 1981). As a general rule, temperatures are warmer near the lake edge (see map 3.4).

The Titicaca region is a huge geological basin that sits between two mountain ranges, the Cordillera Real and the Cordillera Blanca. Lake Titicaca is approximately 8,500 square kilometers in size. There is the large lake, referred to as Titicaca or Lago Mayor,

and the small lake, called Huiñamarca. Within Lago Mayor are a number of islands, some of which are quite large, including Amantaní, Taquile, and the Island of the Sun. Huiñamarca has a number of inhabited islands as well, including Intja, Pariti, Taquiri, Chipi, and Qhehuaya (see Solc 1969 for an ethnography of these latter islands). The lowest part of the region is the surface of the lake itself, at 3,810 m.a.s.l. (meters above sea level). The south-central altiplano zone toward Lake Poopó is slightly lower in elevation. The vast bulk of the Titicaca region is above 3,800 meters. The total hydrological drainage covers about 50,000 square kilometers, and the cultural influences of the lake cultures extend even farther into the Amazonian side of the cordilleras.

Several geographical classifications exist for the region. I generally follow the work of Pulgar Vidal (n.d.), who divides the Titicaca Basin into two broad agricultural and ecological regions called the *suni* and *puna*. The suni is between 3,800 and 4,000 m.a.s.l. The higher and drier puna is between 4,000 and 4,800 m.a.s.l. The suni represents the upper limit of plant agriculture; the puna is a grazing zone for the extensive camelid herds owned by many Titicaca Basin peoples.

Pulgar Vidal (n.d.: 95–98) notes the large variety of agricultural products grown in the suni, including many varieties of tubers, legumes, and chenopods. Flores Ochoa and Paz Flores (1983) have documented the use in the suni zone of *qocha,* small, water-filled depressions or lakes in the altiplano used by modern farmers and herders. It is likely that they were used by Prehispanic populations as well. The lake itself provides an important additional economic resource base on a scale unique in the Andes.

The major plant agricultural product of both zones is the potato, which can be grown up to the snowline (Pulgar Vidal n.d.: 111). Optimal yields occur in the warmer suni zones and in the lower puna. Other important plant foods include *olluco* or *ullucu,* oca, quinoa, *mashwa,* and *tarwi* (Hastorf 1993: 110–117). The most important animal product of the puna is the camelid, particularly the llama and the alpaca. Camelids provide wool and meat and serve as pack animals. The virtually unique capacity of the Titicaca Basin to support such large camelid herds has contributed to its position as a major center of civilization in the Americas.

There are other classifications of altiplano geography. Carl Troll (1968: 48) divides the higher vegetative region into the *puna brava* and the puna. The Troll classification is an ecological one, useful for the study of plant communities. In the puna brava (between 4,500 and 5,300 m.a.s.l.) vegetation is intermittent, composed of plants adapted to a short growing season (Graf 1981: 353). The puna is between 3,800 and 4,500 m.a.s.l. in the Troll classification. Another classification by Tosi (1960) lists eight zones for the Titicaca region, a typology based on the Holdridge system.

The classifications of Pulgar Vidal, Troll, and so forth were not designed for anthropological research. The basic puna/suni distinction of Pulgar Vidal is a good first approximation of the broad agricultural/

pastoral zones and is the most useful of the existing classifications. From a cultural perspective, however, a variety of distinct geographical zones are important in understanding the region's prehistory. A very useful alternative to the ecological classifications is the indigenous categories of land. Years of fieldwork have reinforced the observation that Aymara farmers and herders possess an extremely sophisticated and subtle understanding of their environment that differs in important aspects from those of professional agronomists and geographers.

Perhaps the first published attempt at constructing a typology of soils and land types was that of Harry Tschopik, whose pioneering work on Aymara ethnography was conducted in the 1940s and 1950s. In an important section in his review of Aymara culture (1946: 513), Tschopik distinguishes four types of arable land classified by the Aymara farmers themselves. Although he worked in the immediate area outside Chucuito, numerous text references indicate that he accumulated data from throughout the region. The four land use categories are as follows:

1. Valley-bottom fields. Tschopik's informants said that these soils are the best in the region. They are located at the base of the many *quebradas* (or gullies) that cut the hills toward the lake.

2. Lake-edge fields. These fields are considered to have the second-best soils for agriculture. Canals are used to water these fields today.

3. Hillside fields. These extensive areas have thin and rocky soils, according to Tschopik's informants. These areas are heavily terraced today and are cultivated on a long-fallow system.

4. The flat pampas. These areas away from the lake shore are considered the worst soils, according to Tschopik, who says that irrigation is not practiced in this region. However, working some fifty years later, I have noticed canals in such areas,[7] although they are used today largely for animal pasturing.

There are very few cultivated fields in the flat pampas, except for those near rivers. The canals provide water to pasture land and for some marginal agriculture.

Tschopik's land/soil classification does not take into account the use of raised fields as described by later scholars (Erickson 1988, 1993, 1994; Rivera Sundt 1989; Smith, Denevan, and Hamilton 1968). Raised fields are labor-intensive constructions built in swampy land to improve planting conditions. Essentially, they are large mounds of earth raised above water level and designed to provide a moist planting surface. Raised fields, which were built in various forms, were concentrated along the lake edge, along rivers, and in the low pampas near the lake and in the river floodplains.[8]

There is no indigenous use of raised-field agriculture today, and this explains Tschopik's silence about this technique. However, archaeological evidence indicates extensive use of this technology in the past. Factoring in the use of raised-field agriculture alters the optimal land use categories for Prehispanic populations. According to Tschopik, the flat pampas away from the fields, for instance, are the worst land for agriculture, but they would be the most productive if converted to raised-field agriculture according to work on experimental raised fields (e.g., Erickson 1993). It is apparent that the finest lands in the absence of raised fields, the valley-bottom and lake-edge areas, are restricted in areal extent and confined to the zones near the lake.

Ludovico Bertonio's dictionary provides an insight into the linguistic categories of Aymara geography and farming as used in the early seventeenth century. The Aymara language distinguished among several different types of landscapes based largely upon climate, as seen in the appendix. Bertonio also lists a number of terms for different soil types and farming practices. There is a much greater variety and complexity of land types in Bertonio's dictionary than in Tschopik's typology. Some of Bertonio's definitions and farming terms, particularly those for land or soil *(tierra),* include very specific references to soil quality, such as its ability to be plowed, whether raised fields can be used successfully, soil fertility, porosity, and the like.

A recent study by Onofre (in Stanish et al. 1997) provides a typology of soil and land types by Aymara farmers in the Juli area. Onofre defined nine types based on several factors. Table 3.1 outlines six of these types and reveals a very subtle and sophisticated understanding of agricultural land and soil by contemporary Aymara farmers. The perception and the reality of these land types likely were important settlement determinants in the past, as they are today.

The following typology (see table 3.2) of geographical zones was developed to address archaeological problems using the broad outlines of the Pulgar Vidal system, the work of Onofre, and field observations around the Titicaca Basin. The typology uses several criteria, including topography, human land use, altitude, and vegetation. The typology serves to emphasize the great diversity of the geographical zones in the Titicaca Basin and is, in my opinion, the best way to define the environmental context of the development of complex society in the region.

· Low grassland pampas. These flat plains with a thick grass cover are located in the suni and are usually found next to the lake. Low grassland pampas are the prime areas for raised-field agriculture, particularly where rivers are not entrenched. Water is essential to the successful construction of raised fields, and riverine fields are highly productive. In pampas without rivers, or where rivers are entrenched, raised-field segments are associated with canals, aqueducts, and other water delivery systems.[9] Pampa lands often have qocha, particularly on the northwest side of the lake. Binford and Kolata (1996: 49) note both are

TABLE 3.1
Soil Types According to Aymara Informants

Factor	Type A	Type B	Type C	Type D	Type E	Type F
COLOR	Red	Black/gray	Brown/gray	Clear gray/ brown	White	Brown
TEXTURE	Clayey	Clayey	Sandy loam	Sandy	Clayey with rocks	Clayey with rocks
WATER RETENTION	Good/bad	Regular	Bad	Regular/poor	Regular	Poor
PRESENCE OF ROCKS	Few	Few	Few	Few	Few	Many
WILD PLANTS[a]	Kora, kentu, cebadilla, chijchipa, muni muni, ichu, amicaraya	Kora, muni muni	Kora, llapa	Kora, totora, kentu, muni muni, cebadilla	Kora, chijchipa	All types of wild plants
GEOGRAPHY	Low areas or pampas, hillsides	Low areas or pampas, quebradas	Terraces, quebradas, pampas	Pampas, lake edge, river edge	All areas	High areas, hills; rarely in pampas
CULTIVARS	Papa dulce, maize, oats, vegetables	Papa negra, waka lajra, beans, barley	Pakoya, chikilla, papa negra, beans	Barley, beans, papa blanca	Papa amarga (luk'i)	Mainly oca
SOIL QUALITY	Good	Good	Regular	Regular	Poor	Regular/poor
CLIMATE	Temperate/ cold	Temperate/ cold	Cold	Temperate/ cold	Cold	Cold
FERTILITY	Regular/good	Good	Regular	Regular	Poor	Regular/poor
RAISED FIELDS	Few	Few	None	Many	Some	None

SOURCE: Onofre in Stanish et al. 1997.

[a] These wild plants are herbs or industrial plants that have economic value to the Aymara farmers.

TABLE 3.2

Agro-Ecological Zones in the Titicaca Basin

Low grassland pampas
High grassland pampas
Bofedales
Desert pampas
Riverine environments
Terraced hills
Nonterraced hillsides
Valley pockets
Islands
Littorals
Yungas
Reed beds *(totorales)*

used for agriculture and also as sources of drinking water for pasturing animals. Qocha are very important for agriculture today, and archaeological survey indicates that they were important settlement determinants in the past (Albarracin-Jordan and Mathews 1990).

Pampas are today used as primary grazing areas. Near the lake, most of the herds consist of cattle, sheep, and goats, all European introductions. Away from the lake in the highland pampas, people graze camelids as well. In H. Tschopik's study (1946) referred to above, pampas are considered to be the least productive for agriculture, possessing the worst soils and poorest growing conditions. This was not the information provided to Onofre, however. In his study, farmers recognized two types of soils that occur in the pampas, as well as in other areas, that are the best for cultivation. Under the appropriate conditions, pampas can be converted into the most productive agricultural zones with raised-field agriculture. The major low grasslands in the Titicaca region include the Pucara area and the Huatta pampas in the north, the Ilave Peninsula and Acora

plains in the west, the large Pomata and Zepita pampas in the southwest, and the Desaguadero, Guaqui, and Koani pampas in the south.[10]

· High grassland pampas. These pampas are higher in the puna, away from the immediate lake region, above 4,000 m.a.s.l. They tend to be rolling hills with low grass cover and are often quite dry unless near water sources. They are found throughout the Titicaca puna. Grassland pampas are sparsely populated today, as they were in the past, but they are principal areas of animal pasturing.

· *Bofedales.* These are small areas of swampy land created by collections of groundwater. They have stands of sedges and grasses and are primary grazing areas. They were favored locations for the Archaic hunting and gathering populations and continue to be very rich and coveted for pasture and settlement (Aldenderfer 1989). Bofedales are found in both the puna and suni zones. In the lower areas, around 3,800–3,900 m.a.s.l., the bofedales are extremely productive pasture areas.

· Desert pampas. These are found in the south of the Titicaca Basin, particularly south of Desaguadero, where there is substantially less rainfall and other water than in the rest of the basin. Characterized by sparse stands of grasses in a sandy topsoil, desert pampas are unproductive. Economic activities are restricted to areas of qochas and in restricted areas where springs occasionally flow from hillsides. Prehistoric population densities were low in these environments, as they are today.

· Riverine environments. Several major rivers and a number of smaller ones flow into the Titicaca Basin. These riverine environments are very productive. There are relict raised fields on nearly all of the rivers in the north, west, and south Titicaca Basin, and some limited field areas on the east side of the basin as well. In particular, the Ilave, Desaguadero, Arapa, Illpa, Koani, and Tiwanaku Rivers and the Pomata pampa have substantial raised-field segments. The surveys of Mark Aldenderfer and associates indicate that the river environments were prime areas of Archaic settlements prior to around 2000 B.C. These continued to be areas of intense human settlement and land use through the later periods.

· Terraced hills. These areas represent the largest total territory of the habitable zones in the Titicaca Basin. The vast majority of the habitation areas are restricted to the hills below 4,000 or 4,100 m.a.s.l. In particular, the hills near or adjacent to the lake are most popular. The terraced hills produce a wide variety of crops, particularly tubers and grains. Houses are also built on the terraces, with small hamlets and single-family households built adjacent to agricultural fields. According to Onofre's study, the most fertile land is found on the low hillside, an observation consistent with contemporary settlement patterns. The terraced hills were optimal from one perspective: they were useful for both agriculture and habitation.

· Nonterraced hillsides. Most of the Titicaca Basin is ringed with hillsides that have never been terraced. One reason is the simple topographical fact that many are too steep, but other factors include erosion, an orientation bad for solar radiation, poor soils, and distance from water. These areas are used for pasture today, as they were in the past, and have little human settlement.

· Valley pockets. Small, well-watered areas in the terraced hill zone, these pockets are occasionally protected from chilling winds and are naturally oriented to capture solar energy. The topography is often conducive to irrigation, and springs can be exploited for a relatively constant water flow. As a result, these are prime agricultural areas that sustain one of the most valued crops—maize—as well as other altiplano plant foods. Today, maize-grow-

ing regions in the Titicaca Basin include the Island of the Sun, Amantaní Island, Taquile Island, Ichu, areas on the Tiquina Peninsula, areas on the Capachica Peninsula, areas near Moho, and areas near Conima. Nearly all of the maize-growing areas are valley pockets, which inevitably contain the highest density of human settlement today, as they did in the prehistoric and historic past.

The existence of maize-growing areas in the Titicaca Basin remains intriguing given that the region is above the generally assumed altitude limits of maize agriculture. In the fifteenth century, the Little Ice Age set in, beginning a climatic regime colder than the present regime. Prior to this time, the climate would have been more conducive to maize agriculture. The Toledo Tasa, conducted in the first half of the 1570s, contains several references to Titicaca Basin towns paying tribute in maize, including Achacache, Guaqui, Huarina, Pucarani, Carabuco, Arapa, Saman,[11] Asillo, Azángaro, Vilque, and Taraco (Cook 1975).[12]

The Tasa tribute lists vary town by town and were adjusted for the availability of local products. It is highly unlikely that these towns were collecting maize from lower altitudes and then sending it off as tribute. First, most Titicaca Basin towns, including the seats of the principal caciques, did not have to provide maize even though they were in a better position to acquire it through political means. Second, the areas outside the Titicaca Basin where maize grew in abundance, such as Sama, Moquegua, and so forth, were listed separately, with their respective tribute lists. In other words, the evidence suggests that several basin towns were able to grow maize in regular quantities and provide a portion as tribute to the Crown. It is most likely that all of these towns grew their maize in the fertile pockets.

· Islands. There are several large islands and dozens of smaller ones in the lake. The Island of the Sun, Taquile, Amantaní, Pariti, Paco, and other islands are extremely productive due to the ameliorating effect of the large body of water on the islands' microclimates. The surrounding water elevates the ambient temperature and allows for richer growing conditions. All the large islands are populated today, and all that have been investigated had substantial prehistoric settlements as well.

- Littorals. The immediate lake shore is the most heavily occupied area today, as it was in the past. Littorals provide lacustrine resources such as fish, *totora* reed, and other products. In the past, when boat transportation was so important, many lakeside areas also served as ports for the exchange of goods and movement of people. Among the richest locations for settlement were the mouths of rivers, where they discharged into the lake.

- *Yungas.* In Bertonio's dictionary (1956 [1612]: Bk. 1: 448), the word *yunca [yunga]* is defined as a "land in a hot climate," and the term is used to refer to the lowlands in both the eastern and western peripheries of the Titicaca Basin where warm-weather crops can be grown. The valleys of Moquegua, Sama, and Lluta on the western slopes, as well as the Larecaja region of Omasuyu to the east, were often referred to as yungas. On the eastern side, a low tree and high shrub forest can be found within one or two days' walk from the lake. On the western side, warmer climates are found around 2,500 m.a.s.l. Of vital economic importance to the lake area cultures throughout prehistory and history, these areas were the source of lowland products such as coca, maize, wood, and hallucinogens, as well as other foods and products.

- Reed beds. Totora reed beds represent a very significant basin resource (see pages 62–66). Reeds are a major industrial plant used for house roof and wall construction, matting, and boat building, and the roots, referred to in the sixteenth century as *chullu,*

are edible. In a few rare instances, totora beds are used as residential areas, such as the floating islands of the Uru populations in the bay of Puno. Historic information suggests that lake-dwelling peoples were found in the sixteenth century, although there are no data to indicate whether they existed in the prehistoric periods as well.

Paleoecology

The climate of the Titicaca Basin has not been stable. Even in the twentieth century, the lake level fluctuated more than six meters (Roche et al. 1991: 84). One of the principal reasons for such fluctuations is the lake's relatively large drainage area. Although Lake Titicaca itself is approximately 8,500 square kilometers, the entire surface area of the drainage that feeds the lake is almost 50,000 square kilometers. Therefore, small fluctuations in rainfall and other hydrological patterns in this vast area can have a substantial effect on the lake level. Another factor may be tectonic shifts in the basin, which can affect drainage patterns and total water inflows from their sources. Bills et al. (1994), for instance, discovered extremely high levels of tilting in a study of the shorelines of the ancient Lake Minchin, a Pleistocene lake that once covered a vast area that included modern Lake Titicaca.

The overall pattern in the central altiplano is a net tilt upward in the east and downward in the north (Bills et al. 1994: 295). This is consistent with my observations of river entrenchment and meandering in the Titicaca Basin today. This geological factor is probably very important for understanding the patterning of raised-field abandonment. These tectonic processes may also help to explain some of the lake-level fluctuations, although there has been little work on this question to date.

A number of paleoecological reconstructions of the Titicaca Basin climate, lake levels, and vegetation

TABLE 3.3

Wetter and Drier Periods, A.D. 540–1984

Drier Periods	Wetter Periods
1720–1860	1870–1984
1250–1310	1500–1720
650–730	760–1040
570–610	610–650
540–560	

SOURCE: Thompson et al. 1985: 973.

have been created using various distinct data sets. Unfortunately, the methodologies of these studies are not directly comparable, and there are some discrepancies among these paleoecological models.

Data on the paleoecology of the Titicaca region come from a number of projects. First, the Quelccaya ice cap was cored by the Byrd Polar Research Center at Ohio State (Shimada et al. 1991; Thompson et al. 1985; Thompson et al. 1988; Thompson and Mosely-Thompson 1987). The Quelccaya glacier is roughly midway between Cuzco and the northern side of Lake Titicaca, close enough to the Titicaca Basin to allow direct reconstructions of the paleoclimate of the region. Second, the ORSTOM-UMSA[13] project (Wirrmann, Mourguiart, and Oliveira Almeida 1990; Wirrmann, Ybert, and Mourguiart 1991; Ybert 1991) used a series of limnological cores sunk into "the Little Lake" in the southern end of Lake Titicaca, referred to as Lake Huiñamarca, plus one in the bay of Yunguyu.[14] These data bear directly on the ancient climate and lake levels of the Titicaca Basin. Third, the Proyecto Wila Jawira included the coring of Huiñamarca to obtain limnological data on the lake itself to assess correlations between changes in climate and human land use (Binford, Brenner, and Leyden 1996). Fourth, cores taken from post-glacial peat bogs in

higher elevations of the basin by Kurt Graf (1981) were used to derive conclusions about the regional climate through time.

The Quelccaya researchers report that their data are accurate to approximately twenty years (Shimada et al. 1991: 261). Thompson et al. (1985) have reconstructed wet and dry periods from approximately A.D. 540 to the present using the Quelccaya core data. The "standard" is the present day, so a wet or dry period represents a time in which precipitation was substantially greater or less than at present. These data indicate a series of alternating wet/dry periods of around one hundred to two hundred years' duration throughout their sequence. Most significant for the Titicaca region, there were wetter periods in the first half of the seventh century A.D. and from the mid-eighth century to the mid-eleventh century (Ortloff and Kolata 1993: 199). The latter part of the seventh century was drier, and another appreciably drier period occurred from the mid-thirteenth to the beginning of the fourteenth century A.D. (see table 3.3).

The ORSTOM-UMSA project has provided useful interpretations and data on Holocene lake-level changes. Wirrmann, Mourguiart, and Oliveira Almeida (1990: 119–123) and Wirrmann, Ybert, and Mourguiart (1991: 65–67) summarize their reconstructions of lake levels based upon cores from four stations. From 8500 to 5700 B.C., there was a severe lowering of the lake relative to its present level, suggesting drought.[15] From 5700 to 5250 B.C., the lake was even lower, at least fifty meters below present levels. During this period of severe drought, the lake size was 42 percent less than at present, and the volume was about 30 percent less. From 5250 to 2000 B.C., these researchers report a gradual rise in the lake level to around ten to forty-five meters below present levels at the end of this period. From 2000 B.C. to A.D. I, the lake rose to approximately ten meters below present levels. The lake did not reach modern levels

TABLE 3.4

Periods of Low Lake Levels

A.D. 1100–1500

A.D. 1–300

400–200 B.C.

900–800 B.C.

SOURCE: Reported by Abbott, Binford, Brenner, and Kelts 1997: 169.

until after A.D. 1 and before A.D. 1000, according to these climatic reconstructions.[16] A potential problem with these data is that the ORSTOM-UMSA project relied almost exclusively on cores from the Little Lake (Huiñamarca). As a result, there are some difficulties in extrapolating these data to the large lake and the region as a whole.

Kolata's Proyecto Wila Jawira has provided additional limnological data useful for paleoclimatic reconstructions (Abbott, Binford, Brenner, and Kelts 1997; Abbott, Seltzer, Kelts, and Southon 1997; Binford et al. 1997; Binford and Brenner 1989; Leyden 1989). The authors report that these data are consistent with the Quelccaya glacial data (Binford, Brenner, and Leyden 1996: 95; Ortloff and Kolata 1993: 200; Kolata and Ortloff 1996b), although one major discrepancy is with the 7700–3650 B.P. period. Here, the ORSTOM data suggest a significantly lower lake, but the data presented by Binford, Brenner, and Leyden (1996: 95) suggest otherwise. Most significant for our discussion here is that the Wila Jawira group defined several major periods in which the lake was significantly lower than the overflow level and during which drought conditions obtained. Periods of drought, as reported by recent paleolimnological work, are illustrated in table 3.4.

A major paleoclimatic event detected by this work is a drought that began around A.D. 1100. As we will see, this post–A.D. 1000 drought is considered the proximate cause of Tiwanaku agricultural collapse by

some scholars (Binford et al. 1997; Ortloff and Kolata 1993; Kolata and Ortloff 1996b). In fact, Kolata and Ortloff and Binford et al. argue that this drought was so severe that it was a major factor in the collapse of the Tiwanaku state itself.

David Browman (1986: 11) synthesized many of these sources of climatic data into a reconstruction of wet/dry periods from 1450 B.C. (radiocarbon years). His reconstruction corresponds well with the Quelccaya data, with one discrepancy: Browman states that the period from A.D. 600–950 was wetter than the modern climate, and the Quelccaya researchers describe a dry period from A.D. 650–730. This minor discrepancy could be a result of scale; that is, the glacial core constructions include shorter periods that fit within the larger blocks of time suggested by Browman.

For some time periods, the paleoclimate reconstructions are generally consistent. There is general agreement that around four thousand years ago, the Titicaca Basin was wetter. Argollo and Mourguiart (2000) suggest that wetter conditions, relative to the present, began around 3,900 years ago and have continued to the present day (and see Mourguiart et al. 1998). Similar conclusions are presented by Talbi et al. (1999), who argue that the most arid conditions existed between 6000 and 2000 B.C., with rainfall 18 percent lower than at present.

Another area of agreement is the Little Ice Age. The existence of an appreciably colder period during the sixteenth through the nineteenth centuries is accepted by many paleoecologists (Thompson and Mosely-Thompson 1987: 105–107; Thompson et al. 1988: 763) and carries important implications for modeling the later prehistory of the Titicaca region. Thompson and Mosely-Thompson (1987: 105) suggest that the onset of this period began around A.D. 1490 and peaked around the 1520s. They argue that precipitation increased at the onset of the Little Ice Age around 1490 but that the colder temperatures did not begin until the 1520s. Both the beginning and end of the Little Ice Age were very abrupt, as indicated by distinct and dramatic increases in the climate indices in the cores. The end of the Little Ice Age is placed at 1880, when the climate began to warm again (Thompson et al. 1986). According to this reconstruction, the early sixteenth century would have been warmer than today, and beginning in the first third of the 1500s, temperatures would have become progressively cooler until the nineteenth century.

Some historical data also indicate that the sixteenth century was warmer than today's climate. As mentioned above, the Toledo Tasa, compiled in the mid-1570s, lists several northern Titicaca Basin towns as providing maize as tribute to the Spanish administration. The climate must have been warmer than it is today to permit maize cultivation in this region, given the scale suggested by the historical data. Archaeological evidence is still sparse, but Bermann (1994: 185) discovered maize kernels in Tiwanaku contexts. Although these could have been imported, their discovery in nonelite domestic contexts raises the possibility of maize cultivation at the site.

The cultural significance of this cold and wet period is that it began slightly after the conquest of the area by the Inca state. The relative abruptness of the onset and the severity of the climate change represent an altered ecological context for Inca state expansion from that found in the earlier Altiplano or Late Intermediate period. The existence of a drought around one thousand years ago seems to be fairly noncontroversial as well. Most paleoclimatic reconstructions describe this as a drier period.

It is clear that much more work must be conducted on the paleoclimate of the Titicaca Basin. With some important exceptions, the contradictory interpretations, the generally overly long time periods, and the high degree of standard error make these data useful for only broad correlations. The farther we go back in time, the less certain are the reconstructions. These data and interpretations, although very compelling, must be considered preliminary and subject to future revision.

The Ethnography and Ethnohistory of the Titicaca Basin

The great early Spanish historian Pedro de Cieza de León wrote that the Inca province of the south-central Andes, known as the Collao, was one of the richest and most densely populated provinces in all of Peru. The heartland of the Collao is the Titicaca Basin. During the sixteenth century, the early Spanish historians referred to a number of peoples and languages in the region, the most notable being the Aymara, Pukina, Quechua, and Uruquilla. In this chapter, I discuss the ethnography of the Titicaca region and describe the most important aspects of political, social, and economic organization and lifeways as they relate to archaeological interpretation. This chapter also reviews the extensive knowledge of the protohistoric and historic Aymara "kingdoms" that scholars have assembled over the last five hundred years. Finally, I examine the linguistic, historical, and ethnographic evidence surrounding the

other, less extensive languages or ethnic groups relevant to understanding the region's prehistoric past.

Scholars who have worked among the Aymara and Quechua peoples of the Titicaca Basin are continually confronted with the richness of their extraordinary cultures, which would be impossible to convey in one book, let alone a single chapter. In this section, I therefore confine the discussion to those features of Aymara and Quechua culture (focusing largely on the former) that are relevant to helping us understand and interpret the prehistoric political economy of the basin's cultures. This direct historical approach has its dangers, of course, and must be used with caution. However, an examination of the archaeological record as well as the contemporary and historical past indicates that much can be learned by combining both sources of information (Marcus and Flannery 1994).

Another focus of the chapter is the historical linguistic work that has been conducted in the region over the past several generations. This rich body of linguistic data and theory, of which archaeologists have failed to take full advantage, is an invaluable resource for archaeological model building for the period from at least A.D. 1100 onward, and possibly before. As I will demonstrate below, although some historical linguistic reconstructions of the protohistoric past differ sharply from archaeological ones, these data sets are inherently compatible and should be combined to produce better models.

Historical Documents for the Titicaca Basin

Several sixteenth-century documents provide important information on the economy, society, political structure, language, and culture of the Titicaca region immediately after the Spanish Conquest. Of course, the general histories of Bernabé Cobo, Cieza, Guamán Poma, and others are invaluable when we control for and understand the effect of Inca and Spanish biases. Other documents include the official inspections, or *visitas,* conducted by the Spanish Crown. Two of these are particularly useful: the Diez de San Miguel Visita and the Francisco Toledo Tasa.[1] Another document, *Historia del Santuario de Nuestra Señora de Copacabana* by Ramos Gavilán, written in 1621, also provides important data from the Copacabana Peninsula region.

The official report of a royal inspection of the Lupaqa province made by Garci Diez de San Miguel, an official of the Spanish Crown, represents one of the finest Spanish Colonial–period documents of the Andes. In many ways, this Visita represents the first comprehensive ethnography of a major ethnic group in the Titicaca Basin. Arriving in the basin in 1566–1567, Diez de San Miguel sought to document the status of the people in one of the principal señoríos, or principalities, of the region.

The Lupaqa were one of the few ethnic groups in the Andes not granted to individual Spaniards in encomienda (Murra 1964). This rich and powerful indigenous polity was maintained as a Crown holding directly under royal control and protection. Unlike other native populations under the encomienda system, the Lupaqa paid taxes directly to the Spanish Crown and therefore maintained a relatively high degree of autonomy (Stanish 2000). This economic fact underlies the purpose of the Visita: Garci Diez de San Miguel was sent to record the population of ablebodied tributaries and determine earnings from herding, farming, and other economic activities in order to assess their capacity to pay taxes (Diez de San Miguel 1964 [1567]: x, 5, 10).

Pertinent information in the Visita includes declarations of all subject towns to Martín Curi and Martín Cusi, the *principales* of the Hanansaya and Hurinsaya moieties. Other types of socioeconomic information include a list of all ayllus in the subject populations, the number of Catholic priests in each town, payments to the Church, the nature of tribute during the Inca occupation, the size of camelid holdings, earnings from various economic activities, and the resources controlled by various elite.

The Visita provides an excellent window on the political and economic structure of the Lupaqa region about a generation after the Conquest. Of particular value are the differences in answers given by the Spaniards and the local Aymara elite. All documents, including the Visita, are replete with subjective biases. Diez de San Miguel was a tax collector, and the Aymara elite were trying to hide their wealth during the inspection and at the same time exaggerating the resources and influence they had enjoyed during the Inca and pre-Inca periods. Furthermore, many of the Spaniards were guilty of theft, battery against Indians, and cheating the Spanish Crown as well. Individuals thus displayed their self-interest and represented themselves in the best light. Despite these problems, or perhaps because of them, the Visita of

1567 constitutes an ethnological document of every-day indigenous life far superior to the classic histories (Stanish 1989b). I refer to it throughout this chapter, and also draw heavily from it for chapters 9 and 10, on the Altiplano and Inca periods.

Another superb source of data for Aymara culture in the Early Colonial period is the dictionary of Ludovico Bertonio published in 1612. This Italian-born Jesuit arrived in Lima in 1581 and began his career in the Titicaca region, living and working out of the major town of Juli in 1585 (Albó and Layo 1984: 228–229). Bertonio compiled an extensive vocabulary of the Aymara language that is justifiably one of the most famous and important documents of its age. The appendix of this book contains a selected list of words from the dictionary that shed light on early seventeenth-century Aymara social, political, religious, and economic life.

The Collao

The circum-Titicaca region is referred to as the Collao in early historic texts. The term *Collao,* according to H. Tschopik (1947: 503), is probably a Spanish corruption of *Colla,* the term denoting the region's principal ethnic and political group. Collasuyu, in fact, translates as the "quarter of the Colla" and was the Inca term for the rich southern quarter of their empire. In modern usage, the term *Colla* refers to both the people and geographical region of the protohistoric and historic "kingdom" *(señorío)* that was located on the north side of Lake Titicaca. In archaic usage, the term *Collao* can also refer to the entire circum-Titicaca region, particularly, but not exclusively, where Aymara was the predominant language.[2]

Cieza sets the northern boundary of the Titicaca Basin at Ayaviri (Cieza 1553, chapter 91). Other writers place it at the famous pass at La Raya, several days' walk north of Lake Arapa. A natural geographical boundary between the Cuzco and Titicaca regions, this pass is also a cultural boundary.

Cieza says that in the south, the boundary is the town of Caracollo, and it is significant that the twin Inca roads that ran north-south along each side of the lake may have been joined by a branch road at the town of Caracollo (Julien 1983: 24).[3] This could represent a demarcation of the southern boundary of the Collao.

The ancient name of Lake Titicaca is not known. Given the region's numerous and competing polities during the protohistoric period (the century or so before the European conquest), it is possible that the lake had no single, commonly accepted name even at the time the Spaniards arrived. The word *titi* is an Aymara term for puma *(gato montes),* according to Bertonio (1956 [1612]: Bk. 2: 353). It is also listed as meaning "lead" *(plomo)* (Bk. 2: 353) or as "puma," "lead," or "a heavy metal" in some modern dictionaries (e.g., de Lucca 1987: 155). The word *caca* or *kaka* is listed as "white or gray hairs of the head" (Bertonio 1956: Bk. 2: 32). The term *k'ak'a* is defined in a modern dictionary as "crack or fissure" or, alternatively, "comb of a bird," as used in the Omasuyu province (de Lucca 1987: 90). Two of Weston La Barre's informants said that the proper name of the lake was *titiq'aq'a,* meaning "gray discolored, lead-colored puma," based on a sacred carved rock found on the Island of the Sun (La Barre 1948: 208–209).

Not all early named references of the lake include the term *titi* and/or *caca.* According to Diego de Alcobasa, the lake's ancient name was Chuquivitu (as cited by Garcilaso, Book III, chap. 1; and see La Barre 1948: 208). *Chuqui* is defined by Bertonio as "lance" (1956: Bk. 2: 93) and *vittu* is listed as the point *(punta)* of a hill (Bk. 2: 389). In modern usage, the large lake is occasionally referred to as Lake Chucuito, and the small lake to the south is called Huiñamarca. The large lake also is occasionally referred to as Lago Mayor, and the small lake as Lago Menor.

A set of words in Bertonio's dictionary provides what I believe to be the key to the origin of the name Titicaca. Under the entry *Thakhsi cala,* Bertonio lists the definition "*piedra* fundamental," evoking theological themes (Bk. 2: 343; Bk. 1: 367). The word *cala* is consistently listed as "rock." *Thakhsi* is defined as "horizon, or end of the earth" and as "*cimiento.*" I believe the most logical explanation for the origin of the name Titicaca is that it is a corruption of the term *thakhsi cala,* the fifteenth- to sixteenth-century name of the sacred rock on the Island of the Sun (Bauer and Stanish 2001). The Island of the Sun was, and occasionally still is, also known as Isla Titicaca, the name often used by the early Spanish writers. And the name of the sacred rock area was used for the island as a whole. Therefore, the word *thakhsi cala* was corrupted into *titicala* and *titicaca.* Given that there was probably no common name for the lake in the sixteenth century, it is likely that the Spaniards used the name of the site of the most important indigenous shrine in the region, the Island of the Sun, as the name for the lake as well.[4]

Demography

The first population estimates for the Titicaca region are reported in the Diez de San Miguel Visita for the Chucuito province, the ancestral seat of the Lupaqa señorío. According to the Visita, the census of the seven *cabeceras,* or major settlements, and some other landholdings outside the area was based on a quipu from the Inca occupation. Diez de San Miguel questioned Don Martín Cari, the principal head of the Hanansaya moiety, about the number of tributaries under his authority. According to the official record seen by Diez de San Miguel (1964: 64), Martín Cari had an Inca quipu that had census data.

The basis of the Inca political economy was the mit'a, or labor service tax (Julien 1983; Murra 1982). The census, which served as the basis for labor recruitment from the Lupaqa region, largely divided the population into two dual, overlapping categories (see table 4.1). The upper moiety (Hanansaya) and lower moiety (Hurinsaya) of each town were further broken down into Aymara peoples and Uru peoples.

The Hanansaya/Hurinsaya system was probably an ancient Andean principle used and maintained by the Inca in conquered provinces. Membership in either moiety does not seem to have affected the level of tribute exacted by the state. According to several testimonies in the Visita, the principal able-bodied tributary was the Aymara male, between approximately thirty and sixty years old. The category of "Aymara" from both Hanansaya and Hurinsaya therefore represents mature male heads of households who had access to agricultural land and camelid pasture. Aymara could pay tribute either in labor, as in the pre-Spanish Andean mode, in kind, or in money, the latter an effect of Spanish changes in the economy.

According to the Visita census, there were almost 16,000 Aymara tributaries, a little more than 4,000 Uru, and approximately 331 colonists from outside the Lupaqa area. These colonists, or mitima, were also categorized as either "Indians" or "Uru," indicating their status as landed taxpayers or non-landed poor, respectively. Extrapolating from these data and assuming each male taxpayer represented about five additional people (wives, children, and elderly non-taxpayers), during the last Inca census there were about 100,000 people in the Chucuito province (Murra 1968).

According to Bouysse-Cassagne (1987b: 84–85), the Inca census listed 680,000 persons for Lupaqas, Charcas, Caracaras, Carangas, and Quillacas. By including the rest of the region, she arrived at a figure of 1.6 million people for the entire Collao. These figures differ from those of Rosenblat, who suggested only 800,000 people for all of Bolivia at the time of contact (Rosenblat 1967).

All of these demographic reconstructions correspond fairly well to the impressionistic census of one of Diez de San Miguel's witnesses, a Spaniard named Alonso de Buitrago who was a resident of Chucuito (Diez de San Miguel 1964: 53). The population of the area was large and dense. Table 4.2 gives Buitrago's

TABLE 4.1

Census of Lupaqa Tribute Payers from the Diez de San Miguel Visita in 1567

	Hanansaya		Hurinsaya		Other	Total
	Aymara	Uru	Aymara	Uru		
CHUCUITO	1,233	500	1,384	347	–	3,464
ACORA	1,221	440	1,207	378	–	3,246
ILAVE	Hanansaya and Hurinsaya combined. Aymara: 1,470; Uru: 1,070					2,540
JULI	1,438	58	1,804	256	153[a]/158[b]	3,867
POMATA	1,663	110	1,341	183	20[c]	3,317
YUNGUYU	Hanansaya and Hurinsaya combined. Aymara: 1,039; Uru: 381					1,420
ZEPITA	1,112	186	866	120	–	2,284
TOTAL	Aymara: 15,778		Uru: 4,029		Other: 331	20,138

[a] Chinchasuyu mitimas listed as "Indians" of Hanansaya moiety.
[b] Chinchasuyu mitimas listed as "Uru" of Hanansaya moiety.
[c] Canas mitimas. Witnesses listed conflicting figures.

estimates of population for each of the towns of the Lupaqa cabeceras and affiliated towns. His estimate of total taxpayers is about twenty thousand, a figure consistent with the other censuses.

The Toledo Tasa provides additional demographic data for areas around the basin. For the province of Chucuito ("Chucuyto"), the Tasa lists 17,779 tribute-paying males between eighteen and fifty years old who would correspond to the Lupaqa polity (Cook 1975: 78). Of this figure, 4,054 are listed as "Uru" and the rest as "Aymaraes," "mitimaes," or "yungas." The total population of the Chucuito province in the mid-1570s, as listed by the Toledo Tasa, is 74,988 persons (Cook 1975: 79).

Bouysse-Cassagne (1986: 202) calculates that 260,000 people were classified as Aymara in the Toledo Tasa, a figure that represents about 70 percent of the region's total population. It is generally consistent with the Diez de San Miguel Visita figure of 100,000 for the Lupaqa province alone, assuming that the Colla province to the north was more or less similar in population density to the Lupaqa region, and that the remaining people were distributed around the lake area. Drawing on all of these sources, we can suggest a population of about 200,000 to 400,000 individuals in the Titicaca region during the Inca period.

The first modern census of the circum-Titicaca region is found in an early ethnography by David Forbes (1870: 200–202). He gives a figure of between

TABLE 4.2

Lupaqa Census of Alonso de Buitrago in the Diez de San Miguel Visita in 1567

Town	Aymara Tributaries	Uru Tributaries	Total
CHUCUITO	2,500	800	3,300
ACORA	2,500	900	3,400
ILAVE	1,500	1,400	2,900
JULI	4,000	300–400	4,300–4,400
POMATA	3,500	150–200	3,650–3,700
ZEPITA AND YUNGUYU	3,000	?	3,000
MOQUEGUA	900	?	900
LARECAJA	?	?	?
CAPINOTA	?	?	?
CHHICANOMA	?	?	?
TOTAL	17,900	3,550–3,700	21,450–21,600

750,000 and 870,000 Aymara for Peru and Bolivia, a figure that Tschopik (1947: 504) considered too high. Later, Marroquin (1944: 1) noted that the Peruvian department of Puno had 600,000 people in the 1940s. Tschopik (1947: 504, 506) suggested figures of approximately 500,000 to 750,000 Aymara-speakers between the mid-nineteenth century and 1935, basing this in part on a manuscript by La Barre, who reported a figure of around 600,000 in 1935.

Contemporary Settlement Patterns

The basic sociological and economic unit of Aymara culture is the household, and this is reflected in the construction of discrete household clusters in rural communities. The normative pattern of Aymara household construction appears to be a set of three, four, or five rectangular structures built around a common patio area. The structures house a nuclear, modified nuclear, or extended family.

Aymara villages maintain this normative structure of the household. Villages are an aggregation of household compounds. Even in aggregated villages, households are spatially separated, and such villages appear to have only slightly higher population densities than hamlets with individual and separate households. This observation has been used as an ex-

TABLE 4.3

Sixteenth-Century Settlement Hierarchy as
Suggested by Entries in Bertonio's Dictionary

LEVEL 1	City—*haccha marca*
LEVEL 2	Village—*marca*
	Unprotected village—*cchihita* or *laccaa marca*
LEVEL 3	Small village—*coto*
LEVEL 4	Hamlet—*coto coto marca*
	Tambo (way station)—*corpa uta*

plicit assumption in my calculation of population size in the systematic survey data discussed below.

Modern cities and towns are denser in population, and there is a concomitant change in household size and configuration. In new *pueblos jóvenes*—sections of towns that house the most recent immigrants, such as Juli, Ilave, and Yunguyu—individual households are built along streets. People still try to maintain small patios and separate structures for individual households where possible, but the population density of urbanized areas is significantly higher than that of villages.

The major settlement determinants on the southwestern side of Lake Titicaca are proximity to agricultural and pasture land and roads, and access to the lake edge. Rivers are also more densely populated than other areas. Overall, the pattern is one of dispersed hamlets and small villages at the edge of the lake and along the rivers. The clear favored choice of settlement for nonurban populations is, not surprisingly, near the lake on the best agricultural land.

Bertonio's sixteenth-century dictionary provides insight into the settlement categories of the Early Colonial Aymara. There is a multilevel site size hierarchy evident from the terms used at the time. I suggest that it is at least a four-level settlement size system, as recognized by the indigenous informants

in the early post-Inca period (see table 4.3). For instance, the largest settlement was referred to as *haccha marca,* meaning literally "great place" and translated as *ciudad,* or "city." Below that is a *marca,* meaning "place or village." A separate term, *cchihita* or *laccaa marca,* was defined as "unprotected village." The term *coto* was defined as "small village," and *coto coto marca* as "hamlet" *(aldea).* A single tambo was called *corpa uta.* The use of the term *uta* (house) suggests that tambos at this time were very small and consisted of a single structure. Bertonio also lists the words for *fortress* as *queyna* or *pucara.* A fortress could be any size larger than a hamlet.

In other words, we see that the populations of the sixteenth century recognized at least four levels of settlement size: (1) town, or *marca,* (2) village and unprotected village, (3) small village, or *coto,* and (4) individual households in a hamlet or a small, single-purpose set of structures or structure such as a tambo. This typology is generally consistent with the archaeological settlement data and is consistent with the site sizes derived from the Late Horizon settlement patterns.

Ethnic Groups in the Titicaca Basin

Understanding ethnicity in contemporary society is difficult, but trying to define it in the archaeological record is even more so, and highly controversial. The processes by which individuals identify with different ethnic groups vary greatly throughout the ethnographic and historical literature. Compounding the problem in the Andes is the lack of direct correspondence between ethnic group affiliation and language (Mannheim 1991: 50).

The complex nature of language and ethnicity is demonstrated by the Titicaca Basin data. The descendants of the protohistoric fifteenth-century peoples who populated the largest and most powerful Titicaca Basin polities are the Aymara. Most scholars believe that the earlier cultures of the basin, such as Tiwanaku, were also Aymara-speakers, although there is some disagreement. There is no question, however, that the Aymara-speakers of the Titicaca Basin dominated the region's political landscape for at least five hundred years prior to the Spanish Conquest and were the principal ethnic and language group in the Prehispanic south-central Andes.

Two other ethnic and/or language groups were found in the Titicaca Basin in the sixteenth century: the Quechua and Uru. Quechua-speakers are found throughout the Peruvian and Bolivian side of the basin. Those in the south part of the basin are likely descended from transplanted colonists from the Inca empire who adopted the basin as their home. Those in the north Titicaca region are almost certainly native to the region and were living there prior to the Inca conquest.

The Uru are much more enigmatic; in fact, they do not even constitute an ethnic group in the same way that the Aymara and Quechua do. Determining the origin and history of the Uru—perennially marginalized and oppressed people—remains one of the most vexing problems in Titicaca Basin linguistics and anthropology.

Smaller ethnic groups and/or languages in the region include the Pukina, Uruquilla, Chipaya, and the Choquela. Pukina is now an extinct language. In the sixteenth century, however, it was widespread in the south-central Andes (Browman 1994). Uruquilla is another language that was much more widespread in the past. Finally, sixteenth-century documents make reference to people who lived outside the political control of any groups inhabiting the sparsely populated puna above the lake. These renegades or "wild people" are collectively referred to as Choquela. Chipaya is an enigmatic language associated with cultures of the same name in the south Titicaca Basin.

One of the outstanding characteristics of the Titicaca region is that populations are characteristically multi- or bilingual. In sixteenth- and early-seven-teenth-century documents, particularly in the church surveys conducted to know what languages were spoken in each town, it was rare to find a place where only one language was spoken. In most villages, at least two, or even three, different languages were spoken, often including Aymara, Pukina, Quechua, and Uruquilla. It is still very common to meet people who speak Quechua, Aymara, and Spanish.

Aymara

Aymara peoples call their language *haque aru* or *aqi aru,* meaning "language of the people" or "language of the Indians" (Bertonio 1956: Bk. 1: 288) or simply "human language" (Hardman-de-Bautista 1988). The greatest concentration of modern Aymara-speakers in the Titicaca Basin is along the lake shore, particularly on the western and southern sides. They cluster in two Titicaca Basin cities, Puno and Juliaca, and are dispersed in a number of towns, villages, and hamlets throughout the region. Most of the larger towns on the Peruvian side are also listed in sixteenth-century documents as former Lupaqa or Colla settlements. These include Hatuncolla, Chucuito, Acora, Ilave, Juli, Pomata, Zepita, Yunguyu, and Desaguadero. Among the many large towns on the Bolivian side are Escoma, Kasani, Ancoraimes, Guaqui, and Copacabana (see maps 3.2 and 4.1).

The relationship between the Aymara and Quechua languages has been a controversial topic for centuries. According to Mannheim (1991: 37), early Spanish writers argued that these two common lengua generales of Peru were related, a hypothesis consistently repeated by various authors with little or spurious evidence. Mannheim (1991: 37) ultimately concludes that "the similarities can best be accounted for by contact and mutual borrowing rather than by common descent." In fact, Quechua and Aymara belong to distinct language families and are substantially different. Aymara belongs to the family Jaqi/Aru, according to Mannheim and other linguists (e.g., in Mannheim 1991: 39). The repeated assertion

MAP 4.1. The Titicaca Basin. Adapted from Wirrmann 1991 and Boulange and Aquize Jaen 1981.

by Spanish writers that the two languages were similar and related is most likely explained by the desire to maintain the image of the Andes as a unified culture area, an ideological assertion that would have reinforced the political unification of the former Inca empire by the Spanish state.

The origin of Aymara-speakers in the Titicaca region is another subject of considerable debate. Generally, linguists and anthropologists using linguistic data have argued that Aymara-speakers arrived relatively late in prehistory, during the Altiplano period (A.D. 1100–1450), as aggressors into territory set-

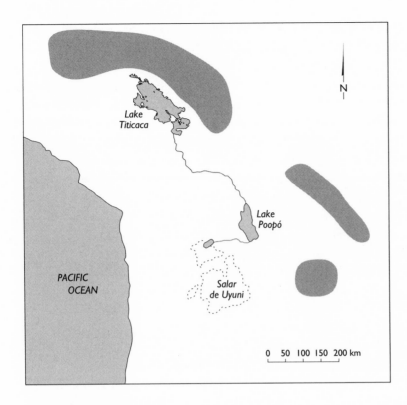

MAP 4.2. Distribution of Quechua (shaded areas) in the sixteenth century. Data derived from church catechisms and adapted from Bouysse-Cassagne (1975: map 2).

tled by Pukina-speakers (Bouysse-Cassagne 1987a, 1987b, 1992; Torero 1987; Wachtel 1987). With the exception of Shady and Torero, scholars explicitly argue for a southern origin of the Aymara. Many cite early documents that recount the Aymara immigration from Coquiabo, generally thought to be in Chile. Torero, in contrast, argues that they arrived from the area of modern Lima. Several linguists argue that the prehistoric cultures of Pucara and Tiwanaku, plus the sixteenth-century Colla, were Pukina-speakers who were ultimately displaced by the Aymara (see chapter 9).

Quechua

In dozens of regions throughout the Titicaca Basin, Quechua is the dominant language. Map 4.2 shows the location of Quechua-speakers in the Titicaca Basin in the sixteenth century based on data derived from church catechisms and adapted from Bouysse-

Cassagne (1975: map 2). The distribution of Quechua in the east, west, and south Titicaca Basin in this period suggests a location near the Umasuyu road system, a pattern consistent with the hypothesis that the Quechua-speakers were the product of Inca colonization policies in the fifteenth century, placed there for military, strategic, and economic purposes. The modern distribution of Quechua in the northern basin probably represents the ancestral distribution of Quechua from at least the Altiplano period, and probably earlier. The existence of Quechua in the Titicaca Basin is the least difficult to explain: those who spoke Quechua south of Paucarcolla were most certainly settled there by the Inca state.

The Uru

One of the most enigmatic groups in the Titicaca region is known as the Uru.[5] The modern Uru are a famous tourist attraction, living on artificial islands in Lake Titicaca and subsisting on fishing and tourist income. They speak Aymara, however, and in fact, most have houses in Puno.

Although the Aymara have been the subject of vicious racist invective throughout the centuries, the Uru have been treated even worse. La Barre (1941: 500–502) listed some of the descriptions of the Uru by the mid-twentieth century: J. de la Acosta said that the Uru were "brutish" and not even human, and even Garcilaso de la Vega, one of the more sympathetic writers on indigenous culture of the Colonial period, called them rude and stupid in his *Comentarios Reales*. Bertonio notes throughout his dictionary that the Uru were despised by all, and were of less intelligence than others. The writer Rigoberto Paredes (1956: 25) called them despicable and unintelligent. The European traveler Paul Walle (1914) said that "the [Uru] face is lifeless and without expression; it betrays hardly a sign of intelligence."

The celebrated Bolivian archaeologist Arturo Posnansky despised the Aymara (see below). Given his characterization of the Aymara, the dominant indigenous group in Bolivia, it is no surprise that he considered the Uru to be semihuman as well (Posnansky 1937: 90). Métraux (1936) compared the Uru to the Aymara and found them both lacking in human qualities, possessing "the apathy and heaviness of spirit which renders the altiplano Indian so downright hateful." La Barre, however, seemed to like the Uru and contrasted them with the Aymara, whom he did not like: "the Uru [are] vastly more sympathetic than the former [Aymara] truculent, hate filled group" (La Barre 1941: 502).

Apart from the small groups of Aymara-speaking Uru living on the islands outside Puno, Uru enclaves no longer exist in the Titicaca Basin. La Barre (1941: 493–494) listed a number of Uru enclaves in the nineteenth century, but these also appear to have been enculturated into the dominant Aymara society.

The Uru are traditionally described as impoverished and marginal members of Titicaca Basin so-

ciety. They are often associated with fishing and water. The Diez de San Miguel Visita refers to the Uru as poor and landless. According to Martín Cari, "There are five other ayllu of fishermen Indians that are called by another name, Uros; they are poor people who do not have farms but subsist only by fishing and by going about *[andando]* in the lake" (Diez de San Miguel 1964: 14). Likewise, Ruiz de Estrada, the *corregidor* of Chucuito, testified that "the Aymaras that are the rich Indians that have twice as much cattle as the Uros have because the Uros are poor fishermen" (Diez de San Miguel 1964: 53). The association of fishing with poverty is curious, given the fact that coastal Andean populations held fishers in higher regard and exported dried fish into the *sierra* (e.g., Marcus 1987: 400; Marcus, Sommer, and Glew 1999; Rostworowski 1978–80).

Uru tribute obligations listed in the Diez de San Miguel Visita and the Toledo Tasa provide insight into their socioeconomic and political status. Uru rarely, if ever, held political office in Colonial-period Aymara society. All local officials were drawn from males categorized as Aymara. Whereas the Aymara were sometimes able to fulfill their tribute obligations to the Spanish Crown with goods and even money, the Uru more often than not were taxed exclusively in labor. In the Diez de San Miguel Visita, local witnesses testified that

these Uros that do not go to Potosí serve in the tambos like the Aymaraes and that these Uros gather lake grass [totora] for the tambos and that also they help in the fields of the caciques and they give fish for the tribute to the priests and when they build churches they [the Urus] perform the labor and they go to the yungas for wood and they do not pay anything else because they are poor. (Diez de San Miguel 1964: 196)

Linguistically and conceptually, the Uru were consistently associated with the lake and, more specifically, with water. For instance, one word in Berto-nio's dictionary, *uma haque,* is defined as "anyone that deals with the sea, or lake, such as mariners, Uru, etc." (Bk. 2: 374). The word *uma* is the Aymara term for water, and the word *haque* means "people." In a similar manner, one definition of Uru is "a nation of poor Indians that ordinarily are fishermen" (Berto-nio 1956: Bk. 2: 380).

In the Diez de San Miguel Visita, the Uru of the Chucuito province comprised anywhere from 8 per-cent of the total number of taxpayers in the town of Pomata to a maximum of 42 percent in Ilave. Over-all, they comprised about 20 percent of the total pop-ulation of adult males in the Lupaqa region (Murra 1964: 427).[6] Virtually all towns had some Uru.

The language of the Uru in the sixteenth century (and before) remains controversial. Early anthropol-ogists believed the language of the Uru was Pukina. Later, La Barre argued that the Uru and Chipaya, an-other very small ethnic group in the southern Titi-caca Basin, spoke Pukina, "yet nowadays Puqina is spoken by only a . . . remnant in the Desaguadero swamps, the Uru, and by their linguistic congeners of the Lake Poopó region, the Chipaya" (La Barre 1948: 20). He furthermore argued that the "uroquil-las of the early chroniclers appears to have meant the Uru" and that the evidence indicated the Uru spoke Pukina (La Barre 1941: 499). La Barre therefore con-cluded that the Uru, Chipayas, and Uruquillas were all Pukina-speakers and formed a distinct ethnic and linguistic group from the Aymara and Quechua (La Barre 1941: 499–500). Wachtel (1986: 284), however, does not consider this an established fact, and Bouysse-Cassagne (1986: 206) and Julien (1983: 62) argue that Pukina and Uru populations spoke dif-ferent languages. Julien believes that Uruquilla and Uru-Chipaya are the same language, and that the so-called Uru language (as distinct from the Uru people) referred to in the historical texts was actually Uru-quilla (see below). Browman (1994: 237) argues that the term *Urukilla* was used in pre-1600 documents

to refer to Uru in the southwest basin and that the terms *Huchusuma* and *Ochosuma* refer to the Uru.

At first analysis, it would appear that the Uru were merely an impoverished ethnic group speaking their own language and existing on the margins of the dom-inant Aymara society, but there are other possibili-ties. One of the most fascinating hypotheses con-cerning the Uru was initially suggested by Camacho (1943) and Murra (1964: 427), and elaborated by Bouysse-Cassagne (1976: 99), Julien (1983), Mann-heim (1991: 50), Torero (1987: 332–338), and Wachtel (1986). These scholars argue that *Uru* was used to des-ignate social status and tax category, not ethnicity; thus the Uru were simply Aymara-speakers placed in a different socioeconomic and, by extension, tax cat-egory. In Mannheim's words, "Uru designated an or-ganizational and functional position in the economy, rather than a language" (1991: 50). As Browman notes, recalling Bittman's (1979) observation, "the reference of Uru was merely to people of a similar subsistence system and 'same miserable existence'" (Browman 1994: 238). Likewise, Mannheim and Julien conclude that neither *Aymara* nor *Uru* correlates with ethnic-ity or language. In Julien's words:

> The tasa of Toledo classifies the entire population of the Lake Titicaca region into two groups: Aymara and Uru. . . . People classified as Uru were located in a ma-jority of the encomiendas listed in the tasa. It is clear from the tasa that some of the people classified as Uru spoke Puquina, while others spoke Aymara. Moreover, some people classified as Aymara spoke Puquina. . . . The distribution of people in two tax categories does not correspond in any meaningful way with the dis-tribution of languages in the area. (Julien 1983: 52–53)

As Julien (1983: 55) and others have noted, in the Toledo Tasa and the Diez de San Miguel Visita, all native people in the Titicaca region were classified as either Aymara, Uru, or foreign colonists (mitima) de-spite the existence of other languages. It is extremely rare that someone is listed as speaking only Uru without some qualifying information suggesting that they spoke other languages.

The Diez de San Miguel Visita offers additional support for this hypothesis. As noted above, Diez de San Miguel divided the populations of all Lupaqa towns into Hanansaya and Hurinsaya groups, following the dual division of upper and lower moieties. In the case of Juli, he recorded the upper and lower groups, further dividing these into Aymara and Uru, as he did for all other towns. To this, however, he added, "and from Chinchasuyo of the said town of Juli that are mitimaes put there by the Inca from the said moiety of Anansaya 153 Indians and of Uros of the same moiety 158 Indians" (Diez de San Miguel 1964: 65). What is significant here is that the tribute-paying Chinchasuyu people, who were not Aymara-speakers, were referred to simply as *indios* and placed in the Hanansaya, or upper moiety. This is the only case in the list of the seven towns where the terms *Uru* or *Aymara* were not used to designate a group of tribute payers. This makes sense because this group did not speak Aymara, or at least were not native to the land. Yet the same Hanansaya moiety contained a second group of Chinchasuyu natives who were termed *Uru*. In other words, a group of non-Aymara-speaking foreigners from the northern quarter of the Inca empire were referred to as either indios or Uru. In this case, it seems evident that the Uru designation was assigned not because of their language or ethnicity but because they were poor and paid a lower tribute; *indio*, in contrast, referred to a wealthier group.

These data must be understood in the context of the changes introduced by the Spanish administration. One of the most significant changes was a gradual transformation of the pre-Spanish Andean tax system of mit'a labor (Stanish 2000; Stern 1982). As the Spanish administration took root, the new elite increasingly permitted or encouraged their subjects to pay in money or kind, as opposed to paying with their labor.

One of the strongest pieces of evidence for Uru being a tax category rather than an ethnic one is a case where a group of apparently wealthy Uru petitioned the state to be reclassified as Aymara (Julien 1983: 55). If reclassified, however, the Uru would have to pay more taxes. Why would anybody seek to pay more tribute unless such it conferred certain advantages? The answer may be contained in a very important section in the Diez de San Miguel Visita. Questioning Ruiz de Estrada, the corregidor of the Chucuito province, about the organization of the region's tambos, Diez de San Miguel was told that "each town serves its tambo and that this service is usually done by the Uros Indians because they are poor" (Diez de San Miguel 1964: 52). As a mistreated, poor minority, the Uru were relegated to menial tasks within the taxation system, but a reclassification to Aymara status permitted them to meet their tribute obligations by providing goods, such as wool and camelids, instead of labor. Once free from labor obligations, individual "Aymara" households could amass additional wealth from their herds and fields. Thus, although an Aymara designation required a higher tax rate, it also conferred certain privileges and a higher status worth claiming. Over time, there would have been a distinct advantage to paying taxes in kind as opposed to paying in labor, and this would account for the seemingly illogical request on the part of some Uru to be reclassified as Aymara.

A reference in the Toledo Tasa also indicates that Uru were generally expected to pay tax in labor, but Aymara were able to substitute money or goods in kind: "and discounted from the said 4,054 Urus that were registered as tribute payers are the 579 Urus of Cepita and Yunguyu who claim to be *[se refutan]* Aymaras and the 400 that go to the mines of Potosí and 91 Uruquillas of Huchusuma who are counted as this for being poor" (Cook 1975: 79).

These data support the idea that Uru was a social designation, not an ethnic one. The term was used to indicate a poor, landless peasant at the bottom of

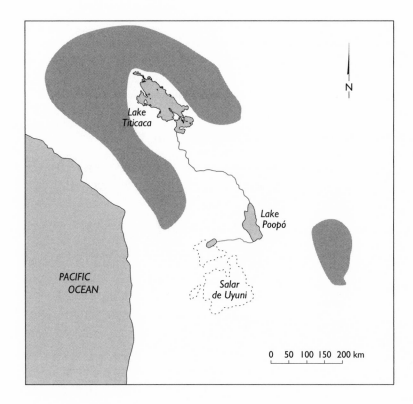

MAP 4.3. Distribution of Pukina (shaded areas) in the sixteenth century.

the indigenous social hierarchy who did not pay taxes in animals or wool but rather provided labor for his tribute obligations. Based on my own reading of the historic documents, I believe that Uru was not a language, nor was it an ethnic or linguistic division, but rather that it was a social and political one. Furthermore, as a social category, it was mutable.

Pukina

Although the Pukina language is almost extinct and little is known about it,[7] sixteenth-century documents indicate it was widely spoken in the south-central Andes (see map 4.3). It was one of the lenguas generales of Peru, along with Quechua and Aymara. I accept the position of linguists who argue that Quechua and Aymara belong to separate language families (Hardman-de-Bautista 1978; Mannheim 1991: 39). There is a substantial literature on these two

languages, and their syntax and lexicon is relatively well understood. The situation with Pukina is different. There is no comprehensive lexicon, and very little of its grammar and vocabulary are known. The only Pukina vocabulary compiled from original speakers was found in Geronimo de Ore's *Rituale seu Manuale Peruanum,* published in Naples in 1607. This book contained about thirty pages in Pukina, including the Lord's Prayer, with translations into other languages (La Barre 1941: 496).[8] However, details concerning Pukina's distribution, structure, and sociological correlates remain obscure (see Mannheim 1991: 47–48). Browman (1994) even questions whether the language was widely spoken.

Linking the Uru "ethnic" group with the Pukina language has been a common hypothesis in the anthropological and linguistic literature (e.g., de la Grasserie 1894 and Brinton 1901).[9] Using data from the Ore manuscript, many early scholars concluded that Pukina was the language of the Uru. La Barre argued that "prima facie evidence indicates that Uru and Puquina are the same" and, furthermore, that the "uroquillas of the early chroniclers appears to have meant the Uru" (La Barre 1941: 499). Métraux (1936) agreed that Pukina and Uru were the same linguistic group. Like La Barre, he considered Pukina closely related to the Chipaya "language" of the more southern Lake Poopó, a fact that led him to propose a Uro-Chipaya language. He noted that the Uru of the village of Ancoaqui referred to themselves as Bukina or Pukina (La Barre 1941: 500).

The counterargument, that the Uru were not Pukina-speakers, also has a long history in the literature. Uhle told Chamberlain in 1896 that the Uru of Iruitu that he had studied were linguistically identical to the Uru of the Carangas (Chipaya), but he went on to note that "the Puquina-Uro of Raoul de la Grasserie is totally different from my Uro" (as quoted in La Barre 1941: 497). Garcilaso de la Vega (1989) listed "the Puquinas, Collas, Urus, Yuncas, and other Indian nations," implicitly suggesting that Uru and Pukinas were distinct.

Torero (1987) has conducted the most extensive work on the Pukina and other languages in the Titicaca region. He unequivocally states that there is no genetic connection between Pukina and the other three languages (Quechua, Aymara, and Uruquilla) and that people classified as Uru spoke all of these languages. Bouysse-Cassagne (1987a, 1987b) has presented corroborating evidence that language and ethnicity were indeed very fluid, and that there is no direct correlation between Uru and Pukina. Murra (1988: 52) has pointed out that most people identifiable as Uru today speak Aymara, with the exception of the Chipaya to the south.

In sum, during the Spanish Conquest in the early to mid-sixteenth century, there were three major languages in the central Andes—Quechua, Aymara, Pukina—as well as a number of lesser ones, such as

Uruquilla. The Uru peoples in the Titicaca Basin area were not primarily Pukina-speakers. Rather, the term *Uru* referred to a social and taxation category, and was applied to poor people who spoke Pukina, Aymara, and/or Uruquilla.

PUKINA AND THE MODERN KALLAWAYA

There are no Pukina-speakers today, with the possible exception of the indigenous itinerant medical doctors known as the Kallawaya (Girault 1966, 1989), who speak a secret language among themselves (Ponce 1969b: 148; Torero 1987: 330).[10] Several linguists and anthropologists believe that this is actually a form of Pukina and have presented convincing evidence based on a comparison of the lexicon of the Kallawaya language with the vocabulary found in the Ore manuscript. However, as both Ponce (1969b: 148) and Bouysse-Cassagne (1987b: 125–126) recognize, the syntax of Kallawaya is similar to that of Quechua. According to Mannheim (1991: 114), the Kallawaya of Bolivia speak a form of Quechuanized Pukina. In other words, the secret language of the Kallawaya, purportedly the closest existing language to Pukina, is grammatically similar to Quechua, with a vocabulary that is distinct from Quechua and Aymara and that is related to the Pukina of Ore. This is a crucial observation. If the Kallawaya secret language is indeed Pukina, or at least a dialect of it, then Pukina is a rare mixed language, with a grammar related to Quechua and a vocabulary related to Pukina.

PUKINA DISTRIBUTION

We can reconstruct the distribution of Pukina in the sixteenth century using documents of that era and contemporary toponyms (e.g., Bouysse-Cassagne 1975; Linares Malaga 1982). Bouysse-Cassagne (1991: 491) and Torero (1987) argue that Pukina was a linguistically coherent unit that was widely distributed in the circum-Titicaca region in the sixteenth century. The language was spoken in La Raya and

Cuzco; to the south in Ayaviri, Caracollo, the Oma-suyu region, Arequipa, and Arica; and along the Pacific Coast. Pukina was in essence wedged between Quechua and Aymara in an arclike pattern in the northern and eastern Titicaca region west toward the Pacific and then south along the western coastal valleys. Bouysse-Cassagne links the language of Pukina with the cultural unit of the Colla. She suggests that the cultures of Pucara, Tiwanaku, and Hatuncolla (the Colla señorío) spoke Pukina (Bouysse-Cassagne 1991: 491).

Torero argues that the original language of the Tiwanaku state was Pukina and that Aymara-speakers migrated from the central Peruvian coast, penetrating the Titicaca region around A.D. 1300 with a violent conquest (Torero 1987). Building on Torero's original hypotheses, Bouysse-Cassagne offers a fascinating theory for the distribution of Pukina and other languages in the Titicaca region. Using strictly linguistic evidence, she argues that there have been four major waves of migration into the region. The first migrants were the Uru who spoke Uruquilla (Bouysse-Cassagne 1987b: 128–136). The second wave was composed of Pukina who created the Tiwanaku state. The third stage was the Aymara migration, who called everybody else Uru and who created the twelfth- to fifteenth-century señoríos, or kingdoms. in the circum-Titicaca region. Finally, Quechua-speakers arrived with the Inca imperial conquest and were found in small pockets around the area.

Kolata argues that Pukina or proto-Pukina was one of at least two ancestral languages in the Tiwanaku state: "If there were dominant actors in this Tiwanaku state culture, they were, most likely, of Aymara or Pukina descent. One of these two languages was Tiwanaku's elite lingua franca, or court language" (Kolata 1993: 241). The linking of Pukina with the Tiwanaku polity has been most strongly argued by linguists using a comparative approach who cite the limited distribution of that language vis-à-vis Aymara. That is, Pukina is older, less widely distributed

than Aymara, and therefore associated with the last great political entity prior to the protohistoric señoríos of the sixteenth century.

There are some problems with this reconstruction, however. The most obvious objection is that Pukina was not spoken in the Tiwanaku Valley in the sixteenth century—a very odd fact if it were the language of the state that collapsed in the twelfth century and which was not replaced with any complex polity. In fact, the closest known Pukina-speakers in the sixteenth century were in Huarina. Furthermore, there are very few Pukina toponyms in the Tiwanaku Valley; the vast majority are Spanish, Aymara, and Quechua. Finally, the distribution of Pukina-speakers of the sixteenth century as well as the apparent distribution of Pukina toponyms bear little relation to the distribution of Tiwanaku sites in the central Andes as a whole.

In contrast, Aymara was the language of the Tiwanaku Valley and surrounding areas in the sixteenth century, and there was no post-Tiwanaku polity of sufficient complexity to have forced themselves into the area. Likewise, the distribution of the mature Tiwanaku state circa the tenth century is generally consistent with the distribution of Aymara-speakers. I agree with Browman (1994) that it is very likely that a form of proto-Aymara was the dominant language of the Tiwanaku state.

In chapter 9, I outline a model of Pukina function and extinction.

Uruquilla or Chipaya

In the sixteenth century, the Toledo Tasa and the Diez de San Miguel Visita noted the presence of an ethnic group called "Huruquilla" in small pockets along the southern and southwestern Lake Titicaca shores. Map 4.4 shows the location of Uruquilla-speakers in the Titicaca Basin in the sixteenth century.

Some anthropologists have identified the Uruquilla with the Chipaya, one of the basin's lesser-known ethnic groups. As mentioned above, the eth-

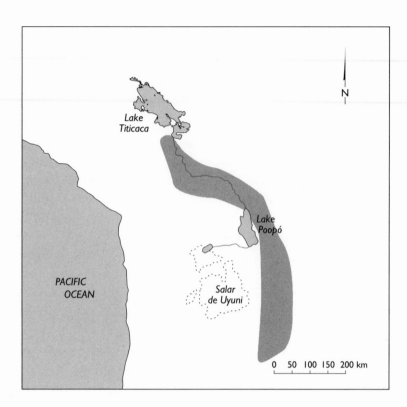

MAP 4.4. Distribution of Uruquilla
(shaded areas) in the sixteenth century.

nologist Weston La Barre believed that the Chipaya and Uru spoke Pukina (Torero 1987; La Barre 1948: 20). Vellard suggested that Uruquilla and Pukina were dialects of the same language (in Bouysse-Cassagne 1987b: 117). Both Bouysse-Cassagne (1986: 206; 1987b: 127) and Julien (1983: 62) disagree and argue that Pukina and Uru populations spoke different languages. According to Bouysse-Cassagne (1987b: 117), "puquina and uruquilla are two distinct languages, that were still spoken in the sixteenth century in two distinct geographical locations." Likewise, Torero felt that Pukina and Uruquilla were two distinct languages. Julien argues that Uruquilla is the same as Uru-Chipaya, a conclusion with which I agree based on linguistic, archaeological, and historical data.

The location of early historic Uruquilla-speakers, as reconstructed from Spanish tax lists, and the apparent linguistic similarity between Uruquilla and Pukina (in contrast to the different language family of Jaqi /Aru to which Aymara belongs),[11] suggests to some linguists relatively recent (post–A.D. 1000) contact of Aymara and non-Aymara-speakers in the circum-Titicaca Basin (e.g., see Albó 1987; Torero 1987). Based on these historical linguistic patterns, we can hypothesize that the twelfth-to-fifteenth-century distribution of Uruquilla-speakers would have been much more extensive and would have covered the area southeast of the Desaguadero River into what is today extreme southeastern Peru, northwestern Bolivia, and northern Chile. A comprehensive archaeological study of this area remains to be completed.

Choquela

The early historic documents make occasional references to groups of hunters who lived in the puna away from the settled towns. In Bertonio's dictionary, the name *Choquela* was defined as "wild or renegade people *[cimarrona]* who live in the puna sustaining themselves by hunting" (Bk. 2: 89). In this particular reference in Bertonio, the term *lari lari* is listed as a synonym or related word, suggesting that these people were renegades who had evaded the political authorities: *lari lari* is defined by Bertonio (Bk. 2: 191) as "people of the puna that do not recognize any cacique" and as "wild people." Likewise, the term *lari larikhatha* is a verb that means "to become wild again *[volverse cimarrón]*" and "to live voluntarily like this [in a wild state]" (Bk. 2: 191). Perhaps most fascinating of all, a synonym of *lari lari* is *lari uru* (Bk. 2: 191).[12] The linkage of the term *uru* with *lari* to refer to those "voluntarily" living in a wild state outside the control of political authorities corroborates the hypothesis that the term *Uru* constitutes a social status and not an ethnic one based on language or culture.

Other terms in Bertonio's dictionary designate people living outside established villages and political structures. *Huacora* and *kita* are defined as "wild person" or "fugitive" (Bk. 2: 142). In another section, he combines the two words as *kitha huacora,* defined as "wild, said of men and animals" (Bk. 2: 303). This may also explain, in part, the occasional linking of "animal" with "Uru" in other contexts. Similarly, the words *kitahaque* (*haque* and *jaque* mean "people" or "pairs") and *sallca* are defined as "wild person." The verb *kithastha* is defined as "to walk or go about wild" (Bk. 2: 306).

An Aymara hunting ritual dance described by Tschopik (1946: 566–567) and Cuentas Ormachea (1982) is called Çoqela, Choquela, or Chokela. This ceremony was practiced in Juli, Ichu, Chucuito and western Bolivia in the early to mid-twentieth century, according to Bandelier (1910: 103) and Tschopik (1946: 567; 1951). Huidobro, Arce, and Quispe (1994: 74) describe a Choquela dance on the Island of the Sun that commemorates the ritual hunting of the *vicuña* after the harvest. Tschopik notes that the dance takes place on hilltops and includes ritual hunting songs and pantomimes of the hunt. At the end of the

ceremony, the vicuña is killed. It is fascinating that the sixteenth-century word to describe "wild" hunters is the same as that for a ritual hunting ceremony of the twentieth century. Although this twentieth-century ethnography certainly does not prove the existence of pre-sixteenth-century hunting peoples, it suggests that the term *Choquela* is associated with such lifeways.

The best description of the modern Choquela in the altiplano is by Cuentas Ormachea (1982: 55–57). He notes that the term has various meanings but that it is strongly connected with a propitiatory dance and communal hunting of wild animals. He notes that the dance is found only in Aymara-speaking communities of the altiplano, including towns as far north as Huancané and as far south as Pizacoma. Cuentas's article stands as the definitive discussion of the Choquela. What is significant for our discussion here is that the term *Choquela* is intimately linked with hunting and wild animals, and is evocative of those people living in the puna away from the towns and villages of the populated lake edge.

Other Ethnic Groups

The Toledo Tasa refers to indigenous populations by a number of terms that mix language, geographical origin, and social status. People are referred to as Uruquilla, Aymara, Uru, mitimas, Chinchasuyus, indios, Hatunrunas, Yanaconas, Carangas, Moxos, and so forth. The word *Yanacona* refers to people belonging to a servile social category in the Inca state. *Hatunruna* or *Hatunluna* is a term that translates in Quechua as *hombres grandes.* In fact, they constituted the majority of peasant peoples in the Inca state and provided the vast bulk of mit'a labor (Rostworowski 1988: 214). Mitimas were transplanted colonists. Those from Chinchasuyu, the northwest province of the Inca state, were referred to "Chinchasuyu mitimaes" in the Toledo Tasa. Designations such as Carangas, Moxos, Canas, Canchis, and so forth refer to ethnic groups from particular regions in the circum-

Titicaca basin and neighboring areas. *Moxos* referred to people from the eastern lowlands; *Carangas,* to those from the southernmost areas of the Titicaca region; and *Canas* and *Canchis,* to people from the northern basin. Uruquilla, as already discussed above, was a language spoken in the southern Pacajes and Carangas areas in the altiplano. As discussed above, Uru was a social class designation. In short, it is essential to realize that any particular term used to denote a group of people could have been based on language, geographical origin, and/or social status.

Agriculture, Pastoralism, and Lake Exploitation: The Subsistence Triad of the Titicaca Basin Endogenous Economy

The economic mainstays of the twentieth-century Aymara were camelid pastoralism and rain-fed agriculture, both augmented by the hunting of fowl and fishing in the lake and rivers. During the nineteenth century, liberal land reform challenged earlier land tenure practices (Stanish 1989b) but does not seem to have appreciably altered basic subsistence pursuits. In contrast, since the turn of the twentieth century, the Aymara have been increasingly incorporated into the market economy. Market exchange, particularly between Peru and Bolivia, has become a major economic activity for the region's Aymara populations and has had a major impact on settlement distribution and subsistence activities over the last two or three generations. This is a pattern that goes back to the Early Colonial period as well, when Aymara elite traded extensively in the south-central Andes (e.g., Miño Grijalva 1984).

Agriculture and animal pastoralism remain the principal local economic activities. There are two agricultural seasons in the Titicaca region, dictated by rainfall. The wet season falls between October and April, and the dry season lasts from May to September. According to Tschopik (1947: 512), the wet season is also referred to as "green time" or "rainy

time," and the dry season as "dry time" or "ice time." La Barre described names for four seasons instead of two, and refers to another system with five seasons (La Barre 1948). According to modern ethnographies, the principal distinction made by Aymara farmers is between wet and dry seasons. Loza B. (1972: 71) relates that the Aymara recognize three climatic seasons—a rainy season, or summer, called Jallupacha; a dry and cold winter, called Autipacha; and a beginning of the agricultural year, or spring, called Lapakapacha. Undoubtedly, these culturally specific classifications of the seasons vary across space and time. The constancy of the wet/dry regime, however, makes it likely that most or all such classifications were based on this distinction to some degree.

The most important indigenous crops are chenopods (quinoa *[Chenopodium quinoa],* qañiwa *[Chenopodium* sp.]), tubers (numerous varieties of potatoes, oca, and ullucu), and legumes known as *habas (Vicia faba).*[13] Since the Spanish Conquest, barley and wheat have been added to the list of crop plants cultivated by Aymara farmers (Tschopik 1947: 514). The Andean peoples are justifiably famous for cultivating a vast variety of potatoes that have evolved over the millennia. Tschopik quotes an unpublished manuscript by La Barre that lists 209 different names for potatoes in Bolivia (Tschopik 1947: 513). Tschopik himself counted fifty varieties in the Chucuito district alone. Bertonio lists some two dozen specific names of potatoes under the general term *papa.* Of these, twelve were described as high quality and best known in the area, six were described as low quality, and others were either neutral in quality or had other distinguishing characteristics. Bertonio also lists several distinct terms for potatoes depending on how they were prepared.

As mentioned above, maize is still occasionally grown near the lake edge, although in very small quantities and under special environmental conditions. It is not a staple crop today but may have been in the past, particularly before the Little Ice Age be-gan in the fifteenth century. Pulgar Vidal (n.d.: 80, fn. 4) notes that maize grows very well as high as 3,200 m.a.s.l. and suggests that its upper limit is 3,500 meters—that is, the upper limit of the Quechua zone in his land use categories. Several early historians mention that maize grown in the Titicaca region was considered a special crop possessing sacred qualities, and that maize from the Island of the Sun was the most sacred of all. The following passage from Gar-cilaso is perhaps the most literary of those in the early histories:

> They [the Inca] flattened the island [of the Sun] as much as possible . . . and made terraces which they cov-ered with good fertile soil brought from a distance so as to bear maize. . . . On these terraces they sowed the seeds and by dint of great care grew a few cobs which were sent to the Inca as sacred objects. He took them to the temple of the Sun and sent them to the chosen virgins in Cuzco, and ordered them to be taken to other temples and convents throughout the kingdom . . . so that all might enjoy the grain sent from heaven. (Gar-cilaso de la Vega 1989: 191)

Minor crop plants in the Titicaca region include European imports such as onions, garlic, and the like, grown in kitchen gardens (Tschopik 1947: 513). The main industrial plant is the totora reed *(Scirpus tatora),* which grows in the swampy land near the lake.

Raised-Field Agriculture

Throughout the Titicaca region, there are vast tracts of relict or fossil raised fields (see map 4.5). It is clear that prior to the modern period, raised field agri-cultural production was an important component of area economic life. Following Denevan and Turner (1974: 24), a raised field is defined broadly as any artificially elevated land surface designed to improve cultivating conditions. Raised fields are labor-intensive relative to the rain-fed terrace agri-culture practiced by peasant farmers today and in the recent historical past (although see Erickson 1994 for a differing opinion). Likewise, experimental data indicate that raised fields are more productive than contemporary systems, at least in the first several years of use.

The first systematic and intensive archaeological field research on Titicaca Basin raised fields was con-ducted by Clark Erickson (1988), who excavated sev-eral mounds and field segments near the modern town of Huatta in the north basin. He concluded that the Huatta fields began functioning around 1000 B.C. and were an integral component of Prehispanic economies for millennia. Research on the southern side of Lake Titicaca has been published by Gray Graffam, John Janusek, Alan Kolata, James Mathews, Charles Ortloff, Oswaldo Rivera, and Matthew Sed-don. The conclusions of Kolata and Ortloff regard-ing the maximum periods of use for raised fields dif-fer from Erickson's, but they also corroborate the observation that they were fundamental to the Pre-hispanic political economies.

There is some evidence in Bertonio's dictionary that raised fields were in use in the Early Colonial period, although this is not corroborated by the ar-chaeological data. The appendix lists a number of agricultural terms found in this early-seventeenth-century document, several of which refer directly to *camellones,* translated as "raised field." Informants to-day have stated to me that *waru waru* refers to the large constructions used in the past and the large ones being reconstructed today. In the Juli area, raised fields are referred to by informants as *jake kolli* (Onofre, in Stanish et al. 1997: 125). In contrast, *suka colla* refers to the much smaller furrows used to cre-ate pasture near the lake edge. The confusion in the early literature may be related to this more subtle dis-tinction used by farmers today.[14]

Throughout the 1980s and early 1990s, there have been extensive efforts to rehabilitate raised field agri-cultural production. Despite their popularity with

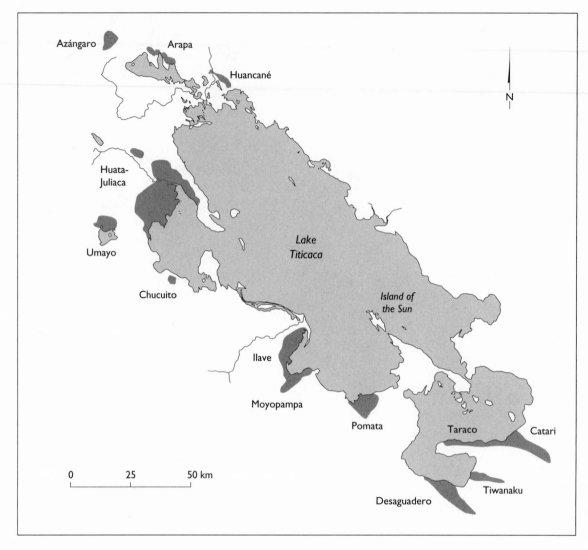

MAP 4.5. Distribution of raised-field areas (shaded areas) in the Titicaca Basin. Adapted from Erickson 1988, Seddon 1994, Smith et al. 1968, and Stanish 1994.

agronomists and archaeologists, however, there are no self-supporting raised fields in the region today apart from a few experimental fields begun by outside aid projects. Although virtually every Aymara farmer is familiar with the use and construction of raised fields, they do not construct them on their own. When asked, informants in the Juli area consistently responded that building raised fields "was not worth the effort." Although they were more than happy to be paid by outsiders to construct the fields, they explicitly stated that the time and labor invested in raised field construction left it an inefficient economic activity. Raised fields appear to be largely an archaeological phenomenon whose voluntary incorporation into modern Aymara farming practices remains problematic.

Terrace Agriculture

Today, virtually all plant agriculture consists of rainfed terrace agriculture, occasionally augmented by simple canal irrigation. The Titicaca Basin is covered with artificial agricultural terraces, with the ancient terraces tending to follow the land's natural contours.[15] They are stone-faced constructions designed to create a level planting surface, retain rain water, and prevent erosion. They are used primarily to grow crops and support pasture for animals, but terraces are also used as foundations for modern houses. A good number of terraces in the region have archaeological remains on their surface as well.

Because the water of Lake Titicaca is slightly saline, with salt concentrations higher in the south, it is not usable for irrigation. The water that runs from the springs and aquifers is fresh, however, as is the groundwater that collects in front of the lake. It is therefore necessary to move water from subterranean sources and springs to farming areas using canals and aqueducts. Although most of the fields in the Titicaca area receive only rainfall, a significant percentage of terraces are irrigated with spring-fed canals.

One of the misperceptions about the extensive terrace systems in the Andes is that they were built by the Inca. Such views derive from early writers like Garcilaso who imply that most of the great construction feats in the Andes were attributable to the last empire. Of course, it is extremely difficult to date the construction of agricultural terraces, but several lines of indirect evidence strongly suggest that the first agricultural terraces were constructed as early as the Middle Formative period, about 1000 B.C. This problem is addressed in subsequent chapters.

Pastoralism

The keeping of domestic animals has been one of the mainstays of Titicaca Basin economies from the earliest periods for which we have data. The principal domesticated animals are camelids (llama and alpaca), along with cows, sheep, and goats introduced from the Old World. Data from the sixteenth century suggest that approximately 20 percent of the population was engaged in pasturing animals (Graffam 1990, 1992), although this appears to have been a historical high compared with earlier periods (Stanish 1994). Today, most of the animals kept near the lake are European imports, and camelids are pastured in the higher puna lands above 4,000 meters or so.

Camelids provide meat and wool and also serve as pack animals. In fact, their role as pack animals was extremely important for the development of early exchange in the Titicaca Basin. Many of the great geoglyphs, or giant ground drawings, of the Atacama and southern Peruvian coastal deserts were probably associated with camelid pack trains as early as the Upper Formative in the region (circa 400 B.C.–A.D. 400), and likely even earlier.

Increased reliance on pastoralism is one of the principal responses to the drought conditions that periodically affect the region. Animals can graze on natural grasses and other plants that grow under severe drought conditions, and they can be moved to well-watered areas. The butchered meat can be freeze-dried (into *charqui,* or jerky) and stored for extended periods, and wool can be used and exchanged for other products.

Lake Exploitation

The most important economic resource from Lake Titicaca is fish. Orlove (1986) estimates the total modern annual catch on the Peruvian side alone to be more than eight thousand metric tons of fish—a significant figure given that nearly this entire amount is harvested by individual fishers organized at the community or household level.

There are both endemic and introduced fish species in Lake Titicaca.[16] Levieil and Orlove (1990), Orlove (1986), and Parenti (1984) note that the lake contains more than twenty species of *Orestias,* the main endemic genus harvested by modern fishers. They also note that Aymara fishers distinguish four main *Orestias* types. Another endemic is *Trychomyc-terus,* a catfish genus that accounts for less than 4 percent of the endemic harvest (Orlove 1986). The two main introduced species are the rainbow trout and the silverside, or *pejerrey,* introduced in the middle of the twentieth century (Orlove 1986).

Aymara populations today and in the historic past heavily exploited the rich lake ecosystem. Aquatic resources included fish and fowl. According to Tschopik, men usually do the fishing, although he notes no formal taboos against women doing the work (Tschopik 1947: 521). I have noted work parties in the lake planting totora reeds near Juli, on the Peruvian side, and all of these groups were composed exclusively of the young male members of the community.

Among the Uru and certain communities of Aymara, fishing remains the most important subsistence activity (and see Tschopik 1947: 521). The existence of such fishing communities attests to the existence of a fairly strong exchange system with concomitant economic specialization. In contemporary Titicaca Basin society, this exchange is mediated through both market and nonmarket mechanisms. As Tschopik (1947: 521) notes, each Aymara community has exclusive rights to exploit the lake near its village(s). In the Juli area, informants confirmed this principle of property rights and told me that the areas for harvesting fish, planting totora, and gathering lake seaweed for cattle feed were rigidly demarcated by known boundaries that pertained to individual communities. The boundaries were often marked in the lake with totora reed poles.

Nets dragged from small watercraft comprise the most common modern fishing practice. Tschopik reports that the Aymara preferred to fish on moonless nights (Tschopik 1947: 522), and La Barre notes that the Uru preferred moonlit ones (La Barre 1941: 510). I myself have observed people setting up nets and harvesting fish at virtually all times of the day and night. Thin rope, twine, and nylon fishing line are all purchased in the various marketplaces. Earlier, Tschopik (1947: 523) listed and illustrated several types of baskets made out of totora reed that were used to catch fish.

Reeds *(Scirpus tatora)* and algae (or, more specifically, the aquatic plants *Elodea, Myriophyllum,* and *Potamogeton)* are important industrial plants used for construction and cattle fodder (Levieil and Orlove 1990). Reeds are used to construct boats, mats, roofing materials, fish weirs, walls, and artisan goods. Tschopik mentions that occasionally the roots and shoots of the totora are eaten raw as well (Tschopik 1947: 513). In Bertonio's dictionary, totora reeds are also said to be edible: the word *chullu* is defined as "the white part of the totora reed near the root, that is good to eat" (Bk. 2: 92).

Reed beds, along with fishing areas, are found around the lake. They are jealously protected by local communities and recently have been a source of intercommunal conflict (Levieil and Orlove 1990). They are planted, cared for, and harvested by individual villagers, usually organized by kin groups. In the Juli region, communities routinely organize men to plant and care for the crops. Fishing is a more individualized activity, although fishing rights are coordinated above the household. The care of these aquatic resources represents one of the few purely economic activities organized at a community level at the present, although my informants tell me that individual households also stake out reed beds in some restricted and marginal areas of the lake.

Prehispanic Andean Political Economy

The concepts of political economy allow us to model the evolution of complex society in the archaeological record. This theoretical framework assumes that people make strategic decisions within a particular cultural, historical, and physical environmental context. This section outlines the particular context in which the complex Andean political economies evolved.

In earlier publications, I outlined some of the features of central Andean political economies prior to the Spanish Conquest (Stanish 1992, 1994, 1997). One of the key features of Andean economies is the absence of any true market mechanisms and the predominance of reciprocity, redistribution, tribute, and nonmarket trade. There is little documentary evidence of competitive feasting, although the famous cargos, in which prominent individuals sponsored fiestas, are most likely an example of such a mechanism.

Reciprocity

As with any society, reciprocal relationships permeate Andean life. Reciprocal exchange occurs between households, and the degree to which that reciprocity is deferred may be a function of the degree of kin relatedness. Agriculture land is farmed with the "borrowed" labor of kin and friends, and that labor must be reciprocated. The same is true for house raising and terrace construction. In communal labor projects for an entire village, such as totora planting and canal cleaning, the individual contributions of labor per household are carefully recorded, and each household is expected to contribute its share. Reciprocity is the economic basis of village life in the Andes (Alberti and Mayer 1974) and throughout the agrarian world. It is conducted without coercive political authority, and disputes are resolved by leaders recognized by the community for their religious expertise (e.g., see Huidobro, Arce, and Quispe 1994).

Redistribution

A variety of documents from the early part of the Spanish Conquest of the Andes illustrates the nature of redistributive relationships between political authorities and nonelite. Many documents describe po-

litical and economic relationships that most likely reflect immediate and not-so-immediate pre-Conquest cultural norms. The following quote from the Diez de San Miguel Visita describing the obligations of the Aymara people to their local political leaders presents a classic case of redistribution in which the obligations of the caciques' subjects were spelled out by the subjects themselves.

> They were asked what services and tribute they would give today to don Felipe Cauana, their cacique, and they said that the Indians of this *parcialidad* [moiety division] work twenty topos of land each year and in other years when it rains they work thirty topos . . . and that the cacique provides the seeds and gives them food on the days that they work, [food] such as potatoes, coca, chicha, quinoa, and meat sometimes and other times other things, and that these fields were cultivated and improved until they cleaned and harvested it [the produce] and he put it in his house. (Diez de San Miguel 1964: 94)

This quotation highlights how the moiety was obligated to provide workers to the cacique for his lands. In return, he gave the workers food and coca (an exotic commodity in this region) on the days that they worked. The amount of food and coca provided by the cacique represents a small portion of the total wealth created by the labor provided. This relationship is a classic redistributive one couched in culturally specific terms: people provide labor and in return are provided food and exotic goods that are not equal in value to the amount of wealth represented by their labor. This entire complex structure of nested obligations and the concomitant economic asymmetries existed in a nonmarket context.

Caciques had additional responsibilities and obligations to their subjects that served to complete the redistributive transaction over the long term. Caciques were expected to provide for periodic feasts, and this was perhaps one of their most important functions. Feasts involved the whole community, however that community was defined, and were occasions for the ritual and real redistribution of goods. One of the most important of these goods was chicha beer, a slightly alcoholic beverage made from maize.[17] Hastorf and Johannessen (1993) and Morris (1979) have discussed the significance of maize beer as a symbolic food imbued with political meaning. In their view, "chicha was at the nexus of reciprocal gift giving, economic production, changing symbolic systems, and political stratification" (Hastorf and Johannessen 1993: 133). Feasting and redistribution of commodities such as chicha were one means of reinforcing the political power of the caciques and related elite.

Chicha was not the only commodity redistributed in feasts in Titicaca Basin society. In the Diez de San Miguel Visita, Martín Cari, the principal cacique of the Lupaqa, explains what had happened to all of the animals that other witnesses had observed on his community's land. He is quoted as saying that the "surplus" animals that multiplied in the "community" herds were used in "the holidays [pascuas] and principal fiestas of the year [when] people come together with the principal cacique, the leaders of the community and other Indians to eat [the surplus meat]" (Diez de San Miguel 1964: 23). Thus camelid meat was part of the politically ritualized redistribution in Titicaca Basin feasts.

In Prehispanic Andean society, complex societies were characterized by an elaborate hierarchy of social and political units that were bound together by rules of redistribution. The minimal socioeconomic group was the household (Stanish 1992: 16–28). Households were divided and grouped into ayllu. The ayllu is difficult to define, but most definitions characterize it as a landholding social unit defined by fictive or consanguine kinship. A number of ayllu composed a moiety, or *saya*. Ideally, there were two saya, an upper one called Hanansaya (or *alasaya*), and a lower one called Hurinsaya (or *maasaya*). This division is an expression of the widespread Andean

principle of duality. The head of each saya in Titicaca Basin society is referred to as the cacique in sixteenth-century texts. The cacique of the upper moiety represents the highest political authority in these contexts. In even more complex political organizations, one upper moiety emerges as paramount among several others. In this latter case, the head of the paramount upper moiety represents the highest political authority.

It is instructive to look at the relationship between the Inca state and the Lupaqa cacique, as suggested by data in the Visita, to understand the structure of Inca-local authority relationships in this polity. What is evident is that this relationship was structurally similar to that between the cacique and his subjects in the ayllu. When Diez de San Miguel asked Martín Cari what tribute he paid to the Inca, he replied in a manner almost identical to that of his own subjects when asked about their tribute to him. Martín Cari said that "as principal cacique he gave to the Inca fifty or sixty pieces of cloth each year and he gave two hundred or three hundred young camelids [ovejas] so that he could feed people going off to fight and other things and that also he gave from his own house to these people fish and sandals and fifty or one hundred fanegas of maize and fifty baskets of coca" (Diez de San Miguel 1964: 22). In short, the manipulation of redistributive economic relationships among the elite and their retainers, most notably of exotic goods and commodities, stands at the core of the development of Prehispanic Andean complex societies. Unequal redistribution resulting in material asymmetries between elite and commoners was the economic and institutional means by which elites maintained their paramount position in their communities.

The ideological aspects of elite control are represented in Andean society in a number of ways, particularly through the manipulation of redistributive and reciprocal relationships. Even though redistributive relationships were inherently unequal, elites were obligated to present them as just and proper within their cultural contexts. Ideology was one mechanism by which these relationships were promoted. One of the most important components of elite use of ideology is large feasts. The successful fulfillment by the commoners of labor obligation permitted them to participate in elite-sponsored feasts, which in turn ensured their access to goods and rituals not otherwise available to them. In this sense, the reciprocal nature of the relationship between elite and commoner was ideologically reinforced, even if it was an economic and social fiction.

Competitive Feasting

Most of the documentary sources for the Andes were based on information obtained during or after the collapse of the Inca state. In this political context, competition among individual local rulers was suppressed by the authorities. Competitive feasting, a behavior most pronounced in peer-polity contexts with many homologous political entities, was not present in the sixteenth-century Andes, as the Spanish chroniclers also noted.

Competitive feasting was most certainly an aspect of Prehispanic Andean life, as it was in most other cultures around the world. Ethnographic, historical, and archaeological data give hints of such behavior prior to the emergence of the Inca state, although such competitive ceremonialism was not as strong as it was in other nonstate societies. Evidence of feasting areas in the archaeological record is vast. Histories describe local lords providing numerous ceremonies. The ethnographic record documents countless instances where local elites supported pilgrimages, religious festivities, and the like.

Trade

I have maintained that virtually all trade in the Prehispanic Andes conforms to that which Polanyi referred to as "administered trade" (Stanish 1992: 14).

There is little evidence for the existence of market-based exchange in the Andes, except possibly on the far north coast (Sandweiss 1992), and virtually no evidence for such exchange in the highlands prior to European contact.

In the sixteenth century at least, and probably before the Spanish Conquest, caciques controlled most interregional trade in highly valued exotic goods. There were exceptions, of course, such as the obsidian trade that extended from the Archaic period to the Altiplano period millennia later. However, obsidian is small and light, and easily moved by down-the-line trade. The bulk of the exotic goods had to be transported through potentially hostile territory, and trading expeditions required the labor of dozens of people.

The Diez de San Miguel Visita reports that caciques organized laborers from their political groups to send camelid pack trains to Cuzco, the lower maize- and coca-growing valleys of the yungas, and the mining center of Potosí to trade various goods for products not available in the Titicaca Basin. A portion of these exotic goods would then be redistributed to the community during periodic feasts. From a political economic perspective, people provided labor to the cacique for trading expeditions, thereby creating substantial wealth that could not have been obtained by individual households. The transport of certain commodities substantially added to their value. Maize, for instance, was several times more valuable in the Titicaca Basin, where it cannot be grown in any abundance, than it was in the lower valleys such as Sama, on the western slope of the Pacific watershed (see table 4.4). This huge value differential was appropriated by the elite, and a portion of this wealth was returned to the commoners in feasts.

Tribute

The available historical documents also provide insight into the nature of tribute relationships be-

TABLE 4.4

Prices of Selected Commodities
in the Diez de San Miguel Visita

(In pesos and tomines)

In the Titicaca Basin	
One fanega of flour	5–8 p.
One fanega of maize	5–6 p.
One fanega of *chuño*	4–7 p.
One camelid	5–6 p.
One pig	3½–4 p.
One fanega of potatoes	2 p.
One bird *(perdiz)*	½ t.
Fish and eggs	*"vale poco"* (of little value)
In the Sama Valley	
One cotton manta	4 p.
One jug of wine	4 p.
One fanega of wheat	1½–1¾ p.
One fanega of maize	7 t.
Small basket of cotton	3 t.

NOTE: p. = peso, t. = tomín (8 tomines = 1 peso).

tween complex and powerful states and their subject populations:

> He was asked what tribute they gave to the Inca in his time and he said that they gave him three thousand Indians for wars sometimes and other times they gave him all the Indians that he wanted to make walls and houses and to serve his household and children for sacrifice and maidens for his household and for the Sun and the Moon and the thunders and cloth and they worked many fields for him and they gave him gold from Chuquiabo and silver from the mines of Porco and they gave him lead as tribute as well and a brown glaze that is called limpi and copper and feathers and all that he wished to ask for they gave him as their lord and many birds and charqui and ducks from the lake they sent fish that arrived in Cuzco from here in two

days that is a distance of sixty leagues and the first mature quinua that was carried by one hundred Indians. (Diez de San Miguel 1964: 39)[18]

These tribute relationships continued into the Spanish Colonial period, and documents such as the Diez de San Miguel Visita and the Toledo Tasa provide detailed information on the quantity and type of goods and labor provided. Tribute was an integral part of imperial political economies in the ancient Andes, as it was in most ancient states around the world.

The Model of Zonal Complementarity or Vertical Control

Bernabé Cobo is possibly the first Andeanist to describe the relationship between the Andean environment and the political economy:

> It is necessary to presuppose the existence of an ancient custom of these people, and it is that when some province did not produce certain foods, especially none of their bread, which was maize, but was suitable for other uses, special arrangements were made. For example, due to the extreme cold, the provinces of Collao do not produce maize or other seeds or fruits of temperate lands, but they are very abundant in pasture lands and most appropriate for raising livestock and producing *papas* [potatoes], from which *chuño,* their substitute for bread, is made, as well as some other roots. For the inhabitants of these provinces, the Inca had picked out lands which lie in the hot valleys of the seacoast on one side and on the other side of the mountains toward the Andes; in these temperate valleys they plant the crops that they lack in their own lands. (Cobo 1983 [1653]: 192)

This passage reveals how the vertically stratified ecological zones in the Andes affect the ways in which people exploit the landscape, a process described in other documents as well. In 1964, Waldemar Espinoza S. published a transcription of the Diez de San

Miguel Visita, which was first published in 1567. Appended to the Visita is an article by John V. Murra that presents for the first time in a comprehensive manner his model of verticality or zonal complementarity. In two critical publications in 1968 and 1972, Murra restated the model of zonal complementarity, establishing it as the principal theoretical framework for analyzing Andean political economy for three decades.

The basic principle behind this model is that the vertical stratification of ecological zones in the Andes profoundly affected the political and economic strategies of Prehispanic populations. The traditional model is characterized by the direct control of colonial lands by polities outside their core region or home territory (Stanish 1992: 3). Populations strategically locate their colonies to control a diverse set of ecological zones, allowing the various complementary ecozones to be exploited by a single polity. Hypothetically, the resulting distribution of colonies creates an archipelago of landholdings over various ecological zones. The overlap of archipelagos results in a complex patchwork of different ethnic groups and political units.

Murra based his theory partly on data from the Diez de San Miguel Visita. Specifically, he demonstrated that the Lupaqa of the sixteenth century controlled lands in a number of lower valleys to the east and west of the Titicaca region (Stanish 1989a, 1989b, 1992). These areas included the Sama, Moquegua, Capinota, Larecaja, and Lluta regions.[19] The following passage from the Visita is typical: "Each year the majority of Indians go to Sama, Moquegua, Capinota and Cuzco . . . for maize, *aji* and other staples that do not grow in this province and from which they barter cattle, cloth, wool and charqui" (Diez de San Miguel 1964: 208).

The verticality model as presented by Murra is consistent with the observation that central Andean economies did not have any developed market mechanisms. In Murra's model, the relationship between the home territories and their colonies was mediated through mechanisms of redistribution and reciprocity (Murra 1985b: 16). In the case of the Lupaqa, the relationship between the elite of the home territory and their colonies appears to have been largely redistributive; it was characterized by the Spanish historians as the payment of tribute. We also can surmise that existing alongside this colonial relationship were family-level reciprocal ones, with the families in lowland colonies exchanging foodstuffs for wool, freeze-dried meat (charqui), potatoes *(chuño)*, lake fish, and other commodities from the Titicaca region.

Although the model of zonal complementarity has been a powerful theoretical tool for understanding Andean societies, I reject one of its central tenets: that it is a process unique to the Andes. In fact, the cultural processes in the Andes can be modeled like those in other parts of the world. In this sense, I take a comparative approach in analyzing the development of political and economic complexity. Clearly, the geographical characteristics of the central Andes profoundly affected the development of complex society, but by rejecting the uniqueness of the verticality ideal (see Forman 1978; Van Buren 1996), we can redirect our attention from defining a unique Andean mode of production to modeling the anthropological processes that underlie the origins and evolution of complex society.

The History of Archaeological Research in the Titicaca Basin

This chapter traces the historical development of Titicaca Basin archaeology. This survey begins in the mid-sixteenth century and seeks to convey an understanding of basin prehistory during this immediate post-European contact period. For each subsequent era, the results of the archaeological and historical research will be summarized. Several other good reviews of the history of research in the region already exist. In particular, I recommend Cook 1994, Lumbreras and Mujica 1982b, and Ponce 1991a, 1991b.

Archaeological interpretation is affected by political and ideological factors because it involves the writing of history that is intimately connected with discovering and creating ethnic identity, encouragement of cultural pride, the political aspirations of nation-states, and so on. In virtually all instances where descendants survive, the production of history is po-

litically charged (e.g., see Patterson 1986). The archaeology of the Titicaca Basin in particular, and the New World in general, has been notoriously susceptible to political and ideological influences throughout its five-hundred-year history. This is because the history of the New World populations has generally not been written by Native Americans themselves but by Europeans or their New World descendants. These scholars were writing in highly charged political, social, and ideological climates, and their interpretations must be evaluated in this light.

Since the fifteenth century, the Aymara people have been assaulted continually by more powerful foreigners. The conquest of the Aymara kingdoms in the fifteenth century by the Inca was followed by their equally brutal oppression by Europeans, as well as by their descendants who made up the elite Peruvian and Bolivian classes. Despite these pressures, the Aymara have maintained their cultural identity as the region's dominant minority ethnic group. This fierce independence has spawned strong reactions against them from both the cultural elite of the Andean republics as well as foreign travelers, naturalists, and scientists. In fact, the Aymara people of the Titicaca Basin have the dubious distinction of being one of the most maligned ethnic groups in the Americas. Throughout history, professional and amateur naturalists, foreign and national, have reacted negatively to the Aymaras' failure to conform to expected standards of behavior of subjugated "Indians." Simply put, when one combines a racist bias against an ethnic group with the power to write that group's history, the result must be assessed with utmost care.

The great Adolph Bandelier, for instance, is one of the most important figures in the formative years of Americanist archaeology, yet he was almost apoplectic in his hate for the Aymara for reasons that I do not fully comprehend. Bandelier's contempt is particularly curious in light of his other work with indigenous groups throughout the New World, about whom he usually writes with admiration and respect. But Bandelier was not alone in his dislike for the Aymara. The celebrated archaeologist Arturo Posnansky was deeply prejudiced as well. Even as late as the 1940s, the great Harry Tschopik, in his encyclopedic survey of Aymara culture for the *Handbook of South American Indians,* began by saying that the terms "'dull,' 'stolid,' and 'unimaginative' . . . in the opinion of the writer, add up to give a general picture of the way in which Aymara culture today strikes the outsider" (Tschopik 1947: 501). Much is left to be said on the construction of Aymara identity as presented to the outside world by anthropologists and non-anthropologists that is outside the scope of this book. However, I feel compelled to note that after fifteen years of work in the region, I have found the vast majority of Aymara people to be warm, decent,

and extremely generous after I had earned their trust. The origin of this stereotype baffles me.

It is useful to divide the research of the Titicaca region into three historical periods: (1) from the Spanish Conquest to the late eighteenth century, (2) from the late eighteenth century to approximately World War I, and (3) from World War I to the mid-twentieth century. From the end of Word War I to the mid-twentieth century, Titicaca Basin archaeology essentially enters its contemporary period. Research from the mid-twentieth century to the present is largely dealt with in later chapters.

From the Conquest to the Late Eighteenth Century

The conceptual foundation of Andean history remained little changed from the Conquest to the European Enlightenment. Colonial-period Andean history and prehistory were amalgams of two great traditions. One tradition was that of the various indigenous histories, in a sense codified and given official status by the Inca and then Spanish intellectual elite. Like all empires in world history, the Inca state supported an intellectual class that developed ideologies supportive of their political expansion. The second tradition, of course, was that of the sixteenth-century Iberian scholars as they rode the wave of conquest into the New World.

As Hamilton (1983: xviii–xix) has pointed out, the early historians of the Andes, such as Bernabé Cobo, Pedro de Cieza de León, and Guamán Poma, were deeply rooted in several traditions: the Bible, the early Christian fathers, Aristotle, and Pliny. Their historical reference was firmly within the Old Testament, and any interpretations of the history of New World peoples had to be consistent with these traditions. In the jargon of today, we would say that all data had to fit within this Scholastic or pre-Enlightenment paradigm.

It is important to realize that the Spaniards dealt almost exclusively with the Inca elite and virtually excluded other ethnic groups from their compilations of historical events, leading to a Cuzco-centered perspective. Many of our conceptions of the past therefore derive from the official histories collected by Spanish administrators and priests during this period. As a result, the history of Peru in the Colonial period reflected the political, social, and economic interests of both the Inca elite who provided the information and the Spanish officials who recorded their words.

One of the great historians of Andean society is Cieza, who was probably born in 1521, the year that Cortés was conquering the Aztec empire. He arrived in the Americas as a relatively young man. His *Crónica del Perú* is one of the best and earliest systematic observations of Andean people, culture, and history. Cieza ranks as one of the first serious non-indigenous scholars to visit the Titicaca Basin.

Cieza's observations of the Titicaca region represent some of the first European views of this important province of Tawantinsuyu. Chapter 99 of the *Crónica* includes the following description of the Colla ethnic group and their territory in the north basin:

This region [of Peru], that is called Collas, is the largest and most populous region, as I see it, of all of Peru. . . . To the east are the mountains of the Andes; and to the west are the headwaters of the snowcapped sierra and their slopes that stop at the sea in the south. Apart from the land that they [the Collas] occupy with their towns and small farms, there are great stretches of unpopulated wilderness that are full of wild game. The Collao is quite flat and in many areas there are well-watered rivers; and in these plains there are beautiful and spacious meadows that always have good pasture, and at times are very lush, however in the summer it dries up like in Spain. The winter begins in October and lasts until April. The nights and the days are practically the same, and it is colder here than in any part of Peru,

apart from the highlands and sierra, which makes it seem like it is part of the highlands; and it is certain that if this Collao land was a low valley like Jauja or Choquiabo that could provide maize, then it would be the best and richest of the better part of the Indies. Walking in the plains of Collao is difficult due to the winds; but when there is no wind and the sun is strong, it is a great pleasure to look at the beautiful meadows so populated; but, as it is so cold maize does not grow here nor are there any types of trees. (Cieza 1553: chapter 99)

In the same chapter Cieza noted that "in ancient times the Colla region was very populated and there were great towns. Next to the towns were their fields where they grew their crops." Cieza personally visited archaeological sites such as Tiwanaku, Hatuncolla, and Pucara. His observations on Tiwanaku and other ancient Andean settlements constitute some of the first recorded suggestions about the antiquity of the site and rank him as one of the first great antiquarians or early archaeologists of the Americas.

Tiaguanaco is not a large town, but it is mentioned for the large buildings found there that are certainly notable things to see. Near one of the principal lodges is an artificial hill built *[armado]* over large stone foundations. Further on from this hill are two stone idols in human form . . . that are so large that they appear to be small giants and it is seen that they have long clothing that is different from that seen in the local people today. . . . Near these stone statues is another building whose antiquity and lack of inscriptions *[letras]* is cause for not knowing who made such great foundations nor how much time has passed since they were made.

There are other things that I could say about Tiaguanaco that were not mentioned in order that I am not detained, however I conclude that for me this ancient ruin *[antiqualla]* is the oldest in all of Peru; thus, before the Incas reigned many buildings like these were made. (Cieza 1553: chapter 105)

Cieza is the first European observer known to document the ruins and recognize that they were older than the Incas. Of course, Cieza was almost certainly reflecting the beliefs of the local people, as well as those of his informants. The observation that Tiwanaku was earlier than the Inca empire was implicit in the official histories told to the Spaniards by the Inca elite. For instance, Cobo relates the story of Pachacuti's impression of Tiwanaku in his campaign in Collasuyu: "Pachacuti saw the magnificent buildings of Tiaguanaco, and the stonework of these structures amazed him because he had never seen that type of building before; and he commanded that his men should carefully observe and take note of that building method, because he wanted the construction projects in Cuzco to be of that same type of workmanship" (Cobo 1983 [1653]: 141).

Tiwanaku was not the only archaeological site in the Titicaca Basin discussed by the early historians. Cieza also briefly described the pyramids of Pucara, the site of Hatuncolla, and the Inca ruins on the Island of the Sun (Cieza 1553: chapter 102). Concerning Pucara, Cieza says that he spent one day there "looking at all of it." He notes that in ancient times the site was a great population center but that in his time almost no one was living there. He also described some of the stone stelae at the site. Another site that Cobo visited and accurately described was Pucara Juli, the large, fortified Altiplano-period site outside the modern town of Juli (Cobo 1983: 140), and he confirmed many of the observations of Cieza about Tiwanaku.

The work of the early historians formed the basis of our understanding of Titicaca Basin history that survives to the present day. By the end of the seventeenth century, the Titicaca Basin had been recognized as one of the most important areas of the pre-Inca Andes. There was a strong grasp of the historical importance of certain sites in Cieza's work, and, in fact, he correctly assessed the relative antiquity of several major sites.

The Late Eighteenth Century to the End of the Nineteenth Century: The Natural History Paradigm

One of the first great modern histories of the New World was written, ironically enough, by a near-blind North American who never visited Peru. William Prescott's monumental *Conquest of Mexico* was soon followed by the equally monumental *Conquest of Peru.* Prescott's work was a popular hit, particularly in the Americas. Another book, *The Manners, Customs, and Antiquities of the Indians of North and South America,* written in 1846 by S. G. Goodrich, was a surprisingly accurate restatement of the early historical writings of Garcilaso de la Vega. These books initiated great interest in the ancient cultures of the Spanish New World, particularly those in Mexico and Peru at a time when there was also an explosion of interest in the natural sciences. One result was the undertaking of the many great naturalist expeditions into the Americas during the 1800s. Particularly in the Americas, during this period archaeology became one of the natural histories, a tradition that survives to the present.

The nature of Spanish natural history in the Colonial period is far richer and more diverse than commonly thought (e.g., see Willey and Sabloff 1980: 12–33). In the mid- to late 1700s, a number of botanical, zoological, and geological expeditions supported by the Spanish Crown (Goodman 1992: 222–242) brought large quantities of specimens to Europe for study. The European Enlightenment created the intellectual context for the first modern natural historical research in the Americas, and archaeological research was a central discipline in these efforts.

Archaeological research from approximately the last decades of the eighteenth century to World War I can be characterized as one conducted in the context of a natural history paradigm. This period overlaps with what Willey and Sabloff (1980) call "the

Classificatory-Descriptive period," which they characterize as one in which "the principal focus of the new period was on the description of archaeological materials, especially architecture and monuments, and rudimentary classification of these materials" (Willey and Sabloff 1980: 34). This research was characterized by generally sound empirical observations, by the standards of the time, and by the building of museum collections throughout Europe and North America.

Despite the politically and racially charged nature of this era of intellectual history, the natural history paradigm provided a rich understanding of the New World past in general and of the Titicaca Basin in particular. The naturalist Alcide Dessalines D'Orbigny visited the area in 1833 and offered some descriptions of Tiwanaku and other monuments in the area in his book *El hombre americano*. Charles Wiener (1880) provided important observations and images of the region in his classic work, *Pérou et Bolivie: Récit de voyage*. Mariano Eduardo de Rivero and Johann Jakob von Tschudi (1855: 292–299) published brief descriptions of a few Titicaca Basin sites, including Hatuncolla, Tiwanaku, the Islands of the Sun and Moon, and Sillustani, but many of their descriptions are inaccurate. For instance, they placed Hatuncolla and Sillustani, the latter referred to as "Clustoni," adjacent to each other—a rather substantial factual error even by nineteenth-century standards. Their drawings of Tiwanaku and Pilco Kayma on the Island of the Sun are incorrect, showing a number of hills that do not exist. Rivero and Tschudi drew most of their accounts from Cieza and appear to have had drawings made from either a poor memory or from an inaccurate informant.

Ephraim Squier visited the Titicaca region in the mid-nineteenth century. He dedicated a large part of his book *Peru: Incidents of Travel and Exploration in the Land of the Incas* to describing the area's ruins (Squier 1877: 272–402). He spent considerable time making observations and included descriptions of Tiwanaku, sites on the Islands of the Sun and Moon, the chulpas of Acora (also known as Molloko) and Sillustani, the Inca Uyu at Chucuito, and other sites. Like those of his predecessors, some of his drawings were inaccurate. However, his work was somewhat more systematic than that of earlier writers and has proven a valuable primary source for information on sites that have since been destroyed or severely damaged.

One of the most outstanding figures in the archaeology of South America in the late nineteenth to early twentieth century was Max Uhle (Willey and Sabloff 1980: 68), a distinguished German citizen who was a philologist, cultural anthropologist, and archaeologist. While working at the Dresden Museum, he collaborated with Alphons Stübel on a lavishly illustrated publication entitled *Die Ruinenstaette von Tiahuanaco*, which was published in 1892 and set the stage for future research on the site of Tiwanaku.

As Willey and Sabloff point out, Uhle had become very familiar with the Tiwanaku art style prior to his work with Stübel. As a result, he recognized it to be a pre-Inca horizon marker found throughout the central Andes. Tiwanaku-like pottery was found along the coast in a number of sites studied by Uhle. The sites that were called Coastal Tiahuanaco were much later recognized as part of the distinct Wari culture centered in Ayacucho.

Naturalists who worked in the Titicaca Basin during the nineteenth century developed a consensus on two very important issues that would greatly influence future research. The first and very unfortunate conclusion was that the Aymara were too inferior a race to have created a complex civilization, particularly that represented by Tiwanaku. The second conclusion was that the altiplano environment was too inhospitable to support civilization. Nadaillac echoes the conclusion of many naturalists: "One thing we think certain: such monuments [Tiwanaku] cannot be the remains of a civilization of local growth, nor can a race, unaided, have developed from its own genius such architectural knowledge. We share the conclusion of Angrand,[1] that the civilization of which the remaining ruins bear the impress, could not have taken its rise on these frozen table-lands" (Nadaillac 1969 [1885]: 406).

Squier was of the opinion that Tiwanaku was a temple or religious center, not the capital of a large polity. Like Nadaillac and others of the time, he based his conclusion on the fact that the altiplano was simply too harsh for "nurturing or sustaining a large population" (Squier 1877: 300). The notion that Tiwanaku was an uninhabited ceremonial center was firmly established in the literature among the early naturalists by the turn of the century.

Along with the conclusions that the Titicaca Basin and the people who populated it were incapable of fostering and creating civilization, the nineteenth-century naturalists left a strong racist imprint on Titicaca Basin archaeological and ethnographic research. Theories of race migrations as the source of cultural evolution were common in nineteenth-century Europe and America. This particular theory was very strongly adhered to by many in Titicaca Basin studies.

In short, this period of research was a double-edged scientific sword. On one hand, it was characterized by some sound empirical description and the discovery of new sites and art styles. Scholars popularized the Titicaca Basin cultures and developed some interesting theories to account for stylistic links to other parts of the Andes. On the other, the work in this time essentially solidified a racist interpretation of Aymara prehistory dominated by theories of racial inferiority, migrations of new racial stocks, and the like. It was in this intellectual and social context that the modern period of archaeological research began.

The Early Twentieth Century to the Modern Era

The late nineteenth century was a time of intense, albeit superficial, research at the site of Tiwanaku. The Conde G. de Créqui-Montfort spent three months at the site excavating the architectural core (see Cook 1994: 39). Likewise, Erland Nordenskiöld published some ethnographic and archaeological observations about Tiwanaku culture after the turn of the century (Nordenskiöld 1917).

One of the most flamboyant figures in early-twentieth-century altiplano archaeology was Arturo Posnansky, a Bolivian national born in Germany. He was extremely proud of Bolivia, and his staunch nationalism permeated all of his work. Unfortunately, like all too many of his peers, he also projected a cold racism against the Aymara majority in Bolivia. Although many of his ideas are truly bizarre, he nevertheless had the greatest impact on Titicaca Basin archaeology for his time.

In 1912, Posnansky published his *Guía General Ilustrada para la Investigación de los Monumentos Prehistóricos de Tihuanacu e Islas del Sol y la Luna,* in which he offered a number of his more outlandish ideas and theories. He argued, for instance, that during its main occupation, Tiwanaku was actually on the coast and had risen 3,800 meters over time by tectonic action (Posnansky 1912: 1–2). He also suggested that the chemical composition of Lake Poopó and the Pacific Ocean were similar, an argument that was important to him because he felt that he had to explain how a great civilization could have been created in the cold, windswept environment of the altiplano. With tectonic uplift, he did not have to explain this. He simply accepted as fact that the city was built in a more conducive tropical climate.

Posnansky also suggested five epochs for altiplano culture history beginning between ten thousand and eleven thousand years ago (when Tiwanaku was much lower in a tropical zone) and ending with the Incas' arrival in the last epoch. The great stone burial towers, or *chulpas,* of the altiplano originated in this period. Posnansky even suggested that the Incas originated in China, noting that in some communities in Bolivia and Peru the native language is understood only by Chinese immigrants (1912: 46).

We must understand Posnansky's book through the filter of his most basic presuppositions about the nature of human society. Like many of his contemporaries who accepted the evolutionary philosophy of the day, Posnansky saw all societies as inevitably evolving from an archaic, primitive stage to a classic one, which in turn eventually decays into a decadent stage. As we will see, this Toynbee-like view of world history was implicitly shared by other important figures in Titicaca Basin archaeology as well, including the great North American archaeologist Wendell Bennett.

Adolph Bandelier (1910, 1911) published an important book on the Islands of the Sun and Moon as well as an article on Tiwanaku. During his four months of research on the islands, Bandelier excavated more than twenty sites, concentrating largely on cemeteries. He made no systematic attempt to record all of the prehistoric sites on the island but visited only those that interested him (Bandelier 1910: 165). Bandelier's work demonstrated that there had been a substantial Inca presence on the island, but also an extensive pre-Inca settlement that he simply called Chullpa. Bandelier did not describe the Tiwanaku materials that he found, although he clearly made reference to the Tiwanaku style that had been previously defined by Uhle and Stübel. At any rate, his work on the islands identified the widespread influence of the Inca and Tiwanaku cultures, and demonstrated archaeologically that the pilgrimage center described by sixteenth-century documents was indeed accurate.

Philip Ainsworth Means's *Ancient Civilizations of the Andes,* published in 1931, remains an important synthesis of Andean prehistory for its time. At the time, Tiwanaku was considered one of the most important pre-Inca cultures in the Andes, and Means accepted Posnansky's two-stage chronology for the occupation of Tiwanaku (the first two periods in his five-period sequence): "in spite of the fantastic quality of some of his [Posnansky's] ideas, we owe a great debt because of his having shown quite clearly that there were two successive and easily distinguishable cultural periods at the site" (Means 1931: 112). Means refers to these stages as Tiahuanaco I and Tiahuanaco II. One great question, therefore, was, What were the absolute dates of these two periods?

In 1931 Means came up with dates for these periods by examining historical accounts and using some very dubious assumptions. He does not provide many details but claims to have analyzed the work of Early Colonial historians and chroniclers to derive a date for the transition between Posnansky's early and late periods: A.D. 600. Ironically, he arrived at the what we now accept as the date (give or take a century or so) of the beginning of major Tiwanaku expansion throughout the Titicaca Basin and beyond.

The Early Modern Era: Big Sites and Big Chronologies

With the pioneering work of Wendell Bennett, Gregorio Cordero Miranda, Alfred Kidder II, Carlos Ponce Sanginés, Julio Tello, Luis Valcárcel, José Franco Inojosa, Marion Tschopik, and Emilio Vásquez, Titicaca Basin archaeological research entered its modern era and began pursuing a new set of interests. The early archaeologists of this modern era combined the old space-time systematic tradition with a new focus on broader questions of cultural process and explanation. This combination of goals and strategies marks the modern era. As early as the sixteenth century, Spanish scholars were concerned with broader questions, and we may presume that Andean scholars before them had similar goals. But these earlier scholars sought to answer questions by means that we now view as unscientific; that is, teleological or tendentious attempts to accumulate observations to prove immutable ideologies. The later space-time systematists accepted a scientific methodology, even if some of them were concerned with narrow problems of chronology and style distribution. However, these narrow problems were always pursued with an aim to understand larger historical ones. What is taken to be the defining characteristic of the modern era is the pursuit of larger problems using good scientific field methods as pioneered by these twentieth-century scholars.

The early modern scholars focused on the great monuments and big sites, such as Tiwanaku, Pucara, and Sillustani. They also concentrated on art styles found on monoliths, pottery, and occasionally textiles from the coast. One of the most direct effects of this work was to isolate certain sites in the region as representative of different cultural periods. This was particularly important before the advent of radiocarbon dating, when the age of a site was defined through stratigraphic and iconographic analysis. Each of these major sites served to highlight the different periods of human occupation in the Titicaca region and became core databases of space-time systematics research.

Tiwanaku

The first systematic investigations of Tiwanaku were conducted by Uhle and Stübel and, slightly later, by Posnansky around the turn of the century. As mentioned above, Posnansky suggested a somewhat fanciful five-stage sequence for altiplano civilization and divided Tiwanaku chronology into two very long periods that fit into this framework. In 1939, Alfred Kroeber offered an Andean-wide chronology of ancient Peruvian art styles (Kroeber 1939) that included three periods: Primitive, Middle, and Late. The Primitive period included the cultures of Nasca, Paracas, Moche, and Chavín; the Middle period was represented by Tiwanaku (the site of Wari had yet to be discovered, and Wari styles were lumped with Tiwanaku); and the Late period was characterized by Inca styles.

The beginning of modern systematic archaeological investigations at Tiwanaku began with the work of Wendell Bennett in the 1930s and 1940s, which represents the second watershed in Titicaca Basin archaeology, the first being Posnansky's research. The normally staid professor ended his 1934 report with a soft jab at his colleagues: "One hopes that the days of treasure hunting and wild subjective speculation on history have passed" (Bennett 1934: 491).

Bennett was a scientist and very much the product of his time. His interest was similar to so many of his colleagues: historical reconstructions of ancient cultures. His method, of course, was space-time systematics. The purpose of archaeology was to define various cultural styles in space and time and build a cultural historical chronology for Tiwanaku. As a scientist, his method of ending wild speculation and treasure hunting was to slowly dig small holes in garbage pits, rather than quickly digging large holes in cemeteries. His goal was to define ceramic chronologies and tie these in, if possible, to discrete construction features. His method differed markedly from most of his predecessors and contemporaries, and made him one of the first scientific archaeologists to work in the region.

Bennett received permission from the Bolivian government to excavate ten pits on any area of Tiwanaku that he chose. Each pit was not to exceed ten square meters, but he was allowed to go as deep as the strata allowed (Bennett 1934: 361). Bennett's goals were well-defined: he would look for stratified middens or superimposed house floors and then analyze the sequence of pottery styles. In effect, he set out to refine Posnansky's Tiahuanaco I and Tiahuanaco II framework into a more empirically sound chronology.

Bennett's results had an effect on Titicaca Basin archaeology that has lasted to the present day. From his ten excavation units, Bennett recovered 14,500 sherds, of which 2,210 were decorated pieces (Bennett 1936: 392, table 2). From these fragments, he identified twenty different design elements. Based upon these data and the associated archaeological strata in the pits, Bennett offered four periods for the Tiwanaku sequence: Early Tiahuanaco (or pre-Tiahuanaco), Classic Tiahuanaco, Decadent Tiahuanaco, and Post-Tiahuanaco (Bennett 1934: 445).

Bennett's lowest strata were stratigraphically under his Classic levels. These lowest levels contained a very high percentage (90 percent) of plain wares in pits number 5 and 8. He considered these strata to represent a separate and early cultural period, and therefore named it Early Tiahuanaco (Bennett 1934: 448–453). In both pits, the Early Tiwanaku levels were at the bottom of a long stratigraphic sequence (Bennett 1934: 380, 384, 389). He also noted the presence of ash pits and hearths in these levels, strongly suggesting that the unit was undisturbed.

Bennett identified a number of vessel shapes that occurred exclusively in the Early Tiwanaku period, including horizontal rim handle bowls and dishes, shallow open bowls, a small flaring-rim olla, and several other shapes. The significance of Bennett's work was that he isolated a cultural level that antedated his Classic and Decadent levels, and had what he believed was a distinctive set of ceramic markers. Most important, Bennett's Early Tiahuanaco corresponded to the time period that we now recognize as existing prior to the development of Tiwanaku as an expansive archaic state.

It was in this research context that the celebrated Bolivian archaeologist Carlos Ponce Sanginés began systematic and intensive research at Tiwanaku, directing massive excavations at the site in conjunction with the Centro de Investigaciones Arqueológicas de Tiwanaku (CIAT). As seen in the photographs in the fourth edition of his book *Tiwanaku: Espacio, Tiempo y Cultura* (1981), Ponce and his team excavated a substantial number of large units outside the Kalasasaya enclosure (photo 45, p. 175) as well as seventy-three units (Ponce 1976: 5; 1981) in the interior of the structure (1981: photo 44, p. 175).

One of the objectives of Ponce's Kalasasaya excavations was to discover stratigraphic levels predating the main structure and, therefore, to define occupations prior to what Bennett had discovered (Ponce 1976: 5). Under the platform of the main structure, Ponce discovered two habitation levels, both below the fill of the Kalasasaya and separated by a sterile stratum (1976: 5). Ponce reports finding a number of intact features associated with these levels, similar perhaps to Bennett's discovery of ash pits and hearths.

The CIAT excavations at the Kalasasaya also provided abundant carbon samples for absolute dating. Based on these data, Ponce constructed his five-phase sequence (I–V). Ponce (1981: 128, table 1) published sixteen dates for Tiwanaku I and Tiwanaku II that range from 580 ± 200 B.C. to A.D. 320 ± 130. One outlier date of 1580 ± 120 B.C. should be discounted as contaminated or out of context. Ponce derived an average date of 237 B.C. for Tiwanaku I and A.D. 43 for Tiwanaku II (the Tiwanaku I date would be 153 B.C. if the 1580 B.C. date is discounted). The first two phases offered by Ponce were argued to be earlier than Bennett's Early Tianuanaco. Although Ponce never explicitly acknowledges it, his phases of Tiwanaku III–V essentially correspond to Bennett's Early, Classic, and Decadent periods, respectively.

The work of Bennett and Ponce at Tiwanaku set the stage for research in the region for decades. Ponce's five-phase sequence for Tiwanaku was in many ways a refinement of Bennett's general chronological framework for the Titicaca region as a whole. By the 1960s, the Bennett-Ponce chronology was firmly established as the most generally accepted framework in Titicaca Basin archaeology (see figure 5.1).

Pucara

Pucara is another great archaeological site and icon of Titicaca Basin archaeology.[2] Like Tiwanaku, Pucara was first described by Cieza in the seventeenth century. He considered it a major *huaca,* or sacred place, and recognized its importance and antiquity. In the twentieth century, Pucara was scientifically

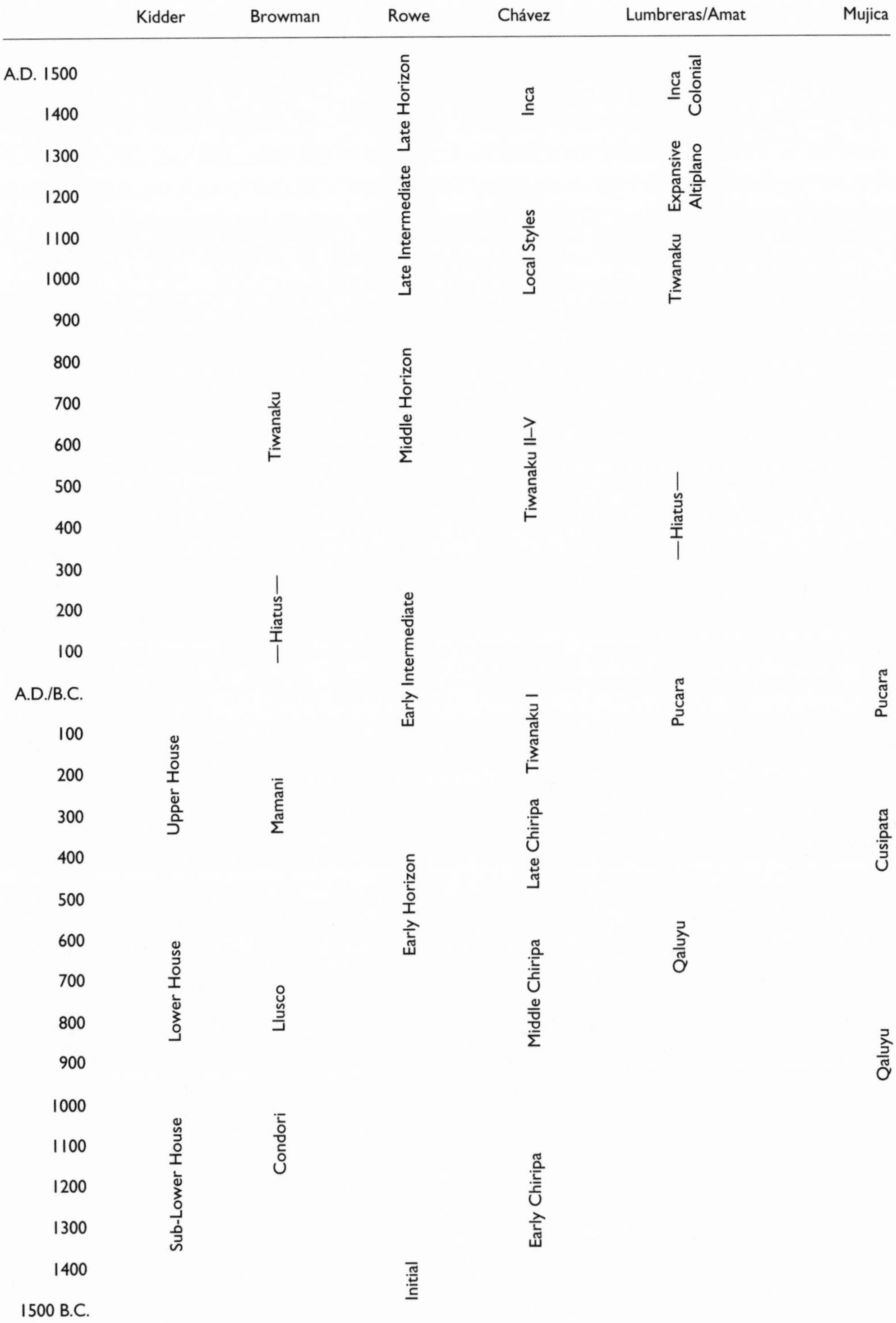

Years	Kidder	Browman	Rowe	Chávez	Lumbreras/Amat	Mujica
A.D. 1500			Late Horizon	Inca	Inca / Colonial	
1400						
1300			Late Intermediate		Expansive Altiplano	
1200				Local Styles		
1100						
1000					Tiwanaku	
900						
800		Tiwanaku	Middle Horizon			
700				Tiwanaku II–V		
600						
500					—Hiatus—	
400						
300		—Hiatus—				
200			Early Intermediate			
100						
A.D./B.C.				Tiwanaku I	Pucara	Pucara
100	Upper House	Mamani				
200						
300				Late Chiripa		Cusipata
400						
500			Early Horizon			
600	Lower House			Middle Chiripa	Qaluyu	
700		Llusco				
800						
900						Qaluyu
1000						
1100	Sub-Lower House	Condori		Early Chiripa		
1200						
1300						
1400			Initial			
1500 B.C.						

FIGURE 5.1. Earlier chronologies utilized in the Titicaca region.

rediscovered, and information about it was published by Valcárcel (1925). His work emphasized the iconographic similarities between Pucara styles and regional styles around the Andes, and also demonstrated that Pucara was the center of this major early art style.

Kidder also worked at Pucara at around the same time. Franco Inojosa (1940: 129–135) summarized the results of Kidder's work here. He reported large areas of midden deposits, almost two kilometers in length, in front of the site that contained camelid bone, deer antlers, quinoa seeds, obsidian, camelid dung, and projectile points. He also described evidence of human sacrifice and reported on the fabulous stone sculptures. Franco Inojosa correctly concluded that Pucara was a very large pre-Inca site. He noted that the ruins "are not contiguous [agrupadas]" and that the entire site area, including the thousands of 'mines' [minas] of clay, covered about one square kilometer (Franco Inojosa 1940: 129–135). He argued that Pucara culture had wide influence, including a great part of the altiplano, Nuñoa, Asillo, Taraco, Ilave, Arapa, and other areas, perhaps even Nasca.

Franco Inojosa indicated that excavations in "various areas" revealed ceramics indicating the existence of three stages of culture: Inca, an Intermediate stage characterized as *behetria* (without lords), and, finally, at the lowest levels, Pucara (Franco Inojosa 1940: 129). In other words, he concluded that the site was predated the Inca and was most likely contemporary with Tiwanaku. With its impressive art styles, Pucara became emblematic of the pre-Tiwanaku cultures of the north basin.

Hatuncolla

Hatuncolla, one of the principal administrative centers of the Inca empire, was described in the early chronicles, and Cieza described it as one of the most important towns of the Collao: the Incas "adorned this town with buildings and many storehouses, a place where tribute was sent from the surrounding countryside, where there was a temple to the Sun, with many mamaconas and priests, a great number of mitima colonists and warriors placed there to guard the province" (Cieza 1553: chapter 102). Juan de Betanzos (1996: 152) wrote that it was here that Topa Inca met with his generals who had come from the coast via Arequipa. Hatuncolla was also described by Garcilaso as a "town ennobled with great and splendid buildings, apart from the temple of the Sun and the house of the virgins" (Garcilaso 1989: 110). One of the principal Inca towns in the basin, Hatuncolla was a favorite stop of nineteenth-century travelers and naturalists.

Sillustani

Sillustani is one of the most famous ancient burial grounds in the Americas (Pardo 1942). Located next to Lake Umayo in the northwestern Titicaca Basin between Puno and Juliaca, the site sits on a large, flat massif dominated by huge burial towers known as chulpas. Chulpas are found throughout the Titicaca Basin and beyond, at least as far north as Huancavelica. The Titicaca region, however, has been famous since the sixteenth century as the center of the most spectacular chulpas. Those at Sillustani are constructed of stone masonry, and the tallest reaches several meters in height. These chulpas have been visited and described for generations, beginning with the early chroniclers.

There is little doubt that the chulpas are burial towers. Three of the major Spanish chroniclers—Bernabé Cobo (1990 [1653]), Pedro de Cieza de León (1553), and Felipe Guamán Poma de Ayala (1980 [1616])—provided descriptions and/or drawings of chulpas as burial chambers. Cobo even noted that indigenous graves vary throughout the Andes, but that the aboveground chulpas are most typical of the Colla in the Titicaca Basin (Rydén 1947: 408–409). The early Spanish travelers and Crown officials originally described the stone and adobe towers as mausoleums for dead nobility. Aboveground indigenous "houses of the dead" were described and illustrated in historic texts by Guamán Poma de Ayala (1980: 262–265, 268–272). Cieza (1976: 274) also commented that these towers were most remarkable in the Titicaca Basin, and he unequivocally described them as tombs: "the most notable thing to see in Collao, in my view, are the graves of the dead . . . made of small, four-cornered towers, some of stone and others of earth and stone, some wide and others narrow." Likewise, Cobo (1990: 248–249) ascribed the chulpas to the Colla and described them at great length as burial towers.

In the twentieth century, Bandelier (1905) published a paper on Sillustani and concluded that some of the large chulpas were Inca qolcas, or storehouses, but that conclusion has since been rejected. Vásquez described Sillustani and compared it with other sites in the region (e.g., Vásquez 1937a, 1937b, 1939, 1940). Virtually all of the chulpas had been looted by the mid-nineteenth century. The few that have been excavated indicate that they are burial towers. Excavation data include samples of the small chulpas (Stanish 1985), the large ones (Ruiz Estrada 1976), and intermediate-sized ones (Nordenskiöld 1906; Rivera Casanovas 1989; and see Isbell 1997). By mid-century, Sillustani was recognized as a major post-Tiwanaku site with many chulpas built in Inca and pre-Inca styles, and that it represented the most spectacular of the many chulpa sites in the Andes.

Chiripa

Bennett was the first archaeologist to publish results of research from the site of Chiripa, which is on the Taraco Peninsula, over the mountain range on the northern side of the Tiwanaku Valley. Bennett's work identified Chiripa as the type site in the southern Titicaca Basin for his pre-Decadent Tiwanaku cultures. Bennett first excavated for five weeks at the site in the 1933–1934 season, naming the culture Chiripa based on ceramic and architectural data. He cut a large trench across the mound and several other trenches north of it, and sank a number of test pits in the site area (Bennett 1936: 413, 415). Initially, Bennett placed Chiripa between Classic and Decadent Tiwanaku in his chronology (Bennett 1936: 332), based on an excavation at Pajchiri, where he thought he had found a Chiripa level above a Classic Tiwanaku one. Later, Bennett (1948a) corrected this error and correctly placed the entire Chiripa sequence earlier than Classic Tiwanaku. By mid-century, Chiripa had become emblematic of the pre-Tiwanaku sites in the southern Titicaca Basin.

Over the decades after Bennett, a number of archaeologists have worked at Chiripa, including Browman (1978b), Chávez (1988), Kidder (1967), Ponce, Cordero, and others. Most recently, Christine Hastorf (1999a, 1999b) and her team have conducted the most systematic research to date. Described below, this work has greatly expanded our knowledge of the region's pre-Tiwanaku periods.

Chucuito

On the western shore of Lake Titicaca, in Peru, Chucuito was mentioned prominently in historical documents as the capital of the immediate pre-Inca Lupaqa señorío, or kingdom. Along with Sillustani, Chucuito was one of the principal sites used to define Titicaca Basin chronology. Marion Tschopik lived in Chucuito in the 1940s and excavated at a number of sites, including Chucuito itself. Most notable is her excavation at the large stone building of Inca Uyu, the temple near the center of the town. Tschopik's work (1946) indicated that Chucuito was a major Inca site, and along with the large Late Horizon chulpas of Sillustani and Hatuncolla, it became exemplary of Inca occupation in the Titicaca region.

Tanka Tanka

This site, a massive fortress, is in the far southwestern part of the Titicaca region, in the dry grasslands away from the lake. It was described by Vásquez, Carpio, and Velazco (1935) and Vásquez (1940), and referred to by Romero in his summary of Puno (Romero 1928). Tanka Tanka is a very impressive site with massive fortification walls, chulpas, and abundant pottery on the surface. The site was used to typify the region's post-Tiwanaku, pre-Inca periods.

Regional Approaches in Titicaca Basin Archaeology

Modern settlement archaeology began (quite arguably) with the Virú Valley survey project directed by Gordon Willey (1974) in the 1940s. Before this path-breaking work, archaeologists in the Titicaca Basin had conducted many surface reconnaissances, which are arbitrary walkovers of an area in order to locate sites. A systematic survey, in contrast, provides, at least in theory, a complete characterization of the surface remains in a study area. Systematic surveys can be full regional coverage (100 percent), or they can use sampling techniques to produce a statistically reliable characterization of the entire area (Stanish 2001a). Whether systematic or not, reconnaissances shift the research foci from individual sites to regional concerns. Reconnaissance is particularly useful in areas where we have little knowledge of the range and nature of the archaeological remains. They serve to define broad patterns of settlement and artifact style distribution, and to generate hypotheses for future testing.

In this sense, Cieza represents the first nonindigenous scholar with archaeological interests to reconnoiter the Titicaca region, describing sites such as Pucara, Tiwanaku, Pukara Juli, Copacabana, and so forth. The first modern reconnaissances in the region were conducted by José Maria Franco Inojosa and Alejandro González (1936), Emilio Vásquez (1939), Alfred Kidder II (1943), and Marion Tschopik (1946) in the 1930s and 1940s. Vásquez (1940: 143–150) described several important sites in the Peruvian part of the basin, such as Sillustani, Cutimbo, Kacha Kacha, Tanka Tanka, Siraya, Maukallajta, Cheka, Wilakolla,

and Taraco. He described the cut stones at Cheka known as El Baño del Inka and the monoliths in the north near Huancané and Pucara, and he provided schematic descriptions of other sites.

Late reconnaissances include that of Gregorio Cordero (1971), who worked around the town of Pucarani and located a number of important sites. Oswaldo Rivera Sundt (1978) reconnoitered the Copacabana Peninsula and the Island of the Sun, and located a number of sites, particularly Inca sites. His archaeological work discovered late occupations on the peninsula, confirming much information in the historical documents. Felix Tapia Pineda (1978a, 1978b) reported on a number of sites from Nuñoa, in the northern extreme of the Titicaca region, and described a substantial complex of Altiplano-period sites, such as Jatun Pukara, Maukka Llajta, and others. Tapia published photographs of well-preserved fieldstone chulpas that appeared to date to the Altiplano period, and he described several Altiplano-period fortified sites, indicating that the Nuñoa region was the northernmost extension of this site type. Maximo Neira Avendaño (1967) reconnoitered the northern basin and described a number of sites in an unpublished manuscript. In the southwestern Titicaca region, Hyslop (1976) used a reconnaissance strategy to identify sites mentioned in historic texts. His work was designed to find sites from all agricultural periods, and to characterize the settlement patterns for each period. He located several dozen large sites and noted a number of small ones.

In the early 1980s the Instituto Nacional de Arqueología of Bolivia conducted an important reconnaissance on the eastern side of the lake (Faldín 1990; Portugal O. 1991). Portugal reports discovering a number of sites in the Camacho province, including significant sites from the Middle Formative, Upper Formative, Tiwanaku, Altiplano, and Inca periods. The reconnaissance identified sites farther east toward Iskanwaya, and the existence of Tiwanaku sites, or at least the presence of Tiwanaku fine wares, on contemporary sites in the lower elevations of the lake's eastern side. Sergio Chávez (1988) also reconnoitered the far northern Titicaca Basin in a systematic effort to locate early sites. His work provided invaluable data on the distribution of Pucara-contemporary sites throughout the region.

Systematic Surveys

In the 1990s, archaeologists began employing full coverage settlement surveys in the Titicaca Basin. The term *full coverage* is used in the sense described by Parsons (1990: 11) to mean a complete pedestrian survey of a region. Full regional coverage field methodologies vary slightly, but all include a comprehensive survey with a trained crew of archaeologists walking close enough to each other to locate all surface sites.

The first systematic full coverage survey of any region in the Titicaca Basin was conducted in the Tiwanaku Valley by Juan Albarracin-Jordan and James Mathews (1990) for their dissertation projects. Mathews surveyed the midvalley area, from approximately 6 kilometers east of Tiwanaku to approximately 6 kilometers west, between the two east-west trending mountain ranges on either side of the valley. The lower valley was surveyed by Albarracin-Jordan from the west side of Tiwanaku to the lake shore. In total, approximately 400 square kilometers were surveyed in the Tiwanaku Valley, providing invaluable settlement data from the Formative period through the Early Colonial period.

The second area that has been systematically and intensively surveyed is on the Peruvian side of the lake, from a few kilometers northwest of Juli to about 2 kilometers east of Pomata (Stanish et al. 1997). The survey covered approximately 360 square kilometers from an area north of Juli to just south of the town of Pomata. The survey included an area up to 14 kilometers away from the lake, in the puna.

The Island of the Sun was intensively and systematically surveyed by Brian Bauer, Oswaldo Rivera Sundt, and Charles Stanish in 1994 and 1995. The island is small (approximately 11 kilometers long, and 1 to 2 kilometers wide), and the survey took only ten weeks. Approximately 180 sites were discovered, several of them dating as early as 2000 B.C., indicating a pre-Formative use of the island by Late Archaic hunters, fishers, and collectors. Subsequent occupations included a substantial Early Formative through Inca occupation.

Other surveys in the region include that of the Pampa Koani by Graffam (1990, 1992) and a later survey of the area by Kolata, Janusek, and Seddon. Designed to test models of raised-field use and their cultural associations, these surveys demonstrated that there were vast areas of raised fields and associated settlements in the area and that raised-field agriculture had been an integral component of the endogenous economies of Titicaca Basin cultures.

Stages, Periods, and Phases: Building a Chronology for the Titicaca Region

Cultural chronologies can be classified into at least two types: evolutionary and historical. Evolutionary chronologies can also be described as developmental and are made up of stages that define a set of cultural features common to all societies within that stage. In contrast, historical frameworks are chronological and are traditionally composed of absolute time periods.

Developmental chronologies presuppose an evolutionary dynamic inherent to all societies, with a local cultural sequence representing a manifestation of some processes common to all societies. The classic evolutionary frameworks include stage names such as Archaic, Formative, Pre-Classic, Imperialistic, Regional Developmental, and the like. These frameworks presuppose that societies at each particular stage share similar cultural characteristics. In this sense, two contemporary societies may be in different stages. For instance, in the late nineteenth century, we could say that Europe and North America were in an Industrial stage, while many poorer non-Western nations were in an Advanced Agricultural or Incipient Industrial stage. The Industrial and Advanced Agricultural societies would be contemporary but would be distinguished by their relative position in an evolutionary framework based on a set of evolutionary characteristics.

Developmental frameworks are useful in a number of ways, particularly because a stage designation also implies certain organizational and structural characteristics of any society at any given stage. These characteristics are defined a priori, consistent with the particular epistemological and theoretical assumptions and conclusions of the scientific paradigm under which they are defined. The most powerful feature of developmental frameworks is placement of a society in a broader explanatory context. Explanation is the fundamental underpinning of anthropological archaeology in general, and of more than a generation of modern archaeological and historical science in particular. Such stage concepts permit us to compare and contrast the structural characteristics of cultures from various time periods and locations.

The principal weakness of developmental stage frameworks is their failure to explain contemporary variation between different societies in an adequate manner. These frameworks also have trouble dealing with the peaks and falls of political complexity (e.g., see Marcus 1992a). As Linda Cordell (1984: 85) points out in her discussion of Southwestern U.S. archaeology: "Any scheme of classification that minimizes or ignores these kinds of variation will not represent a faithful rendering of the diversity that can characterize the archaeological record." Developmental frameworks also strongly favor presumptions of autochthonous evolution, including gradual changes from one stage to the next, a common assumption of processual archaeology but not necessarily an inherent characteristic of society. As a result, such frameworks have difficulty dealing with

rapid transitions, particularly migrations, conquests, and so forth, which are not as easily dealt with in traditional evolutionary frameworks.

Historical or chronological frameworks, in contrast, do not presuppose larger cultural processes operating in all societies, although they do not necessarily rule them out. As a result, it is not necessary to subsume local cultural sequences into broader frameworks; instead, the archaeologist's job is to faithfully reconstruct the time and space relationships between different prehistoric cultures. One of the great strengths of historical frameworks is that the precise date of any culture can be easily defined relative to all other cultures. Historical frameworks also do not presuppose gradual transitions between periods, although such transitions are entirely possible. Consequently, cultural processes such as migrations and other sudden changes in human organization can be readily dealt with in traditional historical frameworks. The negative aspects of historical frameworks include an emphasis on cultural history to the exclusion of processual explanation, and a tendency to promote particularistic (in the sense defined by Harris [1968]) explanations of cultural change.

When deciding which type of framework to use, it is important to take into account the positive and negative aspects of each type, and the goals of the scientific analysis. In my view, historical and developmental frameworks are complementary and necessary in any comprehensive archaeological study.

It is vitally important to realize that a chronology itself constitutes a series of hypothetical relationships between and among prehistoric cultures in space and time. As a hypothesis, it is designed to be tested, refined, and rejected as research progresses. Both historical and developmental chronologies are heuristic tools that have different applications, and they should be used as the need exists. They are not truths to be discovered but hypotheses to be tested.

Modern research in the Andes and Titicaca Basin has provided several chronologies. Some of these were designed for larger areas encompassing the Titicaca Basin (Lumbreras 1974a). Others were not explicitly intended for use in the Titicaca Basin but nevertheless have been used to order the archaeological materials. Still others were built from archaeological data from the Titicaca region (Lumbreras and Amat 1968; Lumbreras 1974b; and the Bennett-Ponce sequence).

In 1968 Lumbreras and Amat proposed a five-period sequence for the western and northern sides of the Titicaca region (see figure 5.1) that relied to some extent on Ponce's and Bennett's work. This framework synthesized the data for the region up to that time, including a number of carbon-14 dates from Kidder's excavation materials from Pucara; his reconnaissance south of Puno; and the work of Tello and Ponce and reconnaissances by Amat, Lumbreras, Mujica, and others. Lumbreras also used museum collections to establish stylistic links between the Titicaca cultures and others outside the basin.

The first period in the Lumbreras/Amat sequence is a preagricultural one called Hunter/Gatherer dated to sometime before 800 B.C. Given that settled villages had already formed in the central Andean highlands and coastal areas in the third millennium B.C., the date of 800 B.C. for a preagricultural lifeway was surprisingly recent for the Titicaca region. The first settled populations in the Lumbreras/Amat sequence were found during the Early Ceramic–Agriculturalists period, divided into two phases: Qaluyu (800–500 B.C.) and Pucara (200 B.C.–A.D. 200). Lumbreras and Amat indicate an occupational gap for the region between 500 and 200 B.C., a problem addressed years later by other scholars.

Lumbreras and Amat also argued for a "great hiatus" between A.D. 200 and 700 in the north, and possibly in the western lake region as well. This would roughly correspond to the Classic and Expansive, or Tiwanaku IV and V periods, in the Bennett-Ponce chronology. Lumbreras and Amat cautiously noted that it was unclear if this hiatus represents a true abandonment of the area, or if it is merely a result of the lack of research. Regardless, they note that there is "no vestige of human society in the area" during this period (Lumbreras and Amat 1968: 84).

The next period in the Lumbreras/Amat chronology is Tiwanaku, dated to A.D. 900–1300. At the time they published their chronology, there was little in the way of systematic research in the western Titicaca area, with the exception of Kidder's reconnaissance. Lumbreras and Amat noted the existence of ostensibly Late Tiwanaku pottery in private collections from the Puno area, which they interpreted as evidence of a regionally integrated state system during this period. This was a significant observation and constituted a new model for settlement in the north basin for this time period. Lumbreras and Amat also suggested that there had been a collapse of Pucara culture, a generalized abandonment of the region, and a reoccupation of the area during Tiwanaku expansive times.

The following Lumbreras/Amat period is the Expansive Altiplano. No dates are provided, but it is described as post-Tiwanaku and pre-Inca, placing it between A.D. 1300 and approximately A.D. 1450, using their terminal date for Tiwanaku and the generally accepted date of Inca expansion—the Late Horizon in the Ica sequence, as described by John Rowe and Dorothy Menzel. The collapse of Tiwanaku is now placed around A.D. 1000–1100. The Expansive Altiplano period would therefore correspond to the protohistoric Aymara kingdoms of Colla, Lupaqa, Pacajes, and Omasuyu territories. The final Prehispanic period in the Lumbreras/Amat sequence is called Inca Colonial.

The Lumbreras/Amat sequence has been modified by several later research projects. Excavations conducted under the auspices of UNESCO in the 1970s discovered that the Kalasasaya temple at Pucara, known to date to the Pucara period (200 B.C.–A.D. 200 in the Lumbreras/Amat sequence), was built on an earlier temple (Lynch 1981: 203–204) that dated to 800–200 B.C., putting it in the earlier part of the Lumbreras/Amat sequence, in the Qaluyu period.

This discovery was also important because it filled in the three-hundred-year gap between the Qaluyu and Pucara phases. These data demonstrated continuity between these two building periods and cultures.

Later work, as described in the following chapters, has altered the chronology of cultures in the Titicaca region. In practice, most chronologies in the central Andes contain elements of both evolutionary and historical frameworks. An example of such a chronology is Lumbreras's (1974a) general Andean system, a seven-period chronology for the entire Peruvian central Andes, including the Titicaca region. Of the seven periods, five are overtly developmental: the Formative period, the Regional Development period, and so on. Two of the periods, in contrast, are historical: the Wari Empire and the Empire of Tawantinsuyu. At first, this appears to be contradictory. However, the cultural effect of Wari and Inca expansion was to truncate local political development and incorporate various polities into the imperial spheres of influence. Thus the end of the Formative (a developmental stage) can actually be viewed as a historical period as well, presuming that Wari and Tiwanaku expansion was relatively fast. In other words, the expansion of these imperial systems effectively ended Formative lifeways throughout the central Andes. The historical period corresponds to a developmental stage and could be called, for instance, a stage of imperial expansion.

The Ponce chronology also contains elements of both historical and evolutionary periods and stages. Numbered Tiwanaku I through V and given specific dates, the Ponce sequence at first appears to be a strictly historical chronology. However, in *Tiwanaku: Espacio, Tiempo y Cultura*, Ponce (1972: 75–85) assigns developmental qualities to each period. Tiwanaku I and Tiwanaku II, for instance, were argued to be "formative" in character. Tiwanaku III and IV, in contrast, were characterized as "the second stage of a fully urban character." The final stage, Tiwanaku V, was expansionist or "imperial" in character. The Ponce framework, therefore, combines an implicit evolutionary dynamic with a series of absolute dates.

Another great modern chronology of the central Andes that has been used extensively in the Titicaca Basin is that proposed by Rowe (1960). Rowe adopted a concept known as the *horizon style*, vaguely similar to that used by Willey in 1948 and presaged by Uhle, Tello, and Valcárcel (see Lumbreras 1974a: 7–13; Rice 1993: 2–5). The horizon framework is strictly a historical chronology that draws on the rich tradition of space-time systematics. As Rice aptly describes the horizon concept, it is "a classificatory term originally intended to place a particular constellation of cultural traits in time and space" (Rice 1993: 1). The horizon concept presumes that certain cultural traits spread rapidly from a point of origin, and that these traits can be used to date a particular culture relative to others.

As used by Rowe, the horizon framework for the Andes is derived from a type sequence from the Ica Valley on the south Peruvian coast. Each period is absolutely dated with reference to the Ica materials. A horizon represents the rapid and widespread distribution of an art style associated with a particular culture or cultural tradition, such as Chavín (Early Horizon), Wari and Tiwanaku (Middle Horizon), and Inca (Late Horizon). The horizon framework presupposes that materials from a particular horizon are roughly contemporary across space. The horizon chronology is therefore an appropriate framework for ordering all archaeological materials in the area where the styles typical of the horizon are found.

The question, then, is, What is the most appropriate chronological framework for the Titicaca region? There is no right answer. The choice depends on the types of questions being asked, and the types of data being used.

Many scholars have used the Rowe chronology for the Titicaca Basin with great success (Burger, Chávez, and Chávez 2000; Erickson 1988; S. Chávez 1992; K. Chávez 1988, among many others), but I consider this chronology difficult to adapt to the Titicaca Basin. For instance, the first monumental architecture on the Peruvian coast dates to perhaps 3000 B.C., but the first corporate architecture in the basin was not built until at least 1500 B.C. or, probably, even later. The dates for the Early Horizon and Early Intermediate period likewise do not correspond to cultural developments in the area. Tiwanaku expansion occurred around A.D. 650 and ended around A.D. 1100, a century or two different from the Middle Horizon and Late Intermediate periods. I have therefore adopted a dual chronological system that formalizes both historical and evolutionary approaches in central Andean archaeology in general, and the Titicaca Basin in particular. It incorporates the broad evolutionary chronology proposed by Lumbreras that is applicable to the Titicaca Basin as a whole, and local historical chronologies for different areas such as the Juli region, the Desaguadero area, the Tiwanaku area, the northern Titicaca Basin, and so forth. Certain features of the Ica sequence are retained, such as the Tiwanaku and Inca periods, which generally correlate to the Middle Horizon and Late Horizon respectively, but I have altered this sequence to fit the Titicaca Basin cultural history according to recent data.

The general chronology is divided into eight periods: Late Archaic (circa 5000–2000 B.C.), Early Formative (circa 2000–1300 B.C.), Middle Formative (1300–500 B.C.), Upper Formative (500 B.C.–A.D. 400), Expansive Tiwanaku (A.D. 400–1100), Altiplano (A.D. 1100–1450), Expansive Inca (A.D. 1450–1532), and Early Spanish Colonial (A.D. 1532–1700). Alongside the general chronology are the local historical ones, providing a dual system for every area. The chronologies are shown in figure 5.2.

Site Types in the Titicaca Basin

Over the last hundred or so years of archaeological research, a number of important sites in the Titicaca Basin have been described. Nearly all of these reports have concentrated on large ceremonial or administrative sites and did not include the far more numerous habitation sites. Therefore, despite this fairly extensive literature, there is no site typology for the Titicaca Basin.

The purpose of a typology is to order materials in such a way as to make meaningful comparisons for specific analytical purposes. The following typology was constructed to deal with regional questions of political, economic, and social organization (see table 5.1). It uses the systematic survey data from the Juli-Pomata area, as well as reconnaissance from other regions. The typology is considered useful for the entire region, but it is recognized that additional site types may be discovered. Sites are divided into two broad categories: habitation and nonhabitation. Habitation sites are broken down into urban and nonurban. Nonhabitation sites are divided into a number of types, such as cemeteries, special-function sites, and so forth.

The typology is devised to make meaningful comparisons between and within periods. Therefore, site size, although extremely important, is specified in relative terms; that is, site size relative to contemporary sites of that period. In this system, a ten-hectare site in A.D. 200 would be much higher in the hierarchy of sites than a twenty-hectare site in A.D. 1500.

Habitation Sites: Urban

The nature of Andean urbanism has been a subject of considerable debate. An absolute definition of the term *urban* remains an elusive goal. At one end, sites such as Pucara in the far northern Titicaca region are considered urban (Rowe 1963), and at the other end, some archaeologists would consider only sites such as Chan Chan and Cuzco as Andean urban centers. A more conservative definition is adopted here.

PRIMARY URBAN CENTERS

These centers are defined as (1) sites housing a substantial percentage of nonagriculturalists, (2) sites that are substantially larger than other contemporary

	North	West	South	Island of the Sun	Stage	Ica Sequence
A.D. 1500	Inca	Inca	Inca	Inca	Expansive Inca	Late Horizon
						Late Intermediate
1000	Colla Late Huaña	Lupaqa	Pacajes	Altiplano states	Regional period	
	Tiwanaku	Tiwanaku	Tiwanaku V	Tiwanaku	Expansive Tiwanaku	Middle Horizon
500			Tiwanaku IV			
	Early Huaña	Late Sillumocco	Qeya	Late Titinhuayani	Upper Formative	Early Intermediate period
A.D./B.C.	Pucara		Kalasasaya Late Chiripa			
500	Cusipata	Early Sillumocco	Middle Chiripa	Early Titinhuayani	Middle Formative	Early Horizon
1000	Qaluyu	Pasiri	Early Chiripa	Pasiri		
1500					Early Formative	
2000 B.C.					Late Archaic	

FIGURE 5.2. Chronologies of the Titicaca region.

TABLE 5.1

Site Types in the Titicaca Basin for All Time Periods

HABITATION SITES: URBAN	Primary urban centers
	Secondary urban centers
	Tertiary urban centers
HABITATION SITES: NONURBAN	Primate regional centers
	Primary regional centers
	Secondary regional centers
	Inhabited major pukaras
	Large villages
	Small villages
	Hamlets
NONHABITATION SITES	Noninhabited pukaras (refuge sites)
	Cemeteries
	Ceremonial sites:
	Carved rocks
	Apachetas
	Water ritual sites
	Pilgrimage sites
MISCELLANEOUS SITE TYPES	Petroglyphs/rock art
	Agricultural features (raised fields, causeways/corrals, etc.)
	Caves and rock shelters
	Roads/bridges
	Quarries/mineral sources/clay sources

sites of that period, and (3) evidence of a very high degree of labor mobilization and/or control. *Substantially larger* is intended to mean that the site should be a rank order higher than other sites in the region. These sites should have corporate architecture, evidence of elite buildings, and extensive nonelite habitation areas. A key indicator of labor mobilization is a planned urban settlement. The ability to construct a planned city with roads, precincts, and the like is a key archaeological indicator of labor mobilization. It can further be argued that such labor mobilization is possible only in state-level societies. By these criteria, there was only one primary urban center in the prehistoric Titicaca Basin—the site of Tiwanaku in its Tiwanaku IV and V periods.

SECONDARY URBAN CENTERS

Relatively large urbanized sites significantly smaller than any contemporary primary urban center, secondary urban centers are rare, and the term refers principally to the large, sprawling concentrations of people typical of the Late Horizon and Early Colonial periods at sites such as Hatuncolla and Paucarcolla. These sites are secondary in rank because Cuzco filled the position as the highest-ranking urban center within this polity.

Secondary urban sites are defined as those that contain a significant percentage of nonagricultural laborers and are at least half as large as a primary urban center. By this definition, secondary urban sites appeared only relatively late in the Titicaca region, during the Inca occupation. In the Juli-Pomata region, they housed about 15 percent of the total population in the Late Horizon and Early Colonial periods (Stanish et al. 1997).

TERTIARY URBAN CENTERS

Found only in the Inca period, tertiary urban centers are relatively small (around five hectares) urban concentrations almost always located on the road system. The term *urban* in this context may not be completely appropriate, as many of these sites most likely functioned as large tambos and/or as other minor administrative centers during the Inca occupation. Historical data suggest that the majority of the population in these towns were largely agriculturalists who also attended to special, nonagricultural functions. The similarity in architectural plan to larger secondary regional centers and their decidedly nonagricultural functions in the Inca state are reasons to include these as the lowest urban tier during the Inca occupation.

Habitation Sites: Nonurban

PRIMATE REGIONAL CENTERS

These centers contain a large concentration of agriculturalists and some attached specialists, and are an order of magnitude larger than the next larger primary regional centers. There are only two such sites in the Titicaca Basin, in one time period: the sites of Pucara and Tiwanaku during the Upper Formative. The development of huge, but nonurban, centers is due to a special set of factors hypothesized for the immediate pre-Tiwanaku periods (detailed below).

PRIMARY REGIONAL CENTERS

Defined as sites that are substantially larger than contemporary sites in the area, nonurban primary regional centers have evidence of constructions requiring labor organization of some complexity. Many primary regional centers in the south and southwest Titicaca region are built on low and generally indefensible natural hills surrounded by domestic residences on terraces. The corporate architecture is almost always found on the hilltop. In the Juli-Pomata survey, we have called these Type 3 sites, referring to these specific characteristics. The site of Incatunuhuiri as described by Kidder (1943: 49) is a example of this site type for the Upper Formative period (Pucara itself would be the largest, nonurban primate center), and sites such as Lukurmata, Simillake, and Palermo would be primary regional centers in the Tiwanaku period.

In some cases, corporate architecture is found in the form of an artificial mound. If the mound is larger than 2,500 square meters (approximately 50 by 50 meters at its base), it is what we have called a Type 1 mound. Type 1 mounds were built with artificial fill that was used to construct non-domestic architectural features. The Type 1 sites represent a considerable labor investment and an elite/political/ceremonial center. The mounds are not just collapsed structures but represent considerable quantities of fill intentionally used to create architectural features. In this typology, the sites of Chiripa and Qaluyu would be large Type 1 sites and also primary regional centers in the pre-Tiwanaku periods.

SECONDARY REGIONAL CENTERS

These centers are sites with domestic residences and some corporate architecture. Secondary regional centers, at least in the west and south, are more commonly found as Type 3 sites, defined as a low hill with corporate architecture on top, and surrounded by domestic terraces. All of these sites date to Tiwanaku or earlier. Type 3 secondary regional centers are found throughout the Titicaca Basin and appear to have been a favored location for regional elites during the Tiwanaku and earlier periods.

OTHER NONURBAN HABITATION SITES

People in the Titicaca Basin lived in a variety of settlement types outside the regional centers. The most common type is referred to as the Type 4 domestic terrace (Stanish et al. 1997). Vast areas of terraced hillsides can be found throughout the region. Most were built for agricultural purposes and are still used in this way. In a few instances, however, terraces were utilized as platforms for houses. The construction of both kinds of terraces is similar, as is their purpose: their level surface either prevents soil erosion or provides a flat surface for structures.

Many modern examples of domestic terraces are found in the region. People today still build their houses on terraced hillsides. The modern pattern of settlement is one of shifting terrace use over generations. A house compound is constructed on a ter-

FIGURE 5.3. Slab-cist tomb from the Huancané area, northern Titicaca Basin. Photograph by the author.

race and is utilized for a few generations. Eventually, the compound is abandoned, and a new set of structures is built nearby on other terraces. The former compound area is then plowed under and used for agriculture.

Another nonurban habitation type is the hamlet or village in the pampas; these villages are built near a river or on the lake edge on flat land. In the past, these kinds of settlements were found throughout the region; evidence is found in the large number of archaeological sites along the major rivers that flow into the lake. These sites were built up over time in a manner similar to tells in the arid areas of the Near East.

Nonhabitation Sites

CEMETERIES

There are a number of tomb types in the Titicaca Basin:

· Cist or shaft tombs. Ranging in size from shallow pits to one-meter-deep shafts, cist tombs are completely belowground constructions. Mouth diameters are thirty-five to fifty centimeters, although some are larger, and cists usually have stone slabs or capstones on top. Cist tombs appear to be the most common type of tomb in the study area. Most

tombs are stone-lined but are not exceptionally well made. Belowground cist tombs rarely contained more than two individuals and usually contained only one, as is demonstrated by excavations of cist tombs in the region (Stanish 1985) and by the quantity of human remains on the surface of looted cemeteries. Rarely found in isolation, cist tombs are usually in aggregated cemetery areas very close to habitation sites. They date to all periods.

· Slab-cist tombs (see figure 5.3). These aboveground constructions, first described by M. Tschopik (1946: 19), are all post-Tiwanaku in date. Slab-cist tombs range in diameter from fifty centimeters to two meters and are characterized by an encircling ring of stone slabs on the surface. The large slabs are uncut but of more or less uniform size, and are set upright around the tomb. In some cases, the belowground depression is very slight, perhaps only twenty centimeters or so, but in others, there is a fairly deep shaft. At present, all slab-cist tombs date to the post-Tiwanaku periods. There is good evidence that in many cases Tiwanaku and Upper Formative temples or other elite buildings were looted for the slabs for use in later tombs. Like cist tombs, slab-cist tombs are generally found clustered in cemetery areas near habitation sites.

FIGURE 5.4. Igloo chulpa. Photograph by the author.

FIGURE 5.5. Adobe chulpa at Sillustani. Photograph by the author.

FIGURE 5.6. Late Horizon chulpa near Pilcuyo, western Titicaca Basin. Photograph by the author.

· Chulpas. These are fully aboveground tombs (Hyslop 1977). The term *chulpa* is listed in Bertonio's dictionary as a "grave or basket where they put the dead" (1956 [1612]: Bk. 1: 430). However, a much more common term in his dictionary is *amaya uta,* defined as a "burial in the ancient manner" or a "grave like a house on the ground." The term *amaya uta* literally means "house of the soul"; Guamán Poma uses the term, or derivatives of it, for aboveground chulpas. He also labels some chulpalike constructions *pucullo.* We continue to use the term *chulpa* because it is so deeply entrenched in the scientific literature, even though it is not the most appropriate term given what we now know.

Hyslop (1977) describes several chulpa types that have been discovered on survey as well, such as adobe, igloo style, *pirca* stonework style, Inca stonework style, and the like (see figures 5.4–5.6).[3] Hyslop also provided a chronological typology of chulpas, suggesting that the "rustic" igloo type and pirca chulpas were earlier, and the large chulpas with Inca-style stonework were later.

Most of the chulpa tombs in the Titicaca Basin have been destroyed through centuries of looting. An obscure reference by the nineteenth-century European naturalist Marquis de Nadaillac suggests that chulpas were much more common in his time than today. For instance, describing Acora, he says, "One vast plain is covered with stones placed erect . . . hence the towers or chulpas which, mixed with megaliths, cover the whole plain of Acora" (Nadaillac 1969 [1885]: 424–426). Today, apart from the large cut-stone chulpas on the ridge away from town, the region around Acora shows little evidence of chulpas. Nadaillac goes on to say that "everywhere they [chulpas] form one of the characteristic features of the landscape."

Chulpas are often isolated from habitation areas and found on ridgetops and sides, hilltops, and along roads or trails. The significance of this remains to be fully investigated. In his typology of chulpa tomb types, Hyslop (1977: 154) argues that chulpa building began in the Altiplano period, a conclusion corroborated by recent data (see table 5.2; also see chapter 9).

· Intrusive tombs in pampa mounds or rock piles. The abandoned pampa mounds were convenient places for burials. A number of rock piles have tombs in them as well, similar to the intrusive tombs in the artificial mounds. The tombs tend to be isolated cist or slab-cist tombs.

CAVE BURIALS

One of the enigmas in Titicaca Basin research was the curious reference by Bertonio to chulpas as baskets *(serones)*. In the 1990s, however, archaeologists apparently solved that riddle after discovering cave burials with mummies wrapped in totora reed (see Sagárnaga 1993: 56). The first such cave burial in the western basin was discovered by looters and reporters at a cave called Molino-Chilacachi (de la Vega et al. 1995). This cave is inland from the lake near Acora. The excavations of the cave, directed by Edmundo de la Vega and Kirk Lawrence Frye, yielded sixty-two mummy baskets that had been disturbed, but the mummies apparently had been placed in a fetal position and then wrapped in reeds. Nearly all of the diagnostic objects in the cave were Altiplano period.

This is a new burial practice documented for the immediate Titicaca Basin, although museums in La Paz and Tiwanaku have similar burials from the southern circum-lake areas. Mark Aldenderfer (personal communication 1995) has discovered several more such caves in the upper Ilave region while on survey. In short, the cave burial pattern appears to be fairly widespread in the puna grazing areas, and current data suggest that it is restricted to a period after approximately the twelfth century A.D.

TABLE 5.2
Chart of Tomb Types per Period in the Titicaca Basin

	Inca	Altiplano	Tiwanaku	"U" Form	"M" Form	"E" Form
FINE CUT-STONE CHULPAS	X	–	–	–	–	–
ADOBE CHULPAS	X	X	–	–	–	–
LARGE FIELDSTONE CHULPAS	X	X	–	–	–	–
IGLOO CHULPAS	–	X	–	–	–	–
SLAB-CIST TOMBS	X	X	–	–	–	–
CAVE BURIALS	X	X	X	?	?	?
BELOWGROUND CIST TOMBS	X	X	X	X	X	X

NOTE: X = present; ? = possible; – = no evidence.

PUKARAS

These are the classic hilltop, fortified sites found throughout the altiplano and described by Hyslop (1976: 110). The largest pukaras usually have architecture surrounded by at least three massive defensive walls. There are two types of pukaras: major ones (see figures 5.7–5.8), characterized by some resident population and massive wall architecture, and minor ones (as in figure 5.9), characterized by few artifacts or architectural remains in a much smaller walled area. These site types are discussed at greater length in chapter 9.

Ceremonial Sites

CARVED ROCKS

Natural rock outcrops that have been carved with irregular steps are common in the Cuzco area, and most seem to date to the Late Horizon. Outside Cuzco, they are less common and generally found along major roads. Hyslop (1990: 120–121) suggests that the individual shelves were used for offerings in purification rituals. In the Titicaca Basin, carved rock outcrops have been located in Copacabana, Huancané, and Tiwanaku, near Juli, and along the western shores of the lake (Arkush 1999a). There are undoubtedly many more throughout the region.

APACHETAS

These intentionally placed piles of rocks were used for domestic ritual and perhaps for marking field or community boundaries. Apachetas are common throughout the Titicaca region and virtually impossible to date accurately.

WATER RITUAL AND PILGRIMAGE SITES

The many carved stones found throughout the Titicaca region are most likely associated with water ritual and ritual offerings of liquids or solid objects.

FIGURE 5.7. Major pukara on the Island of the Sun, Bolivia. Photograph by the author.

FIGURE 5.8. Major pukara walls at Tanka Tanka, in the southern lake area. Photograph by the author.

FIGURE 5.9. Minor pukara near Juli, western Titicaca Basin. Photograph by the author.

Almost all these stones are probably Inca in date, based on comparisons with carved stones in the Cuzco area. Such sites are discussed at length by Hyslop (1990: 102–128). In the Titicaca region, the largest number of these carved stones is found in and around the town of Copacabana. Arkush (1999b) has documented the existence of additional carved stones around the southern Titicaca Basin. These carved stones generally follow the western, or Urqusuyu, road, which branches off at Copacabana and ultimately leads to the Island of the Sun. It is likely that these sites were part of the pilgrimage route and functioned as ritual areas for offerings of the pilgrims.

Miscellaneous Site Types

Petroglyphs are found throughout the Titicaca Basin in virtually all areas that have been investigated. Raised fields are recognized as a distinct site type. Relict fields, defined as raised-field constructions no longer in use, are found throughout the Titicaca Basin and are concentrated on the northwestern, western, and southwestern sides of the lake, where the flatter topography is most conducive to the construction of these agricultural features. Caves and rock shelters are rare near the lake but more common above 4,200 m.a.s.l. or so. Prehistoric road segments constitute another site type, as do bridges. Rock quarries, at least one copper source, clay sources, a possible mica source for pottery tempering, corrals, and causeways have also been found.

· · · · ·

In short, a wide variety of site types can be found in the Titicaca region. These range from small habitation sites to urban settlements to ritual and agricultural constructions.

The Origins and Elaboration of Rank in the Early and Middle Formative Periods

The First Settled Villages of the Early Formative Period, circa 2000 to 1300 B.C.

The beginning of the Early Formative period is defined as the time when the first sedentary populations living in permanent villages developed in the Titicaca Basin. The previous Late Archaic period was characterized by relatively small, semisedentary populations pursuing an economy based on a mix of hunting, plant collecting, horticulture, fishing, and animal domestication. Mark Aldenderfer (1989, 1998) describes patterns of decreasing mobility, resource intensification, and settlement shifts that emerged by the end of the Late Archaic period, prior to the emergence of more complex social organization. The Early Formative societies that developed in this context were characterized by sedentism, specialization, hierarchy, and demographic growth (Aldenderfer 1989: 133).

Over more than two millennia, the Early Formative cultures of the circum-Titicaca Basin developed successful plant agricultural systems, maintained domesticated animal herds, consistently exploited the lake resources, and established permanent villages. Of course, there is no discrete beginning to the Early Formative period, as there is no specific end to the Archaic. The transition from Late Archaic to Early Formative lifeways was a long process, not an event.

James Brown (1985) and Jeanne Arnold (1993) have pointed out that sedentary populations can be maintained by nonagricultural subsistence strategies, at least in North America. Michael Moseley (1975, 1992) has persuasively argued that in the Andes, maritime resources supported complex, sedentary societies in the preceramic periods on the coast. The same appears to be true for the Titicaca region, particularly given the rich resource base provided by the lake and rivers that run into the lake. The Early Formative period represents the establishment of village life in the region but does not necessarily imply the existence of fully developed agriculture, pastoralism, and the abandonment of hunting, fishing, and plant collecting. Rather, the process from a predominantly nomadic to a predominantly sedentary way of life evolved over millennia and included a variety of subsistence strategies.

In the Titicaca Basin, the shift to sedentism was not necessarily based on agriculture and domesticated animals. On the Pacific coast in the central Andes, sedentism and elaborate monument construction preceded the development of plant food agriculture. In theory, the rich lake edge and freshwater riverine environments should have provided sufficient resource concentration to permit the development of permanent villages, as it did on the Peruvian coast in the late preceramic period. For instance, Aldenderfer (1989) argues that the Late Archaic site of Quelcatani was a residential camp. The population lived in semipermanent settlements with domestic structures and probably maintained domesticated camelids. In other words, we can expect many sites with Late Archaic diagnostics to also have features characteristic of the Early Formative, and vice versa. This period would have been transitional between an Archaic lifeway of predominantly hunting, foraging, and fishing to a more sedentary one with the adoption of agriculture as the principal source of food.

We can also hypothesize substantial variation of the economies in the Late Archaic throughout the Titicaca Basin. Lake and river-edge areas appear to have been used more intensively, but the puna areas away from these water sources were sparsely populated. This hypothesis is based on the recent work of Aldenderfer (1998) in the Río Ilave region, as well as on the analysis of settlement data from the Juli-Pomata region (Stanish et al. 1997).

The development of permanent residential structures aggregated in sedentary villages is the defining characteristic of an Early Formative lifeway, but the transition to dependence on agricultural or intensive horticultural, lacustrine, and/or riverine resources was a long and uneven process. Archaeologists stress different characteristics as important in this process. The existence of fully sedentary villages is not so important in and of itself; the cultural concomitants of established village life are more significant. The existence of a sedentary village implies a reliance on stable food sources such as agriculture, or at least intensive horticulture, intensive lake or river exploitation, possible territorial marking, and population levels substantially above that of a mobile hunting and collecting economy.

At the end of the Late Archaic, there clearly was a major change in the lifeways of the Titicaca Basin peoples that is related to this sedentism process. As Browman (1984: 119) notes, "Shortly after 2000 B.C. some new shifts appear in the archaeological record, including the adoption of new technologies such as ceramics, the development of new techniques in architecture, and the increasing reliance upon a wide range of domesticated plants." In the Titicaca Basin, the Early Formative hamlets and small villages were undifferentiated settlements of probably no more than a few dozen households: the sites were small, similar to each other, and had little internal architectural variation. Virtually everywhere that survey and reconnaissance have been conducted within a few kilometers of the lake, a few Early Formative sites have been found (e.g., Stanish et al. 1997; Albarracin-Jordan and Mathews 1990); river edges were also favored locations. It is therefore a reasonable hypothesis that these early villages were spread throughout the basin, principally along the lake edge and rivers, with a lower density of sites elsewhere. Of course, this hypothesis remains to be tested with future research.

At present, the evidence suggests that the cultures of the first settled villages, at least in the southern Titicaca Basin, developed directly out of the existing Late Archaic populations and were not the result of the migration. This conclusion is based on several excavations (discussed below) in which Late Archaic materials underlay Early Formative ones without any discernible disjunction in site occupation. In other words, the most parsimonious working hypothesis at this point is that there was no migration of agriculturalists from another area; rather, the Early Formative lifeway developed out of the Late Archaic period one around 2000 B.C.

The period during which small migratory groups experimented with permanent or semipermanent settlements in particularly rich ecological zones, such as the lake edge where bofedales were found and along the major rivers that flow into the lake, was probably a long one. Contemporary with these initial settlements would have been others engaged in a fully mobile lifestyle, providing a complex mosaic of differing subsistence strategies and settlement patterns. Binford, Brenner, and Leyden (1996: 106) suggest that prior to 3,400 years ago, there was insufficient precipitation in the region to support extensive agriculture. It was only with the increase in long-term net rainfall at that time that agriculture was possible.

Work on this crucial time period has been limited. As recently as 1990, we could identify only a handful of published Archaic sites in the entire region. Since that time, systematic survey and reconnaissance have identified hundreds of Middle and Late Archaic sites. There is no question that the Titicaca Basin supported an Archaic population since the Middle Archaic, and a very large Early Formative population beginning around 2000 B.C.

Absolute Chronology

The beginning of the Early Formative is defined as the appearance of permanent human settlements in which agriculture or intensive horticulture, intensive fishing, and the keeping of domesticated animals (predominantly camelids and guinea pigs) constituted a significant portion of the economy. Political organization of the Early Formative is best characterized as small, undifferentiated villages lacking any regional integration. This lifestyle continued from at least 2000 B.C. to approximately 1300 B.C. in the Titicaca region, with a variation of as many as several centuries depending upon the region and culture. The Early Formative ends with the development of ranked societies, and these later Middle Formative polities began developing as early as 1300 B.C. (during the Qaluyu period in the north, for instance).

Prior to work in Juli and the work of Mark Aldenderfer in the high puna near Mazocruz, the earliest settled villages were identified by dating the earliest ceramic assemblages at sites such as Qaluyu and Chiripa (Chávez 1977). Browman (1980: 113) identified several ceramic types that were the earliest known at the time, including his Chiripa Condori and a type from Pizacoma called the Kalikantu style, which dates to around 1300 B.C. Kalikantu style pottery, according to Browman (quoting Mujica), is "almost identical" to the Condori ceramics. Lynch (1981) identified a type of pottery called Ramis ware that represents the earliest pottery found at Pucara. Described as having thick geometric incisions with post-fire paint, Ramis ware is most likely related to Qaluyu traditions. The earliest pottery at Chiripa dates to around 1500–1000 B.C. (Whitehead 1999). The Early Qaluyu phase at the type site begins circa 1300 B.C. (Browman 1980).[1] These dates are consistent with early pottery levels at other sites in the region. Corrected, these would date to the fifteenth century B.C. These dates are also consistent with Chávez's (1977: 159) suggestion that the earliest pottery-using peoples were in the altiplano (south of Cuzco) around 1400 B.C.

Because Qaluyu and Chiripa were political and/or ceremonial centers, the decorated pottery is expected to be generally of higher quality, nondomestic types. For years we have suspected that an earlier type of domestic pottery antedates the pottery traditions at the major sites. One question facing archaeologists, therefore, centers on the nature and date of the earliest pottery in the Titicaca region.

At present, the earliest pottery in the Titicaca Basin has been identified by Steadman (forthcoming) at the site of Quelcatani, which was excavated by Aldenderfer. A carbon-14 date of 3660 ± 60 B.P. (which calibrates to circa 2000 B.C.) is associated with several fragments of pottery. Although insufficient to define a period and pottery type, these data are the first evidence for the emergence of pottery making in the Titicaca region in the beginning of the second millennium B.C.

Research by Stanish et al. (2002) on the Island of the Sun included excavations at several sites, two of which, Ch'uxuqullu and Titinhuayani, contain very early occupations dating back to 2000 B.P. Analysis of surface and excavation data from all other sites on the island indicates that these two sites are representative of the earliest occupations on the largest island in Lake Titicaca.

A stratigraphic cut at Ch'uxuqullu provided data on the earliest pottery on the island. Located in the community of Challa, in the middle of the island, Ch'uxuqullu is an open-air site on a low knoll above several springs in a low valley above the lake. The site itself is relatively small, covering no more than a quarter-hectare. Three Late Archaic/Early Formative projectile points found on the surface indicate a Late Archaic occupation.

A two-meter-deep midden from the site was excavated in 1995. A carbon date from the first pottery-bearing level is 3100 ± 45 B.P.[2] Although the sample size is small, it is instructive that the earliest pottery-bearing levels have around 90 percent fiber tempering, and that there is a gradual replacement of the assemblage with sand and mica tempering through the sequence. Certainly, pottery of the first stratigraphic levels is typical of the early pottery from the mainland.

Near Ch'uxuqullu is a very large site known as Titinhuayani. Esteban Quelima excavated several units at the top of Titinhuayani, and the sequence he discovered parallels that from Ch'uxuqullu, beginning with a preceramic (Late Archaic) occupation and continuing in an unbroken sequence up to the Upper Formative or Tiwanaku period. The earliest ceramic-bearing levels at Titinhuayani contain substantially more pottery fragments than those at Ch'uxuqullu and provide a better sample. In these earliest levels, the ceramic assemblage again contains about 90 percent poorly fired, unslipped pottery with heavy fiber and grit temper, a few of these same wares with a red slip, and about 5 to 10 percent well-fired sand-tempered wares.

The Pasiri Pottery Tradition

We use the term *Pasiri* to identify the earliest pottery in at least the southwest Titicaca Basin. As demonstrated above, this pottery is as least as old as the earliest pottery from Chiripa and Qaluyu, and the carbon-14 dates from Ch'uxuqullu and Quelcatani indicate that it is probably older. The Pasiri ceramic assemblage (see Stanish et al. 1997: figures 14–15) is defined by paste and surface treatment characteristics from sherds that directly overlay aceramic Late Archaic strata in at least four sites that were test excavated. The vast majority of sherds are poorly fired, unslipped, with heavy inclusions of fiber and coarse sand. We do not have any complete vessels, nor many rims. The few rims collected appear to be from thickened rim, slightly flaring ollas and slightly thinner jar forms. Alongside these poorly fired fiber-tempered sherds are a few (around 10 percent) sand-tempered, better-fired wares that are occasionally painted red (see figure 6.1).

Surface collections in the Juli-Pomata area support the proposition that the Pasiri pottery is the earliest ceramic assemblage so far defined in the region. First, the distribution of this ceramic type is not very widespread; it is found in less than a dozen sites in the

FIGURE 6.2. Qaluyu pottery. Photograph by the author.

FIGURE 6.1. Pasiri pottery from the Island of the Sun.
Photograph by the author.

Juli-Pomata intensive survey region. Of these sites, at least six have Late Archaic occupations. In fact, in every multicomponent Late Archaic site, Pasiri ceramics also occur, a fact that suggests that the ceramic type is quite early.

Analysis of the ceramic assemblage at Tumatumani (Steadman 1994) supports this chronological placement of the Pasiri assemblage. With several thousand fragments analyzed, no Pasiri ceramic diagnostics were discovered. This is significant because Tumatumani has a substantial Early Sillumocco (Middle Formative) component with fiber-tempered pottery and represents a huge sample. These data suggest that the Pasiri assemblage is not a poorly fired subset of the Middle Formative fiber-tempered wares but is chronologically distinct. In

fact, the Pasiri ceramic assemblage is not found on most sites that date to the Middle Formative, as indicated by Qaluyu and Chiripa pottery (see figures 6.2 and 6.3). In no case did we find a Late Archaic component without Pasiri ceramics, but it is very common to find Middle Formative sites without Pasiri ceramics. In other words, the Pasiri ceramic type is consistently found on Middle Formative sites only if there is a Late Archaic occupation, but many sites with Middle Formative occupations lack Pasiri ceramics.

Another site on the Island of the Sun supports the definition of the Pasiri assemblage as well. This unnamed site is a very small single-component site on the western end of the island. It is a very dense concentration of fiber-tempered pottery, virtually all of

FIGURE 6.3. Chiripa pottery. Photograph by the author.

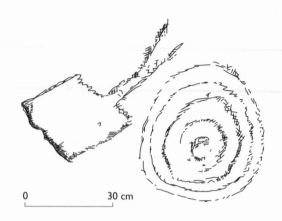

FIGURE 6.4. Petroglyph from San Bartolomé-Wiscachani, outside Juli. Photograph by the author.

which would be classified as Pasiri. The several hundred sherds on the surface are extremely consistent in style. Single-component sites are strong evidence that the ceramic assemblage is not a functional or technological subset of a broader ceramic tradition but a chronologically distinct type associated with a single occupation.

The Site of San Bartolomé-Wiscachani

Very few Early Formative sites have been found and intensively investigated in the Titicaca region. Furthermore, the Pasiri ceramic assemblage is known only from the south and southwestern Titicaca region; we do not know what the earliest ceramics associated with the earliest settled villages look like elsewhere around the lake. This is complicated by the fact that the sites that have been found are, for the most part, buried under later, more massive constructions. To date, the most thoroughly investigated site from the Pasiri tradition without a major post-Pasiri occupation is San Bartolomé-Wiscachani (shown on map 6.1), which is on the high promontory south of Juli. This extremely important site is one of the very few known to have a late Early For-

mative occupation and no substantial later ones. Diagnostic Late Archaic points indicate an occupation as early as 4000–2000 B.C. Diagnostic pottery is Early Formative in date, although some small concentrations of later pottery have been found. In other words, the surface features of the site most likely date to the latest occupation in the late Early Formative.

A very important architectural feature of San Bartolomé-Wiscachani is the domestic terraces that cover the entire site and almost certainly contained habitation structures. The terraces cover about one hectare and extend to an open area at the top of the site that has a small circular depression several meters in diameter. Near the depression is a petroglyph (figure 6.4) that appears to depict a square or rectangular depression and a line that leads to a spiral. The spiral may represent a hill, and the line a path. If this interpretation is accurate, the petroglyph could very well depict a ritual pathway from a sunken court area to a hill, which would make it the earliest evidence of ritual behavior in the circum-Titicaca Basin among settled villagers. This proposition, of course, remains speculative.

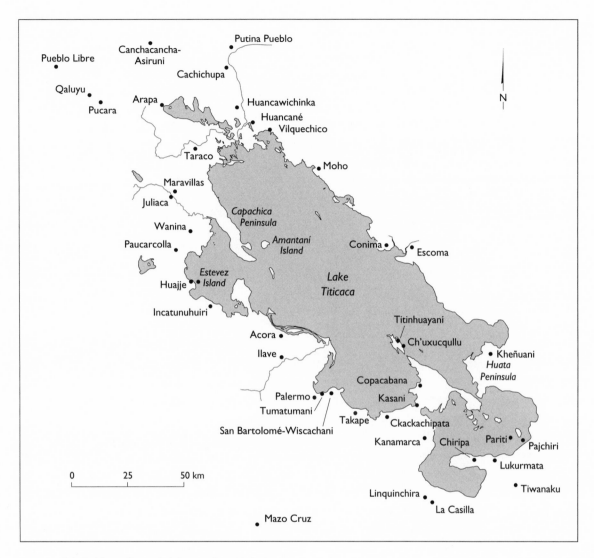

MAP 6.1. Selected Formative-period sites mentioned in text.

The site has several carved stone protuberances as well. Two of these align almost precisely with the highest peak in the eastern Cordillera. Given the importance of mountain worship in Andean society (Reinhard 1983, 1985), and presuming the interpretation of this alignment is accurate, the San Bartolomé-Wiscachani data may represent the earliest evidence for this mountain worship tradition in the circum-Titicaca Basin.

Settlement Patterns

The distribution of Pasiri-period sites in the Juli-Pomata region is seen in map 6.2. A most salient characteristic of this pattern is a generally even distribution of settlements along the lake edge, with a slight clustering of sites in the Moyopampa area, the region's richest ecological zone. The slight clustering of the earliest village sites in the Moyopampa region

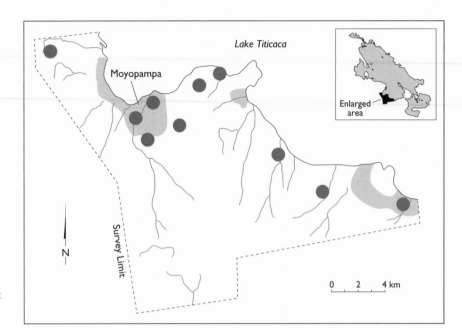

MAP 6.2. Pasiri-period (Early Formative) settlement patterns in the Juli-Pomata survey area.

is most parsimoniously explained by a resource-optimizing strategy with a higher spacing of settlement (i.e., less dense) in areas of fewer resources.

For now, the definition of Pasiri ceramics must be at the assemblage level. As a result, it is impossible to accurately estimate the average site sizes for this period using intensive walkovers on multicomponent sites. However, in the five sites with Early Formative occupations and without significant later occupations, the average site size is less than one hectare (0.80 hectare). The average site size of the later Middle Formative occupations is only slightly larger (0.92 hectare), so it is safe to deduce from these data that the Pasiri sites were, on average, no larger than one hectare, and probably much smaller.

The nature of the distribution of Early Formative–period sites on the Island of the Sun roughly parallels that found in the Juli-Pomata area in that they are evenly distributed with a concentration in the most productive areas (see map 6.3). Sites are concentrated along the lake edge and near wet areas and springs. As with the Juli-Pomata area, many Early

Formative sites are associated with Late Archaic occupations.

Early Exchange in the Titicaca Region

Lisa Cipolla's analysis of lithic materials from the excavations at Ch'uxuqullu and Titinhuayani on the Island of the Sun (Stanish et al. 2002) indicates that there was a vigorous stool tool industry and exchange network in the region by Late Archaic and Early Formative times. By-products of lithic tool manufacture were discovered in the undisturbed aceramic levels of both sites. The aceramic levels of Ch'uxuqullu contained twenty chert or quartz flakes that represent various stages of biface reduction. One quartzite core, a clear indication of tool manufacture, was found in the lowest level of the dated unit. The lowest stratigraphic level at the site of Titinhuayani contained by-products of lithic manufacturing as well as ten obsidian flakes representing middle stage lithic manufacture and one broken basalt projectile point that had been reworked.

The obsidian, andesite, and basalt from both sites

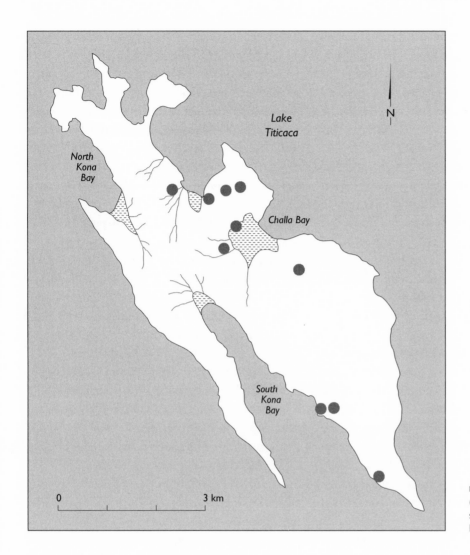

MAP 6.3. Early Formative
(circa 1500–1000 B.C.)
settlement pattern on the
Island of the Sun.

do not naturally occur on the island. Analysis of the lithic materials indicates that the earliest inhabitants used local materials to manufacture most of their tool kit but imported finished basalt and andesite tools from the mainland. Likewise, the presence of obsidian flakes representing a middle stage of the manufacturing process indicates that the inhabitants imported obsidian in either its raw material form or as preformed blanks. Source analysis of the obsidian by Richard Burger and Michael Glascock (in Stanish et al. 2002) indicates that all fragments analyzed came

from the Colca Valley near Arequipa. In other words, we can hypothesize a brisk down-the-line trade of obsidian during the Early Formative from a distance of more than a week's travel. In this model, a relatively simple system of reciprocal exchange resulted in the widespread distribution of this highly portable and valuable commodity.

The work from the Island of the Sun indicates that Late Archaic peoples were actively boating around the lake and expanding into rich lacustrine ecological zones by the beginning of the second millennium

B.C. Thus, by the Early Formative, boating around the lake shore was most likely a well-established technology. This would have substantially added to the economic mainstay of the inhabitants, and would have made settlement along the lake edge during this period even more attractive.

Summary

The Early Formative lifeways slowly developed out of the Late Archaic hunting, gathering, foraging, and incipient agricultural economies around the turn of the second millennium B.C. This was a process, not an event, and the definition of the time period is by necessity arbitrary. The degree to which the adoption of pottery is indicative of sedentism is, of course, debatable. Analysis of the midden from the excavations of Ch'uxuqullu on the Island of the Sun shows little obvious change between the preceramic and ceramic levels. At this site at least, people lived for several hundred years off of the lake shore and adjacent bofedal resources. Pottery was first used in very small quantities, and there is no obvious change in the midden composition after the introduction of ceramic technology on the site. It is as likely, in fact, that the preceramic levels were the remains from a sedentary population as it is that the ceramic-period remains were from semisedentary populations. As Prudence Rice (1999: 28) notes, nonagricultural peoples in the ethnographic record frequently use pottery, so it is perfectly likely that the first use of pottery at the site of Ch'uxuqullu was by a nonagricultural population.

Settlement pattern data also suggest that the introduction of pottery in and of itself was not a transformational event in the life of the Titicaca Basin peoples. Rather, pottery appears to represent a technological innovation that was added to the repertoire of the Titicaca Basin peoples at this time. This is not to minimize the value of ceramic technology: it allowed for better storage of foodstuffs and was a superior cooking technology.

The Early Formative represents the establishment of settled villages in the Titicaca region. There is at present no evidence for political ranking at these sites: all sites are small (less than one hectare) and therefore not differentiated by size. There is little evidence for wealth differences in artifacts, burials, and so forth. Admittedly, current data are sparse. However, by analogy to organizationally similar societies around the world in space and time, it is most likely that the Early Formative–period societies were characterized by very moderate social rank (religious specialists, for instance) but no political or economic ranking of any significance. Where there is systematic data, such as in the Juli-Pomata and Tiwanaku areas, Early Formative sites are distributed evenly across the landscape in a pattern that optimized natural resources, and settlement choice does not appear to have been influenced by political factors.

One of the major questions for the Formative period in the Titicaca region is, When did the economic triad of pastoralism, agriculture, and lake exploitation begin? The Early Formative, of course, is the logical place to begin to search for the origins of these strategies. A more appropriate question is, What was the relative importance of each of these economic strategies in each of the periods in the region? The distribution of Pasiri-period sites in the Juli-Pomata region suggests a strong reliance on lake resources—presumably fish, fowl, and totora reeds (the roots of the totora were eaten)—because virtually all sites were located in such a manner as to exploit the lake. Aldenderfer, in fact, refers to the latest Archaic-period sites with evidence of sedentism as "Lacustrine Archaic," suggesting a heavy reliance on fish and fowl from Lake Titicaca as the primary resource (Aldenderfer, personal communication 1996). Again, the maritime hypothesis of Moseley (1975) for the Andean coast may be modified and applied. The extremely productive lake edge and/or rivers would have supported greater populations than those areas where there were only agro-pastoral economies. Settlement data in which sites are concentrated along the lake edge and along the rivers, plus the evidence of intensive use of the Island of the Sun in Late Archaic and Early Formative times, support this model.

By the end of the Late Archaic in the south-central Andes, populations had most likely developed fairly sophisticated knowledge of domesticated and semi-domestic plants. The Pasiri sites in the Juli-Pomata region are near the lake edge in a pattern that later populations would use for the optimization of agricultural resources (the best land is near the lake edge); this location also granted them access to lake resources. We can hypothesize a simple rain-fed agriculture without any intensification techniques used by later populations. There is no evidence of raised-field agriculture during this time period, nor any evidence of the use of canals or other water-control devices.

Subsistence in the Early Formative was mixed: wild plant collecting, hunting, and fishing constituted important components of the economy, along with agriculture and the keeping of domestic animals. These observations are based on analysis of site locations and excavated materials. It is significant, however, that there are no major freshwater rivers in the Juli-Pomata survey area. Aldenderfer (1998) discovered along the Ilave River hundreds of Late Archaic and Early Formative sites that extend well into the puna regions. The geographical location of these sites suggests a heavy reliance on pastoralism and river exploitation, perhaps in a manner not unlike that along the lake edge. Hunting and collecting were most likely a major component of the Early Formative economy in the Titicaca Basin, although the extent to which various settlements continued to use wild resources remains to be defined. For the earliest occupation (200 B.C.–A.D. 50) of the site of Lukurmata, Bermann (1990: 76) discovered significant quantities of deer, fish, and bird refuse. Based on comparative data from similar cultural contexts from around the Andes and the world, it is likely that hunting and collecting were a very important component of the diet.

This is inferred from the very low population densities of the Pasiri-period populations, and the likelihood of substantial deer, camelid, and other wild fauna available for exploitation.

In sum, the evidence indicates that the Early Formative was a dynamic period in the Titicaca Basin in which an increasing reliance on cultivated plants and lake resources profoundly changed the nature of society. Small populations settled in permanent villages, and settlement patterns indicate that people concentrated on the richer ecological zones near the lake and along the rivers. There was a brisk trade in obsidian and most likely other commodities as well. The evidence, as reported in Stanish et al. 2002, indicates that the Early Formative people exploited the lake edge with balsa (reed) boats. The economy was therefore mixed, with agriculture, hunting, fishing, and lake edge exploitation all used during this period. Within this context, during the Early Formative at least two distinct cultural areas were already forming, thus setting the stage for the emergence of ranked society in the Titicaca Basin.

The Evolution of Ranked Society in the Middle Formative Period, circa 1300 to 500 B.C.

The Middle Formative represents the establishment of ranked society in the Titicaca Basin. It is during this period that there is evidence of corporate labor organization well above the capacities of individual households. The result of this more complex labor organization is particularly evident in the development of elaborate architecture on a few sites that were larger than their contemporaries, and where we also see the development of specialized ceramic and stone art traditions. Settlement data from the Island of the Sun suggest that terrace agriculture was used by the Middle Formative people. Raised-field agriculture, a more intensive technique, was probably used as well. Raised fields provided for agricultural production in more restricted areas that allowed the concomitant concentrations of larger numbers of people into nucleated settlements.

This more complex organization promoted the emergence of site size ranking and the development of primary regional centers, the first in the Titicaca Basin. In the Middle Formative, certain sites became elite civic-ceremonial centers with allied commoner populations. These regional centers were characterized by the first appearance of sunken courts, the production of stelae, elaborate mounded sites, and other indications of differential rank. Contemporary with these regional centers were the villages and hamlets linked to the regional centers by political, ideological, social, and economic relationships. The Middle Formative represents the emergence in the region of the first elites with the capacity to mobilize labor beyond the household level. The ramifications of this new elite organization extended to settlement patterns, architecture, art, regional economic relationships, and political organization.

Absolute Chronology

The Middle Formative societies flourished from about 1300 B.C. (at Qaluyu in the north and at Early and Middle Chiripa–related sites in the southern Pacajes region) to 500 B.C., when the Upper Formative societies were established. At Chiripa, the Middle Formative is represented by the Early and Middle Chiripa period and early Late Chiripa period of K. Chávez (1988) or by the Llusco and Late Mamani phases of Browman (1978b: 807). In this book I use the revised Middle Formative dates reported by Whitehead (1992: 20) from the Taraco Archaeological Project: : Early Chiripa (1500–1000 B.C.), Middle Chiripa (1000–800 B.C.), and early Late Chiripa (800–500 B.C.).

Alfred Kidder II and Manuel Chávez Ballón excavated some test units at the site of Qaluyu in the 1950s, obtaining two dates reported in Chávez 1977 (157): 3043 B.P. ± 124 and 2590 B.P. ± 117. The mid-

point of the calibration of the first date is about 1250 B.C., and the midpoint of the second calibrated date is about 650 B.C.[3] Chávez obtained other radiocarbon dates from ceramic-bearing levels at the site that ranged from approximately 1360 B.C. (uncalibrated) to 1063 B.C. (uncalibrated). The early date is consistent with early pottery from other sites in the Titicaca Basin (see page 102). The Middle Formative period at Qaluyu is represented by the Early Qaluyu phase and dates to circa 1300–500 B.C. (Browman 1980; Chávez 1977).

In other areas of the Titicaca Basin, the Middle Formative lifeways began later. In the Juli area, the Early Sillumocco period represents the Middle Formative–period occupation. Early Sillumocco dates to approximately 900–200 B.C. based on stylistic analyses of ceramics by Steadman (1994) and a single carbon-14 date at the site of Palermo, a major Middle Formative site in the region (Stanish et al. 1997).

Steadman (1995: 541, 544) excavated at the Late Archaic– through Upper Formative–period site of Camata, a few kilometers south of Chucuito and discovered a sequence beginning around 1700 B.C. with preceramic remains. In the levels that dated to around 1300 B.C., Qaluyu-related materials were found directly above the Archaic ones. The Middle Formative at Camata is therefore represented by the Early Qaluyu 1 and 2 phases (circa 1300–900 B.C.) through Late Qaluyu 1 and 2 (circa 900 B.C.–750 B.C.).

Principal Middle Formative Sites

The Juli-Pomata survey data (Stanish et al. 1997) provide good information on site size distributions in the Middle Formative. Figure 6.5 illustrates that there were three site sizes, with the vast majority of the sites (80 percent) between 0.01 and 1.25 hectares. Four sites are 2.0 to 3.0 hectares, and one site is at least 4.0 hectares. These data, plus observations on other sites throughout the region, suggest that there are only three habitation site types in the Middle Formative: large villages with corporate architecture

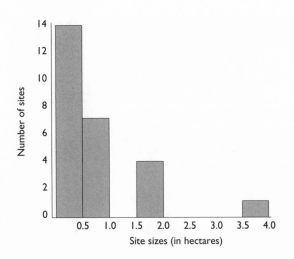

FIGURE 6.5. Site size distribution of Middle Formative sites in the Juli-Pomata survey area.

TABLE 6.1

Habitation Site Types per Period
in the Titicaca Basin

EARLY FORMATIVE	Small villages
	Hamlets
MIDDLE FORMATIVE	Primary regional centers
	Villages
	Hamlets
UPPER FORMATIVE	Primate regional centers (Tiwanaku and Pucara)
	Primary regional centers
	Secondary regional centers
	Large villages
	Small villages
	Hamlets
TIWANAKU	Primary urban center (Tiwanaku)
	Primary regional centers
	Secondary regional centers
	Large villages
	Small villages
	Hamlets
ALTIPLANO	Primary regional centers
	Large villages
	Small villages
	Hamlets
INCA	Primary urban center (Cuzco)
	Secondary urban centers
	Tertiary urban centers
	Large villages
	Small villages
	Hamlets

(primary regional centers), large villages without corporate architecture, and small hamlets (see table 6.1). The villages and hamlets were domestic agricultural, pastoral, hunting, collecting, and fishing settlements linked to the primary regional centers, a pattern that represents an elaboration of the Early Formative–period settlements.

Middle Formative Primary Regional Centers

Primary regional centers in the Middle Formative appear to have been fairly small and are defined by the presence of corporate architecture above that of the household, and site sizes significantly larger than the vast bulk of the settlements. Most centers appear to be no more than ten hectares and average around five hectares during this period. Using these criteria, we can identify a number of primary regional centers in the Titicaca region during the Middle Formative period, which are described below.

CANCHACANCHA-ASIRUNI

The site of Canchacancha-Asiruni was first published by Chávez and Chávez (1970) as a site found earlier

FIGURE 6.6. Site of Canchacancha-Asiruni, in the Azángaro Valley. Photograph by the author.

by Chávez Ballón (see figures 6.6–6.8). It is northeast of Azángaro, a few kilometers from the old hacienda house of Tintiri.[4] The site is huge by Middle Formative standards, covering at least twelve hectares. It is composed of a series of compounds with probable sunken courts and stelae in the centers. The compounds are not architecturally planned but represent a series of architecturally similar units that aggregated over time. Excavations in similar compounds at the site of Cachichupa by Aimée Plourde (1999) have confirmed the existence of this architectural form in the Middle Formative period.

Canchacancha-Asiruni has Middle and possibly early Upper Formative–period stelae on the surface. Some of the stelae, as first reported by Chávez and Chávez (1970), were some of the largest known Formative-period sculptures in the north basin outside Pucara. What is significant about the surface blocks on the site is the large number of stones that appear to have been shaped in the form of stelae but not decorated with complex motifs.

Canchacancha-Asiruni is one of the most important Middle Formative sites in the northern Titicaca Basin. The large number of surface stelae (including carved, uncarved, and partially carved ones), the large enclosures, and the site's large size indicate that it

was a very important political center. In fact, Canchacancha-Asiruni is larger than Qaluyu itself and may be the largest Middle Formative–period site in the northern Titicaca Basin outside the Pucara Valley.

QALUYU

The site of Qaluyu was discovered by Chávez Ballón in conjunction with a project directed by Julio Tello (Chávez 1977: 8). The Qaluyu pottery style was identified independently by both Chávez Ballón, who described the materials from Qaluyu itself, and John Rowe, who identified Qaluyu material from the site of Qaqachupa outside Ayaviri at this time (Rowe 1956: 144). The Qaluyu pottery style and associated culture were recognized soon thereafter as a major pre-Pucara tradition. Rowe (1963) described the type site as a large habitation mound with refuse that covers "several acres in extent." Lumbreras (1974a: 57) notes that it appears to have been "an agglutinated village," and he also describes the site as one with a "strong tendency towards population concentration, but one without evidence of urbanism" (Lumbreras 1981: 201).

Qaluyu is a large Type 1 mound in our typology developed in the Juli-Pomata area (see figures 6.9 and 6.10). The Middle Formative–period occupation at

FIGURE 6.7. Stela from Canchacancha-Asiruni. Note looter's hole where the sunken court is most likely located. Photograph by the author.

FIGURE 6.8. Uncarved stela from Canchacancha-Asiruni. Photograph by the author.

FIGURE 6.9. Site of Qaluyu, showing recent road cut and construction episodes. Photograph by the author.

the site dates from 1300 B.C. to around 500 B.C. (Chávez 1977: 154). Preliminary mapping of the site by Programa Collasuyu indicates that it was at least seven hectares, and probably larger. There is substantial evidence of corporate construction throughout the mound area of the site. A modern road cut has exposed a several-meter-high artificial fill that extends across the entire width of the site. Several low terraces were built on at least the north and south sides. These terraces have remains of domestic artifacts and were most likely habitation areas. The surface features also indicate that there were at least five, and probably several more, sunken courts, which were built with large shaped blocks. Figure 6.9 shows several of these blocks that had recently been looted from a sunken court area. The blocks are similar in form to other contemporary sites with stone-lined sunken courts. A set of cardinally oriented structures on the west side of the site may date to either the latest occupation of Qaluyu or to the period when the site dominated the region; that is, if the later Pucara occupation was restricted to the mound proper, then these structures could date to Qaluyu times. The nature of these structures suggests the existence of discrete compounds with interior rooms.

What we can now say is that Qaluyu was one of the largest Middle Formative–period sites in the Pucara Valley (Pucara itself most likely being larger), although it is smaller than Canchacancha-Asiruni. Qaluyu was characterized by a large mound built with fill over a number of construction episodes. This mound supported a number of sunken court complexes that do not appear to have been constructed under any architectural plan. The courts appear to have been slowly added, growing by accretion over time in a manner similar to Canchacancha-Asiruni. Associated with these sunken courts are possible contemporary structures, along with a substantial domestic area along the sides.

We can now suggest that the type site was actually a peripheral settlement in the Qaluyu polity. Recent work by Plourde and Stanish in the Putina Valley (upper Huancané) discovered two major Qaluyu sites in strategic locations on the route to the eastern slopes (Plourde 1999; Stanish and Plourde 2000). The quantity and quality of Qaluyu materials at both Cachichupa and Putina Pueblo is substantially higher than in the Qaluyu type site itself. Karen Chávez (1977: 1020) noted that in her excavations at Qaluyu, the archaeological material was "less

FIGURE 6.10. Sunken court at Qaluyu. Photograph by the author.

dense" than at either Marcavalle or Pikicallepata. She furthermore notes the similarities between the later Qaluyu pottery (circa 1000 B.C.) and her Marcavalle Phase B (Chávez 1977: 1021), suggesting strong stylistic links as far north as Cuzco. Recent discoveries by Rolando Paredes (personal communication) in Ayaviri at the site of Pueblo Libre (near the site of Qaqachupa) confirm that there were dense Qaluyu settlements in this region as well.[5] The data so far indicate that the core of Qaluyu pottery distribution is to the north and/or east of Qaluyu itself, although Pucara may have the largest Qaluyu site in the region.

In short, we still do not know which site, if any, was the principal Qaluyu center in the Titicaca region. It is possible that a large primary regional center for Qaluyu exists and remains undiscovered, or that the major center is under the later constructions of Qaluyu. It is also possible that the style was adopted by a number of polities from Cuzco to the northern edge of Lake Titicaca and that, as one of the first complex polities in the Titicaca region, Qaluyu did not have the strong settlement hierarchy found in later periods.

PUCARA

The Middle Formative at Pucara is represented by the pre-Pucara phase of Qaluyu. There is also a likely pre-Qaluyu phase, located by Ernesto Nakandakari in a plaza area of the site (Wheeler and Mujica 1981: 26). Little is actually known about the nature of the Qaluyu period at the site, except that ceramic fine wares were used in the settlement and that regional relationships existed for a considerable distance. Excavations by archaeologists working with the UNESCO project also discovered that the visible surface temple that dates to the Upper Formative was built over an earlier one (Wheeler and Mujica 1981). Lynch (1981) reports that this earlier temple dates to 800–200 B.C., which would place it squarely within the Middle Formative period, contemporary with the construction of similar structures at the southern Titicaca Basin site of Chiripa.

CHIRIPA

The most famous pre-Tiwanaku site in the southern basin, Chiripa was the center of one of the region's first ranked polities. As mentioned above, the site was first excavated by Bennett in his 1933–1934 season (and see Bandy 1999b). His work revealed a sequence of three or four stratigraphic levels, the earliest of which we can now date to the Middle Formative period (Bennett 1936: 430). The first period identified by Bennett was called Pre-mound. These stratigraphic levels corresponded to the natural contours of the hill, indicating that this occupation was not characterized by any type of corporate construction. According to Bennett (1936: 430), there were "rough stone walls . . . ash beds, stones, fish, animal and human bones, [and] pottery fragments" in this first set of occupational levels. In other words, Bennett discovered a good domestic habitation level on a hill at the Chiripa site with little evidence of intentional alteration of the natural landscape. The data suggest an aggregated village on a low hill above the lake.

The second set of strata, which Bennett grouped into a single cultural period, was characterized by a "circle of houses" with a diameter of approximately thirty-two meters built on an artificial "ridge . . . built specifically for the houses" (Bennett 1936: 430–431). This occupation was ultimately destroyed by fire, and the old surface was covered with adobe bricks. This event left a low mound with a slight depression in the center. The first substantial corporate architecture was built on the site during this "House phase" (Bennett 1936). This would have been the depression noted by Bennett, which was perhaps a sunken court.

Browman's excavations (1981: 414) revealed a pre-Tiwanaku sunken court that Chávez recognizes as one of the earliest court structures in the Titicaca region (K. Chávez 1988: 18). The sunken court is approximately 22 by 23 meters and is 1.5 meters deep. K. Chávez (1988) argues that the site's rectangular structures are associated with this temple and that a storage-temple complex first developed in Chiripa during this period. The mound had been formally walled and faced in the preceding Middle Formative. The site's inhabitants also created a plaza area on the mound proper (Browman 1978b: 808). In the Upper Formative, the plaza area was replaced with a formal walled, semisubterranean temple, a construction technique that was to become typical of elite architecture in the Titicaca area.

Chávez describes the buildings as residential and storage structures with elaborate decorations, including painted walls and red washes, interior yellow clay floors, decorative niches, and double-jamb doorways with step frets (K. Chávez 1988: 19). She further argues that the structures were for a religious elite, with strictly controlled architectural access to the storage areas. The architecture of this complex at Chiripa was reconstructed by Conklin and Moseley (1988: 161). Their reconstruction is very similar to the architecture of the sunken courts at Pucara, as indicated by Kidder's (1943) work and plans provided by K. Chávez (1988). This suggests that the elite architecture at the major regional centers throughout the basin had common architectural features that linked the region as a whole.

Chávez renamed Kidder's and Coe's levels at Chiripa to Early, Middle, and Late. She assigned the Early Chiripa a 1400–900 B.C. date and suggested that the Middle Chiripa dated to 900–600 B.C. The site's Early and Middle Chiripa occupations (which correspond to Bennett's Pre-mound and House phases) represent the Middle Formative–period occupation in the general chronology used here. The Middle Formative is also represented by the structures discovered by Kidder and Coe below Bennett's House-phase level.

The most recent work at the site was directed by Christine Hastorf (1999a) and her colleagues, who also divided the sequence into Early, Middle, and Late Chiripa, assigning the dates listed above. Systematic surface collections by Bandy (1999a) indicate a scatter of Chiripa pottery over 7.5 hectares. As he describes it, this latest work at Chiripa "firmly establishes the existence of large-scale, nucleated habitation at least by the Late Chiripa phase."[6]

Hastorf's team discovered a very important semi-subterranean structure two hundred meters south of the main mound (where Bennett, Coe, and others had excavated previously) that dated to 800–750 B.C. This would fall in the early part of the Late Chiripa period (Whitehead 1999) in the chronology provided by Hastorf's team. It would be in the Middle Chiripa period of Chávez, and would fall squarely in the Middle Formative in the Titicaca Basin–wide chronology used here.

The Llusco structure, as they term it (Hastorf 1999a), is a semisubterranean construction with a plaster floor. It measures approximately eleven by thirteen meters. The walls are constructed with "rounded cobbles and clay" (Paz Soría 1999: 33). Paz Soría (1999: 33) also reports the existence of a "drainage canal, an attached wall, and the presence of a new floor in the interior." Presuming the presence of an adobe superstructure, the Llusco structure would have been an impressive construction. It would have been almost 150 square meters in size, sunken partially into the earth, with plaster walls that may have been painted, a subterranean drainage system, and a well-made white plaster floor. The Llusco structure is one of the earliest such structures known in the region, and its semisubterranean construction presaged the much larger sunken courts of later periods.

It is significant that Hastorf (1999b) reports at least one, and possibly two, more of these structures at Chiripa that are either contemporary with or even earlier than the Llusco structure. Each of these is about thirteen meters on a side, square, and semisubterranean. It is a reasonable hypothesis that other similar structures exist at Chiripa and at other similar sites around the basin.

Several domestic terraces with heavy concentrations of domestic remains are below the mound on the lakeside at Chiripa. Although almost never reported until the work of Hastorf (1999a), the existence of these domestic terraces indicates that Chiripa was not an isolated and "empty" temple site but a more complex settlement that included elite residences, corporate constructions in the form of elaborate ceremonial architecture, and substantial nonelite domestic areas surrounding the elite/ceremonial core.

TIWANAKU

Current evidence indicates that the first occupation at the site of Tiwanaku began by at least 800 B.C., and probably earlier. If not contaminated, the one carbon-14 date in the sixteenth century B.C. that Ponce published would suggest an Early Formative–period occupation on the site. The Middle Formative period at Tiwanaku is occasionally referred to as Tiwanaku I by scholars who assume that this period extends back to the early date obtained by Ponce. Alternatively, it is referred to as Chiripa based on the existence of pottery manufactured in a generalized Middle Formative style (e.g., Portugal O. 1992).

I believe that the Tiwanaku I/II occupation (referred to here as the Kalasasaya period) began around 300 B.C. and no earlier. Therefore, the Middle Formative period at Tiwanaku itself remains unnamed in my reconstruction. We know little about the architecture and size of the Middle Formative occupation at the site because it was followed by the massive building programs of the later Tiwanaku capital. Nevertheless, the work of Portugal O. (1992: 50), who has published a very useful map of several Middle Formative–period deposits at the site, indicates that a major site existed. Also providing evidence of a Middle Formative occupation is Arellano (1991: 277), who reports that Chiripa pottery was found in the bottom half of his excavations at the base of the Akapana pyramid. Extensive future excavations will be required to reveal the nature of this early occupation.

PALERMO

The site of Palermo is near the town of Juli, in the Lupaqa region of the Titicaca Basin. The site itself is on the side of Pukara Juli, adjacent to an old hacienda that lends its name to the site. It has an Early Sillumocco (Middle Formative)–period component that covers about four hectares. Palermo is a classic example of an elite center characterized by massive domestic terraces that climb to an artificially altered hilltop. There is corporate architecture, including a sunken court and a probable stone enclosure on the hilltop, probably built during the Upper Formative and rebuilt in the Tiwanaku period (see chapter 7). Based on current evidence, the best hypothetical reconstruction of the architectural sequence at the site includes a substantial Middle Formative occupation with some sort of corporate architecture, like the Llusco structure in Chiripa, that was rebuilt in later occupations.

Excavations at Palermo above the sunken court indicate two major construction periods separated by a clay floor. Below the floor, only pre-Tiwanaku Early Sillumocco pottery incorporated into fill was discovered; from it a single carbon-14 date of 2810 ± 80 was obtained.[7] This date calibrates to 940 ± 110 B.C., the very beginning of the Early Sillumocco period. A date obtained from the floor surface was 2180 ± 80, calibrated to 210 ± 150 B.C.,[8] indicating it was constructed in the Early Sillumocco/Late Sillumocco transition.

Palermo is between two major aqueducts that lead into the raised-field area immediately below the site. One aqueduct now runs to a spring used to water a church-run agricultural research station and produces a large quantity of water throughout the year.

TITINHUAYANI

The site of Titinhuayani is in the Challa area, in the center of the Island of the Sun. It was mapped and excavated by Esteban Quelima, in conjunction with the Island of the Sun Archaeological Project (Bauer and Stanish 2001). Titinhuayani, the major Middle Formative–period site on the island, is estimated to cover approximately three hectares.

The site has evidence of elaborate corporate architecture, including stone-faced terrace walls, a sunken court, and extensive burial areas. The surface features of the site appear to indicate an architectural history roughly similar to that of Chiripa: a Middle Formative occupation with some corporate architecture and subsequent rebuilding episodes. Surface pottery is of exceptional quality, including well-made Middle Formative, Upper Formative, and Tiwanaku fine wares. A section of relict raised fields is found on the pampa below the site. Bandelier (1910: 172) spent little time at this site, but he notes in passing that he "excavated a number of graves, obtaining skulls, pottery of the coarser kind, and one skull trephined on the forehead." After finding the small adjacent site of Qeya Kollu Chico to be richer in intact graves, he concentrated his excavations there.

There has been some looting of Titinhuayani, and a modern cemetery covers about one hectare on the site. Nonetheless, the terrace walls and many interior walls are intact. Exposed cuts on the hillsides reveal deep stratified midden areas with abundant carbon and organic remains. Cut stones on the surface suggest that intact plaza areas or sunken courts will be found below the surface. Excavations by Quelima in this flat area on the hilltop indicate an initial Late Archaic occupation with abundant obsidian, an Early Formative, Middle Formative, Upper Formative occupation, and a light Tiwanaku occupation. The major period of construction is in the Upper and (possibly Middle) Formative periods.

CKACKACHIPATA

Ckackachipata is the largest confirmed Middle Formative site discovered in the southern Titicaca Basin between Santiago Chambilla, just south of Ilave, and the Desaguadero area on the Peruvian side. Nearly the entire peninsula that juts into the lake is covered with domestic terraces and artifacts, most of which date to the Middle Formative. There are moderate scatters of Upper Formative, possibly a very light Tiwanaku occupation, and light scatters of Late Horizon pottery as well. There is no surface evidence of corporate architecture on the site, but the wide terraces leading up to a flat area with heavy concentrations of artifacts is suggestive of corporate constructions. These would include sunken courts and artificially flattened enclosure areas.

The total site area covers at least nine hectares, of which we estimate about five to seven hectares were occupied during the Middle Formative. This would make the Middle Formative occupation at Ckackachipata larger than that of the Middle Formative at Palermo in the Juli area. It is significant that Ckackachipata is about the size of Chiripa in the Formative period. Chiripa is considered to be one of the most important Middle Formative sites. As Ckackachipata is similar at least in size to Chiripa, it may be one of the most important regional centers of this time period in the south.

IMICATE

The site of Imicate was first reported by Hyslop (1976: 384), who described it as "located on a knoll about 2 kilometers from the lake." He also noted the existence of stone blocks on the surface that "were probably in the Tiwanaku style. One may be an eroded statue." The site is approximately one and a half kilometers from the Checca Checca–Yunguyu highway. On the road from the highway to the community of Imicate is a standing rock, probably a cut stone from now-destroyed corporate architecture at Imicate, and probably the block referred to by Hyslop. This mound is at least three meters above the natural ground surface, and the site is at least five hectares, and possibly larger. The substantial initial Middle Formative–period occupation was followed

by occupations during the Upper Formative, Tiwanaku, Altiplano, and Inca periods. The site was a primary regional center in the Middle Formative.

KANAMARCA

On a very wide, low hill north of the Zepita-Yunguyu road, near the village of Calacota, is the site of Kanamarca. There is now a school on the northern end of the site, and the Río Calacota runs directly east of it. Kanamarca is one of the most prominent natural hills that juts into the lake, and the site contains surface diagnostics from the Middle Formative, Upper Formative, Tiwanaku, and Late Horizon periods. The habitation area of the Middle Formative occupation appears to be at least three hectares, although no systematic work has been conducted. The hill is heavily plowed, and there is only the trace of some very wide, large, and low domestic terraces. The huge, unshaped andesite blocks on the site are typical of those used in Tiwanaku architecture, but they also occur naturally in this area. It is likely, however, that these blocks were used in Tiwanaku or Upper Formative constructions, and this occupation probably has obscured much of the site's Middle Formative occupation. Regardless, the widespread distribution of Middle Formative pottery on the surface indicates a major site, one that was a primary regional center.

PAUCARCOLLA–SANTA BARBARA

There was a substantial Middle Formative occupation at the site of Paucarcolla–Santa Barbara. Diagnostics on the surface include Qaluyu or Qaluyu-related incised wares. The total area of the Middle Formative occupation appears to be at least four hectares in size and possibly much larger. More-intensive work at this site could demonstrate that it was comparable in size to Chiripa or Ckackachipata during the Middle Formative. This appears to be the case, based on a surface reconnaissance. The site is associated with a large raised-field complex in the pampa below, and agricultural implements abound on the surface. Although the site has no obvious corporate architecture, there may be some sunken courts on terraces high up the hill.

YANAPATA-CANINSAYA

First reported by Hyslop (1976: 255–257), Yanapata is about one kilometer from the crossroads where the Yanapata road branches off from the Yunguyu-Zepita highway. It is a half-kilometer from the plaza in modern Yanapata. Hyslop (1976: 255) described it as being on "a hill pointing northward toward Lake Titicaca which is less than 1 km. away." He also noted two badly eroded monoliths on the surface, one of which had been recently placed upright by the local landowners. The upright stela is about three meters in height, squarish, and approximately twenty by forty centimeters on a side. Hyslop felt that the remains of a human figure could possibly be seen on the upright stela, and he noted the presence of building stones and other cut stone blocks typical of Tiwanaku and Upper Formative sites in the region. Our observations of the site are generally consistent with those of Hyslop. The habitation area of Yanapata is at least three hectares (Hyslop estimated the site area at five hectares.) In our typology, the site is a Type 1 mounded site, with a probable aboriginal corporate construction on the hilltop where the stelae are now found (Stanish et al. 1997: 101–102).

Caninsaya is a large Type 3 and Type 1 site near the town of Yanapata, on the low, flat, wide lake plain in front of Lake Huiñamarca. There are two distinct architectural components on the site: a major domestic hillside site west of the road that covers about three to four hectares, and a second mounded area east of the road that covers about two to three hectares. In total, the habitation and ceremonial areas cover four to seven hectares. Caninsaya has two cut stone stelae that fit into the Formative-period sculpture traditions defined by Chávez and Chávez (1975). The motifs include a Late and/or Middle Chiripa–style face, llamas, some geometric patterns, and possible snake designs (and see Portugal O. 1981). The stelae are very significant in that they indicate the site was an elite center (Stanish et al. 1997: 88–90).

HUAJJE

The site of Huajje is a rare and very large U-shaped mound in Puno Bay opposite Esteves Island. The site was identified in 1997 by Programa Collasuyu, and little work has been completed. The mound is about 450 meters long and perhaps 75 meters wide, making it the largest corporate construction in Puno Bay. Pottery fragments on the surface indicate occupations from at least the Middle Formative up to the Tiwanaku period. The U-shaped structure at the site is emblematic of the Initial and Early Horizon on the Pacific coast, but such structures are not common in the Titicaca Basin. Without excavations, it is impossible to know if the U-shaped mound at Huajje was constructed in the Middle Formative; however, we know that a U-shaped mound at Tumatumani almost certainly dates to this time period, and the best hypothesis at present is that the mound at Huajje was built at this time as well. Along with other sites in Puno Bay, Huajje is hypothesized to represent a distinctive polity by at least the late Middle Formative.

Middle Formative Villages and Hamlets

Dozens of Middle Formative villages have been discovered in the region. One site, known as Takape, stands out because it is one of the rare Early and Middle Formative sites without later occupations. Takape is in the Huancani area, near Pomata. The Early Formative occupation is impossible to define without excavations. The site's existing architecture is most likely Middle Formative and covers about 2.75 hectares. Lacking later occupations, the site provides insight into the nature of a large Middle Formative village.

The site is on the top and sides of a low ridge between two watercourses: the Río Chachacomani and the Río Takape. It now has a rounded, mound-like appearance, a result of the collapse of the Middle Formative–period structures. The architecture appears to have been tightly compact and aggregated, with a possible court in the center of several domestic structures. The domestic architecture appears to be characterized by round structures, but this observation is somewhat speculative, based on the existence of circular depressions and analogies to sites of similar time periods in the Moquegua Valley. If this observation is correct, then we can surmise that Middle Formative villages in this area were tightly packed and aggregated, with round structures arranged into patio groups around a central court.

Among the other Middle Formative villages that stand out is Tacapisi, on the southern side of Ccapia Mountain. This important site is a little more than one kilometer from Copani, on a high ridge about two hundred meters from the road. The ridge is between two small quebradas, or rivers. The hilltop was occupied during the Late Archaic, Early Formative, and Middle Formative periods. Below the ridge and terraces is an Upper Formative and Inca occupation. The habitation area of the site covers about one to two hectares. Beginning near the road is a series of about four to six terraces that rise to the top of the ridge. At the top of the hill is a low, flat area that appears to have been artificially leveled and may have contained corporate architecture; if so, it would be a secondary regional center in our site typology. This area is badly disturbed, however. The artifacts on the upper terraces and the ridgetop are overwhelmingly Middle Formative, and the lower terraces contain artifacts from the Upper Formative and Inca period.

The site of Kalatirawi was discovered during survey by the Juli-Pomata Project on the southwestern side of the lake. This moderately sized Type 2 mound, in the Moyopampa near the Río Salado, covers approximately twenty to thirty meters. It contains oc-

cupations from the Early Sillumocco to the Early Colonial period. It is not an artificially constructed platform mound like Tumatumani. Rather, it is most likely consists of a series of structures that collapsed over at least two millennia. The site is very significant because it has diagnostic ceramics from all periods in the Juli-Pomata region, including the Middle Formative, but there is no surviving architecture. It is also significant because it is a pampa mound site with a Middle Formative occupation. This is rare in the region but indicates that small villages or hamlets were already being founded in the pampa grasslands in the Middle Formative.

The site of Linquinchira has a Middle Formative occupation that is significant because it is on the Desaguadero River. First recorded by Hyslop, the site is "on the eastern and southern edge of a rock outcrop 100 meters west of the Desaguadero River" (Hyslop 1976: 261–262). It is about five hectares in size, and "the eastern side is principally a large platform 50 by 100 m. with piles of stones on it possibly indicating habitations. The southern section of the site has a number of cist graves and at its western end there is a platform of about 50 by 50 m. with cist graves in it" (Hyslop 1976: 261). This cemetery area was included in Hyslop's site size calculation. The size of the habitation area is estimated at about two hectares, with the large platform noted by Hyslop as the principal location of aboriginal domestic structures (Stanish et al. 1997). Linquinchira is a Type 4 site in our regional typology (Stanish et al. 1997), characterized by large, wide domestic terraces and an absence of corporate architecture. The large platform noted by Hyslop is a very large domestic terrace, and smaller ones are located along the eastern hillside of Vilamaya, down to the modern road.

The artifact density of Linquinchira is quite high. Surface artifacts include post–Late Archaic projectile points, a finely made nonprojectile lithic assemblage using a wide variety of nonlocal materials, copper ore, andesite hoes and adzes, and well-made ceramic artifacts. The principal occupations were during the Middle Formative, Upper Formative, and Tiwanaku periods. The site is adjacent to prime raised-field agricultural land, and a major aqueduct about five hundred meters south of the site fed the raised fields near Quintuvincolla. This aqueduct is also associated with the site of Chicane to the south. Along with other sites in the region, Linquinchira indicates that there were substantial occupations in the Desaguadero River area during the Middle Formative period, but the primary regional center of the Desaguadero River area has not been located. It is possible that it is on the Bolivian side of the river or that the nearby site of Simillake has a Middle Formative–period component, which would make it a likely primary regional center.

The site of Tumatumani is part of the elite/ceremonial complex of sites in the Juli area during the Middle Formative. As with so many multicomponent sites in the region, the Middle Formative occupation has been obscured by the later occupations, particularly the Upper Formative (Late Sillumocco) and Tiwanaku occupations (Stanish and Steadman 1994). At Tumatumani, the distribution of Middle Formative (Early Sillumocco) ceramics defines the maximum extent of the occupation as approximately 2.5 hectares. Excavations at the site indicate at least two periods of corporate construction during the Upper Formative and Tiwanaku periods but no evidence of such constructions during the Middle Formative. One reconstruction of the site history (Stanish and Steadman 1994) suggests that the initial occupation was a small, early Middle Formative–period one on a low hill. The site's U-shaped mound suggests a very early corporate construction but was not excavated, so there is no settlement history for that part of the site. It is quite possible that Tumatumani was the primary regional center early on in the Middle Formative in the Juli area, with Palermo usurping its paramount position in the later Middle Formative, but this hypothesis remains conjectural and subject to future research. At present, it is uncertain if Tumatumani was a major primary regional center during the Middle Formative or merely a small village in prime agricultural and lake-edge land linked to a primary center in Palermo.

Kasani is the border town between Peru and Bolivia on the road from Yunguyu to Copacabana. At the Colonial-period arch north of the church is a Type 3 site, literally divided by the border, with Middle Formative, Upper Formative, and possibly Tiwanaku pottery on the surface. Being a border area, the site is heavily damaged, but surface features suggest a typical Type 3 site with domestic terraces and probable corporate constructions. This may also be the source of the Kasani stela published by Chávez and Chávez (1975: figure 13).

On the Huata Peninsula in the south, in Bolivia, is Khañuani, a site with a substantial Middle Formative–period occupation. It has some later materials as well, but the principal occupation appears to be contemporary with Early and Middle Chiripa. There are no Tiwanaku diagnostics on the site. The habitation area of the site is about one-half hectare, or about seventy by seventy meters. There is a low wall around the site, and inside is a squarish, sunken area, probably a court, about sixteen meters on a side. Above this depression is a platform that measures about seven by twenty-three meters. Both the court and the platform walls were built with fieldstones. Khañuani is typical of the many sites that were abandoned in the late Middle Formative in the Titicaca region. The dynamics of this abandonment process are addressed in chapter 11.

Middle Formative Settlement Patterns

THE JULI-POMATA REGION

The local Middle Formative occupation in the Juli-Pomata region is called Early Sillumocco. The word *Sillumocco* (Fingernail Hill) is a local toponym for the site a few kilometers due west of Juli. The Sillumocco

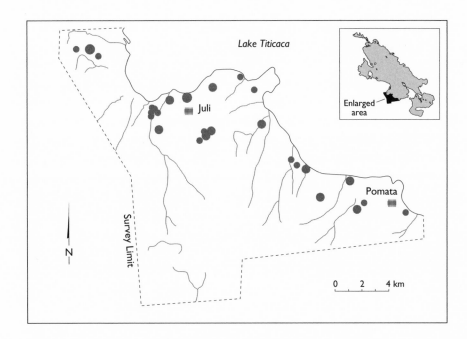

MAP 6.4. Early Sillumocco settlement pattern in the Juli-Pomata survey area.

period was named after this site (in Stanish et al. 1997), a low hilltop settlement with a large semi-subterranean structure at the top of the hill. The term *Sillumocco* thus refers to the culture, the type site, and the associated ceramic assemblage in the Juli-Pomata area during the Formative period. Early Sillumocco spans the end of the Middle Formative and the early Upper Formative, and also the Qaluyu, Cusipata (Mujica 1987), Chiripa Llusco, and Chiripa Mamani periods.

The Early Sillumocco settlement pattern (shown in map 6.4) reveals a preference for the lake shore, which was occupied by fully 85 percent of the total population living below 4,000 meters, as calculated by total habitation area per period. Three sites in the puna constitute the remaining 15 percent of the population. It is significant that the largest cluster of Early Sillumocco sites is on low hills in, or on the periphery of, the Moyopampa raised-field system. In fact, 41 percent of the population, as calculated by total habitation area, was located within one kilometer of the raised-field areas (see table 6.2).

Settlements were generally spread evenly along the lake shore, but there is some clustering of sites, particularly in the raised-field areas and richer riverine environments. The latter, of course, would have been agriculturally rich zones with or without raised fields. In other words, the Middle Formative settlement pattern suggests that these populations optimized ecological resources.

The survey data strongly suggest that raised-field agriculture was an important component of the Early Sillumocco economy. The first substantial occupation of Palermo, which is directly between two aqueducts that feed the raised fields, was in the Early Sillumocco period, and control of these freshwater sources was likely a major settlement determinant. Raised fields are also found in the Pomata area and the Challapampa zone due west of Pomata. Each of these areas has some Middle Formative settlement. In summary, the Middle Formative settlement pattern is characterized by a lakeside focus, the absence of fortified settlements, a general concentration of almost half of the population (41 percent) in the

TABLE 6.2

Population Table from the Juli-Pomata Survey

	Middle Formative	Upper Formative	Tiwanaku	Altiplano	Inca	Early Colonial
TOTAL POPULATION (HECTARES)[a]	23.04	32.72	62.86	74.16	178.49	153.75
TOTAL NUMBER OF SITES	25	19	41	140	242	224
MEAN SIZE OF ALL SITES (HECTARES)	0.92	1.72	1.53	0.53	0.73	0.69
TOTAL NUMBER OF SITES IN RAISED-FIELD AREAS	11	12	17	44	48	43
POPULATION INDEX OF RAISED-FIELD ZONE (HECTARES)	9.49	22.71	35.74	21.04	25.15	15.18
MEAN SIZE OF SITES IN RAISED FIELDS (HECTARES)	0.86	1.89	2.10	0.48	0.52	0.35
POPULATION INDEX OF RAISED FIELDS AS PERCENTAGE OF TOTAL	41	69	57	28	14	10
TOTAL NUMBER OF SITES IN NON-RAISED-FIELD SUNI	11	6	21	75	143	124
POPULATION INDEX OF NON-RAISED-FIELD SUNI (HECTARES)	10.20	8.01	24.53	42.64	118.62	99.89
MEAN SIZE OF SITES IN NON-RAISED-FIELD SUNI (HECTARES)	0.93	1.33	1.16	0.57	0.83	0.80
POPULATION INDEX OF NON-RAISED-FIELD SUNI AS PERCENTAGE OF TOTAL	44	24	39	57	66	65
TOTAL NUMBER OF SITES IN PUNA	3	1	3	21	51	57
POPULATION INDEX OF PUNA (HECTARES)	3.40	2.00	2.59	10.48	34.72	38.68
MEAN SIZE OF SITES IN PUNA (HECTARES)	1.13	2.00	0.86	0.50	0.68	0.68
POPULATION INDEX OF PUNA AS PERCENTAGE OF TOTAL	15	6	4	14	19	25

[a] The total area of settlement is an index for the population.

TABLE 6.3

Middle Formative Sites from
the Juli-Pomata Survey Area

Site Number	Size (in hectares)
212	4.00
342	2.75
001	2.50
333	2.00
457	2.00
158	1.00
261	1.00
383	1.00
365	1.00
347	1.00
349	1.00
022	0.90
210	0.50
282	0.50
278	0.50
321	0.50
422	0.50
372	0.25
113	0.25
450	0.09
451	0.09
208	0.06
499	0.05
500	0.05
220	0.04
133	0.01

NOTE: Numbers are from the site registry in Stanish et al. 1997; sites
with Early Formative component are underlined.

raised-field areas, and no evidence of formal of
camelid pasturing.

The Juli-Pomata data also illustrate another very
important feature of the settlement dynamics of the
Formative period. Table 6.3 illustrates that none of
the Early Formative sites in the Juli-Pomata survey
were abandoned in the Middle Formative. All growth
in the Middle Formative occurred at existing sites and
by the addition of new sites. In contrast to later periods, there was no abandonment of settlements in
this area during the Middle Formative.

Of the five sites that are two hectares or larger,
three were preexisting Early Formative settlements,
and two were established in the Middle Formative.
An interesting pattern is that all of the very small
hamlets were newly founded in the Middle Formative, and only seven of the twenty-one sites smaller
than two hectares had Early Formative components.
In other words, 66 percent of the smaller sites in
the Middle Formative were newly founded. This settlement continuity between the Early and Middle
Formative suggests that there was no migration of
population into the area, and that as the political
economy became more complex, existing settlements
became the elite-dominated regional centers.

During the Middle Formative, settlements clustered around these regional centers in a pattern that
deviated from the strict environmental optimization
strategies of the past. A general two-tiered ranking
of site types, and a three-tiered ranking of size,
emerged in the settlement patterns of the Middle
Formative. The regional centers became the locus of
the production and erection of stone stelae and other
stone art, and the production of finely made serving
and drinking vessels, ceramic trumpets, and probably other elite art.

THE TIWANAKU REGION

Formative-period settlements in the Tiwanaku Valley proper are dated from 1500 B.C. to A.D. 100 by
Mathews (1992: 133–155), who identifies three cultures
in the area: Chiripa-related, Tiwanaku I/II or Kalasasaya, and a new culture represented by a ceramic
assemblage named Early Formative Lateral Banded
Incised. Albarracin-Jordan (1996a) also located in the

region a number of Formative sites that he dates to the same period. Both Mathews and Albarracin-Jordan discovered clusters of Formative-period sites in the Tiwanaku Valley. This can be interpreted in several ways. The most parsimonious explanation is that the Middle Formative of the Tiwanaku Valley was similar to that of the Juli-Pomata region, with sites spaced more or less evenly across the landscape and some clustering in the richest areas. The evidence from the Tiwanaku Valley is consistent with observations elsewhere that the Middle Formative peoples were beginning to form settlement clusters around larger sites with corporate architecture.

THE ISLAND OF THE SUN

The cultural development on the Island of the Sun parallels that of the mainland in a number of ways. By at least 800 B.C., and probably as early as 1100 B.C., a moderately complex society (relative to the Early Formative) developed. It was organizationally similar to the Middle Formative societies on the mainland. Around this time, there appeared a new set of ceramic diagnostics related to the generalized elite pottery style of the Middle Formative and early Upper Formative periods in the region known as Chiripa. Chiripa-like pottery is found throughout the southern and southwestern Titicaca Basin, from at least the Ilave and Escoma Rivers in the north to areas well south of the lake into Bolivia and extreme northern Chile. The diagnostics on the Island of the Sun can be dated with reference to earlier work by Alconini (1993), Bermann (1994), Browman (1978b), Mohr (1966), Janusek (1994), and Steadman (1994), among others, which indicates that by at least this time period, the island was in the general cultural orbit traditionally characterized as Chiripa.

I call this period and the associated culture Early Titinhuayani, after the large site in the center of the island, in the community of Challa. Early Titinhuayani refers to the local expression of the Middle Formative period of the Titicaca Basin as a whole. Based on stylistic comparisons to the mainland, Early Titinhuayani dates are bracketed between 1100 and 200 B.C., with peak populations probably after 800 B.C., a date also based on similarities to mainland patterns.

The settlement pattern indicates that some major changes occurred between the Early and Middle Formative, including a substantial increase in the number of sites and the total population (see map 6.5). As with the Titicaca Basin in general, there is evidence of the development of site size hierarchies and the emergence of ranked society. The two basic Middle Formative site types on the island are villages and hamlets. The villages range from one to slightly less than four hectares in size, and the hamlets are less than one hectare and may be as small as a single household.

The largest site during this time period was most likely Titinhuayani, then a regional center about 4 to 5 hectares in size. Another contemporary site on the island covers about 3.75 hectares, but the settlement is scattered, and there is no evidence of corporate architecture. It is most likely a large village attached to Titinhuayani. There are several other larger village sites on the island during this period.

Four, and possibly five, Middle Formative settlement clusters on the island may represent some sort of political division (see map 6.5). This is an important pattern that suggests the emergence of politically and geographically bounded groups centered on the larger villages. This interpretation is supported by the absence of sites in the southern Challa area, which is very productive agriculturally, with no obvious impediments to human occupation. Later peoples constructed many sites there, attesting to its productivity, but Middle Formative populations chose not to live there, leaving an unoccupied area between the Challa cluster of sites and the southernmost group on the island. This is a classic indicator of a social and/or political boundary.

Another important change between the Early and

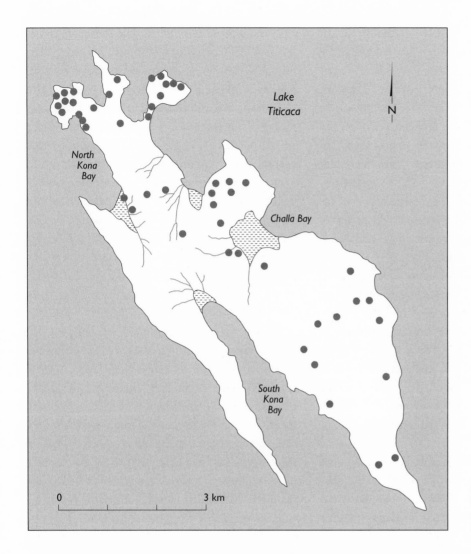

MAP 6.5. Middle Formative–period settlement on the Island of the Sun.

Middle Formative periods is that sites were established well away from the lake shore in the Middle Formative, although other lakeside and springside sites continued to be exploited. The most logical explanation for this pattern is the adoption of terrace agriculture, particularly for the Kalabaya Peninsula and the northernmost site cluster in the Titikala area. There are large areas of relict or in-use terraces in these zones, which could not be exploited effectively for any period of time without the use of terraces.

This shift of population away from the lake is consistent with paleoclimatic reconstructions of the Titicaca Basin environment for this time. Data from studies by Wirrmann, Ybert, and Mourguiart (1991) indicate that the period around 1000 B.C. was either "wetter than today" or characterized by a "progressive rise of the lake level," indicating wetter conditions. Likewise, Kolata and Ortloff (1996a: 109–110) argue that "only with an increase in long-term net precipitation beginning about 3400–3000 B.P. was there sufficient moisture to support intensive agriculture."

If such a climate shift did occur, it would have

made terrace agriculture feasible and highly productive for the first time in the region, particularly if the early agriculture was combined with lake exploitation. It is also likely that there was a significant reduction in the wild animals available for hunting by this time, a result of demographic increases on the island and its relatively low carrying capacity. In other words, an increase in precipitation, a population increase, and the shrinking of wild resources may have provided the context for the emergence of intensive agriculture and the development of settlement clusters possibly representing political boundaries during the Middle Formative.

As with the Early Formative–period sites, there is evidence in the excavations for a vigorous exchange in lithic raw materials during the Middle Formative. The general similarities in the ceramic styles between the mainland and the Early Titinhuayani styles on the island further indicate strong cultural linkages. Thus, it appears that during the Early Titinhuayani period, the island was part of the general cultural developments of the southern Titicaca Basin and not an isolated area.

The settlement pattern data indicate that one of the site clusters is in the Titikala area. Ten sites with Middle Formative diagnostics were discovered on the island's northern peninsula. The existence of a cluster of sites near the future Sacred Rock of the Inca (see chapter 10) raises the question of whether the area was used as a huaca by the Early Titinhuayani peoples. Although intensive site excavations would be needed to answer this question, several observations suggest that the area was not ritually significant in this period. For instance, there is no special site that was constructed; the sizes and nature of the sites in the Titikala area parallel those in the other areas of the island. Furthermore, the sites are all associated with terraced areas or are near the lake, a distribution explainable by economic factors. They are all situated to exploit the agricultural and lake resources of the northern peninsula of the island.

In sum, it is most likely that the Early Titinhuayani sites were sedentary populations engaged in fishing, agriculture, and economic exchange with the mainland. There is no evidence to suggest that the Titikala area was ritually significant at this time. Although there clearly was a major occupation in the northern side of the island, the sites are not significantly different in surface characteristics and settlement distribution from other areas of the island at the time. The Early Titinhuayani settlement of the Titikala area can be explained by economic factors, but future excavations could alter this conclusion by demonstrating qualitative differences between sites in the Titikala area and the other sites on the island.

Art Styles and Emergent Elite Ideologies

The first ranked societies in the Titicaca region developed during the Middle Formative, and it is not surprising that there is a concomitant elaboration in art and architectural styles. In models of simple chiefly society, the emergence of rank is intimately associated with the production of status-validating ideologies, architecture, and material goods. Based on this model, it has been hypothesized that the ceramic, stone, bone, and probably textile art traditions developed by Middle Formative cultures were associated with emerging elite lineages that had some degree of control over the domestic labor of their communities. This labor was tapped to produce goods and architecture that reinforced the lineage's status, and these goods, in turn, were circulated to maintain the economic relationship between chiefs and commoners as part of the politico-religious system characteristic of simple chiefly societies. As discussed above, the distribution of fine-ware ceramic vessels is one of the best archaeological indicators of this political economic process. Two excellent examples of fine wares are the classic styles of Chiripa and Qaluyu.

Chiripa, which is better known than Qaluyu, is characterized by red-slipped, thick-walled, flat-bottomed vessels tempered with fiber. Decoration includes geometric designs in white, yellow, and black. Chiripa-style pottery is distributed over a wide area, south from the Pacajes area and north to the Ilave and Escoma Rivers, east into Iskanwaya and the *ceja de selva* (Faldín 1991), and west into the Pacific valleys. Moseley (1992: 146–148) argues for a diffusion of this ceramic technology, based on fiber tempering, throughout a very large area including north-central Bolivia, southern Peru, and northern Chile.

There is virtually no fiber-tempered pottery in the north. All Formative pottery is sand- and/or mica-tempered in this area. Reconnaissance throughout the northern basin suggests that the Qaluyu style is as widespread as Chiripa. It is, of course, found at the type site but is found in even greater densities in the Ayaviri area, where Rowe first described the style. Aimée Plourde has discovered substantial Qaluyu fragments at the site of Cachichupa in the Putina area. Systematic survey of that valley discovered several sites with Qaluyu pottery, most notably the site of Putina under the modern town. This large mound covers at least eight hectares and was a major Qaluyu center (Stanish and Plourde 2000). Qaluyu pottery is also found at the site of Canchacancha-Asiruni in the Azángaro area (Stanish et al. 2000). Steadman (1995) has discovered a Qaluyu-related assemblage at the site of Camata, just south of Chucuito. The number of decorated pieces is extremely low (Steadman 1995: 157), and the assemblage shows clear evidence of local manufacture and influence. This is a similar pattern seen at Tumatumani near Juli. In other words, the site of Camata is a local Middle Formative site without any evidence of formal ties to Qaluyu.

In short, both Chiripa and Qaluyu pottery appear to have been widespread. These two areas are most notably defined by the use of fiber tempering in Chiripa pottery and by the exclusive use of mica and sand tempering in the north, where Qaluyu was located. The widespread distribution of a pottery style does not, however, imply the existence of a correspondingly widespread political entity. There is lit-

tle evidence for any centralized political institutions beyond simple chiefly societies in this period.

A PROPOSED SEQUENCE OF ELITE STELAE AND ARCHITECTURE FOR THE FORMATIVE PERIOD

The Early Middle Formative Period   Throughout the Titicaca Basin there are multicomponent sites with occupations that began in the Early Formative and continued through the Upper Formative. In some cases, these sites even have Late Archaic diagnostic projectile points, suggesting continuous occupations from 2000 B.C. through Pucara or even Late Huaña/ Tiwanaku times. We have discovered numerous uncarved stone slabs on these sites that range from fifty centimeters to several meters in length and are approximately thirty to seventy-five centimeters wide. We have also discovered flat, slightly polished andesite or basalt hoes of considerable size (up to one meter long). I hypothesize that many of these huancas and other uncarved stones were the first stelae of the Titicaca region and that they were associated with the first elite, nondomestic architecture, which consisted of small, well-made, plastered, squarish structures such as those described by Hastorf (1999a) and her colleagues at Chiripa.

The huancas found on small sites with Middle Formative pottery are flat and polished, and it is likely that these, and possibly wooden ones as well, were painted and set inside the small structures. This hypothesis remains to be tested; however, the association of these small stones with small sites, as well as their abundance on later sites, supports the proposition that they were found in or near the well-made structures of the period. Many of the smaller stones that are not polished are made of softer materials such as sandstone. The stela at Tariachi is one example (see figures 6.11 and 6.12). It is common to interpret these as partially eroded ashlars for the construction of courts and other buildings on the Pucara, Chiripa, and Tiwanaku sites. However, many of these stones

FIGURE 6.11. Uncarved stela at the site of Tariachi, near Juliaca. Photograph by the author.

found on sites such as Incatunuhuiri, Chiripa, Canchacancha-Asiruni, Qaluyu, Pajchiri, and so on are distinguished by irregular shapes. This, and other features such as length-to-width ratios, suggests that some of these stones were used as early stelae and later incorporated into court constructions. At Lukurmata, for instance, a decidedly pre-Tiwanaku motif on a stone, possibly a carved slab, was incorporated into the sunken court that dates to Tiwanaku times (Rivera Sundt 1989: 67).[9] Reuse of building stones is very common in later periods in the region, particularly the use of Tiwanaku and Pucara carved stones in later chulpa burial towers.

Stones like those found on the surface of the site of La Casilla, in the Desaguadero River area, are true ashlars (Stanish et al. 1997: 106, figure 81). This site has Upper Formative and Tiwanaku diagnostics on the surface, and the function of the stone is not in question because it is so similar to sunken court stones in the area. It has sharp edges and flat faces. Other stones are different and may represent the earliest stelae in the region.

The Late Middle Formative Period   Sometime during the late Middle Formative period and continuing on into the Upper Formative in the Titicaca region, a new ideology emerged that Chávez and Chávez (1975: 57) and K. Chávez (1988: 17) have called the Yaya-Mama religious tradition. The tradition takes its name from a stela discovered in Taraco on the north side of the lake (Chávez and Chávez 1975: 85, figure 1). One stone slab in Yaya-Mama style was found by Kidder and Coe (Kidder 1967 [1956]) at Chiripa in good stratigraphic context: ten centimeters above a Middle Chiripa structure and below a Late Chiripa one (in K. Chávez 1988: 21). The slab thus appears to be Middle Chiripa in date, although Chávez argues that it is more probably Late Chiripa. According to K. Chávez (1988: 21), the Yaya-Mama tradition is pre-Classic Pucara (roughly contemporary with the Cusipata phase) in date, in the late Early Horizon. It is roughly contemporary with at least part of the Kalasasaya period in the south basin, Chiripa Llusco, and the early part of Chiripa Mamani, and the late Early Sillumocco. Yaya-Mama stelae are found around the lake area. One weathered monolith from the Cochabamba area, well away from the lake, was published by Dick Ibarra Grasso (1994: 445) and appears to belong to this tradition as well; he describes it as "the earliest" found in Bolivia

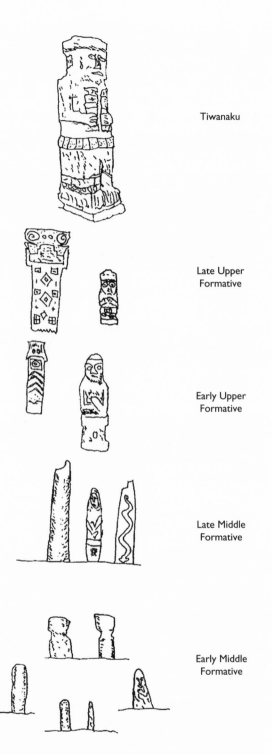

FIGURE 6.12. A hypothetical sequence of elite stelae in the Titicaca Basin. Drawing by the author.

and assigns it a date of 500 B.C., which would fit with the Yaya-Mama tradition as described by Chávez and Chávez (1975).

Yaya-Mama stone sculpture is one of the most prominent features of this tradition. The significant characteristics as noted by Chávez and Chávez (1975: 57–59) are: (1) sculpture is not in the round but in the form of stelae and slabs; (2) motifs are predominantly heads or faces with projecting appendages, undulating serpents, anthropomorphic figures, checkered crosses, four-legged animals in profile, frogs or toads, rings, and forked serpent tongues; and (3) the composition of sculpture is characterized by a mixture of motifs and the use of opposition and symmetry; stelae tend to be carved on all four sides.

Also associated with this tradition is a new set of ritual paraphernalia in which the principal artifact is a ceramic trumpet made with grass molds. Kidder (1943) illustrates one from the north basin. Several fragments of these trumpets were found at the site of Tumatumani (Stanish and Steadman 1994), and trumpet fragments have been found in most areas of the basin. K. Chávez (1988) notes that the Yaya-Mama trumpets have post-fired red and white paint rubbed into shallow incisions, and this same technique was discovered on unslipped incised wares at Tumatumani. These ceramic fragments appear to come from incense burners, and instead of red and white paint, the paint is red and yellow. It may be that white paint was used as well, but these fugitive pigments did not preserve. The ceramic style from Tumatumani is very similar to early Tiwanaku-related *incensarios* from Cuzco as described by Chávez (1985). It appears that the Yaya-Mama ritual paraphernalia includes unslipped incised incense burners as well.

S. Chávez (1988: 28) characterizes the Yaya-Mama style as indicative of "a religious movement that unified a number of diverse local groups." Although I agree that the Yaya-Mama style has religious components, it can be argued that it is more than just a religion and represents the emergence of a new elite ideology associated with a profound change in the sociological and political structure of Titicaca Basin society: the development of social and political ranking. The Yaya-Mama tradition permeated many aspects of life. It is associated with the emergence of new architectural and art styles as well as a new ritual artifact complex. These features included the new stone sculptural style, a temple-storage architectural complex, the distinctive set of ritual paraphernalia, and a "supernaturalistic" iconography (S. Chávez 1988: 17).

The Yaya-Mama religious tradition represents the first elite ideology of ranked societies in the region that had pan-Titicaca Basin significance. For the first time, a few people in a few settlements constructed small but fine buildings, created elaborate ceramic artifacts, *and* erected carved-stone stelae. I believe that the existence of stelae on a site represents the emergence of an elite that was identifying with a larger, pan-regional ideology. Stela construction was rare, restricted to a few dozen or so sites around the Titicaca Basin. It is likely that the existence of a stone stela indicated that a particular site was a regionally important center with a resident elite actively engaged in the political competition of the time.

CAN WE "READ" YAYA-MAMA STELAE?

The obvious answer to this question is no. Yaya-Mama stelae are not like their counterparts in the Maya area, which contain readable inscriptions. However, a careful analysis of available stelae indicates a patterned variation in style, suggesting that some motifs are associated with individual persons or, more likely, elite lineages or some other corporate groups. The Yaya-Mama–type stela, for instance, is a squarish stone slab approximately two meters long. One face is an anthropomorphic representation with objects on his/her head, two bent arms, an unidentified figure, a probable belt, legs, and another unidentified motif. This posture is almost exactly reproduced on an opposing face; one difference is an absence of two dots near the navel area, and there is a slight variation in the collar. On the other two faces, the motifs from top to bottom depict the same unidentified figure, a two-headed serpent, a belt represented as a continuation from the other faces, and another serpent.

Five other Yaya-Mama stelae of this type are drawn by Chávez and Chávez (1975). All of these have elements common to the type stela: an anthropomorphic figure, serpents, crossed arms, and at least one unidentified figure. The positions of these motifs vary somewhat, but one relationship seems to be constant: in each case where the drawing is sufficiently detailed (Chávez and Chávez 1975: figures 3–6), a variable motif always appears under the crossed arms of the anthropomorphic figure. These variable motifs include opposing felines, a face with protruding rays, a cross, and an unidentified motif (see figure 6.13).

There are two important observations to be made about these data. First, some of the motifs—serpents, human figures, and crossed arms—are consistently found in all sufficiently detailed stelae. Second, a variable motif is always placed under the crossed arms. A plausible interpretation is that the common elements symbolize a widespread belief or phenomenon, but the one variable motif, always in the same position, symbolizes a local or individualized phenomenon and/or belief.

It is likely that the suite of constant motifs constitutes a shared set of symbols of the Yaya-Mama tradition (Steadman 1997) that associate a local elite with a wider, pan-Titicaca tradition. The variable motifs found under the crossed arms are best interpreted as images associated with a local phenomenon. If the stelae are products of emergent elite groups typical of simple chiefly societies, then it could be that the local phenomenon represented by this variable motif is most likely a particular emergent elite group.

FIGURE 6.13. Variable motifs on Yaya-Mama stelae. Drawing by the author.

The stelae likely served to publicly announce that a particular elite group was part of a wider political and ideological system and to link emergent elite with established elite groups elsewhere in the region. The Yaya-Mama tradition is the material manifestation of a modest elite class that first developed in this period. As the first expression of the ideology of rank in the Titicaca region, it is best seen as a politico-religious movement adopted by emergent chiefs. These data accord well with models of elite formation in which art (and the ideologies behind them) are manipulated for political purposes. This is a process that led to a widespread art style linking a number of ranked individuals over a wide area.

The architecture of the late Middle Formative changes as well. At Chiripa, during the Llusco phase, formal facing was added to the large mound on at least three sides (Browman 1978b: 808), and additional walls were built. Work at the site indicates that during this period the architecture included a number of structures, presumably residential, around the mound, with a possible plaza area in the center. The structures are well constructed and most certainly required the coordinated labor of individuals beyond a household level—again, a pattern consistent with the existence of an elite capable of organizing community-wide labor.

Economic Production

The economic triad of pastoralism, lake exploitation, and agriculture (both rain-fed terrace and raised-field systems) was fully in place during the Middle Formative period. In fact, one of the period's hallmarks is the stabilization of economic production around these strategies, and a decreased reliance on hunting and wild plant collecting. The data from the surveys and excavation suggest that raised-field agriculture began in the Middle Formative, coincident with the development of simple chiefly society in the region. Evidence from at least two projects in the Titicaca Basin support this hypothesis. In his research near Huatta in the north basin, Erickson (1988: iv) excavated fields with datable pottery indicating that the fields were used before 1000 B.C. Certainly, during this early agricultural period, people were living in the Huatta pampas. These areas are ecologically marginal for most types of agriculture, with the exception of raised-field technologies, which convert the pampa into a very productive landscape. As a result, the mere existence of a substantial Middle Formative–period occupation in the Huatta pampas is good evidence for their use as raised fields.

The second project with data suggesting a Middle Formative–period date for raised-field agriculture is the Juli-Pomata survey (Stanish et al. 1997). These survey data provide a regional perspective on raised-field agricultural use and indicate a general distribution of Middle Formative sites around raised-field segments. Of the total population in the survey area during the Middle Formative, 41 percent lived within one kilometer of raised-field areas. This contrasts with other periods in which raised fields were not used, such as the Inca period, in which only 14 percent lived in this zone. The settlement data also suggest that there was no formal organization of raised-field production; production was most likely organized at the household or ayllu level.

Archaeological evidence from the Titicaca Basin also indicates that terrace agriculture probably began by Middle Formative times. Although dating terraces is extremely difficult, we can use the distribution of sites and their association with terraces to infer the dates of terraces. The distribution of Middle Formative sites on the Island of the Sun and the Juli-Pomata area correlates with the location of major terrace blocks. The most likely hypothesis at present is that terrace agriculture began in the Middle Formative throughout the Titicaca region.

LAND USE PATTERNS

The location of settlement in any region can be used to approximate the relative importance of any particular ecological zone; for example, the percentage of the population living in a raised field area provides a good indication of the importance of raised fields in the economy in question. This method assumes, of course, that each zone is used predominantly for one economic activity. Even when this is not entirely true (people near a raised-field area could obviously maintain some terraced fields, and vice versa), the location of settlement can define the principal economic activity of the population. For example, people today living above four thousand meters are overwhelmingly pastoralists, and those living near terraced land away from the lake are overwhelmingly terrace agriculturists. This is simply a question of optimization of labor and natural resources. In the absence of extraordinary noneconomic settlement determinants such as conflict or other political pressures, it is assumed that agricultural populations will generally conform to optimal settlement models. It can likewise be presumed that an optimization model characterized the raised-field areas as well.

Given these assumptions, a population index can be derived using total habitation area for all sites during any period in the survey area. In the Juli-Pomata survey (Stanish et al. 1997), a total habitation area of 23.21 hectares was calculated throughout the entire region for the Early Sillumocco period (circa 800–200 B.C.), the local manifestation of the Middle Formative. Of this total habitation area, 7.66 hectares, or 33 percent, were in the raised-field zone. The rest of the population was divided among the non–raised-field suni (50 percent) and puna (17 percent) (Stanish 1994).

The Juli-Pomata survey data (Stanish et al. 1997) provide a baseline for assessing Middle Formative–period subsistence strategies. The ratio between raised-field land use, rain-fed agriculture, and camelid production is the most even and balanced during the Early Sillumocco compared with any other time period in the region. This ratio is 3:5:2 in the Early Sillumocco. The ratios were virtually reversed in the subsequent Late Sillumocco period, which was characterized by a much more complex political structure. The disposition of settlement in this earlier context suggests a domestic economy geared to low-risk, low-productivity strategies relative to achievable levels. In other words, the populations were more evenly divided among the three economic regions than during any other period. Even so, the bulk of population remained in the terrace agriculture/lakeside zone.

Albarracin-Jordan and Mathew's (1990) survey of the Tiwanaku Valley provides additional data on Middle Formative economy. Although they used only one large Formative period (circa 1500–100 B.C.), most of the sites of this time period are in the foothills near terraced landscapes today. Another cluster is around the future site of Tiwanaku, on what would have been a river flowing through the main part of the upper valley. Their data support a conclusion drawn from the Juli-Pomata survey that the population of this period maintained a risk-avoidance strategy that relied on terrace, possibly raised-field, and riverine agriculture. Pasturing of animals is also suggested by the proximity of sites to the grass-covered valley bottom. Curiously,

there were few sites near the lake shore and a noticeable absence of sites in the low valley, so lowered lake levels could not account for this pattern. That is, if the lake were higher at the time, the lake-edge sites would have been found higher in the valleys' low portions, at the original lake edge. The Tiwanaku Valley survey data therefore support a model of Formative-period land use strategies that concentrated on raised-field and terrace agriculture, plus camelid pasturing.

REGIONAL EXCHANGE

There was a brisk exchange of goods throughout the Titicaca Basin in the Middle Formative. The northern Titicaca Basin during the Middle Formative maintained strong links with the Cuzco region. Lumbreras (1974a: 57) has noted that the shapes of domestic Qaluyu vessels are similar to Chanapata and Marcavalle pottery. Likewise, K. Chávez has identified the links between the two regions in certain decorated ceramic styles (K. Chávez 1988: 24). Lumbreras hypothesizes a regional culture that includes Qaluyu, Marcavalle, and Pikicallepata and that extended from the Cuzco region to the northern Titicaca Basin (Lumbreras 1981: 201). Silverman (1996: 112) has even noted similarities between early Qaluyu pottery and styles of Initial-period pottery from as far away as Acarí on the Peruvian coast.

The lower reaches of the eastern basin area were already being exploited by lakeside polities at this time. In the Titicaca Basin, Middle Formative–style pottery has been located on settlements near rivers and along existing roads and trails in the Omasuyu and Larecaja areas (Faldín 1990, 1991). Fiber-tempered, red-slipped pottery is common in the region. This pottery tradition, commonly called Chiripa after the type site, was also found in the southwest and southern Titicaca Basin. In fact, current data indicate that a generalized fiber-tempered pottery tradition extended throughout the southern half of the circum-Titicaca Basin in the Middle Formative.

Fiber tempering in pottery began in the Early Formative in the south basin. By the Middle Formative, particularly in its later phases, fiber-tempered pastes were used to manufacture ritually and/or politically significant vessels. The classic flat-bottomed Chiripa bowls, for instance, are beautifully executed in deep red slips. This tradition was found throughout the southern Titicaca region, and all the pottery was locally manufactured. By the late Middle Formative, fiber-tempered pottery was manufactured throughout the southern circum-Titicaca Basin. The geographical limits of this ware are not completely known. It appears that the Ilave and Escoma Rivers were the northernmost area of local manufacture of fiber-tempered ware in the west and east basin, respectively. As mentioned, well-made fiber-tempered pottery is also found in the Larecaja and Omasuyu areas to the east, and in Moquegua to the west, where it is known as Huaracane. In short, the so-called Chiripa pottery was actually a very widespread tradition in the south that began in the Early Formative and continued through the Middle Formative. The distribution of this tradition most likely represents the extent of an exchange network throughout the southern circum-Titicaca Basin.

Summary

The Middle Formative period in the Titicaca Basin was characterized by the development of the region's first ranked societies. During the Early Formative,

sites were small, homogeneous, and scattered over the landscape in a manner that optimized natural resources. During the Middle Formative, some of these sites grew in size relative to the rest of the villages in their immediate area. These larger sites became the regional centers characterized by the construction of walled mounds with corporate architecture and a suite of ritual artifacts.

The Middle Formative witnessed the formation of two cultural traditions in the north and south Titicaca Basin: the Chiripa and Qaluyu. One hallmark of these cultures is the development of nondomestic, well-made structures throughout the region. As exemplified by those discovered by Hastorf (1999a) and her team at Chiripa, these buildings were small, carefully constructed, and most likely the product of a supra-household labor organization.

This new corporate architecture developed throughout the Titicaca Basin; the north and south regions were particularly precocious. It was accompanied by the production and use of carved stelae and a new suite of artifacts that has been called the Yaya-Mama tradition by Karen Chávez and Sergio Chávez (1975). In short, the development of ranked societies in the region at this time is materially evident in the creation of a new architectural style, the development of fancy pottery traditions, the carving and erecting of stelae, and the development of at least a two-tiered site size hierarchy.

The Rise of Competitive Peer Polities in the Upper Formative Period

During the Upper Formative period (500 B.C.–A.D. 400), highly ranked societies developed in some areas of the Titicaca region. Prior to this time, the Titicaca Basin societies were demographically small and were not characterized by significant social and political hierarchies beyond that of simple ranked societies, as evident in Qaluyu, Chiripa, Early Sillumocco, and so forth. The adoption of social and political hierarchies, paralleled almost certainly by an economic hierarchy, marks the transition from the Middle to the Upper Formative period in the Titicaca region.

The Upper Formative is therefore defined as the period in which complex ranked societies developed and were the dominant political organization in the region. This is an important point to emphasize: complex ranked societies were the *dominant* political organization in the region, but this evolution of complexity was an uneven process. In many areas of the basin, there were polities that maintained political economies typical of the Early and Middle Formative lifeways and did not develop markedly ranked political economies. But a number of very complex chiefdoms did develop in the region at this time, the two largest being Pucara and Tiwanaku. Apart from these two polities, we can isolate perhaps a dozen smaller regional centers that date to the Upper Formative period as well. Based on interpretations of survey and reconnaissance data and my observations from other areas in the region, I hypothesize that there are at least two dozen additional regional centers still to be described. Each of these represented the center of autonomous or semiautonomous polities. The relationship between these polities was competitive, and alliance-formation was one means of competition. The archaeological data from these

Upper Formative sites conform well with our understanding of complex chiefly societies and incipient state societies, particularly in regard to the development of elite alliances, conflict between polities, absorption of neighbors, peer-polity interactions, and control of exchange.

Absolute Chronology

The first complex, ranked societies appear to have developed in the Pucara and Tiwanaku/Chiripa regions, the traditional centers of political power in the basin. At Chiripa, during the late Late Chiripa period, there was construction of complex architecture that is interpreted to be indicative of political ranking above that of the preceding Middle Formative times. I believe that the latter periods of Pucara (circa 100 B.C.–A.D. 300) represent the apex of complex chiefly, nonstate organization in the region. In the Juli area, the construction of a sunken court complex at Palermo represents the development of the architectural features associated with other chiefly Upper Formative cultures. A carbon-14 date from an initial Late Sillumocco (Upper Formative) floor at the site was 230 B.C. ± 80 (Stanish et al. 1997).

In the Tiwanaku Valley, we have a much better sequence than for any other area in the Titicaca Basin, based on the work of Albarracin-Jordan, Alconini, Kolata, Mathews, Ponce, Rivera, and others. Here we are able to divide the Upper Formative into early and late phases. The early Upper Formative is represented mainly by Chiripa or Chiripa-related sites that date to the Late Chiripa period. The first substantial occupation characterized by a ranked political organization in the Tiwanaku Valley, according to Albarracin-Jordan and Mathews (1990), appears to have been around the middle of the first millennium B.C. and was culturally associated with the Chiripa polity.

Around 300–100 B.C., the Chiripa-related sites were replaced by another complex society that is referred to as Kalasasaya (also known as Tiwanaku I/II) (Mathews 1992: 117). The dates of the latest Kalasasaya occupation are poorly known, but I believe that it continued up to circa A.D. 300. I therefore agree with Mathews (1992), who sees a sequence of Chiripa-related occupations to about 100 B.C., followed by the Kalasasaya period. There was also the Qeya period, dated to around A.D. 200–500. It also represents the late Upper Formative of Tiwanaku. The relationship between Kalasasaya and Qeya is not clear.

There are at least two distinct traditions in the Kalasasaya period that I believe are chronological. Ponce's only published carbon-14 date associated with an archaeological feature with identifiable pottery is a Tiwanaku I cache dated to A.D. 299 (Ponce 1976), substantially later than the date claimed for the period by Ponce. The red-yellow incised pottery with representational designs is stylistically related to Pucara and would be more or less consistent with this late date. The designs, on the other hand, deviate enough from styles from the Pucara heartland (see figure 7.1) to make them a distinct tradition. Other pottery identified as Tiwanaku I, however, is associated with the pre-Pucara traditions of the Titicaca Basin. At any rate, once these stylistic problems are sorted out, I believe we will see a sequence of Chiripa-related, Kalasasaya, and finally Qeya, prior to Tiwanaku expansion during its later periods. This chronology is virtually identical to that presented by Willey (1971: 85) in his book *An Introduction to American Archaeology*. Of course, this chronology remains hypothetical and subject to revision. The A.D. 299 date for the Tiwanaku I pottery is problematic. At present, there are two possible relationships between Qeya and Kalasasaya: one is that they are sequential, the second is that they were contemporary for at least part of the time.

Late Chiripa and Kalasasaya represent the early Upper Formative occupation in the southern Titicaca or Pacajes region. Kalasasaya developed relatively

FIGURE 7.1. Pucara pottery. Photograph by the author.

late in the Titicaca region and overlaps with the later phases of Pucara, and other local sequences. The earliest dates for Kalasasaya are not well established. In my opinion, what we now recognize as Tiwanaku I or Kalasasaya would be no earlier than 300 B.C. This conclusion is based on pottery characteristics consistent with post-200 B.C. dates from the rest of the region (e.g., see Steadman 1994). Yet there are earlier ceramic traditions and occupations at the urban site that have yet to be adequately defined. In short, the best absolute dates that can be suggested for Kalasasaya are approximately 300 B.C.–A.D. 200.

Following the Kalasasaya period is the Qeya period, which is included as part of the late Upper Formative because we are fairly certain that it extends up to around A.D. 400, and current data suggest that the Kalasasaya period does not extend that late. Bermann argues that at Lukurmata, the last Tiwanaku III occupation lasted until the sixth century A.D. (Bermann 1990: 189; 1994: 131). Based on her work at the site of Camata near Chucuito, Steadman

(1995: 544) places Qeya contemporary with the Late Pucara phase circa A.D. 100–400. Janusek (1994: 100) dates Qeya from A.D. 100 to 400 and argues that the transition between Tiwanaku III and IV is in the fifth century A.D. (Janusek 1994: 95). It is likely that Qeya extends up to A.D. 500, as suggested by Bermann, with the major period of Tiwanaku expansion beginning in the seventh century or later.

There is some question as to the reliability of the Qeya diagnostics, and whether we can appropriately speak of a Qeya occupation at the site of Tiwanaku itself, or if it was a lake-focused polity (Paul Goldstein, personal communication 1993). Qeya pottery has been reported from the site, but there are few illustrations. In fact, Qeya is quite rare from the surface of the Island of the Sun (see page 152), and it is possible that the area where it was manufactured is somewhere in the Copacabana or Huatta Peninsula (Bolivia) region. The best chronology that can be offered at present is the sequence from Chiripa-related to Kalasasaya to Qeya, recognizing some potential overlap in these phases.

The north Titicaca Basin sequence is more difficult to describe because of a lack of research. Franquemont (1986: 2) reports Kidder's dates for the classic Pucara–style pottery obtained in the Huayapata excavations east of the main mound as ranging from 2101 ± 108 B.P. to 1847 ± 106 B.P. The earlier Cusipata phase, which appears to be associated with some significant corporate construction, dates to around 500–200 B.C. and, according to Wheeler and Mujica (1981: 34), is probably a derivation of the Marcavalle tradition to the north. Mujica (1988: 79) has divided the Pucara sequence into three phases: Initial (500–200 B.C.), Middle (200 B.C.–A.D. 100) and Late (A.D. 100–300). These dates were corroborated at Camata by Steadman, who dates the Initial Pucara phase to 400–300 B.C., with Pucara 1 through Late Pucara dating to 300 B.C.–A.D. 400 (Steadman 1995: 544).

I consider the Upper Formative of Pucara to be

at its full cultural development between approximately 200 B.C. and A.D. 200. Around the third or fourth century A.D., the site of Pucara apparently declined as a regional center. It is significant that for the latest Pucara phase at Camata, in the fourth and fifth centuries, Steadman (1995: 510) notes "an increased presence of southern Basin-related ceramics at the site." In other words, the Camata data support the hypothesis that there was a decline in Pucara regional influence around the fourth century and a concomitant increase in influence from the south.

There is a question as to what the political and cultural landscape of the north basin looked liked between the collapse of Pucara and the expansion of Tiwanaku—a period that would correspond to the late Upper Formative in the region. It is hypothesized that a Pucara-derived polity in the north, called Early Huaña, existed from the end of Pucara dominance to the Tiwanaku period in the area. This period and polity are discussed below.

Political Organization of the Upper Formative Period

One of the defining characteristics of the Upper Formative is that markedly ranked societies dominated the political landscape of the Titicaca Basin. There are several key archaeological indices of the development of a complex political organization in the Titicaca region: construction of walled sunken court areas on a larger scale than that in the Middle Formative; enclosed plaza areas, or kalasasayas; artificial mountains, or akapanas; marked site size hierarchies; abandonment of small sites for larger ones (Stanish 1999); elaboration of stone sculpture; and the production of finely made ceramic serving vessels and other elite ceramic artifacts.

Significant settlement changes occurred during the Upper Formative. A typology is particularly useful when it serves to highlight key organizational characteristics of a time period as they relate to important anthropological questions. From this point of view, it is instructive that there were no urban centers in the Upper Formative as defined in the criteria outlined above. However, a new phenomenon did arise: the growth of two sites, Tiwanaku and Pucara, into huge, nonurban aggregations of elite and retainer populations into primate regional centers. This term borrows from discussions of "primate cities," or those that "overwhelmingly" dominate their settlement hierarchy (Millon 1988: 138; and see Adams 1988: 28). In the case of Pucara and, most certainly, Tiwanaku during the middle Upper Formative, they were an order of magnitude larger than any other center in the Titicaca region (see table 6.1).

Pucara and Tiwanaku during the Upper Formative are not considered urban; this term is reserved for settlements with certain characteristics not found at these sites in the Upper Formative, the two most important being planned architecture and large numbers of nonelite nonagriculturalists. By these criteria, the only Prehispanic urban sites in the Titicaca Basin were Tiwanaku during its Tiwanaku Expansive period and several Inca-period settlements. The term *primate nonurban center* serves both to emphasize the large relative size of these settlements and to indicate that they were not of sufficient complexity to be considered premodern cities. The nature of Pucara settlement is discussed below.

In addition to the two primate centers, there were several smaller centers about 10 hectares in size. Settlement data from the Juli-Pomata survey (Stanish et al. 1997) provide an insight into site size distributions during the Upper Formative in areas outside Pucara and Tiwanaku control. Figure 7.2 indicates four discrete site sizes: a major regional center over 10 hectares (Palermo), smaller sites around 4 hectares and 2 hectares, and sites less than 1.5 hectares in size. The vast majority of sites fall into the last category. The site size distribution curve of the Upper Formative is similar to that of the Middle Formative, with the exception of an additional level in the Upper Forma-

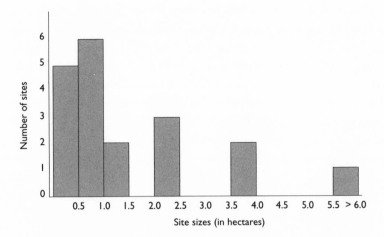

FIGURE 7.2. Site size distribution of Upper Formative sites in the Juli-Pomata survey area.

tive. Also, the absolute numbers are larger; that is, the largest Upper Formative site is more than twice the size of the largest Middle Formative site, and so forth.

During the Upper Formative there were only two primate centers, a number of primary regional centers, and several smaller primary regional centers (see table 6.1). These centers, in turn, were surrounded by smaller secondary centers, villages, and hamlets. The regional centers were the areas of fine-ware pottery production, stone sculpture manufacture, political and ritual feasts, and the organization of regional exchange. They are hypothesized to have been the main residence of autonomous or semiautonomous polities linked by a variety of mechanisms to other elites in the region.

In other words, Pucara and Tiwanaku during the Upper Formative successfully pulled relatively large numbers of nonagricultural populations into aggregated, nonurban, nonplanned settlements. At the beginning of the Upper Formative, the rest of the region's population probably remained largely agricultural, living in hamlets, villages, and regional centers. The political landscape was dynamic, with alliances and conflicts constantly shifting. By the end of the Upper Formative, a large part of the Titicaca region was linked, in turn, to the two primate cen-

ters by social, political, economic, and ideological alliances. However, even at the end of the Upper Formative, substantial areas of the Titicaca region were outside the direct control of either Pucara or Tiwanaku.

The primary regional centers during the Upper Formative are defined by the presence of what is referred to as the Kalasasaya Complex. This architectural complex is characterized by the presence of stone-lined sunken courts, a Kalasasaya-like stone enclosure, and in many cases, an adjacent hill that was a pyramid. These three elements are found on a number of Upper Formative–period settlement systems in the region. Beginning in the early Middle Formative at sites such as Chiripa, Pucara, and probably Tiwanaku, these architectural features reach their full expression in the Tiwanaku period at the capital. However, it is likely that they reached their maximum distribution as centers of regional polities in the Upper Formative period.

Another essential characteristic of regional centers is the presence of cut-stone stelae, which represent an elaboration of the Yaya-Mama tradition. Stela manufacture was rare, restricted to perhaps a few dozen sites around the basin. Upper Formative–period stelae were a material manifestation of elite political, social, and ideological power. They are particularly common near and in Tiwanaku and Pucara but are found throughout the region.

I interpret these regional centers to have been the home of semiautonomous or autonomous chiefly societies associated with either Pucara or Tiwanaku. There is substantial variation in space and time between these centers throughout the region. Not unexpectedly, the northern primary regional centers were more closely affiliated with Pucara traditions, and the southern centers were more allied with those of Tiwanaku. In the following pages, I review most of the known primary regional centers of the Titicaca region during the Upper Formative that have been adequately published.

Elite pottery styles are one of the best means of archaeologically defining the distribution of Upper Formative–period polities. This pottery was intentionally designed for ritual feasts, for exchange with other elites, for distribution to commoner populations as part of the reciprocal labor/goods exchange relationship, and possibly for other kinds of ceremonies. It is likely that the regional centers were the loci for pottery manufacture, although this proposition remains to be tested. The existence of a distinct style of pottery at secondary centers and smaller sites serves to define the settlement network of a particular polity.

Work by Steadman (1994) indicates that the vast bulk of Upper Formative–period pottery, at least in the south, was locally made, probably in the primary regional centers. At the site of Tumatumani, Steadman noted that a substantial percentage of Late Sillumocco pottery was local or semilocal, with only a fraction imported from elsewhere. The semilocal pottery may well have been produced in secondary centers. It is likely, though not sufficiently tested at this point, that this pattern holds for the Upper Formative polities in the region in general.

In short, autonomous Upper Formative–period polities are identified by the existence of a primate or primary regional center characterized by a large population and the existence of corporate architecture. The production of stelae is another hallmark of an autonomous primary regional center of an Upper Formative polity. Regional centers controlled the production of fine-ware pottery and other highly valued objects. Surrounding the primary regional centers were secondary centers, villages, and hamlets. Based on the distribution of several distinct pottery styles and distribution of known primary regional centers, it appears that at least a dozen polities existed in the Upper Formative period.

The Primate Regional Centers of
Pucara and Tiwanaku

The sites of Pucara and Tiwanaku were by far the largest regional centers in the Titicaca Basin. According to Lumbreras (1981: 202), the development of the complex chiefdoms of the Upper Formative was accompanied by the development of true urban centers: "the urban process developed and led to the construction of that immense ceremonial center known by the name of Pukara." Rowe (1963: 6) also characterized the site of Pucara as urban, but I disagree with the use of that term for Pucara at this time period. Nevertheless, I agree with Lumbreras and Rowe that these sites were significantly larger than any earlier ones in the region.

Pucara remains one of the most important and least published major sites in the Titicaca Basin (see figure 7.3). Erickson (1988) estimates the site to be approximately four square kilometers in size, but this includes the total area surrounding the central core and associated mounds near the river. If the methodology developed for the Juli-Pomata survey (Stanish et al. 1997) is used, the habitation area of Pucara is found to be no larger than two hundred hectares (two square kilometers) at its height during the late Upper Formative period. This estimate includes the central architectural core and the surrounding area with surface materials. Consistent with the observations

FIGURE 7.3. Site of Pucara. Photograph by the author.

of Franco Inojosa (1940), several areas appear not to have Upper Formative occupations, which accounts for the lower estimate of habitation area size than given by other researchers. The upper limit of my estimate includes all areas with possible buried Upper Formative occupations. There are additional mounds and other refuse areas near the river, as mentioned by Kidder, but these were not counted in my total habitation area estimate given the existence of nonoccupied areas between these mounds and the central architectural core.

The main architectural feature of Pucara is a series of large terraces that lead up to a flat area with two exposed sunken courts (see figure 7.4). There is another large court immediately to the north. The largest exposed court measures approximately 16 by 16 meters and is 2.2 meters deep (K. Chávez 1988; Kidder 1943; Palao B. 1995). The walls of the court were constructed with large cut slabs set upright, a typical pattern for this period.

In front of the large terraced construction is a dense habitation area. To the front of the site, toward the modern town, is a series of mounds that most likely had sunken courts as well. Directly south of this area are at least three other mounds with evidence of sunken courts. Habitation areas have been found near and on these mound areas, and domestic refuse is found toward the modern road.

There is some compelling evidence that the courts were used for large-scale competitive feasts and human sacrifice, two practices that would be intimately linked to the existence of an elite. Chávez (1992) discusses the existence of one hundred human mandible and skull parts from a single "ritual" area in Kidder's excavations. This would have been Kidder's "area IV," in what was most likely one of a number of sunken court complexes in front of the main terraces. The most likely interpretation is that the remains are those of war captives or other sacrificial victims buried, or reburied, during a politically important ceremony. The sacrifice of these individuals is similar to patterns associated with the Moche, the first archaic state in the Andes, on the Peruvian coast several hundred years later. Other interpretations are possible, but the location of so many bodies in an obvious public area is very strong evidence for ritualized sacrifice in a context of intense elite conflict. The site had three very large courts and a number of smaller ones, each of which may have functioned at the same time to host feasts, ceremonies, and other rites associated with building elite factions.

Pucara is not a planned site like the later Tiwa-

FIGURE 7.4. Sunken court at Pucara.
Photograph by the author.

naku capital or the Inca-period urban sites that dot the Titicaca Basin. It is, in contrast, a very large concentration of architectural complexes composed of residential and other structures of unknown function built around sunken courts of various sizes, from the very large ones at the top of the main mound to the smaller courts on the low mounds to the east. Without excavations, it is impossible to define additional courts at the site, but if the analogy to the Llusco structure at Chiripa is valid for Pucara, there are many other much smaller nonresidential structures at the site that predate the Pucara Classic period. At its height in the Upper Formative period, Pucara was an aggregation of habitation areas and sunken court complexes that covered approximately two square kilometers. It was, in many ways, an elaboration on a massive scale of the Middle Formative pattern seen at sites such as Chiripa, Qaluyu, and Canchacancha-Asiruni.

THE DISTRIBUTION OF PUCARA IN THE TITICACA BASIN

The reconnaissances of Kidder, Rowe, and Chávez and our own work with Programa Collasuyu serve to define the regional distribution of Pucara materials in the north Titicaca Basin. Confirmed areas or sites with Pucara materials that Kidder (1943: 17–19) found include Arapa, Moho, Taraco, and Ayrampuni. Pucara stonework has been recovered from Qaluyu (Rowe 1958, 1963), a site that also has a substantial Pucara component. Rowe mentions that Chávez Ballón discovered a large Pucara site at the hacienda of Tintiri, between Azángaro and Muñani, which is apparently the site referred to as Canchacancha-Asiruni by Chávez and Chávez (1970). Rowe (1958) illustrates a Pucara statue from Chumbivilcas in the southern part of Cuzco province, and S. Chávez (1988) and Núñez del Prado (1972) discovered Pucara or Pucara-related materials in reconnaissances of that same area.

The site of Maravillas, just north of Juliaca, has been known for years but has not been published. The site is huge, with domestic terraces, several architectural complexes in the pampa, a large raised-field area, several mounds to the north, and a number of linear features with early tombs. There is a dense scatter of Upper Formative diagnostics on the surface. The site may be one of the most important regional centers in the Upper Formative and deserves much more attention before it is destroyed by encroaching urban sprawl.

To the south is the large site of Incatunuhuiri, on a high hill between Puno and Chucuito in the Ichu Valley. It was first reported by Kidder. It is a classic Type 3 site with a large number of domestic and agricultural terraces below a civic-ceremonial area. On top of the hill is a sunken court and monoliths carved in pre-Tiwanaku styles. Incatunuhuiri appears to be the farthest site to the south with any significant density of Pucara-related pottery. Several other sites with Pucara materials have been found between Incatunuhuiri and Pucara on the west side of the basin, including Cerro Cupe, off the road to Hatuncolla. This Type 3 site has about six major domestic terraces with a high quantity of debris and covers approximately two hectares. Pucara pottery is found over the surface. At the top of the site is an area that could have had corporate architecture.

Across the Huatta pampa from Cerro Cupe is another recently discovered site with Pucara materials on the surface. The site of Wanina is two and a half kilometers from Huatta on the road to the southeast. It has dense habitation refuse on the last two hills that jut into the pampa on the southeast side. Wanina is a Type 3 site that may be as large as five hectares in size.

The Capachica Peninsula has been reconnoitered by Luperio Onofre and several of his students and visited by members of Programa Collasuyu (Luque López and Canahua Saga 1997; Stanish et al. 2000). There are a number of pre-Altiplano-period sites on the peninsula. One, called Cotos,[1] is on the northern side of the peninsula near the town of the same name, on the higher part of a ridge that separates a bay from the lake. The site has an impressive density of pottery, particularly Upper Formative, Altiplano, and Inca. We noted a number of local Upper Formative plain wares, some incised Pucara-like pieces, and flat-bottomed bowls. There is also a high density of obsidian flakes on the surface. Cotos is possibly a Type 3 site, although the existence of ceremonial architecture on the hilltop could not be confirmed. Certainly, there are several large and well-made domestic terraces on three sides of the hill. The site has about two to four hectares of domestic residence, of which we roughly estimate that approximately two hectares was occupied during the Upper Formative.

On the south side of the Capachica Peninsula is a monolith first described by Hoyt (1975) (see figure 7.5). As she notes, the sculptural tradition is Pucara. The monolith is similar in style to the famous Arapa stela located to the north. Local informants indicate that their ancestors brought the stela from elsewhere, but they could not say precisely where. Our reconnaissance failed to locate an Upper Formative site nearby, but large areas along the base of the hill fit the geographical and topographical characteristics for a Type 3 site.

These data help to define, in broad terms, the limits of Pucara control and influence in the Titicaca Basin and beyond (see map 7.1). The southern limit of *direct control* in the west basin is somewhere near Incatunuhuiri. Kidder described Pucara-affiliated sculpture in the east on the Huata Peninsula, near Conima at the site of Lailuyu (see page 156). Current data indicate that the limit of Pucara influence in the east basin is the Suches River. I do not believe that any site north of La Raya Pass or south of the Suches and Ilave Rivers was politically controlled by the Pucara polity in the sense of participating in an integrated political economy headed by a resident elite at the primate center. Certainly, Pucara-like pottery has been found far outside this area, as far west as Moquegua (Goldstein 2000) and as far south as the Pacajes region in Bolivia. Some Pucara or Pucara-like artifacts are reported from northern Chile (Mujica 1985; Muñoz 1983a; Rivera 1991). However, the densities of the Pucara materials, as well as the existence of other contemporary fine-ware pottery on the

FIGURE 7.5. Hoyt monolith from the Capachica Peninsula. Photograph by the author.

sites not in Pucara style, indicate that the sites were not incorporated into the Pucara polity. An example in this case would be the zone-incised pottery of the Pacajes or Tiwanaku area at this time. Although this style was part of a generalized ceramic tradition in the south-central Andes, I believe the pottery from this area is sufficiently different to distinguish it from Pucara to the north. Furthermore, the existence of Pucara sites outside the northern Titicaca Basin is problematic. The Pucara pieces found on the sites were most likely the result of exchange, not a direct political relationship.

TIWANAKU DURING THE UPPER FORMATIVE PERIOD

The nature of Tiwanaku during its Upper Formative periods is a subject of considerable debate. The huge subsequent Tiwanaku-period occupations on the site have obscured the earlier periods, particularly the Upper Formative period. Ponce (1969b, 1972, 1995) argues that major building episodes at the site began in his Tiwanaku III period (Upper Formative), which he refers to as an urban stage, but he offers little archaeological evidence for this hypothesis.

The work of Ponce, Portugal, Kolata, Manzanilla, Bennett, Janusek, Rivera, Alconini, and others provides some evidence for the distribution of pre-Tiwanaku IV materials at the site. The existence of Upper Formative–period monoliths suggests that it was a major center at that time, although in theory these could have been brought in at a later date, like the Arapa stela (Chávez 1984). Recent excavations (Alconini 1993; Janusek 1994; Manzanilla 1992) suggest that the major buildings on the site today date to the Tiwanaku period, well after Upper Formative times. Janusek (1994: 329) has stated that the greatest urban expansion of the site occurred around A.D. 600–800. Based on these limited data and some inferences from the surface remains, it is hypothesized that Tiwanaku was similar in scale to Pucara during the Upper Formative.

Something can be learned from the settlement patterns of the middle and lower Tiwanaku Valley (Albarracin-Jordan 1992; Mathews 1992). The pattern of the Formative sites indicates that Tiwanaku was the largest site in the valley, with several smaller regional centers scattered down to the lake. Albarracin-Jordan's and Mathews's survey detected a number of Forma-

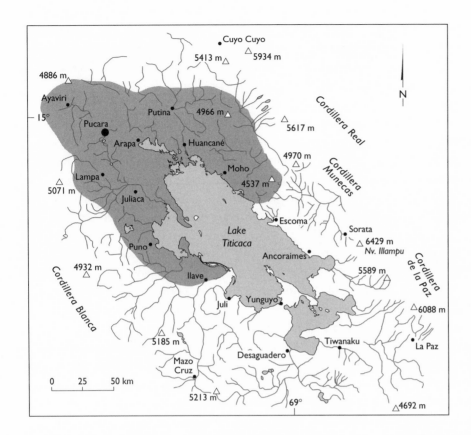

MAP 7.1. Hypothesized distribution (shaded area) of Pucara control and influence at its height, circa A.D. 100–200.

tive sites around the periphery of Tiwanaku itself. The settlement pattern also indicates a process of site aggregation during the Qeya period, when the number of sites in the valley dropped substantially and the population became concentrated near the site of Tiwanaku. In other words, settlement data from outside the site of Tiwanaku itself provide indirect evidence that it was a substantial regional center at the time.

A number of problems with the Tiwanaku settlement data center on the identification of the Qeya ceramics and the lack of other contemporary diagnostics. A more refined ceramic chronology could possibly alter these settlement patterns for this particular period, and could include many more sites in the Qeya period. On the other hand, the dramatic decrease in total sites in the Tiwanaku Valley outside

Tiwanaku itself appears to be real, and the concentration of sites into the center is consistent with patterns from the Juli-Pomata area during a similar transition from the Middle to the Upper Formative period. McAndrews (1995) has analyzed data from the region and notes that this process is common in other similar contexts of incipient urbanism, with Teotihuacán being a particularly salient example.

The pottery of the Upper Formative period of Tiwanaku is poorly known. Qeya and Qeya-related styles have been traditionally used to define this period in the region, but more recent research indicates that it is quite rare. Steadman (1994) has published Qeya-related pottery styles from the site of Tumatumani, near Juli, but she discovered very few examples. Qeya pottery was found in very limited quantities by Bauer and Stanish (2001) on the Island of the Sun, where it was first identified by Wallace (1957). The distribution of Qeya-related pottery to the north and east has not been published. My own nonsystematic reconnaissance in the Omasuyu region suggests that it is not found in the Conima to the north. The distribution of Qeya to the south and southeast is unknown (or at least unpublished).

The Upper Formative settlement pattern in the Tiwanaku Valley has been defined by Albarracin-Jordan (1996), Albarracin-Jordan and Mathews (1990), and Mathews (1992: 127–137). Mathews discovered twenty-five Chiripa-related sites located "almost exclusively along the slopes of the hills bordering the north and south sides of the valley" between 3,850 and 4,000 m.a.s.l (Mathews 1992: 127–128).

Mathews (1992: 128) notes that the Formative settlements are clustered, and that "these clusters consist of three to eight sites in close association, separated by distances of roughly three kilometers. In several cases . . . the clusters are composed of one larger, centrally-located site, often with recognizable architectural features such as walls and terraces surrounded by several sites." As Mathews notes, the Chiripa-related sites do not appear to be randomly located, "but rather suggest a higher degree of settlement organization" (Mathews 1992: 128). This pattern is interpreted to be a classic feature of ranked society, with each cluster representing a complex of one site with corporate architecture, and associated sites that housed allied factions. Albarracin-Jordan's (1996) survey in the lower Tiwanaku Valley discovered a settlement pattern similar to the one Mathews found in the midvalley. Many Formative sites were grouped in clusters and located next to raised-field agricultural areas.

Smaller Polities in the Upper Formative Period

Regional settlement data indicate that there were two regional centers in the Titicaca Basin by the late Upper Formative that were an order of magnitude larger than any other site in the region: Pucara and Tiwa-

naku. These extremely large sites are referred to as primate centers, a term that indicates their demographic size and political and economic power compared to contemporary sites in the region (see table 7.1).

The distribution of Pucara and Qeya sites and pottery throughout the Titicaca Basin does not suggest strong political control by either the Pucara or an early Tiwanaku polity outside their home territories. At Tumatumani, for instance, there were only a few dozen fragments of Qeya pottery out of several thousand studied (Stanish and Steadman 1994). The Qeya pottery was imported into the site. During the Late Sillumocco or Upper Formative period at Tumatumani, there was a local pottery manufacturing tradition that borrowed from both the north and the south. Likewise, a local polychrome was manufactured in the northern Pucara tradition. However, there is very little actual Pucara pottery on the site. The data suggest that the Late Sillumocco Polychrome was locally manufactured and that Late Sillumocco-Qeya pottery was a minor trade ware. The site of Tumatumani was part of an autonomous political entity outside the control of either the Early Tiwanaku or Pucara polities.

The same model holds for other sites in the region. Using the criteria above, it's possible to identify several primary regional centers that were not under the control of either Pucara or Early Tiwanaku. Each of these centers is believed to be the primary site of an autonomous or semiautonomous polity that coexisted with Pucara and Early Tiwanaku during the Upper Formative.[2]

THE SILLUMOCCO POLITY

This polity is centered on the site of Palermo, the primary regional center outside the Juli area, adjacent to Pukara Juli (see map 7.2). Two other sites, Tumatumani and Sillumocco-Huaquina, represent secondary regional centers of this polity (Stanish et al. 1997). The Upper Formative (Late Sillumocco)–period occupation at Palermo is represented by sub-

TABLE 7.1

Estimated Size of Selected
Upper Formative Regional Centers

Site	Size (in hectares)
Pucara	ca. 100–200
Tiwanaku	> 100?
Paucarcolla–Santa Barbara	> 12
Lukurmata	> 10
Palermo	10
Ckackachipata	7–9
Chiripa	7
Incatunuhuiri	< 10
Quellamarka	?
Putina	5–10
Cachichupa[a]	5–10
Southern Ccapia polity[b]	5–10
Northern Ccapia polity[c]	5–10
Huajje	> 5
Punanave	> 5
Taraco	> 5
Maravillas	> 5
Huancahuichinka	5
Titinhuayani	4–5
Chingani Alto[d]	> 4
Pajchiri	> 4
Titimani	> 2
Pariti	?
Asiruni	?
Sarapa	?
Kusijata	?

[a] See Plourde 1999.
[b] Either Kanamarca or Amaizana China.
[c] Probably Yanapata and/or Caninsaya, but possibly Imicate.
[d] This refers to the site area defined by Portugal (1989) that includes Pujiti, Guerra Pata, and Misituta.

stantial corporate architecture and a domestic residence area of about ten hectares. A semisubterranean court at the top of the hill is fifteen by fifteen meters. It is assumed to date to the Late Sillumocco (although it could possibly be a Tiwanaku-period construction) based on stratigraphic associations with a cut into the top of the hill. The court is lined with shaped but uncut stones, and it contains a stone doorway that is very similar to one found at Lukurmata, Bolivia (see pages 179–180). At the top of the site is a small, rounded hilltop that may have been an Akapana-like structure, albeit on a very small scale. The base of the hilltop today is no more than twenty by twenty meters.

The site of Tumatumani is next to Lake Titicaca near the modern town of Juli (Stanish and Steadman 1994). It is a large artificially mounded site, representative of a secondary regional center. The site covers 5.3 hectares and is composed of two mounds. The formal architecture of the west mound includes a low platform with a second, smaller platform built on top of the first. The east mound, in contrast, is shaped like an elongated U or horseshoe and is 150 meters at its maximum length.

The major occupations at Tumatumani include a Late Sillumocco occupation and a second reconstruction of the site by the Tiwanaku state. The Late Sillumocco occupation is about four hectares in size and includes both mounds. During this period, the architecture included a two-layered platform mound to the west and the enhancement of an earlier U-shaped mound to the east.

The site of Sillumocco-Huaquina is described in greater detail in the next chapter. Because a major reconstruction of the site occurred in the Tiwanaku period, it is difficult to distinguish the Upper Formative–period occupation without substantial excavations. What we do know is that Sillumocco-Huaquina is a classic Type 3 site, characterized by a low hill with domestic terraces leading up to a semisubterranean square structure on the hilltop. This temple area most

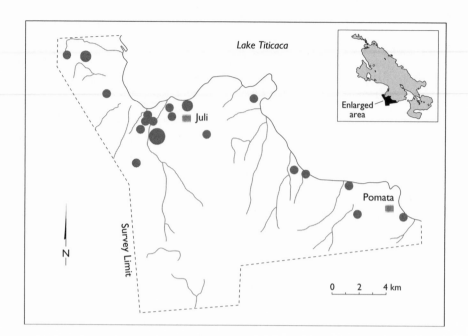

MAP 7.2. Late Sillumocco (Upper Formative) settlement distribution in the Juli-Pomata survey area.

likely dates to the Late Sillumocco and Tiwanaku periods. The site was excavated by de la Vega (1997). The subterranean construction is built with uncut fieldstones. It is very badly damaged, and the excavators were not able to define it very well, but surface evidence in the form of some apparently in situ blocks and the size of the depression allowed them to estimate the structure as approximately nine by nine meters in size. As at the site of Palermo, there is a higher open area that corresponds to a Kalasasaya-like enclosure.

The Juli-Pomata survey identified nineteen sites that date to the Late Sillumocco period. Most of these would correspond to the Sillumocco polity based on the location of the primary and secondary regional centers. Those sites near Pomata in the southern end of the survey zone, in contrast, were more likely associated with another contemporary polity, that of Ckackachipata in the Pomata pampa area.

The Late Sillumocco period in the southwestern Titicaca Basin is characterized by a small reduction in the total number of sites and an increase in mean

site size from the Early Sillumocco (see map 7.2 and table 7.2). Total population increased, and there was a major concentration of population in the raised-field areas, increasing from 41 percent of the population to almost 70 percent. Land use in the puna was much reduced, with less than 6 percent of the total population concentrated in one relatively large site called Hanco Vilque. The obvious conclusion from these settlement data is that natural population increase was directed toward the raised-field areas, and additional existing populations were also pulled into this economic activity.

During the Late Sillumocco period, there is a distinctive site size hierarchy. Significantly, a calculation of total habitation area indicates that more than half of the population during the period lived in mounded sites, a figure up 20 percent from the earlier period (see table 7.2). Since the Juli-Pomata survey stopped just north of the other primary regional center of Ckackachipata, these figures are actually biased to the low end. In reality, if this other primary regional center and its associated secondary regional

TABLE 7.2
Population per Habitation Site Type per Period in the Juli-Pomata Survey Area

Type	Middle Formative	Upper Formative	Tiwanaku	Altiplano	Late Horizon	Early Colonial
1	3	5.5	9.05	1.25	4	3
	13%	16%	14%	1%	2%	1%
2	0.53	0.69	5.35	11.88	13.97	9.60
	*	*	8%	16%	7%	6%
3	5	12	23.75	4.25	6	3.5
	21%	36%	37%	5%	3%	2%
4	14.41	14.53	23.9	51.38	112.04	100.56
	62%	44%	38%	69%	62%	65%
6	0	0	0.2	5.17	14.99	9.4
	0%	0%	*	6%	8%	6%
7	0	0	0	0	27	27
	0%	0%	0%	0%	15%	17%

NOTE: The data reflect the population as measured by total habitation area in hectares and the relative population size as a percentage of the total. Fortified sites (Type 5) were not counted in this tabulation, and therefore percentages do not equal 100%.
* Less than 1%.

centers had been included in the survey area, the figure may well have approached 65 percent of the population living in the regional centers during the Upper Formative.

THE LATE CKACKACHIPATA POLITY

The large Middle Formative occupation at Ckackachipata continued in the Upper Formative. Systematic reconnaissance in the area (Stanish et al. 1997: 90) discovered several Upper Formative sites in the Chatuma area immediately west of Ckackachipata. These sites are associated with the extensive raised-field area in the Pomata pampa. Ckackachipata is be-

lieved to have been a primary regional center with about a dozen affiliated settlements, such as Llaquepa Mancja, Camuna, and others in the region. The Ckackachipata polity was associated with a highly productive raised-field area, numerous nucleated settlements, and a concomitantly large population.

At present, the southern Ccapia region is included in the Ckackachipata polity. We cannot determine the degree to which these sites were autonomous or part of a larger political organization. The sites of Amaizana China and Kanamarca are on the southern side of Cerro Ccapia, in the southern Titicaca Basin. One of these sites was a regional center in the

Upper Formative period.[3] Amaizana China is a little more than one kilometer south of the school at Isani. It is about five hundred meters from the lake, with a total habitation and ceremonial area of at least six hectares.

Amaizana China sits on a narrow hill or ridge that runs more or less perpendicular toward the lake. There are at least three to four very wide domestic terraces on the lake side, and an extensive area of generally flat habitation area on the crest. Large andesite blocks on the hilltop indicate that there was a corporate construction of some sort, most likely a sunken court and/or formally faced stone terraces. Several sites in the northern Ccapia area were also part of a larger political organization in the Upper Formative period. There are two large sites on the northern side of Cerro Ccapia—Qeñuani and Imicate—that may have been the regional centers of an Upper Formative polity.

THE TITINHUAYANI POLITY

Titinhuayani, the primary regional center on the Island of the Sun, is in the community of Challa. It was a major Middle Formative regional center that continued to be the primary regional center in the Upper Formative. The site is large by island standards, covering about four hectares, with extensive domestic terrace areas around the hilltop. Excavations by Esteban Quelima of the Universidad Mayor de San Andrés indicate that the top of the hill was built and rebuilt several times prior to the Tiwanaku period. Excavation profiles show large fill events designed to modify the natural contours of the hill early on (after a long Late Archaic through Middle Formative–period occupation), with subsequent efforts to modify or enlarge the already existing architecture. The hill area was intentionally filled with soil and midden. The intent seems to have been to create a large flat area with some sort of corporate architecture in the middle. Cut stones around the area

suggest that a sunken court or perhaps an enclosure of some sort was built on the hilltop.

The Upper Formative (Late Titinhuayani) settlement pattern on the Island of the Sun is seen in map 7.3. The number of sites decreases from forty-eight to thirty-one, a reduction of about one-third, from the Middle Formative to the Upper Formative periods. It is significant that the total number of sites is almost twice that of the entire Juli-Pomata region, yet the total area of the island is an order of magnitude smaller. The methodologies of the two surveys were identical. The survey data therefore indicate that although site sizes were smaller, the total number of sites was substantially greater on the Island of the Sun than it was on the mainland, at least as represented by the data from the Juli-Pomata survey.

Mean site size increased from the Middle Formative to the Upper Formative, and factoring in the different lengths of the periods, there was an overall increase in population as determined by total habitation site size per period. This general pattern is evident in other areas of the basin that have been intensively surveyed for this time period (Albarracin-Jordan and Mathews 1990; Stanish et al. 1997). In other words, the settlement pattern during the Late Titinhuayani period indicates that there was a nucleation of a growing population into larger and fewer settlements, a pattern similar to that in the Juli-Pomata mainland area.

The earlier clustering of sites in the Early Titinhuayani period (see pages 126–128) continued in the Late Titinhuayani period and intensified as people lived in fewer but larger sites around the larger centers. Sites continued to be located near agricultural terraces. Settlement around the raised-field system in the Challa area increased dramatically. Certainly, the location of three of the four large sites during the period around the Challa area suggests that raised fields were an important settlement determinant in the Upper Formative, a pattern consistent with that in the Juli-Pomata area (Stanish 1994). In both of

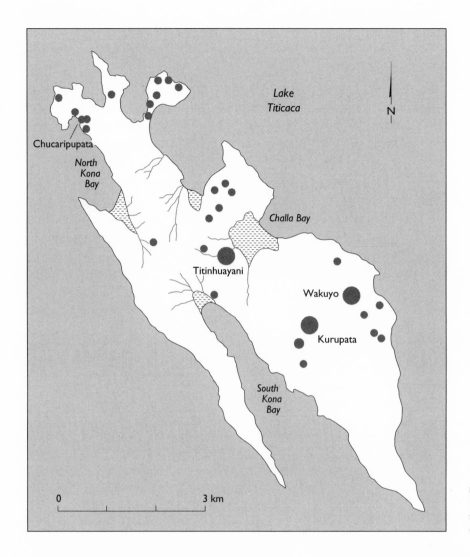

MAP 7.3. Late Titinhuayani (Upper Formative) settlement pattern on the Island of the Sun.

these areas, the highest percentage concentration of the population in the raised fields areas occurred in the Upper Formative periods.

Apart from the type site of Titinhuayani, two other large sites on the island were occupied in the Upper Formative period: Wakuyo and Pukara. Each of these sites was approximately four hectares in size during this time. Wakuyo (Perrín Pando 1957), which is on the southeastern side of the island near the border of Challa and Yumani, is a classic Upper For-

mative site built on a low hill with domestic terraces around its base. Abundant surface pottery, including a large quantity of decorated pieces, indicates that the site was an important secondary center in the regional settlement system.

The nature of the political organization on the Island of the Sun during the Upper Formative is unclear. Analogies to the mainland during this period would suggest a unified political entity, but these expectations are not supported by the settlement data.

In a context of political unification, a breakdown in the settlement clustering and a distribution of sites for optimal economic maximization would be expected, as would the rise of one center of a qualitatively larger size than any of the others. It is possible that future research will reveal that Titinhuayani is indeed larger than four hectares (the total hill area with surface pottery is about seven or eight hectares) and that the other sites are smaller. However, surface evidence suggests a pattern of three sites of roughly similar size located in two settlement clusters. These data therefore do not indicate an overarching political unity centered in one site, although the nature of that political organization remains unknown. Rather, the data suggest a cluster of moderately sized sites in the Challa area. At present, it appears there was an emergent elite in the Challa area who lived in the three sites of Titinhuayani, Wakuyo, and Pukara, with a fourth important ritual center near Chucaripupata.

The site of Chucaripupata is in this context extremely important. It is located in the Titikala or Sacred Rock area, so named because the Inca empire maintained a huaca, or pilgrimage shrine, at a large sandstone rock. Work conducted by Matthew Seddon has demonstrated that the domestic area of Chucaripupata during the Upper Formative is not as large as we calculated from the survey data. However, his work indicates that the area was used for ritual feasting (see Seddon 1998). The site was first noted by the Swiss archaeologist Adolph Bandelier in 1895 during his fieldwork on the island, and he accurately described the site as a quadrangular platform "lined by walls and surrounded by lower terraces on three sides" in his book (Bandelier 1910: 225). Excavations by Seddon confirm the existence of a Late Titinhuayani occupation at this important site. Three other sites were found in the Titikala area during this time period as well. The settlement shift from the Middle Formative (Early Titinhuayani) period in the Titikala area is significant. Several sites were abandoned, but the total population in the area, adjusted for length of time and calculated by total site size, slightly increased, although the numbers are statistically even.[4]

The evidence indicates no nucleation of population into any major settlement in the Titikala area during the Late Titinhuayani, although Chucaripupata was a major ritual center most likely controlled by the Challa-area Titinhuayani polity. It is possible that the Challa area was coalescing as the political center of power, with the Titikala area emerging as a ritual center focused on Chucaripupata. One model would therefore be the emergence of a weak political centralization on the island, with the political elite nucleating in the Challa area while retaining a local huaca near the Sacred Rock area.

THE TITIMANI POLITY

The site of Titimani is approximately three and a half kilometers southeast of the modern town of Escoma (Portugal O. 1993: 27–30). It has a sunken court that measures approximately fourteen by seventeen and a half meters. Portugal says that the site covers at least two hectares, and my own observations suggest that it is at least twice that size if one includes the domestic component. At least one red sandstone monolith was discovered on the site, as well as a number of other cut or shaped blocks. The pottery discovered in association with this site is affiliated with the Chiripa tradition, a style that conforms well to the architecture of the semisubterranean court.

Other sites in the Titimani/Escoma area date to the Upper Formative. Titimani almost certainly represents a primary regional center. Along with the other sites in the area, the Escoma region supported a complex polity during the at least the Upper Formative period.

THE SANTIAGO DE HUATA POLITY

The peninsula of Santiago de Huata has numerous Upper Formative–period sites (Carlos Lemuz, personal communication 1999). A number of pre-Tiwanaku stelae of ambiguous provenience are found in the plaza of the town of Santiago de Huata. Max Portugal Ortíz has located a number of sites south of the town that have stelae and/or corporate architecture in Upper Formative–period traditions. In the area referred to as Chingani Alto, he (Portugal O. 1988a) reports finding three sites or localities with carved stone and monoliths. These three areas are referred to as Misituta, Guerra Pata, and Pujiti. One monolith at Pujiti is huge at 3.7 meters in length, and is characterized by the diagnostic notched top of pre-Tiwanaku-period stelae. Pottery in the area is in the Chiripa style. Likewise, much of the stonework has motifs related to the broad Upper Formative traditions of which Chiripa is most noteworthy. However, many of the stelae, particularly those in the plaza in Santiago de Huata, are without question stylistically very distinct and suggest a strong local tradition.

Other Possible Upper Formative–Period Centers in the Southern Titicaca Basin

A number of large sites in the Titicaca Basin have substantial Upper Formative–period occupations. We can hypothesize, based on analogies to the better-studied areas in the south and west, that these were primary regional centers of polities of some size related in some way to the emergent Tiwanaku polity. The site of Mocachi, on the southern Copacabana Peninsula, has some classic Yaya-Mama stelae along with a large sunken court complex (Casanova 1942). Pottery styles from the site range in date from the Middle Formative through Inca periods, and there are dense Upper Formative and Tiwanaku remains. The site has not been adequately investigated, but it was probably a regional center in the Upper Formative. Likewise, the site of Ollaraya in the far south near the bay of Pajano has a Middle Formative occupation of indeterminate size and a large Upper Formative one. The site has cut-stone blocks, substan-

tial habitation areas surrounding the top of the site, and additional evidence of corporate construction.

Close to Tiwanaku is the site of Quellamarka, which was excavated by Portugal in the 1970s. It is described as a complex of rectangular structures with a platform and a large domestic settlement area (Bermann 1990: 170). Portugal describes two levels from the site, with one containing Tiwanaku III materials. Other sites in the southern Titicaca region include Pajchiri, the island of Pariti, and sites along the Escoma River. These and other yet-undiscovered sites in the region were most likely primary regional centers during the Upper Formative, and related in a variety of ways to the southern Early Tiwanaku polity.

Upper Formative–Period Polities in the Northern Titicaca Basin

In the north, the sites of Taraco and Saman are the most likely regional centers affiliated with the Pucara polity in this rich northern region. The Taraco area is replete with Formative-period stelae. Kidder reported a number of Formative statues and stelae from the town of Taraco (Kidder 1943: plate III, nos. 1–6; plate IV, nos. 1–3, 5–8, 10–13; and plate V, nos. 1–7). He also illustrated two pieces from Saman, just a few kilometers away (Kidder 1943: plate IV, nos. 4, 9). Several of these have Upper Formative stylistic canons and suggest the presence of a primary regional center in the area affiliated with Pucara in the middle to late Upper Formative.

Other northern Titicaca Basin regional centers were most likely located in the Arapa and Huancané areas. The area around this small lake has a number of Formative-period sites, and the Arapa region was most certainly an Upper Formative–period polity of some importance incorporated into the Pucara polity. The regional center for the Huancané area is about seven kilometers outside town at the hill of Huancahuichinka. Discovered in reconnaissance by members of Programa Collasuyu, the site is on the long ridge to the west, away from the lake from the town of Huancané. The landowner excavated a hole at the top and discovered two monoliths about fifty centimeters wide and ten to twelve centimeters thick. The monoliths are Formative in date, and apparently carved on only one side.

On the eastern side of the lake, Kidder discovered some Pucara-like statues at the site of Lailuyu, near Conima, on the border with Bolivia (Kidder 1943: plate VI, nos. 8–10). Kidder reports finding similar statues on the site near another peninsula named Huata that had a large (sixty-five by fifty meters) platform on top of a terrace. There are a number of Upper Formative sites in the Moho region as well that most likely were associated with Pucara.

Upper Formative–Period Interactions in the South-Central Andes

Archaeologists for decades have noted the similarities between the three art traditions of Paracas, Kalasasaya, and Pucara. Lumbreras (1974a: 87), for instance, refers to these three styles as comprising an "isolated group" that shares "a number of distinctive decorative features, including the use of polychrome painting." Moseley (1992: 150) agrees, although he appropriately characterizes the stylistic relationship as "generic," emphasizing that the similarities are not precise. Certainly, the absolute dates of these three cultures at least partially coincide. Silverman (1996: 124–126) argues that the stylistic relationships between the Yaya-Mama iconography on the stelae and contemporary Ica textile designs are so strong that they reflect the borrowing or adoption of religious ideologies from the Titicaca Basin to the south coast of Peru. Cook (1994: 189) agrees that the available evidence supports the existence of an extensive cultural exchange network between the areas on the south coast producing Ocucaje and Nasca styles and those in the altiplano producing Pucara styles. The Paracas style begins a few centuries before Pucara and Ka-

lasasaya pottery manufacture, but all three styles were contemporary from 200 B.C. to A.D. 100.[5]

One of the most distinctive features of the ceramic tradition is the use of a decorative technique referred to as zone incised. In this technique, single-color motifs were outlined with prefire incisions, creating a striking design pattern on pottery. Red, black, yellow, and white were the principal colors. In the Paracas tradition, a resin was applied to the surface. In Kalasasaya and Pucara, vessels were finely burnished. Felines are depicted in all three pottery traditions and appear to be particularly significant (see Chávez 1992).

Zone-incised pottery of this general type is found in large quantities in Ica, the north Titicaca Basin, and the Tiwanaku area. A few fragments have been found in Moquegua (Disselhoff 1968; Feldman 1989), and in the Arequipa area (J. Chávez, personal communication 1987). It is also found in small quantities on the western lake edge at the site of Tumatumani in Peru, where it is referred to as Sillumocco Polychrome Incised (Stanish and Steadman 1994: 55). In her meticulous analysis of the Sillumocco Polychrome Incised fragments, Steadman concluded that this pottery type is "contemporary . . . with both Pucara and Qalasasaya but [is] a local or semilocal production from near Juli, belonging to what was probably a pan-Titicaca tradition of non-fiber-tempered polychrome incised ceramics during the Upper Formative period" (in Stanish and Steadman 1994: 55). It is significant that many of the most striking motifs from Pucara and Paracas styles were not found in the Sillumocco Polychrome examples.

A similar pattern in which a small number of zone-incised fragments were found in a local assemblage outside Pucara, Paracas, and Tiwanaku is in the Moquegua Valley. Robert Feldman (1989) reports finding some fragments of a locally produced zone-incised pottery style at two sites in the midvalley during the pre-Tiwanaku Trapiche phase. He notes the similarities of the fragments to Pucara pieces and describes the period as a time in which people in the

Moquegua area were "making variants of Pukara pottery and textiles" (Feldman 1989: 213). In fact, the total percentage of zone-incised pottery on the Moquegua sites is exceedingly small, comparable to that in Tumatumani and elsewhere outside the Pucara and Tiwanaku areas.

The Relationship between Pucara and Early Tiwanaku

One of the most difficult and interesting problems of the Upper Formative period of the Titicaca Basin is the relationship between the sites and cultures of Pucara and Tiwanaku. Several scholars have argued for a direct relationship between the two. S. Chávez (1988: 37) has suggested that with the collapse and abandonment of Pucara, there were population shifts to the north toward Cuzco and south to Tiwanaku. Chávez's hypothesis implies a migration of Pucara peoples to the Tiwanaku area, a model that would explain the artistic continuities of Pucara and Tiwanaku. Likewise, Anita Cook (1994: 184–205) has suggested that some similarities between the two cultures' art traditions indicate an indirect relationship, and Conklin (1997: 375) notes that Wari tunics are based "entirely" on Tiwanaku ones, suggesting a direct relationship in at least some artistic motifs. Cook (1994: 185) does note, however, the unexpected lack of similarity between Pucara deities and motifs on stonework in Tiwanaku. Rather, she sees the similarities of some Wari and Pucara motifs as indirect, influenced from Paracas on the coast.

As already mentioned, the southernmost limits of Pucara were the Ríos Ilave and Suches, far from Tiwanaku's core territory. Early Tiwanaku (Qeya period) influence did not extend beyond the southern Titicaca Basin. In fact, several other semiautonomous polities were located between Pucara and Tiwanaku during the Upper Formative (see chapter 11). There are later Tiwanaku sites in the Pucara area in the north, but there are no Pucara sites in Tiwanaku territory in the south.

The relationship between these two polities must be assessed in relation to the dates for the end of Pucara and beginning of Tiwanaku. The data suggest strongly that Tiwanaku did not expand outside its core territory until at least the sixth or even seventh century A.D., and maybe even later. Likewise, the data from Pucara suggest that it collapsed as a regional polity around the third century A.D. Given present data, it appears that Pucara collapsed well before the emergence of Tiwanaku as an expansive polity. This collapse would have occurred around A.D. 200, fully four hundred years prior to Tiwanaku expansion to the north.

Why did Pucara collapse? First we have to define with some precision what we mean by *collapse*. There was clearly a cessation of Pucara pottery and stelae production, and major building at the site of Pucara slowed or halted at this time. Systematic settlement data are not available, but limited reconnaissance suggests that there was a dispersal of settlement, and not a population abandonment (discussed further below). In short, the collapse of Pucara does not appear to have been a demographic one but a collapse of the elite political economy that had previously been able to mobilize labor for commodity production and architectural works.

It is probable that the drought in the Titicaca region around A.D. 100 (described by Abbott, Binford, Brenner, and Kelts 1997: 178) made the extensive raised-field areas too dry to support this intensive agricultural technique. Unlike the southern Titicaca Basin, where canal irrigation mitigated the effects of drought, the topography and entrenchment of rivers in the north made this unfeasible. The northern basin cultures adapted to the drought through intensification of camelid pastoralism and dispersal of settlement. This process was inimical to the type of settlement nucleation and labor mobilization necessary to maintain regional centers like Pucara.

Settlement evidence also supports this model. In the south, Tiwanaku occupations were usually built directly over Upper Formative ones, a process that included the reconstruction of corporate architecture (for example, at the sites of Tumatumani, Palermo, Lukurmata, Chiripa, and Sillumocco-Huaquina). In fact, most Upper Formative regional centers in the south have correspondingly large Tiwanaku occupations. In the north, however, Tiwanaku occupations are rarely found directly on Pucara sites. At Incatunuhuiri, for instance, the architectural core of the site was apparently not altered by the Tiwanaku settlement, which was on the lower terraces of the former regional center (K. Frye, personal communication 1997). Other Upper Formative sites in the region were either abandoned without Tiwanaku occupations, or existed outside the Tiwanaku orbit. In short, the combined settlement and excavation data indicate little direct contact between Pucara and Tiwanaku.

The late Upper Formative period (circa A.D. 400) in the northern basin was characterized by major shifts in settlement and political organization from earlier periods. As early as 1974, Lumbreras hinted at a serious problem with the ceramic chronology in the northern basin between the cessation of Pucara pottery and the beginning of Tiwanaku pottery. He even suggested (Lumbreras 1974a: 89) that Pucara pottery could have continued up to as late as A.D. 800 before being replaced by Tiwanaku pottery.

Over the past several years, nonsystematic reconnaissance and systematic survey in the northern Titicaca Basin have been conducted by members of Programa Collasuyu, who have discovered dozens of major sites. This work essentially substantiates Lumbreras's observation about an absence of Qeya and Early Tiwanaku IV pottery in the region. Some later Tiwanaku pottery was found on a number of sites in what is a restricted geographical area (see chapter 8), and Pucara pottery or Pucara-affiliated styles were also found around the region. However, very few sites north of Pucara have sufficient quantities of Tiwanaku

pottery to suggest a Tiwanaku occupation (see Stanish et al. 1997 for a discussion of this methodological issue). In short, there is no known Tiwanaku III (Qeya) pottery in the area. Late Tiwanaku and Tiwanaku V settlements are restricted to enclaves in a few areas along the two roads on the sides of the lake, and along the road to Cuzco. Outside these areas, there are no Tiwanaku sites yet identified in patterns typical of the Puno region or areas south of the Río Ilave in the Tiwanaku heartland.

Numerous sites, including Huancahuichinka, have Middle Formative pottery, Pucara or Pucara-related pottery, Altiplano-period pottery, and occasionally Inca-period examples as well. It is certainly possible that there was a major abandonment of area sites with the cessation of Pucara pottery production and the dispersal of settlement, and then a reoccupation of these large sites with the advent of the Altiplano period. However, can this apparent hiatus be explained with another model? The more parsimonious explanation is that our ceramic chronology is not accurate, and that Tiwanaku III, or Qeya, pottery is not a diagnostic for this time period in the extreme north, between the collapse of Pucara and the expansion of Tiwanaku circa A.D. 600. In other words, it is more likely that sites like Huancahuichinka, near rich agricultural and pasture lands and away from the major road system, were continuously occupied and that our ceramic chronology is unable to distinguish between the occupations contemporary with Tiwanaku III and Tiwanaku IV. It is also important to note that these sites have Altiplano-period pottery. Since the Altiplano period was a time of generalized conflict around the region, sites of this period would have been located in defensible areas. We therefore cannot explain the supposed hiatus in occupation as a result of warfare after Pucara collapse. That is, an explanation that sees the rise of conflict coincident with Pucara collapse, leading to settlement abandonment for the post-

Pucara periods, is belied by the Altiplano-period settlement patterns.

I hypothesize a fluid political landscape after Pucara collapse in which small, Pucara-derived polities focused on intensive agro-pastoral economies as the raised-field areas collapsed, particularly rain-fed fields in the northern Huatta area and near Pucara itself prior to Tiwanaku expansion. Raised fields did continue to be worked next to sites such as Maravillas near Juliaca and along the Ramis River but generally receded in areas where fields could not be watered with canals. With the collapse of the Pucara political economy, stelae production also ceased, as most manufacture of decorated pottery in the Pucara tradition. The culture that developed is hypothesized to be one that responded to the drought conditions by concentrating on the riverine areas and lake edges, and utilizing the pampas for pasture. Called Early Huaña (*huaña* means "drought" in Aymara), this culture dates from the end of Pucara influence to the expansion of Tiwanaku into the area around A.D. 600.

Early Huaña sites are similar to Pucara sites in the region. They are commonly Type 1 and Type 3 sites, located on hills near the rivers and on the low mounds lining the rivers in the north. Early Huaña pottery is poorly known. Initial reconnaissance by Programa Collasuyu indicates that the pottery assemblage includes a distinct style derived from Pucara plain wares. Thickened-rimmed bowls with flat bottoms are one diagnostic. The red slip on a sand-and-mica-tempered paste that Kidder called Pucara Red also is found on these sites. There is no elaborate decorated pottery style associated with this assemblage, which may reflect the collapse of the centralized polities during this time.

The polities associated with the Early Huaña culture have not been defined because of a lack of systematic survey and good chronological controls, but nonsystematic reconnaissance suggests that there were a number of interacting, autonomous polities

like those of the west and south basin areas. Large sites in the Moho, Huancané, Taraco/Saman, and Juliaca areas are hypothesized to have been primary regional centers during this period. It is hypothesized that Huaña cultures continued to coexist in some areas with the Tiwanaku-affiliated populations through the Tiwanaku period circa A.D. 600–1100. The Tiwanaku-contemporary culture that coexisted with the Tiwanaku occupation in the north is referred to as the Late Huaña culture.

A Hypothesis for the Location of Tiwanaku and Pucara

By the end of the Upper Formative, Tiwanaku was the largest site in the Titicaca Basin. A few centuries earlier, Pucara had developed a complex polity that influenced other peoples living in the northern half of the Titicaca Basin. There were no other comparable polities of such size during the Upper Formative. Virtually all of the known primary regional centers in the Upper Formative are found near the lake, which is the agriculturally richest zone in the region.[6] Yet, the two primate regional centers in the region developed away from the lake by a considerable distance. This suggests that factors other than a lakeside location were on the optimal settlement choice for these political centers.

The locations of the two primate centers of the Upper Formative—Tiwanaku and Pucara—have several common factors, all of which appear to co-occur only in these two areas. Thus, it appears that the development of political complexity at Pucara and Tiwanaku was due in part to their favored geographical locations, relative to their competitors in the area, for optimal economic production and exchange. The northwestern and southeastern Titicaca Basin areas have several geographical and ecological features that only co-occur in these zones: a proximity to prime raised-field agricultural land, location on a major river, proximity to extensive camelid grazing lands, and direct access to the major lake within one day's walk (via the smaller, attached Lakes Arapa and Huiñamarca). Furthermore, each area had unimpeded access to the western slopes of the Pacific watershed and the eastern lowlands. That is, people living in these two areas were able to travel directly east and west without having to cross territory controlled by contemporary complex polities. All other groups living on the western and eastern shores of the lake would have had to cross one of these two areas (northeast or southwest) of high population densities and complex polities, or make extraordinarily long treks to the far south to have access to both sides of the Andes.

It is significant that all of these characteristics co-occurred only in the far southeastern and northwestern Titicaca Basin areas and not in any other part of the basin. These areas are large, of course, covering hundreds of square kilometers. It can therefore be argued that the areas roughly bounded by the Desaguadero and Catari River drainages in the southeast, and the areas of the Pucara/Ramis and Azángaro drainages in the northeast, were the richest zones in the Titicaca Basin in terms of Prehispanic economic production and exchange.

It is no surprise that the northwestern and southeastern areas were the first to develop complex polities, as defined by the presence of corporate architecture, specialized craft production, and regionally dominant art styles such as Qaluyu and Chiripa. For most of the geographical factors common to Pucara and Tiwanaku, there is empirical evidence to support the observation that each was important in their development. Several projects have demonstrated the importance of raised-field agriculture, for instance, in the altiplano environment (Erickson 1988; Graffam 1992; Kolata 1986; Stanish 1994). The importance of river location for the successful delivery of fresh water to field systems has been suggested as well (Lennon 1983). The huge economic effect of the extensive camelid herds of the Titicaca Basin has been demonstrated for Tiwanaku, Pucara, and other contemporary and later cultures in the region (Browman 1984; Lynch 1983; Murra 1968). Obsidian from the Arequipa area indicates access to the western slopes of the Andes from very early on. Neither Tiwanaku nor Pucara is located on the lake edge, but each is less than a day's walk from a major body of water. Tiwanaku is twenty kilometers from Lake Huiñamarca, and Pucara is about forty-five kilometers from Lake Arapa. Finally, settlement surveys and excavations have demonstrated the existence of Pucara-related and Early Tiwanaku–related (Late Chiripa–affiliated) materials in several western slope drainages, indicating access to these regions through exchange and/or colonies (Berenguer, Castro, and Silva 1980; Browman 1981; Feldman 1989; Goldstein 2000; Lumbreras and Mujica 1982a; Mujica 1985).

The major difference between the Tiwanaku and Pucara areas is the location of political competitors. Pucara was between the Titicaca Basin polities to the south and the complex polities of the circum-Cuzco and Chumbivilcas region to the north (S. Chávez 1988). Tiwanaku, in contrast, had a distinct advantage with no political competitors to the south. It is probably not a coincidence that Tiwanaku was the southernmost complex polity in the Titicaca Basin and ultimately emerged as the successful competitor of the Upper Formative period that developed into a fully integrated state system in the first millennium A.D.

Upper Formative–Period Art and Political Competition

An emerging elite [at Pucara] was manipulating symbols of power for personal gain, in some instances using visual terrorism to do so. By controlling powerful supernatural images, this emerging elite assured themselves access to supernatural, political, and economic power, the ability to control labor and have greater access to resources. Directly or indirectly, the emerging elite must also have closely controlled the production of these symbols of power on pottery, an important medium on which they were depicted.

Sergio Chávez, "The Conventionalized Rules in Pucara Pottery Technology and Iconography: Implications for Socio-Political Developments in the Northern Lake Titicaca Basin," 1992, p. 11

The shift from Middle Formative to Upper Formative lifeways in the Titicaca Basin involved a number of profound cultural changes that are reflected in the art styles, particularly sculpture and pottery. In the several hundred years of transition to Upper Formative lifeways, the Yaya-Mama stone sculptural style evolved into the Pucara and Early Tiwanaku traditions. Stone sculpture found at Pucara was executed in several styles, including anthropomorphic sculptures,[7] stelae with predominantly geometric designs,[8] sculpture with predominantly naturalistic designs,[9] "squatting" human sculpture,[10] and smaller carvings. Similar stone carving traditions are found in the southern Titicaca Basin associated with the site and culture of Early Tiwanaku or Kalasasaya, particularly the anthropomorphic statues.

It is significant that the Upper Formative traditions were characterized by anthropomorphic sculptures that were executed with shared canons, in a manner similar to the Yaya-Mama tradition. Both northern and southern Titicaca Basin sculpture traditions produced statues with human faces and a common set of icons, such as large eyes, headbands, belts, and trophy heads. Some of these icons were later incorporated into the much larger Tiwanaku monoliths, indicating that the conceptions behind these motifs continued into the Tiwanaku state (and see Isbell and Cook 1987).

Perhaps the most dramatic change from earlier artistic traditions was the adoption and emphasis in the Upper Formative on the trophy head motif. In the earlier Yaya-Mama tradition, there were no trophy heads. By Upper Formative times, artisans were consistently using the trophy head motif in stone, ceramic, and textile arts, and its symbolic power in the region cannot be overstated.

The presentation of trophy heads was a theme in Inca culture depicted in many historical sources; this theme has strong cultural links with the people of the region. As late as the early 1630s, Antonio de la Calancha relates how a band of island-dwelling Uru were raiding settlements in the southern and western basin (in Wachtel 1986: 302–306). The cacique of Chucuito ordered them to cease, and they refused. Five of the Uru were captured and executed in Zepita, and "their heads were exhibited at the entrance to the bridge over the Desaguadero [River]" (Wachtel 1986: 302). It is probable that the journey from Zepita to Desaguadero involved a procession of sorts by the victors. Given that the punitive measures up to this point had been directed by an indigenous authority, the public display of the captured heads is significant. Even more fascinating is the counterattack by the Uru. According to Calancha, as related by Wachtel, they named a new leader who was the son of a *brujo*. Instead of seeking revenge against other settlements, they attacked the Desaguadero bridge and recaptured the trophy heads. Calancha noted that "they licked the blood on the stakes on which the heads had been exposed," after which the exasperated cacique "begged them to obey him" (in Wachtel 1986: 303). Eventually, the cacique was forced to get help from the corregidor of Pacajes, and, through this Spanish authority, reinforcements from Oruro, Potosí, Cochabamba, and La Plata. In 1677, the corregidores of Chucuito and Pacajes finally ended the rebellion. Unlike the traditional cacique, who had the rebels beheaded and their heads displayed, the Spaniards had the Uru hanged or sentenced them to forced labor in the mines (Wachtel 1986: 304).

The significance of these fascinating events is the way in which local Aymara lords tried to use the decapitated heads as part of establishing their political and military authority over the rebellious Uru. Equally compelling is the Urus' counterattack to get the heads back, the success of which we may presume sent an equally powerful message to the cacique.

Documentary evidence indicates that a similar pattern of decapitating enemies was common among the Inca and their adversaries. It was the most profound statement of ultimate military triumph over, and humiliation of, vanquished enemies. Pachacuti's treatment of the defeated Chanca after the battle of Xaquixaguana is another example. According to Betanzos (in Rostworowski 1988: 50), he hanged them *(ahorcar)*, placed their heads on high poles, and then burnt their bodies. What is significant here is that although the bodies were burnt, the heads were kept as trophies.

In another case related by Sarmiento, Pachacuti actually had a building where trophy heads were kept. After the conquest of the Collas, Pachacuti returned to Cuzco, where he celebrated by cutting off the heads of his principal enemies, which he placed in a house called Llaxaguasi (in Rostworowski 1988: 100).

The trophy heads depicted in Pucara and Early Tiwanaku art relate to their symbolic power in reinforcing traditional authority and also reflect conflict in the region at this time. It is no coincidence that the development of complex societies in the region was accompanied by the practice of taking trophy heads. The most plausible explanation is that the iconography depicts actual conflict between elite groups, as in the Moche culture, and is not merely symbolic, as earlier scholars believed (e.g., see Donnan and McClelland 1999). One of the concomitants of the development of complex, hierarchical polities in the Titicaca Basin is the intensification of conflict between elite groups.

Production and Interregional Exchange

In theory, the establishment of complex, ranked society in the Titicaca Basin would be associated with the widening of exchange networks between elite groups, even in an environment of conflict. Although data are sparse, there is evidence that precisely this process occurred during the Upper Formative, a period of substantial interregional exchange in a variety of status-validating objects such as obsidian, sodalite, turquoise, marine shell, and other objects.

According to Bermann, the Qeya or Tiwanaku III levels at Lukurmata indicated the existence of long-distance networks for the exchange marine shell, obsidian, and sodalite (Bermann 1990: 186). At Chiripa, Browman (1978) found little evidence for extensive interregional exchange in the first two phases, Condori and Llusco. In the Upper Formative Mamani phase, however, Browman (1978b: 809) notes that "there is considerable evidence of trade in status-validating objects, particularly semiprecious stones and metal items, from the north end of Lake Titicaca to the Cochabamba valley, indicating that a fairly extensive llama caravan, as well documented later, had begun to be established."

Evidence of interregional trade between the Sillumocco polity and neighboring groups was found at the site of Tumatumani near Juli, where systematic surface collections and excavations recovered several nonlocal obsidian fragments dated to the Upper Formative and Tiwanaku Expansive periods. Seddon analyzed the lithic artifacts from the site and concluded that the obsidian projectile points were manufactured elsewhere: "while obsidian projectile points comprise 3 percent of the type collection, the percentage of obsidian debitage does not exceed 1 percent in any subsamples. In fact, only 33 obsidian flakes in total were recovered. This indicates that manufacture of the obsidian artifacts probably occurred elsewhere" (Seddon, in Stanish and Steadman 1994). Also, Steadman (1994) notes that a significant percentage of the pottery was not produced at the site.

The Titicaca Basin exchange networks appear to have reached well beyond the lake area. In the Middle Formative period, a fiber-tempered ceramic tradition was distributed throughout the south half of the basin and beyond, but virtually all ceramic artifacts were locally produced. In the Upper Formative period, these patterns intensified and qualitatively changed into extensive exchange relationships of high-valued objects.

In Moquegua, northern Chile, Arequipa, and possibly other areas, ceramic traditions are identified with Pucara in the Titicaca Basin. In Moquegua, the Trapiche period represents a time in which local populations maintained contacts, or possibly coexisted with, Pucara peoples (Feldman 1989). Feldman maintains that sufficient variation exists between classic Pucara and the Trapiche ceramic style in Moquegua to suggest that the Trapiche populations were local residents in contact with the Titicaca region (Feldman 1989: 216; 1996).

Pottery and textiles executed in the Pucara tradition have been found in northern Chile as well. Mario Rivera (1984) suggests that Pucara influence is evident in the Alto Ramírez phase, and argues for relationships between contemporary Kalasasaya (Tiwanaku I/II), Chiripa Mamani, and Wankarani. Guillermo Focacci (1983: 111) proposes that the Alto Ramírez settlements represent altiplano colonists, a proposition supported by Kolata (1983: 275). Mujica (1985: 111), in contrast, rejects the hypothesis of Pucara colonization in northern Chile, citing the "lack of sculptures, typical altiplano pottery or even villages." I agree with Mujica, and see the existence of Pucara-related objects in the northern Chile as evidence for widespread distribution of elite ideologies and complex exchange relationships, not actual colonization.

In short, the evidence for exchange within and beyond the Titicaca Basin is very strong. Settlement evidence indicates that the road system was in place along the lake by this period, at least on the western side. Highly valued objects were exchanged around the area from substantial distances. In a context of both conflict and alliance, a brisk exchange of exotic goods flourished in the region in the Upper Formative.

Land Use Patterns and Raised Fields in the Upper Formative Period

Settlement pattern analysis from the Juli-Pomata survey has provided quantitative data on economic land use during the Upper Formative period. The distribution of Late Sillumocco populations over the three principal economic zones—raised-field areas, rain-fed terrace agricultural areas, and pasture lands—indicates a concentration of the population into the raised-field areas (Stanish 1994). In the survey region, almost 63 percent of the population was living within one kilometer of raised-field agricultural zones. It is also significant that the percent of the population living in the puna dropped from 17 percent to less than 7 percent between the Early and Late Sillumocco periods. There was also a 20 percent drop in the relative population living in the rain-fed terrace agriculture areas. We calculated a land use ratio of 6:3:1, representing raised fields, rain-fed agriculture, and puna land use, respectively. This contrasts sharply with the Early Sillumocco ratio of 3:5:2. These data indicate that raised fields dramatically increased in importance during the Late Sillumocco period. Although a natural growth rate could account for some of this increase, most of the population growth in the raised-field areas is most likely explained by the movement of people from the puna and non-raised-field areas to raised-field zones. In other words, there is very strong evidence of intensive use of raised-field agriculture during the Upper Formative in the Juli-Pomata area. This observation is also supported for other areas of the basin. Erickson argues for extensive use of fields in the pre-Middle Horizon periods in the Huata area (Erickson 1988), and Graffam's work indicates raised-field use in the Upper Formative of the Pampa Koani (Graffam 1992).

Survey and excavation data indicate that another major economic activity was the keeping of camelids.

Excavations in Upper Formative–period contexts routinely find large quantities of butchered camelid bone. The distribution of sites in the period indicates use of the lands above 4,000 m.a.s.l., even though total population and/or land use decreased to its lowest, at least in the Juli-Pomata survey area (see table 7.2).

Summary

Earlier interpretations of the Upper Formative period in the Titicaca Basin have focused on the sites of Pucara and Tiwanaku. This perspective has led to an inaccurate view of the millennium prior to Tiwanaku emergence as a time dominated by two nuclear civilizations that divided the region into two roughly equal spheres. Challenging that view is evidence that in the early Upper Formative, numerous autonomous and semiautonomous polities developed complex political, economic, ideological, and social organizations. These polities were centered on the primary regional centers and satellite communities known as secondary regional centers. These centers were characterized by sites with corporate architecture, usually in the form of pyramid mounds, sunken courts, and extensive areas of domestic residence. Stone stelae were erected at these centers, which were also the loci of fine-ware pottery production, other commodity production, and, perhaps most important, large-scale feasting.

By at least 200 B.C., Pucara and Tiwanaku had emerged as primate regional centers. These two settlements were large concentrations of people living in a fairly elaborate architectural complex. Pucara-related settlements and artifacts are found throughout the circum-Titicaca Basin and beyond. The actual area of direct political control or alliance by the Pucara peoples was much more restricted, but still quite large: around twenty thousand square kilometers from the Ilave and Escoma Rivers in the south to the Ayaviri region in the north. The Upper Formative period in Tiwanaku is less well known, but at this time its maximum distribution appears to have been similar to that of Pucara. Coexisting in the areas between these two polities were other autonomous groups, all of which created a fluid and unstable political landscape.

The First State of Tiwanaku

The late Upper Formative period in the circum-Titicaca Basin was a politically dynamic time that provided the context for the emergence of an expansive archaic state. By A.D. 400 or so, dozens of polities of varying sizes and complexity existed in the region. Intense competition was the norm, as evidenced in iconography and other indices of conflict. This competition took many forms, including military conflict, strategic alliances, competitive feasting and ceremonialism, the co-option of exchange networks, and the intensification of economic production. It is no surprise that a state such as Tiwanaku developed out of this political context. With the collapse of Pucara several centuries before, the political field was opened for the development of its rival in the southern Titicaca Basin. The emergence of Tiwanaku, out of its Qeya- and Chiripa-derived predecessors, ushers in the Expansive Tiwanaku period

and represents the development of the first archaic state of the Titicaca region.

It is important to emphasize that the term *Expansive Tiwanaku* refers to the post-Qeya (post–Tiwanaku III or post–Early Tiwanaku) period, when the Tiwanaku state expanded out of its core territory in the southern Titicaca Basin. The use of the terms *Early Tiwanaku* or *Tiwanaku I, II, and III* has resulted in some confusion in the literature. As stylistic or chronological designations, these terms are fine (but see Janusek 1994 for a revision of the Tiwanaku IV and V "style"). However, the use of the numerical sequence for pre–Tiwanaku IV, or even the use of the term *Early Tiwanaku*, obscures the profound sociopolitical changes that occurred in the southern basin in the middle of the first millennium A.D.

Prior to Tiwanaku IV, in the Bennett-Ponce sequence, the site and culture of Tiwanaku were one of a number of complex polities in the region. Probably about a century or so after A.D. 400, a great transformation occurred in Tiwanaku society. The urban capital was built, a new polychrome pottery style was created, existing stone sculptural traditions were elaborated into a qualitatively distinct style, and the political organization of the culture shifted from a chiefly society to an archaic state. The processes seen in Tiwanaku cultural history are similar to those of the Moche and Wari. In short, the Tiwanaku peoples created a new phenomenon, never before seen in the Titicaca region.

The numerical chronology Tiwanaku I–V does not reflect this change. Tiwanaku III or Early Tiwanaku, as a sociopolitical phenomenon, is as different from Tiwanaku IV as Gallinazo is from Moche, or Huarpa is from Wari. To imply that the Tiwanaku state extends back to pre–Tiwanaku IV is false. For this reason, we choose to abandon the use of Tiwanaku I and Tiwanaku III, except perhaps at the site of Tiwanaku itself. In their place, I have adopted *Kalasasaya* and *Qeya* as a conscious attempt to distinguish the pre-state and state periods in the region. In short, the Upper Formative ended around A.D. 400, when Tiwanaku developed out of Qeya- and Chiripa-derived settlements in the southern Titicaca Basin and emerged as a conquest state overwhelming its Titicaca Basin rivals. The beginning of Tiwanaku as an expansive archaic state polity marks the end of the Upper Formative in the Titicaca region and the beginning of the Expansive Tiwanaku period in the south-central Andes.

Absolute Chronology

The site of Tiwanaku was one of the earliest monuments in the Andes to capture the attention of early chroniclers. By Cobo's account, even the great Pachacuti was impressed by the stoneworking of the ruins in the late fifteenth century. The early Spanish historians had already commented on the impressive ru-

ined buildings and had speculated on the importance of the site to Andean prehistory. By the end of the seventeenth century, scholars had decided that Tiwanaku was a culture that had prospered well before the Inca. By the turn of the nineteenth century, Tiwanaku had been studied by a number of scholars, and nineteenth-century natural historians recognized that the site was pre-Inca as well. Uhle created his Tiwanaku Horizon, and Posnansky argued for some extremely old dates for the site and culture.

Work in the early to mid-twentieth century focused on the chronology of the site itself, and by the 1970s, the Tiwanaku chronology provided the framework for understanding the culture history of the Titicaca Basin as a whole. More work has been done on the later Tiwanaku chronology (Tiwanaku IV and V) than virtually any other culture in the Titicaca region, with the possible exception of Chiripa. Tiwanaku culture and art are so central to south-central Andean prehistory that that there has been a tendency to treat the Tiwanaku sequence much like the Ica master sequence on the Peruvian south coast and to tie in all other cultural histories to Tiwanaku. Although it certainly is the most impressive culture of the prehistoric south-central Andes after the Upper Formative, the tendency to correlate other cultures to Tiwanaku prior to its expansive period has been ill-advised; prior to its expansive period in Tiwanaku IV times, the area was home to impressive, but local, polities without much influence beyond the Pacajes region. Only after Tiwanaku began its expansionist policies outside its core territory are comparisons of other regions to Tiwanaku meaningful for problems other than those that are purely chronological.

In the 1930s, Bennett developed the first scientifically documented ceramic chronology for the Expansive Tiwanaku culture. Based on his ten excavation units and 14,500 sherds, he identified twenty different design elements. Bennett then formalized a stylistic distinction in Tiwanaku ceramic art that had been implicit in much of Posnansky's work, the distinction between Classic and Decadent styles:

> If design is treated without regard for stratigraphic position of sherds, two styles, which might be called "classic" and "decadent," are immediately evident. Like the colors, the design elements are essentially uniform throughout Tiahuanaco ware. However, in the colors, a division in brilliance is noted, and in the designs a division in style is noted. . . . A division of color treatment into a rich, varied group and a drab, restricted group . . . [characterizes] the Classic-Decadent distinction. (Bennett 1934: 403)

Bennett's typological distinction at this point was without controversy. He had created a typology based on ceramic style, particularly the use of base colors and design motifs. Bennett then immediately went on to make a tenuous logical leap: he suggested that the Classic and Decadent styles were not just a stylistic distinction but a chronological one. As the names imply, the Classic was suggested to be earlier than the Decadent styles. On the same page, Bennett implied that this chronology was based on independent data—the relative position of stratigraphic units: "The distinction in style and color is readily observed, but the establishment of chronological distinction will be left for the section on cultural stratification" (Bennett 1934: 403). Yet, in the very next paragraph, his own choice of chronological terms betrays his implicit assumption that this stylistic distinction was also a chronological one: "A brief review of some of the salient features of Tiahuanaco style may serve to distinguish two periods, Classic and Decadent . . . a more detailed study would reveal the introduction of new design elements and the elimination of old motives in the Decadent phase." From this page on in Bennett's book, he continually couples the Classic and Decadent styles with the chronological designation of *period,* even though no stratigraphic corroboration had yet been offered. After this, Bennett argues that

his stylistic distinction was indeed supported by stratigraphic data: "the distinction [between Classic and Decadent] is substantiated by stratigraphic proof. Classic levels are stratigraphically lower than Decadent, higher than Early" (Bennett 1934: 453).

A critical reading of Bennett's monograph reveals that his data were not as unambiguous as he suggested. At the outset, he admits that the chronological distinction in terms of vessel shape was not supported by the excavation data: "The shapes have already been classified into Classic and Decadent types. This division is not absolutely borne out by the stratigraphic evidence" (Bennett 1934: 455).

For chronological purposes, this left only surface treatment, particularly paint color and design motifs, as a variable useful for seriating the Classic and Decadent phases. In his excavations, only two pits (numbers 5 and 8) out of the ten were either not mixed or undisturbed (actually, 20 percent is a very good percentage as far as semirandom testing goes). Another way to view these data is that in eight out of the ten pits, Classic and Decadent sherds were found in the same levels, sometimes in very similar proportions. Even Bennett admitted that 25 percent of the sherds in Classic levels were Decadent, although he felt that this was more than sufficient to prove the chronological accuracy of the Classic/ Decadent distinction (Bennett 1934: 455). Likewise, the upper levels (the hypothetical Decadent strata) contained at best 70 percent Decadent sherds and 28 percent Classic ones (Bennett 1934: 456).

In summary, there is little doubt that a stylistic distinction within the Tiwanaku ceramic assemblage exists, and that Bennett's stylistic typology works very well. The chronological utility of this typology remains in doubt, however. Only two of his units provided good stratigraphy. Even his best levels from these two units were mixed. It is also important to remember that Bennett's units were thick (fifty centimeters) by today's standards, and the question remains as to whether smaller levels would have yielded more homogeneous ceramic counts or if the same degree of mixing would have resulted. It is therefore possible that the two styles reflect synchronic functional or status differences, and not chronological ones. In fact, work by Alconini (1993) and Janusek (1994) has demonstrated that the Classic and Decadent styles are not chronologically useful. Their work (described below) has served to revise the sequence with the addition of other criteria.

Writing in 1948, the celebrated anthropologist Alfred Kroeber made an important observation about Bennett's work that must be kept in mind when reading the latter's monographs. Kroeber compared Bennett's interpretation of south Titicaca Basin prehistory to that of the historian Arnold Toynbee: "Another query that began to strike me as Bennett read his paper . . . was how far schemes of development like these also exemplify or imply general schemes of historic evolution of civilization—the most famous . . . being that of Toynbee?" (Kroeber 1948: 116). Bennett, as did many of his contemporaries such as Posnansky, presumed an inherent tendency for society in general, and art styles in particular, to degrade through time in a life-cycle pattern. It was therefore patently obvious to him that the Classic-Decadent stylistic distinction reflected a chronological distinction as well. Yet, by today's standards, his data are insufficient to demonstrate this.

As mentioned earlier, Carlos Ponce and Gregorio Cordero excavated extensive areas at the site of Tiwanaku in the 1950s and 1960s. Ponce constructed the most often-cited ceramic chronology for the site, composed of five periods referred to as Tiwanaku I through V, respectively. The validity of Tiwanaku II has been dismissed above. As mentioned in the last chapter, Tiwanaku I is referred to in this volume as Kalasasaya, and Tiwanaku III is referred to as Qeya. Ponce's Tiwanaku III and Tiwanaku IV correspond very closely to Bennett's Early Tiwanaku and Classic Tiwanaku, respectively (Chávez 1985: 137 fn. 1; Janusek 1994: 92). Classic Tiwanaku, as understood

by Bennett, and Tiwanaku IV, as utilized by Ponce, are essentially equivalent and correspond to the beginning of the Tiwanaku IV and V periods in the chronology used here. In other words, the term *Tiwanaku* refers *only* to the state-level society that began an expansionist process in the first part of the first millennium A.D. in the Titicaca region. Prior to this period, the direct antecedents of the Tiwanaku state in the Pacajes area were complex, nonstate societies referred to here as Qeya and Kalasasaya.

Pottery assemblages stylistically identified as Tiwanaku IV at the provincial site of Lukurmata are dated to between A.D. 400 and 800 by Bermann (1990: 205). These dates are confirmed by Goldstein's (1993a, 1993b) work at the Moquegua Valley Tiwanaku site of Omo. Likewise, Bermann dates Tiwanaku V to A.D. 800–1200 (Bermann 1990: 323). Kolata offers similar dates for the two periods. Data from the most recent work of Alconini (1993) and Janusek (1994, 1999) on the Tiwanaku ceramic chronology has made it possible to define with much greater precision the ceramic styles first named by Bennett.

Janusek (1994: 90–101) notes emphatically that there is no Tiwanaku IV or Tiwanaku V style: "After excavating in Tiwanaku IV–V strata for years, I say with confidence that . . . there is no Tiwanaku IV style, and no Tiwanaku V style" (Janusek 1994: 92). The analysis has to be at the assemblage level, therefore, and not at the individual-object level. Work in the western Titicaca Basin also supports this contention. I found, after several seasons of work, that we could not distinguish between Tiwanaku IV and V at the individual sherd level (see figure 8.1). Rather, the assigning of a period had to be at the assemblage level, and even here, given the limited number of Tiwanaku motifs and shapes, we could only define a site as Tiwanaku "expansive." In short, we lumped both Tiwanaku IV and V into the same chronological category (Stanish et al. 1997: 12).

The best synthesis of the data for the Tiwanaku

FIGURE 8.1. Tiwanaku pottery. Reproduced courtesy of the Fowler Museum of Cultural History, University of California, Los Angeles.

chronology is found in Janusek 1994 and Alconini 1993. Their chronology is based on a variety of data, including seriation of ceramic vessels, associated political and/or architectural changes at Tiwanaku, and a number of radiocarbon dates (Janusek 1994: 94). They divide Tiwanaku IV–V into four periods: Early Tiwanaku IV (circa A.D. 400–600), Late Tiwanaku IV (circa 600–800), Early Tiwanaku V (circa 800–1000), and Late Tiwanaku V (circa 1000–1100) (Janusek 1994: 95, 100). I believe this to be the best chronology at the present.

Expansive Archaic State Settlement Patterns

The development of Tiwanaku as an expansive state represents a new cultural phenomenon in the Titicaca region. In the earlier Upper Formative period,

complex polities were much smaller, generally covering a territory of no more than one or two days' travel from the principal site of the polity. Complex chiefly societies are regional polities composed of various alliances between groups in a territory that is fairly restricted. There is no real state control of discrete territorial units in any conventional sense but a series of shifting alliances between the paramount lineage heads and neighboring groups. The relatively small territories and political uniformity of complex and simple chiefdoms allows us to use a single model of settlement distribution for these polities.

The rules of political geography change dramatically in the evolution from complex chiefdoms to archaic states. In expansive states the territories are much larger and include numerous political and ethnic groups whose relationships with the center vary considerably from one group to the next. The state forcibly incorporates different ethnic groups, coopts others, makes strong or fragile political and/or economic arrangements with some, and so forth. In some cases, local labor is rigidly controlled by a foreign elite, whereas in others, a local elite mediates between the center and the local population. It is impossible to characterize the settlement pattern of archaic states by a single model.

Given this complexity, it is necessary to develop a typology of political geography for archaic states such as Tiwanaku at its height. Four different regions are recognized, defined by their geographical distance from the center and the nature of their political and economic relationship with it: the core territory, the heartland, the provinces, and the periphery.

The core territory is defined as the immediate surrounding territory of the principal settlement. It is also the ancestral territory of the paramount lineage of the ethnic group of the predecessor polity. In general terms, the core zone is within one day's travel from the principal center. The core territory of Tiwanaku is hypothesized to include the Tiwanaku Valley and to extend about twenty-five kilometers from the site. This would include the Catari Valley to the north and the southern Desaguadero River region. In effect, this definition more or less coincides with what Binford and Kolata have described as the "Tiwanaku sustaining area," which includes the Pampa Koani, the Tiwanaku Valley, and the Machaca Valley (Binford and Kolata 1996: 50).

The heartland includes the territory of the allied lineages and neighboring chiefdoms or states incorporated early in the expansion process. Based on my reading of historically documented expansive states, the heartland encompasses an area of about two days' distance from the capital. The case of the *Incas de Privilegio,* as discussed by Brian Bauer, provides an excellent example of this political geographical type. According to Bauer's reading of the early histories, the status of Inca de Privilegio was awarded by the Inca in Cuzco to groups "immediately outside of the Cuzco Valley" who were non-noble, "tribute-paying subjects and lower-level citizens of the Inca state" (Bauer 1992a: 15).

The heartland is expected to be an integral part of the state political economy, and the settlement pattern should reflect its close political and economic ties to the core territory. In the case of Tiwanaku, it is hypothesized that the heartland's boundaries in the north are the Río Ilave on the western side and the Río Suches near Escoma on the east. This area would include the Sillumocco (Juli and surrounding region), Copacabana, and Escoma areas, all of which are within a relatively short distance of Tiwanaku but possessed distinctive political systems immediately prior to Tiwanaku expansion. It is important to note that the lake altered the "radius" of two days' travel from the capital of Tiwanaku because it was a waterway that provided both obstacles and opportunities for travel and communication. Lake Titicaca is a very difficult body of water to navigate and did not necessarily facilitate communication. The winds are severe and unpredictable. The water is very cold, and exposure in the lake leads to death in a short time.

However, in a context of internecine warfare, the lake would have been outside the direct control of any one polity, making it possible to boat around a potentially hostile group instead of walking around it.

The provinces include territories that were conquered or allied, forcibly or otherwise, to the core territory. Their political and economic structures are highly varied in archaic states. Furthermore, unlike European conceptions of the political geography of modern and recent states, preindustrial archaic states tend to control pockets of territory in their provinces, creating a mosaic of direct and indirect control mechanisms combined with independent and semidependent territories. Control is highly varied through time, with some areas shifting in and out of autonomy status and titular or de facto authority by the state. By definition, a province is a region over which the state has potential military control, but the state may or may not choose to exercise that control. The settlement pattern of the provinces is highly varied, determined by a number of political, economic, ecological, strategic, and historical factors. The potential provincial territory of Tiwanaku is vast, covering an area of 300,000 to 400,000 square kilometers, based on the distribution of Tiwanaku pottery (principally Tiwanaku IV or V) in the south-central Andean region.

The periphery includes the areas beyond the state's ability to control. It differs from a province in that certain factors make state control unfeasible or highly tenuous. Generally, simple distance from the core can become so great as to make a sustained military effort too costly. It is therefore no surprise that the Inca state was obsessed with building roads and storehouses, which decreased the time it took to travel to the provinces and provided logistical support for armies on the march. It is also not surprising that the Inca state periphery was ringed with forts, attesting to the tenuous nature of Inca control there.

Peripheral areas can be very important to archaic

states. If economic incentives exist, the state will generally arrange some type of exchange relationship with peripheries, giving rise to ports of trade, long-distance trading groups (such as the *mindala* in Ecuador during Inca hegemony), and so on. The settlement patterns in peripheral areas are expected to be highly varied, and reflect an interplay between the local political and economic settlement determinants and the strategic and/or economic concerns of the state-level polity.

In recent years, anthropologists have borrowed from and expanded on world systems or core-periphery models. Although these models have helped to define the structure of premodern empires, a major weakness is that they are often too static to explain the dynamic relationship between a political center and peripheral areas over time. In other words, what is peripheral at one point in time eventually may become part of a core. Of course, it is also true that what is peripheral to one group of people may be quite central to another. In this light, a critique of world systems theory has emphasized the important and often active role that peripheries play in the regional political landscape of states. The dynamic relationship between different areas involves a whole host of linkages, including social networks, economic exchanges, political alliances, and strategic ties. Formerly peripheral territories are often transformed into regional centers, integrated by very complex political and economic relationships with the imperial capital and with other regional centers. Thus, the relationship between core and periphery is best conceived of as a fluid continuum continually transformed in the expansion process. Schreiber describes this "dynamic element" of expanding empires, noting that "groups that once lay in the outer periphery become client states as the empire expands . . . and as the imperial boundary changes, core/periphery relations are also in a state of flux" (Schreiber 1992: 13).

Comparative data indicate that this continuum reflects the dynamics of empire building in a wide variety of historical contexts. To take one example, Daphne Nash (1987: 88–89) argues for four "concentric" zones of imperial influence around the late Roman Republic's capital: a heartland consisting of Rome and Italy, directly administered provinces outside Italy, allies and official "friends" (or at times enemies) of the senatorial elite, and the remote periphery from which critical goods were acquired. Through time, the process of Roman empire building involved the transformation of allies, enemies, and peripheral populations into provincial territories under the aegis of the complex and heterogeneous political structure of the Roman state. Nash notes the fluid relationship between core and periphery in the Roman case: "By annexing provincial territory, the frontier that separated directly administered Roman territories from the outside world moved forward repeatedly, bringing progressively more remote societies into contact with the Mediterranean world" (Nash 1987: 88).

At any particular point in time, therefore, an expansive polity will be characterized by a heterogeneous set of relationships between core, heartland, provincial, and peripheral territories. No empire, no matter how mature, is monolithic and uniformly integrated with all of its constituent parts. This seems to be particularly true for archaic or first-generation states like Tiwanaku, where control of distant territories is not necessarily continuous and monolithic.

The furthest reaches of Tiwanaku influence around A.D. 900–1000 represent the peripheral areas of the state. The northernmost limit of Tiwanaku influence, according to S. Chávez (1988: 38), was in the Azángaro area in the northern Titicaca Basin. He believes that Sicuani was the frontier with Wari to the north. However, Tiwanaku or Tiwanaku-influenced pottery has been found as far north as Cuzco (Bauer 1999: 145), and it appears that some kind of exchange, perhaps indirect, was taking place between these two areas. To the west, the famous case of Cerro Baúl in Moquegua (Lumbreras, Mujica, and

Vera 1982; Moseley et. al 1991) apparently represents a Wari intrusion into Tiwanaku territory. Tiwanaku sites are found in the Arequipa area, and the northwestern limit appears to be the Majes drainage. Tiwanaku materials are found as far south as San Pedro de Atacama, which appears to have been a trading outpost given the lack of evidence for Tiwanaku colonization of the desert oasis.

Core Territory: The Circum-Tiwanaku Valley

The Urban Capital of the Tiwanaku State

The capital of the Tiwanaku state was in the Bolivian altiplano, in the middle of the Tiwanaku Valley, approximately twenty kilometers from the lake. At its height, Tiwanaku was home to a powerful elite and a massive concentration of people living in and surrounding an impressive architectural core of pyramids, palaces, streets, and state buildings. Surrounding the core of the capital was an urban settlement of nonelite artisans, laborers, and farmers who lived in adobe structures up and down the valley.

This vast, planned urban capital sprawled over the altiplano landscape in the southern Titicaca Basin in the majestic Tiwanaku Valley. Current estimates suggest that the total urban settlement covered four to six square kilometers, and had a population ranging from thirty thousand to sixty thousand (Janusek 1999: 112; Kolata and Ponce 1992: 332). The valley between Tiwanaku and the lake was also heavily populated during the Tiwanaku IV and V periods (Albarracin-Jordan and Mathews 1990; Albarracin-Jordan 1996a; Mathews 1992). The combined population of these settlements and the capital at Tiwanaku's height was the greatest concentration of people in the Andes south of Cuzco prior to the Spanish Conquest in the sixteenth century.

As the capital city of an expansive archaic state, Tiwanaku was more than an urban concentration of artisans, commoners, and political elite. The site itself served as the architectural representation of the power of a state with influence over a vast area in the south-central Andes, and it is dominated by a large, terraced, stone-faced pyramid in its urban core. Known as the Akapana, this construction measures 197 by 257 meters at its base and is 16.5 meters high (Manzanilla 1992: 22). There were six stone-faced terraces that outlined the hill. The Akapana was shaped like a half Andean cross (this shape is shown in figure 8.2) with a cross-shaped sunken court on its top (Escalante 1994; Kolata 1993: 104).

The Akapana is a huge construction and was most certainly one of the principal political and sacred public areas in the capital. Significantly, there were "distinctly secular structures" built at the top of the pyramid that Kolata (1993: 117) interprets as domestic residences of an elite. Substantial quantities of domestic refuse were found in middens associated with these rectangular structures, which were built with finely cut stones and faced inward toward a patio area in a manner not unlike that of the much smaller and earlier buildings at Chiripa. Structures were also discovered by Oswaldo Rivera on the lower terraces, indicating that much of the Akapana housed elite populations. The Akapana is interpreted as an artificial sacred mountain by Kolata (1993) and Reinhard (1991), an interpretation with which I agree, but I would add that there was a substantial elite residence on the artificial sacred mountain of the capital, a political and social statement of not insubstantial effect. It is also significant that the shape of the Akapana is reproduced throughout Tiwanaku art and architecture, attesting to the importance of this motif.

Adjacent to the north face of the Akapana is a large walled enclosure known as the Kalasasaya, which measures approximately 120 by 130 meters and is slightly elevated above the ground surface (Kolata 1993: 143). There is also a sunken court in the enclosure, along with a series of structures of unknown function. The walls are built with massive,

FIGURE 8.2. Andean cross. Photograph by the author.

upright stone blocks and smaller shaped stones, giving the enclosure a monumental appearance. Monolithic stone sculpture such as the Bennett and Ponce stelae were found in the Kalasasaya, and it is possible they were placed there during the height of the capital. The Kalasasaya was cardinally oriented, and there may be some simple astronomical alignments to the architecture, specifically the equinoxes (Kolata 1993: 143). A staircase on the east provides access to this impressive architectural complex. Even with this staircase, however, the architectural plan restricts access to the interior of the Kalasasaya, which is believed to have functioned as a locus for elite-directed religious and/or political ritual, as suggested by the large space, possible storage structures, and analogies to other walled public areas in the Andes.

Below the Kalasasaya is the semi-subterranean sunken court (see figure 8.3). This stone-lined construction is almost square, measuring approximately twenty-six by twenty-eight meters, and built partially below the ground surface. As in the Kalasasaya, stelae were found in the court. The sunken court has tenoned heads along the side of the walls.[1] The court

was reconstructed by Bolivian archaeologists in the 1970s, of course, so we are not completely certain of its original architecture. However, the existing walls appear to be a reasonably faithful reconstruction of the original architecture. According to Chávez and Chávez (1975), Kolata (1993: 141–42), and Moseley (1990b: 29), the tenoned heads were representations of captured huacas of various villages and subject polities of the Tiwanaku state at its height, probably contemporary with the carving of the Bennett and Ponce stelae. Although this remains conjecture, it is significant that the heads were placed in the sunken court below the Kalasasaya in a visible location. The court would have been particularly visible from the side and top of the Akapana pyramid. This visibility is consistent with a an emphasis on the display of state power through ritual.

One of the most salient characteristics of the tenoned heads is their variability, which suggests that they represent some kind of individual entities. The most obvious interpretation is that they represent trophy heads of individual people, as depicted occasionally on Tiwanaku art. They might also represent the symbols of individuals (huacas) associated with

FIGURE 8.3. Sunken court at Tiwanaku. Photograph by the author.

particular villages or towns captured by Tiwanaku. Alternatively, they could represent individual towns or villages themselves, with the physical location materialized in an anthropomorphic fashion. Along with the Akapana and Kalasasaya, the sunken court formed a political-religious complex that was used for important rituals that promoted the state power vested in the elite of Tiwanaku.

The sunken court, and possibly the Kalasasaya, may have housed captured stelae that also represented incorporated huacas. One of the most interesting discoveries in Titicaca Basin archaeology was the identification by Sergio Chávez of the Arapa stela as half of the Thunderbolt stela found in Tiwanaku (Chávez 1984). The Arapa stela is from the town of the same name, about 250 kilometers northwest of Tiwanaku in the northern basin. The stela was broken, and about half of it was moved to Tiwanaku by boat or a land route along the lake edge. This half was placed in the architectural core of Tiwanaku. The stela is in Upper Formative–period style and therefore predates the development of Tiwanaku as an expansive state by at least two centuries. The date of the stela is well-established, based on stylistic com-

parisons with sculpture from other sites in this tradition. This suggests the stela was brought to Tiwanaku long after it was carved. Stelae have important sociopolitical ramifications for villages today, and it is likely that the Arapa stela was being used by a polity long after it was carved.

Interpretations of the significance of this particular act vary, but if the Thunderbolt stela is evidence of huaca capture, it supports the argument that Tiwanaku was an expansionist state. Throughout the Andes, anthropologists and historians have noted the significance of huacas to communities or political groups, and the capture of such symbols has profound political significance not only in the Andes but throughout the world.

A little less than a kilometer southwest of the Akapana is the architectural complex known as the Pumapunku (literally, "door or gate of the puma" in Aymara). It is a mound that once housed elaborate stone and adobe architecture, and its subterranean canals suggest that the complex, in at least the phase represented by the surviving architecture, was planned and constructed at one time. There are two sets of stairs on the east and west sides of the Pumapunku, much like the Akapana (Kolata 1993: 97). Kolata, in fact, considers the Pumapunku to be the architectural counterpart of the Akapana, with both serving as the architectural center of a sacred urban landscape. During the height of the city, these two elevated structures would have dominated the architectural core of the city.

Excavations by the Proyecto Wila Jawira discovered elaborate decorative sculpture and painting in the Pumapunku. Kolata (1993: 99) describes the eastern court as having elaborate carved door jambs, lintels, sculptures, and the like. He even suggests that this was the original location of the beautiful Puerta del Sol, now found in the Kalasasaya. The cut masonry that graced the exterior of the Pumapunku is unrivaled at the city. In short, the Pumapunku was perhaps the second most significant architectural monument at Tiwanaku, if considered in terms of labor input, artistic effort, workmanship, and size.

The Putuni is directly west of the Kalasasaya and is the spatial counterpart to the semi-subterranean court to the east. The Putuni, in Kolata's words, is a "Palace of the Lords." He accurately notes that the architecture stands out from other architecture on the site and is characterized by a slightly elevated platform with a sunken court or plaza area (Kolata 1993: 149). The Putuni appears to have been a residential area with additional functions, and the fact that it is architecturally linked to the Kalasasaya is significant. The Putuni almost certainly housed some of the most elite members of Tiwanaku society.

East of the semi-subterranean temple is the area known as Kantatayita. Little systematic work has been published on this sector of the site, but it is known to have architectural constructions similar to the Putuni. Huge blocks lie on the surface, and what is most likely an architectural model carved in a monolithic block is found in this area. According to Ponce (1995: 243), a large decorated lintel was discovered in the Kantatayita area. Likewise, the architectural complexes known as the Kherikala and Chunchukala have complex cut-stone buildings. According to Kolata, all of these complexes have characteristics that identify them as nonresidential (Kolata 1993: 104).

The available data, particularly the underground sewer system and cardinally oriented layout of many of the buildings, indicate that the capital of Tiwanaku at its height in the eighth or ninth century A.D. was a planned city built in a relatively short period of time. Furthermore, a substantial pre-Tiwanaku IV occupation at the site indicates that in a relatively short time period, the inhabitants rebuilt the urban center. The architects who planned the site were able to draw off a huge labor pool, one that would have been essential for creating and transporting the large stone blocks used in the construction of the city's core. These massive blocks would have required years of work by an enormous and skilled group of artisans, and some of the blocks were brought from quarries twenty or more kilometers away.

There was a very dense population outside Tiwanaku's architectural core. Janusek's excavation, one-half kilometer east of the architectural core in the area called AKE2, indicated dense residential structures that dated to his late Tiwanaku IV and Tiwanaku V. These structures were on top of sterile, undisturbed strata, indicating that the first expansion of an urban nature in this area occurred in the Tiwanaku IV period, after Tiwanaku III or Qeya, and that the site was not occupied during the Upper Formative. However, the Tiwanaku IV–V occupation was substantial. This excavation produced evidence for "common domestic activities" (Janusek 1994: 141), indicating that the area was intensively used for nonceremonial, nonelite purposes.

There are numerous unpublished reports of excavations conducted outside the protected park area of the site where there is exposed dense architecture. According to Ponce (1995: 244), Javier Escalante excavated a 228-square-meter area in a sector called Lakkaraña. This area, to the north of the architec-

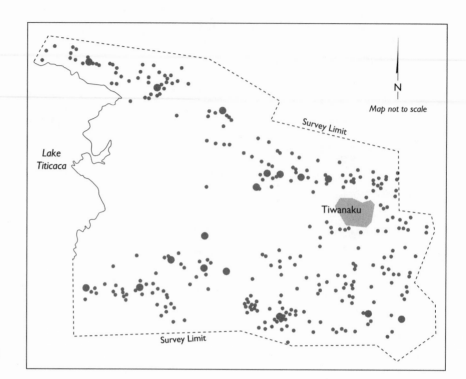

MAP 8.1. Distribution of settlement in the Tiwanaku Valley during the height of Tiwanaku. Adapted from Albarracin-Jordan 1996 and Mathews 1992.

tural core near the old road, had a Tiwanaku wall, two structures (one round and one rectangular), and domestic refuse. These data clearly indicate that domestic subsurface residential structures are to be found in areas of the site without evidence of surface architecture. Portugal Ortíz excavated near this area and discovered the remains of a painted mural "similar to that found in the excavations in the interior patio of the Kalasasaya" (Ponce 1995: 244; Portugal O. 1992: figure 16).

The survey of the Tiwanaku Valley conducted by Albarracin-Jordan and Mathews indicates that nearly the entire area from Tiwanaku itself to the lake was inhabited by a dense conglomeration of settlement. By the criteria used in Mesoamerica to define sites, this section of the valley, perhaps around twenty square kilometers, would be considered one site. Map 8.1, adapted from the surveys of Albarracin-Jordan

(1996) and Mathews (1992), shows the settlement densities near the urban core and in the valley down to the lake edge.

One significant characteristic of the site is that most of the buildings in the city outside the architectural core were built with an adobe superstructure with rock foundations. Subsequent deterioration of the building walls, along with substantial soil-forming processes in the altiplano, has served to obscure the vast habitation areas associated with the site. An appropriate analogy would be the site of Chan Chan on the coast of Peru, where most of the buildings were adobe. If that capital of the Chimú kingdom were in a climate similar to Tiwanaku, little would remain of the structure walls. The central architectural core of the site would be preserved, but the rest of the habitation areas would have been eroded and covered with soil. At Tiwanaku, whenever test excavations are conducted outside the architectural core, habitation and domestic midden remains are found, and the modern town is replete with pottery sherds from the Tiwanaku period. Thus, the nature of the architectural construction techniques and the high rainfall of the Tiwanaku area have obscured the monumentality of the site.

One can also argue that the proper analogy for Tiwanaku, in terms of political and economic scale, would be a polity like the Chimú capital. Chan Chan was about the same size as Tiwanaku, both physically and demographically, and capital of a state that controlled a substantial territory (see table 8.1). Both maintained satellite communities or colonies. Chan Chan had a divine kingship, and the iconographic evidence from Tiwanaku suggests that it too had such a political system. Both societies had marked social classes and both incorporated polities, either voluntarily or otherwise, through a variety of means to create expansive polities of some proportion.

Primary Regional Centers in the Core Territory

Defining a Tiwanaku site outside the Tiwanaku Valley is a difficult methodological issue. The question is, What criteria does one use to define a site that was incorporated into the Tiwanaku political orbit? This issue stands at the center of the debate regarding the nature of the Tiwanaku state; that is, a site with Tiwanaku pottery outside the basin could be an autonomous settlement that imported or copied Tiwanaku iconography, but it was not necessarily part of the Tiwanaku state system. In other words, how does one distinguish among a colony, an affiliated settlement, and a trading partner? Adding to the complexity is the fact that, throughout its history, a site could have been sequentially all three.

Assuming for the moment that Tiwanaku was indeed complex enough to potentially send out colonies, a Tiwanaku-contemporary site in the region could have had a number of possible political and economic relationships to the core territory in the Tiwanaku Valley:

1. The site may have had no relationship with Tiwanaku at all.

2. The site may have had an economic exchange relationship but was not politically incorporated into the Tiwanaku orbit, meaning that the individuals on the site may have produced surplus wealth for exchange with individuals from Tiwanaku, but that the Tiwanaku elite had no control over that production.

3. The elite on the site may have been culturally (ideologically, politically, and sociologically) part of the Tiwanaku elite, either as subordinate members of an elite Tiwanaku hierarchy through marriage or fictive kinship, or as direct administrators placed there by the state after the local elite were removed.

4. A substantial part or all of the population of the site may have moved from the Tiwanaku core as colonizers.

Obviously, a site without any Tiwanaku materials has no evidence of any political and economic relationship to the Tiwanaku state. A site with a low density of high-status Tiwanaku goods and no other material indicator supports the second type of relationship defined above. The Atacama desert oasis of San Pedro de Atacama represents this kind of site.

In earlier publications, I outlined some criteria for defining colonies of larger polities (Stanish 1992; Stanish et al. 1997). This methodology relied upon the definition of the normative domestic household type in the core and hypothesized colonial settlement. Domestic objects and architecture are very useful for defining the cultural affiliations between settlements. For the Tiwanaku period, other criteria can be used as well. First, there should be a significant

TABLE 8.1
Major Prehispanic Urban Centers in the Americas

City	Estimated Area (in square kilometers)	Estimated Population	References
TENOCHTITLÁN	12–15	160,000–200,000	Sanders and Webster 1988
TEOTIHUACÁN	18	125,000	Sanders and Webster 1988
CUZCO	10	125,000	Agurto 1980; Hyslop 1990: 64–65
TIKAL	5–10	60,000	Marcus (personal communication)
CHAN CHAN	6	50,000	Moseley and Mackey 1973: 328
TIWANAKU	4–6	30,000–60,000	Kolata and Ponce 1992: 332
WARI	5	20,000–70,000	Isbell et al. 1991; Isbell 1988: 173
TULA	10.75–13	30,000–40,000	Diehl 1983: 58
CALAKMUL	1.75 +	50,000	Folan et al. 1995
HUÁNUCO PAMPA	2	30,000 (?)	Morris and Thompson 1985: 86
COPÁN	2.5	18,000–25,000	Sanders and Webster 1988
SAYIL	3.45	10,858	Tourtellot et al. 1990: 248, 261
PIKILLACTA	2	?	McEwan 1991: 100

quantity of Tiwanaku fine wares on the site. The presence of keros, tazones, and incensarios indicates an affiliation with some aspects of Tiwanaku political beliefs, and possibly a more formal political relationship. Furthermore, there should be no other fineware pottery styles on the site. This criterion is extremely important. In the Upper Formative period and before it, all primary regional centers and most smaller sites had both locally or semilocally produced fine wares that identified the site as distinct from adjacent contemporary polities, as well as nonlocal fine wares imported from other polities, indicating some kind of exchange relationship. During the Tiwanaku period, Tiwanaku-affiliated sites do not contain pottery of any other style associated with a distinct polity in the Titicaca Basin. Not coincidentally, this is very similar to the pattern found on Inca sites during the Late Horizon.

An additional criterion is the use of Tiwanaku architectural motifs in sites outside the capital. In the previous Upper Formative period, there was a general replication of pan-Titicaca Basin architectural styles but significant regional variation. In the Tiwanaku period, there is a standardization of architectural canons on a number of sites throughout the region. Finally, apart from these stylistic criteria, there are others such as settlement shifts coincident with the appearance of Tiwanaku materials in the area, major architectural building, economic shifts, and so forth.

Lukurmata

The site of Lukurmata was test excavated by Bennett in the 1930s. Kolata and Rivera also worked at the site in the mid-1980s, and Bermann wrote a book on his excavations at a major domestic area (Bermann 1994). The Tiwanaku occupation of the site includes a large sunken court on a hill adjacent to the lake. There were also monoliths discovered at the site that were subsequently moved to La Paz (Bennett 1936: 493). Below the corporate architectural core of the site is a series of domestic areas that cover more than 150 hectares (Stanish 1989c). This huge size makes Lukurmata both an anomaly in the Titicaca Basin (where other Tiwanaku sites are less than 20 hectares) and the largest known Tiwanaku site outside the capital itself.

As discussed above, there was a major Upper Formative occupation on the site of Lukurmata. The architecture was reworked during the Tiwanaku period into one of the principal sites in the core territory. The sunken court was rebuilt using blocks from what was most certainly a Upper Formative one. The monoliths on the site are executed in Tiwanaku styles, one of the few examples of stone sculpture manufactured outside Tiwanaku itself during the height of the state.

Secondary Regional Centers in the Core Territory

Secondary regional centers, as defined above, are sites with domestic residence and corporate architecture. In the Tiwanaku period, as in the preceding periods, secondary regional centers were found on Type 1 and Type 3 sites only in the Juli-Pomata survey area. This pattern holds throughout the south and western regions of the basin. In both cases, the intent seems to have been to locate the corporate architecture on a high area surrounded by residences. In only a few cases does one find evidence of corporate architecture on a hillside. Almost always, cut-stone blocks or remains of the actual wall are found at the top of a hill.

The best-known secondary regional center in the core territory is Chiripa. As discussed above, Bennett's excavations there revealed four distinct occupational levels. Bennett's "Decadent Tiahuanaco period," defined by the artifacts associated with this level, was characterized by the construction of a semisubterranean, stone-lined temple (Bennett 1936: 431). Subsequent work indicated that this temple was actually built in the Tiwanaku III or Qeya period (K. Chávez 1988). Nevertheless, work by Hastorf (1999b) indicates a substantial Tiwanaku occupation at the site that covered at least thirteen hectares. As Bandy notes, Chiripa was as large or larger than any other Tiwanaku site in the valley with the exception of the capital itself (Bandy 1999a).

Other regional centers in the core territory include the sites of Quellamarka, Wancané, Taquiri, and most likely Sulikata (e.g., see Kolata 1985; Lumbreras and Mujica 1982a). Each of these sites has substantial Tiwanaku pottery, corporate architecture in apparently Tiwanaku styles, and habitation zones covering large areas. All of them could be primary or secondary regional centers of substantial size and complexity.

Summary: The Core Territory

The core territory of Tiwanaku is hypothesized to include the Tiwanaku Valley and most of the Catari

Valley to the north, as well as the area south of Tiwanaku to the Desaguadero River. The site of Lukurmata, on the southern edge of the Catari pampa, was a huge primary center during the Tiwanaku occupation and the largest nonurban site in the region at any point in history. Binford and Kolata (1996: 48) argue that the combined population of the Tiwanaku and Catari Valleys during the height of Tiwanaku was between 285,000 and 570,000, a truly massive number of people concentrated in these two areas. Kolata and Ortloff (1996a) argue that the entire Tiwanaku core was geared to intensive agricultural production, with raised-field agriculture as the cornerstone of the endogenous Tiwanaku economy that supported these large numbers.

Primary Regional Centers in the Heartland

Oje (Ojje, Llojepaya, Chocupercas)

The site of Oje is on the southern side of the Copacabana Peninsula. Portugal and Ibarra Grasso (1957: 42) refer to it as a Tiwanaku temple with a pyramidal structure measuring 87 by 123 meters and 3.5 to 4.0 meters in height. They note that there are cut stones on the surface as well as stelae. Uhle first reported the site, and Bennett also described the temple area. Judging by the amount of corporate architecture, the site of Oje was likely a primary regional center with a substantial population during the Tiwanaku periods.

Simillake

The site of Simillake, first mentioned by Posnansky (1938), is in the middle of the Desaguadero River, on the Peruvian side in the totora beds. At the time of Posnansky's visit, Simillake was a small island that he described as being less than five hectares in size. He also noted that the island was occasionally submerged. Posnansky observed a sunken court construction that measured more than fifty meters on a

side, and he suggested that it was built in a manner "typical of the Kalasasaya" at Tiwanaku. Photographs taken at the time of Posnansky's visit indicate cut-stone blocks on the surface that are very typical of those used in sunken court constructions elsewhere in the altiplano. He also included a photograph of what appears to be a Tiwanaku cut-stone monolith on the site (Posnansky 1938: figure 109). Simillake would have been a major site, particularly given the large Kalasasaya construction, and most likely was a primary regional center in the Tiwanaku settlement system.

Amaizana China

This large Upper Formative–period and Tiwanaku site (described above) has large andesite blocks on the top of the hill, indicating that there was a corporate construction of some sort, most likely a sunken court and/or formally faced stone terraces. The blocks are in Tiwanaku style and suggest a major sunken temple and Kalasasaya construction at the site. The remains of a possible platform can be detected at the top of the hill, but the site is very badly disturbed. The site was almost certainly a primary regional center in the Tiwanaku period.

Kanamarca

The major occupation of Kanamarca (whose Middle and Upper Formative–period occupations are described above) appears to have been during the Tiwanaku period, as indicated by the huge Tiwanaku-style andesite blocks on the surface. These are some of the largest cut blocks found in the Titicaca Basin, and they suggest a corporate construction of considerable importance.

The habitation area covered seven to ten hectares during the Tiwanaku period, and the site is located next to a probable raised-field area, one of the few on this side of the lake. I was unable to examine the pampa for any obvious relict raised fields; however, the area is low and swampy and has topographical features similar to those of raised-field areas in the region. Most notably, there is a large, circular depression in the pampa very similar to the reservoir described by Kolata and Ortloff at the major Tiwanaku site of Pajchiri in Bolivia (Ortloff and Kolata 1989).

Palermo

The site of Palermo is the largest Late Sillumocco (Upper Formative)– and Tiwanaku-period settlement in the Juli-Pomata area. The Tiwanaku occupation is represented by a probable rebuilding of the corporate architecture, originally built in the preceding Late Sillumocco (Upper Formative) period. Excavations at the Kalasasaya area on the site have provided a chronological sequence of the constructions in this probable enclosure area. About a meter of Early Sillumocco construction fill was discovered below a floor constructed in the Late Sillumocco period. Above this floor was a level of unconsolidated midden, a substantial quantity of burned vegetal matter, and larger rocks, all associated with the Tiwanaku occupation. The features in this level indicated post-occupational collapse and burning. The burning could also represent a violent episode in which structures on the floor surface were destroyed. Higher up in this post-floor level was a thick lens of camelid dung, which suggests that the site was used as a corral after the principal occupation represented by the floor. This interpretation is supported by the existence of a canal that runs from the side of Pukara Juli into the sunken court area.

The semi-subterranean sunken court at the top of the hill measures fifteen by fifteen meters and was most likely built in the preceding Late Sillumocco period (see pages 148–151). As with the site of Lukurmata, however, the sunken court appears to have been used in the Tiwanaku period as well. First, the last major occupation of the site was during the Tiwanaku period, as indicated by the extensive distribution of diagnostic pottery fragments on the site. The

court was not covered with fill and not destroyed in antiquity, so it is most likely that it was used during the last major occupation of the site. Furthermore, the Tiwanaku levels at the excavations, including the domestic structures on the sides, were also intact and appear to be contemporary with the last use of the temple area. Future excavations at this important site can easily resolve these issues.

Islands of the Sun and Moon

There was a substantial Tiwanaku occupation on the Islands of the Sun and Moon. On the Island of the Moon, Bauer (as reported in Bauer and Stanish 2001) located Tiwanaku pottery and intact levels under the Inca construction known as the Iñak Uyu. On the Island of the Sun, systematic survey located twenty-eight Tiwanaku sites (see below). Of these, two stand out as potential regional centers: Chucaripupata and Wakuyo. Wakuyo was test excavated by Perrín Pando (1957), who discovered good Tiwanaku pottery from tombs on the site. Survey of the area indicates that the site was several hectares in size.

The site of Chucaripupata is another large Tiwanaku site on the Island of the Sun. It has been extensively studied by Seddon (1998). The site is approximately one hundred meters southeast of the Titikala rock in the northern part of the island. The surface features are largely Tiwanaku in date. Bandelier, the first to report the site, described it as an "irregular quadrangle . . . platform lined by walls and surrounded by lower terraces on three sides, whereas in the northeast it abuts against a higher plane on the flanks of Muro-Kato" (Bandelier 1910: 225). Murokata is a large hill east of the site that is similar to the Titikala rock in appearance.

On the northern and southern sides of the platform, descending down the original ridge, is a series of large terraces. There are no terraces on the western, or lake-edge, portion of the site, as the terrain is too steep. The first terrace down from the upper platform on both the northern and southern sides is a specially constructed terrace. This system of walls forms a first terrace at either side of the site that is explicitly architecturally linked with the upper platform.

According to Seddon, the site includes a walled upper platform and descending lower terraces as described by Bandelier. The upper platform, which is approximately sixty by sixty meters, forming an irregular square, has a slight slope from the middle to either side, with a drop in altitude of about one and a half meters from the middle of the platform to the northern and southern edges. As Bandelier noted, this may originally have been level. Bedrock is visible on the surface at the western, or lake-edge, portion of this platform.

Excavations by Seddon indicate a substantial corporate construction on the site, including a huge double-faced wall. The high quality of ceramic artifacts indicates an important ritual locus with a substantial domestic component on the lower terraces. Seddon interprets the site as a major Tiwanaku ritual center during Tiwanaku IV and Tiwanaku V times. Seddon's work and the survey data strongly suggest that Tiwanaku controlled the entire island and that the Sacred Rock or Titikala area, the famous Inca pilgrimage destination, was a major ritual center in Tiwanaku times as well.

Secondary Regional Centers in the Heartland

There are a number of known secondary regional centers in the Tiwanaku heartland, particularly on the Peruvian side, where systematic survey has been conducted (see map 8.2). A few of them have been excavated, intensively surface collected, and/or mapped. The site of Sillumocco-Huaquina is about three and a half hectares in size (Stanish et al. 1997). One fascinating aspect of the site is that the entire mound of Sillumocco-Huaquina was altered in the Tiwanaku period into what appears to be a classic Tiwanaku cross shape. Excavations by de la Vega

(1997) indicate that the last large reconstruction of the mound was during the Tiwanaku period, the last major occupation on the site. The shape may very well be a miniature Akapana. Sillumocco-Huaquina is therefore a replica of the corporate architecture at Tiwanaku, and was one of several regional centers in the Juli area during the Tiwanaku period.

The site of Tumuku is near the lake edge a few kilometers south of the town of Juli. Tumuku is the name of a large hill in the Chokasuyu or Kajje area. On top of this large hill is a multicomponent site with a significant Tiwanaku occupation. At the very top is a semi-subterranean sunken court very similar to those found at other sites such as Sillumocco-Huaquina and Palermo. The court is stone-lined on four sides. It is, unfortunately, difficult to measure but is no more than twenty by twenty meters, and probably much smaller. It is at least several meters long on a side and appears to be roughly square. The site itself covered about four hectares in the Tiwanaku period.

Qeñuani (Fortina Vinto), described above as a regional center during the Upper Formative, was a secondary regional center during the Tiwanaku period. A rectangular structure on top of the site measures approximately twenty by twenty-five meters and appears to be at least as late as Tiwanaku in date, given that the Tiwanaku period constituted the last major use of the site. The Tiwanaku occupation was at least four, and possibly as much as six, hectares in size.

Dozens of sites that have not been investigated by professional archaeologists or that have received only a cursory examination could be primary regional centers. On the island of Pariti, for instance, Bennett (1936: 446) reports numerous cut and dressed blocks and slabs, and his excavations there in the 1930s uncovered Tiwanaku pottery and gold from a number of trenches. Collections at the American Museum of Natural History made by Bennett at this site contain keros in classic Tiwanaku styles. Although he did not find any structures, it is most likely that a major

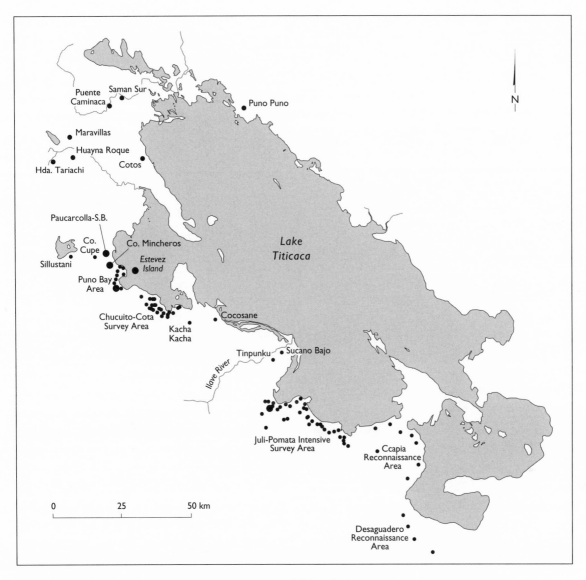

MAP 8.2. Known Tiwanaku sites in the Peruvian (west-southwestern) Titicaca Basin.

Tiwanaku center existed on the island during the height of Tiwanaku expansion.

The site of Pajchiri is another large Tiwanaku site that has not been adequately investigated. Bennett (1934) worked at the site in his 1933–1934 season, and the site may have been visited by Uhle. There is a large structure on the site constructed with cut-stone blocks, and substantial Tiwanaku remains were discovered on the surface and in the excavations. There is little doubt that Pajchiri is a major Tiwanaku regional center of great size. Work by Ortloff and Kolata (1989) discovered a large reservoir below the residential area that was associated with aqueducts and walled canals.

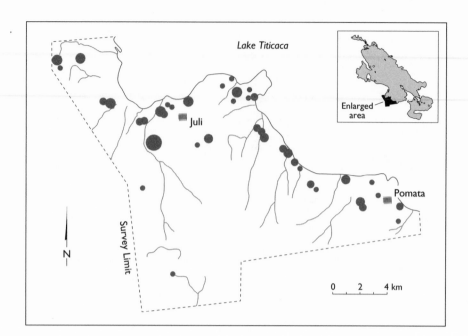

MAP 8.3. Tiwanaku settle-
ment patterns in the Juli-
Pomata survey area.

The Tiwanaku Settlement Pattern
in the Juli-Pomata Area

As shown in map 8.3, one of the most striking features in the Tiwanaku settlement pattern in the Juli-
Pomata region is the continuity from the Late Sillumocco pattern. With the exception of one small site,
all major Late Sillumocco sites continued to be occupied in the Tiwanaku period. Most significant, nine
of the ten sites that were abandoned were small. Of
course, it is likely that the subsequent Tiwanaku occupation served to obscure the size of the earlier Sillumocco occupation. On the other hand, the three
regional centers of Tumatumani, Palermo, and Sillumocco all continued to be occupied. The general site
size distribution remained relatively constant from the
earlier period (see figure 8.4). Excavations in Tumatumani revealed that the Tiwanaku occupation was
characterized by the rebuilding of an earlier Late Sillumocco stepped pyramid complex. Recently completed excavations at Palermo confirm this historical
pattern for that important regional center as well.

Twenty-two new sites were founded in the Tiwanaku period, including the site of Tumuku, a regional
center in the Kajje area between Chokasuyu and El
Molino, and the unnamed site number 444 in the
Moyopampa. The Tiwanaku settlement pattern in
the Juli-Pomata area is characterized by a lakeside settlement focus and the absence of fortified settlements, patterns identical to the earlier Late Sillumocco pattern. Sites were clustered near raised-field
areas. In most respects, the Tiwanaku pattern was an
elaboration of the existing Late Sillumocco one. It is
most likely that the Tiwanaku state expanded into
an already complex political and economic system
dominated by the Late Sillumocco peoples.

The Tiwanaku Settlement Pattern
on the Island of the Sun

The Islands of the Sun and Moon were one of the
first areas to be controlled by this expanding Tiwanaku polity. Absolute dates of the initial Tiwanaku
occupation obtained by Seddon (1998) from Chucaripupata fall in the mid- to late seventh century

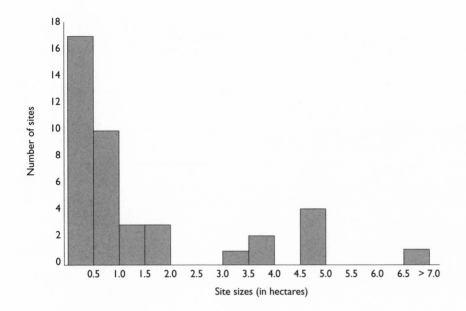

FIGURE 8.4. Site size distribution of Tiwanaku settlements in the Juli-Pomata survey region.

A.D. We have known that there was a Tiwanaku occupation on the Islands of the Sun and Moon for more than a hundred years. As early as the turn of the century, Bandelier recovered a number of Tiwanaku pottery vessels from the islands and surrounding countryside, such as the Copacabana Peninsula and Escoma. These vessels are all executed in Tiwanaku-style canons, and some of them could have been manufactured in Tiwanaku itself. These data indicate that all stylistic innovation derived from the Tiwanaku area during this time. This contrasts with the earlier Upper Formative, in which art styles were derived from around the lake area, as well as exhibiting substantial local variation. In other words, the dominant cultural influence as indicated in Tiwanaku-period art styles is from Tiwanaku alone.

Our research (Bauer and Stanish 2001) confirmed a significant Tiwanaku occupation on the Islands of the Sun and Moon. Twenty-eight Tiwanaku sites were identified on the Island of the Sun (see map 8.4), and a few sites on the Island of the Moon. The combined data make it clear that the islands were a fun-

damental part of the Tiwanaku polity and indicate that the islands had been incorporated into the Tiwanaku state by A.D. 650 or so.

The settlement pattern during the Tiwanaku period on the Island of the Sun supports the model of an integrated political entity for the entire island population. Unlike settlement during the Upper Formative period, there were no settlement clusters, and combined with the increase in mean site size, this pattern suggests that the entire island was a single political entity. As mentioned above, it is possible that there was a single political entity in the Upper Formative as well, but this remains speculative. In the Tiwanaku period, the evidence for a centralized political organization is quite strong.

Two sites emerged as the dominant settlements on the island during the Tiwanaku period: Chucaripupata and Wakuyo. Although Wakuyo has no remaining architecture, several observations suggest that it was a major site with elaborate architecture. The site is located on a low hill, surrounded by terraces with a high density of pottery on the surface, indicating that they were domestic terraces (that is,

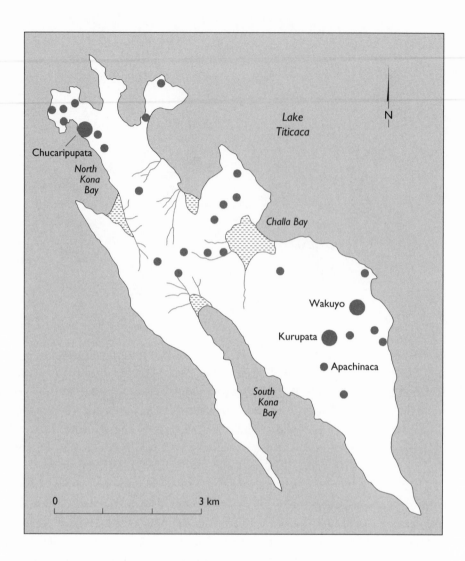

MAP 8.4. Tiwanaku settlement pattern (circa A.D. 600–1100) on the Island of the Sun.

they were used at one point as floor surfaces for houses). This pattern is typical of other Upper Formative and Tiwanaku sites in the region. The hill has been modified to create a flat surface above the domestic terraces. If it follows the pattern of other sites, the flat area most likely supported a walled enclosure area and a small sunken court. As mentioned above, Perrín Pando (1957) excavated at the site and discovered several classic Tiwanaku pottery vessels. He also noted that the hill was artificial and that he had discovered at least one major wall on the site.

Tiwanaku Provincial Territories

The Puno Area

The Bay of Puno is in the northwest side of Lake Titicaca. The bay itself is fairly large (about five hundred square kilometers) and is defined by the Capachica Peninsula to the north and a second peninsula to the south, dominated by Cerro Coaraya. Mario Núñez (1977) published a brief review of the known Tiwanaku sites in the Puno area. A number of sites have since been destroyed or are now covered by modern constructions. They were identified by the presence of Tiwanaku diagnostics recovered from rescue work, or as a by-product of construction activities. Tiwanaku sites include one on the present site of the Colegio Nacional in Puno, in Barrio José Antonio Encinas: the site of Huajjsapata, three hundred meters from Plaza de Armas; the site of Molloqo Mata, near the lake off the main highway south of Puno (Molloqo Mata was also visited by Hyslop 1976); and Punanave, above Puno on the road to Moquegua. Núñez also notes that Tiwanaku artifacts were located on Isla Salinas and, of course, on the large Tiwanaku site of Isla Esteves.

The principal Tiwanaku center in the Puno area was Isla Esteves (Núñez and Paredes 1978). The island is in the north part of the bay, less than one kilometer from the mainland. In the 1970s, the island was partially bulldozed to construct a tourist hotel. During that time, Mario Núñez supervised a brief rescue effort on the island. His work revealed a large area of domestic architecture along terraces on the western side of the island, facing the town of Puno. He also discovered camelid offerings, extensive midden areas, a line of subterranean storage cists, burials, canals, and large ceramic storage vessels.

Recent work directed by de la Vega and Chávez has confirmed the earlier work of Núñez and clarified the nature of the domestic area. The site of Isla Esteves covered at least ten hectares, and there is evidence of corporate architecture. Excavations in the domestic areas revealed very high-quality pottery associated with well-constructed habitation areas. These structures were directly below a low, flat area on the crest of the hill that may have been a Kalasasaya area. This is inferred by the flat topography that was evident before the hotel construction, and which appeared to be partially artificial; if so, it would fit the pattern of site construction for Tiwanaku sites.

In the past several years, several additional sites have been located in the Puno area. The largest of these is directly across the lake from Isla Esteves. Huajje is a very large mound, possibly built in a very long U shape. The mound on the east side of the site is a mostly artificial construction built as three platforms on top of each other. The top platform has what appears to be a sunken area, approximately 20 by 20 meters in size. The east face of the site, toward the railroad tracks, is almost 400 meters long. The site is about 100 to 150 meters wide, making it about 4 to 6 hectares in size. The site has abundant Tiwanaku pottery that is extremely fine in manufacture. Some of the fragments may well have been imports.

Small Tiwanaku sites are found south of Puno on the road, as well as in the surrounding hills above town. Tiwanaku sites are also located to the immediate north of the Esteves area, along the foothills that line the pampa adjacent to the lake. The site of Chuchuparqui is on the road north from Isla Esteves, along the hill adjacent to the railroad tracks and lake edge; it is a modest domestic terraced hill site, approximately three to four hectares in size. Toclomara is located at the curve on the same road as Chuchuparqui. It is a domestic terrace site with a number of occupations, including a major Tiwanaku one at least three hectares in size.

Above Puno on the modern (and presumably ancient) road to the Moquegua Valley is the site of Punanave, first discovered by Mario Núñez. The site is huge, with a very dense distribution of artifacts on the surface. Punanave is actually a series of domestic terraces covering an area of perhaps twelve or more hectares. There is abundant worked, raw, and waste debris from basalt and other stone materials on the surface. Pottery fragment densities are quite high, and there are also pieces of raw copper ore on the surface. The site is huge by Tiwanaku provincial standards, yet there is no surface evidence of corporate architecture. The site is best interpreted as a significant domestic site with evidence of specialized lithic production. It is an aggregation of domestic residences without evidence of elite, ritual, or any other kind of nondomestic architecture.

In short, the Puno Bay area is replete with Tiwanaku sites. This area was an enclave of Tiwanaku settlement, with the site of Isla Esteves as the principal regional center. Tiwanaku sites are associated with raised fields to the north of the bay area proper, and it is likely that the shores near Puno also had these intensive agricultural constructions. The town of Puno itself is on the Inca Urqusuyu road, and there was an extensive Tiwanaku settlement in the present-day town. The Puno Bay Tiwanaku enclave is, in fact, the largest and most densely populated Tiwanaku enclave yet discovered in the north Titicaca Basin.

The Island of Amantaní

This island is not geographically associated with any particular Tiwanaku enclave, and it has not been intensively investigated; our knowledge is based on unsystematic survey and some brief reports. Niles (1988) has written an article describing the Pachatata Amantaní, a high hill with a sunken court at the top. The sunken court is built with fieldstones and measures about fourteen by fourteen meters. It is not oriented in cardinal directions.

The overall style of the sunken court is Tiwanaku, albeit with some significant differences. Typically, Tiwanaku is the semi-subterranean construction, a corner doorway that is virtually identical to that found at Lukurmata, and a stairway similar to that at Tiwanaku itself. On the other hand, the second stairway is not typical of Tiwanaku canons, nor is the fieldstone construction of the court. The outside wall, an obvious modern construction, appears to be built on Prehispanic foundation stones. If this outer foundation wall is indeed Prehispanic, then it is not a typical Tiwanaku construction. Finally, there is no evidence of a Tiwanaku occupation on the hillside below Pachatata, although Niles reports finding some Tiwanaku pottery in the region (Niles 1988: figures 6 and 7). Without intensive excavations it is difficult to know the precise architectural history of the temple construction. At the present time, there are two viable hypotheses about this enigmatic construction: (1) that it is a temple that was originally built as a Tiwanaku construction, with a rebuilding of the area by the Inca, or (2) that the temple is Inca, Early Colonial, or Modern in date, and is not a Tiwanaku-period construction.

Across from Pachatata is the Pachamama hill, on which there is a circular structure several meters in diameter with five concentric walls inside. Edmundo de la Vega has pointed out that the walls are possibly similar to the circular structures as Sillustani. There are no sherds associated with the immediate site area, but the north face of the hill is full of Inca pottery. The construction today is associated with the Pachatata, but this circular structure is not a typical Tiwanaku construction.

Nonsystematic reconnaissance of about one-third of the island indicated that there are abundant Inca fine wares surrounding the Pachatata and Pachamama hills. To date, despite several concerted attempts, no Tiwanaku habitation site has been located on the island, and virtually no Tiwanaku pottery has been observed on the surface. The island deserves intensive research. Although I do not accept "empty" ceremonial centers as a valid prehistoric settlement type in the Titicaca Basin, if there is any candidate that might prove this position incorrect, then it is the Pachatata during the Tiwanaku period.

The Paucarcolla Area

Several Tiwanaku sites have been reported in the area north of Puno near Paucarcolla. Rosanna Revilla B. and Mauro Uriarte P. (1985: 86–95) report finding Tiwanaku levels in their excavations at the site of Sillustani. They also note the presence of Tiwanaku ceramics on a site called Patas, two kilometers north of Sillustani. Likewise, they found "miscellaneous" fragments at the site of Cerro Ale, three kilometers north of Sillustani.

Steadman (1995) notes a significant Tiwanaku occupation at the site of Paucarcolla-Santa Barbara, adjacent to the town of Paucarcolla. Unsystematic survey of this site suggests that it was one of the largest Tiwanaku primary regional centers outside the core territory: at least twelve hectares during the Tiwanaku period and most likely larger. The Tiwanaku pottery fragments found on the surface are of exceptional quality. The site of Paucarcolla-Santa Barbara is hypothesized to be the regional center for a number of Tiwanaku sites in the south Huatta or Paucarcolla pampa raised-field areas. The site of Cerro Cupe, mentioned above, is on the road north of Paucarcolla-Santa Barbara and has a Tiwanaku component covering about two hectares. Another site discovered by Erickson in the Huatta pampa also has a Tiwanaku component.

In short, we can suggest an additional Tiwanaku enclave centered on the site of Paucarcolla-Santa Barbara that would have included several other smaller sites. This complex is on the principal road and is ideally situated to exploit the raised-field areas nearby. It is significant that the sites of Paucarcolla-Santa Barbara and Cerro Cupe have very high quantities of andesite and basalt hoes on the surface. Settlement of the Paucarcolla-Santa Barbara area appears to have been designed to maximize agricultural potential and maintain the economic trade links to the north.

The Juliaca Area

A large Tiwanaku site just north of Juliaca is the site known as Maravillas, which is at least five hectares in size, and possibly much larger. The site is next to the modern road and adjacent to a huge relict raised-field system. Large room blocks are evident on the low area below the hill, while at least some domestic terraces were occupied above. A low natural hill appears to have been modified with midden fill on the northern end of the site and may have been a civic-ceremonial construction associated with the Tiwanaku occupation. Finally, another Tiwanaku site has been reported by John Rowe (1956) at Huayna Roque near Juliaca.

Other Areas in the Titicaca Basin

The data suggest a number of Tiwanaku enclaves in the northern and northeast Titicaca Basin. We have known about the existence of Tiwanaku materials in the Ramis River, Huancané and Moho areas since at least the publication of Kidder (1943) and Tschopik (1946). There are also several Tiwanaku sites on the east side of the lake in the Omasuyu area.[2] There has not been much systematic work on the Tiwanaku occupation in this area with the exception of a survey conducted by the Instituto Nacional de Cultura of La Paz. Three Tiwanaku sites were found: two habitation sites and one cemetery (Faldín A. 1990: 87). Informal reconnaissance indicates that there are many more Tiwanaku sites near the lake, particularly in the Escoma region. The Tiwanaku occupation of the Omasuyu/Escoma area appears to have been similar or greater in population density to the Juli-Pomata area on the Peruvian side. These data suggest a major Tiwanaku provincial territory along the lake edge, with a particularly strong concentration of sites in the Escoma area along the Río Suches.

The Moquegua Tiwanaku Settlement System

The Moquegua Valley is about 150 kilometers from the Titicaca Basin, a walk of a few days. It is one of the principal valleys south of Arequipa and constituted one of the major provincial territories of the Tiwanaku state. There has been substantial research on the Tiwanaku occupation of the Moquegua Valley. Work by members of Programa Contisuyu in the 1980s and 1990s has defined a massive Tiwanaku presence in the valley, particularly during the Tiwanaku IV and V periods.

For the period immediately prior to the Tiwanaku occupation, McAndrews (1995) has described a very large number of relatively small sites that date to the Huancarane period (roughly equivalent to the Middle and Upper Formative periods in the Titicaca region). The Huancarane sites are distributed along the river in a pattern that suggests that agricultural maximization strategies were the major settlement determinants. Sites line an extensive set of canals that water the peripheries of the valley. The Huancarane population appears to have been a local one, derived from earlier, less complex societies that developed in this western slope drainage.

The first Tiwanaku occupation began in the late Tiwanaku IV period, characterized by a number of small sites along the agriculturally rich valley floor. These sites are small, but they are interpreted by Goldstein (1993a: 31) as being Tiwanaku colonies. According to Goldstein, sites such as M-12 represent small colonial enclaves in a context of local settlements. Goldstein bases his arguments on architectural and ceramic data from the sites. In particular, the Tiwanaku pottery styles are virtual reproductions of the Tiwanaku altiplano style, if not actual imports in some cases.

Around A.D. 750, there was an "explosion" of Tiwanaku V or Tiwanaku Expansive–related sites in the valley, according to Goldstein (1989a, 1989b, 1993a). In particular, the site complex of Omo, in the midvalley of the Moquegua drainage, represents a massive Tiwanaku colony. The local Tiwanaku V occupation is called the Chen Chen phase, named after a site immediately adjacent to the modern town of Moquegua. At Omo, the Chen Chen phase is found at the site of M-10, which has a major ceremonial structure described by Goldstein as "a set of three adobe-walled courts built on a stepped terreplane" with a "sunken central walled area surrounded by rectangular rooms" (Goldstein 1993a: 32). This architectural complex had a "striking facade of finely dressed stone," and a "rhomboidal

cemetery" area attached to the main platform construction. Associated with the ceremonial architecture is an area of at least nine hectares of domestic residence, characterized by sets of buildings with small plaza areas.

I agree with Goldstein and see the settlement dynamics of the Moquegua Valley as indicative of a transformation from a "loosely integrated string of colonies to a centrally governed provincial system" (Goldstein 1993a: 42). In other words, the Moquegua data elegantly define the creation of a provincial territory of Tiwanaku in an agriculturally productive and populated valley far away from the core territory. The initial occupation of Tiwanaku was characterized by small colonies among local populations. Over time, the local population was drawn into a Tiwanaku-controlled "breadbasket" complete with classic Tiwanaku civic-ceremonial architecture and a probable resident elite population.

Goldstein (1993a: 24) notes the profound similarities between the Omo corporate architecture and that at the capital itself, complete with "terraced platforms, sunken courts and doorways that restricted access"—key features of Tiwanaku elite-ceremonial architecture. In fact, he describes the Omo temple complex as a "miniaturized representation" of the homeland capital, a "mountain-like terraced platform [that] . . . played a significant role in the reproduction of Tiwanaku's ideology of power." Kolata agrees and observes that Omo "replicates the basic canons of Tiwanaku ceremonial architecture" (Kolata 1993: 267).

Significantly, there was a profound change in virtually all archaeological indicators in the Moquegua Valley during the Tiwanaku period, including settlement pattern shifts, architectural changes, and ceramic style changes to Tiwanaku canons. The data from Moquegua indicate a Tiwanaku colonial enclave of substantial proportions. Ironically, the archaeological data are stronger for the Tiwanaku presence in Moquegua than they are for the Inca, but we know from historical sources that this valley was a major Inca province.

The Tiwanaku Periphery

Cochabamba

Historic documents describe the Cochabamba area as one of the great colonies of the Inca state (Caballero 1984: 67; Wachtel 1982). It is a prime maize-producing zone and is relatively close to the Titicaca Basin, within several days' walking distance from the southeastern side of the lake. The combination of these factors indicates that the region was an important area for the complex polities of the Titicaca region.

The archaeological data for the earlier periods are far more ambiguous than data for the Inca period, however. The Tiwanaku pottery in Cochabamba is particularly distinctive and appears to represent a local style linked to Tiwanaku elite canons. This Cochabamba style was first defined by Bennett (1936). Caballero (1984: 71) suggests that the limit of Tiwanaku direct control is north of Cochabamba, although she offers no data for this hypothesis. She lists a series of sites with Tiwanaku-like ceramics in the Cochabamba area.

Anderson and Cespedes Paz (1998) have conducted extensive work in the region. They report that during the Middle Horizon there was a substantial change in the pottery assemblage in the Cochabamba Valley coincident with the Tiwanaku occupation: "The first clear and substantive transformation that occurred with Tiwanaku is that there was a vast increase in the number of types of painted ceramic styles that appeared including the appearance of imported Tiwanaku ceramics such as [the] black on red flaring bowl." Along with the importation of Tiwanaku pottery was a change in the local utilitarian wares as well. Anderson and Cespedes Paz report that the firing technologies shift to Tiwanaku types as well. These data strongly suggest that this foreign influence reached down to the level of household

production, which is more typical of actual colonization than long-distance exchange (Stanish 1992). Finally, a Tiwanaku-like hallucinogenic complex of artifacts began in the valley coincident with the appearance of Tiwanaku materials (Anderson and Cespedes Paz 1998: 4).

Higueras-Hare (1996) has also conducted extensive work in the region and concludes that that Tiwanaku influence was weak. However, my interpretation of his data suggests the contrary, that the area was linked to Tiwanaku by a variety of cultural ties. The data from the Cochabamba region indicate that there were substantial changes in settlement patterns, ceramic technology and style, ritual, and burial practices coincident with the beginning of Tiwanaku influence. These data suggest that Cochabamba was a direct enclave of the Tiwanaku state, the only one in the southeastern Titicaca Basin yet identified.

Larecaja/Muñecas (Mollo Area)

A number of sites with Tiwanaku-affiliated pottery have been discovered as far away as the Larecaja region of Bolivia. Work conducted by the Instituto Nacional de Cultura located a number of sites with Tiwanaku pottery in the Llika drainage of Muñecas and Larecaja. According to Faldín:

> The expansion of the Tiwanaku culture is typically represented by pottery remains of which we have located in 19 sites . . . also, evidence [for Tiwanaku presence] was found in the form of architectural or funerary remains especially in the valleys of Larecaja or Muñecas in the department of La Paz. The 19 sites represent mature or imperial Tiwanaku, that is to say in the Tiwanaku IV or V periods. . . . The ceramic remains from the sites of Muchha Cruz and Tambo Kusi are the most representative of the Classic period. (Faldín A. 1990: 79–80)

The pottery from these sites is related to the Cochabamba styles and is characterized by Tiwanaku-derived motifs and a narrow base form. The large number of domestic sites and large quantity of fine Tiwanaku pottery, combined with an apparent absence of a contemporary non-Tiwanaku ceramic tradition, would suggest that the Larecaja/Muñecas area was colonized by Tiwanaku.

Arequipa

A number of sites in the Arequipa area have Tiwanaku pottery on the surface. The Majes River valley appears to be the northernmost extension of Tiwanaku influence. It is significant that there are Wari sites in the area as well. Unfortunately, very little work has been published on the Tiwanaku occupation of the Arequipa area. It is significant that a major source of obsidian for Tiwanaku was located in the Colca Valley near Chivay (Burger et al. 1998), a source most likely controlled by Arequipa-area polities. We do not know the nature of Tiwanaku presence in the region, but the little evidence accumulated and published to date suggests a Tiwanaku enclave. This proposition remains to be tested with future research.

Far Southern Peru/Northern Chile Coast

The valleys of Caplina, Lluta, Sama, Locumba, and Azapa comprise the western coastal valleys of the south-central Andes. There are a number of Tiwanaku-affiliated sites throughout these valleys (Berenguer, Castro and Silva 1980; Berenguer and Dauelsberg 1988; Focacci 1969, 1982; Mujica 1985; Mujica, Rivera, and Lynch 1983; Muñoz O. 1983b; Vela Velarde 1992). With the exception of Azapa, there have been few systematic tests of the political and economic relationships between this area and the altiplano. In the case of Azapa, Goldstein conducted reconnaissance and reviewed the existing evidence for the Tiwanaku occupation and concluded that there was "a small altiplano Tiwanaku colonial presence, among a far more numerous local substrate. Although actual Tiwanaku residence was limited to ex-

tremely small enclaves, privileged Tiwanaku styles in material culture supplanted local preferences" (Goldstein 1995–1996: 67). Goldstein points out the differences between Azapa and Moquegua. In the latter, the colony was characterized by the construction of large corporate architecture. In Azapa, he suggests that the relationship between the Tiwanaku agents and the local population was based on "diplomacy and subtle interaction." In other words, the Tiwanaku presence in Azapa, according to Goldstein, was qualitatively distinct from that in Moquegua. Tiwanaku presence in Azapa is best seen as a kind of barrio of foreigners permitted by the local people, for whatever reason, to live and interact in the region.

We do not know if there was a direct political relationship between the other southern valleys and Tiwanaku. Present data suggest that the other valleys were not directly incorporated into the Tiwanaku political orbit but did maintain economic and possibly social relations with the capital. Regardless of the precise relationship between Tiwanaku and these areas, there is no doubt that Tiwanaku had access to minerals, agricultural products, ores, and human labor of the western coastal valleys in at least its later stages of expansion. These sites, at the very least, were part of an integrated political network designed to secure economic access to the western slopes.

San Pedro de Atacama

There is general agreement that San Pedro de Atacama was not a colony of Tiwanaku but an autonomous polity economically linked to the Tiwanaku state (Orellana 1985; Winter, Benavente J. A., and Massone M. 1985; but see Oakland 1993). Berenguer, Castro, and Silva (1980) have noted that in San Pedro, Tiwanaku artifacts tend to be of a more ritual nature, including gold keros, hats, and the like. Snuff tablets are very common and make up what Constantino Torres and William Conklin (1995: 79) describe as "intimate and portable" Tiwanaku art in this desert oasis. Instead of a colonial presence, most scholars have suggested an interaction sphere model for the relationship between San Pedro and Tiwanaku. The nature of this interaction has been suggested to range from shared iconographic styles to more formal exchange relationships. This indirect, noncolonial model is supported by the large number of foreign objects in tombs, with the most common objects being Tiwanaku in style (Torres and Conklin 1995: 83). Such a pattern of exotic artifact distribution in funerary contexts, instead of domestic ones, fits the criteria that I believe support models of exchange, not colonization (Stanish 1989a, 1992).

My own interpretation is that Tiwanaku maintained an exchange relationship with the San Pedro elite (and see Orellana R. 1985). Torres and Conklin (1995: 96) argue that trade was not a component of this relationship. They point out that there is little that the population of San Pedro could have traded back, with the possible exception of salt and copper. I agree that these two commodities are available in the Titicaca Basin and are unlikely trade goods. Certain portable minerals may have been important, particularly sodalite. However, the most important commodity that San Pedro has is its location and water. This oasis would have been a prime rest area for camelid caravans. There would have been a strong economic incentive for Tiwanaku traders to exchange high-valued commodities for access to food, water, and rest in a manner similar to other strategically located desert oases around the world. From this perspective, the ability to create and maintain long-distance exchange relationships with an area as distant as San Pedro indicates a complex political and economic organization in the Tiwanaku state.

Cuzco Area

The site of Batan Urqo contains pottery that is in a Tiwanaku style, and other Tiwanaku-like pottery is found in the Cuzco area (Bauer 1999: 145). There is little doubt that these pieces were trade wares and do not represent Tiwanaku colonies. Cuzco represents the northernmost extension of Tiwanaku materials and is squarely within the Tiwanaku periphery and in the Wari heartland. Tiwanaku did not directly control territory farther north than Juliaca. The presence of Tiwanaku and Tiwanaku-related pottery north of this area is best interpreted to represent exchange patterns between the core and heartland of Tiwanaku in the Titicaca Basin and its periphery.

Tiwanaku Economic Patterns

Raised-Field Agriculture and the Tiwanaku State

Raised-field production is considered to be one of the primary, if not the most important, economic underpinnings of the Tiwanaku state. There was little or no indigenous raised-field use in the Titicaca Basin in the 1990s, except for those field tracts sponsored by outside institutions. Raised fields appear to be largely an archaeological phenomenon, one associated most directly with the Tiwanaku state and pre-Tiwanaku complex polities.

The Juli-Pomata settlement survey provides the best quantitative data on the relationship between raised fields and the Tiwanaku state. Analysis of the data indicates that the major use of raised fields is correlated with the rise and collapse of complex political systems, the exception being that of the Inca state. During the Early Sillumocco (Middle Formative), for instance, in which political organization was not complex, the percentage of raised-field populations compared with non-raised-field ones was approximately 41 percent to 59 percent. During the Late Sillumocco and Tiwanaku periods, during which complex chiefly and archaic state political systems dominated the region's cultural landscape, this pattern was almost reversed, with 57 to 69 percent of the population living in the raised-field areas, and 31 to 43 percent in the non-raised-field areas. At its height, 69 percent of the Late Sillumocco population was living in the raised-field zone. This figure drops in the Tiwanaku period, but the absolute number of people increased in the field areas, suggesting, perhaps, that the productive limits of raised-field agriculture had been reached.

I believe that the Late Sillumocco– and Tiwanaku-period settlement distribution represented a strategy by complex polities designed to maximize agricultural production (see Stanish 1994). During these two periods, large settlements were strategically located along the periphery of the fields in association with aqueducts and canals. Roughly 57 to 69 percent of the population was concentrated in raised-field areas, with only a small fraction (4 to 6 percent) in the puna. It is very likely that the elite during these periods maintained extensive camelid populations in areas more suited to large-scale herding. In these periods, the political elite organized labor to extract surplus; the most effective means of extracting surplus in the Tiwanaku period was to intensify existing technologies, specifically raised-field agriculture.

Contrary to the hydraulic hypothesis of an earlier generation, the elite were not necessary for management of the raised fields. Rather, they either provided incentives or coerced the nonelite populations into increasing agricultural production using existing raised-field technology. Raised fields in complex political contexts represented by the Late Sillumocco and Tiwanaku periods are best understood as a form of staple finance as defined by Earle and D'Altroy (1992; Johnson and Earle 1987) for Andean political economies.

The data indicate that the Tiwanaku state utilized raised fields as one of the primary components of its economic strategies in the heartland. There is very strong evidence that the vast majority of raised fields in the western and southern Titicaca Basin were built or co-opted by Tiwanaku after A.D. 600. Furthermore, it is no coincidence that the major Tiwanaku enclaves were all located next to raised-field areas.

Rain-Fed Agriculture

All of the available evidence suggests that rain-fed terrace agriculture was a major component of the Tiwa-

naku economy. This conclusion is based largely upon settlement distribution in areas that could only support agriculture on terraces, as in the Juli-Pomata region. I have suggested above that terraced agriculture began as early as the Middle Formative. It is not surprising, therefore, that Tiwanaku sites consistently are located near agricultural terraces. It is also telling that many Tiwanaku domestic structures were built on terraces, indicating that the leveling of steep slopes was a principal engineering and architectural technique in the region.

Camelid Raising

There is abundant evidence of intensive camelid use during the Tiwanaku period. Excavations at the site of Tiwanaku itself indicate a heavy reliance on camelid meat. Excavations at other sites, from Tumatumani (Stanish and Steadman 1994) in the western Titicaca Basin to Pucara in the north, discovered butchered camelid remains throughout the archaeological levels (Franco Inojosa 1940).

Based on the archaeological record, there is little doubt that camelids were used for wool, food, and as pack animals from very early on. The significant question is when did the corralling and maintenance of large herds begin? In the Juli-Pomata survey, the total percentage of the population living in the puna grazing lands was lowest during the Upper Formative and Tiwanaku periods (around 5 percent). This suggests either that larger herds were kept elsewhere, or that the populations maintained extensive relationships with herders much farther out in the puna. The areas about five to fifteen kilometers away from the lake were optimal areas for grazing. Here vast areas of pampa could support large herds, and it is here that the existence of large "state" herds is hypothesized.

Commodity Production

There is significant evidence of obsidian tool manufacture in the Tiwanaku IV and V periods throughout the Titicaca region. The site of Tumatumani near Juli has a number of obsidian artifacts that date to the Late Formative and Tiwanaku IV and V periods. Seddon (1994) analyzed the lithic artifacts from the site and concluded that the obsidian projectile points were manufactured elsewhere. It is significant that the patterns for the Upper Formative period seem to hold for the Tiwanaku period as well. In other words, the people at Tumatumani received obsidian bifaces from an exchange network in the region.

Albarracin-Jordan (1992: 175, 225) has located a site in the lower Tiwanaku Valley that has abundant surface obsidian. Excavations at the site of LV-109 (also named Obsidiana) indicated a sporadic occupation from the late Tiwanaku IV period through the post-Tiwanaku Early Pacajes. Albarracin-Jordan did not discover any workshop area, but the surface indications suggest a focus on obsidian tool production. Also, the site of Punanave was a major workshop for basalt, andesite, and possibly other lithic raw materials.

Metal tools and objects of art were manufactured at Tiwanaku. The builders of Tiwanaku used metal clamps to hold the large blocks together (Ponce 1994). Graffam (1992) has discussed at length the great copper deposits in the Atacama Desert of Chile. He has discovered a number of sites with copper ores and evidence of smelting dating back to pre-Tiwanaku times. Based on these data, Graffam and others have suggested that the northern Chilean desert and foothills were a major source of copper for the Tiwanaku state (Graffam, Rivera, and Carevič 1996). There has been insufficient research on the sources of Tiwanaku copper to state definitively where the sources were for metalworking. One copper source has recently been discovered near the Desaguadero River at a site called Chincane. The source is eroding out of a small quebrada that cuts through the hilly flanks facing the river. A major (four-hectare) Tiwanaku habitation known as La Casilla is approximately one kilometer away (Stanish et al. 1997) and also has abundant copper ore lying on the surface. These two sites have not been intensively investigated; however, the complex is a likely source for Tiwanaku copper.

Although systematic analysis of excavation data remains in a very preliminary state, there is evidence of highly specialized ceramic production areas at the site of Tiwanaku and satellite settlements. Rivera C. (1994) has identified a sector of Tiwanaku itself, known as Chiji Jawira, which was probably a ceramic workshop. It is a low mound, covering an area slightly larger than one hectare. According to Rivera, the site has a high density of pottery and wasters on the surface, and excavations revealed the remains of domestic activity as well. The evidence in the excavations suggests that firing techniques were relatively informal, using shallow pits and dung and grass as fuels. The existence of adobe building foundations also supports the notion that there were specialized potters living in the Chiji Jawira. Importantly, Rivera notes that the area was occupied in late Tiwanaku IV and Tiwanaku V times, from approximately A.D. 700 to 1000. This would correspond to the height of Tiwanaku expansion throughout the Titicaca region.

Janusek (1999) argues that the Chiji Jawira data indicate the existence of a specialized craft production area. He characterizes the residents as "a group that performed both domestic and craft activities. Situated in the far outskirts of Tiwanaku, it [Chiji Jawira] was ideally located for ceramic production, near a semipermanent water supply and down site from the prevailing northwest winds" (Janusek 1999: 114–115). Based on a detailed analysis of pottery styles, cranial deformation, botanical remains, and other data, Janusek argues that the Chiji Jawira people were able to maintain their own social identity in this urban environment. The pottery is stylistically linked to the Cochabamba area to the southeast, raising the real possibility that residents from a distant part of the circum-Titicaca Basin were living on the outskirts of Tiwanaku, maintaining a distinctive regional identity in their own "barrio" and participating in the state political economy through the specialized manufacture of pottery.

Janusek (1993, 1999) has identified a bone pan pipe or flute *(sikus,* or *zampoñas)* production area at the site of Lukurmata. He argues that this represents a case of specialized production at the domestic level— most likely specialists attached to an elite group at the urban site. The excavated area, known as Misitón I, dates to around A.D. 800. The manufacture of this highly specialized product in what appears to be an artisan area in an otherwise domestic context is quite significant. It suggests that one group of people were engaged in an economic activity other than agriculture or pastoralism for a significant percentage of their time. It also suggests that the Tiwanaku state induced economic intensification at secondary centers such as Lukurmata in what otherwise were domestic areas.

There was a brisk trade between Tiwanaku and its provincial and peripheral territories. Research has indicated that Tiwanaku imported obsidian, copper, sodalite, and possibly maize. We can only surmise what Tiwanaku provided in return. Certainly, the fine Tiwanaku textiles recovered from sites on the coast would most likely have been a highly prized commodity. Likewise, Tiwanaku pottery and possibly wooden objects, such as *rapé* (or snuff) tablets, would have been highly prized.

Hallucinogens were an important commodity imported by the Tiwanaku state. Analysis of residue from rapé tablets from coastal Chile unequivocally demonstrate that mescaline-type plants were used by Tiwanaku populations (Torres 1985). There is a whole complex of drug paraphernalia associated with Tiwanaku and post-Tiwanaku populations in the south-central Andes. Kolata interprets a flowering plant on the Bennett stela at Tiwanaku to be a hallucinogenic cactus (Berenguer 1985; Kolata 1993: 139); it was placed there alongside maize, a llama, a kero, and other motifs of profound importance to Tiwanaku

society. Wassen discovered a cave dated to be roughly contemporary with Tiwanaku that had implements associated with hallucinogenic substances (Wassen 1972). It seems likely that these drugs were provided to lower elite and commoners in the great feasts that would have periodically occurred at the site of Tiwanaku and other primary and secondary regional centers. As such, they would constitute an important component in the complex exchange relationships between elite and commoner, and would have been an important exotic commodity imported by the Tiwanaku polity during its height.

Lake Exploitation

Virtually every Tiwanaku midden excavated in the Titicaca region contains abundant fish remains. Likewise, most Tiwanaku sites in the Juli-Pomata area are within a few kilometers of the lake. It is obvious that the lake was a major resource for the Tiwanaku peoples. We can surmise that it provided not only fish but also totora reeds for construction and food, algae for fodder and possibly fertilizer, and other goods as well. There has been insufficient work on the paleofaunal and paleobotanical remains from Tiwanaku contexts, but there is little doubt that the lake was a major source of food and industrial plants during the Tiwanaku period in the region.

Historical Relationships between Upper Formative Polities and Tiwanaku

The most important observation concerning the relationship between the Upper Formative– and Tiwanaku-period cultures is that they were highly varied across the south-central Andes. In some areas, there was great continuity between the Upper Formative polities and the appearance of Tiwanaku state influence; in others, there was little continuity.

The strongest continuity between Upper Formative cultures and Tiwanaku is in the Titicaca Basin south of the Ilave River in the west, and south of the

Suches River in the east. This corresponds to the core and heartland territory of Tiwanaku. This observation is supported by research at sites such as Chiripa, Lukurmata, Pajchiri, and the regional centers in the Juli-Pomata area. Here, there is substantial continuity in architectural, economic, settlement, artistic, and political patterns. Excavations in Tumatumani and Sillumocco-Huaquina near Juli, for instance, demonstrate that the Tiwanaku occupation was characterized by the rebuilding of earlier Late Sillumocco stepped pyramids. That is, there were two distinct construction episodes that dated to Late Sillumocco and Tiwanaku times. Recently completed excavations at Palermo (de la Vega 1997) confirm this historical pattern for this regional center as well. These data support the hypothesis that the Tiwanaku state expanded into an already complex political and economic system south of the Ilave River and incorporated these into a complex, and highly organized political and economic system.

In contrast, Steadman (1995) notes that Tiwanaku sites north of the Ilave tend to be much reduced in size (the Puno Bay is an exception) and complexity compared to the Upper Formative settlements that preceded them. In his survey, Frye noted that the site of Incatunuhuiri had a major Upper Formative occupation but that the Tiwanaku settlement had been restricted to the basal terraces.

The northern Titicaca Basin presents one of the most interesting problems regarding Tiwanaku expansion. Mujica (1978) sees the development of Tiwanaku out of Pukara, which in turn had developed out of Chiripa. This model assumes a more or less direct historical sequence of these three cultures, based upon a stylistic analysis of the ceramic and other iconographic styles in the immediate pre-Tiwanaku cultures. However, it can be argued that Pucara, Late Chiripa, and Kalasasaya were at least partially contemporary, and that Late Chiripa, or a Chiripa-derived culture, and Kalasasaya were the antecedents to Qeya in the southern basin. Pucara col-

lapsed around A.D. 200, contemporary with the beginning of Qeya. I would agree in part with Mujica and see the collapse of Pucara as correlated with the development of Tiwanaku as a polity that expanded out of its core territory. However, the data suggest that there was an indirect relationship at best because of Tiwanaku's inability to act as a major competitor to Pucara prior to the latter's collapse. If competition did occur between Pucara at its height and the early period of Tiwanaku expansion, it would have occurred in the periphery of both polities' area of influence.

If we accept that the collapse of Pucara occurred no later than A.D. 400, and that the Tiwanaku state did not have political control of the area north of Ilave except for some enclaves in Puno and along the road system up to Juliaca, then there existed a polity that continued after Pucara collapsed and survived as a contemporary to Tiwanaku in the northern basin. This polity was outside Tiwanaku control and developed directly into the Colla señorío of the twelfth to fifteenth centuries A.D. This polity was Late Huaña.

The existence of a Pucara-derived polity that existed between approximately A.D. 600 and 1100 and that was independent from Tiwanaku (or, for that matter, Wari to the north) is supported by settlement and ceramic data. It is hypothesized that Tiwanaku enclaves existed within or adjacent to autonomous polities and that some economic exchange was carried on between these polities, collectively referred to as the Late Huaña culture, and the Tiwanaku enclaves.

The Late Huaña culture developed directly out of the Early Huaña culture described above for the Upper Formative period. The Wari site of Cerro Baúl in Moquegua serves as an appropriate analogy for the type of political and economic interaction of these groups. In this model, a foreign state polity establishes an enclave and road network in a particular area. That polity has sufficient resources to control the road and its colony but has insufficient resources or lacks the resolve to control the territory as a province. The enclave remains relatively isolated from the rest of the area, with few formal political and economic relationships with the local populations. Without formal relationships, there is little or no circulation of ritually and politically significant objects, such as pottery, textiles, carved stone, and the like. Therefore, there would be little Tiwanaku pottery found outside the enclaves.

At present, there is little systematic data that describes the Late Huaña cultural materials. A number of sites that have Middle and Upper Formative pottery fragments also have Altiplano-period styles and an occasional Tiwanaku fragment. Assuming that the sites were continuously occupied, the pottery assemblage is most likely a derivative of the Early Huaña styles defined above. The occasional Tiwanaku fragments are compelling. The site of Unocollo, for instance, located on the Río Ayabacas northwest of Juliaca, is a good example (Stanish et al. 1999). This site is very similar to Tiwanaku domestic Type 3 and Type 4 sites in the region. It is built on a hillside, with several large, wide domestic terraces that face a major river. Pottery from the site includes a handful of decorated, locally made Tiwanaku sherds, numerous Late Intermediate fragments, and domestic and other better-made types that are not Late Intermediate period. These latter fragments have pastes similar to Upper Formative and Tiwanaku types but are not decorated. I suggest that this is the Late Huaña assemblage, a date confirmed by the presence of a few Tiwanaku fragments. The Late Huaña assemblage is not characterized by substantial numbers of local decorated polychromes, perhaps due to the fact that the political economy of these sites was not sufficiently complex to support pottery specialization.

It is also possible that some pottery types traditionally viewed as only Altiplano period in date may actually date to Late Huaña and/or Altiplano. This is particularly true for several variants of the Collao black-on-red type first described by Tschopik (1946).

Our reconnaissance has discovered a wide range of styles that fit within this general type, which Tschopik called a series. These data suggest that some of the black-on-red types, particularly those jar forms that have very straight sides that are similar to Tiwanaku keros, are most likely Late Huaña in date. A number of sites have pottery that is suggestive of kero forms but is undecorated and poorly manufactured. These are most likely Late Huaña in date. Given the existence of the Tiwanaku enclaves that were confined to a limited geographical area, there would have been some kind of local Middle Horizon culture, but the nature of this culture remains to be defined.

The Ideology of Imperial Expansion: Art and Architecture

Ceramic art, textile art, and architecture were some of the great achievements of the Tiwanaku peoples. The most dramatic artistic development in the Tiwanaku period is the use of several ancient symbols in the central Andes. The dominant symbols in classic Tiwanaku-period art include an anthropomorphic motif called the Staff God (Front-Face Deity) and several zoomorphic motifs, including the puma, condor, and llama. These symbols are found on a variety of media including ceramic vessels, textiles, stone, wood, and bone. Tiwanaku art thus represents the creation of a coherent system of elite symbols associated with an expansive polity. Cook has convincingly argued that the Staff God represents a symbol correlated to the development of expansionist states in the central Andes, including Chavín, Tiwanaku, and Wari (Cook 1994).

Tiwanaku architectural style is derived from earlier Upper Formative cultures in the region. The unique contribution of Tiwanaku is the transformation of these elements into an imperial artistic style imposed on subject populations throughout the Titicaca region and beyond.[3] Tiwanaku, like most states throughout the Andes, reworked these ancient elements into a recognizable set of canons that conveyed Tiwanaku power throughout the south-central Andes. In this light, it is significant that the collapse of Tiwanaku paralleled the collapse of these architectural and artistic canons. The post-Tiwanaku señoríos of the Colla, Lupaqa, and Pacajes did not construct pyramids, enclosures, or subterranean courts. At Palermo, for instance, the post-Tiwanaku population used the sunken court as a corral. It is also significant that there is no Tiwanaku monolithic sculpture outside the core territory. These monoliths were intimately associated with the ruling elite at Tiwanaku itself and in its immediate core territory. Tiwanaku monoliths are found at the capital, Lukurmata, Khonko Wancané, Quellamarka, and a few other sites in the core territory but not elsewhere. This contrasts with the Upper Formative period, in which Pucara and Early Tiwanaku sculpture was found around the basin. In short, these architectural and artistic elements were intimately tied to the existence of numerous complex political systems in the Titicaca Basin of which Tiwanaku was the most successful. When Tiwanaku came to dominate the political landscape, monolithic stone working ceased in areas outside Tiwanaku's core.

Tiwanaku Provincial Pottery Styles

Tiwanaku provincial pottery, at least in the Juli-Pomata area, was locally produced imitations of the imperial style. One of the hallmarks of the Tiwanaku occupation in the area is that all stylistic borrowing on pottery was from Tiwanaku. There is no obvious local innovation in style. In other words, coincident with the expansion of Tiwanaku in at least this area, the source of all artistic canons shifted to Tiwanaku itself.

The Tiwanaku pottery is characterized by predominantly black-on-red or black-on-orange decorations, Tiwanaku polychromes, and black and white decorations on red or orange slips. The most com-

mon shapes are keros and tazones. Keros are found with and without bands around the body. Incense burners are also a common item in the Tiwanaku ceramic assemblage in the region.

The vast majority of Tiwanaku pottery in the Juli-Pomata area would be classified as Tiwanaku IV and Tiwanaku V in the Bennett-Ponce typology. Significantly, the repertoire of designs from these surface finds is quite limited compared with those published by Bennett (1934), Ponce (1981), Alconini (1993), and Janusek (1994) for Tiwanaku sites in the core territory. The typical Tiwanaku base slips—red, orange, and brown—are found on all sites. Polished black ware (Bennett 1934: 396) is very rare, and virtually no incised black wares were found on survey, although a few were found in excavations at the site of Sillumocco-Huaquina. Black, orange, and white are used in the designs, generally as independent design elements. This latter design practice is described by Bennett as a characteristic of the Decadent, or latest, phase of Tiwanaku (Bennett 1934: 456).

The two most common decorative motifs on the Tiwanaku materials from the study area are the perpendicular wavy line and the step pattern. Flamingo motifs are also found in the survey area; Bennett (1934: 401–402) considered these bird designs to be late. Occasionally, keros and tazones have interior decoration on the rim, particularly the common perpendicular wavy line. We found very few typical classic Tiwanaku designs such as condors, trophy heads, and front-face deities. Only a small fraction of the pieces showed evidence of having more than three colors ("two-color ware" in Bennett's stylistic classification [1934: 397–398]). Plastic decoration on Tiwanaku forms includes a number of pieces characterized by raised punctuate necklace decorations identical to those described by Bermann (1990: 503) from Lukurmata in Bolivia. We also found olla or jar handles with a raised cross motif. This motif is also found in Moquegua in Tiwanaku-related contexts (Stanish 1991: 30).

The nature of the pottery in the Juli-Pomata region suggests a polity incorporated into the Tiwanaku orbit relatively early in the expansion process, probably around A.D. 600. A small fraction of the decorated Tiwanaku fine-ware pottery in the Juli-Pomata region was not local, and the same observation holds for the assemblage from Isla Esteves. It is most likely that the state canons of ceramic art were expressed in pieces manufactured by local potters, but a small but significant number of pieces were from either the capital of Tiwanaku itself, or from a production center outside these two provincial territories.

Goldstein (1989b) also found a variety of Tiwanaku styles in the Tiwanaku colony of Omo in the Moquegua Valley. In other enclaves, such as in the Puno area, there appears to be a greater variety of Tiwanaku pottery. Thus there appear to be some differences in the repertoire of design elements and forms in each of the enclaves, the significance of which we do not understand. Local potters either chose certain styles over others, or were given a restricted range of styles to produce for local use. It is likely that the differences in pottery styles in each of the enclaves reflects the varied nature by which the state interacted with these areas.

Possible Tiwanaku Tomb Styles

To date, all documented Tiwanaku tombs are belowground, round cist tombs. There is some compelling evidence from the Island of the Sun that Tiwanaku and Formative tombs were more elaborate. Bandelier first described the site of Sicuyu (1910: 228), where he noted that "the entire promontory, on its upper plane, which stands twenty feet above the Lake, contains stone cysts [sic] of Chullpa type. . . . they are all quadrangular; then they are encased by thin slabs set upright in the ground, and most of them had covers." The existence of quadrangular tombs is rare indeed, and judging by some of Bandelier's drawings, these were in fact rectangular slab-cist tombs with

covers. These have not been noted on any survey to date in the Titicaca region.

In our survey of this site (Bauer and Stanish 2001), we discovered only Tiwanaku and pre-Tiwanaku pottery on the surface. If Bandelier's observation about the tomb architecture is correct, then we have the only Middle Formative– and Tiwanaku-period tombs ever fully described for a site outside a large population center. Our research revealed that all traces of the upright slabs had been lost or incorporated into modern walls and agricultural terraces. These data would suggest that, in fact, these pre-Altiplano-period tombs were rectangular, slab-lined, and possibly even slightly above ground. This would contrast substantially with the more common round, belowground cist tombs known for earlier periods, and suggests that Tiwanaku tombs were distinct from later tomb styles.

Pilgrimage Route to the Island of the Sun

The Tiwanaku state developed a rich suite of art and architectural canons that represented a state ideology. Tiwanaku state art and architecture comprised a codified set of beliefs that served the interests of Tiwanaku's elite as well as provincial supporters. There is also evidence that the Tiwanaku state created the first state-sponsored pilgrimage destination in the southern Titicaca Basin. Documents from the sixteenth and seventeenth centuries, as well as archaeological research on the Inca state, indicate that the Islands of the Sun and Moon were the final destination for a great pan-Andean pilgrimage route at the time of Spanish contact. Archaeological evidence suggests that the Tiwanaku state also maintained a pilgrimage center on the islands.

The Island of the Sun area was first used in a systematic manner as a ritual pilgrimage destination by the Tiwanaku state. Survey data, as seen in map 8.4, indicate a number of Tiwanaku sites in a line between Apachinaca and Chucaripupata, the latter of which is located near the Sacred Rock. This pattern is highly suggestive of a road and would therefore constitute the first evidence for any kind of formalized pilgrimage route from the historically known landing place on the south of the island to the Sacred Rock area in the north. In fact, these sites are found along a modern trail that has stone walls in a number of sections. These walls are from the original road. Where sections of the Prehispanic road exist, it is approximately two meters wide, begins at least at Apachinaca, continues along the ridge above Challa and Kasapata, and drops down to the area of Chucaripupata. Curiously, there is no line of Tiwanaku sites along the low, eastern side of the island where the Inca road was constructed much later.

It is during the Tiwanaku period that the first major site with corporate architecture was constructed in the Titikala area: the site of Chucaripupata. It is also significant that the population of the northern end of the island increased along with a simultaneous aggregation of population into Chucaripupata. In the Tiwanaku period, therefore, there were two principal population centers on the Island of the Sun. One can best be interpreted as the political center, in the Challa area. The second center was the site of Chucaripupata, best interpreted as the focus of political and religious ritual.

Excavations from the Island of the Moon indicate that the site of Iñak Uyu was occupied in the Tiwanaku period as well (Bauer and Stanish 2001). There is solid evidence of a major Tiwanaku occupation beneath the Inca one. This is significant in that both the Island of the Moon and the Titikala area were used during the Tiwanaku period. The fact that substantial numbers of ritually significant objects dating to the Tiwanaku period (incensarios, finely made keros, and so forth) were discovered at Iñak Uyu supports the hypothesis that a ritual pilgrimage complex had been established on the island at least by Tiwanaku times.

The accumulated data strongly suggest that the Islands of the Sun and Moon were incorporated into the Tiwanaku state around the middle of the first millennium A.D. Simultaneous with the control of the islands was the creation of the first formalized pilgrimage route in the region. Prior to this time, the Titikala area and the Island of the Moon were important huacas in the local Upper Formative polity, but there is no evidence of a pan-regional pilgrimage complex of significance beyond the islands and Copacabana area. In the Tiwanaku period, in contrast, the ritual destination complex, complete with major architectural constructions and possible attendant populations, was first established. The incorporation of the Islands of the Sun and Moon and the creation of a pilgrimage route would have been an integral part of the process of Tiwanaku imperialism as it expanded throughout the Titicaca region and beyond.

The Relationship between Wari and Tiwanaku

As early as 1553, Cieza proposed that Tiwanaku and Wari were built by the same people (Cieza 1959 [1553]: 458; and see Isbell and McEwan 1991: 1; and Schreiber 1992: 80). Andeanists are very familiar with the subsequent history of research on "Coastal Tiahuanaco," Wari sites that were lumped in as part of the Tiwanaku phenomenon, particularly by Uhle and Kroeber, based on some vague similarities in design motifs on pottery. The discovery of the Pacheco cache of Wari pottery in Nasca by Tello further convinced many that Tiwanaku was the origin of this style (Isbell and McEwan 1991: 3). With the later work by Tello, and the publication of the site by Rowe, Collier, and Willey in 1950, the differences in Wari and Tiwanaku styles became more obvious. Schreiber nicely sums up these differences:

> There is a clear distinction between the distribution of Wari styles, and the distribution of Tiwanaku styles. Although the two cultures shared certain aspects of iconography (Cook 1985), there are important stylistic differences between the respective depictions, and they

are expressed in largely different media. The primary examples of Tiwanaku iconography are expressed in stone sculpture. In the case of Wari, such stone carving is unknown, and the iconography is expressed in an entirely different medium: ceramics. . . . Tiwanaku iconography was expressed in a nonportable medium: to see it, one had to go to the center. Wari iconography, on the other hand, was expressed in portable media: it could be transported long distances and seen by people who would never go to the center. The iconography of Tiwanaku also contrasts with that of Wari in that it is closely associated with medicinal (or drug-related) paraphernalia: snuff tablets, bone tubes, and so forth. These artifacts are unknown in the Wari sphere, and this aspect of Tiwanaku culture further distinguishes it from the Wari culture. (Schreiber 1992: 79)

Although one could argue that Tiwanaku pottery and wooden snuff tablets indeed carry state iconography as well, it is true that Tiwanaku stonework and architecture are the most pronounced expression of its art. There are other differences as well. One of the most dramatic is that Wari built many of their settlements with stone walls, whereas all Tiwanaku sites outside the capital, and most of the capital itself, were constructed with adobe superstructures over stone foundations. At the capital of Tiwanaku, the major buildings were indeed faced or built with stone. But fully three-quarters of the site was constructed with adobe.

These contrasting building styles are not just a response to environmental conditions. It is true that adobe is probably a superior building material in the altiplano. However, it is not a coincidence that the later Inca peoples constructed their buildings in the Titicaca Basin with stone, yet the local populations continued the Tiwanaku adobe traditions. In Moquegua, at the Tiwanaku colony of Omo, buildings were made from adobe with stone foundations. Yet, at Cerro Baúl, the Wari colony located in essentially the same environment, the stone construction technique was used. Both the Inca and Wari used a cen-

tral highland tradition of stone wall construction (*pirca*), with Tiwanaku using cut stones only in very special buildings. There is, to my knowledge, no standing Tiwanaku building made of uncut fieldstone or pirca architecture. Certainly, there is nothing that approaches the kind of architecture built during the so-called Great Walls Construction Phase of Wari (Isbell, Brewster-Wray, and Spickard 1993: 51). The vast majority of Tiwanaku construction was executed in the altiplano tradition of adobe walls on low stone foundations only one or two courses high.

Isbell, Brewster-Wray, and Spickard (1993: 50) suggest that the semisubterranean temple at Moraduchayuq was constructed by Tiwanaku masons. They also note, however, the significant differences in this temple from those at Tiwanaku. Based upon Knobloch's (1991) date for iconographic changes at Wari, they argue that "Tiahuanaco stone technology was adopted briefly without any evidence for the adoption of religious ideology or social organization that would accompany influential elites, whether religious or secular" (Isbell, Brewster-Wray, and Spickard 1993: 50).

The pottery from Wari and Tiwanaku both draw off some earlier iconographic traditions, but the repertoire of Tiwanaku motifs is substantially different from Wari (see Alconini 1993). Likewise, the forms are very different (Conklin 1991: 290). Although both Wari and Tiwanaku fine-ware pottery probably functioned, in part, as a component of reciprocal relationships between elite and commoner, the difference in forms suggests that the pottery was used in different social and political contexts, reflecting contrasting modes of state organization.

Regarding the architecture of the two cultures, Conklin (1991: 286) notes that "the diagnostic elements of Huari empire architecture seem to be entirely different from those of Tiahuanaco." In particular, he notes that Wari attempted to create self-contained architectural spaces rather than "place[s] of ritual passage" as evident in Tiwanaku. Of course, it is possible that similar self-contained architecture, constructed in adobe, could have characterized the area outside the architectural core and Tiwanaku. In fact, work by Janusek (1994, 1999) and others at Tiwanaku and Lukurmata has uncovered large areas of residential architecture that may have been built in a series of self-contained compounds. But Conklin's significant point is that the architectural core of Tiwanaku indicates a level of site planning designed for ritual movement that is not evident in Wari.

The distribution of Wari and Tiwanaku artifacts throughout the central Andes overlaps in only a few places—Moquegua and Arequipa being the most notable examples—and in at least the Moquegua area, the physical separation is quite dramatic. By and large, both polities appear to have controlled areas outside each other's territory. The Wari and Tiwanaku states are best interpreted as two virtually autonomous polities that coexisted for several hundred years without any significant interaction between them.

Summary

At the beginning of the first millennium A.D., Tiwanaku and Pucara were the two great powers in the Titicaca Basin. By A.D. 400, Tiwanaku stood alone. By A.D. 650, Tiwanaku had become a great capital city, and the Tiwanaku polity had expanded outside its core territory. The site of Lukurmata came under Tiwanaku sway around A.D. 600 (Janusek 1999:

116). The Tiwanaku peoples incorporated the Island of the Sun by the mid-seventh century and established the Esteves Island center around the same time (Núñez and Paredes 1978). At about the same time, or even a bit earlier, a Tiwanaku colony was established in Moquegua (Goldstein 1993a: 31). By A.D. 800–900, Tiwanaku dominated a large area across the south-central Andes, and artifacts had been distributed over a vast area.

Tiwanaku in the seventh century A.D. represented the first fully developed archaic state in the Titicaca Basin. The earlier Upper Formative–period polities of Early Tiwanaku and Pucara were very complex indeed, but it is only with the site and culture of Tiwanaku that we see unmistakable characteristics of state political organization: a large, planned urban capital with a substantial nonagricultural population, an identifiable canon of state architecture that was replicated in colonies well outside the core territory, the establishment of a road system to link those colonies, and an overall capacity to marshal the labor of substantial numbers of people. By A.D. 1000 at the latest, the colony in Moquegua had collapsed. Raised-field construction dropped significantly (Seddon 1994: 153–154; Stanish 1994), construction at the site itself was reduced, and many Tiwanaku settlements were abandoned. By A.D. 1100, Tiwanaku had declined as a regional power, a process that set the cultural stage for the rise of the Aymara señoríos.

The Rise of Complex Agro-Pastoral Societies in the Altiplano Period

One of the first great historians of Peru, Pedro de Cieza de León, considered the Titicaca Basin one of the most important regions in all of the Indies. By the time Cieza visited the area, the Inca empire had controlled the region for about two generations. The physical and cultural landscape that the first Western historians saw in the sixteenth century was primarily defined by the pre-Inca peoples of the Titicaca Basin. By and large, the peoples of Collasuyu, as the circum-Titicaca Basin was known in the Inca empire, were Aymara-speakers who had created several large and powerful kingdoms, or señoríos, prior to Inca conquest.

In chapter 99 of his *Crónica del Perú,* Cieza said that the Collao was perhaps the most populous region in Peru. He commented on the numerous herds of camelids (referred to as *ganado,* or "cattle," in older texts). He noted the existence of large towns along the lake edge and vast expanses of underpopulated territory away from the lake. He suggested that if the Titicaca Basin had been in a better climate (such as one of the lower valleys where maize could be grown), it would have been the best and richest land in all of the Indies.

Most of what we know about the great pre-Inca Aymara señoríos of the Titicaca Basin comes from the information recorded by Cieza, Cobo, and other early historians. In one of his most important quotes about the pre-Inca peoples, Cieza relates:

> Before the Inca reigned, according to many Indians from Collao, there was in their province two great lords [señores], one named Zapana and the other Cari, and these señores conquered many pucaras that are their fortifications, and that one of them entered Lake Titicaca, and found on the major island [Isla del Sol]

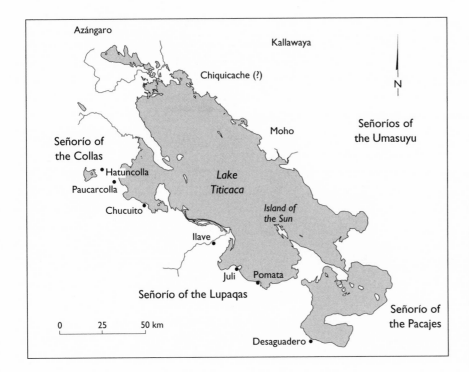

MAP 9.1. Sixteenth-century political and ethnic boundaries in the Titicaca Basin, as derived from historical documents. Adapted from Cieza, Juan de Betanzos, Bouysse-Cassagne 1986, Julien 1983, Saignes 1986, Spurling 1992, and Torero 1987.

bearded white people with whom they fought and put all of them to death. And more people say, that after [these events], there were great battles with the Canas and Canchis. (Cieza 1553: chapter 100)

Cieza was an astute observer. Along with his work, which provided a great deal of first-hand information, was that of Bernabé Cobo, Guamán Poma de Ayala, Garcilaso de la Vega, Ramos Gavilán, Juan de Betanzos, and others who described the peoples of the Titicaca Basin. Historical data from such sources make it possible to define a number of distinct political divisions within the circum-Titicaca region during the sixteenth century that almost certainly reflect some of the pre-Inca boundaries. Map 9.1, adapted from several sources (Bouysse-Cassagne 1986; Julien 1983; Saignes 1986; Spurling 1992; and Torero 1987), shows the distribution of these divisions. These boundaries, of course, existed before the

Early Spanish period. Julien (1983) has convincingly argued that these divisions reflect Inca provincial boundaries, which, in turn, reflected the pre-Inca political-ethnic landscape. In other words, it is a safe assumption that these divisions reflect the general outlines of the Altiplano- and Inca-period cultural landscape in the circum-Titicaca region.

The largest cultural geographical division in Titicaca Basin society is that of Umasuyu/Urqusuyu. In the most superficial terms, Umasuyu corresponds geographically to the eastern and northeastern side of the lake, and Urqusuyu refers to the western and northwestern side. These concepts, however, are more than a geographical division: they refer to a series of dualities vital to Andean political and social geography. *Urqu*, or *orqo*, implies masculinity, "mountainness," dryness, solid, and high (Kolata 1993: 8). In Bertonio's dictionary, *orqo* is defined as "the masculine sex in all of the brute animals" (1956 [1612]:

205

Bk. 2: 239). In contrast, *uma* refers to femininity, water, wetness, passivity, and lowness (Bouysse-Cassagne 1986: 202; Kolata 1993: 8; Wachtel 1986). The term *uma* is the Aymara word for water (Bertonio 1956: Bk. 2: 374), but, curiously, it also refers to the water in the swale of a raised field (see pages 63–64). The conceptual boundary between these two concepts was the lake itself, expressed in the term *taypi*.

The two largest political groups mentioned in the sixteenth-century texts were the Lupaqa and the Colla. These señoríos figure prominently in the oral and written histories of the region, as the two protagonists engaged in a great military struggle immediately prior to Inca conquest of the region. To the south was the Pacajes, an area that included the ancestral home of the Tiwanaku state. Other, smaller polities included the Canas and the Cachi to the far north, the very poorly understood Omasuyu to the east (referred to as the Kallawaya area by Escalante M. 1994: 329), and the Carangas to the south (Bouysse-Cassagne 1986, 1987b). Spurling (1992: 41) notes that Betanzos was the only historian to mention a pre-Inca polity called Caquesani that was near the Arapa Peninsula in the north. Spurling also notes that Betanzos identified four northern provinces of the Titicaca Basin, including Azángaro, Chiquicache, Moho, and Kallawaya (later Carabaya) (Betanzos 1996: 95; Spurling 1992: 56). If Betanzos is correct, the northeastern and eastern side of the lake would have been divided into a number of divisions that were smaller than the those on the western side. However, his reference to these "provinces," although specific, is also casual, so this information must be used with some caution.

The dictionary compiled by Bertonio provides information on political offices in Aymara society during the sixteenth century. He lists a number of terms in use in the Early Colonial period that indicate a rich vocabulary for political and social rank. Many of these terms are found in the appendix of this book.

One implication of these data is that the Lupaqa and Colla were complex societies; that is, señoríos, or "kingdoms." This is reinforced by several quotes by Cieza, including his statement that "the principal señores are always well attended and when they are on the road they are carried on litters" (1553: chapter 100). Carrying the elite in litters was considered one of the marks of kingship in Andean society. Although the idea that the Aymara kingdoms were complex political entities has been generally accepted by historians and archaeologists alike, as discussed below, this may not be the case.

Absolute Chronology

The collapse of Tiwanaku political organization and the prolonged drought of the twelfth century provided the context for the development of the Aymara señoríos of the twelfth through fifteenth centuries. These small polities relied extensively on camelid herds as well as rain-fed terrace agriculture. Although earlier cultures kept large herds, the Altiplano-period peoples intensified the use of the puna grazing lands, resulting in a much more dispersed settlement system.

The Altiplano period is also known as the *auca runa,* or "time of war." One of the principal settlements characteristic of this time was the development of hilltop fortified sites called pukaras (see pages 96–98), which were built throughout the Titicaca Basin (with a few notable exceptions). Warfare was one of the primary settlement determinants during this period. It was during the Altiplano period that the modern Aymara economic way of life came into being, characterized by a heavy reliance on animal herds, nonintensive farming, lake exploitation, and regional trade.

The historical chronological terms *Altiplano period* (Hyslop 1976; Stanish et al. 1997), *Late Intermediate period* (e.g., Rowe 1962; K. Chávez 1988), and *Regional Development Stage* (Lumbreras 1974a) can be used interchangeably in the Titicaca region. This era is defined as the time between the collapse of Tiwanaku influence and the conquest of the Titicaca Basin by the Inca empire. The term *Altiplano period* was originally used by Lumbreras (1974a) and Hyslop (1976, 1977). Lumbreras also refers to the stage designation *Regional States* for this time period for the central Andes as a whole (Lumbreras 1974a: 179) and the Altiplano period for the Titicaca Basin. Lumbreras's use of the term *Regional States* emphasizes the pan-Andean effects of the collapse of the Middle Horizon states of Tiwanaku and Wari, leading to the emergence of new, local polities instead of larger, expansive ones. This same process is evident in the Titicaca region, and, unlike in the earlier and later periods, the Titicaca Basin during the Altiplano period was relatively free of outside influences (Hyslop 1984: 117). I use the term *Altiplano period* for the entire circum-Titicaca region for the period after the Tiwanaku collapse and before the incursions of the Inca state.

The Altiplano period is significant for archaeological research in that it represents a protohistoric period whose major events are referred to in later historic documents. It is also a sufficiently "young" time, relative to the ethnographic present, for which historical linguists have offered hypothetical reconstructions of population movements as reconstructed from language distributions. In the case of the Titicaca Basin, sixteenth-century histories discuss the Aymara señoríos, translated variously as "kingdoms," "chiefdoms," "manors," "feudal estates," or "domains," that surrounded the lake region. They also contain references to other ethnic groups and/or languages, such as the Uru, Uruquilla, Pukina, and Quechua. Because of these written histories, for the Altiplano period we can for the first time correlate specific historical references with archaeological data.

Guamán Poma describes the pre-Inca periods throughout the central Andes as *auca runa,* or the age of warriors and a time of strife. This undoubt-

edly reflected the official histories of the Inca state, which often sought to denigrate the earlier cultures that they had conquered. Although the construction of hill forts has a long tradition in the central Andes, the number of such forts dramatically increased in the Late Intermediate period. This suggests a relatively high level of internecine conflict during this period. The Altiplano period in the Titicaca Basin is no exception.

The Altiplano period begins with the collapse of the Tiwanaku state and ends with the Inca conquest of the Titicaca Basin. The end of Tiwanaku control is determined by the cessation of the manufacture of Tiwanaku pottery in the south-central Andes. As discussed above, the end of the manufacture of Tiwanaku pottery represents not just the end of an art style but the collapse of a political and economic system integrating an expansive state. Likewise, Inca control can be identified by the presence of Inca ceramics or by local pottery manufactured by Titicaca Basin peoples under Inca domination. As we will see, both the Tiwanaku and Inca ceramic types are easily distinguishable. With some notable exceptions, Tiwanaku iconographic motifs and vessel shapes did not continue into the post-Tiwanaku periods and it is therefore relatively simple to define the end of this ceramic tradition.

The absolute dates of the collapse of the Tiwanaku state vary from region to region in the south-central Andes. In the core Pacajes area of Tiwanaku itself, Tiwanaku ceramics may have been manufactured up to as late as A.D. 1200. In other areas of the south-central Andes, in contrast, the Tiwanaku occupation ended three hundred years earlier. An appropriate example here would be the Moquegua drainage in far southern Peru, where the local, post-Tiwanaku Tumilaca period most likely began around A.D. 1000 (Bermann et al. 1989: 270), perhaps even earlier. Carbon-14 dates from Late Tiwanaku raised fields near Lukurmata suggest a terminal date around A.D. 1000. Mathews obtained dates from terminal Tiwanaku V in the Tiwanaku Valley that are about A.D. 1100 as well. In sum, in the Titicaca Basin proper, the end of the Tiwanaku state control occurred between A.D. 1000 and 1200.

Carbon-14 dates from the Estuquiña-Inca–period sites in Moquegua help pinpoint the date of Inca expansion in the south-central Andes in general, and help bracket the date of expansion into the Titicaca region in particular. One date from the Estuquiña-Inca site of Porobaya in the upper Moquegua Valley is 490 ± 80 B.P. The calibrated date is A.D. 1427.[1] At the site of Torata Alta, an Inca site, the carbon date associated with a Late Horizon feature is 380 ± 90 B.P., which calibrates to A.D. 1474.[2]

These absolute dates fit relatively well with the traditional chronology of Inca expansion as suggested by Rowe (1946) and as modified by Bauer (1992a: 41). Viracocha Inca is said to have ruled from A.D. 1438 to 1471 (Rowe 1946: 203). It therefore appears that the Inca state expanded out of its homeland in the late fourteenth or early fifteenth century and conquered the Titicaca Basin. Actual Inca political control of the region appears to be around A.D. 1450, possibly a bit earlier. The Altiplano period therefore falls between approximately A.D. 1100–1450. Of course, Inca rule ended in 1532 with the Spanish conquest of the Inca state.

The Inca conquest of the Titicaca Basin proper likely occurred sometime between A.D. 1420 and 1490, although this so-called conquest probably occurred over an extended period. It is important, however, to make the distinction between actual Inca geopolitical control and the prior period during which there was Inca influence in the form of trade, alliances via intermediaries to the north, and possible abortive military campaigns.

The Protohistoric Aymara Señoríos

The Colla and the Lupaqa were the largest and most powerful polities in the Titicaca Basin during the im-

mediate pre-Inca periods. The Colla were located from somewhere slightly south of the Puno area to the Canas and Canchis areas in the north. The Colla capital is often said to be the town of Hatuncolla, although it appears that the actual Altiplano-period site was the pre-Inca settlement behind the modern town. The great chulpa cemetery site and the hypothesized pilgrimage destination of Sillustani was in Colla territory as well.

The Lupaqa capital was in the Chucuito area. The Lupaqa area bordered the Colla in the north and extended as far south as the Desaguadero bridge. The Lupaqa also apparently controlled the Island of the Sun prior to Inca conquest, although the evidence for this remains somewhat tenuous.

The Pacajes area was the ancestral home of the Tiwanaku state. The post-Tiwanaku occupation of the Pacajes was focused on the Tiwanaku Valley and immediate surroundings, but the cultural region extended to the south and east. To the east of the lake were the Omasuyu and Larecaja regions. These areas are very poorly known, but limited archaeological work indicates a vigorous Altiplano-period occupation throughout the region.

Site Typology of the Altiplano Period

The settlement changes that occurred during the Altiplano period in the Titicaca Basin were profound. Primary regional centers focused on fortified sites called major pukaras, secondary regional centers essentially disappeared, and the majority of the population dispersed into small villages and hamlets. In other words, the settlement pattern shifted to one of large sites on and around the large pukaras, and a plethora of small sites.

John Hyslop first emphasized the profoundly different nature of the Altiplano-period settlement patterns from earlier ones. His path-breaking survey work, published in 1976, defined the Altiplano macropattern, a synthesis of the settlement and cultural characteristics that typify the Late Intermediate period in the Lupaqa region. The Altiplano macropattern is characterized by sites with walled habitation and/or burial areas, chulpa burial towers, an increase in pastoralism, and distinctive ceramic types. Hyslop emphasized fortified pukaras as a focus of settlement. In this model, the low, lakeside sites typical of the Tiwanaku period were abandoned in favor of the higher, fortified sites in the hills that ring the lake, although some lakeside Altiplano-period sites continued to be occupied (Hyslop 1976: 99–137).

In the Juli-Pomata survey (Stanish et al. 1997), we discovered that the Altiplano-period settlement pattern was more complex than originally suggested by Hyslop. Most important is the fact that during the Altiplano period, most sites were not fortified. Rather, the majority of the population lived at the base of, or close to, the fortified hills in small villages and hamlets. Second, many of the fortified sites were not permanently occupied. Excavations by de la Vega (1990) at the huge pukara outside Juli demonstrated that most of the domestic terrace areas were not permanently occupied. Likewise, a sample of a number of nonhabitation structures (most likely storage structures) indicated that they were used only sporadically (de la Vega 1990). These data suggest that many of the pukaras were temporary refuge sites used in times of danger. Some of the largest pukaras had substantial villages and hamlets around their base.

Major and Minor Pukaras

The Juli-Pomata survey provided additional insight into the nature of the Altiplano-period settlement, revealing that there were at least two types of fortified settlements during the Altiplano period. Major pukaras are the massive type, such as Pukara Juli and Tanka Tanka. The minor pukaras are much smaller and much more common.

Major pukaras have substantial walls that encir-

cle a very large area, including some domestic area near the base or, more usually, alongside the lowest defensive wall. These are the classic hilltop, fortified sites found throughout the altiplano and originally described by Bernabé Cobo in the early histories. These sites almost always are surrounded by at least three large defensive walls, and some have as many as six walls. The walled areas of the major pukaras are so huge that they enclosed agricultural areas, pasture areas, and springs. Thus these pukaras would have provided defense for these areas as well as for the population. This would have enabled the inhabitants to withstand a siege for a substantial amount of time. The chronicler Montesinos described an Inca pukara in the north Titicaca Basin: "the whole stronghold formed a cone, and the entire army was within the *andenes* [defensive walls]. The pukara was built, he said, with many "*andenes,* trenches and so on in such a way that they each had but one very narrow entrance . . . all the way up [the hill] . . . where the king had his stores and the necessary supplies" (Montesinos 1991 [1630]: 61).

To date we have identified several major pukaras in the south and southwestern Titicaca Basin: Pukara Juli, Tanapaca, Llaquepa, Huichajaja, Tanka Tanka, and Cerro Carajuana (see map 9.2). Hyslop (1976) described Pukara Juli, Llaquepa, and Tanka Tanka. Vásquez, Carpio, and Velazco (1935) first reported Tanka Tanka as a major fortified settlement. These and other major pukaras in the north basin constituted the primary regional centers of the Altiplano period.

There are two types of minor pukaras. One is characterized by small hills with surrounding defensive walls and very little or no architectural remains. These minor refuge sites are similar to the major pukaras but are considerably smaller and much more numerous. The available data indicate that minor pukaras were not permanently occupied, as evidenced by a lack of permanent habitation structures and little midden refuse. Instead, they appear to have

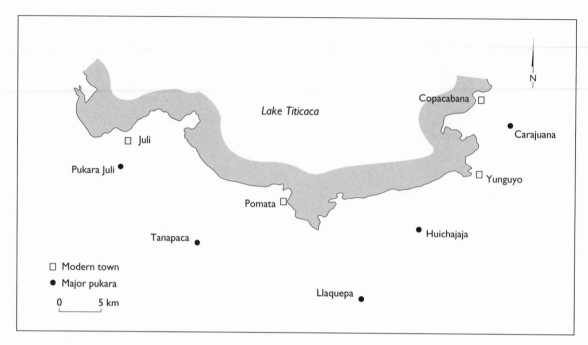

MAP 9.2. Major pukaras in the south.

served strictly as short-term refuge sites for settlements in the immediate area.

The second type of minor pukara is similar to the first but has dense architectural remains near and inside the walls. These pukaras are generally smaller, and most habitation areas are contained within the walls. These minor pukaras appear to have functioned as the major pukaras did, but they had far smaller populations. Domestic structures were built inside the walls, and the populations worked fields and flocks below. Many of these minor pukaras are found on mesas and naturally protected hills. They rarely have more than two hectares of domestic residence, and usually much less.

Reconnaissance and analysis of the artifacts from the inhabited pukaras (major ones and minor ones with domestic remains) suggest that the major pukaras are later, and the inhabited minor ones are earlier. The noninhabited minor pukaras are difficult to date, given the lack of diagnostic sherds on the surface. Major pukaras have little transitional pottery (between Tiwanaku- and Altiplano-period styles) and contain some Late Horizon ceramics. That is, the pukaras that have a late component are characterized by temporary residential sites above the walls and permanent settlements below.

The inhabited minor pukaras, at least in the western basin, appear to be earlier (K. Frye, personal communication 1996), based upon several lines of evidence. Transitional pottery between Tiwanaku and Altiplano styles is occasionally found on these sites, and we have not found Late Horizon chulpas associated with these pukaras. Likewise, on sites such as Cerro Capalla, an inhabited pukara in the Acora region, there are only igloo-style chulpas. This chulpa style is said by Hyslop (1977) to be the first fully aboveground tomb type of the Altiplano period, an observation supported by our data (e.g., Stanish et al. 1997). The occurrence of only early chulpas on the inhabited minor pukaras supports the conclusion that they are earlier.

Primary Regional Centers: The Inhabited Pukaras

PUKARA JULI

The large pukara outside Juli (appropriately named Pukara Juli)[3] was one of the first large archaeological monuments to be described by the Spanish historians (see Hyslop 1976). Cobo, in relating the history of the conquest of the Titicaca region by Pachacuti Inca, describes the fortress outside Juli where the inhabitants took refuge:

> On this expedition the Inca subjugated all the towns and nations surrounding the great Lake Titicaca . . . which were densely populated at that time. Some of the towns defended themselves bravely, and they had many clashes with the Inca before they were subjugated. The Inca subjected many of them to a relentless siege, and they built forts in order to defend themselves, such as those at Caquingora and the one we see on the high hill near the town of Juli, which has five dry stone walls, one inside the other, where the natives took refuge and fought for a long time in defending themselves. (Cobo 1983 [1653]: 140)

The Altiplano-period settlement of Pukara Juli is actually a series of hamlets and villages that surround the large fortified pukara, the classic pattern for these major pukaras. The ceramic materials from the associated settlements appear to be contemporary, but this remains to be tested. There are no habitation sites above 4,200 m.a.s.l. The extensive walls surround several square kilometers of land, a huge area, suggesting that they were intended to surround grazing and agricultural land. A substantial area of land inside the walls is cultivable, and the entire hilltop above four thousand meters is suitable for grazing. There are also springs inside the walls. With all of these resources protected within the pukara's walls, the inhabitants of the region could gather there and survive a long siege if necessary, as suggested by Cobo.

The walls of Pukara Juli are massive. It appears that in antiquity, the principal defensive walls were approximately two meters high and about one and a half meters wide. The construction was a double-wall, rubble-fill technique, making the walls very strong and wide enough for defenders to walk on and move rapidly around the hill. There were five defensive walls placed around the hill, as first correctly described by Cobo several centuries ago.

On the north slope of Pukara Juli is a section of wall that provides some additional insight into the nature of the inhabitants' defensive strategies. At one of the least naturally defensible areas, there is a wide cleared area in front of the slope leading up to a major wall. The rubble from this area was cleared and placed in front of the wall to make the ascent exceedingly difficult, a type of *cheval de frise* technique.[4] Even today, walking on the rubble is extremely difficult, and it was not uncommon for our field crew to trip on the loose boulders piled in front of the wall. Not surprisingly, the area of the rubble contained a high density of throwing stones, evidence of actual conflict at the site of Pukara Juli.

Excavations by de la Vega (1990) in the Yacari-Tuntachawi area of Pukara Juli indicate a preponderance of storage vessel fragments. He discovered double-chambered, undecorated vessels buried on small terraces, and analyzed a number of very small structures (less than one and a half meters in diameter) that he concluded were for storage as well. The site thus appears to have been designed to store food and possibly water, and to protect crops and animals, all of which would have protected the population at the base of the pukara and in the surrounding villages and hamlets during a sustained siege.

CUTIMBO

Another major pukara, known as Cutimbo, is a little more than twenty-two kilometers south of Puno, on a mesa more than four thousand meters above sea level (Hyslop 1976: 341–347). According to Hyslop, the site covers at least twenty-five hectares. He notes that there are many round house foundations (an Altiplano-period architectural style), and rectangular enclosures that may be prehistoric (Hyslop 1976: 341). My own observations confirm those of Hyslop. There is a substantial habitation area at the site, and possibly distinct house clusters along the mesa top.

The site has an enormous number of round structures and chulpas. Many of the chulpas have Inca stonework. The significance of the site is that it may have been the residence and burial grounds of the Lupaqa elite prior to Inca expansion (Hyslop 1976: 160). I interpret the site to be a major regional center built in a defensible location during the Altiplano period. The Inca-style chulpas probably postdate the major occupation of the site.

CARAJUANA

Carajuana is between Yunguyu and Copacabana, on the Bolivian side of the border. It is the largest major pukara in the Titicaca Basin in terms of area enclosed by fortification walls. The site has not been ground-checked by any member of Programa Collasuyu, but the distribution of the walls conforms to those of the major pukaras. It is also significant that the site probably is the "Huana" listed as one of the major huacas of the seventeenth-century Lupaqa by Bertonio.[5]

LLAQUEPA

First reported by Hyslop (1976: 300), the major pukara of Llaquepa is several kilometers southeast of the town of Pomata. It has at least three large walls that encircle a fairly narrow hill up to the summit. Frye (1997) estimates the habitation area of the site to be between eight and ten hectares. Frye mapped the site, and he reports "approximately 600–700 structures within an overall enclosed area of over 50 hectares" (Frye 1997: 133). The site has extensive habitation around the base of the hill.

TANKA TANKA

First reported in 1935 by Vásquez et al., Tanka Tanka is on a very prominent massif that is part of an east-west tending chain of uplifted hills in a very broad pampa. The site has a number of outstanding chulpas built of fieldstone, cut stone, and adobe (Stanish et al. 1997). Hyslop described the massive fortification walls: "The walls are dressed on their exterior and in their bases there are often stones up to 2 m. in height. Walkways 2 m. wide are observed in places behind and below the tops of the walls" (Hyslop 1976: 335). There are five major walls that reach several meters in height and two or so meters wide, with a dense rubble-filled or reinforced construction.

The walls of Tanka Tanka are arguably the most impressive constructions in terms of sheer size of the Altiplano-period peoples in the circum-Titicaca Basin that are still standing. Their massive size may well be a function of the fact the site is not on a very defensible location, at least on the southern exposure. As a result, the inhabitants were forced to build a series of walls to withstand any attacks.

Hyslop (1976) noted the extensive habitation area to the southwest, which has the remains of hundreds of circular structures, and suggested that it covered about one hundred hectares. However, most of the area inside the higher walls does not appear to have been used as permanent habitation, so we have suggested a permanent habitation area of about fifty hectares (Stanish et al. 1997), but even this lower estimate of the residential area of this essentially single-phase Altiplano-period site is enormous. The majority of surface artifacts date to the Altiplano period, although Late Horizon sherds are noted in some areas, particularly near the chulpa burials. Tanka Tanka therefore ranks as one of the largest major pukaras in the southwest Titicaca Basin, if not the largest in total habitation area.

Hyslop (1976) also noted numerous cist tombs in the pampa area below the site, and we corroborated this observation. There probably were hundreds, or thousands, of belowground cist tombs that coexisted with the aboveground chulpas on the site. Of special interest are chulpas that were reconstructed. At least three of them were originally fieldstone igloo types that were redressed with either cut-stone blocks in Inca style or, in one case, with adobe. This fact suggests that an original tomb of an elite was rebuilt or enhanced in the Late Horizon, and yet there are very few Late Horizon artifacts on the surface of the habitation areas. This would suggest that the site was generally abandoned after Inca conquest but that it remained an important ceremonial/burial area for the local Lupaqa elite.

North of Tanka Tanka other massifs rise out of the pampa. One of these, Ichucollo, was described by Hyslop (1976: 296–299). The site contains chulpas, petroglyphs, and associated habitation areas. West of Tanka Tanka are at least two minor pukaras that were not ground-checked. These sites are typical of minor pukaras throughout the region in their wall placement, topographical location, number of walls, and size. The Tanka Tanka and surrounding area was therefore an area of major Altiplano-period settlement.

CHACCHUNE

Chacchune is on the neck of the isthmus that connects the Huata Peninsula to the mainland just south of the town of Conima. It is most likely the site of Chakchuni, first reported by Neira (1967: 155). An Altiplano-period site on a low hill with a series of walls and domestic terraces, it has at least four hectares of domestic residence areas, and may be two or three hectares larger. The architecture is extremely well preserved, including house walls, chulpas, and apparent storage features. On top of the site is an oval or rectangular plaza area. Although small, the site of Chacchune was a densely packed major pukara in the Omasuyu area.

OTHER POSSIBLE MAJOR PUKARAS

There are dozens of other major, or potential major, pukaras in the Titicaca Basin that have not been ground-checked or adequately reported. Analysis of air photos and ground observation indicate substantial numbers of pukaras in the north and northwest basin, particularly around Sillustani. Neira (1967: 121) reported a major fortified site in Cupi, west of Ayaviri, with eleven walls surrounding domestic areas characterized by round structures. In the Huancané area of the northeast basin, pukaras are not as dense, but they can be seen throughout the region, and large ones do exist. About seven kilometers outside Huancané, on the hill surrounded by the communities of Antajahua, Caluyo Miruraya, and Callapani, is a very large pukara with at least five stone walls and similar to Pukara Juli in form. Pukaras in the Colla area in the northern basin are discussed by Rowe (1942), and Squier (1877: 387) reports that the site of Quellenata was a major "hill fortress" on the northeast shore of the lake.

In addition to Chacchune, other pukaras are found on the Omasuyu side of the lake between Moho and Ancoraimes. Neira (1967: 126–133) reports on several probable major pukaras in the Moho area. Cerro Pukara Kollo, about eight kilometers southeast of Moho, is described as having defensive walls, andenes, chulpas, and rectangular storage structures. Merquemarka, above modern Moho, is most likely a major pukara (and see Kidder 1943; Tschopik 1946). Neira also visited Cerro Calvario, approximately thirty kilometers northeast of Moho, in the puna near the village of Occopampa; this site is described as having defensive walls, storage structures, andenes, chulpas, and domestic structures (Neira

1967: 138–140). Directly west of Occopampa, one and a half hours by foot, is the site of Cerro Pucara, which appears to be a major pukara as well. The sites of Huancarani, Paru Paru, and Chasani are other probable major pukaras. Huancarani is northeast of Moho on the Río Huancarani (Neira 1967: 141–142). Paru Paru is reported to be west of Moho (Neira 1967: 143), and Chasani is several hours' walk from Paru Paru. Neira also published the site of Siani, ten kilometers southeast of Conima. He describes it as one of the largest centers in the province of Huancané, covering approximately one square kilometer (Neira 1967: 50). He describes huge areas of habitation structures, chulpas, defensive walls, and terraces. This site is most certainly one of the areas' major pukaras.

Squier (1877: 373) reports a site near Escoma that he describes as "one of the ancient *pucaras,* or hill forts, consisting of a series of five concentric terraces and stone-walls surrounding a conical eminence of great regularity of form." Portugal Ortíz (1991: 34) reports on fortified sites near Carabuco. Finally, Bennett (1933, 1950) mentions possible pukaras in the southeast Titicaca Basin, although they are much rarer there than in other parts of the basin.

With the possible exception of Siani, the eastern Titicaca Basin pukaras tend to be smaller than contemporary sites in the southwest. Like Chacchune, other pukaras in the Omasuyu area tend to be densely packed and built on hillsides and hilltops. They also seem to have functioned differently than those in the rest of the basin. The Omasuyu lakeside pukaras are more like Late Intermediate–period fortified sites on the western slopes of the Andes, where populations lived inside the fortified hilltop sites and farmed land below. In the rest of the Titicaca Basin, pastoralism was a major economic activity. The topography of the Omasuyu lakeside area, however, was not conducive to large camelid herds. Pukaras here did not function as refuge sites for scattered agro-pastoral populations but instead appear to have been permanent habitations for largely agricultural groups. In contrast, in the puna of the Omasuyu area, the western Titicaca Basin pattern of small refuge sites with an occasional large pukara, is found, but not on the same scale. At Iskanwaya (Arellano L. 1975), there are no obvious fortification walls, but the site location and relatively large population densities served to protect the inhabitants.

In the southern Titicaca Basin, pukaras are not as numerous as they are in the rest of the region. There is only one pukara in the Tiwanaku Valley (Albarracin-Jordan and Mathews 1990), which is most likely explained by the large populations that were living in the region after the collapse of the Tiwanaku state. Such large aggregations of people were not in much danger of raiding by small groups, the principal danger to the other populations of the period.

A few typical Titicaca Basin–type pukaras are found as far south as Tiquina. Further south, there are a number of hills with walls that could be pukaras as well, although they would be quite small relative to others in the region. To the southwest are large numbers of pukaras in the southern Chucuito province of Peru. Good refuge sites typical of the Altiplano-period societies of the Titicaca Basin have been noted outside Mazocruz in Chucuito province, well away from the lake. In short, the rise of fortified settlements was a pan–Titicaca Basin phenomenon, and their absence in some areas can be easily explained as the result of high local population densities, where the threat of attack was low.

Minor Pukaras

Characterized by small hills with surrounding defensive walls, minor pukaras are refuge sites that are similar to major pukaras but considerably smaller and much more numerous. Many of the minor pukaras have very few architectural remains, and they almost never had more than three walls; the available data suggest that these minor pukaras were not permanently occupied and were later in date. In contrast, other minor pukaras were permanently occupied, and these sites are much more densely packed with structures. There is considerable evidence of midden and other debris on the surface, indicating a permanent occupation. There are hundreds of minor pukaras throughout the region; some of the more notable ones are described below.

HUICHAJAJA

Located near the modern town of Yunguyu (Hyslop 1976: 307), Huichajaja is a high site, with habitation areas as high as 4,500 m.a.s.l. According to Frye (1997), the site is surrounded by three main walls that encircle about two hectares of domestic residential structures. He reports approximately one hundred structures and describes the architectural pattern as consisting of "circular and ovoid structures measuring from 2.5 to 3.5 meters in exterior diameter." This site is a minor pukara with domestic residences and early pottery on the surface, suggesting that it was an early site established after the collapse of Tiwanaku.

PUKARA CAPALLA

A few kilometers south of Acora on the main highway is Pukara Capalla, mentioned by Tschopik (1946) and Neira (1967) as a large pre-Inca site. It is a huge mesa formation with a number of well-preserved igloo chulpas leading up a ridge to the major pukara. The site has several large defensive walls with doors, and at least two hectares (probably more) of habitation area, reminiscent of Tanka Tanka.

Several diagnostics indicate an early date for this site. The chulpas are all igloo-style, and the sherds appear to be early, including several that have kerolike forms. There are also many straight-sided bowls that could be derived from keros. The only Inca sherds are found at the very top near a well-maintained apacheta. It is safe to conclude that this is an Early Altiplano–period site that was an important fortified habitation during this immediate post-Tiwanaku period. Pukara Capalla, like Huichajaja, is a rare exam-

ple of a transitional site between the Tiwanaku occupation and the later Altiplano-period one.

ZAPACOLLO

Located above Juli, Zapacollo is popularly known as the "sleeping lion" hill. It has two crests, each of which has a modern shrine, or *capilla,* on top. On the northernmost crest is site 019, a minor pukara with two or three low rings of walls encircling the hill in a typical fortification pattern. It appears to have functioned as a temporary refuge site for the populations around the base of the hill. There are no structures visible on the surface, and the intensity of occupation was very low.

The Problem of Hatuncolla and Chucuito

Historical documents suggest that the Colla, one of the Aymara señoríos, had a capital in Hatuncolla ("Hatuncollao" or "great Collao"—see Spurling 1992: 42). Similar suggestions can be found concerning the town of Chucuito, which would have been the capital of the Lupaqa polity. The idea that these were pre-Inca sites can be found in the histories of Cieza and Cobo, among others. According to Cieza, Viracocha Inca and the political head of the Lupaqa, Cari, met in Chucuito to conclude an alliance that preceded the actual conquest of the area by the Inca (see Stanish 1997).

Both sites lack fortifications, and they do not fit the pre-Inca settlement pattern for the region as a whole, with settlement clusters in villages and hamlets associated with a refuge site of some kind. The question, therefore, is whether Hatuncolla and Chucuito, due perhaps to their population size, were atypical of the Altiplano-period settlement pattern as a whole, or whether the documents are inaccurate in this respect.

Hyslop (1976) did not find any pre-Inca remains at Chucuito. This has been confirmed by Frye in his systematic survey of the area, as well as by my own observation. In other words, the archaeological evidence indicates that Chucuito was founded in the Inca period, and not before. The documents do not distinguish between the town of Chucuito and other nearby settlements in the area. Hyslop has suggested that Pucara Chucuito was the pre-Inca residence of the Lupaqa elite. Alternatively, he suggests that Cutimbo could have been a residence of the Lupaqa elite as well, perhaps in the Late Horizon period, with Altiplano-period antecedents. In other words, it is likely that both the pre-Inca pukara and the modern town were referred to as Chucuito in the texts.

Julien's work (1983) indicates that modern Hatuncolla was founded in the Inca period as well. However, a surface survey discovered two sites, called Esturi and Ale, about one kilometer from Hatuncolla, each with abundant pre-Inca diagnostics (Julien 1983: 94, plate 3). According to Julien's map, the total area of midden distribution of the two sites is about eighty hectares, a substantial settlement by Titicaca Basin standards. So although the modern town of Hatuncolla was founded in the Inca period, there may have been a significant occupation very near the site that could have been the Hatuncolla referred to in historic documents. It is therefore likely that references to the pre-Inca capitals of the Lupaqa and the Colla at Chucuito and Hatuncolla refer to the nearby sites of Pucara Chucuito and Esturi/Ale, respectively. The archaeological data indicate that both of the modern towns were founded in the Inca period, and not before.

Villages and Hamlets in the Altiplano Period

The bulk of the population in the Altiplano period lived in villages and hamlets. Many of these sites were adjacent to or very near the pukaras. Settlement data suggest that most Altiplano-period sites were quite small compared with other time periods. In fact, as seen in table 6.2, the mean size of sites in the Altiplano period was only slightly larger than a half hectare, considerably smaller than sites in other periods in that survey region. The systematically collected data suggest a major dispersion of population into small villages and hamlets coincident with the rise of agro-pastoral economies and the collapse of Tiwanaku state influence. There was no demographic collapse; rather, there was a settlement dispersion. Table 7.2 demonstrates that a substantial proportion of the population lived outside the walled sites in the Juli-Pomata region during the Altiplano period.

Systematic Settlement Data

Four systematic surveys in the Titicaca region have provided data on Altiplano-period settlement patterns. In the Juli-Pomata area, which would have been in the Lupaqa señorío, the Altiplano-period settlement pattern has been defined by Stanish et al. (1997). An additional survey by Frye around Chucuito has provided excellent information on the area of the Lupaqa capital. In the southern Pacajes area, Albarracin-Jordan's and Mathews's surveys provide intensive coverage in the Tiwanaku Valley (Albarracin-Jordan 1996a, 1996b; Albarracin-Jordan and Mathews 1990). The Island of the Sun has been surveyed by Bauer, Rivera, and Stanish (Bauer and Stanish 2001). Finally, nonsystematic reconnaissance provides settlement data for the north, northwest, and eastern sides of the lake.

The Altiplano-period settlement pattern in the Juli-Pomata region is shown in map 9.3. Sites continued to be built on the lake shore, as in the previous Tiwanaku period, but there was a notable expansion into the higher puna zones. Fortification walls are found at Pukara Juli, on the San Bartolomé hill, at the large hill due northwest of Pomata, and at two major sites just outside the surveyed area.

Based on analysis of air photos, ground reconnaissance, and the previous research of Hyslop (1976), we have discovered or documented several major pukaras in the south and southwestern Titicaca region that functioned as primary regional centers (see map 9.2). Immediately apparent is the fact that most of

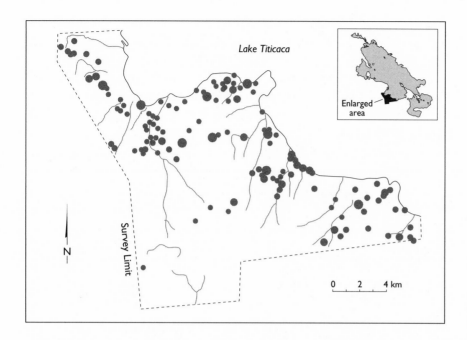

MAP 9.3. Altiplano-period settlement pattern in the Juli-Pomata survey area.

the pukaras are evenly spaced, suggesting some kind of catchment distribution that could have been defined by population levels, natural resources, the need to locate pukaras within a few kilometers of the settlements, or a combination of all of these factors. This pattern is interpreted as a spacing of political groupings with the polities, distributed in such a manner as to exploit the altiplano landscape with rain-fed terrace agriculture and animal husbandry. Most likely, the principal settlement determinants were economic and political, with the need to have a defensible refuge for the scattered settlements balanced by the need to be near lake resources, pasture, and possibly raised-field areas.

The distribution of aboveground tombs in the Juli-Pomata region closely parallels that of the habitation sites and supports this settlement model. The survey failed to discover any major chulpa cemetery areas. Rather, the aboveground tombs appear to conform to a pattern of territorial marking suggested by Hyslop (1976). These data could be interpreted to suggest the formation of distinct political-geographical

units in this period, each associated with one major pukara and possibly one or more small refuge sites.

In the Pacajes area, the settlement pattern for the local Altiplano period, called Early Pacajes, is similar to that of the Juli-Pomata region, characterized by hundreds of small hamlets and villages scattered over the landscape. In this valley, the post-Tiwanaku populations concentrated along the base of the hills (Albarracin-Jordan 1996a, 1996b; Albarracin-Jordan and Mathews 1990). There are no obvious fortified sites, as in the rest of the region to the west and north.

The Island of the Sun was probably linked politically to the Lupaqa señorío. Much of the decorated pottery collected by Bandelier from his excavations fits within the Altiplano-period pottery styles as presently known from other work in the region. The settlement pattern of the Island of the Sun during the Altiplano period indicates a decrease in the population to Late Titinhuayani (Upper Formative) levels. Average site sizes reverted to pre-Tiwanaku levels as well, also typical of the region as a whole. Overall, the settlement pattern on the Island of the

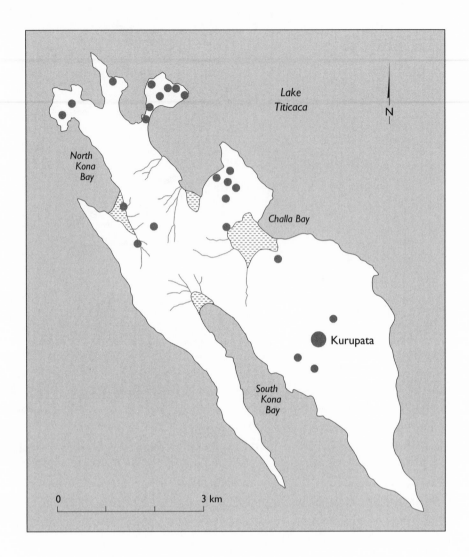

MAP 9.4. Altiplano-period settlement pattern on the Island of the Sun.

Sun indicates an agricultural optimizing pattern, with sites scattered over the island and some clustering in the richest agricultural areas, such as Challa Bay and the Kalabaya Peninsula (see map 9.4).

Settlement in the northern Titikala area, near the Sacred Rock, was reduced to only a minor occupation, but it is significant that some people continued to live there. The sites are not large, and there is no evidence for any special constructions. Excavations in the Titikala area indicate only an Inca occupation, although an ephemeral Altiplano-period one is pos-

sible. The main occupation is site 028, a moderately sized village. There is no evidence of a special site, nor is there any evidence that the earlier Tiwanaku site of Chucaripupata continued to be occupied in the Altiplano period.

There was one major pukara on the island, called Pukara, that had been occupied since the Middle Formative. During the Altiplano period, the site of Pukara was most likely built as the principal fortified site on the Island of the Sun. This refuge site was most likely used by the entire population of the island, including settlements in the far north. Since there was only one major pukara, it is very likely that the entire island was politically unified during this period.

The Altiplano-Period Settlement System

What factors explain the nature and distribution of Altiplano-period sites? Obviously, the salient factor is the development of warfare in the Titicaca Basin that required protection behind the massive walls. Conflict in the region was not new to the first centuries of the second millennium A.D. From at least the third century B.C., the taking of trophy heads and the subjugation of neighbors by military force were common. However, the rise of the Aymara señoríos after the twelfth century correlates with the development of a new style of conflict that necessitated the building of the large pukaras. These pukaras were most likely designed to protect against large-scale aggression by opponents whose tactics included sieges, a common Inca military strategy. The data suggest that it was present in the Titicaca region prior to Inca incursions, and that it first developed with the rise of the Aymara kingdoms.

The evidence indicates that there was a profound shift in aggressive tactics in the Altiplano period from small-scale raiding and trophy taking to larger-scale conflict. The major pukaras were designed to withstand sieges, with walls enclosing massive areas to protect agricultural fields, flocks, and water. The concentric rings of walls are a classic military design used by small populations to defend against larger armies.

In this light, the existence and distribution of the minor pukaras are most intriguing. If most uninhabited minor pukaras were contemporary with the major ones, then two factors may explain their origin. The first possibility is the need to locate major fortified settlements within the viewshed of other major pukaras. The minor pukaras essentially link the views of the major sites. Logically, there is a prob-

lem with a model that has both defended and undefended sites coexisting. That is, one presumes that the need for defended settlements is uniform over a region and that if there is conflict, then all sites should theoretically be defended. This problem centers on the ability of people in the unfortified settlements to retreat to a fortified site quickly enough to escape attackers. Some kind of communication system between regions would seem necessary for such a settlement pattern to be viable.

One possibility is that the populations in at least the southwestern Titicaca region during the Altiplano period employed a system of signal fires. That such a system was used as late as the end of the nineteenth century was confirmed by Bandelier. During his fieldwork on the Island of the Sun, he noted that signal fires were used to warn the local populations of marauding bands during a period of civil strife.

> We noticed, during our stay among them [the Aymara of Isla del Sol] while the civil war in Peru was going on, with what interest the Indians followed the course of events and how surprisingly well informed they were of military movements. When Chilian [sic] troops once trespassed on Bolivian territory and an invasion of Bolivia by them was feared, we obtained the news through our Indians at Challa and at once noticed that the occurrence was not by any means a matter of indifference to them. While the Indian uprising along the Peruvian border continued and negotiations were being carried on secretly between the insurgents and the Indians on the Peninsula of Copacavana, we now and then noticed fire-signals on the mainland both west and east, and it was not very reassuring to see a response flaring up on the summit of Kea-Kollu, the most convenient height for that purpose in the island. (Bandelier 1910: 89)

Bandelier's observations suggest that the use of large signal fires provided an efficient means of communication between settlements of the altiplano. Such a communication system would have readily provided enough time for populations to group inside the defensive walls if there were threat of attack. This practice might also explain the existence of some of the minor pukaras, which may have been strategically placed to visually connect settlements and make communication with signal fires rapid and easy. This would explain why some of the minor pukaras have no evidence of use other than the defensive walls themselves.

It is worth noting that La Barre makes a bolder claim about the use of signal fires but unfortunately offers no corroborative data. Perhaps he had Bandelier's observations in mind: "To gather their fighters the Aymara made smoke signals on the summits, simple smoky signal fires without the use of a blanket as in N. America" (La Barre 1948a: 161). Likewise, H. Tschopik described Aymara warfare in his survey article and claimed that they used signal fires: "In case of sudden attack, the troops were summoned by means of simple smoke signals, fires on mountain peaks, and trumpets" (Tschopik 1947: 549). As did Bandelier, Tschopik presents no evidence, either archaeological or documentary, to support this claim. In fact, it appears that both of them essentially borrowed this idea from Bandelier, who never made any claims that such a practice was Prehispanic.

The Late Intermediate period in the south-central Andes was a time of military innovation in general (see Moseley 1990a). A second explanation for the nature and distribution of the minor pukaras is an Andean variation of a defensive strategy known as "defense-in-depth." The principle behind this strategy is to maintain a number of forts scattered throughout a territory. A well-constructed fortress permits a small group of defenders to hold off a much larger force; thus for every fortress defended, an attacking army must leave a disproportionately large number of troops to invest it. If an army ignores such fortresses, the defenders can counterattack its rear and flanks. In premodern warfare, a cardinal rule was to avoid being outflanked. Therefore, the placement

of many small but well-defended fortresses would theoretically deplete an attacking force's ability to siege a larger pukara.

This strategy is generally associated with societies capable of maintaining mobile armies and may not be commensurate with Altiplano-period social and political organization. However, the basic principle would work against the kinds of military forces a state like the Inca could muster. As Spurling (1992: 49) aptly characterizes it, "The lists of conquests [by the Inca in the Titicaca region] clearly demonstrate the role of siege warfare in Andean military practice; the Inka army marches from fortress to fortress, laying siege to the enemy and eventually defeating them in battle." A defense-in-depth strategy would even be viable against neighbors as strong as the Lupaqa or the Colla. Certainly, the distribution of the minor pukaras fits such a model. The degree to which either signal fires or anti-siege defense strategies were a significant factor in the construction and distribution of the minor pukaras remains to be tested.

Migrations or Autochthonous Origins of the Aymara Señoríos

One of the most important questions regarding the Altiplano period in the Titicaca Basin centers on the origin of the Aymara señoríos. There are two major hypotheses about what caused the dramatic changes in settlement patterns and other archaeological indices during the post-Tiwanaku periods. One hypothesis is that the processes seen in the Altiplano period are typical of local post-imperial cultural landscapes throughout the world and are expected in a political and economic context of imperial fragmentation. The second hypothesis is that new populations migrated into the Titicaca region, at least in the southwestern basin, after the collapse (or perhaps as a cause of the collapse) of the Tiwanaku state. In other words, were the Aymara señoríos created by the migration of new populations in the wake of the

Tiwanaku collapse, or were they the result of local processes internal to the region?

Models of the Autochthonous Origin

The hypothesis that the settlement shifts and archaeological changes in the Altiplano period are due to internal processes, and not a migration of new populations, is the view most accepted by archaeologists at present. That is, most archaeologists believe that the collapse of the Middle Horizon states in the central Andes as a whole was, in broad processual terms, largely responsible for the auca runa, or period of internecine conflict, in the Andes as a whole. In this scenario, the Titicaca Basin data are manifestations of a larger, pan-Andean process of "balkanization" and settlement disruption with the collapse of Tiwanaku and Wari. As the former state systems collapsed, settlements readjusted to politically much less complex polities. Nucleated settlements dispersed, less-intensive agricultural practices were adopted that permitted risk-averse strategies, and strong labor organizations collapsed. Conflict between the politically autonomous, but culturally similar, groups was another outcome of such a process. Therefore, in this model the conflict in the Altiplano period is explained as the result of the collapse of a regional political organization capable of restraining internecine conflict. Once the Tiwanaku state was absent, populations reverted to pre-Tiwanaku patterns of overt competition.

If we accept the hypothesis that the minor inhabited pukaras are earlier than the major pukaras, then we have strong support for the autochthonous model. The smaller inhabited pukaras would therefore represent the Early Altiplano period. These sites show evidence of transitional pottery, including Tiwanaku shapes. The cultural landscape of the immediate post-Tiwanaku era, the Early Altiplano period, would therefore have been characterized by a series of small fortified villages. As the population grew large enough to construct and protect the ma-

jor pukaras, the settlement pattern would have shifted to more complex political organizations centered on these large pukaras. In short, a model of an evolution from the small inhabited pukaras to the larger major pukara–centered polities of the Late Altiplano period would be consistent with a model of the autochthonous origin of the Aymara señoríos.

Models of Aymara Migration

Contemporary archaeologists are very uncomfortable with models that rely on human migrations as explanatory factors. Yet, throughout the history of modern archaeology, the complex problem of human migration has been a recurrent theme. Migration was the implicit or explicit process underlying many of the cultural historical reconstructions prior to the New Archaeology of the 1960s, when many archaeologists downplayed the significance of migrations as an explanatory mechanism in prehistory. This deemphasis can be seen as a direct result of the influence of systems theory and information theory that stressed systemic processes and patterns of autochthonous development over migrations of new ethnic groups as explanatory mechanisms. Also, the association of migrant ethnic groups with fascist political theory in the late nineteenth century, along with its association with the simplistic geographical determinism of the early twentieth century, served to marginalize migration as a viable explanatory mechanism.

Migration is often invoked as an ad hoc explanation for culture change in the absence of other models (Adams, Van Gerven, and Levy 1978: 483), but this is an unscientific and unacceptable use of the concept. A method for modeling migrant populations is necessary, however, given that movement of new populations after the collapse of complex societies is a common phenomenon in history.

The varied nature of migration complicates archaeological studies of this process. Migrations can range in intensity from small populations inhabiting the margins of existing populations to wholesale replacement of existing populations. Complicating social factors (from an archaeological perspective) of intergroup marriage, development of fictive kinship relationships, fluctuating political alliances, and the like make defining the in-migration of new populations very difficult in archaeological contexts. The simplistic association of ceramic artifacts with ethnic groups is not a viable methodology. This is particularly true for the south-central Andes, where ethnicity, language, and cultural affiliation are fluid.

With the availability of good historical and linguistic data that can be combined with archaeological data, migration models are on much firmer logical grounds. In the Titicaca region, the Aymara migration hypothesis is generally not accepted by archaeologists, but it is generally adhered to by a number of linguists and social anthropologists. It has been most forcefully argued by Alfredo Torero:

> The presence of Aymaraes peoples (aymará-speakers) in the Collao and Charcas was relatively recent in the sixteenth century; they arrived three centuries before, apparently in a violent manner, by military conquest advancing from the north toward the southeast along the Cordillera Occidental of the Andes and appropriated for themselves the altiplano territory possibly in the form of diverse señoríos or kingdoms, some of which are mentioned by Ludovico Bertonio in the introduction of his *Vocabulario de la lengua aymará:* Lupacas, Pacases, Carancas, Quillaguas, and Charcas. (Torero 1987: 339)

In Toledo's reconstruction, the central and south-central Andean highlands and coast had four great languages spoken around A.D. 500: Quechua was spoken in the central highlands, Aru (the family to which Aymara belongs) was spoken north of Ayacucho to roughly the pass at La Raya, Pukina from La Raya to the southern edge of Lake Titicaca, and Uruquilla south through the lake district in the altiplano (Torero 1990: 245). Over time, Aru expanded

at the expense of the Pukina- and Uruquilla-speakers, leaving the latter with small enclaves of speakers throughout the southern region of the altiplano. The fundamental premise of Torero's principal conclusion, that the Aymara are recent immigrants, is accepted by other linguists and anthropologists such as Bouysse-Cassagne (1987a, 1987b), Shady (1987), Gisbert (1987), and Wachtel (1987). With the exception of Shady, however, each of these scholars explicitly argues for a southern, not a northern, origin of the Aymara (see map 9.5). The location of proto-Aymara is the subject of a very significant disagreement among linguists; this dispute is illustrated in Torero's reconstruction of language distribution during the Middle Horizon in the Central Andes, as seen in map 9.6.

The basis of the Aymara migration model is the reconstruction of the distribution of indigenous languages in the region for the immediate pre-Inca periods. Bouysse-Cassagne, for instance, argues:

> It is now possible to locate with great precision the ecological areas and the distribution zones of the different groups that spoke Uruquilla, Puquina, Aymara, and Quechua that correspond to different types of cultures. The Urus that were fishers-gatherers, and the Puquinas, pastoralists. The later advance and penetration of languages such as Aymara and Quechua was made at the expense of the linguistic areas of Uruquilla and Puquina. (Bouysse-Cassagne 1987b: 164)

Maps 4.2, 4.3, and 4.4 reproduce the hypothetical distribution of Quechua, Pukina, and Uruquilla in the south-central Andes at the end of the sixteenth century (and see Bouysse-Cassagne 1987b: 163; Browman 1994; Torero 1987: 342). Aymara was spoken in the entire area. Pukina was found throughout the Omasuyu area to the east and in the north and extreme northwest Titicaca Basin, which corresponds to the Collas Urqusuyu and Collas Umasuyu cultural divisions. It also includes the northern part of the Pa-

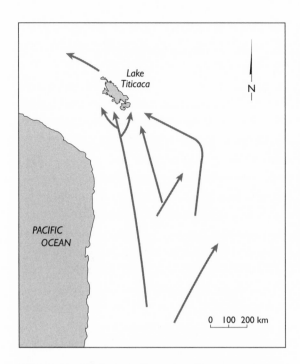

MAP 9.5. Hypothesized migration routes of Aymara-speakers in the post-Tiwanaku period (twelfth century A.D.), according to T. Gisbert. Adapted from Escalante M. (1994: 322).

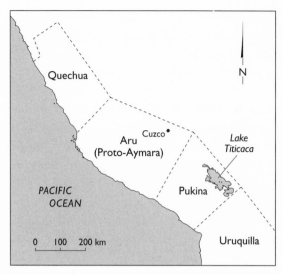

MAP 9.6. Distribution of languages circa A.D. 500, according to Torero 1990.

cajes Umasuyu and possibly Pacajes Urqusuyu, the ancestral area of the Tiwanaku state. These linguistic data suggest a formerly widespread Pukina language with a "wedge" of Aymara-speakers moving in from the south. Supporting the model of a recent immigration of Aymara-speakers is an observation made by Albó that highland Aymara lacks much dialectical differentiation. Albó (1987) emphasizes this fact to support a model of a recent origin of this language in the area as well.

A Model of Pukina Origins, Function, and Distribution

The archaeological data that we now have can be used to evaluate these competing hypotheses. In particular, the survey data from the Juli-Pomata area and from the Tiwanaku Valley are ideally suited for this

problem. The Tiwanaku area, of course, is the ancestral home of the Tiwanaku state and the hypothesized region of Pukina speakers. The Juli-Pomata region, in contrast, is squarely in the Lupaqa heartland, the area of hypothesized migration of Aymara-speakers in the twelfth to fifteenth centuries A.D.

In the Juli-Pomata area, the most dramatic differences between any two cultural periods in the later prehistory of the Titicaca Basin occur between the Tiwanaku and Altiplano periods. The data indicate major shifts in settlement location and site types, with the nucleated and rank size settlement distribution of the Tiwanaku period giving way to numerous small and generally undifferentiated villages and hamlets in the Altiplano period. Fortified sites developed for the first time in the Altiplano period as well. Superficially, these data would suggest that the dramatic changes coincident with collapse of the

Tiwanaku state would support the hypothesis that migrating Aymara speakers displaced the Pukina speakers.

However, other data do not support the Aymara migration model. As already mentioned, the sixteenth-century distribution of Pukina did not include the Tiwanaku Valley, perhaps the strongest evidence against a migration model; that is, it would be surprising that the putative capital of a Pukina-speaking state, Tiwanaku, would have so few Pukina speakers in the home valley in the sixteenth century, even though they continued to exist in areas outside Tiwanaku. Furthermore, although there is a substantial abandonment rate between the Tiwanaku and Altiplano periods as indicated in the Juli-Pomata survey data, numerous sites continued to be occupied.

Another factor that could account for this population dispersal is the climatic changes in the altiplano that occurred around A.D. 1100. This, of course, is the major drought detected in paleolimnological cores (see pages 40–43). A shift from plant agriculture to pastoral economies is a good drought adaptation, and pastoral activities foster settlement dispersion. The pattern evidence in the Tiwanaku/Altiplano-period transition is very similar to that at the end of the Upper Formative in the northern Titicaca Basin area. At this time as well there is evidence for a drought, and there was a concomitant shift from nucleated to dispersed settlements. There is also no evidence for migrations during this period.

The evidence suggests that the changes in the Tiwanaku/Altiplano-period transition are related to factors other than a major migration of new populations into the area. These factors include the collapse of the Tiwanaku state system, which had previously aggregated populations into a relatively small number of settlements. The collapse of Tiwanaku would have led to the dispersal of populations in a settlement shift pattern consistent with the collapse of complex political systems elsewhere in the prein-

dustrial world. Furthermore, the beginning of a major long-term drought would have further exacerbated this process.

A final possibility is that smaller groups of Aymara-speakers immigrated into the region and intermingled with existing populations. The existing linguistic data do not support this, but much remains to be finished.

We are still confronted with explaining the origin and disappearance of Pukina in the south-central Andes. The distribution of Pukina in the sixteenth century generally correlates to the distribution of the Upper Formative Pucara polity. Pucara pottery and textiles have been found in northern Chile. Rivera (1984) suggests that Pucara influence is evident in the Alto Ramírez phase on the coast and argues for relationships between contemporary Kalasasaya, Chiripa Mamani, and Wankarani. Focacci (1983: 111) proposes that the Alto Ramírez settlements represent actual altiplano colonists, a proposition supported by Kolata (1983: 275). Mujica (1985: 111), in contrast, feels that the Pucara colonization in northern Chile is not supported by the data, given the "lack of sculptures, typical altiplano pottery or even villages."

Tiwanaku sites and pottery are distributed over a very large area, including part of the area where Pucara sites and/or artifacts are found (Stanish 1992; Stanish and Steadman 1994). Near the Pucara heartland, for instance, are a number of Tiwanaku sites (Kidder 1943). The northernmost limit of Tiwanaku influence, according to S. Chávez (1988: 38), was in the area of Azángaro. He feels that the Wari state extended south to Sicuani, thereby defining the Wari-Tiwanaku frontier in the north.

In other words, there is good evidence that Tiwanaku politically incorporated or influenced a large part of the former territory of Pucara, even though the latter had collapsed as a complex political entity prior to Tiwanaku expansion. Many sites, such as Incatunuhuiri near Chucuito, have Pucara occupations with subsequent Tiwanaku occupations. In Moquegua, Feldman has defined a local culture that is linked with Pucara, called Huaracane. The Huaracane phase was followed by a major Tiwanaku occupation. At present, the site complex of Omo in Moquegua is the southernmost documented Tiwanaku colony on the coast. South of this area, Tiwanaku influence seems to have been much more indirect. Similar patterns of Pucara-derived cultures being subsequently replaced by Tiwanaku ones are found in Arequipa as well (Stanish 1992: 67–75).

The northern counterpart of the Tiwanaku state was the proto-Quechua speaking Wari, with its capital in the Ayacucho Valley (Bird, Browman, and Durbin 1988). The development and decline of Wari is more or less parallel in time to Tiwanaku at circa A.D. 600–1000. Furthermore, as with Tiwanaku, there is disagreement as to the nature of Wari political economy. I agree with Schreiber (1992: 275), who views Wari as an expansionist state or even empire. Furthermore, there is very little geographic overlap in Wari and Tiwanaku territories, with the exception of the site of Cerro Baúl in Moquegua and the Arequipa areas. Wari and Tiwanaku represent two different expansive states that controlled distinct territories in the central Andes. As Schreiber aptly notes, "Wari and Tiwanaku materials are distinguished both in terms of style and in terms of geographic distribution. Although both cultures pertain to the Middle Horizon, they have separate and discrete spatial distributions" (Schreiber 1992: 82).

In this historical, political, and economic context, the correlation of Pucara sites with the sixteenth-century distribution of Pukina is compelling. I argue that a form of proto-Quechua was most likely the language associated with the Pucara polity as well as the antecedents of the Wari state. Given these observations, I propose the following model. The incorporation of the Pucara-derived polities by Tiwanaku in essence carved out and isolated a group from the main group of proto-Quechua speakers to the north. The political and social barriers created by the conquest of this area by the proto-Aymara (proto-Jaqi) speaking Tiwanaku state promoted the differentiation of this proto-Quechua into what eventually became known as Pukina in the sixteenth century. Tiwanaku influence and control in former Pucara territory continued to grow for several centuries, effectively reinforcing this linguistic barrier and promoting the Jaqi language families (to which Aymara belongs) at the expense of Pukina.

At the time of the Toledo Tasa, Pukina was one of three general languages of Peru. As Torero notes, one hundred years later there are no references to the language (Torero 1987). Pukina rapidly disappeared, while smaller languages survived (e.g., Uruquilla) and the other two general languages flourished. These data strongly suggest that Pukina was somehow fundamentally different from Aymara, Quechua, and the minor languages in the region.

The fundamental difference is that sixteenth-century Pukina was a mixed language that had evolved into a lingua franca and was not the natal language of any significant population. Although it was a very convenient lingua franca in the particular cultural context of the central Andes circa A.D. 1100–1650, with the collapse of the Wari and Tiwanaku states, Pukina was rapidly replaced by Spanish as the preferred lingua franca within two or three generations of Spanish rule. The concept of mixed languages is a major problem in linguistics. I follow Thomason and Kaufmann, who argue that mixed languages are rare but do indeed exist and can be defined (Thomason and Kaufmann 1988: 3). As mentioned above, the data that we have on the Kallawaya suggest that the lexicon of Pukina was different from Quechua or Aymara but that its syntax was structurally similar to Quechua (Bouysse-Cassagne 1987b: 125–126). In other words, Pukina has the principal characteristic of a mixed language.

In short, with the consolidation of power by the Tiwanaku state isolating proto-Quechua speakers for several centuries, Pukina developed as a mixed language. It retained the grammatical structure and some vocabulary of Quechua but borrowed vocabulary from proto-Jaqi and/or other now-extinct languages. As geographically intermediate between Quechua and Aymara, and as a mixed language, it served as the most viable second language in the region characterized by bi- and multilingual populations (Mannheim 1991).

Data from the Toledo Tasa support the hypothesis that Pukina was virtually a second language for almost every region. In the dozens of cases where Pukina was spoken in the circum-Titicaca Basin, all but two were bi- or multilingual populations. In other words, Pukina was almost always spoken in villages with other languages. In contrast, there are numerous instances, in both the Toledo Tasa and in other documents, as well as today, in which villages speak only Quechua and Spanish, or Aymara and Spanish. Furthermore, the two cases may be exceptions that prove the rule. The two villages are Coata and Capachica, in the extreme north in an area that was in the sixteenth century the most likely linguistic boundary between Aymara and Quechua. They were also on or near the Inca road from Cuzco to the south. In other words, the location of supposedly monolingual Pukina-speakers in two villages is precisely where one would expect a contact language to flourish: on the boundary of two distinct languages on a major road system.

The rapid disappearance of Pukina in the late sixteenth and seventeenth centuries occurred as Spanish replaced it as the most viable second language of the central Andes. Unlike Quechua and Aymara, which had large numbers of native speakers, Pukina was most likely a second language used in a specific political and social context during the hegemony of Tiwanaku and during the political fragmentation after the Tiwanaku collapse. As such, it ceased to be used by indigenous populations when Spanish replaced it as the principal lingua franca in the areas of the former Inca empire.

Economic Patterns

The available data indicate a substantial change in economic patterns at a regional level between the Expansive Tiwanaku and the Altiplano periods. Altiplano-period populations shifted from intensive agricultural strategies to extensive ones, relied much more heavily on pastoralism, and possibly reduced interregional trade. All of these changes are associated with the development of the agro-pastoral economies that characterized the Aymara señoríos of the first half of the first millennium A.D.

In the Juli-Pomata region, the land use ratios indicate a major shift away from raised-field agriculture and an increase in the relative importance of rain-fed terrace agriculture and pastoralism. During the Altiplano period, land use patterns reverted to those of the Middle Formative (approximately 30 percent of the population in the raised-field areas, and about 70 percent in non-raised-field areas). The Early Sillumocco– and Altiplano-period settlement patterns represent site distributions characteristic of low-risk labor and resource optimization strategies used by farmers in an ecological context in which raised-field agriculture is feasible. In this pattern, about 30 to 40 percent of the population were located in areas of raised-field production, while about half were in rain-fed terrace areas. The remaining population was in the puna, most certainly tending camelid herds.

During the Altiplano period there was also a shift in settlement choice for exploiting the raised-field system, similar in some ways to that in the Early Sillumocco period. In both periods, settlements were much smaller on average. In the Altiplano period, sites were directly adjacent to smaller sections of the fields. The model offered by Graffam (1992) for the

FIGURE 9.1. Altiplano-period pottery. Photograph by the author.

Pampa Koani fields is also the most appropriate settlement model for the Juli-Pomata fields. In this pattern, individual households are adjacent to small plots of raised fields, and formal canal and aqueduct systems were not significant. It is significant that this pattern also included substantial non-raised-field land use.

The settlement pattern of the Early Sillumocco and Altiplano periods can be explained as one aimed at minimizing risk by diversifying economic activities. The cultures that adopted this strategy were politically no more complex than simple chiefdoms. I interpret this strategy to be one that conformed to Chayanov's rule for domestic economies.

In short, in a context of minimal political centralization, peasant populations pursued economic strategies characterized by underproduction relative to household needs, low surplus, and low labor inputs. These are ideal strategies for long-term survival. Browman (1986: 1) notes that even contemporary altiplano *campesinos* employ risk-reduction strategies rather than maximization ones. Such an observation conforms well to this model in that the collapse of the *hacienda* system, the minimal penetration of the

national market system, and the relative autonomy of the modern Aymara farmer from governmental authorities is precisely the context for the operation of Chayanov's rule.

Altiplano-Period Pottery Styles

Very little is known about Altiplano-period art styles, principally because of two factors. First, fancy stone and ceramic art apparently disappeared during this period. Second, unlike Tiwanaku and Pucara, the Altiplano-period cultures were geographically localized, and there is no representation of their textile art on the coast, where such materials preserve. The best medium of artistic expression that we have for the Altiplano period is pottery (see figure 9.1). A number of pottery traditions have been identified in the Titicaca region that generally correspond to the ethnic and political divisions of the Aymara señoríos of the late prehistoric periods.

THE COLLA REGION

Several distinctive pottery types occur only in this period in the northern Titicaca Basin. These types are distinguished largely by paste and surface decoration. Altiplano-period diagnostics in the Colla region were first mentioned by Kidder (1943: 8) and later defined by M. Tschopik (1946) as the "Collao Series." Most of Tschopik's period attributions are correct based on my observations, although there are problems with the Allita Amaya type. Also, the Sillustani Black-on-red type may be both pre-Inca and Early Inca in date. In the northern Titicaca, the Collao Black-on-red bowls and jars are very common and constitute the principal means of recognizing Altiplano-period sites.

A small number of Altiplano-period diagnostics are classified as Sillustani; they were first identified and named by M. Tschopik (1946: 22–27) and further discussed by Julien (1982), Revilla Becerra and Uriarte Paniagua (1985), and Stanish (1991). This work indicates that Sillustani pottery has both pre-Inca and Inca types. The pre-Inca types are poorly burnished on the exterior, have parallel black lines on red or reddish brown surfaces, and tend to have very thin walls.

THE LUPAQA REGION

Altiplano-period diagnostics in the Juli-Pomata area consist largely of bowls, jars, and olla forms. We have called the most common ware Pucarani, following the work of de la Vega (1990) at Pukara Juli. This locally manufactured ware is Altiplano period in date. De la Vega's typology of the Pucarani ware includes several decorated varieties and five discrete pastes that are found in quantity on Pukara Juli. The paste is semicompact, with temper inclusions of fine to coarse sand. Six types have been recognized: Pucarani Plain, Pucarani Black-on-red, Pucarani Black-and-white-on-red, Pucarani Red-on-orange, Pucarani Red-on-brown, and Pucarani Black-on-orange.

Pucarani decorated bowls are characterized by deep, thin-walled vessels with black decoration on the interior (and see Onofre 1989). Stylistic links can be seen between decorated Pucarani pottery and Hyslop's Tanka Tanka Black-on-orange, several pre-Inca Sillustani types, and the Early Pacajes type identified by Albarracin-Jordan and Mathews (1990) from the Tiwanaku Valley.

SOUTHERN TITICACA
BASIN POTTERY STYLES

In the Desaguadero area and farther south, we discovered an additional Altiplano-period type that we have called Kelluyo (Stanish et al. 1997: 104–108). Diagnostics are exclusively straight-sided bowl forms characterized by typical Altiplano-period design motifs: poorly executed black linear paint on the interior of the vessels. The Kelluyo type most likely is associated with a nonlacustrine Altiplano-period culture that has yet to be adequately studied.

EASTERN BASIN ALTIPLANO-PERIOD
CERAMIC STYLES

From roughly Huancané in the north to at least Conima to the south, the predominant Altiplano-period pottery types are two distinctive wares that are generally referred to Collao pottery. It is characterized by typical Altiplano-period forms with a highly distinctive paste ranging in color from gray to orange, depending on oxidation, and stone temper inclusions of crushed granite and/or limestone.

Hernán Amat (1977: 5) has identified another pottery type called Quequerana, named after the site of the same name near Moho. He describes the pottery as "based in the use of geometric motifs [painted] in brown on a cream paste and decorated with plastic and incised decorations." This pottery is found throughout the area as well, and appears to be a regional variant of the Altiplano-period pottery tradition.

In general, the pottery of the Altiplano period in the immediate lake area shows few stylistic links to the Tiwanaku styles. There are some exceptions, however, such as the occasional kero shapes found in the small inhabited pukaras, and some straight-sided, red-slipped bowls that are similar to Tiwanaku tazones. This pattern is a noticeable contrast with other areas in the circum-Titicaca Basin. The Mollo styles to the east and the Churajón style to the west show much stronger links to Tiwanaku styles (Lumbreras 1974a). Why this is the case remains problematic.

On the surface, Churajón and Mollo could be used as evidence for the Aymara migration hypothesis: the areas where this pottery is distributed roughly coincide with the distribution of Pukina in the sixteenth century. However, there is the very important exception of the immediate northern Titicaca Basin, where Tiwanaku-like styles disappeared quickly but which was an area of Pukina dominance. Furthermore, the Altiplano-period pottery is stylistically consistent and is found beyond the hypothesized limits of Aymara immigration. In fact, these styles first developed in areas where Aymara was not a dominant language; that is, the northern Titicaca Basin where Quechua predominated.

One hypothesis is that the Tiwanaku-like iconographic traditions were maintained in areas where complex political organization was also maintained, and that these traditions disappeared where the agropastoral political economies developed. This would explain the distribution of Tiwanaku-related polychromes in the Mollo and Churajón areas as a result of a more complex labor organization that was capable of manufacturing these commodities. That is, the elite were stronger in these areas and were able to support attached specialists of pottery producers. Their counterparts in the altiplano would have lacked this ability to mobilize labor on such a scale. In short, this hypothesis could be tested by comparing levels of political economic complexity with areas of Tiwanaku-related pottery distributions in the post-Tiwanaku periods. In broad terms, there is indeed a correlation: the polities in the Mollo, Chiribaya, and Churajón areas were more complex than the altiplano cultures at the time.

Funerary Patterns

The most dramatic change in funerary patterns in the Titicaca region occurred in the Altiplano period. This, of course, is the development of aboveground burial tombs. A wide variety of aboveground tomb types in the Titicaca region are defined in chapter 5. It is important to stress that all aboveground tomb types begin in the Altiplano period and not before. At least four types of tombs were used in the Titicaca region during the Altiplano period: belowground cist or shaft tombs, slab-cist tombs or stone-fence graves, chulpas, and cave burials.

The typology that has been developed over the years from the archaeological data is also consistent with terms found in Bertonio's dictionary. These terms indicate a wide variety of above- and below-ground tomb types that were recognized by the Aymara informants in the sixteenth century. For instance, the term *amaya uta,* translated literally as "house of the soul," is defined by Bertonio as "burial in the ancient manner" or "grave like a house on the ground," and probably refers to what we today call chulpas. The term *chulpa,* in contrast, is defined as a "grave or basket where they put the dead." The term *haccha chupimpi imatha* is a verb meaning "to bury with great pomp." In contrast, nonelite or simple burials were defined by the term *imaui,* meaning "grave simply dug in the earth." In other words, the sixteenth-century texts indicate several different types of burial forms for elites and commoners, and archaeological survey and excavation have helped to identify these forms. The typology developed for the Altiplano period is outlined below.

BELOWGROUND CIST OR SHAFT TOMBS

Cist tombs in the Altiplano period appear to be similar to pre-Altiplano–period tombs as described in chapter 5. They are found in abundance throughout the Titicaca Basin and beyond, and probably correspond to the word *imaui* ("common grave") listed in Bertonio's 1612 dictionary.

SLAB-CIST TOMBS OR STONE-FENCE GRAVES

This type of aboveground tomb was first described by M. Tschopik (1946: 19) as a slab-cist tomb, but is referred to by Rydén (1947: 362) and Hyslop (1976) as stone-fence graves. This type of tomb consists of a ring of uncut fieldstone slabs about one meter in diameter, inside of which is usually a low depression in which multiple burials were interred. The word *callca* in Bertonio's dictionary (Bk. 1: 430), defined as a "grave like a box of many stones for burying *principales* under the earth," may refer to slab-cist tombs. This is quite compelling in that slab-cist tombs are aboveground constructions (burial locus visible) but the actual bodies were placed just belowground.

FIGURE 9.2. Pre-Inca chulpa near Pajchiri, Bolivia. Photograph by the author.

Slab-cist tombs are fundamentally different from cist tombs in that they contain multiple burials. They appear to function in a manner similar to that of chulpas in that they are visible markers of the burial area for large numbers of people. Like chulpas, slab-cist tombs are most likely collective burials for corporate groups, probably nonelite extended families.

SMALL FIELDSTONE CHULPAS

The most common completely aboveground tombs in the Titicaca Basin during the Altiplano period are small fieldstone chulpas constructed in the igloo, transitional, and pirca chulpa styles identified by Hyslop (1977). Originally, they would have been about one to five meters in height, and one to two meters in diameter. Both round and square shapes are quite common and are found throughout the Titicaca region. In fact, small fieldstone chulpas are found throughout the central Andes (Isbell 1997). The chulpa illustrated in figure 9.2 is in the Pajchiri area in Bolivia and is an example of an exceptionally well-preserved multichambered tower that dates to the Altiplano period. In spite of the fieldstone construction technique and small base diameter, the chulpa reached over five meters in height. Inside were the remains of three floors, stacked vertically, that housed mummies. It is likely that the chulpa was built sequentially, with each floored chamber representing a nuclear family, probably from an elite group that lived in the area.

LARGE CUT-STONE CHULPAS

Built with Inca-like cut-stone blocks and occasionally decorated with bas-relief carvings, these rare large chulpas can be round or square. There is some question as to whether they are Late Horizon or Altiplano period in date, but they are most likely the amaya uta defined in Bertonio as "burial in the ancient manner" (Bk. 1: 218) and "grave like a house on the ground" (Bk. 1: 430). Translated literally, *amaya uta* means "soul house."

It is possible that large cut-stone chulpas were built in both periods. Some of the best evidence for pre-Inca fine stoneworking comes from the site of Tanka Tanka, which was built initially in the Altiplano period. The fact that the blocks of the fortification walls are reminiscent of the Inca building of Sacsahuaman in Cuzco strongly suggests that this stoneworking technique had its origins, or was used independently, in at least the Lupaqa area prior to Inca expansion. Of course, a literal reading of some chroniclers who claim that Pachacuti ordered his stonemasons to learn from the architectural techniques at Tiwanaku supports this interpretation.

On the other hand, there is no direct evidence that these chulpas are Altiplano period in date. There is a small Late Horizon occupation on Tanka Tanka. Furthermore, several of the chulpas appear to have been fieldstone or igloo chulpas that were subsequently redressed with cut-stone blocks, suggesting reuse in the Late Horizon. Given our lack of knowledge of the dates of these chulpas, I adopt a conservative view and date these to the Late Horizon based on the stoneworking technique. Future work may resolve whether these finely built burial towers are local imitations of Inca stoneworking, an indigenous development of earlier traditions (Tiwanaku or Pucara, for example), or a from introduced by the Inca. These chulpas, in particular, most likely correspond to the amaya uta described by Bertonio. They do indeed look like stone houses and are built in such a manner. They almost always have an east-facing doorway and were built to house a number of bodies over a long period of time.

LARGE FIELDSTONE CHULPAS

Built with uncut, but possibly shaped, blocks, these massive chulpas measure up to three meters in height and three meters in diameter. This type is found throughout the Titicaca Basin but in restricted areas. One of the earliest and best-preserved sets of such chulpas are those at Molloko, about four kilometers south of Acora. Presently, four chulpas appear to be preserved as well as when they were described by Vásquez (1937b). From the drawings in Squier (1877: 352), it appears that the Molloko chulpas were in a similar condition in the nineteenth century. As with the finely cut stone chulpas, fieldstone chulpas traditionally are dated to the Late Horizon. There is no direct dating of these chulpas (all but a few were looted in the Early Colonial period), but it is more likely that these are Altiplano in date as they do not exhibit the fine workmanship associated with the Inca style.

ADOBE CHULPAS

These chulpas appear to be rare north of the Río Ilave, with the exception of a few found in Sillustani (see figures 9.3a–d), those reported by Ruiz Estrada (1978: 799) near Cabanillas, and a few in the Ayaviri area. The existence of adobe chulpas at Sillustani is important because it proves that they can survive the climate of the north basin, where rainfall is higher. Nevertheless, adobe chulpas appear to be primarily a southern Titicaca Basin phenomenon associated with the Carangas and Pacajes areas and the areas around and south of La Paz (Pärssinen 1993; Ponce 1993; Rivera Casanovas 1989; Sagárnaga M. 1993; Trimborn 1993). A number of adobe chulpas are found along the lower Río Desaguadero, and they are found in abundance in the desert grasslands of the south and in the region around Oruro. Adobe chulpas are also common in the lake region to the south, near Lake Poopó.

Adobe chulpas can be either round or rectangular. They have an eastern doorway or niche, just as the stone ones do. Most adobe chulpas are solid adobe wall constructions made with rectangular and conical bricks (Ponce 1993: 153). Some chulpas are fieldstone constructed with adobe plastering on the exterior. There is evidence of painted decorations on chulpa exteriors and interiors (e.g., Pärssinen 1993: 25–26; Squier 1877). Gisbert (1994: 455–457) provides photographs of some stunning painted adobe chulpas in the far south of the circum-Titicaca Basin region, near Lake Sacabaya. The designs are similar to Inca dress as depicted in Guamán Poma, and the architecture of these chulpas is some of the most highly developed in the Titicaca region. The Lake Sacabaya chulpas reinforce the argument that adobe chulpas are most common in the south.

FIGURES 9.3A–D. Chulpas from the site of Sillustani, Peru. Photographs by the author.

*The Chulpa Phenomenon
in the Titicaca Basin and Beyond*

The development of chulpas in the Altiplano period in the Titicaca Basin and the Late Intermediate period in the central Andes in general remains unexplained. As we have seen above, the collapse of Tiwanaku power precipitated numerous changes in basin cultures. Chulpa building began and flourished in the Altiplano period, and continued into the Early Colonial period.

Nordenskiöld (1906) reported several ceramics from chulpa graves that Rydén characterized as Decadent Tiahuanaco (Rydén 1947: 444). Apart from this single reference, virtually all objects recovered from chulpas are post-Tiwanaku in style. Subsequent archaeological research has confirmed the post-Tiwanaku date of all aboveground tombs yet investigated. The pioneering archaeological fieldwork by Bennett (1934), Franco Inojosa and González (1936), Tschopik (1946), Vásquez (1937a, 1937b) and Rydén (1947, 1957) served to reinforce this view with solid archaeological data.[6]

Chulpas are also found sporadically throughout the central Andes, however, and have been reported as far north as Huancavelica (Matos 1960: 316–317), Chavín de Huantar (Burger 1982), and as far south as the Río Loa in Antofagasta (Aldunate and Castro 1981). Numerous chulpas are also found in the Cuzco area and beyond (Franco Inojosa 1937; Gutiérrez Noriega 1935, 1937; Kaufmann-Doig 1983: 538; Kendall 1985), in Apurímac (Arrendo 1942), in the Ayacucho Valley (K. Schreiber, personal communication 1995), and in other areas throughout the central Andes.

The available evidence indicates that chulpas were burial areas for corporate groups. The first controlled excavations of chulpas were conducted by Nordenskiöld (1906) in the early twentieth century. This pioneering naturalist worked on the northeast side of Lake Titicaca in the high valleys of the alti-plano. One of the most striking results of Nordenskiöld's excavations was the discovery of collective burials in the chulpas, in some cases totaling as many as two hundred individuals. Later excavations by other scholars also supported the interpretation that chulpas functioned primarily as multiple burial chambers. Rydén's (1947) work in circum-Titicaca Basin "grave houses" produced numerous instances of multiple burials in stone and adobe chulpas. Although all of the chulpas excavated by Rydén had been looted, numerous human skeletal remains were still present.

Chulpas were the material manifestations of a new ideology that was distinctly non-Tiwanaku and one that was shared by the region's emerging societies. Chulpas varied considerably in architectural style, but the essential principle behind chulpa building remained constant: aboveground tombs became a locus of ritual surrounding corporate elite groups and their ancestors. The doors and wall niches in chulpas suggest that, unlike belowground cist tombs, they were designed for a continual ceremonial reuse and possibly numerous episodes of interment as individuals within the group died. Traditional belowground cist tombs, on the other hand, were used for one event and permanently covered, often under the floor of a domestic structure or in cemeteries. Their use reflects a fundamentally different treatment of the dead that goes back millennia.

ARE CHULPAS ELITE CONSTRUCTIONS?

Chulpa tombs are generally considered to be elite constructions. There is little question that the large chulpas made with finely cut stone and the large fieldstone chulpas in the Titicaca region are the tombs of elite. Our data from the Juli-Pomata survey suggest strongly that both of these massive chulpa types are Late Horizon in date. Furthermore, our data confirm the relatively small numbers of these large chulpas in our survey area (less than 20). What was a surprise from our survey is the relatively large number of small chulpas (approximately 285) and slab-cist tombs (approximately 530). Also, there were undoubtedly numerous chulpas that were destroyed to clear land for agriculture. These smaller chulpas are quite common, and although the vast majority were small igloo-shaped and low fieldstone, there was a fair number of larger ones as well. It appears that aboveground tombs of all types are considerably more common than has been previously recognized.

I have already quoted the European naturalist Marquis de Nadaillac, who suggested that chulpas were much more common than they are today: "chulpas which, mixed with megaliths, cover the whole plain of Acora" (1969 [1885]: 424). Squier's (1877: 351–352) observations are similar to those of Nadaillac. He noted numerous monuments in the Acora plain: "The plain is covered with many rude monuments, small circles and squares of unwrought upright stones, planted in the ground." In the next paragraph, he goes on to say that such monuments are found "in abundance all through the ancient Collao."

I conclude that small aboveground tombs were used by a substantial number of nonelite, but the very large chulpas (above two meters or so) were confined to elite groups. The precise relationship between social class and mortuary practice remains one of the most important topics for future research in the region.

THE SPECIAL SITE OF SILLUSTANI

Sillustani is one of the most famous archaeological monuments in the Titicaca Basin. The site is in Colla territory, due west of the plains between Juliaca and Paucarcolla, near the beautiful lake of Umayo. The site houses a number of spectacular chulpa burial towers. One of the most outstanding features of the burial towers at Sillustani is their variability. We find huge, finely cut stone chulpas built in an Inca style, very poorly constructed ones built in igloo styles, adobe chulpas, and one built in what would appear to be a derived Tiwanaku style.

Sillustani is not just a cemetery. There is a substantial habitation area on the west side of the site. Approximately three hectares of midden are located on the hills flanking the modern entrance to the site under and adjacent to the present-day road. These middens are typically habitation debris containing bone refuse, traces of hearths, many stone flakes, and so forth. Excavations by archaeologists from the National Institute of Culture and the Catholic University in Arequipa indicated that there was a Tiwanaku occupation at the site, followed by later peoples (Revilla B. and Uriarte P. 1985).

Almost all of the chulpa construction techniques at Sillustani are stylistically post-Tiwanaku in date, and there are both pre-Inca and Inca-style chulpas. There is also a number of fortified pukaras surrounding Sillustani that most likely date to the Altiplano period. The great site of Hatuncolla, the capital of the Colla state, is just a few kilometers away. Sillustani is thus associated with a number of Altiplano-period habitation and fortification sites in the area.

Sillustani is a very unusual site in the altiplano. The diversity of chulpa types is astounding, and there is no other site that we know of with such a variety of burial forms. The chulpas are not contemporary either, so the site had to be used for generations. How do we explain this site? One possibility is that Sillustani was a major pilgrimage/burial center in the post-Tiwanaku periods. The adobe chulpas, for instance, are most common in the Pacajes region to the south, and the round, finely cut stone chulpas are more common in the Lupaqa and southern Colla areas. In other words, Sillustani may have functioned as a pan-regional burial center of the great Aymara señoríos during the twelfth through fifteenth centuries before becoming a major pilgrimage and burial center during the Inca occupation. Certainly the existence of pilgrimage destinations is well documented for the Prehispanic Andes in general and the Titicaca Basin in particular. An example is the

Island of the Sun, which the Inca maintained as a pilgrimage destination. As I have discussed above, this pilgrimage center was first used during the Tiwanaku period but apparently was not used in the Altiplano period by any polity off the island itself.

The fact that the collapse of the first pan-Collao pilgrimage shrine on the Island of the Sun coincides with the collapse of Tiwanaku is quite telling. This suggests a political and ritual dynamic in the region in which the most powerful polity maintained a regional shrine. In other words, the Tiwanaku state constructed the first pan-Aymara huaca on the Island of the Sun. The collapse of the Island of the Sun huaca at Chucaripupata (Seddon 1998) correlated with the collapse of the Tiwanaku political structure. The Colla to the north developed as the most powerful polity in the post-Tiwanaku periods. The hypothesis offered here is that with the collapse of the pan–Titicaca Basin pilgrimage destination on the Island of the Sun, there was a shift to Sillustani as the region's primary Aymara ritual destination. This shift would correlate to the decline of the Pacajes (ancestral Tiwanaku) region as the principal political power and a shift to the north in Colla territory. Control of the one pan-regional pilgrimage destination during and after Tiwanaku therefore correlated with the center of political power. The shift from the south, on the Island of the Sun, to the north, at Sillustani, reflected the power shift in the region as a whole. The numerous gold objects recovered by Ruiz Estrada (1976) may

in fact support the notion that this was a pilgrimage destination. Although some of these gold objects may have been Inca period in date, the possibility remains that some were pre-Inca.

Summary

The collapse of the Tiwanaku state ushered in a period in which agro-pastoral economies dominated the cultural landscape of the Titicaca Basin. By A.D. 1200, the concentrated Tiwanaku centers gave way to a highly dispersed settlement pattern. The Titicaca Basin peoples of the Altiplano period built large refuge sites, called *pukaras,* among the many scattered small villages and hamlets.

The nature of Altiplano-period political organization is highly debated. Historic documents suggest that the post-Tiwanaku kingdoms were, indeed, state-level societies with a social and political hierarchy. Archaeological evidence, however, provides a different view of pre-Inca society as one with only moderately ranked political organization. The large pukaras appear to have been the primary settlements, with villages and hamlets politically linked to centers. By these criteria, there were perhaps a dozen or so major pukaras in the region during the fifteenth century. These would correspond to a similar number of autonomous or semiautonomous polities, including the Colla, the Lupaqa, the Pacajes, and several peoples of the eastern basin.

Conquest from Outside

The Inca Occupation of the Titicaca Basin

The Quechua-speaking peoples who lived in the Cuzco region built a mighty conquest state that expanded over an enormous area in a relatively short span of time. Over the centuries, the nature of the Inca state has been defined and redefined, with interpretations ranging from its being a totalitarian state to a benevolent "socialist" empire (Arze 1941; Baudin 1928). In a similar vein, twentieth-century writers interpreted the Inca more as a great redistributive state in which even the poorest citizens were protected from disease and want.

Leaving such romantic illusions aside, it is clear that the principal mechanism of Inca expansion was military conquest. Like virtually every other imperial state in history, the motive for Inca expansion was territorial gain, appropriation of other peoples' resources, and neutralization of potential enemies. A conception of the Inca as a benign state concerned with the commoners' welfare fails the test of scholarship.

The conquest of new territories was often preceded by intense negotiations and political intrigue. After a territory was conquered, the Inca usually instituted their classic incorporation strategies, including the creation or rehabilitation of the road system, the building of way stations, or tambos (tampu), the resettling of colonists (mitima), and the co-option of local political authority. Physical facilities were constructed by using the labor tax, based usually on the decimal system (Julien 1982). One point on which most Andeanists agree is that the extraction of wealth in the Inca state was based on a labor tax and not on tribute-in-kind, as in the Aztec and other early empires worldwide (Julien 1988a: 261–264; La Lone 1982: 294; Murra 1982: 245; 1985b: 15; Stanish 1997). This distinction is subtle, yet important. Murra repeats a statement made many times in the documents that "*curacas* received no tribute of any kind save respect and the working of their fields" (Murra 1980: 92). Goods were indeed collected by the state; however, instead of using a tribute-in-kind system, where the local political economy is left intact and a tribute obligation is imposed, the Inca state expropriated land and used corvée labor to work the land.

Ideology served powerful political purposes in the Inca state. A primary goal of the imperial ideology was to define economic relationships between high nobility, lesser nobility, and commoners, as just in traditional Andean terms (La Lone 1982: 296). The chief means of promoting the ideal of elite generosity was the sponsoring of feasts or the distribution of certain commodities to tribute-payers when actually fulfilling their labor obligations. In these redistributive transactions, maize beer *(chicha),* textiles, and possibly other commodities were redistributed (Hastorf and Johannessen 1993; Morris 1971, 1982). Another major goal of Inca ideology was to present the elite as legitimate rulers of Tawantinsuyu. Origin myths of the Inca state represent an excellent example of this strategy (Bauer 1992a, 1992b; Urton 1990).

In sum, the Inca political economy was based largely on the manipulation and transformation of traditional political and economic mechanisms in Andean society. Reciprocity and redistribution were transformed into an extractive imperial political economy legitimized by the use of myth and ideology. Administered trade relationships were co-opted by the Inca and reworked into a vast commodity producing and transport system. The result was a vast and complex system of resource extraction, unparalleled in Andean history.

Absolute Chronology

The dates of Inca expansion have been fairly well established by historical and archaeological research. As described in the previous chapter, the dates for the end of the Altiplano period define the beginning of Inca expansion. Generally, the first actual control of the Titicaca Basin by the Inca state is dated to around A.D. 1450–1475, which has been corroborated by carbon-14 dates that have been run on Inca-period samples.[1]

In the previous section, we saw that the Titicaca Basin during the fifteenth century A.D. was home to several powerful and independent Aymara señoríos that abruptly lost their independence with the conquest of the region by Tawantinsuyu. One of the most detailed accounts of the Inca conquest of Collasuyu can be found in Bernabé Cobo's and Pedro de Cieza de León's histories. Although details vary, the accounts provide a basic outline of the events leading up to the conquest. Of course, it is unclear how much of the information in the documents represents a mythic history as part of Inca imperial propaganda, and how much represents factual events. As Urton has demonstrated (1990), the histories as recorded by Spanish writers were dramatically influenced by contemporary political and ideological considerations. It is in this light that we must go back to the documented oral histories of the Spanish conquest of the Titicaca Basin as reported by the early Spanish historians.

As mentioned above, the Lupaqa and Colla fought a great battle on the plains of Paucarcolla. The Cari, or king, of the Lupaqa was said to have won this battle, and he returned to Chucuito and negotiated peace with Viracocha Inca.[2] According to one interpretation, Viracocha Inca actually lost in his bid to control the Titicaca region south of the Colla area. But although there may be some doubt as to whether Viracocha Inca established strong control of the region, the chronicles leave little doubt that Pachacuti brought the Titicaca Basin firmly into the Inca orbit. Forced to fight the Colla again near Ayaviri, the Inca defeated them and concluded a peace with the Lupaqa. After the remaining Colla retreated to Pucara, the Inca destroyed the town of Ayaviri and killed a number of people. The Inca then met the Colla

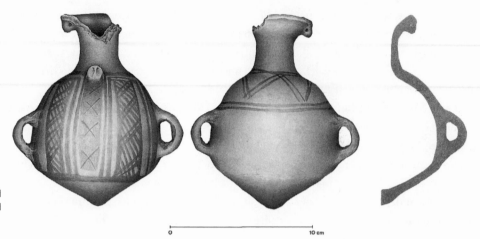

FIGURE 10.1. Inca pottery. Reproduced courtesy of the Field Museum, Chicago, catalog no. 2687.

again, and the Colla were decisively defeated a second time.

Cobo relates that the Lupaqa then concluded an alliance with the Inca: "The cacique of the nation of the Lupaca Indians, who resided in Chucuito, was just as powerful as the cacique of Collao, but he took sounder advice, because he received the Inca in peace and turned over his state to him. Thus the Inca honored him very much and in order to show him more favor, he stayed in Chucuito for a few days" (Cobo 1983 [1653]: 140).

Other polities in the Titicaca Basin did not fare as well as the Lupaqa, according to Cobo. Pachacuti is said to have conquered the Pacajes region, Paucarcolla, Omasuyu, Azángaro, and the Islands of the Sun and Moon. It was during this campaign that Pachacuti is reported to have seen the ruins of the ancient city of Tiwanaku in what appears to have been a triumphal march around the lake.

The chronicles also indicate that the Inca rule in Collao was rife with rebellions by the conquered populations. Cieza refers to one major rebellion that had to be quelled by Pachacuti's successor, Topa Inca. Presuming the accuracy of the traditional chronology, this event would have occurred around 1471, near the end of Pachacuti's reign (Hyslop 1976: 141). The rebellion was apparently a bloody one, with many or all of the Inca administrators killed or expelled. Documents suggest that additional rebellions occurred throughout the Inca reign in Collasuyu, one that was always tenuous at best.

Inca Settlements in the Titicaca Basin

The Titicaca Basin was one of the most important provinces in the Inca state. The Collao had an enormous population and was very rich. Inca sites, in fact, are ubiquitous throughout the basin and are identified by the presence of Local Inca pottery (see figures 10.1 and 10.2).

Secondary Urban Settlements

Archaeological survey data suggest that the population in the Titicaca Basin reached a peak during the Inca period and that it did not reach that level again until the late nineteenth or early twentieth centuries. The population of the Titicaca Basin was most likely one of the densest in the Inca empire at its height in A.D. 1530. It is therefore not surprising that urbanized settlements became a major settlement

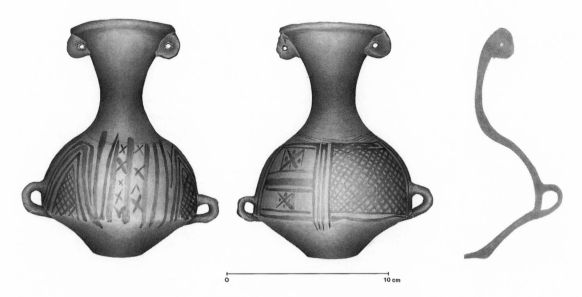

FIGURE 10.2. Inca pottery. Reproduced courtesy of the Field Museum, Chicago, catalog no. 2957.

type in the basin during the Inca period. The capital of the Inca state, of course, was Cuzco, the empire's primary urban center.

It was during the Inca period that, for the first time in the Titicaca region, substantial urban settlements were established outside a capital or core settlement. Tiwanaku, of course, was a huge urban area (by Andean standards) that covered about 6 square kilometers. Outside Tiwanaku, however, sites were dramatically smaller (the one exception being Lukurmata, at around 150 hectares). During the Inca period, this pattern changed: urbanized sites of ten hectares or more were common, and Inca-period urban centers were substantially more extensive than those of any other time period.

I refer to the many Inca urbanized sites as either secondary or tertiary urban centers, as defined in chapter 5 (see table 10.1). Based on several indirect lines of evidence, and some direct evidence, I believe a large percentage of these centers' populations were nonagriculturalists. The documents generally (rarely specifically) refer to these sites as centers of craft specialists and Inca administrators. Also, the vast majority of sites are along the road systems, suggesting state functions distinct from agriculture, such as tambo provisioning, support for the army, and commodity movement. In general, secondary urban centers are larger than ten hectares, with Hatuncolla and Chucuito reaching at least fifty hectares.

Tertiary urban centers in the Incanized Titicaca Basin are numerous, and almost all are along the road system. These sites tend to be around five hectares in size. They, too, functioned as administrative centers, way stations, military garrisons, and the like. The size of tertiary centers is generally related to the area's preexisting population. Therefore, the heavily populated north and west sides of the lake had the largest Inca sites, and the eastern side was characterized by a series of smaller sites along the road system.

Many sites in the Titicaca region that had substantial Inca occupations are also modern towns. One of the primary questions about the Inca occupation

TABLE 10.1

Selected Secondary and Tertiary Urban Centers
in the Titicaca Basin during the Inca Occupation

Secondary Urban Centers[a]	Area (in hectares)
HATUNCOLLA	50–80
CHUCUITO	50–80
PAUCARCOLLA	25
ACORA	25
JULI	20

Tertiary Urban Centers	Area (in hectares)
ZEPITA	11 (Hyslop)
LUNDAYANI	10
GUAQUI	6 (Albarracin-Jordan 1992: 316)
POMATA	5
SULLKAMARKA	5 (Albarracin-Jordan 1992: 321)
PUCARANI	4–8
TARACO	5–10
MOHO	3–5
CONIMA	5 +
HUANCANÉ	5
CARPA	2–5

[a] Primary urban center would be Cuzco.

of the region centers is whether these sites were built by the Inca as new settlements, or whether they were pre-Inca sites that the Inca absorbed and enhanced.

Analysis of regional data strongly indicates that the vast majority of the secondary and tertiary urban centers were built during the Inca period, and not before. It appears that Inca occupation entailed profound changes in settlement, economy, and polity. The site of Hatuncolla, for instance, was one of the most important Inca settlements in the Titicaca Basin proper (Julien 1983). Although Cobo and Cieza said that Hatuncolla was the capital of the Colla polity before Inca expansion, Julien's research at the site provides no evidence of occupation prior to the Inca period (Julien 1983: 107). This latter observation is extremely important. In a survey of the Lupaqa area, Hyslop discovered that the large colonial and modern towns of Chucuito, Acora, Juli, Pomata, Yunguyu, and Zepita also fit this historical pattern: a substantial Inca occupation without a recognizable pre-Inca settlement (Hyslop 1976). This is also the case for Pila Patag, the site of metalworking near Chucuito. In our survey of the Juli-Desaguadero region, this pattern was confirmed for the centers of both Juli and Pomata (Stanish et al. 1997).

Analysis of historical data also suggests that this pattern holds for most major sites in the Titicaca region in the sixteenth century. Table 10.2 lists the sizes of the towns (in number of taxpayers, not total population) from the Toledo Tasa and the Diez de San Miguel Visita. In unsystematic survey, I have examined the surface of several of these sites outside the Juli-Desaguadero survey region, including Conima, Copacabana, Huancané, Moho, Paucarcolla, Pucarani, and Taraco. All sites fit the pattern in which there were major Inca- and Early Colonial–period occupations but no recognizable pre-Inca occupation. This is also the case for smaller Early Colonial–period sites such as Desaguadero and Guaqui (Albarracin-Jordan and Mathews 1990: 162). These combined data indicate that at the dozen major and

TABLE 10.2

Census of Selected Towns from the Toledo Tasa
and the Diez de San Miguel Visita

Town	Total Number of Taxpayers
JULI[a]	3,709
CHUCUITO[a]	3,464
POMATA[a]	3,318
ACORA[a]	3,246
ILAVE[a]	2,540
ZEPITA[a]	2,284
YUNGUYU[a]	1,420
CAPACHICA[b]	1,303
GUAQUI[b]	1,286
PUCARANI[b]	1,227
PAUCARCOLLA[b]	1,003
PUNO[b]	983
TIWANAKU[b]	868
HUANCANÉ[b]	753
HATUNCOLLA[b]	601
VILQUE[b]	325

[a] Figures from the Diez de San Miguel Visita of 1567.
[b] Figures from the Toledo Tasa of 1572.

minor Early Colonial sites studied, 100 percent had a substantial Inca occupation and no pre-Inca one. This represents a sample of about 20 percent of the major sites in the Titicaca area. In other words, the data suggest that most major early-sixteenth-century settlements were originally founded by the Inca state along the road system, and not before.

Secondary Urban Centers in the Northern Colla Area
HATUNCOLLA (ATUNCOLLA)

The site of Hatuncolla was one of the four regional administrative centers in the Inca empire, according to Cieza; the other three were Hatun Xauxa, Pumpu, and Huánuco Pampa (Cieza 1553: 65; Snead 1992: 71).[3] This site was a major center, complete with a state temple, storehouses, and residences for Inca administrators (Julien 1983: 89). Cuzco, of course, was the empire's only primary urban center. Hatuncolla is therefore ranked as a secondary urban center in the typology developed for the Titicaca region (see table 10.1), the largest of the Inca sites of the Collao. Hatuncolla and Chucuito were the largest secondary urban centers in the Titicaca Basin during the Inca occupation.

Hatuncolla is built on a grid pattern, and several cut-stone blocks in Inca style indicate substantial architecture from the Inca occupation. The modern village of Hatuncolla is approximately thirty hectares in size. My calculation of the size of Inca Hatuncolla is fifty to eighty hectares. According to Cieza, Pachacuti used Hatuncolla as a soldier garrison to maintain a military presence in the region (D'Altroy 1992: 76). This documentary evidence supports the notion that Hatuncolla was the center of Inca military and state efforts to control the Collao. In the Toledo Tasa, Hatuncolla was listed as having 601 taxpayers and a total of 2,385 individuals, including people described as "aymaraes," "uros," and "hatunlunas" (see table 10.2). Tribute included silver, animals, *chuño*, cloth, and fish.

Significantly, one of the largest Inca sites was one-sixth the size of Juli by the 1570s. This demonstrates that there was a substantial reduction in the size and importance of Hatuncolla with the collapse of the Inca state. One could conjecture that Hatuncolla was populated by immigrant Inca officials during their occupation, and that the collapse of the state led to an abandonment of this center. At any rate, by the late sixteenth century, Hatuncolla was a minor town in the Titicaca Basin, virtually abandoned like its counterpart in the north, Huánuco Pampa.

PAUCARCOLLA

According to the Toledo Tasa, Paucarcolla was a moderately large Early Colonial settlement with 1,003 taxpayers and more than 4,500 individuals (Cook 1975: 59). The town was divided into Aymaras and Urus, with the latter constituting about 9 percent of the total population. In the Toledo Tasa, it is noted that apart from the usual tribute items such as meat and wool, the people of Paucarcolla also contributed dried fish and salt (Cook 1975: 60). The area was likely an important area for salt production in the Inca period as well, although we have no direct evidence of this.

Paucarcolla had a substantial Inca occupation, as confirmed by my own observations and those of Julien (1981: 144). I calculate that the site area during the Inca occupation was at least twenty-five hectares, placing it in the second rung of site sizes in the basin, below only Chucuito and Hatuncolla (see table 10.1). Systematic analysis of the surface materials would probably indicate that the Inca town was even larger.

Julien (1983) notes that surface materials are similar to the ceramic phases she defined at Hatuncolla, which suggests that Paucarcolla was contemporary with Hatuncolla during its pre-Colonial phases. The similar ceramic artifacts also indicate a common ceramic production area. As at Hatuncolla, there was a pre-Inca occupation above the Inca town: a scatter of Altiplano-period pottery and some aboveground tomb foundations were observed about one kilometer west of the town plaza. Farther west are at least two hills with encircling walls that likely were the pukaras of the area's Altiplano-period peoples. The Inca state appears to have moved these people down a few kilometers and concentrated them into the urban center of Paucarcolla.

In an unsystematic survey at the site, we discovered extensive and deep Inca-period middens containing typical Inca-period refuse such as pottery fragments, burnt bone, charcoal, andesite, basalt tools, and so forth. We also discovered a scatter of raw copper in an eroding midden. Because copper could not have naturally occurred on the site, such a find suggests metalworking as a specialization, but this remains to be tested. Furthermore, a good reddish clay source noted above the town could have been a source for potters.[4]

Tertiary Urban Centers in the Colla Area

ARAPA

The population of Arapa listed in the Toledo Tasa was 5,486. Kidder notes that "in the vicinity of the town itself we found nothing but late sherds; there are also a number of typical Inca building stones in the church and yards of the town" (Kidder 1943: 19). The town today has evidence of Inca pottery in some adobe bricks. The scatter continues south along the road that parallels the river. Exposed middens around the north side of town also have evidence of Inca pottery. Along the Juliaca-Huancané road are numerous small Inca sites as well, suggesting that settlement was densely packed along the Inca road (assuming that it is in the same location as the modern one). Arapa appears to have been a small Inca administrative site, but we have no quantified data to determine its size.

PUNO

Modern construction has made it difficult to define the Inca occupation in Puno from archaeological materials. There is little documentary information that would suggest it was a major Inca center, but Inca artifacts have been noted from construction sites and from occasional isolated finds, such as that reported by Julien for the site of Azoguini, on a high hill north of town (Julien 1981). In unsystematic survey, I discovered a number of Inca sherd scatters around the Puno Bay area. Outside the town proper, numerous terrace sites have been discovered with fine Local Inca pottery. Whether Puno was a secondary urban center during the Inca occupation remains an open question.

OTHER POSSIBLE URBAN CENTERS IN THE COLLA AREA

A number of sites in the Colla region show some indications that they were Inca urban centers. Superficial observations suggest that they fit the pattern of such sites, with Inca materials on the surface, a grid-pattern plan, and Colonial through modern occupations. Among these sites are the towns of Ayaviri, Huancané, Carpa, Moho, Taraco, Conima, and Saman (and see Kidder 1943; Neira 1967; M. Tschopik 1946).

Secondary Urban Centers in the Lupaqa Region

The Diez de San Miguel Visita lists seven Inca cabeceras in the Lupaqa area of the western Titicaca Basin. *Cabecera* is a Spanish term that denotes a major city with administrative functions. In the Visita, the seven major Lupaqa cabeceras were Chucuito, Acora, Ilave, Juli, Pomata, Yunguyu, and Zepita. Table 4.1 provides the census of taxpayers in the Diez de San Miguel Visita by social division, usually moiety, in each town. The largest town was Juli, with Chucuito, Acora, and Pomata each having more than three thousand inhabitants.

Two patterns are evident from these data. First, the seven sites are evenly spaced along the lake shore. Second, the census data indicate that at least in the Early Colonial period, there was little site size dif-

ferentiation between the major centers. The largest site was only twice as large as the smallest, with a deviation of only 840 people for all seven towns. Furthermore, eliminating Yunguyu, a town very close to Copacabana, the deviation for the remaining six was a mere 590. These data suggest a relatively even distribution of population in towns of more or less even size.

CHUCUITO

The most important and presumably the largest of the Inca centers in the Lupaqa region was Chucuito. Chucuito is approximately sixteen kilometers south of Puno on the Puno-Desaguadero highway, and it was directly on the Inca road as well. The site was home to Martín Cari and Martín Cusi, the two principal caciques of the Lupaqa in 1564. The Diez de San Miguel Visita consistently notes that mit'a laborers were sent from the other six towns to Chucuito to provide service in the caciques' households, a fact that highlights the town's importance during this period. In Hyslop's opinion, Chucuito was the Lupaqa capital during Inca times as well (Hyslop 1984: 130).

Hyslop surveyed the site of Chucuito for his dissertation research, and as did Julien at Hatuncolla, he concluded that there was little evidence that Chucuito was occupied before the Inca period, even though he noted several rectangular stone blocks suggestive of Tiwanaku influence (Hyslop 1976: 122–130). Hyslop calculated a total area of about eighty hectares and noted that the site was built on a grid pattern, an Inca architectural style that he calls "orthogonal."

The pottery on the surface is typically Local Inca and Chucuito types. There is no evidence of pre-Inca remains in the village. Occupation is found in the center of town and extends down toward the lake on the other side of the road. Stone blocks are found throughout the town area, suggesting that there were Inca buildings where the modern streets and structures now stand.

One of the most enigmatic buildings in the Titicaca Basin is found at the site of Chucuito. Known as Inka Uyu, this cut-stone structure was first excavated by Tschopik, who described it as built in an "Inca style." According to Hyslop, all the levels that Tschopik excavated had some Spanish colonial glazed wares, and she therefore was not certain of its context (Hyslop 1984: 130); consequently, excavation results have never been published. According to Hyslop, Tschopik was told of another structure called Kurinuyu, east of Inca Uyu.

The cut stone at Inca Uyu is not in a typical Cuzco style and represents a local architectural technique within Inca stylistic canons (B. Bauer, personal communication 1994). Several blocks have an elongated U shape that has counterparts in Inca sites such as Machu Picchu and Ollantaytambo. At these latter sites, the blocks formed the bottom part of niches and windows. We can therefore presume that typical Inca niches and windows characterized this building.[5]

According to Hyslop, Chucuito had two plazas, one where the modern plaza is and the second where the Inca Uyu is found (Hyslop 1990: 197). I calculate a total Inca occupation of around fifty hectares, based on a pedestrian survey in the site area. This would include the entire town and areas to the east. It is possible that Hyslop was able to see more undisturbed areas in the 1970s and that his estimate of eighty hectares is more accurate (see table 10.1). Regardless, the only site comparable to Chucuito in size and importance in the Inca period was Hatuncolla. There is little doubt that Chucuito was the principal site in the Lupaqa area, and one of the major administrative centers in the Titicaca Basin for the Inca state.

ACORA

Hyslop surveyed Acora, noting that the Inca site was under the modern town (1976: 406–408), and calculated a total area of about twenty-five hectares based on the distribution of surface artifacts and the fact that it was the largest site on the Inca road south of Chucuito (Hyslop 1976: 131). He also suggested that the sites of Kacha Kacha B and Qellojani may be the burial grounds of this cabecera. My observations of the site are generally consistent with those of Hyslop. The pottery is typically Local Inca and Chucuito, and covers most of the modern town. There is no evidence of pre-Inca remains in the village.

JULI

Juli was the center of Early Colonial settlement in the Titicaca Basin. According to the early censuses of both Diez de San Miguel and Buitrago (see tables 4.1 and 4.2), it was the largest Early Colonial settlement as determined by total number of tributaries. Archaeological evidence indicates that it was also a major Inca-period settlement. Hyslop surveyed the site and suggested that it was approximately nine hectares in size. I have estimated the total site area to about twenty hectares, a figure that includes Hyslop's site of Juli B (Hyslop 1976: 133, 309–401). Hyslop felt that Lundayani was larger than Juli, and he therefore concluded that Juli itself was most likely just a tambo, and that Lundayani was the cabecera. I can suggest an alternative explanation—that Juli was twice the size of Lundayani, and that Juli was the original cabecera.

Not only is Juli on the Inca road, but a branch of the road went around the hill of Sapacolla behind Juli. The fact that the main road forked at its entrance to Juli and met again in the center of town is further evidence that it was the principal cabecera. Another southern section of the original road was located by Hyslop; this well-paved road heads south out of town toward Pomata.

Juli is built on a grid pattern and was first constructed in the Inca period, and not before. Extensive observations and surface collections have revealed no recognizable pre-Inca occupation. These observations include rescue excavations in town and extensive observations of construction projects throughout the area. During 1992, the Proyecto Lupaqa was asked by the mayor to supervise a small rescue project at a construction site on the east side of town. Excavations revealed a single well-made wall and about fifty centimeters of Spanish colonial and Inca fill. The base of the excavation did not reveal any pre-Inca occupations, confirming an Inca-period founding date for the site.

Tertiary Urban Centers in the Lupaqa Area

LUNDAYANI

Lundayani is several kilometers west of Juli at the head of the Río Salado. The site was first identified in print by Hyslop (1976: 377–380) as a major Inca- and Spanish Colonial–period site. There are some cut stones near Lundayani, possibly the location of a hot spring near Juli (an Inca bath) mentioned by Bertonio in his dictionary as *Huntto uma* ("hot springs or baths in the puna") (1956 [1612]: Bk. 1: 85). The site is between two quebradas and contains a number of standing structures, including round and rectangular ones that led Hyslop to suggest that this could have been a "reduction" of some indigenous Lupaqa populations by the Inca state. That is, rectangular structures are typical of Inca domestic construction styles, and round structures were typical of pre-Inca Lupaqa ones (Hyslop 1976; Stanish, de la Vega, and Frye 1993).

Lundayani has perhaps the earliest Christian church in the Juli region. The town of Juli was one of the most important centers for the Jesuits and the Dominicans (Meiklejohn 1988). Since Lundayani is so close to Juli and has very early Spanish architecture, it too was likely one of the most important towns in the early Colonial period. The church is built in a classic Early Colonial style with adobe and bricks. The significance of Lundayani for the Early Colonial and Inca history of the Juli region cannot be overstated. It appears to be one of the first churches in the region to be built on top of one major Inca-period settlement and near another. As an Inca site, Lundayani remains problematic. Hyslop calculated the size of Lundayani at more than ten hectares and decided that it was larger than Juli. This is not accurate, as our extensive survey of Juli suggests a site of around twenty hectares in size. I agree with Hyslop that Lundayani is around ten hectares, but I see Juli as the principal cabecera during the Inca period in the area. Lundayani was a major secondary settlement associated with the Inca occupation of Juli.

Another compelling feature of Lundayani, one of the few Inca sites not covered by later occupations, is the mixture of local and Inca-style structures. It is entirely possible that most Inca-period sites had such a mix of architectural styles, but I am inclined to see Lundayani as an exception, not the rule. I base this conclusion on observations of the site of Torata Alta in the Moquegua Valley (Stanish and Pritzker 1983), a settlement that is also intact. At Torata Alta, the settlement layout is an Inca orthogonal grid pattern and is more typical of known southern Peruvian Inca architecture such as Juli and the other major towns along the road system.

I have several hypotheses about the nature and function of Lundayani. It could be the location of the Chinchasuyu mitima noted by Diez de San Miguel and other early writers in the area (Diez de San Miguel 1964 [1567]; Murra 1964). Alternatively, it could be that it was the principal residence of the Lupaqa elite, who enjoyed a privileged position in the Inca state. In this hypothesis, the Lupaqa elite were permitted to have a site well away from the Inca road. The location of Lundayani in this hypothesis could be explained as a need to be near the extensive camelid herds for which the Lupaqa elite were famous (Murra 1968). A final hypothesis is that the site was a major tambo on a road leading west to the puna and the coastal valleys of Moquegua, Sama, and/or Lluta. The site is today on a well-traveled road that follows the drainage into the Pasiri puna lands about thirteen kilometers from the lake. Whatever the explanation, Lundayani ranks as one of the most important sites for understanding Inca-local interactions in the area, and it deserves substantially more research.

ZEPITA

Although it is a relatively small town today, Hyslop suggests that Zepita's Inca occupation covered eleven hectares. He also noted that the site was a tambo and cabecera in the Early Colonial period (Hyslop 1976: 136). My observations at the site generally corroborate Hyslop's.

ILAVE

Hyslop did not find Inca remains in Ilave proper, as he did in other towns along the lakeside, and thus concluded that there was not a significant Inca occupation under the modern town. In limited reconnaissance, however, I discovered a number of small Inca-period hamlets along the Río Ilave just south of Ilave. The question remains as to whether it was a secondary urban center or merely a concentration of smaller villages. At present, I am inclined to agree with Hyslop, based upon my observations in the town itself. Ilave most likely was a cluster of small settlements along the road but not an administrative center.

POMATA

Of the cabecera listed in the Diez de San Miguel Visita, Pomata Pueblo is the smallest (Hyslop 1976: 135). The site seems to have been important in the Early Colonial period, but it was not a center on the scale of Juli or Acora in the Inca period. We estimate a total site size of only four to five hectares, based on the distribution of Inca-period pottery in the streets and disturbed areas of the town (Stanish et al. 1997). Pomata has an Inca component but no obvious pre-Inca occupation, although there are some Altiplano-period sherds in the collection of the Juli-Pomata survey. The site was not a secondary urban center by Inca standards but was most likely a major tambo on the Inca road. Next to the Colonial-period church is a modern *mirador,* around which are a number of Inca sherds as well as some shaped blocks.[6] It is possible this site was a ritual area or shine on the pilgrimage route to the Island of the Sun (see pages 273–275).

YUNGUYU

Yunguyu is on the border of Peru and Bolivia. This town was an important stop as a gateway to the Copacabana/Island of the Sun pilgrimage complex maintained by the Inca state. It was here that the actual pilgrimage began, with a check by guards at what is now the border between Peru and Bolivia (Bauer and Stanish 2001). Some Inca sherds are found in the streets and adobe bricks of the town, but the density is not high. The degree to which the site was a major center, or even a tambo, is unclear.

Urban Centers in the Pacajes Region

The Pacajes region is in the southern Titicaca region, northeast of the Río Desaguadero. The term *Pacajes* was used by the early Spanish government and church authorities in a similar manner to that of *Colla, Lupaqa,* and the like.

PUCARANI

The modern town of Pucarani[7] is in the near southern Titicaca Basin, approximately thirteen kilometers from the lake. Pucarani was a major settlement in the Early Colonial period, listed in the Nación of Pacajes Umasuyu in the early encomienda lists (Julien 1983: 18). In the Toledo Tasa, the population is listed as 5,398, which included 1,079 males classified as Aymara and 148 classified as Uru, with the rest being children, elderly people, and women (Cook 1975: 51–52). The town has a substantial Inca occupation as well, as indicated by the high density of Inca-period pottery found in the streets and in adobe brick in the town. The Inca-period pottery in this town is characterized typically by locally made wares.

GUAQUI

Guaqui is on the lake shore, at the eastern end of the Tiwanaku Valley. According to Mercado de Peñaloza (1965 [1583]), Guaqui was said to have been founded by Tupac Yupanqui as an administrative center through the nucleation of six hamlets (Albarracin-Jordan 1992: 34). Albarracin-Jordan (1996a) suggests that Guaqui could have been a port as well and that the inhabitants manufactured ceramics and produced maize. According to the Toledo Tasa, there were 5,800 people in Guaqui in 1573, with 1,286 tax-payers, including 654 Aymara and 632 classified as Uru. In his survey of the lower Tiwanaku Valley, Albarracin-Jordan (1992: 319) argues that the Inca-period occupation is six hectares in size. There is also a variety of cut sandstone blocks in the town, indicative of an Inca occupation.

TIWANAKU

There was a significant Inca occupation at the site of Tiwanaku as evidenced by the substantial and high-quality Inca sherds found in excavations and on the surface. The occupation appears to have been restricted to the former core of the site, suggesting that Tiwanaku was possibly viewed as a minor pilgrimage center as well as an urban habitation during Inca control of the region. A few cut-stone blocks on the surface appear to be Inca in style, typical of the stepped blocks used in rituals (see Arkush 1999b). Certainly, the site of Tiwanaku was symbolically important in the state's political ideology. Inca intellectuals attempted to usurp the ideological authority and prestige of the former Tiwanaku state in a manner reminiscent of Postclassic Mesoamerican states who invoked the authority of the Toltec (Stan-

ish 1997). They did this by linking their founding elite with the site of Tiwanaku, which was most certainly a major Inca ceremonial site, although we have little data on the occupation to date.

Urban Centers in the Omasuyu Region

The Omasuyu region has not been extensively studied, but several modern towns have substantial Inca remains. Moho, for instance, has an Inca town that covered about five hectares (and see Kidder 1943; Neira 1962, 1967). This town was described by Cobo as having a fine Inca storehouse still standing well after the Conquest: "of those [tambos] that are still standing, the best, most spacious, and best maintained that I have seen are the one at Vilcas and the one at the town of Moho . . . in the Bishopric of Chuquiabo" (Cobo 1983: 229).

The town of Conima also has a large distribution of Inca-period materials on the surface. The towns of Escoma, Ancoraimes, and Huarina probably fit the same pattern. That is, they have a major Early Colonial occupation, as demonstrated by data in the Toledo Tasa, with Inca remains on the surface. Other towns in the region most likely fit this pattern as well.

Carpa is particularly interesting because of the existing Inca walls on the site and the excellent preservation of many of the buildings (Kidder 1943; Neira 1962, 1967). The Inca occupation covers less than five hectares, but the remaining architecture is quite impressive. Walls are built in classic Inca provincial styles (see figure 10.3). Pottery on the surface suggests an important provincial administrative center, perhaps a major tambo on the Omasuyu road.

Inca Occupation of the Lake Titicaca Islands

On this expedition the Inca subjugated all the towns and nations surrounding the great lake Titicaca . . . along with the islands of the aforesaid lake, which were densely populated at the time.

Bernabé Cobo, *History of the Inca Empire*, 1983 [1653], p. 140

FIGURE 10.3. Inca walls at the site of Carpa, northeastern Titicaca Basin. Photograph by the author.

The islands in Lake Titicaca were extensively occupied by the Inca state. Occupations on the major islands go back to at least 2000 B.C., as evidenced by the stratigraphic cut on the Island of the Sun at the site of Ch'uxuqullu (Stanish et al. 2002). Survey on the Islands of the Sun and Moon has indicated a substantial Inca presence. Clearly, the principal settlement determinant on the Islands of the Sun and Moon were ritual in nature, but the distribution of sites indicates that agricultural production was equally important.

There is a substantial Inca settlement on Amantaní Island near the two hills of Pachamama and Pachatata. The entire hillside leading up to the two ceremonial sites was a major Inca village. The debris on the surface is quite thick, indicating an intensive domestic settlement. The semi-subterranean court on the hill above the town, known as the Pachatata, is clearly in a pre-Inca style, but it is possible that architectural modifications to the building were made in the Inca period.

Taquile Island has Inca remains scattered over the surface in a pattern similar to that of the lake's other large islands. No work has been published on the is-

land, but it is likely that the Inca occupation was oriented to agricultural production and possibly ritual. At the top of the island's highest hill is a set of Inca-period structures that most probably functioned as storage units. It is possible that these storehouses held maize, which could have been grown on the island at that time.

A number of smaller islands in the lake also have Inca remains, and Isla Quiljata, in the south, may be representative. It is a very prominent island near the lake shore, in the Chatuma area in the far south of the large lake. The island itself rises dramatically out of the lake with very steep sides. Today it is an island, but the lake levels around it are very shallow. In antiquity, and in the recent past, the island was almost certainly connected with the mainland during periods of drought.

A survey of the island revealed only a small Altiplano-period occupation (Stanish et al. 1997). There are a few Pucarani-like sherds, as well as some round or oval structures. The top of the island supported only a modest occupation during the Altiplano period. A few Inca-period sherds suggest either a very small habitation site or perhaps a burial and/or ceremonial area on the summit. Surprisingly, there was no evidence of major Inca ritual activity on the top, as I had expected, such as a major cut-rock outcrop. On the southeast side of the island, in the beach area, is a fairly large Inca village that covers two to three hectares. A number of slab-cist and chulpa tombs are associated with this habitation area. There is no evidence of corporate architecture, and the site is not listed as a major settlement in any documents known for the period. A possible explanation for the site location is the abundant totora reed stands in the lake near the island today. The site could have been a specialized totora-producing and fishing settlement within the Inca settlement system.

Another small island, Pallalla, is northeast of the Island of the Sun. It is a small island, with little area for agriculture. However, the site contains a structure forty-five meters long and six meters wide, with a series of even divisions. The architecture is very similar to that of an Inca *qolca,* or storage structure. Sherds from the island also indicate an Inca site. The exact function of an Inca qolca on such an isolated island is unknown, but it is likely that Pallalla was part of a water pilgrimage route during the Inca period. According to an early visitor, Joseph Pentland, Pallalla was called Isla de los Plateros and had tombs, and possibly gold and silver figurines (Pentland 1827: f. 90). Of course, such figurines are found in a number of ceremonial contexts, including Capaccocha ceremonies that could have been a component of a pilgrimage.

The island of Koa was an important ritual site during the Tiwanaku period (see pages 273–277; and Ponce et al. 1992). It also was an important center during the Inca period, based on a number of Inca-period offerings that were found. The island was possibly along a water pilgrimage route during the Inca period described below.

There are several islands in the little lake (Huiñamarca) that have important Inca remains. Cordero M. (1972) published the first account of the Inca re-

mains on the island of Suriki and on Isla Intja, and the walls on the latter are among the finest examples of Inca architecture in the Titicaca Basin. Likewise, Esteves and Escalante (1994) reported a large Inca occupation on Huiñamarca's Isla Paco. They noted massive terrace complexes associated with an Inca occupation. There is also a structure in front of a cut-stone carving in a rock that appears to have been an Inca temple.

Other Habitation Site Types during the Inca Period

The most common habitation type during the Inca period, the hillside domestic terrace, is similar to that found in earlier periods. This site type is usually less than one hectare in size, with a small concentration of two or three households. There were literally thousands of such sites in the Titicaca Basin during the Inca period. The vast majority of the population in the region lived in either domestic terrace sites or urban settlements. In the Juli-Pomata area, approximately 81 percent of the population lived in these two site types (Stanish et al. 1997: 208).

Three other site types are occasionally found in the Inca period: small lakeside mounded sites, large lakeside mounded sites, and dispersed sites on flat land. These were rare and their residents did not represent a significant portion of the population.

Inca-Period Orthogonal Grid Patterns in Provincial Settlements

The sites of Hatuncolla, Chucuito and Juli (and, possibly, other sites in the Titicaca region) are built in a modified grid pattern that has been called "orthogonal" by Hyslop (1990: 221). The orthogonal plan consists of parallel streets crossed by quasi-perpendicular ones that radiate slightly outward. Hyslop's examples of the pattern include Cuzco, Chincheros, Ollantaytambo, Chucuito, and Hatuncolla (Hyslop 1990: 192–194). Figure 10.4 shows plans of Hatuncolla and Chucuito adapted from Julien (1983) and Hyslop (1990). In both cases, as well as that of Juli

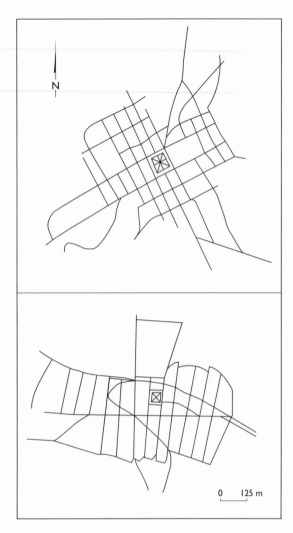

FIGURE 10.4. Plans of Hatuncolla (top) and Chucuito, adapted from Julien 1983 and Hyslop 1990.

and most likely other major towns in the Titicaca region with Inca occupations, there is an orthogonal plan to the settlements.

On superficial examination, the orthogonal plan is reminiscent of the Spanish grid plan used in so many New World settlements. One of the principal questions about the Inca-period archaeology of the south-central Andes is whether this pattern is Inca or Spanish. Some archaeologists working at Torata Alta in Moquegua (P. Rice et al. 1989; Van Buren 1996) have argued that the site's grid pattern is most likely Spanish Colonial in date, a product of Crown reduction policies. One piece of evidence offered is that during excavations they encountered Spanish artifacts in all levels. Curiously, this is similar to Tschopik's excavation at Chucuito, where she found Spanish-period glaze ware fragments in all levels adjacent to the Inca Uyu, an unequivocally Inca-period structure built in a provincial but almost certainly a Cuzco-derived style masonry (Hyslop 1984: 130). Given the brevity of the Inca occupation, and the longevity of the Spanish one in most sites such as Chucuito and Torata Alta, it is not surprising that Colonial artifacts are found mixed with Inca levels.

Gasparini and Margolies (1980: 77) also believe that the grid plan is Inca in origin. They base this on two observations: first, that the Spanish grid never departs from a rigid square pattern, and second, that the orthogonal pattern is clearly typical of Inca architecture as evidenced by the site of Ollantaytambo in the Urubamba Valley near Cuzco. There are dozens of other Inca sites built in a grid pattern throughout the Andes. The private estate of the Inca emperor Huascar in Cuzco, at Calca, is a good example (Niles 1993: 164). This site was built on a grid with existing Inca blocks still in place on some of the walls. The streets were given Spanish names, and the site was reworked for Spanish purposes.

Hyslop (1990: 193, 195, 200), of course, defined the orthogonal pattern and believes that it is Prehispanic. He notes that the orthogonal plan differs from Spanish ones in having plazas off of center. He also reinforces Gasparini and Margolies's observation that the streets on Inca plans are generally not rigidly square like Spanish ones but tend to radiate outward (Hyslop 1990: 221). In the circum-Titicaca region, the sites of Torata Alta, Juli, Hatuncolla, Ilave, and Chu-

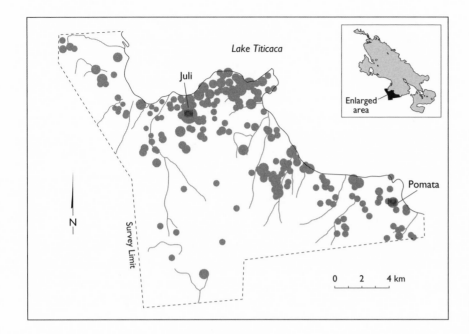

MAP 10.1. Inca-period settlement pattern in the Juli-Pomata survey region.

cuito conform to this Inca pattern, not to the rigid Spanish grid pattern. Julien also argues that the grid pattern in evidence at Hatuncolla is Inca in date, corroborating Hyslop's and Gasparini and Margolies's observations (Julien 1983: 90–92). Clearly, however, some Spanish Colonial modification is evident on all of these sites. Julien notes that the plaza at Hatuncolla was probably cut down into a square shape to conform to Spanish canons of site layout.

Systematic Settlement Data

The first model of Inca-period settlement pattern in the Titicaca Basin was offered by Hyslop in 1976. His Chucuito and Inca macropattern describes the settlement pattern typical of the period of Inca control of the region. Hyslop found fifteen sites dating to this period. He describes them as having Inca and Chucuito ceramics, structures with fine Inca masonry, and locations usually in undefended lakeside areas.

Systematic Data from the Juli-Pomata Region

The survey data from the Juli-Pomata and Tiwanaku areas provide a more detailed characterization of Inca-period settlement patterns. Juli was one of the principal towns of the Lupaqa polity during the sixteenth century when the Diez de San Miguel Visita was conducted. The Juli subdivision was the largest town in population, with more than 19 percent of the total number of taxpayers in Chucuito province. Pomata was the third largest town in population. Both Juli and Pomata had the largest percentage of Aymara taxpayers relative to the poor-taxpayer category of Uru. Throughout the Visita, Juli was consistently listed as the most important town in the region after Chucuito. Therefore, the Juli-Pomata survey provides some of the best systematic data for reconstructing settlement patterns in the Titicaca Basin.

The settlement pattern during the Inca period in the Juli-Pomata survey area is shown in map 10.1. It is immediately apparent that this pattern is dra-

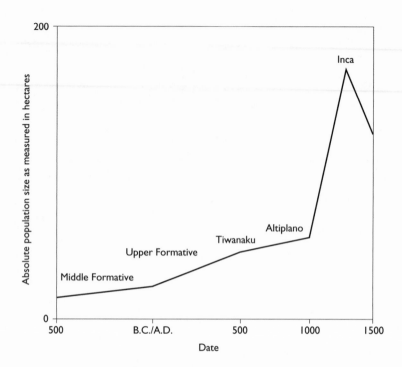

FIGURE 10.5. Population curve for the Juli-Pomata survey area, based on total area of domestic residence, calibrated for length of period.

matically more complex than one would suspect if focusing solely on the Inca centers. There are three major differences in the settlement pattern from the previous Altiplano period: the walled sites were abandoned, larger towns were founded, and raised-field areas were abandoned. Puna land use intensified (19 percent of total population), a process that began in the preceding Altiplano period. A significant percentage of the new population was concentrated into the larger towns. In particular, the towns of Juli and Pomata were founded in this period.

The Inca did not utilize raised-field areas, as indicated by site location and the derived population data (Stanish 1994; also see this volume, page 124). This is most likely related to the altered ecological conditions, specifically drought and lower average temperatures, beginning around the time of the Inca conquest (Graffam 1992; Ortloff and Ko-

lata 1989). The Inca-period settlement pattern is heavily weighted to terrace agricultural and lakeside urbanized areas, suggesting a maximization strategy designed to produce and move commodities, and locate populations in optimal agricultural land.

DEMOGRAPHY

Figure 10.5 presents our calculation of population growth in the Juli-Pomata region over time. The most obvious characteristic is the growth spike in the Inca period after a generally steady growth rate from the Middle Formative (Early Sillumocco) period. This growth rate could not occur from natural population increases alone. The projected population level during the Inca period would be approximately 90 hectares of domestic residence using the previous growth rates from the Middle Formative to Altiplano periods. The actual figure of 179 hectares is almost twice as large. These data leave little doubt that sub-

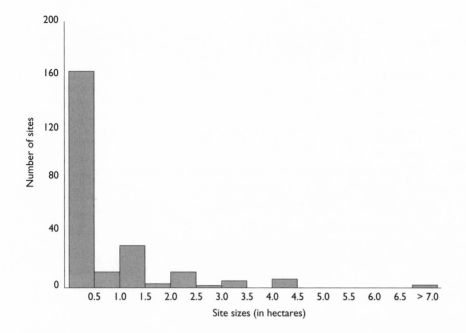

FIGURE 10.6. Site size distributions for the Juli-Pomata survey area during the Inca period.

stantial populations migrated into the Juli-Pomata region during the Inca period.

SITE SIZE DISTRIBUTIONS

Figure 10.6 represents site size distributions for the Juli-Pomata area during the Inca period. It is instructive to compare these distributions with the earlier Tiwanaku- and Altiplano-period ones. The two most significant observations are (1) that the Altiplano- and Inca-period distributions are very similar for sites 2.5 hectares and smaller but quite different for larger sites and (2) that the Tiwanaku-period distribution is dramatically different from the Altiplano-period one. Between the Altiplano and Inca periods, all change in size distribution occurs in the sites larger than 2.5 hectares.

I believe that sites larger than 2.5 hectares were either elite centers, administrative sites, or population concentrations in a context of heightened elite production. The presence or absence of larger sites is best understood as the result of the degree of political centralization or decentralization in the Juli-Pomata re-

gion; that is, in the Tiwanaku and Inca periods, sites larger than 2.5 hectares are common, but they virtually disappear in the Altiplano period, when complex political organization is absent.

In the Tiwanaku period, for instance, there are four distinct site size categories, with a very high percentage of the sites larger than 2.5 hectares (23 percent [7/30]). The shift between the Tiwanaku- and Altiplano-period patterns indicates a general abandonment of sites larger than 2.5 hectares, indicating a profound reorganization of the region's political landscape. The collapse of the Tiwanaku state led to the dramatic abandonment of virtually all large sites in the area, with a concomitant reorganization of the bulk of the nonelite population in the Altiplano period. The absolute number of sites and their total populations increased, indicating that people living in the large Tiwanaku sites moved to smaller, dispersed settlements around the region.

During the Inca occupation, larger sites once again were founded in the region. However, in contrast to the change between the Tiwanaku and Altiplano period, the site size distribution change between the Altiplano and Inca periods for sites smaller than 2.5 hectares remains virtually unchanged. These data indicate that the major change in the Inca period corresponds to the addition of large population concentrations, particularly at sites such as Juli and Pomata, under Inca occupation.

SITE LOCATIONS

For sites smaller than 2.5 hectares, there is little difference between the Inca and the Altiplano periods in terms of location and altitude. However, a number of new sites were added during the Inca period, including sites larger than 2.5 hectares. These sites range in altitude from 3,800 to 4,100 meters, with most near the lake below 3,900 meters. In other words, these data demonstrate that most (twelve of seventeen) of these large sites are near the lake, an optimal location for lake resource exploitation and rain-fed terrace agriculture. Five new large sites, a significant number, were added in the puna, attesting to the importance of camelid grazing in the Inca political economy.

Systematic Settlement Data
from the Tiwanaku Valley

The Inca-period settlement in the Tiwanaku Valley is referred to by Albarracin-Jordan (1996a) and Mathews (1993) as the Inka-Pacajes period. The pattern is very similar to that of the Juli-Pomata area, with a large number of small sites scattered over the landscape, probably to maximize agricultural production, plus a few large centers. Albarracin-Jordan and Mathews suggest that that the Inca occupation did not entail profound changes in the local political economy or settlement patterns (1990: 193); they argue for a more indirect control of the region by the Inca state. However, their settlement data (1990: 215–242) indicate some dramatic changes in the Late Intermediate/Inca transition, suggesting a significant Inca impact. More than 50 percent of the Late Interme-

diate sites, for instance, were abandoned during the Inca occupation, a figure actually higher than that from the Juli-Pomata area. Very significantly, the total number of sites in the Inca period (492) decreased by almost half from the Late Intermediate period (948 sites) but almost rebounded to those levels in the Early Colonial period (836 sites). Likewise, site distribution by ecological zone shifted in the Inca period but returned to almost the precise pre-Inca pattern during the Early Colonial period, at least in the middle Tiwanaku Valley (Mathews 1993). I argue that these data indicate major changes coincident with the Inca occupation, including a major aggregation of settlement that disrupted pre-Inca settlement patterns. The collapse of Inca control in the Early Colonial period permitted the population to revert back to pre-Inca patterns prior to Spanish *reducciones*.

Mathews (1993: 322) has cautiously suggested that there was a population concentration toward the lake, specifically at the site of Guaqui, a hypothesis with which I agree. Documentary evidence indicates that the major center of Guaqui was established by the Inca (Mathews 1993: 319). Mathews notes, for instance, that there was a population reduction of about 60 percent in the middle Tiwanaku Valley in the Inca period. In the lower Tiwanaku Valley, an area that included Guaqui, there were 40 percent more Inca-period sites than in the Middle Valley.

There are some real differences between the Juli-Pomata region and the Tiwanaku Valley during the Inca period. The former area seems to have been more important to the Inca, insofar as the number of people brought into a region reflects its status in the empire. In the Tiwanaku Valley, populations were moved within the region to meet state needs, but in the Juli-Pomata area, people were moved both within and into the region.

Systematic Survey Data from the Island of the Sun

The Island of the Sun was surveyed by Brian Bauer, Oswaldo Rivera, and Charles Stanish in 1994 and

1995 (complete details in Bauer and Stanish 2001). The survey discovered several dozen Inca sites, including small and large habitation sites, and sites with standing architecture that may not have been strictly domestic. Most of the habitation sites were small, nondescript scatters of artifacts, particularly, Inca pottery on domestic terraces associated with good agricultural land. The typical site was less than one hectare in size. There is almost no surviving architecture for these small sites, except, occasionally, stone foundations of walls. Almost all of the sites were isolated from others, and most likely were small hamlets of one or two households. Among the sites that approached one hectare in size were some that may have been clusters of three to five households, and therefore small villages. The nonhabitation sites included ritual centers, tambos (way stations), ports, and tombs. We also discovered the road system used by the Inca pilgrims, but we did not include road segments as sites.

One of the most striking characteristics of the Inca settlement system is the plethora of small sites. On the Island of the Sun, more than sixty sites covered less than one hectare. This pattern was also discovered in the Juli-Pomata region for the Inca period (Stanish 1997) and is characteristic of an imperial control strategy: a generally bimodal distribution of a few large administrative sites with a large number of small villages and hamlets. On the Islands of the Sun and Moon, the major administrative sites were Kasapata, Challapampa, Bandelier's site 100 (or Pukara), and possibly the site of Puncu on the south side of the island, where the rafts from Copacabana landed (see pages 275–277). Even these sites are small by mainland standards, where Hatuncolla and Chucuito cover at least 50 hectares. It is therefore likely that Copacabana was the administrative center responsible for the islands in the Inca empire. We do not know the size of Copacabana during the Inca occupation, but it was at least three times larger than the largest Inca site on the Island of Sun. In other

words, the settlement site size data suggest that the island was not an independent administrative district of the Inca state but was tied to the Copacabana region.

Apart from the lack of large administrative centers, it is significant that the Inca state utilized the same strategy on the island that they had used on the mainland of scattering the bulk of the population into small settlements. A few of the larger sites probably functioned as minor administrative sites. We can interpret these data to suggest that the island's native populations were scattered and the mitimas and other empire-dependent groups were concentrated into the larger settlements.

It is also significant that the bulk of the small Inca settlements were in primary agricultural land. The Island of the Sun was indeed a major ritual and pilgrimage center, but the Inca clearly understood that it had to be provisioned. The settlement data strongly indicate that nearly all the subsistence goods that sustained the people on the island—including the priests, mamacona (chosen women of the Inca), and other ritual specialists—were produced on the island, not brought in from elsewhere. In fact, the distribution of Inca hamlets and villages on the island correlates to the best agricultural land. This pattern is identical to the mainland pattern, as evidenced by the settlement data from the Juli-Pomata survey (Stanish et al. 1997).

There are three important exceptions to this pattern. On the southern side of the island, an impressive set of steps climbs the hill in the middle of the natural "bowl," or small valley. These steps start at the ritual site known today as the Fountain of the Inca. A large number of well-made agricultural terraces flank these steps. Unlike every other part of the island—and for that matter, unlike the entire Juli-Pomata survey area, where such excellent agricultural land exists—there are no Inca hamlets or villages on and between the terraces. In other words, the entire area was crisscrossed with beautiful terraces, but there was no settlement in the fields themselves. The habitation sites were, in fact, on either side of the valley to the east and west, where they were concentrated in great numbers. In these latter areas were also agricultural terraces and associated habitation sites that housed the population that would presumably have worked these fields. The typical pattern for the Titicaca Basin in the Inca period includes a set of agricultural fields and a series of sites that housed the peasant population that worked those fields, but there was a deviation from this pattern in the valley above the Fountain of the Inca.

One way to explain the distribution of settlements on the Island of the Sun is as a function of ritual settlement determinants—that is, the Inca state may have forced people to live away from this particular valley for ritual and/or aesthetic reasons. The entire valley section would have been built with the beautiful terraces, perhaps housing gardens of special maize or other plants, but the peasants who worked these fields appear to have been forbidden to live there. Perhaps it was for ritual reasons, or perhaps it was to leave the area clear of human habitation for aesthetic reasons. Regardless, this small valley was altered to fit the needs of the pilgrimage complex on the entire island.

The second area that does not conform to the optimal pattern of agricultural land use is the western part of the island, where there are huge terraces without any evidence of habitation sites. It is possible that this area was for growing special crops. According to Ramos Gavilán (1988 [1621]: 45), "The Inca tried to grow a plot of coca for the Sun on one of the beaches near the rock of Titicaca," which suggests that the coca was to be used for ritual purposes.[8] The climate in this area is distinct because of the high solar radiation and because the topography protects the terraced areas from wind. The effect was to create a warmer environment, which could have been used to grow nonaltiplano crops.

Titikala is the third area that does not conform to the pattern. Although there is evidence of substantial human settlement, there appears to be no appreciable agricultural sustaining land. A number of sites were discovered in the northern section of the island, most of them small villages or hamlets adjacent to the ritual complex that included the Sacred Rock, the Chicana, and Mama Ojila. Farther north, away from the ritual center, are small hamlets on the Ticani Peninsula. These sites are associated with some modest terracing and probably housed farmers who cultivated maize for ritual use, as well as other crops for the maintenance of the religious specialists that cared for the temple. In other words, the Titikala area proper was not an agricultural zone; the settlement determinants there were strictly ritual, with the subsistence of the inhabitants provided for by the rest of the island.

The number of sites and the total size of the habitation area during the Inca period is extremely high relative to the earlier periods. As in the Juli-Pomata area, this increase cannot be accounted for by natural population growth alone. Even accounting for some minor methodological problems and biases, there is little doubt that people were brought into the area from elsewhere.[9] In the case of the island, documentary evidence indicates that the Inca imported mitima colonists. It is also likely that the Inca brought together the scattered populations of the Altiplano period into lakeside and island locations where they could more effectively be controlled. The island would have been an obvious place to put these settlers to support the ritual specialists.

During the Inca occupation, a cluster of settlements and agricultural features near the southern Kona Bay was used to intensively grow agricultural produce (see map 10.2). The principal site in this cluster is a major Inca one characterized by a walled platform with niches in the walls. The site itself is between two quebradas, each of which was channeled with water diversion walls. These walls narrowed and formed the neck of a larger, oval depression at the

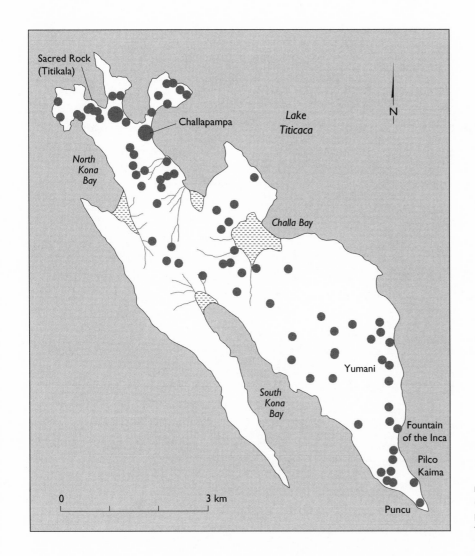

MAP 10.2. Inca-period (A.D. 1450–1532) settlement pattern on the Island of the Sun.

base of the pampa, which most certainly functioned as a tank or reservoir. Below the tank are a series of relict raised fields, which do not cover an extensive area (just a few hectares) but are highly significant.

The existence of raised fields during the Inca period was extremely rare. Most studies indicate that the fields were out of use by the time of the Inca conquest, a period that correlated to the onset of the Little Ice Age. Furthermore, this was a period of extensive and progressive drought, severely restricting the viability of raised-field agriculture. Nevertheless,

there is compelling evidence that these fields near Kona Bay were in use during the Inca occupation. From an environmental perspective, these fields' existence represents an exception that proves the rule. More specifically, it supports a largely ecological explanation of field collapse due to drought and decreased temperatures. The land near the lake edge, particularly in the protected area of the Kona Bay, would have been appreciably warmer than the Titicaca Basin in general. Also, the two quebradas and special reservoir structures would have provided sufficient fresh water to make the fields viable. In other words, the Inca reconstructed the conditions necessary to make the raised fields viable in this atypical and highly conducive environment. The association of this agricultural complex with a niched platform wall is highly suggestive of a special or ritual use of the fields. It thus appears that the Kona Bay field complex was a special agricultural area designed to grow maize and possibly other plants for the pilgrimage center.

Another settlement determinant for the Inca period would have been the road system. As discussed above, the roads were probably in place by the Tiwanaku period, and were probably built from earlier paths and trails that had been used to cross the island for millennia. The Inca were adept at formalizing earlier road systems throughout the Andes, and they did the same on the Island of the Sun. Two principal roads led from the southern side of the island to the Titikala area. One begins in the Yumani area and leads north on high ground on the west side of the island past Apachinaca. It continues along the high ridge, past some small platform constructions, and then descends down to the Titikala area. The second road also begins in the Yumani area and continues on the east side to Apachinaca as well. This road then descends down past the Challa Bay and follows the east side of the island, going past Challapampa, Challa, Kasapata, and finally reaching the Titikala area. Inca sites along these roads were constructed in part to service and/or have access to them.

Local Agricultural Systems during the Inca Occupation

Analysis of the settlement data from the Juli-Pomata region has made it possible to define the relative importance of economic activities over time. Four major economic activities were pursued by populations in the Titicaca Basin: raised-field agriculture, rain-fed terrace agriculture, camelid pastoralism, and ex-

ploitation of lacustrine resources. Each of these activities is linked to site location. The puna zone is ideally suited for camelid pasturing, and only marginal for tuber cultivation. The raised-field zone, confined to the flat pampas inland from the lake and adjacent to rivers, is agriculturally useful only with raised-field constructions, although today it is used for marginal grazing and there are only relict fields. The terraced areas in the suni are divided into two types by contemporary Aymara. The gently sloping areas at the base of the hills that are protected from wind are considered ideal agricultural land, almost as good as raised fields. The hillsides themselves, a second type, are generally considered poor to moderate areas for cultivation (M. Tschopik 1946: 513). What is significant is that each zone provides specific and different economic opportunities. The Juli-Pomata survey data permit us to define the relative use of the four economic strategies by locating the sites and calculating the total habitation area per period (e.g., see Stanish 1994).

Analysis of settlement data revealed several patterns. First, raised-field agriculture disappeared during the Inca period. Settlement data indicate a shift away from the raised-field zones in the survey area to locations in the rain-fed terrace areas and the puna pastoral zones (Stanish 1994). The most parsimonious explanation of the data is that altered ecological conditions—specifically, the onset of lower average temperatures—began around A.D. 1400 and were the primary factors in this economic shift (Graffam 1992; Kolata 1993: 298; Ortloff and Kolata 1989).

Second, there was a substantial shift to the puna pasture lands, particularly when compared with earlier figures. In the Tiwanaku period, about 4 percent of the population lived in the puna, and in the Altiplano period this figure increased to 14 percent. By the Inca period, almost 20 percent of the population was living in the puna.

An Inca-period settlement pattern heavily weighted to terrace agricultural and lakeside urbanized areas suggests a maximization strategy designed to produce and move commodities and to locate populations in optimal agricultural land. The importance of camelid wool in the Inca economy is indicated by the fact that 20 percent of the population lived in the pasture grazing lands.

Why Did the Raised-Field Agricultural System Collapse?

Around the end of the fifteenth century, significant ecological changes occurred in the Titicaca region. The Little Ice Age, a period of lower ambient temperatures, dates from circa A.D. 1480 to the nineteenth century (Graffam 1992: 899). Our data support both Graffam (1990: 248–249) and Ortloff and Kolata's (1993) arguments that raised fields were ecologically unfeasible by the time of the Inca conquest.

The Juli-Pomata settlement data reflect this changed ecological situation. Less than 15 percent of the population lived in the raised-field areas during this period, and most of that population can be accounted for by the presence of a major Inca road that runs through the pampas in areas of former raised fields. The Inca elite pursued alternative staple and wealth finance strategies in the circum-Titicaca region, such as economic specialization and the establishment of agricultural colonies in lowland maize-growing areas (e.g., Murra 1982; Wachtel 1982).

The Inca Qolca

The *qolca,* or storehouse, was one of the principal features of the Inca administrative and military system. Qolcas were stocked with cloth, maize, shoes, and other commodities used to feed and clothe the armies. In one of the earliest documents known to exist from the Spanish conquest, the anonymous "La Conquista del Perú," we are given a description of such qolcas: "They [Hernando de Soto and soldiers] arrived at the village which was large and in some very high houses found a lot of corn and shoes. Other houses were full of wool and more than 500 women

who were doing nothing else than [making] clothing and chicha for the soldiers. In these houses there was a great deal of this chicha" (in Sinclair 1929: 27).

This anonymous document also makes an interesting reference to perhaps another commodity of military value stored in the qolcas. Arriving in Cajamarca, the Spaniards noted a house with trees, reportedly where Atahualpa was staying, and "around this house on every side for a distance of more than half a league the ground was covered with white tents" (Sinclair 1929: 29–30). Accepting the accuracy of this quote, it is evident that at least some soldiers in the Inca army had tents, of either cotton or wool.

The storehouses therefore most likely contained at least cloth for clothes and tents, shoes, corn, and chicha. These commodities were distributed to the soldiers and were used to maintain the army. The Diez de San Miguel Visita makes dozens of references to tambos that were still in use in at least 1567. Diez de San Miguel directly addressed the question of the tambos in a section called "Concerning service to the tambos": "the seven principal towns in the royal road are large and provide substantial labor in servicing the tambos because they give to them totora and firewood to all of the travelers that pass and there are many Indians that are occupied in this" (Diez de San Miguel 1964: 213). In another section of the Visita, corregidor Licenciado Estrada noted that "each town serves its tambo and that this service is usually done by the Uros Indians because they are poor" (Diez de San Miguel 1964: 52). Evidence in the Visita conforms to our generally understood model of the Inca storehouses as having been maintained by local communities as part of their mit'a labor obligations.

Mitimas in the Titicaca Region

… because the Inca kings that ruled this empire were so wise and governed so well … they established things and ordered laws according to their custom, that truly, if it were not for these measures, the greater part of the

people in their kingdom would have toiled with difficulty and would have lived under hardship, as it was before they were governed [by the Inca]. And because in the Collao, and in all of the other Peruvian valleys that were cold and not fertile or bountiful like the warmer regions, they ordered ... that each one let go a certain quantity of Indians with their women to be placed in regions where their caciques indicated and ordered and they worked their fields and grew that which they lacked in their native land ... and they were called mitimaes.

Pedro de Cieza de León,
"La crónica del Perú," chapter 99, 1553

As suggested by Cieza, mitima, or *mitmaqkuna,* were transplanted colonists moved by the Inca state for economic purposes. We now recognize that mitima had other functions as well for military or strategic objectives. Colonists were expected to maintain the dress and other ethnic markers from their home territory. According to Patterson (1991: 77), mitima were not under the control of the local *curaca,* although the latter had to provide for some of their subsistence for two years of their residence. Patterson distinguishes several types of mitima: rebels resettled in the center of the state, loyal settlers placed among potentially rebellious groups, and garrisoned peoples who eventually settled frontier land and resettled underpopulated regions (Patterson 1991: 77, with citations of Cieza, Garcilaso de la Vega, Rostworowski 1988, and Rowe 1946).

Mitima served a number of functions, including increasing agricultural productivity by resettling underpopulated areas (Patterson 1991: 78). In such areas, the strategic value of placing loyal subjects among potentially rebellious ones is obvious, and this practice also sowed distrust and discord among resident peoples under Inca rule. It is much more difficult to unite and organize rebellions among people of different ethnicities, who may have mistrusted each other as much or more than they distrusted the Inca state.

One of the most massive population relocations in the Inca system has been documented by Wachtel (1982) and Julien (1998) in the Cochabamba Valley, in present-day Bolivia. The Cochabamba Valley was conquered by Tupac Yupanqui and heavily colonized by his son, Huayna Capac, who moved in approximately fourteen thousand settlers after expelling the local populations (Wachtel 1982: 199–200). The Cochabamba settlement was a major maize- and coca-producing estate that fed the state armies. Wachtel makes an important distinction between two types of colonists: mitimas were permanent settlers, whereas the *mittayoc* were temporary workers fulfilling their mit'a obligations. Wachtel notes that "the mitimas were given specific supervisory tasks (notably the maintenance of the granaries), while the mittayoc performed the ongoing work, such as sowing and harvesting" (Wachtel 1982: 214). Wachtel also indicated that, along with these foreigners, certain natives remained and took care of royal camelid herds (Wachtel 1982: 217). In this major resettlement, the Inca state utilized permanent colonists, resident mitima workers, temporary mittayoc workers, and local peoples to perform the labor necessary to supply maize to the armies. Aspects of this colonization model can serve as an appropriate analogy for understanding the Titicaca Basin mitima colonies.

There are numerous documented cases of mitima colonists in the Titicaca Basin. Some of the most visible were colonists from Chinchasuyu, the northwest quarter of the Inca empire. This was the most distant region from which mitimas were drawn. One notable colony was near the town of Juli. Here, the Diez de San Miguel Visita discusses the presence of 311 Chinchasuyu colonists. Each taxpayer was a single adult male who probably represented at least five additional persons. In one passage, for instance, Diez de San Miguel noted, "and, likewise, apart from [people from] various nations there are certain Chinchaysuyo Indians that are mitimaes placed there by the Inca" (Diez de San Miguel 1964: 114). Another group of Chinchasuyu colonists lived in Ancoraimes, for which the Toledo Tasa lists 151 "indios tributarios matimaes *[sic]* de Chinchasuyo."

Cobo also mentions, in a general fashion, that a number of people from Chinchasuyu were found in the Collao (Cobo 1983: 191). Murra (1964: 428) warns that Europeans such as Diez de San Miguel incautiously labeled as mitima almost anyone who lived far from their place of birth. However, the fact that the Diez de San Miguel Visita actually lists an origin place (Chinchasuyu) for the colonists is compelling. Also, Cobo, Cieza, Garcilaso, and Ramos Gavilán all mention the Chinchasuyu mitima in the region as well. This also appears to be the case of twenty mitima from Canas located in Pomata, listed in the Diez de San Miguel Visita as part of the upper moiety (Hanansaya) of that town (Diez de San Miguel 1964: 65). Spurling reports on mitima from Huancané, Ancoraimes, Guangasco, Ambaná, and Chuma, towns from Larecaja, and other areas in the eastern lowlands (Spurling 1992: table 2.3).

Julien's ethnohistorical research has isolated a number of other mitima colonies in the region as well (Julien 1983: 82–83). Other Chinchasuyu natives were said to be located in the Umasuyu province of the Colla region (Julien 1983: 82). Julien notes that the entire town of Ayaviri was replaced with mitimas because the Inca had annihilated the town (Julien 1983: 88). Cobo's account of the Inca victory at Ayaviri is relevant here:

> [T]he Inca moved his squadrons and proceeded through those extensive meadows and savannas which are found on the other side of the sierra of Vilcanota; and as he neared Ayavire, the Colla Indians came out to meet him in battle array, inciting the Inca to make war. . . . Seeing that the majority of their men were dead, the Colla Indians lost courage, retreated with as many men as possible, and repaired to Pucará. The Inca destroyed the town of Ayavire, and on his orders, all the people his men could lay hands on were beheaded. (Cobo 1983: 140)

According to Julien, contemporary toponyms may be an indication of mitima status in the Inca period. Both Acora and Chucuito have ayllu named Inca (Julien 1983: 82–83). There is a Canas ayllu in Yunguyu, a Canchis ayllu in Caracoto and Achaya, and a Pacajes ayllu (Caquingora) in Azángaro (Julien 1983: 83). Outside Juli, one of the communities is named Inca Pukara, or "fortress of the Inca." Directly west of Puno about ten kilometers is a town called Chimú in an area that local lore claims was settled by the Chinchasuyu mitima.

Likewise, there were numerous mitima in Copacabana associated with the state religious shrines and pilgrimage center on the Islands of the Sun and Moon (see pages 272–277). The Toledo Tasa divides the entire taxpayer base of Copacabana into 953 mitimas and 88 uros (Cook 1975: 72).

There is a very significant pattern regarding the placement of mitima in the Titicaca region during the Inca occupation. With the exception of the Chinchasuyus and most of the Copacabana mitima, the colonists *in* the Titicaca Basin are generally *from* the Titicaca Basin. Moving populations within a region would not have been of major economic utility. Rather, the rationale for these population movements seems to have been strategic, moving Aymara-, Pukina-, and Uruquilla-speakers around the region to prevent unified resistance to Inca rule. The economic aspect appears to have been ancillary to the strategic one. That is, the Inca could have set up potters, metalworkers, and so forth in any area near a road. The particular relocation of groups within the region suggests a greater concern for strategic considerations, not strictly economic ones.

The Inca Roads in the Lake Region

One of the Inca empire's principal imperial economic and military strategies was the maintenance of a vast network of roads throughout the Andes. In addition to economic and military functions, the road system had administrative and even ideological functions

FIGURE 10.7. Inca-period bridge near the Pajchiri Peninsula, Bolivia. Photograph by the author.

within the Inca state (Hyslop 1984: 2). Much of the empire's road system was not built *de novo* by the Inca. Schreiber (1987) has demonstrated that the so-called Inca road system in the Carhuarazo Valley was actually built earlier by the Wari state. The Inca inherited the trade routes and roads of earlier cultures and used their enormous labor capacity to staff and improve this communication system. The vast system of tambos and the construction of excellent bridges are two examples of this road maintenance policy. The famous "floating" totora bridge across the Río Desaguadero is one Inca construction that lasted into the nineteenth century (Squier 1877: 531). Cieza described the bridge over the Desaguadero as being made of "sheaves of oats" *[de avena]* and being strong enough to hold horses and men. He also said that there were toll-collectors *[portazgueros]* at the bridge

in the time of the Inca. Alongside the bridges were causeways built over swampy land. Today, the remains of such constructions can be seen outside Chucuito (Hyslop 1990), near Sillustani (Julien 1988b), and near Pajchiri in the south (see figure 10.7). The effect of this policy was to give the Inca an enormous strategic advantage against rebellious populations, and the ability to move goods over long distances for relatively low costs.

As one of the most important provinces in the Inca empire, the Titicaca region had two major roads running roughly northwest-southeast along both sides of the lake. The terms *Urqusuyu* and *Umasuyu,* which referred to the large spatial division of Collasuyu, were also used for the names of the two-branched road system in the Titicaca Basin (Julien 1983: 24).

The only systematic study of the Inca road system in the Titicaca region was conducted by John Hyslop, and the following observations are excerpted from his excellent 1984 book. According to Hyslop, the Titicaca roads were three to seven meters wide, with little evidence of margin markers, prepared roadbeds or sidewalls, although these latter features occasionally occurred (Hyslop 1984: 120, 125).

The causeway in Lake Umayo, near Sillustani, is part of the Inca road system. The road is visible slightly to the south in Hatuncolla, and can be picked up five kilometers northwest of Paucarcolla as well. Hyslop notes that Paucarcolla was once an Inca tambo, or way station (Hyslop 1984: 120), and our research indicates that it was a major center. The road entered Puno and went south between the hills and the lake. Hyslop mentions references to an Inca occupation in Puno, and I believe that this is sufficient evidence to indicate that Puno was at least an Inca tambo. The Inca road enters Chucuito and passes into the plaza, known as the Inka Uyu. South of Chucuito the road becomes a causeway for walking across the swampy zone between the Chucuito hills and the lake edge. My own observations suggest that an old aqueduct was reutilized by the Inca as a bed for this causeway. According to Hyslop, the Inca road then goes through all of the main towns of the lakeside altiplano: Acora, Ilave, Juli, Pomata, and Zepita (Hyslop 1984: 121).[10]

The Inca roads are famous for the efficient messenger system of the *chasquis,* the runners who manned posts along the highway system and rapidly carried messages or small goods to all parts of the empire. Cobo specifically mentions small chasqui stations along the Collao royal highways:

> Apart from the tambos and storehouses, along these two royal highways every quarter of a league there were also some huts or small houses built in pairs facing one another near the road, and these huts were only large enough for two men to fit in them. In the provinces of Collao the huts were made of coarse stones without mortar, and they were about the size and shape of an oven for baking bread. . . . In each one of these huts two Indians always resided. . . . They performed the job of runners or messengers, who with incomparable speed carried the orders and commandments of the Inca to the governors and caciques of the whole kingdom. (Cobo 1983: 229)

As noted above, many of the roads were from earlier cultures and had been appropriated by the Inca for their own purposes. Available evidence is ambiguous for the Titicaca road. Hyslop feels that the Titicaca roads were Inca constructions, a conclusion that he bases on the fact that almost all sites on the Inca road were founded in the Inca period (Hyslop 1984: 119). Our survey of the Juli-Pomata region supports the observation that the Altiplano-period Lupaqa sites are not associated with the road system, but that earlier Tiwanaku and Upper Formative–period settlements were along a road. In fact, a significant majority of Tiwanaku sites are within one kilometer of the present road. Aside from the small hamlets and villages, most major Upper Formative and Tiwanaku sites are within one kilometer of the path of the road.

Economic Specialization during the Inca Occupation

There are abundant historical references to economic specialists in the Titicaca region during the Inca occupation. Martín Cari testified that in Chucuito there were "ten ayllos of Aymara Indians that are the best people that are in this town and that there are another two ayllos, one of silver workers and another of potters and there is another five ayllos of fishermen Indians" (Diez de San Miguel 1964: 14). In this case, the economic specialists were grouped into separate ayllu in individual towns.

Many of these ayllu may have been mitima colonists. One possible example of such colonization by economic specialists is a reference to a town of about one hundred state potters and weavers near

Huancané on the northern side of Lake Titicaca (Spurling 1992). Spurling also provides information from an early document in which the cacique of Moho mentions a group of weavers at Conima.

Another reference is to an ayllu of metalworkers at Pila Patag (Platería) between Chucuito and Acora. This site was referred to by Hyslop (1984: 131; 1979: 65–66) in his reconnaissance of the region. The site is twelve hectares in size, according to Hyslop. It has both Inca-period and Early Colonial pottery on the surface. These metalworkers belonged to the Chucuito subdivision of the Lupaqa kingdom, which is mentioned in the Diez de San Miguel Visita of 1567. Julien (1983: 75) refers to this site as Sunicaya: "Sunicaya has been identified as the modern town of Platería."

Diez de San Miguel also refers to another possible ceramic workshop listed as Copi or Cupi in the Visita: "and another town of potters that is named Copi " (Diez de San Miguel 1964: 14). Julien feels that Cupi was within the Chucuito district, a conclusion I agree with based on the data in the Visita. In spite of some effort to identify this site in the field (e.g., Hyslop 1976), the site of Cupi has not been positively located.

According to Murra (1978: 418), there were two groups of economic specialists near Huancané. One was a group of potters called Hupi, and another was a group of weavers called Millerea, and they lived near each other. Murra says that the two groups were placed there by the eleventh Inca, Huayna Capac. These groups of economic specialists were mitimas from the Titicaca region.

MINING OF PRECIOUS METALS

The Collasuyu region provided laborers for what appears to have been one of the Inca empire's major silver mines. Known as Porco, the mine was described by Cieza as a principal source of metal for the Coricancha in Cuzco (Cieza 1553: chapter 108). The Diez de San Miguel Visita contains numerous references to this mine, as exemplified in chapter epigraph. Silver was also mined near Puno in the Colonial period.

The mining of gold and silver was an extremely important economic activity in the Titicaca Basin during the Inca occupation. Gold was a highly valued commodity, used in architecture, elite artwork, ritual objects, and the like. Jean Berthelet makes an important observation that the large quantity of gold and silver captured by the Spaniards attests to the "existence of intensive mining, the mobilization of many workers, and an organization of the mines at the state level" in Tawantinsuyu (Berthelet 1986: 69). During the Spanish Colonial period, there is no question that the circum-Titicaca region was one of the most productive mining areas in South America. It is not surprising that the Inca state likewise exploited the gold and silver of the region.

According to Berthelet (1986: 72), there were two types of mines in the region. As with other forms of real wealth, such as land and water, mining areas were divided into those belonging to the Inca and those belonging to local ethnic groups. The Inca or state mines were concentrated in certain areas, such as Carabaya, Huancané, Chuquiabo, Porco, and so forth, and community mines were scattered in river valleys and quebradas (and see Portugal O. 1972). Documentary evidence suggests that the Inca controlled the more labor-intensive and productive pit mines, but local elite maintained control of placer mines.

The Toledo Tasa lists the taxes collected from various communities in the region. Table 10.3 lists selected towns and their tribute items, including those where gold was collected. Map 10.3 shows towns required to provide gold to the Spanish state in the sixteenth century. The distribution of communities paying tribute in gold corresponds well with Berthelet's reconstruction of the principal gold-producing areas in the Inca period (Berthelet 1986: 73). The ma-

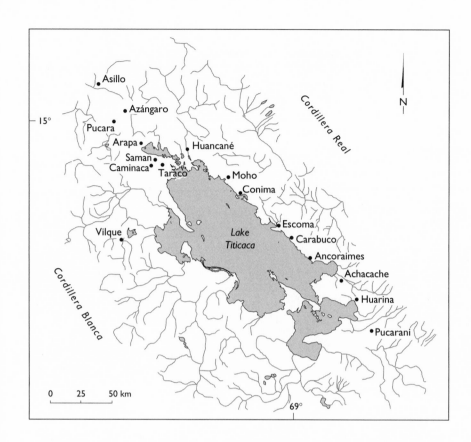

MAP 10.3. Towns required to provide gold as tribute in the sixteenth century, according to the Toledo Tasa. (Nunca and Carabaya are outside map area.)

jor gold placer mines were in the Omasuyu region, to the east and northeast of the lake, and over the cordillera in the Carabaya region. In the 1480s, the Carabaya area was conquered by Tupac Yupanqui, and the Inca laid claim to the gold mines (Berthelet 1986: 74). The gold-producing areas were worked by colonists, as well as by local ethnic groups. At Chuquiabo, it was Huayna Capac, Tupac Yupanqui's successor, who resettled Indians on the site to work the mines (Berthelet 1986: 74). Berthelet locates several other important mines, particularly the silver mines in Porco and Tarapacá, in the far south. Both Porco and Chuquiabo were owned by the Inca (Berthelet 1986: 74). Curiously, the Inca state provided weights and inspectors to assure that the Inca expropriated sufficient quantities of precious metals.

The Inca roads appear to be at least partially associated with the extraction of these metals. The main Inca road in the south, for instance, goes near Chuquiabo and directly to the mining town of Porco. The Omasuyu road obviously skirts the eastern side of the lake, passing a number of towns associated with the Carabaya region. Good sections of the Omasuyu road can still be found. Figure 10.8 is a photograph of a section of road above Moho, on the eastern side of the lake. The road is paved with flagstones and is about two to three meters wide. This represents a section of the principal road on the eastern side, with a number of side roads that most likely went due east to exploit the gold-producing, semitropical regions just a one- or two-day walk away.

TABLE 10.3
Selected Towns and Their Tribute Items as Listed in the Toledo Tasa

Town	Gold	Cloth/Wool	Chuño	Maize	Fish	Animals	Salt
MACHACA		X					
CAPACHICA		X	X		X		
PUCARANI	X	X	X	X			
HUARINA	X	X	X	X	X		
GUAQUI		X	X		X	X	
PUNO		X	X		X	X	
ACHACACHE	X	X	X	X			
HUANCANÉ	X	X	X				
TIWANAKU		X	X		X	X	
PAUCARCOLLA		X	X		X	X	X
COATA		X	X		X		
ANCORAIMES	X	X	X				
COPACABANA		X	X		X		
CARABUCO	X	X	X	X	X		
MOHO/CONIMA	X	X	X		X		
VILQUE	X	X	X	X	X		
CAMINACA	X	X	X	X		X	
MOQUEGUA				X			
ARAPA	X	X	X	X		X	

TABLE 10.3 (CONTINUED)

Selected Towns and Their Tribute Items as Listed in the Toledo Tasa

Town	Gold	Cloth/Wool	Chuño	Maize	Fish	Animals	Salt
SAMAN	X	X	X	X	X	X	
ASILLO	X	X	X	X	X	X	
AZÁNGARO	X	X		X	X	X	
TARACO	X	X	X	X		X	
NUÑOA	X	X	X	X		X	
LAMPA		X				X	
HATUNCOLLA		X	X		X	X	
AYAVIRI/CUPI		X				X	
NICASIO		X			X	X	
CARABAYA	X			X			
PUCARA/QUIPA	X	X				X	

POTTERY PRODUCTION

Inca-period pottery in the Titicaca region has been discussed by several authors, most notably Julien (1983). In the Juli-Pomata area, we defined a number of Inca-period pottery types. Virtually 98 percent of the known sample of Inca-period sherds were locally manufactured. The Local Inca type represents imitations of Cuzco styles manufactured in the Titicaca region. The Chucuito pottery style appears to be a local phenomenon, manufactured for the first time under Inca occupation. Although there are no direct antecedents to the Chucuito decorative styles, many of the motifs are noted in Cuzco Inca pottery. Unlike Chucuito, the Pacajes and Sillustani type motifs do have earlier antecedents in the Titicaca region.

This pattern of the local manufacture of decorated pottery provides insight into the nature of Inca provincial control. D'Altroy and Bishop (1990) analyzed the chemical composition of Inca-period pottery from four areas in the central Andes, including the Titicaca Basin, the Mantaro Valley, Tarma, and Cuzco. They concluded that "distinct sets of pottery were produced and consumed in the three principal regions. Virtually none of the imperial Inka pottery

FIGURE 10.8. Inca road segment near Moho, Peru. Photograph by the author.

tested from the upper Mantaro or Lake Titicaca areas was produced at Cuzco and shipped out."

Stylistic analyses of Inca-period pottery from throughout the Titicaca Basin supports this hypothesis. In the Juli-Pomata region, for instance, Steadman has defined a number of distinct paste types that are either local, semilocal, or exotic regarding their place of manufacture. In the case of the Inca-period pottery, the vast majority of the sample sherds were locally manufactured in a paste used both prior to the Inca occupation and in the Early Colonial period.

Art and Architectural Styles

The most detailed study of changes in pottery style in the Titicaca region as a result of the Inca occupation is the work of Julien (1983) at the site of Hatuncolla. She excavated eleven test units at the site and defined a four-phase ceramic sequence. According to Julien, all materials at the site represent a time in which there was a strong Inca influence at Hatuncolla, indicating that the site was founded during Inca expansion.

In Julien's (1983: 151–153) refined ceramic chronol-

ogy for the Inca occupation of Hatuncolla, there are three pre-Colonial phases, beginning with the founding of the site. In Phase 1 there is a clear influence of Cuzco ceramic traditions imitated in predominantly two local clays alongside a pre-Inca Sillustani-derived assemblage. Some of these are outright imitations, but other borrowing is more subtle. She notes that decorated bowls are the most important in the ceramic assemblage. She also notes a substantial stylistic break from the pre-Inca Sillustani traditions, emphasizing that Inca occupation reached into the stylistic canons of the local population.

For Phase 2, Julien notes a greater variety of rim profiles and decoration. Again, bowls were important, but there were many more shapes that were borrowed from the Cuzco inventory. Only a few of the Sillustani-derived tradition shapes from Phase 1 continued into Phase 2. Phase 3 is the latest Prehispanic ceramic period defined by Julien (1983: 203–230). Shallow bowls continued, but larger bowls were added. Sillustani styles continued, and Julien notes a revival of conservative Sillustani shape features, with fewer Cuzco-Inca shapes. In the first Spanish-influenced phase, Phase 4, Julien notes Cuzco-related surface finishes with wheel-made vessels and a lack of glazed pottery.

In the Juli-Pomata area, the personnel from the Lupaqa Project have defined a number of ceramic types for the Inca period. There are several distinct types of Inca-period diagnostics in the Juli-Pomata, Ccapia, and Desaguadero areas. The most common shape by far is the bowl form, with Inca bottles (known as aryballoids) quite common as well. The most common decorative motif is Local Inca. This latter type is essentially Inca pottery manufactured in the Titicaca Basin, and dates to the Inca period circa A.D. 1450–1532. These pieces are imitations of Cuzco pottery, with bottles and bowls being the predominant forms. In particular, the use of Cuzco motifs and the distinctive double protuberance at the lip of bowls serves to identify this type. Julien notes that the use of local pastes and pigments and the misinterpretation of Cuzco motifs identifies the Local Inca style as locally manufactured in the Titicaca area (Julien 1983: 146). We recognize three subtypes within the Local Inca assemblage: Local Inca Plain, Local Inca Polychrome, and Local Inca Bichrome.

Another Inca-period type is Chucuito. Virtually all Chucuito types are bowl forms. It was first defined by M. Tschopik (1946: 27–31) as two related wares: Chucuito Polychrome and Chucuito Black-on-red. The dominant decorative motifs include animal and plant designs, with human, insect, and geometric designs used as well. The Chucuito ceramics in the Juli-Pomata area are locally manufactured. M. Tschopik (1946: 27) notes that Chucuito pastes are fine textured and tend to be pink or light red. They are sand tempered, with occasional mica inclusions.

Pacajes is a Inca-period type more common in the Desaguadero area and was first reported in detail by Rydén (1957: 235–238) from a number of sites in Bolivia. Albarracin-Jordan and Mathews (1990: 171; and Mathews 1993) refer to this type as Pacajes-Inka and assign it an Inca-period date. This ceramic type is almost certainly associated with the Pacajes region of the south basin.

Pacajes ceramics are easily recognized by the distinctive *llamita* designs (and similar, unrelated shapes) on the interior surface of bowls. Our Pacajes ceramics all appear to be Inca period in date given their similarity to Chucuito and Local Inca bowls. The low occurrence in the region of this type and its greater known density to the south strongly suggest that Pacajes is an exotic import in the Juli-Pomata area. With one exception, all Pacajes examples from the Juli-Desaguadero study area are bowl forms.

Sillustani types are found in both Altiplano and Inca-period contexts, as determined by stratigraphic excavations and stylistic analysis (Julien 1983: 116–125; Stanish 1991: 13–14). Inca-period Sillustani types are fairly easily distinguished by thicker lips, shallower bowl forms, finer exterior burnishing, and more elaborate design motifs. The Inca-period Sillustani type was also first identified and named by M. Tschopik (1946: 22–27), and further discussed by Julien (1982), Revilla Becerra and Uriarte Paniagua (1985), and Stanish (1991). As with the pre-Inca types, virtually all Sillustani diagnostics are bowls. The primary defining characteristic of the Sillustani type is a set of parallel lines along the interior rim of burnished or polished bowls. Tschopik suggested four wares within the Sillustani series: Sillustani Polychrome, Sillustani Brown-on-cream, Sillustani Black-on-red, and Sillustani Black-and-white-on-red. We did not find any polychrome (with one exception that was classified as a possible Chucuito Polychrome) or Sillustani Black-and-white-on-red in the Juli-Pomata area and therefore did not include these in our typology (Stanish et al. 1997). We defined an additional subtype, Sillustani Black-on-orange. Based on paste characteristics, the Sillustani Brown-on-cream is hypothesized to have been imported to the Juli-Pomata area, but the Black-on-orange and Black-on-red were most likely locally made.

There are some relatively strong geographic associations between major Inca-period pottery styles and polities in the Titicaca region. For instance, the Chucuito ceramic style is clearly associated with the Lupaqa polity (Hyslop 1976: 147; Stanish et al. 1997). The Sillustani ceramic style is associated with the Colla area to the north and northwest. The Pacajes style is found in the Pacajes region in the south and extreme southwest (Albarracin-Jordan 1992: 313; Portugal O. 1988b; Stanish et al. 1997).

Regional Relationships

In chapter 2, the concept of zonal complementarity, or verticality, was introduced as it applies to the Lupaqa state, in particular, and the Titicaca Basin Altiplano and Inca periods in general. One of the best archaeological methods for testing the zonal complementarity model is in a hypothesized colonial territory. In 1983–1985, research was conducted on Late Intermediate–period settlements in the Moquegua region of southern Peru, one of the principal regions in the south-central Andes where the Lupaqa were said to have maintained colonies in the sixteenth century (Pease 1982a; Murra 1968). Additional research by Bürgi (1993) and Conrad and Webster (1989) has greatly expanded our knowledge of this important valley.

The results of this research are available in great detail elsewhere (Bürgi 1993; Conrad and Webster 1989; Stanish 1989a, 1989b, 1992), so I will only briefly summarize them here. The intensive excavations and survey of the Otora Valley of the Moquegua drainage indicate that Lupaqa control was not evident until the Inca period, coincident with the Inca occupation of the region. Prior to the establishment of Inca-Lupaqa administrative sites, the mid to upper sierra region in Moquegua (above about 2,000 m.a.s.l.) was controlled by independent political groups collectively known as Estuquiña. Estuquiña sites were fortified and had evidence of a local elite that engaged in vigorous exchange with the coastal areas and the northern Titicaca Basin. Specifically, the main exchange partners appear to have been the Colla, as evidenced by the abundance of Sillustani pottery found in domestic and nondomestic contexts on Estuquiña sites (Stanish 1989a, 1992). In short, the Moquegua data suggest that the northern Titicaca Basin Colla groups were displaced as the primary group in the region by Inca and Lupaqa elite who maintained administrative centers there.

THE EIGHTH CABECERA?
THE SITE OF TORATA ALTA IN MOQUEGUA

The large Inca and Early Colonial–period site of Torata Alta is one of the most important sites outside the Titicaca Basin for understanding the nature of Inca rule in the basin itself. Torata Alta, in the upper reaches of the mid-Moquegua Valley in the Torata Valley, is built on a grid pattern and has a major Inca occupation and a smaller Early Colonial one (Stanish and Pritzker 1983).

The data suggest that the site was constructed in the Inca period, and served as the region's major administrative center. It is possibly the site mentioned by several chroniclers, as cited by Murra in his seminal 1968 article. The fact that the majority of the Chucuito pottery fits into Julien's Phase 3 (with a few from Phase 2) in her sequence from Hatuncolla also strongly supports a pre-Colonial founding date (Julien 1983: plates 12, 33, 34).

As noted above, the grid pattern is typical of many Inca sites in the south-central Andes. Furthermore, the Inca-period ceramics are overwhelmingly Chucuito in style, and suggest a strong connection with the Lupaqa subdivision of the Inca province in the Titicaca Basin. Van Buren (1996) notes that the Chucuito ceramics are virtually identical to Titicaca Basin ones.

Documentary evidence also suggests that the Torata area was part of the Lupaqa province as understood within the model of zonal complementarity as a true archipelago. We can suggest the following hypothesis: that the site of Torata Alta was one of the Lupaqa-controlled territories granted to the Lupaqa under Inca domination. There is no evidence of Lupaqa control prior to Inca occupation in the Moquegua drainage. I have suggested previously that the first Lupaqa presence in the Moquegua drainage is correlated to initial Inca geopolitical control of the Moquegua drainage (Stanish 1989a: 319). Prior to the Inca occupation, in the Late Intermediate period, the Moquegua area was controlled—or at the very least, the exchange relationships were controlled—by the Colla polity. Coincident with the conquest and annihilation of the Colla as a significant political power, the Lupaqa were given lands in the Moquegua area. The Lupaqa took advantage of their privileged position within the Inca state to appropriate the Moquegua region, acting as indirect administrators for this important and productive valley. Torata Alta was constructed in conjunction with Lupaqa authorities and served the interests of the newly elevated Lupaqa elite as well as those of their patrons, the Inca state. The fact that the site was built with Inca architectural patterns, but that artifactual styles were linked with the Lupaqa, strongly supports the historically documented alliance between the Lupaqa and the Inca. In short, the Inca militarily conquered the Moquegua Valley and used Lupaqa elite to administer the province. Such an interpretation is consistent with historical data suggesting that the Lupaqa "owned" lands in the western yungas, with the Moquegua Valley representing an archetypal example of this Inca-Lupaqa alliance. The repeated assertions of the Lupaqa in the Diez de San Miguel Visita that they were the rightful owners of yunga colonies in the Spanish Colonial period *prior* to the Inca were, in my opinion, a legal fiction to lay claim to these lands in the context of Spanish legal norms (Stanish 2000).

INCA CHULPA TOMB SITES

There are a number of sites with fine cut-stone chulpas in the Titicaca region. One of these is Molloko, first reported by Squier (1877) and described as the chulpas of Acora. These chulpas are built in classic Inca-period style. Chulpas at Molloko have a cornice, an architectural feature also found at Sillustani and other sites. On the sides of one of the chulpas at Molloko is a low relief of two viscachas.[11] Snakes are depicted on another chulpa, and on a third, pumas. The chulpas at Molloko were associated with Inca settlements in the Acora region.

Another cluster of finely made chulpas is found in the Challapampa area just north of Pomata. These Inca-period chulpas, first reported by H. Tschopik (1946: 506), are found along the north side of the hill that rings the low pampa zone. There is a substantial settlement in the Challapampa area (also referred to as Huancani) that includes a number of Inca-period sites. The chulpas are not directly associated with any particular site. They are very near the Urqusuyu road and are along a probable branch of the road that went around the marshy area nearby. The chulpas were placed in such a manner that they would have been visible from the road, suggesting an intentional placement similar to that of Molloko.

Inca Ideology and State Control in the Titicaca Basin

When he came into Colla, he advanced as far as Chucuito, where the rulers of the land had gathered to celebrate a feast in his honor; and with the order he had established there was such an abundance of supplies that there was plenty for the 300,000 men who made up his army. Some of the lords of the Colla offered to go themselves with the Inca, and with those he chose, he went out on the lake of Titicaca, and praised those who had put up the buildings his father had ordered constructed for the excellence of their work. He performed great sacrifices in the temple, and bestowed rich gifts on the idol and the priests, as befitted the great lord he was.

Pedro de Cieza de León,
Crónica del Perú, 1959 [1553], p. 244

With the conquest of this perennially rebellious area, the Inca elite attempted to ideologically associate themselves with sacred places in the Titicaca region and to forge a genealogical link with their predecessor state, Tiwanaku. This was the cornerstone of their ideological strategies in the region. Cobo, for instance, describes the temple at Tiwanaku as "a universal guaca and shrine" believed by the residents of Collao to be "in the middle of the world, and that the people who repopulated the world after flood came out of this place" (Cobo 1990 [1653]: 100). Likewise, one of the creation myths of the Inca state emphasized the sacredness of Lake Titicaca as the origin place of the first Inca, Manco Capac (Cobo 1983: 103–105). According to Cobo, the temples on the islands were considered the third most important shrine in their empire, on par with other ceremonial sites such as Pachacamac (Cobo 1990: 91). According to Cieza, these temples were built by the orders of Pachacuti during his triumphal victory march through Collasuyu (Cieza 1959 [1553]: 233).

Cobo relates one Inca myth in which the creator god Ticiviracocha "made all things in Tiaguanaco, where they pretend that he resided" (Cobo 1983: 104–105). This version continues with an explicit linking of Tiwanaku with the founding elite of the Inca state: Ticiviracocha created the Sun, who in turn told Manco Capac that he and his descendants would conquer many lands and peoples, and be great rulers (Cobo 1983: 105). Manco Capac then traveled to Cuzco via Pacariqtambo, another principal origin place in Inca myth (Bauer 1992a: 29–33). As Bauer (1992a: 29) notes, the descendants of this mythical founder then became the Inca of Royal Blood. This myth therefore links two origin places in Inca social and political history: Pacariqtambo near Cuzco, where the royal lineages were created, and Lake Titicaca, the ancestral home of the earlier Tiwanaku civilization, where the mythical founder was born and received divine authority. In other words, the creator god and the Sun, originating in the ancient capital of Tiwanaku, provide ideological legitimacy for the Inca elite lineages and their subsequent conquests.

Cieza (1959 [1553]: 284) parenthetically notes that "the first Incas talked of setting up their court and capital here in Tiahuanacu," providing us the most explicit and direct statement of an Inca attempt to establish an early genealogical linkage with the empire of Tiwanaku. Likewise, the claim that Manco Inca, the son of Huayna Capac, was born in Tiwanaku represents an attempt to associate the Inca royal lineages with the site of Tiwanaku, if not with the actual rulers of that ancient and revered state. In this light, it is significant that the conqueror Pachacuti also took pains to visit Tiwanaku in his march around Collasuyu, and then ordered his architects to copy the architectural styles of the then-ruined city (Cieza 1959 [1553]: 284; Cobo 1983: 141; Cobo 1990: 104).

Copacabana and the Island of the Sun

The town of Copacabana houses one of the greatest Christian pilgrimage centers in South America: the great church and hilltop shrine with its stations of the cross. The founding of these religious institutions in the Copacabana region is no coincidence. The entire area from Yunguyu on the current Peru/Bolivia border to the Island of the Sun was one large ritual area created by the Inca state (Bauer and Stanish 2001).

A very special use of mitimas was connected with the state religious temple on the Island of the Sun. The entire peninsula of Copacabana was apparently replaced with colonists from dozens of different ethnic groups from across the empire (Cobo 1990: 94). The original population from Copacabana was sent to Yunguyu, the town immediately adjacent to the peninsula, on what is now the Peruvian side of the Peru-Bolivia border (Ramos Gavilán 1988 [1621]). They may also have been responsible for the cut-stone shrines just outside Copacabana (see figure 10.9). The 1589 chronicle *Historia del Santuario de Nuestra Señora de Copacabana,* by Ramos Gavilán, specifically states that people from more than forty

FIGURE 10.9. Inca cut stone in Copacabana. Photograph by the author.

different *naciones* from around the empire were sent to Copacabana:

> Here [in Copacabana] the Inca transplanted (taking them from their place of birth) Anacuscos, Hurincuscos, Ingas, Chinchaisuyos, Quitos, Pastos, Chachapoyas, Cañares, Cayambis, Latas, Caxamarcas, Guamachucos, Guaylas, Yauyos, Ancaras, Quichuas, Mayos, Guancas, Andesuyos, Condesuyos, Chancas, Aymaras, Ianaguaras, Chumbivilcas, Padrechilques, Collaguas, Hubinas, Canches, Canas, Quivarguaros, Lupacas, Capancos, Pucopucos, Pacajes, Iungas, Carangas, Quillacas, Chichas, Soras, Copayapos, Colliyungas, Guánucos, y Huruquillas. (Ramos Gavilán 1988 [1621]: 84–85)

Several of these groups were from the high-status "Inca by privilege" as well as additional groups from subject, non-Quechua peoples from the empire (Bauer 1992a: 32; Zuidema 1983: 73). Incas by privilege were Quechua-speaking peoples from the Cuzco area who were given this special status by the Inca state. The mitimas of Copacabana were responsible for the administration and care of the major temples on the Island of the Sun and Moon dedicated to the glory of the Inca state (Julien 1983: 88). They may

also have been responsible for the cut-stone shrines just outside Copacabana. Cobo says that there were human and material sacrifices, pilgrimages, and other state-sanctioned ceremonies at these sites (Cobo 1990: 91–99).

An Imperial Pilgrimage Route

Historical and archaeological data indicate that there was a major state-sponsored pilgrimage route to the Copacabana Peninsula and ultimately to the Island of the Sun. Documents indicate that actual Inca emperors visited the Islands of the Sun and Moon, and it is logical that a major pilgrimage route was followed, beginning in Cuzco, continuing through to the south Titicaca Basin via the Urqusuyu road and ending at the Island of the Sun in southern Lake Titicaca. Such a long route is not uncommon in ancient states. From the Delian League and Rome in the Classical world through the fragmented states of medieval Christendom in Europe, to the pilgrimages in the Hindu and Moslem states, religious elite reworked a particularly sacred area into the endpoint of a physical and spiritual journey that transformed a pilgrim from a member of a local ethnic group or village into a participant in a larger state system. The

Inca were masters of this type of ideological manipulation, drawing on earlier traditions and creating new ones to suit the needs of their empire.

Archaeological reconnaissance and survey have located several ritual sites in the Titicaca Basin that are likely associated with this pilgrimage route. Throughout the basin there are numerous Inca cut-stone rocks and rock outcrops, almost all of which are on the main road system crossing the area from north to south. Cut stones are a prominent feature of Inca ritual throughout the empire. Extensive and elaborate cut stones are found around the Cuzco area, particularly at such sites as Kenko. As Hyslop (1990) has noted, the function and importance of these cut stones varied throughout the empire; in some cases they were extremely elaborate carved boulders. In the Titicaca Basin, there are several cut-stone rock outcrops in what is almost certainly an Inca style.

There appear to have been three main types of stone carving in the Inca state. One is the elaborate carving of large boulders with fancy motifs. None of these have been located in the Titicaca Basin, to my knowledge, but they are common in the Cuzco region. The second type is small boulders with carved depressions. The third type is large outcrops cut in asymmetrical steplike patterns; the Intihuatana stone at Machu Picchu is the most visited and well-known. Examples of this latter type of steplike carvings are found in the Titicaca Basin and appear to have functioned as stops along the pilgrimage route to the Island of the Sun, with each having certain ritual requirements.

One such cut stone, known as the Inca's Chair, is near Santiago Chambilla, between Ilave and Juli. It was described by Squier (1877: 350), Romero (1928: 59), and others years ago, and has been a major tourist stop for decades. Squier's drawings are not quite accurate, and he implies that natural uplifted sandstone formation and terraced interiors were all part of the complex. This interpretation remains questionable, and Squier's drawing typically exaggerates the com-

plexity of the site. The steps or platforms of the cut stone are irregularly shaped and cut in the typical Inca style of finely hewn stone. Again, Squier's drawing is inaccurate in this regard, making the stones appear to be more formal than they truly are.

It is significant that the site is directly adjacent to the modern and presumably Inca-period road. If this road was part of the ritual walk to the Island of the Sun and Copacabana, the Inca's Chair would have been part of this elaborate pilgrimage route, as would the enigmatic site of Altarani.

In the same geological formation, and only a few kilometers from the Inca's Chair, is Altarani, first published in some detail by Hyslop (1976: 352; 1977: 161). His description matches observations of the Juli-Pomata survey, except that we (Stanish et al. 1997) included the entire Bebedero rock outcrop with an earlier Tiwanaku and Upper Formative platform and presumably carved niche as one site. The carving is best described as a small inverted trapezoidal or T-shaped niche inside an upside-down, square U shape. It is geometric in form. The carving, about seven meters high and about fourteen meters wide,[12] is unfinished, suggesting that the site was abandoned during preparation of this niche. This is evidenced by the uncompleted flanking section on the north side of the cut-stone face. If the niche was an Inca construction, it is possible that the architects abandoned their work at the time of the Spanish Conquest. Hyslop (1977: 161) argued that the niche represented a carved chulpa facade constructed in the Altiplano period. This is not established, however, and the carving could be associated with the probable cut stone at the Inca's Chair. The Inca occupation at this site supports the interpretation of the niche as Inca in date. An alternative hypothesis is that the carving was completed during the Tiwanaku or the Late Sillumocco period. Hyslop himself notes that the "doorway has a T-shape reminiscent of a Tiwanaku sculptural motif" (Hyslop 1977: 161–162). It is also trapezoidal in shape and appears to be a modification of Inca architectural canons as well.

The Copacabana–Islands of the Sun and Moon Ritual Complex

The final destination in the Inca pilgrimage was the Titikala, or Sacred Rock, area on the northern side of the Island of the Sun (see map 10.2). To get to the island, pilgrims had to go through a series of sacred areas, beginning in Yunguyu and continuing through Copacabana (Bauer and Stanish 2001), which was a major town in the Inca period. Although its exact dimensions remain unknown, the high density of Inca-period ceramic fragments found in the alleys and adobe bricks of the town indicate a major Inca occupation. The town layout conforms to an orthogonal grid pattern. There is also a typical plaza, which is probably on top of the Inca one. The famous Catholic church facing the plaza probably was built over an Inca temple, although this observation remains untested. In short, the surface data strongly suggest that Copacabana was founded in the Inca period.

Copacabana houses several of the most famous cut stones in the region. The shrine to the Virgen de Copacabana, adjacent to town, also may have had some Inca cut stones, but the site has been heavily altered by the Christian shrine complex. The town was one of the most famous Catholic pilgrimage centers throughout the Colonial and Republican periods, and it continues to be a major shrine. It is no surprise that Copacabana was a major center on the Island of the Sun and Moon pilgrimage route, and the elaborate cut stones were most certainly associated with this ritual center. Hyslop suggests that the Copacabana cut stones had the most elaborate set of steps or shelves outside the Cuzco area, with the exception of the massive Inca site of Samaipata in Bolivia.

The first archaeological research on the Island of the Sun was conducted by Ephraim Squier in the nineteenth century. The first intensive research was conducted by Adolph Bandelier in 1894, who, during his four months of research, conducted excavations at more than twenty sites, concentrating largely on cemeteries. Bandelier (1910: 165) made no systematic attempt to record all of the prehistoric sites on the island, visiting only those that interested him. Despite this, his work demonstrated that there was a substantial Inca presence on the island, as well as an extensive pre-Inca settlement that he simply called Chullpa.

Hyslop (1990: 75–80), using information from Cobo, Ramos Gavilán, Cieza (1959 [1553], 1976) and Calancha, as well as later writers such as Bandelier (1910) and Squier (1877), correlated many of the Inca settlements and structures on the Island of the Sun with these historical accounts. He suggested that a group of Inca buildings to the east of the Sacred Rock represents the Temple of the Sun as described by Cobo, Ramos Gavilán, and Calancha. Furthermore, he suggested that an elaborate set of structures adjacent to the Titikala, currently called Chincana, represents the labyrinth-like storehouse that the chroniclers locate near the rock.

The Island of the Sun was one of the three most important huacas in the Inca empire, surpassed only by the Coricancha in Cuzco and possibly Pachacamac on the north coast of Peru. The huaca was actually a series of ancient temples, the largest of which stood beside the Sacred Rock of the sun, a reddish-brown sandstone formation that rises several meters above the land and is on the far northern end of the island. The finest descriptions of the island come from the priests who lived along the shores of Lake Titicaca during the early seventeenth century. These include the writings of Cobo (1983, 1990) and the works of two Augustinians, Ramos Gavilán (1988 [1621]) and Calancha (1981 [1638]).

Cobo stresses that the Inca maintained large facilities on the island for the worship of the Sacred Rock, the site of large pilgrimages. There is a long tradition of pilgrimage centers in the Andes (Silverman

1990, 1994), and the Island of the Sun was one of the most important at the time of Spanish contact.

Because the Island of the Sun was a major center for the Inca, facilities were maintained by individuals brought in as mitimas directly from Cuzco, the capital. Cobo, who states that the Inca transported two thousand colonists to the island, writes: "[the Inca] brought in other people from Cuzco, in whom he could put the trust that the gravity of the case required. He made a moderate-sized town one league from the temple, and the majority of the inhabitants were mitimaes of Inca blood and lineage" (Cobo 1990: 94 [Bk. 13: chap. 18]). Ramos Gavilán (1988 [1621: chap. 12]), is even more specific and states that these colonists represented the forty-two groups of Inca by Privilege, individuals of some status in the empire who lived in the Cuzco region (Zuidema 1983: 73–74; Bauer 1992a: 18–35).

Cobo's descriptions of the Island of the Sun are supported by those of Ramos Gavilán (1988 [1621]) and Calancha (1981 [1638]). Cobo describes the Sacred Rock, or Titikala, a temple to the Sun and other deities, and a large labyrinth-like structure that housed the Mamacona ("chosen women" of the Inca who attended the shrines).

Julien (1993: 186) has argued that the Copacabana/Island of the Sun area was a special provincial territory in the Inca state reserved for the most important religious centers or estate holdings. According to her reconstruction from documentary sources, the Island of the Sun was one of several local huacas taken over by the Inca and replaced with mitima.

Archaeological research (see pages 254–258) indicates a huge Inca presence on the island (see map 10.2). All of the sites mentioned by the early documents were located, and scores of additional hamlets were discovered. The archaeological evidence is unambiguous: the Inca clearly controlled the Islands of the Sun and Moon. They relocated existing settlements on the islands, most likely importing mitimas, as described in the early historical documents. The

Island of the Sun was a major pilgrimage destination in the Inca empire, which appropriated an already sacred area for the peoples of the Titicaca Basin and converted it into a shrine that supported the sanctity of Inca control. The state invested a huge amount of resources in the maintenance of the shrine complex as part of its imperial expansion into Collasuyu.

A Water Pilgrimage Route?

The existence of a major ritual pilgrimage route from Cuzco to the Island of the Sun is little disputed. It would have followed the Urqusuyu road along the western edge of the lake before crossing into the Copacabana Peninsula and ending up at the origin place of the Sun on the Island of the Sun at the Titikala temple. There is some suggestion that there was also a water route, as suggested by archaeological data. This is a speculative suggestion but deserves some attention.

In the 1980s, several diving expeditions discovered Inca and Tiwanaku materials on a submerged ridge next to the island of Koa, north of the Island of the Sun (Ponce et. al. 1992; Reinhard 1993). Reinhard describes a number of ritual objects recovered from the ridge, including cut andesite boxes containing figurines and animal bones, spondylus shell, gold objects, and pottery. In Reinhard's well-informed opinion, the andesite boxes were of Inca origin and most likely were made to be lowered onto the underwater ridge (Reinhard 1992a: 128). In other words, this particular ridge adjacent to the small island was a place of worship in which objects were intentionally offered in a manner identical to that of objects left along a land pilgrimage route.

Several other islands in the lake have Inca remains and may have been ritually important. As mentioned above, Pallalla was described by Pentland in the early nineteenth century as having gold and silver offerings (and see Reinhard 1992a: 135). In our survey of the Island of the Sun, we also covered the islands in the immediate vicinity, including Pallalla, where, as described above, we discovered the foundations of a probable *qolca,* or storage structure. A qolca on an island so small suggests a ritual function, an observation supported by the remains of ceremonial activities reported by Reinhard (1992a, 1992b) off the nearby island of Koa.

Summary

The Titicaca Basin was the demographic and cultural center of the Inca quarter of Collasuyu. According to the historical accounts of Cobo (1983) and Cieza (1959 [1553]), the first incursion into the Titicaca region was initiated by the early (and possibly apocryphal) emperor known as Viracocha Inca, most likely in the middle of the fifteenth century. This Inca encountered two large, complex polities in the western Titicaca Basin—the Lupaqa and Colla—along with several smaller political groups such as the Pacajes and those of the Omasuyu regions.

At the time of Inca expansion into this region, the Lupaqa and Colla were bitter enemies engaged in nondecisive conflict. It is recorded that Viracocha Inca negotiated with both sides, trying to manipulate them for his own political advantage (Cieza 1959 [1553]: 215–216). Fearing an alliance between the Lupaqa and the Inca, the Colla initiated a battle with the Lupaqa at Paucarcolla (Cieza 1959 [1553]: 219). The Lupaqa won this battle, and their king, known as Cari, negotiated a peace with Viracocha Inca.

These mytho-heroic histories suggest that the actual incorporation of the region was accomplished by the son of Viracocha Inca, Pachacuti (Cieza 1959 [1553]: 232–235). Pachacuti initiated a new campaign in the Titicaca region and was forced to fight the still autonomous Collas. The Colla fought and lost a battle with the Inca near the town of Ayaviri. The Colla retreated to the town of Pucara while the Inca destroyed Ayaviri, killing most of the population (Cieza 1959 [1553]: 232). Cobo (1983: 140) relates that then the Lupaqa king "received the Inca in peace and turned over his state to him."

Certainly by A.D. 1500, and most likely earlier, the Inca had incorporated the Titicaca Basin as one of its most productive provinces through a variety of strategies: the establishment of military garrisons, the massive resettlement of people into more strategic and economically more efficient areas, the use of mitima colonists, the co-option of the local elite, and the appropriation of ideological authority.

The Evolution of Complex Society in the Titicaca Basin

Social power derives from the political control of economic production and exchange. This control is exercised through a variety of mechanisms ranging from voluntary organizations held together by mutually beneficial reciprocal relationships, to outright coercion by an entrenched elite. The initial development of organization where some groups control production and exchange results in ranked society. In the Titicaca Basin, politically ranked societies developed for the first time in the Middle Formative period. Robert Carneiro (1998) argues that the most salient characteristic of chiefdom development is the formation of intervillage polities and the loss of individual autonomy for some of these settlements. From this perspective, the Middle Formative period can be understood as the development of the first political organizations in the region that transcended the village level. It is also significant that the north-south division of the entire basin, first seen in the Early Formative, continues into the Middle Formative period. There is excavation evidence for the first substantial site architecture in the Chiripa and Qaluyu areas. The pottery from these areas is distinctive, and two distinct areas of distribution of non-fiber- and fiber-tempered decorated and undecorated wares are evident in the north and south basin, respectively.

One of the earliest corporate architectural constructions is found at Chiripa and dates to the Middle Chiripa period: the depression, first identified by Bennett (1936), was most likely a sunken court. Work by Hastorf (1999a) and her team supports this interpretation. At the site of Titinhuayani on the Island of the Sun, excavations by Quelima (see Bauer and Stanish 2001) indicated substantial remodeling of the site in late Middle Formative and Upper Formative times. The construction features included the leveling of part of the hill, the construction of what appears to be stone-walled areas, and possibly sunken courts or enclosures. Similar patterns are seen at the site of Palermo and Sillumocco-Huaquina near Juli as well.

In the early Middle Formative times, elites were numerous and were found throughout the Titicaca Basin. In the ethnographic examples described around the world, chiefly societies have many elite families. Flannery (1998: 21) notes that in a chiefly village of one thousand people, one can find as many as fifteen chiefly families, each having elite residences with some kind of public architecture. The residences of the elites most likely represented the heads of lineages in each of the larger villages. These villages, in turn, had political alliances with other villages in the region. As a result, we would expect to find numerous small courts in many villages around the region, each belonging to, or associated with, a lineage.

The earliest elite architectural construction type in the Titicaca Basin is hypothesized to be the small, squarish sunken court. The Llusco structure, discovered by Hastorf (1999a), is typical of dozens of known small sunken courts around the Titicaca Basin. Other structures similar to, and roughly contemporary with, the Llusco structure have been found in the Tiwanaku Valley by Mathews (1992: 69) at the site of T'ijini Pata and possibly at the site of Allkamari by Albarracin-Jordan (1996a: 105–109). Sunken courts that possibly date to the early Middle Formative are found at the site of Sillumocco-Huaquina in the Juli area, and at Titimani in the southeast basin (Portugal O. 1988a). Reconnaissance indicates that there are numerous sunken courts throughout the Titicaca Basin that may date to this period as well.

Persuasive Means of Elite Emergence

The sites with sunken courts became the original primary regional centers and were the focus of emergent elite efforts to attract retainers or attached specialists. The Middle Formative was the first time that people were able to organize the labor of others beyond the household level. In this sense, the court complexes became the material means by which these societies began to overcome the inherent productivity limits as embodied in Chayanov's rule. As Paz Soría (1999) points out for the Llusco structure at Chiripa, it likely required coordinated labor beyond a single household. The same can be said for the two other structures as the site. The question then is, why did the elite develop in the first place, and how were they able to attract other people to their primary regional centers?

The model proposed here is that the origins of rank in the Titicaca Basin are intimately linked with elite-directed feasting and ceremony at these centers during Middle Formative–period times. It is hypothesized that the regional centers were the settlements where elites and commoners intensified and formalized these reciprocal relationships. The sunken courts and associated architecture were the center of these political rituals. Following the theoretical framework outlined above, the emergent Titicaca Basin elite engaged in a number of strategies to attract followers. The northern and southern areas of the basin had the first courts. Since there were settlements throughout the basin, I hypothesize that the Chiripa and Pucara areas had favorable noncultural features that promoted elite emergence.

There is little evidence for coercion either by intentional elite behavior or by exogenous factors such as resource stress, population growth, and the like. Population densities were quite low relative to later ones. Certainly, the population levels were nowhere near the carrying capacity of the environment and levels of technological development in the Middle Formative. Furthermore, there is little evidence of conflict in the Titicaca Basin during this period. Therefore, there is at present no evidence that populations were forced to aggregate into these centers from fear of raiding or other dangers from neighboring groups. Finally, the regional centers show no evidence of intra-settlement conflict. Quite to the contrary, the regional centers are smaller, and individual families do not seem to have been segregated into separate areas of elite and nonelite. There is no evidence of the physical segregation of groups on these sites.

What was the nature of the reciprocal relationships between emergent elite and nonelite in the Middle Formative? In the model presented here, the elite competed for commoner support by organizing their labor to provide goods and ceremonies not available to individuals. Elites used the organized labor of multiple households to create economies of scale, to intensify production above the levels inherent in Chayanov's rule, and to create larger-scale organizations capable of activities above household-level capacities. The net effect was an economic surplus that was used by the elite to perpetuate these relationships. For instance, the elite used the labor to build and maintain the sunken courts, to maintain part-time artisans to produce the stone and ceramic objects (and probably textiles as well), and to mount trading expeditions outside the region.

The goods obtained and manufactured by this reorganized labor were redistributed to the population in competitive feasts and other ceremonies. It is hypothesized that exotic goods, particularly coca and other similar substances, were obtained from the lowlands. The formation of elite alliances as evidenced in the distribution of Yaya-Mama art styles could have facilitated this exchange. Based on ethnographic and ethnohistorical analogies, such alliances could include complex marriage ties and elaborate elite gift giving, strategies that created a complex set of reciprocal debt obligations among these groups (Marcus, personal communication 1999).

The existence of long-distance exchange patterns throughout the area is supported by the presence of Titicaca Basin Middle Formative–period pottery styles in the eastern and western sides of the Titicaca region. It is also significant that it was during the Middle Formative that elaborate pottery styles developed around the region. How did these beautiful pottery vessels function? The first observation is that the vessels are rare and were locally produced. Second, they are shaped in such a way as to suggest a drinking/serving function. Furthermore, as in the production of stelae, certain canons were followed in manufacture, but most, if not all, of the assemblages are locally produced. Many vessels show signs of curation, including repair holes on used vessels. The distribution of fine-ware sherds near cemetery areas suggests that they were commonly buried with the dead. It is likely, therefore, that these vessels were extremely valuable until the person who "owned" them died. Then, they had no value except as a grave good. In other words, these were not alienable goods but only had value in the possession of a particular person. In death, they would have possibly had the same function as in life, being used for eating, drinking, and feasting in the afterlife.

It is possible that the development of these fineware pottery styles was another persuasive strategy of elites. By organizing pottery production, elites were able to produce fine wares not readily manufactured by individual households. The flat-bottomed bowls were used in politically ritualized feasts, where exotic or mass-produced goods were distributed by elites to their followers. Feasting in general, and alcohol drinking in particular, is associated, I believe, with the flat-bottomed bowls. This phenomenon represents a key process of elite formation in the Middle Formative.

Michael Dietler's discussion of the appearance of Mediterranean imports in Iron Age France provides a useful analogy for understanding the nature of this process:

The traditional explanatory framework for this archaeological material [from the Mediterranean], particularly in southern France, has been the somewhat nebulous concept known as "Hellenization" . . . , a sort of progressive general emulation of "civilized" customs by "barbarians" as a natural and inevitable response to contact. . . . [In reality] the overall pattern of cultural borrowing and material imports . . . seems curiously at odds with the idea of blanket emulation of Greek culture. In fact, from the very first contacts, this pattern remained limited, specific, and consistent: it was overwhelmingly dominated by wine and wine-drinking gear. . . . As Appadurai has indicated, demand [for goods by the Iron Age French cultures] cannot in any case be assumed to be a natural response to the availability of goods. It must be understood, rather, as the "political logic of consumption," a feature of the overall political economy. (Dietler 1990: 356–357)

The political landscape of the Middle Formative was one of numerous competing and cooperating elite families, all attempting to persuade commoners to participate in their political and economic system. Each of the scores of primary regional centers in the Titicaca Basin possessed aspiring elites competing with others to increase their factions. It is no coincidence that in the few centuries during which ranked society emerged in the region, the Yaya-Mama stelae, the fancy pottery, and corporate architecture essentially coevolved. The objects and the architecture were used by these elites to maintain their factions. Ultimately, only a few elite organizations were successful. Sites like Khañuani on the Huata Peninsula in the south basin are representative of successful Middle Formative elite centers but ultimately Upper Formative–period failures. Khañuani appears to be a largely Middle Formative–period site with some minor later occupations. The corporate architecture is modest, consisting of a probable single court and platform. We can assume that there was a monolith of some sort in the court, based on comparisons to similar sites that have been excavated in the region. This site, along with several dozen others in the region, was a center of political

ritual, feasting, ceremony, and faction building. In time, Khañuani and most of the other sites of similar scale and complexity were unable to successfully compete with the soon-to-be larger center in Chingani, a few kilometers to the south. Chingani most likely began as a regional center like Khañuani in the Middle Formative but emerged as a primary center in the Upper Formative, absorbing the surrounding elite alliances, including Khañuani. In these sites can be seen the operation of the emergence of complex ranked societies throughout the region.

In the model presented here, numerous methods were employed by elites to attract commoner populations into their political sphere for the first time in the Middle Formative, particularly the hosting of feasts in and around the sunken court areas. This process represented the beginning of formal reciprocal relationships between elite and commoner, with the latter exchanging a part of their labor for assets provided by the elite. The organization of craft specialists to produce fine wares and other goods, plus the ability of the elite to mobilize or support labor for heightened economic production and exchange, lay at the core of emergence of complex society in the Titicaca region.

The Upper Formative Period

There is substantial evidence that several strategies were successfully used by elite groups during the Upper Formative period. The Juli-Pomata survey data provide evidence on the degree of agricultural intensification throughout the sequence. Raised fields are a labor-intensive technique relative to rain-fed terrace agriculture and pastoralism. It is not coincidental that the highest level of raised-field use as a percentage of total agricultural land use peaked during the Upper Formative, when almost 70 percent of the population was living less than ten minutes' walk from the raised-field areas; in the entire history of the region, this is the highest percentage of the total population utilizing raised-field agriculture. These survey data strongly support the proposition that labor was mobilized for the intensification of agricultural production above household organizational levels.

Browman (1978b) has documented the existence of long-distance exchange at Chiripa during the Mamani phase. He notes that there is "considerable evidence of trade in status-validating objects" and emphasizes trade in semiprecious stones and metal. Browman argues for extensive trade networks using llama caravans from the north end of Lake Titicaca to the Cochabamba Valley. There is also evidence of interregional trade between the Late Sillumocco polity and neighboring areas. Similar patterns of exotic goods at Chiripa in its latest Formative phases have been documented by Hastorf (1999a). The widespread distribution of Pucara and Pucara-like pottery to the western Pacific slopes attests to the range of trade during this time. The similarly widespread distribution of Chiripa styles to the southeast and southwest, as well as the distribution of Kalasasaya pottery outside the Tiwanaku/Taraco Peninsula area, is additional evidence of extensive exchange contacts.

A compelling argument can be made that the Titicaca Basin elite during the Upper Formative created the first widespread, pan-ethnic ideologies as indicated in art, architecture, and portable objects. I believe that these beliefs were expressed in iconographic traditions such as the Late Chiripa, Early Tiwanaku, and Pucara stone carvings. Elites in chiefly societies adopt iconographic motifs in their art as an attempt to identify with foreign groups, enhancing their power. The adoption of such foreign icons by emerging elite explains the existence of locally manufactured, highly valued ceramic imitations of nonlocal styles. In the Juli-Pomata region, for instance, locally manufactured Late Sillumocco pottery included imitations of southern Titicaca Basin styles (i.e., Chiripa). In the north, Pucara art flourished over a wide area. Again, this was an elaboration of

Middle Formative–period patterns. Stelae production became more restricted, with the stelae larger and much more labor intensive; pottery fine wares were produced and distributed over the area of Pucara influence in the north and Late Chiripa/Qeya in the south; and the sunken court tradition intensified substantially.

As mentioned above, there is substantial evidence of interelite conflict among the Upper Formative Titicaca Basin polities. Apart from the manufacture of projectile points (which could also be used for hunting), the most obvious indication is the existence of trophy-head motifs on Pucara, Early Tiwanaku, and Pucara-related pottery and stelae. It is unlikely that these depictions are purely symbolic; evidence suggests that the capture and decapitation of individuals was likely a major form of elite power aggrandizement during the Upper Formative. As Marcus (1992b: 435) points out, competition in the form of endemic raiding is a hallmark of early ranked societies. In state emergence, the "humiliation and sacrifice of rivals" is a prominent feature of the political landscape. Such tactics were almost certainly a feature of the Upper Formative Titicaca Basin.

The ability to raid other villages and possibly regional centers is predicated on the capacity of the elite to organize commoners for expeditions. The use of such conflict is at once both a persuasive and coercive strategy. It is persuasive because an elite can provide retainers an opportunity for booty capture, status enhancement, and so forth if they participate in raids. It is obviously coercive from the perspective of the vanquished groups. However, like the Preclassic Maya, the Norsemen, and other raiding chiefly or early state societies around the world, this militarism did not result in territorial expansion until the end of the Upper Formative.

People in the Upper Formative period created complex labor organizations that overcame the inherent limits of Chayanov's rule. Populations lived closer to raised-field areas, an intensive form of agriculture that provides for sustained surplus. Artisans created beautiful goods such as pottery and textiles. This heightened economic production above household levels was maintained by the use of ritual and feasting facilities—temples, courts, enclosures—and the redistribution of highly valued goods. The rapid elaboration of these Upper Formative–period centers, in a context of moderate to low population growth and no sustained environmental pressures, is explained as a result of intense feasting and ceremony by competing elites. Goods were manufactured by artisans or were imported from the east and west and redistributed in these periodic feasts. Elites developed pan-regional ideologies that served to integrate them into a larger network in which alliance and trade could flourish. Conversely, these groups also competed with each other, as evidenced by the trophy-head iconography and other evidence of conflict.

The Rise of Competitive Peer Polities

Whether the latest Upper Formative polities of Pucara and Tiwanaku were complex chiefdoms or states is a semantic distinction of little analytical value. By my definition of state-level societies, Tiwanaku would have been the first state in the region (Stanish 2001b). What is important is that the process of complex political organization building was uneven and relatively long by historical reckoning, perhaps three centuries or more. By the end of the period, and the collapse of Pucara, very complex polities had come and gone in the region. All of these were characterized by systematic and organized conflict with their neighbors.

The model that best characterizes the Upper Formative political landscape is a series of autonomous and semiautonomous polities that developed complex sociopolitical, economic, and ideological organizations. This model is similar to what Renfrew (1986: 1, 7) has described as "peer polity interaction," defined as "strong interactions between . . . autonomous socio-political units within [a] region"

combined with the elements of "factional competition" as defined by Brumfiel (1994), in which two of these polities—Tiwanaku and Pucara—emerged as the most successful competitors in the late Upper Formative.

The model of late prehistoric Mississippian societies in the southeastern United States represents a good analogy for the Upper Formative in the Lake Titicaca Basin, at least in its early periods. Anderson describes the political landscape at the time of European contact:

> The early sources provide a number of specific details about the operation of settlement and organizational hierarchies. Large numbers of towns were tied together in the more complex, geographically extensive polities, which were characterized by at least two administrative/decision-making levels occupied by primary chiefs and their retinues and lesser chiefs and their retinues. . . . A three-level settlement hierarchy consisting of major ceremonial and political centers, larger villages/small centers, and scattered small hamlets or villages is documented. . . .
>
> The most complex southeastern polities were geographically extensive, covering thousands of square kilometers, with subsidiary towns and polities held together through alliance networks and the use or threat of force. (Anderson 1994: 63)

In other words, in the early Upper Formative, there were more or less equivalent polities characterized by competition for resources and retainers. As Brumfiel (1994: 10) notes, competition involves not only conflict between elites but also coalition or alliance formation. Alliances are strategic, and they form and dissolve as different elite groups vie for resources, political authority, and labor. Central to this model is the existence of large-scale competitive feasting and use of labor. There is substantial evidence for this economic mechanism in the Upper Formative. The large deposit in Area 4 of Pucara, excavated by Kidder, has already been mentioned.

The emphasis of this model is that the polities are politically autonomous but interact along a number of different axes, including economic, sociological, political, ritual, and so on. Alliances can form and break with some regularity. As a result of this interaction, there tend to be numerous material and organizational similarities between these polities, leading to the type of "modular regularity" described by Cherry (1986: 19). However, unlike that which occurs with the development of fully integrated state organizations possessing coercive powers and the ability to draw on substantial numbers of commoner labor, there is no evidence of "highly structured control hierarchies" (Cherry 1986: 19). Such a model explains the shared architectural and art traditions of the various polities in the region, which remained politically autonomous.

Throughout most of the Upper Formative, the peer-polity relationships held. However, the incessant elite competition eventually led to the emergence of two polities that grew to an order of magnitude larger than their competitors. By the late Upper Formative, Tiwanaku and Pucara had emerged as the primate centers. By A.D. 100 or so, Pucara and Tiwanaku had consolidated power in the north and south basin areas, respectively. They constituted a heretofore unknown phenomenon in the region: the development of powerful regional polities that had control or influence well outside two days' travel from their home territory.

We know little about the nature of Tiwanaku during the Upper Formative period because the massive later occupation of the site by the Tiwanaku state has obscured any remains. However, I believe Pucara's surface architecture is an appropriate analogy for contemporary Tiwanaku as well. Pucara as it exists today is an architectural snapshot of its height about A.D. 200, and this pattern is the best hypothetical reconstruction of Tiwanaku at the same time.

One of the key characteristics of Pucara is that it is not a planned site, as Tiwanaku would be several hundred years later. Its architectural plan is instead an aggregation of temple complexes without any evidence of central planning. Some of these complexes are substantially larger than others, most notably the highest area with the three large sunken courts. Below this area are a number of smaller complexes defined by the presence of a semi-subterranean sunken court. At least ten such complexes are suggested by the topography and surface characteristics of this site, most of which has not been excavated.

This pattern can be interpreted to be an outcome of Upper Formative–period political economies: Pucara became a primate center that pulled in allied elite from around the northern basin. Each of the individual temple complexes at Pucara is similar to the corporate architecture at the other primary regional centers. In effect, these elite constructed temple complexes at the primate center, effectively moving their primary residences from the smaller regional centers. I hypothesize that attached specialists moved with elite from their home territories. Over time, a hierarchy of elites developed at Pucara itself, materially manifest in the larger temple complexes on the hill above and the smaller complexes below. The habitations of the nonelite were below and outside the architectural core of the site on the pampa.

Assuming the validity of this hypothesis, a qualitative shift occurred in the power of Titicaca Basin elite with the ability of local elites to live away from their home centers but continue to maintain the political and economic relationships with attached commoners. The marked site size hierarchy developed at this time. In other words, the elite political economy became institutionalized to the point where elites did not have to actively, on a day-to-day basis, compete for support of commoner populations. Pucara and, by implication, contemporary Tiwanaku had achieved a level of organization at the threshold of early states. These are the only two sites in the Titicaca region exhibiting this level of complexity. Elites had cemented the political and economic relationships to the point where they could move their primary residence. The act of moving to Pucara and Tiwanaku, in turn, served to increase the ability of elite to maintain these relationships. By living in the primate center, the local elite had even greater access to commodities, artisans, and other goods and labor that further fueled the relationships between commoner, attached specialists, and elite. The process of state building is vividly evident in the architectural layout of Pucara. This process, in fact, constituted the context in which Tiwanaku emerged as the first fully integrated expansionist state polity in the Titicaca Basin.

Tiwanaku

The nature of Tiwanaku's political and economic organization has been a constant theme in Andean prehistory. In an excellent book, Albarracin-Jordan (1996a: 74–76) defines four models of the Tiwanaku state: (1) the Urban Revolution model, (2) the Altiplano model, (3) the Centralized Bureaucracy model, and (4) the Local Autonomy model. He then offers his own model for the structure of Tiwanaku based on a segmentary, nested hierarchy organization. These five models nicely define the range of existing conceptions of Tiwanaku from a small, decentralized chiefly society to that of a centralized imperial state.

The "Urban Revolution" and "Centralized Bureaucracy" models are structurally similar. In both, Tiwanaku is viewed as a small Inca empire possessing most of the organizational structures of Tawantinsuyu, including mit'a laborers, a military organization, a complex labor tax system, the holding of provincial territories, and so on (e.g., see Ponce 1976; Kolata 1986, 1993; Tapia Pineda 1978c). That is, these models view the Tiwanaku polity as built on

the same militaristic and expansionist principles as those of the Inca, but on a smaller scale. These scholars argue that Tiwanaku was a conquest state, employing coercive and ideological power to bring groups within its orbit.

Kolata (1993: 101) has suggested a complex dual social, political, economic, and ideological organization for Tiwanaku. He sees the origin of this duality in the merging of pastoralist proto-Aymara populations with Pukina-speaking agriculturalists in the Tiwanaku region. Following Duviols's (1973) model from the central highlands of Peru, Kolata accepts many of the immigration hypotheses of linguists. According to this model, Tiwanaku state ideology and social structure served to order this "contradiction" of two elite groups. Kolata also accepts the existence of Uru- and/or Uru-Chipaya-speaking populations in the Tiwanaku state as well. These latter populations would have occupied a specialized economic niche as lake foragers. There is a problem in that the Tiwanaku organization is argued to be dualistic, when there are actually three major ethnic groups in his model. Kolata resolves this problem by arguing that the Uru populations did not enjoy the same status as the Pukina and proto-Aymara populations; the elite of Tiwanaku are argued to have been largely composed of the pastoralists and farmers, not the fishers.

In Kolata's model, the Tiwanaku peoples built a bureaucratic, imperial state based on these principles of duality. Tiwanaku was a polity with a four-level size hierarchy of sites, with the capital of Tiwanaku at the top (Kolata 1993: 223). Politically, the Tiwanaku state was an empire that engaged in predatory expansion. Kolata is careful not to view Tiwanaku as a smaller version of the Inca state, however. He notes that military coercion was just one of several strategies used by the Tiwanaku state to expand (Kolata 1993: 226–227).

In this bureaucratic model of the Tiwanaku state,

agricultural production and resource extraction were coordinated by state agents. Tiwanaku engineers built causeways, canals, aqueducts, reservoirs, terraces, and raised fields to maximize agricultural production. The state also established colonies in the lower altitudes to control commodities, particularly coca. Organized trading expeditions reached the ends of empire and state-directed workshops produced commodities.

In the "Altiplano model" proposed by Browman (1978a, 1984), Tiwanaku is a state made up of traders. This model is based on the environmental reality of the stratified ecozones that characterize the Andes. Basing his arguments on the models of zonal complementarity of Murra, Pease, and others, Browman makes a compelling case that Tiwanaku developed as a response to the needs of moving goods over these ecological zones. The strength of this model is that it is based on empirical data (historical and ethnographic) and is embedded in a well-developed theoretical framework of zonal complementarity. The model's weakness is that it assumes market mechanisms were used in the Tiwanaku state. This pushes an ethnographic phenomenon, market exchange—which is most likely a result of European influences—back to a fairly remote prehistoric period. There is, in fact, little evidence for the existence of true price-fixing market mechanisms in the central Andes prior to European contact. In its intellectual context, the Altiplano model is a middle ground between centralized and noncentralized conceptions of the Tiwanaku state.

Albarracin-Jordan's model is a most fascinating formulation that represents a second middle-ground formulation. It is based on empirical data of cultures that actually existed (historical and ethnographic), is embedded in a well-developed theoretical framework of segmentary lineage theory, and incorporates archaeological data. He suggests that the Tiwanaku state was composed of a series of nested hierarchies based fundamentally on the ayllu but with a supra-ayllu organization vested in the *marca*. He argues for a structure of "confederated" ayllus ultimately organized at the level of the marca:

> In the past, groups of ayllus, organized in confederations, also were divided into two sections [alasaya and masaya]. This binary segmentation, nevertheless, functioned as a single unit *[unidad]*, being two complementary poles. Each section of the confederation was represented by a jacha mallku qapac, or supreme leader, who had reciprocal obligations to the people of his moiety *[parcialidad]*. (Albarracin-Jordan 1996a: 53)

> Although the ayllu, in its distinct organizational levels, is characterized principally by a hierarchy at the service of the collectivity, the marka best exemplifies this principle, not only because the various ayllus converged in it, but because in its structure it integrates various ethnic groups. . . .
>
> Ethnohistoric data that support an inclusive hierarchical composition of markas are found in the documents [about Guaqui]. . . . Guaqui . . . was divided into four sections, each one composed of four ayllus and represented by a leader. Each ayllu, in turn, had its own representative. (Albarracin-Jordan 1996a: 70)

Albarracin-Jordan uses the nested ayllu-marca model to explain Tiwanaku. After conducting an extensive analysis of the settlement data from the Tiwanaku Valley and beyond, he concluded that marcas and ayllus integrated the Tiwanaku state. He does not view militarism as an integrative mechanism of Tiwanaku (Albarracin-Jordan 1996a: 218); instead, he sees the creation of the Tiwanaku phenomenon as a form of voluntary or noncoercive participation cemented with ritual.

Albarracin-Jordan deserves credit for proposing a model based on ethnographic and historical data, and then assessing it with archaeological data. The model ultimately is hierarchical, albeit without the concomitant associations of power and control, and the question as to whether it was coercive or not can be reduced to mere semantics (ideological coercion, superstructural determinism, and so on).

At the other extreme are the "local autonomy" models that view Tiwanaku as a congregation of farmers who voluntarily constructed a "big village" (Tiwanaku) and then spread an art style, and supposedly a concomitant religion, to other areas. In these models, massive agricultural and architectural projects such as raised-field systems and large pyramids do not require a centralized state or even a hierarchy of any kind. Most of these models are based primarily on a deconstructionist critique and do not provide models of their own. Some scholars have suggested that Tiwanaku was not a hierarchical polity of any sort, and that it did not possess a political organization of any real complexity. They suggest that such statist interpretations derive from contemporary political ideologies associated with Bolivian nationalism, which has its origins, I suppose, with Posnansky at the turn of the century. This critique represents a type of postmodernist critique that is simply not explanatory; instead of offering an alternative, empirically based model to explain the archaeological record, it merely attempts to associate a theory with an existing and completely unrelated hegemonic ideology. Therefore, the state model can be dismissed without recourse to the task of amassing data to refute it.

Since almost all proponents of these extreme conceptions of Tiwanaku have failed to publish (at the time of this writing) any coherent definition of what they think the political and economic structure of Tiwanaku was (as opposed to what it was not), it is necessary to cull information from their critiques of others to understand their positions (e.g., Isbell 1995). For this class of model, the Tiwanaku phenomenon represents the voluntary or noncoercive spread of an art style and its concomitant ideology among the various peoples of the south-central Andes. Tiwanaku was not a state or empire but a social phenomenon mediated by kinship and ritual. The integration of the Tiwanaku polity, according to these models, was achieved through strictly voluntary means integrated at an ayllu or even family level.

This notion of Tiwanaku has a long pedigree in Andean scholarship. More than a century ago, when Andean archaeology was characterized by few data but creative minds, some scholars argued that Tiwanaku was nothing more than the center of a religious cult similar to Pachacamac. As late as 1987, the ethnographer Sallnow could argue for such a model of Tiwanaku: "Despite the evident sophistication of its urban élite and their ability to mobilize labor on a vast scale, the dominion of Tiwanaku did not rest on military conquest so much as on the peaceful diffusion of its prestigious religious ideas coupled with the stimulation of extensive interregional trade. Its cult, carried out of the heartlands by merchant missionaries and pilgrims, syncretized with local cults and traditions" (Sallnow 1987: 22).

We can not only excuse Sallnow as an ethnographer unfamiliar with the archaeological data but compliment him on his attempt to make sense out of the contradictory and sparse archaeological literature. However, the notion of Tiwanaku-as-oracle-center, like Tikal for the central Petén, has been discounted after systematic field research at the site and surrounding areas revealed the site's urban nature and the complex political and economic structure that supported it.

The principal problems with the local autonomy models are that (1) there exist no viable historical or ethnographic analogies for such models, and (2) they fail to explain the profound and substantial changes in art, architecture, settlement patterning, political organization, and economy concomitant with the appearance of Tiwanaku materials in many (though not all) regions in which they are found. There is no historical example to my knowledge of an urban center as large and complex as Tiwanaku that existed in a political and economic structure integrated solely by religion. For that matter, I know of no historical example of any complex political entity integrated by religion without an economic infrastructure of substantial proportions. Even the Vatican in the premodern era had a huge bureaucracy that controlled estates and other wealth-producing entities that by virtually any definition was a multiethnic state, albeit one with fluid geographical boundaries and a much more explicit ideology of power than its peers.

These models also fail to explain why many local art traditions as far away as Moquegua are replaced by Tiwanaku styles, and they utterly ignore the empirical fact that the changes in the archaeological record in the pre-Tiwanaku/Tiwanaku transition in many areas are actually more profound than that for the pre-Inca/Inca transition in the same region. They conveniently ignore the urban character of Tiwanaku itself, apparently dismissing it as merely a large "village" of fifty thousand or so people.

Another common critique of state models of Tiwanaku is to claim that all statist, hierarchical, and militaristic elements of traditional Aymara or indigenous society are related to changes introduced by European contact. Of course, this somewhat naive position ignores the pre-Spanish Inca state, which virtually no one would deny had statist, militaristic, and hierarchical qualities. Leaving aside the Inca example as perhaps not a good one for the south-central Andes, the notion that there were no socioeconomic classes and no intergroup conflict in traditional Aymara society is confounded by the enormous range and diversity of indigenous class-laden and militaristic terms reported in Bertonio's dictionary of 1612.

Bertonio's dictionary contains a number of words that refer to class status, hierarchy, warfare, and conquest. It is significant that virtually all these terms are Aymara in origin; they are not Spanish loan words. Where a Spanish introduction was necessary (such as the word *vacacamana*), the Aymara showed a great capacity to incorporate the word in their language structure. For a people supposedly different from most of the world's cultures in their lack of class distinctions and reluctance to make war, the Aymara had a truly rich vocabulary for expressing these concepts. Terms include *anca mayco*, defined as "tyrant," and *ccapaca suti*, defined as "royal name or tremendous sovereign." The word *ccapaca* is described as "royal seat or site *[asiento]*," "king," "señor," or simply "a rich person." Significantly, Bertonio notes that *ccapaca* was "an ancient term not in use anymore." The term *warmi apu* meant "woman with vassals."

Other words that denote hereditary class distinctions include *ccapaca wila*, defined as "royal blood"; *mayco hatha*, defined as "royal caste"; *lampa*, describing a litter in which the ancient caciques were carried; and *mayco uta*, or "royal house." Political classes are evident in words such as *haqueni* or *mallku*, meaning "señor over vassals"; *haqueha*, meaning "vassal"; *ina haquenaca*, or "crowd or mob of plebeians"; and a number of terms derived from *yana*, meaning "servant."

Militaristic terms include *auca*, or "enemy that makes war"; *aucasiña*, meaning "weapon"; *aucasiri*, denoting "soldier"; *aucasitha*, defined as "to fight or make war"; *collukhatha* and *tucuskhatha*, defined as "to destroy towns or residents of some province"; *haquechatha*, defined as "to conquer people"; *micchi aattasita haque*, meaning "one who carries a bow and arrow"; *pucara*, which of course means "fortress" in both Quechua and Aymara; *ttorokhthapitatha* or *aucathapitatha*, defined as "when armies meet to fight"; and *vinuna fampparpaatka*, defined as "to demolish an army."

There is also a small, but growing, body of direct archaeological data for the use of spearthrowers in Tiwanaku. Owen (1998) discovered a copper spearthrower in a single-component Tiwanaku IV site in the Moquegua Valley, near the Wari site of Cerro Baúl. He notes that the Tiwanaku colonists in the midvalley also made lithic points, and small, triangular, and often stemmed points are found in association with Tiwanaku in the Titicaca Basin as well. Owen concludes that the adoption of the bow was not a major technological breakthrough in south-central Andean society; instead, spearthrower and bow and arrow technology coexisted. One hypothesis is that the bow was used for hunting, and the spearthrower for combat. Certainly, there is little doubt that bow and/or spearthrowing technology existed in the Tiwanaku state, but their use as a military tactic remains to be demonstrated.

The model proposed by Albarracin-Jordan is the only one of the nonbureaucratic state models (albeit a modified one, to include hierarchy) to use a coherent ethnographic and historical database. His model still provides for hierarchical organization, particular in Tiwanaku's latest phase (Albarracin-Jordan 1996a: 261–296). Even so, the big problem with the ayllu/marca-based analogy is that it is derived from sixteenth-century and later ethnographic and historical texts. These texts describe the ayllu/marca structure in what is already a state context. That is, the ethnographic and historical analogs used to build this nested hierarchy model were never independent political and economic entities functioning outside a state context. In the case of the sixteenth-century texts, the nested hierarchies existed either as the remnants of an Inca imperial organization or as a functioning structure within the Spanish state. Throughout the rest of the historical and ethnographic present, local communities all existed within a Colonial or independent state (Bolivia or Peru). In spite of the fact that the state may have been weak at times, it still provided a supra-regional legal, political, economic, religious, and even social framework. One simply cannot dismiss the influence of a Spanish colonial or national administration on the ayllu and supra-ayllu organization.

This same mistake is made in reference to the ability of ayllu- and village-level organizations to build complex agricultural systems such as raised fields. Some archaeologists and agronomists who have re-

habilitated raised fields argue that it is done within strictly a village-level context. They use this argument to support models of Tiwanaku raised-field production as conducted at the village or ayllu level, suggesting that the Tiwanaku elite did not exercise any control over agricultural production. Yet they fail to recognize that modern rehabilitation projects are carried out in the context of a modern state that sustains a market and a legal system, and which enforces police powers. Furthermore, the projects are all funded and directed by outsiders who provide resources and organization far beyond the capacity of a village. The outside projects themselves function as a centralizing, decision-making, resource-providing, and conflict-resolving institution. That is, they function as an elite, statelike organization with both persuasive and coercive economic powers, albeit on a small scale. In short, if the fields were indeed feasible at the village level, the villagers would have rehabilitated them long ago on their own.

As I have suggested in an earlier publication (Stanish 1994), there is no doubt as to the ability of peasant farmers to build complex and intensive agricultural systems. Historically and ethnographically, however, it is very rare. Most intensive agricultural systems are built within hierarchically organized systems of some sort. Hierarchies can be created in a variety of ways, and not just through the use of raw physical power, as so many postmodern archaeologists naively believe. The real question is not *whether* peasant farmers in a nonhierarchical political context can organize intensive agricultural systems but *when* and under *what* conditions farmers intensify production. I have argued previously that hierarchical political systems provide the context to overcome the inherent limitations of Chayanov's rule (Stanish 1994) and create the incentives and/or coerce populations into intensifying production by adopting maximizing strategies at the expense of risk-avoidance ones. The Tiwanaku state, as well as its complex predecessors, did indeed provide the context for agricultural intensification and combined both persuasive and coercive means to achieve it.

Tiwanaku as an Expansionist Polity

Tiwanaku is best viewed as an expansionist state, but it was not as complex as the Inca state in either scale (the Inca expanded over one million square kilometers of territory) or organization. A better analogy for the political and economic scale of Tiwanaku is the Chimú or Wari polities. I base this conclusion on a number of empirical observations and theoretical considerations. In the first instance, although I agree in theory that nonhierarchical peasant societies can indeed self-organize themselves for "state" projects such as the construction of massive agricultural works, urban centers, and the like, the actual historical or ethnographic cases are rare to nonexistent. To suggest that the urban concentration of Tiwanaku and its vast area of colonies and formal economic relationships over an area of about 400,000 square kilometers could have been maintained for centuries only by organized ayllu without any formal state authority is without empirical or theoretical foundation.

Several empirical observations strongly support the conclusion that Tiwanaku was an expansionist state system. First, sites found throughout the south-central Andes reproduce a very distinctive Tiwanaku art and architectural style. This pattern constitutes strong evidence for some kind of political control of a region. Niles (1987) describes the development of an imperial style of architecture in the Inca state: "The architecture of empire included the creation of a state aesthetic with little tolerance of variation from official standards, which resulted in a recognizable and seemingly uniform architectural style throughout the Inca domain" (Niles 1987: 1). In the case of Tiwanaku, we see the same process. Sites such as Omo, Sillumocco-Huaquina, Pajchiri, Isla Esteves, and others are built in an architectural style that exhibits canons from Tiwanaku. The construction of such sites strongly suggests the operation of coercive

strategies in the expansion of Tiwanaku well outside its core territory, albeit on a qualitatively smaller scale than that of Tawantinsuyu.

Second, the distribution of elite pottery outside the core represents a radical change from the Upper Formative throughout the Titicaca Basin and beyond. There is a consistent pattern in which all stylistic borrowing is from one area: in this case, the Tiwanaku Valley. In earlier periods, stylistic borrowing was from many areas, and was combined with local innovation in ceramic styles. During the Tiwanaku period, no areas with Tiwanaku pottery developed distinctive styles alongside that of the state canon: all pottery styles in the Tiwanaku period were based on Tiwanaku canons. It is not surprising that this identical empirical pattern occurred with Inca expansion as well.

Third, the settlement patterns in at least three areas indicate the incorporation of territories in a classic coercive, imperial pattern. In the Juli-Pomata area, there is an increase in the population, the establishment of new sites, the intensification of agricultural production, the formalization of the road system, and the resettlement of a major proportion of the population. In Puno, there is evidence for the establishment of Tiwanaku temples on Esteves Island, the specialization of production, the intensification of agriculture in Paucarcolla, the formalization of the road system, the co-opting of local elite, and the resettling of local populations. In the Moquegua Valley, there is a similar pattern coincident with the Tiwanaku occupation. The first Tiwanaku occupation begins in the Tiwanaku IV period with a number of sites along the agriculturally rich valley floor. These sites are small but are interpreted by Goldstein (1993a: 31) as being Tiwanaku colonies. According to Goldstein, sites such as M-12 ("M" refers to Moquegua) represent small colonial enclaves in a context of local settlements. Goldstein bases his arguments on architectural and ceramic data from the sites. In particular, the Tiwanaku pottery styles are virtual reproductions of the Tiwanaku Altiplano style, if not actual imports in some cases.

I agree with Goldstein and see the settlement dynamics of the Moquegua Valley as indicative of a transformation from a "loosely integrated string of colonies to a centrally governed provincial system" (Goldstein 1993a: 42). In other words, the Moquegua data elegantly define the creation of a provincial territory of Tiwanaku in an agriculturally productive and populated valley far from the core territory. The initial occupation of Tiwanaku was characterized by small colonies among local populations. Over time, the local population was drawn into a Tiwanaku-controlled "breadbasket," complete with classic Tiwanaku civic-ceremonial architecture and probable resident elite population.

Many modern scholars who have worked directly on Tiwanaku political organization have argued that it was at least a complex state with regional control, and at most a conquest empire. Ortloff and Kolata state flatly that Tiwanaku was an empire, based on the criteria established by Schreiber: "This territorial expansion and control of lower altitude zones which began in the latter portions of the Tiwanaku IV phase (c. A.D. 400–750) qualifies the mature Tiwanaku state as a true imperial system" (Ortloff and Kolata 1993: 196–197). Bermann (1994: 154) characterizes Tiwanaku at its height as "the urban capital of a powerful polity that would dominate the south-central Andes for the next five centuries." In short, the accumulated data support the model of Tiwanaku as a complex expansionist state that incorporated peoples from around the south-central Andes.

Aymara Señorío Segmentary Political Organization

Two factors appear to be key in understanding the processes responsible for the origin of the Aymara señoríos. First, as noted above, the collapse of the Tiwanaku state led to a dispersal of settlement in the region and the virtual collapse of any major nucle-

ated sites. Second, the severe and sustained drought that occurred around the turn of the millennium lowered the productivity of plant agriculture, particularly intensive cultivation with raised fields (Kolata 1993; Stanish 1994). These two conditions promoted the rise of the agro-pastoral economies of the period. As mentioned above, the adoption of pastoralism is an excellent response to drought conditions since this provides economic flexibility and avoids risks associated with large-scale agricultural systems. Likewise, the shift away from low-fallow raised-field systems to high-fallow terrace agriculture promoted settlement dispersal. In other words, the drought of the eleventh century A.D. had similar effects as the drought of the second century A.D. In both cases, there was a shift to more extensive agricultural and animal husbandry that worked against settlement nucleation.

Agro-pastoral societies such as the Aymara señoríos are suited for a segmentary structure, a type of organization not characteristic of any other polity either prior to or after the Altiplano-period Aymara señoríos. Albarracin-Jordan (1996a, 1996b) has suggested that the Tiwanaku state utilized elements of this organization, but not on the scale of the Aymara señoríos. A segmentary organization is intimately linked with the economic mainstays of Aymara society: camelid pastoralism and nonintensive plant agriculture. Segmentary lineage theory is a controversial concept in anthropology. Some scholars have suggested that certain state-level societies were segmentary. John Fox, for instance, argues that the Quichí Maya were characterized by segmentary lineages. As he notes, this type of organization was abstracted from African ethnographic cases and was used to describe "'tribal level' congregations of lineages that maintain their own estates. They amalgamate into uneasy successively higher alliances of mechanical solidarity type segments when threatened by other peoples or when penetrating into new territories" (Fox 1987: 4).

Marcus and Feinman (1998: 7–10) have argued that the term "segmentary states" is an oxymoron because the basic process inherent in segmentary systems—fissioning—cannot be a characteristic of a state. In fact, segmentary societies in the ethnographic literature are decidedly not state level, and they appear to be associated largely with societies with a large pastoral component, such as the Altiplano-period señoríos.

In some complex chiefdoms, lineages can retain substantial autonomy over the domestic economy, but some chiefly lineages control more wealth and labor than other lineages, even if this is not institutionalized. They are entitled to tax/tribute in the form of labor or goods, but given the lack of non-kin-based political institutions, chiefly positions tend to be highly fluid and unstable. In other words, in nonsegmentary societies, there is an economic hierarchy of lineages that parallels the political hierarchy. In segmentary systems, political office exists but is not paralleled by an economic hierarchy of the lineages themselves, although there may be a substantial wealth hierarchy within the lineage.

One of the outstanding features of segmentary organization is that the society is capable of forming very large cooperative labor organizations when necessary, but these organizations are highly unstable. Threats from foreigners, in particular, induce complex labor organization for specific tasks, such as fighting, but quickly break down on kinship lines after the threat has passed.

Evidence in the Diez de San Miguel Visita supports a model of segmentary political organization of the pre-Inca Lupaqa. Although it is true that the Visita was written in 1567, and that the Lupaqa had been incorporated into larger imperial systems for two or three generations, the political and economic relationships revealed in this document highlight the features of a segmentary lineage organization.

The highest political authorities in the Lupaqa during this early Spanish Colonial period were Martín Cari and Martín Cusi, the principal caciques of the upper and lower moieties, respectively. These individuals lived in Chucuito, the recognized capital of the Lupaqa kingdom. Yet, it is extraordinary that the town of Chucuito was no larger than any other Late Horizon/early Early Colonial–period site. In fact, the population of Chucuito as listed in the Diez de San Miguel was smaller than that of Juli, and just slightly larger than that of Acora, Ilave, Pomata, and Zepita (see tables 10.1 and 10.2). In the Buitrago census (see table 4.2), Chucuito was smaller than Acora, Juli, and Pomata. Regardless of the small fluctuations in the numbers, the main point is that the town of Chucuito in the early Early Colonial period was approximately the same size as the other towns in the area and did not constitute a primate center. This contrasts with its size in the Inca period, when Chucuito was twice the size of the next largest center. A viable model is that the Inca substantially reworked the political and economic landscape, giving it a more traditional hierarchy. With the relaxation of Inca control in the early Spanish Colonial period (i.e., pre-Toledo reductions), the Aymara señoríos reverted back to pre-Inca patterns. This pattern is evident in both the Juli-Pomata and Tiwanaku Valley survey data. The end of the Spanish civil wars and Viceroy Toledo's assertion of state power saw a second "reversion" to Inca patterns after the late sixteenth century.

The ethnohistorical data also suggest that the households of Martín Cari and Martín Cusi were not substantially richer than those of other moiety heads in the Early Colonial period. Their status derived from the fact that they had access to labor sent to them by other lesser caciques. That is, all taxed labor was controlled by other lineages, not directly by Martín Cari and Martín Cusi. During the Early Colonial period, in fact, Martín Cari and Martín Cusi complained that the traditional labor obligations were not being met by the other moiety heads, perhaps an insight into their minimal authority by this time. Curiously, the "traditional" authority that they speak of was, in reality, imposed upon the area by the Inca.

I interpret these data to mean that these labor obligations were enforced by the Spanish authorities, and the implication is that the local populations would not have provided it otherwise. The Lupaqa paramounts had no retainers, no warriors, no big household, or any other evidence of substantial differential economic power, even under the early Spanish state. All they had was political authority to force labor obligations within the aegis of the Spanish state, and presumably before this, the Inca state.

In sum, the pattern for the sixteenth-century Lupaqa is one of semiautonomous towns composed of lineages divided into moieties based on ayllu—an organization based exclusively on kinship. Martín Cari and Martín Cusi were not substantially richer than the other ayllu heads but had a permanent tribute of labor and goods granted to them by the Spaniards, and presumably the Inca. It appears that an integral feature of the Inca and Spanish imperial economies was the naming of local authorities to exact tribute from the population. This was not a characteristic of the pre-Inca Altiplano-period populations.

As mentioned above, Albarracin-Jordan (1996a, 1996b) has argued that a segmentary organization characterized the Tiwanaku state. His model is vaguely similar to what I propose for the later Aymara señoríos. A loosely organized set of polities explains many of the apparent contradictions in the archaeological and historic data. Such a political and economic structure would explain the capacity of the Lupaqa and the Colla to amass substantial numbers of retainers to fight wars and build fortified settlements, and the lack of archaeological indicators of marked elite classes, including traditional capital cities. The Aymara could build massive defensive sites such as Tanka Tanka, Carajuana, and Pukara Juli but could not organize labor to build an elite house or to make fancy pottery or textiles or carved stone.

This type of organization would further explain the ability of the Lupaqa elite to quickly adapt to the Inca and Spanish states' demands for labor taxes while appearing in the documents as relatively powerless vis-à-vis their society at large. This model of pre-Inca political organization remains to be tested more fully. At present, it stands as the best model of Altiplano-period political and economic organization.

The Inca Period

A central question concerning the nature of the Inca occupation of the Titicaca Basin is the degree to which it involved dramatic changes in the existing political economy of the region's indigenous polities: in this case, the Aymara señoríos. The question can be rephrased to ask whether Inca statecraft left the indigenous political economies intact, and simply added a new level of political control, or if it entailed substantial changes. In theories of preindustrial imperial expansion, this classic distinction between direct and indirect control strategies is well developed. I note here the discussion of Robert Santley and Rani Alexander (1992) and Terence D'Altroy (1992), and their discussion of territorial and hegemonic imperial strategies, concepts based on the earlier work of S. Noah Eisenstadt (1963), Ross Hassig (1985), and Edward Luttwak (1976). They argue for a continuum of imperial strategies, called a "territorial-hegemonic" model. At one end, territorial strategies "entail more-direct occupation and governing of subject territories," and the hegemonic strategy "entails a core polity (usually a state) and client polities that are responsible, with varying degrees of autonomy, for implementing imperial policy, extracting resources for imperial consumption, and providing security" (D'Altroy 1992: 19).

This continuum represents a useful framework for assessing the nature of imperial control in any area. It also reflects the differing views of Inca statecraft in the literature. Julien (1982), among others, argues that the Inca occupation involved substantial changes in the region's political economy. Her work has demonstrated that the Colla capital, Hatuncolla, north of Lupaqa territory, was initially founded in the Late Horizon (Julien 1983). The founding of such a large settlement is indicative to Julien of a profound change in the Colla settlement system, and presumably the political economy, during the Inca occupation. Furthermore, Julien considers the operation of the Inca decimal administrative system to be additional evidence for direct imperial control by the Inca state.

A very different view of Inca rule of the Titicaca Basin has been suggested by Pease (1982b) and Murra (1982). Citing predominantly ethnohistorical sources, particularly the Diez de San Miguel Visita, these authors see minimal Inca intervention in the political economy of at least the Lupaqa señorío. The substance of this argument is that the Lupaqa state was already sufficiently complex to permit an indirect rule of sorts, in which Inca authorities "did not change the Lupaqa's traditional means of obtaining resources. . . . Tawantinsuyu superimposed its economic system on that of the Lupaqa" (Pease 1982b: 185). If we extend this model to the Collao as a whole, then the Inca occupation would have been more like that for the north coast of Peru, where indirect means predominated.

The research conducted in the last two decades supports a model of major political and economic reorganization by the Inca in the Titicaca region (Stanish 1997). Survey data support a model of Inca statecraft in the Lupaqa area characterized by substantial alterations in the political economy of the Altiplano-period patterns. The Tiwanaku Valley data are equally compelling for substantial changes in the local political economy coincident with the Inca occupation (Albarracin-Jordan 1996a; Albarracin-Jordan and Mathews 1990). Original settlements were moved, new populations were brought in as mitimas, and urban settlements were established. Road systems, probably originally formalized in the Tiwanaku period, were heavily used for classic imperial purposes, such as military movements, population control, and the movement of goods. In short, the Inca period represents the reimposition of a centralized political control in the region after the hiatus of the Altiplano period.

. . . . .

The prehistory of the Titicaca region represents the expression of cultural processes found in other areas of the world. However, these processes played out in a unique cultural and historical context that nurtured the development of ranked societies, states, and empires. Titicaca Basin prehistory does not represent the unfolding of a universal set of cultural laws that inevitably worked to create complex society. Rather, this is a history of human beings making decisions within the constraints and opportunities provided to them by their physical and cultural environment.

Selected Terms from the 1612
Aymara Dictionary of Ludovico Bertonio

All translations are by the author.

People, Ethnicity

Cani, koli: "women Indians from Camata, Mala and Moquegua" (Bk. 1: 280)

Chiy chiy: "dance of the Uros" (Bk. 2: 84)

Choquela, *see* Lari lari: "wild people who live in the puna sustaining themselves by hunting" (Bk. 2: 89)

Choquela, lari lari: "vicuña hunter who lives in the puna" (Bk. 1: 107)

Haque aro: "language of the Indians" (Bk. 1: 288)

Huacora, kita; "wild person, fugitive" (Bk. 2: 142)

Huasara, ttantata cchinchata: "depopulated" (Bk. 1: 183)

Itu haque: "Indians from Larecaja" (Bk. 1: 280)

Kaska aro: "elegant language" (Bk. 1: 203)

Kita, huacora, sallca: "wild person" *(cimarrón)* (Bk. 1: 160)

Kitahaque, sallca: "wild person" (Bk. 2: 306)

Kitha huacora: "wild; said of men and animals" (Bk. 2: 303)

Kithastha: "to walk or go about wild" (Bk. 2: 303)

Koli haque: "Yungas Indians found near *[hazia]* Moquegua" (Bk. 1: 280; Bk. 2: 56)

Lari: "mother's brother's uncle and almost all of the male relatives on the mother's side are called 'lari'" (Bk. 2: 191)

Lari lari: "people of the puna who do not recognize any cacique"; "wild people" *(cimarrón)* (Bk. 2: 191) (Bk. 1: 290)

Lari larikhatha, lari uru: "to revert to a wild state" *(volverse cimarrón);* "to live voluntarily like this" (Bk. 2: 191)

Taqquena isapaui aro, taqquena haquitata: "language that everybody knows" (Bk. 1: 288)

Thaa vraquenquiti, suni haque: *"serrano"* [highlander] (Bk. 1: 430)

Social and Political Structure

Alasaa: "a *parcialidad* of the Indians whose opposite is Maasaa" (Bk. 2: 9)

Anca mayco: "tyrant" (Bk. 1: 449)

Arcani: "mit'a laborer to serve a tambo or way station" (Bk. 2: 24)

Apu: *"corregidor"* [governor] (Bk. 1: 143)

Apu cancaña: *"señorío"* [kingdom, chiefdom] (Bk. 2: 24)

Arcatha, mittasitha: "to serve the tambo" (Bk. 1: 430)

Aylluchasitha: "to unite in an ayllu" (Bk. 1: 461)

Callca: "grave like a box of many stones for burying *principales* under the earth" (Bk. 1: 430)

Ccapaca: "royal seat or site *[asiento]*" (Bk. 1: 75); "king," "señor," or simply "a rich person" [According to Bertonio, this is an ancient term no longer in use.] (Bk. 2: 42)

Ccapaca suti: "royal name or tremendous sovereign" (Bk. 2: 42)

Ccapaca wila: "royal blood" (Bk. 2: 42)

Cchihita, laccaa marca: "unprotected village" (Bk. 1: 387)

Chasqui uta: "house of the chasqui" (Bk. 1: 120)

Coto: "small village" (Bk. 1: 387)

Coto coto marca: *"aldea"* (Bk. 1: 36)

Haccha marca: "city" (Bk. 1: 161)

Haccu cancaña: "authority" (Bk. 1: 32)

Hakhllaña: "election" (Bk. 1: 203)

Haque: "common Indian" (Bk. 1: 280)

Haqueha: "vassal" (Bk. 1: 465)

Haquení: *"señor* over vassals" (Bk. 1: 430)

Haqueni: *"encomendero* of Indians" (Bk. 1: 210); *"señor* of vassals" (Bk. 1: 430)

Haquicani: "one who is in charge of sending people for work *[jornada]"* (Bk. 1: 203)

Hatha: "caste," "family," "ayllu," "seeds of plants, men, and all of the animals" (Bk. 2: 124; Bk. 1: 121)

Hilacata: "ayllu head" (Bk. 2: 133)

Hisquiquiri, hisquivila: *"hidalgo"* (Bk. 1: 264)

Huakhcha: "poor person and also orphan without father or mother" (Bk. 2: 144)

Huarcuri matha: "to go to pay the *tasa,* or to work in Potosí" (Bk. 1: 284)

Huskotaro camatha: "to be of the tribute-payers" (Bk. 1: 232)

Ina haquenaca: "crowd or mob of plebeians" (Bk. 1: 460)

Iñaca: "woman of the Cuzco caste" (Bk. 1: 325)

Lampa: "a litter that the ancient caciques were carried in" (Bk. 2: 188)

Lari lari: "people of the puna who do not recognize any cacique"; "wild people *[cimarrón]"* (Bk. 2: 191)

Mallco, mayco: "cacique, or *señor* over vassals" (Bk. 2: 212, 2: 220); "illustrious man" (Bk. 1: 227)

Mamani: "district or province" (Bk. 1: 194)

Mamani, vraque: "province of some nation" (Bk. 1: 387)

Marca: "place or village" (Bk. 1: 295; Bk. 1: 371; Bk. 1: 387)

Marca marca: "populations of many towns" (Bk. 1: 371; Bk. 1: 387)

Marca marcani: "populated, land of many towns" (Bk. 1: 371)

Mayco hatha: "royal caste" (Bk. 2: 124)

Maycoñahisqui: "to administer a domain *[cacicazgo]"* (Bk. 1: 19)

Mayco uta: "royal house" (Bk. 1: 120)

Mitta, arca: "mita of the tambo" (Bk. 1: 318)

Mittalitha: "collection to give to the tambo" (Bk. 1: 402)

Mittani: "one obligated to do his turn for community things" (Bk. 1: 203)

Ñusta: "noble women of Cuzco" (Bk. 1: 325)

Phattachiri, phattiri: *"mayordomo* who distributes the animals *[ganado]"* (Bk. 1: 311)

Pillu: "crown of kings" (Bk. 1: 143)

Pucaracamana: *"alcalde* of a fortress" (Bk. 1: 36)

Pusisuu haqueni: "monarch, ruler" (Bk. 1: 320)

Reyana haqpa: "vassals of the king" (Bk. 1: 465)

Saapiyri: "fiscal" or "protector" or "office holder of the same type" (Bk. 2: 304)

Sasiri ccapaca: "The brother of the Inca" (Bk. 2: 311)

Sukatha, apanocatha: "to pay tribute" (Bk. 1: 343)

Tata auqui, hutuui auqui: "lineage head" (Bk. 1: 105)

Thokhrisirapiri, camachisirapiri: "administrator of a dignitary" (Bk. 1: 19)

Ttalla, ppasña, ccapkhomi: "noble woman" (Bk. 1: 325); "princess" (Bk. 1: 384)

Tupu: "royal road" (Bk. 1: 113)

Vacacamana: *"mayordomo* of cattle" (Bk. 1: 19, 310)

Warmi apu: "woman with vassals" (Bk. 1: 325; Bk. 1: 430)

Yana, siruiri: "servant" (Bk. 1: 149)

Yanani: "*señor* of servants" (Bk. 1: 430)

Warfare

Aputaquiqhuiuithaltaña: "rebellion" (Bk. 1: 400)

Auca: "enemy that makes war" (Bk. 1: 111)

Auca chuymacatiri: "rebel" (Bk. 1: 400)

Auca huallpatha: "to prepare for war" (Bk. 2: 145)

Aucasiña: "weapon" (Bk. 1: 68); "war" (Bk. 1: 255)

Aucasiri: "soldier" (Bk. 1: 255)

Aucasitha: "to fight or make war" (Bk. 1: 255)

Aucasiui: "war or field" (Bk. 1: 255)

Collukhatha, tucuskhatha: "to destroy towns or residents of some province" (Bk. 1: 73)

Haquechatha, haquechasitha: "to conquer people" (Bk. 1: 137)

Micchattatha: "bow and arrow" (Bk. 1: 67)

Micchi: "arrow for shooting" (Bk. 1: 243)

Micchi aattasita haque: "one who carries a bow and arrow" (Bk. 2: 221)

Micchiri: "bowman" (Bk. 1: 243)

Micchitha: "to shoot with a bow *[arco]*" (Bk. 2: 221)

Pucara camana: "*alcalde* of a fortress" (Bk. 1: 36)

Queyna, pucara: "fortress" (Bk. 1: 121)

Ttorokhthapitatha, aucathapitatha: "when armies meet to fight" (Bk. 1: 210)

Vinuna fampparpaatka: "to demolish an army" (Bk. 1: 189)

Geography

Collo collo: "adjacent hills" (Bk. 1: 159)

Hapu laka: "dry or sunny land" (Bk. 1: 448)

Kinku: "land in a rainy climate *[temporal]*" (Bk. 1: 448)

Pampa: "country or land that is away from the town" (Bk. 1: 114)

Puna: "suni" (Bk. 1: 388)

Taypitta: "in the middle" (Bk. 1: 107)

Taypi yuca: "land in a moderate climate" (Bk. 1: 448)

Vyaya: "land abundant in everything" (Bk. 1: 448)

Yunca: "land in a hot climate" (Bk. 1: 448)

Agriculture

Alli mara: "fertile year" (Bk. 2: 10)

Amphuta aynacha: "very uneven *[fragosa]* land" (Bk. 1: 448)

Callpa: "Land that has not fallowed long enough" (Bk. 1: 448)

Canglla canglla (cchapicchapi): "Land or soil full of spines *[espinas]*" [This probably refers to secondary growth of pasture land with ichu grasses.] (Bk. 1: 448)

Ccauri: "totora reed root" (Bk. 2: 43)

Cchaco cchacco: "soil good for clay or adobe *[barro]*" (Bk. 1: 448)

Cchapicchapi: "soil full of spines" (Bk. 1: 448)

Cchaycata cchullq: "land difficult to till" (Bk. 1: 448)

Ccollintatha huachantatha kimintatha: "to plow the soil very deeply" (Bk. 1: 66)

Ccolliquipatha, sucaquipatha, mutaquipatha: "to plow a lot of land" (Bk. 1: 66)

Ccollitha: "to till or plow the soil" (Bk. 1: 66)

Ccuchi: "pig"; Kita ccuchi: "wild pig" (Bk. 1: 388)

Challcachallca: "land tilled to pieces *[pedaços]*" (Bk. 1: 448)

Collca: "granaries to store food," "granaries of the Inca" (Bk. 1: 460)

Collitonco: "black maize" (Bk. 1: 310)

Cucathasuca ccollitha: "to plow with raised fields" (Bk. 1: 66) (*and see* Suca)

Hanko yapu: "soil good for sowing" (Bk. 1: 448)

Hassa, sulltta vraque: "soft soil" (Bk. 2: 124)

Huaña: "time of great drought" (Bk. 1: 448)

Huarikasaa: "time of frost" (Bk. 1: 448)

Irpa, larca: "acequia" (Bk. 1: 16)

Kay: "land good for irrigation *[regadio]*" (Bk. 1: 448)

Kusa: "chicha" (Bk. 1: 161)

Lahkra lahkra kaka: "land with many cracks or fissures *[grietas]*" (Bk. 1: 448)

Larcachatha: "to make a canal" (Bk. 1: 16; Bk. 2: 191)

Llutapu: "precious chicha" (Bk. 1: 161)

Lustotha, añancotha: "to weed an entire or great part of a chacra" (Bk. 1: 68)

Maccha: "time of infertility *[esterilidad]*" (Bk. 1: 448)

Morocchi: "hard maize" (Bk. 1: 310)

Morochitonco: "hard maize" (Bk. 1: 198)

Mottitha: "to cook maize" (Bk. 1: 148)

Muta: "land good to till without raised fields *[camellones]*" (Bk. 1: 448)

Mutatha: "to till a field without raised fields" (Bk. 2: 323)

Mutatha, muta ccollitha: "to plow without raised fields" (Bk. 1: 66, 448)

Parakhra: "land bad for sowing" (Bk. 1: 448)

Pata pata, patarana: "*andenes* on hills" (Bk. 1: 52)

Pincha: "canal" (Bk. 1: 114)

Piura: "granaries for quinoa or maize" (Bk. 1: 460)

Ppakhra: "barren land without trees or grasses *[yerbas]*" (Bk. 1: 449)

Puruma: "land never or rarely sown" (Bk. 1: 448)

Quilla yapu: "coca farm" (Bk. 1: 253)

Sehke: "granaries for *chuño;* it is made of reeds" (Bk. 1: 460)

Sillpiratha: "shallow plowing" (Bk. 1: 66)

Suca: "land good to till with raised fields" (Bk. 1: 448); "an actual raised field" (Bk. 2: 322)

Sucatha: "to till a field using raised fields" (Bk. 2: 323); "to make raised fields" (Bk. 1: 112)

Sultha: "land soft for plowing" (Bk. 1: 448)

Thikhrasi pacha: "time of much water or rain *[agua]*" (Bk. 1: 448)

Totora: "reed" (Bk. 1: 275)

Ttokho ttokho: "land with many pits *[hoyos]*" (Bk. 1: 448)

Uma: the common word for water; also "the swale between raised fields" (Bk. 2: 322)

Uma irpatha: "to make a canal" (Bk. 2: 375)

Uma larca: "canal" (Bk. 2: 375)

Vilachatha: "to plow a little bit of land in the middle of unworked land . . . This is a poor person's word." (Bk. 1: 66)

Vraque: "soil or land" (Bk. 1: 439)

Yapu: "farm or field" (Bk. 1: 253); "land for sowing" (Bk. 1: 448)

Yapuchatha: "to plow or to improve the chacra" (Bk. 1: 66)

Potato Types

Good quality: puma coyllu, amajaa, ahuachucham ppatticalla, nayrappoco, allca hamacorani, kusku, vila kapi, huatoca, apichu ccullukauna

Bad quality: pacokhahua, iurama, choquhinchu, choquephitu, luki, cchaara

White and long: surimana

Moist: cchiqui

Wild: apharu

Those that lose quality *(bondad):* hanka amcca

Like a sweet potato *(batata):* apilla

Early *(tempranas):* ccochi

Scaly: choco choco

Purple inside: cchapina

Very small, wild: ipiamca

Those that bud when others are sown from still being in the ground: kea

Those that remain small from the frost: llullu

Those that resist the frost: luki, hakhayari

Cured in water: tunta

Cured in the sun and frost: cchuño

Cooked: ccati

Roasted in coals: sirque

Roasted in an oven: at time of gathering, huakha; at time of sowing, hapu

Roasted and wrinkled: sonco huakha

Elongated: sucuya luki

Very large (monstruosas): llallahua

Religion/Ritual

Amaya uta: "burial in the ancient manner" (Bk. 1: 218); "grave like a house on the ground" (Bk. 1: 430)

Chullpa: "grave or basket where they put the dead" (Bk. 1: 430); "grave where they put their dead" (Bk. 2: 92)

Haccha chupimpi imatha: " to bury with great pomp" (Bk. 1: 430)

Huakanaca, tatanaca: "huacas or idols" (Bk. 1: 254)

Huákona vllatha, huanko cchaatha: "to divinate using a guinea pig [cuy]" (Bk. 1: 18)

Huntto uma: "hot springs or baths in the puna" (Bk. 1: 85)

Husnu: "altar of the huacas made of worked stone as seen in the puna" (Bk. 1: 41)

Imatha: "to bury" (Bk. 1: 430)

Imaui: "grave simply dug in the earth" (Bk. 1: 430)

Phokhpocollo: "famous shrine [adoratorio] in the puna of the Lupaqas" (Bk. 1: 21)

Sanctonaca hamppatiui: "shrine [adoratorio or humilladero] of the Christians" (Bk. 1: 21)

Sasitha (safitha): several meanings, one of which is "As in the ancient way to abstain from using salt or aji when eating meat at the death of relatives [Hazer abftinencia al modo antiquo comiendo carne, y qualquiera otra cofa, fin fal, ni axi, en la muerte de fus parientes]" (Bk. 2: 311)

Technology

Aythitha: "to refine metals by washing them [lavandolos]" (Bk. 1: 23)

Cala chaca: "stone bridge" (Bk. 1: 387)

Caycu, saraya: "fence with many doors to capture [coger] vicuñas" (Bk. 1: 157)

Cchuaatha: "to refine metal" (Bk. 1: 16)

Choqkhtara, collqukhtara sirca: "rich gold or silver mine" (Bk. 1: 317)

Choque: "gold" (Bk. 1: 341)

Choqueccoya: "gold mine" (Bk. 1: 341)

Corpa uta: "tambo" (Bk. 1: 441)

Huampu: "boat" (Bk. 1: 87)

Huayraatha: "to refine metals with fire" (Bk. 1: 23)

Inca tupu: "an Inca league; it is one and a half of a Castilian one" (Bk. 1: 288)

Llica: "net to hunt birds [pájaros]" (Bk. 1: 405)

Llucu: "net to hunt viscachas, rabbits, etc." (Bk. 1: 405)

Mama sirca, ccoya: "mine" (Bk. 1: 317)

Molloko uta: "round house" (Bk. 1: 120)

Saraya: "trap to catch vicuñas" (Bk. 1: 456)

Sau chaca: "wooden bridge" (Bk. 1: 387)

Tica: "adobe" (Bk. 1: 20)

Tumantatha: "to surround vicuñas with a rope to catch them" (Bk. 1: 416)

Tumi: "knife of the Indians" (Bk. 1: 151)

Virakhocha topu: "an ordinary league" (Bk. 1: 288)

Yauri: "copper" (Bk. 1: 124)

Notes

Chapter 1. Ancient Collasuyu

1. This figure is almost certainly an exaggeration.
2. *Ayllu* are kin-based landholding groups made up of a number of households.

Chapter 2. The Evolution of Political Economies

1. "Neolithic" refers to the Old World. "Formative" or "Preclassic" would be roughly equivalent in the Americas.
2. It is true that the variation between the two is a continuous one, and that any typological breaks in a continuous distribution is inherently arbitrary. However, such typological distinctions are commonly made in science, and they serve important methodological and comparative purposes.
3. I view technology as part of the economy and will elaborate below.
4. For consistency, I should use the term complex or ranked *political economies* instead of complex or ranked *societies* since the latter covers, in theory, all social relationships. Likewise, I should use only *political economic evolution* instead of *cultural evolution*. However, for stylistic purposes, I will use the term *complex* or *ranked societies* since it is so widely used in the literature, and I will use the term *cultural evolution* to follow established convention. The context in which these terms are used should therefore be unambiguous.
5. In earlier publications (Stanish 1989b, 1992), I qualify the use of the term *household,* making the distinction between it and the term *family.*
6. I thank Lawrence Coben for help in this section.

7. These ethnographic and historical data have been formalized into archaeological models of complex chiefly and state formation for a variety of areas from around the world, including the Mississippian (Anderson 1994: 75–76), Mesoamerica (Clark and Blake 1994), the Andes (Morris 1979), and many others (see the edited volume by Brumfiel and Fox [1994]; and see Marcus and Flannery 1996).

Chapter 3. The Geography and Paleoecology of the Titicaca Basin

1. *Tawantinsuyu* is translated by Mannheim (1991: 18) as "the parts that in their fourness make up a whole."
2. Wari is also spelled Huari.
3. The four general languages *(lenguas generales)* of Peru were Quechua, Aymara, Pukina, and Mochica (also referred to as Moche and Yunga) (Mannheim 1991: 34). Quechua was spoken in the north and central highlands, Aymara and Pukina in the south, and Mochica on the north coast. The expansion of the Inca state in the fifteenth and sixteenth centuries was responsible for spreading Quechua dialects across the Andes.
4. Among the various spellings of Tiwanaku are Tiahuanaco, Tiaguanaco, Tiwanacu, Tihuanacu, Tiwanako, and Tiahuanucu.
5. It is no coincidence that Aymara was initially described by some Spaniards as Quechua, despite the fact that the two are in different language families (Mannheim 1991: 6). This apparent confusion highlights the fact that Spanish writers either unconsciously viewed all Andean peoples as

culturally similar or consciously sought to maintain the political fiction of the underlying unity of the Andean peoples.

6. Lake Titicaca is occasionally referred to as Lake Chucuito or Lago Mayor in early texts.

7. Field observations by the author in the Juli area, 1988–1995; Pomata area, 1991–1995; and several areas between these two towns, 1991–1995.

8. Raised fields are also known as *waru waru* in Quechua and *suka colla* in Aymara.

9. In this book, an aqueduct is merely an earth-banked, slightly raised canal.

10. There is a Santiago de Huatta town on the Huatta Peninsula in the southeast Titicaca Basin in Bolivia, a Huata town and pampa in the northwest basin in Peru, and a Huata Peninsula near Conima in Bolivia.

11. Spelled *Caman* in the Visita and other early texts.

12. There is a town of Taraco in Bolivia in the southeast Titicaca Basin, and a town of Taraco in the north basin in Peru.

13. ORSTOM—Institut Français de Recherche Scientifique pour le Développement en Cooperation; UMSA—Universidad Mayor de San Andrés.

14. Lake Huiñamarca is also spelled or referred to as Huiñamarka, Huayna Marka, Winay Marca, Winay Marka, "the Little Lake," and Lago Menor.

15. I have converted the reported B.P. dates into B.C. dates for consistency throughout this book. I usually subtracted 2,000 years from the B.P. dates when the level of specificity was in millennia. Where highly specific dates are provided, I subtracted 1,950 years.

16. There are some discrepancies in the dates given in the two publications cited, probably as a result of more cores analyzed and reported on in the 1991 publication. I therefore follow this later publication.

Chapter 4. The Ethnography and Ethnohistory of the Titicaca Basin

1. When referring specifically to the Diez de San Miguel Visita, I capitalize *Visita* if used alone.

2. Berthelet (1986: 84) points out that the word *ccoya* (or *q'oya*) in Bertonio's dictionary is defined as a "mine" or "a gallery from which one extracts metal." Although precious

metals were extracted from Collasuyu by the Inca state, there is no evidence that the term for this quarter derived from anything other than the ethnic group of the Colla.

3. Hyslop notes that the existence of this branch remains hypothetical but that Julien's map may be more accurate than alternatives (Hyslop 1984: 264).

4. See the appendix for page references to these terms in Bertonio.

5. La Barre (1941) lists a dozen additional synonyms used for these people, the most common being Uro or Uros.

6. And see tables 4.1 and 4.2.

7. Pukina is also referred to by other names, particularly when it is assumed that it is an Uru language or a variant of Uruquilla. Variant names include Puquina, Poquina, Bokina, Uro, Ochomazo, Uchumi, Kjotsuni, Uroculla, Oroquilla, and Yuracare (see Manelis de Klein 1973).

8. In 1590, Alonso de Barzana, a Jesuit, wrote a lexicon of Pukina that has been lost (Torero 1987: 343).

9. And see La Barre (1941: 496) for a more detailed historical summary.

10. Kallawaya is also spelled Callawaya and Qallawaya.

11. Following Mannheim 1991.

12. A fascinating additional observation concerns the definition of the word *lari* in Bertonio's (1612) dictionary: "mother's brother's uncle and almost all of the male relatives on the mother's side are called 'lari.'" This is outside of my expertise, but it raises the possibility of linking the concept of "wild and renegade" with female descent.

13. See Pulgar Vidal n.d. for an extensive list of altiplano crop plants.

14. My informants include several farmers from Chatuma (near Pomata), from the Juli district, and from Ichu (near Chucuito).

15. In contrast, modern terraces built under the direction of nonlocal agronomists tend to be more uniform in construction style and do not often follow the natural hill contours. Although they initially look very impressive, they tend to erode very quickly. Although not useful for agriculture, their existence does at least provide a source of humor for the local farmers, as do the "rehabilitated," but unfortunately dried-up and useless, raised-field tracts that also dot the landscape.

16. Lake Titicaca is sometimes referred to as Lake Chucuito in older texts. Chucuito is also spelled Chuquito by

some contemporary authors. Albó and Layo (1989: 224) spell it Chukuwitu.

17. Maize actually grows very well on the Island of the Sun and in some restricted pockets in the Titicaca region. It apparently grew in a number of areas of the Titicaca region in the sixteenth century. However, the quantities grown in the altiplano were substantially smaller than the quantities grown in the lower valleys. Maize was not a major crop in the altiplano.

18. Don Pedro Cutimbo, cacique of Anansaya of Chucuito, as told to Visitador Garci Diez de San Miguel in 1567.

19. Sama is also spelled Zama; Moquegua is also spelled Moqueghua and is also called Osmore (e.g., Rice, Stanish, and Scarr 1989).

Chapter 5. The History of Archaeological Research in the Titicaca Basin

1. Leonce Angrand 1866/1867.

2. Pucara is also spelled Pukara. Qaluyu is also occasionally spelled Qaluyo. Pucara is the name of the town near the site of the same name. It is, as well, a completely unrelated term, meaning "fortress" in both Aymara and Quechua (and is spelled "pukara" in this volume). Its use in the sense of "fortress" is applied to the post-Tiwanaku site types characterized by fortification walls. *Pucara* is a very common toponym in the region and is usually, but not always, a good indicator of either a Late Intermediate–period hill fort or an Inca and modern capilla or religious shrine.

3. *Pirca* refers to fieldstone wall construction.

Chapter 6. The Origins and Elaboration of Rank in the Early and Middle Formative Periods

1. We were able to map about 50 percent of the area of Qaluyu. One landowner did not give us permission, and we therefore were unable to complete the map. Unfortunately, there are a number of possible sunken court areas and other architectural features in the area where we were forbidden to walk.

2. Dates from the four carbon samples from this site are:

3780 ± 170 B.P. (Teledyne I-18,314; wood charcoal); 2770 ± 100 B.P. (Teledyne I-18,402; wood charcoal); 2110 ± 100 B.P. (Teledyne I-18,401; wood charcoal); and 3100 ± 45 B.P. (NSF Arizona AMS facility #AA37210, FM 0.6798 ± 0.0037, wood charcoal). The samples were treated for the removal of carbonates and humic acids. The Libby half-life of 5,568 years was used to calculate the ages. Dates were corrected using University of Washington Quaternary Isotope Lab Radiocarbon Calibration Program Rev 3.03c, method A. The minimum of calibrated age ranges for I-18,314 at one sigma are cal B.C. 2430 (2136, 2078, 2072) 1835. The calibrated age range at one sigma for sample I-18,402 is cal B.C. 987–956. The calibrated age range at one sigma for sample I-18,401 is cal B.C. 193–cal A.D. 60. The calibrated range for AA37210 is cal B.C. 1426 (1393, 1327, 1324) 1316.

3. The Oxcal calibration program was used for these calculations. The first date of 3043 B.P. ± 124 ranges at the 68.2 percent confidence level to 1440–1110 B.C. and 1600–900 B.C. at the 95.4 percent confidence level. The date 2590 B.P. ± 117 ranges between 840–510 B.C. at the 66.1 percent confidence level and 1000–400 B.C. at a 95.4 percent confidence level. Note that Chávez (1977) reported these with the then-accepted 5,760 half-life.

4. The site is also referred to as Tintiri.

5. Pueblo Libre is also referred to as Balsas Pata.

6. Chiripa Condori is more or less equivalent to Early Chiripa, dated circa 1400–900 B.C., according to K. Chávez (1988: 18).

7. Teledyne I-17,545, wood; sample number 212–165.2.

8. Teledyne I-17,572, wood; sample number 212–054.

9. This corresponds to "block 9" in Rivera Sundt's report (1989). He notes that the block was curiously placed in such a way that it could not have been viewed by the users of the Tiwanaku-period temple. I personally observed this stone while acting as field director for the Proyecto Wila Jawira in Lukurmata in 1986.

Chapter 7. The Rise of Competitive Peer Polities in the Upper Formative Period

1. Also spelled Ccotos.

2. It is important to emphasize that this list of regional centers is far from exhaustive. These represent only sites

that have been ground-checked or previously published. There are most certainly many more such primary regional centers and associated polities in the region that existed prior to Tiwanaku expansion.

3. It is important to remember that not all large sites have been found outside the intensively surveyed areas. Reconnaissance methodologies have been outlined in Stanish et al. 1997. We believe that we found most of the big sites but most certainly missed others. Therefore, the definition of a regional polity outside the intensively surveyed areas remains speculative.

4. There are several Early Titinhuayani sites in the Titikala area that total 5.85 hectares in size. There are four Late Titinhuayani sites in the Titikala cluster that total 4.15 hectares in size. Adjusting for the length of the period, the figure is statistically the same population size.

5. Lumbreras (1974a: 89) wrote that Tiwanaku I or Kalasasaya was slightly earlier than Paracas and Pucara, based on a carbon date of 239 ± 130 B.C. published by Ponce. However, as discussed above, other data indicate that the Kalasasaya style actually continued into the first millennium A.D.

6. Probable exceptions would include the Putina, Azángaro, and Ayaviri river valleys. These areas have not been extensively explored, but Kidder's work (1943) indicates sites of considerable complexity.

7. For example, see Kidder 1943: plate II, nos. 1, 3–7; plate III, no. 3; plate V, nos. 1–3; plate VI, nos. 3, 4, 8–10.

8. For example, see ibid.: plate VI, nos. 1–2; plate VII, nos. 10–11.

9. For example, see ibid.: plate II, nos. 8–9; plate IV, nos. 1–6; plate VII, nos. 8–9.

10. For example, see ibid.: plate III, nos. 1–6.

Chapter 8. The First State of Tiwanaku

1. A tenon is a projection at the back of a sculpture used to join it to a wall.

2. The term *Omasuyu* in early texts included most of the eastern side of the lake. For this discussion, I restrict the use of the term to a portion of this area on the southeast side of Lake Titicaca.

3. The Tiwanaku site of Omo in the Moquegua Valley, excavated and mapped by Goldstein (1989b), also has an Akapana-like hill, a kalasasaya area, and a round, sunken depression that could be a court.

Chapter 9. The Rise of Complex Agro-Pastoral Societies in the Altiplano Period

1. Using CALIB radiocarbon calibration program. Teledyne I-15,086 (in Stanish and Rice 1989: 8).

2. Using CALIB radiocarbon calibration program. Beta-22436 (in Stanish and Rice 1989: 8).

3. Tschopik (1946) and de la Vega (1990) occasionally refer to Pukara Juli as "Pucarani." Pucarani is also the name of an Altiplano-period ceramic style and the name of a large Inca, Early Colonial, and modern town in Bolivia. I retain the name first used by Bernabé Cobo.

4. I thank Lawrence Keeley for the information regarding this defensive technique. *Chevaux de frise* are defensive techniques used to slow down or stop attacking troops.

5. In Bertonio's (1612) Aymara dictionary, there is a reference to the "most well-known Lupaqa huacas," listed as Ano Ano, Pachapaqui, Ccapia, Huana, Hatucachi, and Phokhpocollo. Ccapia, of course, is the huge mountain that dominates the southwestern Titicaca Basin, and Huana most likely refers to Cerro Carajuana. Ccapia is surrounded by Altiplano-period sites, including the two pukaras of Llaquepa and Huichajaja. Cerro Carajuana is the largest pukara in the altiplano in total area encircled by defensive walls. We have not been able to locate the other huacas listed in the dictionary.

6. Both Rydén (1947) and M. Tschopik (1946) offered preliminary typologies of chulpas. Their research defined a pre-Inca, post-Tiwanaku culture known as Colla or Chullpa, and, as the name suggests, placed the beginning of chulpa construction in this intermediate period after the collapse of the Tiwanaku state and prior to Inca expansion. Rydén even defined a ceramic style associated with the burial towers and named it "chulpa."

Chapter 10. Conquest from Outside

1. Terence D'Altroy and Brian Bauer (personal communication from Bauer 1998) report that some carbon-14 dates suggest an expansion slightly earlier, about A.D. 1420.

2. The term *Cari* refers to both the title and the name of the Colla king.

3. The word *Hatuncolla* most likely means Hatun Collao, or Great Collao.

4. The clay source was discovered by C. Herhan.

5. There are some phallic-shaped cut stones in the Inca Uyu. Most of the smaller stones are probably authentic. However, the more elaborate ones are probably not Prehispanic but apparently were commissioned by a collector and assembled in the Inca Uyu sometime in the twentieth century. They have since become a New Age phenomenon on the tourist circuit.

6. A *mirador* is a walled, high area with aesthetic views of the landscape.

7. Pucarani is also spelled Pucarane.

8. "En una destas playas vezina a la peña Titicaca intentó el Inga sembrar una chácara de Coca para el Sol" (Ramos Gavilán 1988 [1621]: 45).

9. Some factors that may artificially inflate the Inca-period population include the ubiquity and distinctiveness of Inca pottery diagnostics, and better preservation of sites because of the later time period. Both factors were dealt with in the analysis. Even with the biases, however, it is clear that there was a major increase in population on the island.

10. Chucuito is also spelled Chuquito, and is referred to on rare occasions as Chuquiuito in older texts. Ilave is also spelled Hilave or Ylave in the Diez de San Miguel Visita. Juli is variously spelled as Xuli or Xule in early texts and is possibly the town referred to as Hila Haui or Lundayani. The town of Pomata has also been referred to as Pomanta, and the town of Zepita is alternatively spelled as Cipita, Cepita, or Sepita, particularly in older texts.

11. Mountain viscachas *(Lagidium viscacia)* are rodents found throughout the Titicaca region.

12. Hyslop (1977: 161) says that the niche is seven by eight meters in dimension. However, he appears to have not included the unfinished carving flanking the deeper niches in his width estimate. The total width of the carving is in reality fourteen meters, but the width of the inverted U is consistent with Hyslop's original measurements.

References Cited

Abbott, Mark B., M. Binford, M. Brenner, and K. Kelts. 1997. "A 3500 [14]C High-Resolution Record of Water-Level Changes in Lake Titicaca, Bolivia/Peru." *Quaternary Research* 47: 169–180.

Abbott, Mark B., Geoffrey O. Seltzer, Kerry R. Kelts, and John Southon. 1997. "Holocene Paleohydrology of the Tropical Andes from Lake Records." *Quaternary Research* 47: 70–80.

Adams, Robert McC. 1988. "Contexts of Civilizational Collapse: A Mesopotamian View." In *The Collapse of Ancient States and Civilizations,* ed. N. Yoffee and G. Cowgill, pp. 20–43. University of Arizona Press, Tucson.

Adams, William Y., Dennis P. Van Gerven, and Richard S. Levy. 1978. "The Retreat from Migrationism." *Annual Review of Anthropology* 7: 483–532.

Agurto Calvo, Santiago. 1980. "Cusco. Traxa urbana de la ciudad Inca, proyecto-Per 39." Report, UNESCO. Instituto Nacional de Cultural del Perú, Imprenta Offset Color S.R.I., Cuzco, Peru.

Albarracin-Jordan, Juan. 1991. "Petroglifos en el valle bajo de Tiwanaku, Bolivia." *Sociedad de Investigación de Arte Rupestre de Bolivia* 5: 35–56.

———. 1992. "Prehispanic and Early Colonial Settlement Patterns in the Lower Tiwanaku Valley, Bolivia." Ph.D. diss., Department of Anthropology, Southern Methodist University.

———. 1996a. *Tiwanaku: Arqueología Regional y Dinamica Segmentaria.* Editores Plural, La Paz, Bolivia.

———. 1996b. "Tiwanaku Settlement System: The Integration of Nested Hierarchies in the Lower Tiwanaku Valley." *Latin American Antiquity* 7 (3): 183–210.

Albarracin-Jordan, Juan, and James Edward Mathews. 1990. *Asentamientos Prehispanicos del Valle de Tiwanaku.* Vol. 1. Producciones CIMA, La Paz, Bolivia.

Alberti, Giorgio, and Enrique Mayer. 1974. "Reciprocidad Andina: Ayer y hoy." In *Reciprocidad e Intercambio en los Andes Peruanos,* ed. G. Alberti and E. Mayer, pp. 13–33. Instituto de Estudios Peruanos, Lima, Peru.

Albó, Xavier. 1987. Comments on "Lenguas y pueblos altiplánicos en torno al siglo XVI" by A. Torero. In *Revista Andina* 5 (2): 375–376.

Albó, Xavier, and Félix Layo. 1984. "Ludovico Bertonio (1557–1625): Fuente única al mundo Aymara temprano." *Revista Andina* 2 (1): 223–264.

Alconini Mujica, Sonia. 1993. "La cerámica de la pirámide akapana y su contexto social en el estado de Tiwanaku." Tesis de Licenciatura, Universidad Mayor de San Andrés, La Paz, Bolivia.

Aldenderfer, Mark. 1989. "Archaic Period Settlement Patterns in the High Sierra of the Osmore Basin." In *Ecology, Settlement, and History in the Osmore Drainage, Peru,* ed. D. Rice, C. Stanish, and P. Scarr, pp. 129–166. British Archaeological Reports International Series, Oxford.

———. 1998. *Montane Foragers: Asana and the South-Central Andean Archaic.* University of Iowa Press, Iowa City.

Aldenderfer, Mark, and Charles Stanish. 1993. "Domestic Architecture, Household, and the Past in the South-Central Andes." In *Domestic Architecture in South Central Andean Prehistory,* ed. Mark Aldenderfer, pp. 1–12. University of Iowa Press, Iowa City.

Aldunate, Carlos, and Victoria Castro. 1981. *Las Chullpa de Toconce y Su Relación con el Poblamiento Altiplanico en el Loa Superior Periodo Tardio.* Ediciones Kultrún Ltda., Santiago, Chile.

Amat Olazabal, Hernán. 1977. "Los reinos altiplánicos del Titicaca." *Rumi* (1977): 1–8.

Anderson, David G. 1994. "Factional Competition and the Political Evolution of Mississippian Chiefdoms in the Southeastern United States." In *Factional Competition and Political Development in the New World,* ed. E. M. Brumfiel and J. W. Fox, pp. 61–76. Cambridge University Press, Cambridge.

Anderson, Karen, and Ricardo Cespedes Paz. 1998. "Late Formative to Middle Horizon Transition in Cochabamba, Bolivia." Paper presented at the annual meeting of the Society for American Archaeology, Seattle, Washington.

Angrand, Léonce. 1866. *Lettre sur les Antiquités de Tiaguanaco.* J. Claye, Paris.

Arellano Lopes, Jorge C. 1975. *La Ciudadela Prehispánica de Iskanwaya.* Publicación no. 6, n.s., Centro de Investigaciones Arqueológicas, La Paz, Bolivia.

———. 1991. "The New Cultural Contexts of Tiahuanaco." In *Huari Administrative Structure: Prehistoric Monumental Architecture and State Government,* ed. W. H. Isbell and G. McEwan, pp. 259–280. Dumbarton Oaks, Washington, D.C.

Argollo, J., and Philippe Mourguiart. 2000. "Late Quaternary Climate History of the Bolivian Altiplano." *Quaternary International* 72: 37–51.

Arkush, Elizabeth Nelson. 1999a. "Pilgrims and Emperors: Inca Ceremonial Sites in the Southwestern Lake Titicaca Basin, Peru." Paper presented at the annual meeting of the Society for American Archaeology, Chicago.

———. 1999b. "Small Inca Ceremonial Sites in the Southwest Lake Titicaca Basin, Peru." Master's thesis, Department of Anthropology, University of California, Los Angeles.

Arnold, Jeanne. 1993. "Labor and the Rise of Complex Hunter-Gatherers." *Journal of Anthropological Archaeology* 12: 75–119.

Arrendo, Sofía. 1942. "Las ruinas de Marcansaya." *Revista del Instituto Arqueológico* 4 (10–11): 52–65. Cuzco, Peru.

Arze, José Antonio. 1941. "Fué socialista o comunista el imperio incaico?" *Revista del Instituto de Sociología Boliviana,* no. 1. Sucre, Bolivia.

Bandelier, Adolph. 1905. "The Aboriginal Ruins at Sillustani, Peru." *American Anthropologist,* n.s., 7: 49–69.

———. 1910. *The Islands of Titicaca and Koati.* The Hispanic Society of America, New York.

———. 1911. "The Ruins at Tiahuanaco." *American Antiquarian Society Proceedings,* no. 21.

Bandy, Matthew. 1999a. "Systematic Surface Collection." In *Early Settlement at Chiripa, Bolivia,* ed. C. Hastorf, pp. 23–26. Contributions of the University of California Archaeological Research Facility, Berkeley.

———. 1999b. "History of Investigations at the Site of Chiripa." In *Early Settlement at Chiripa, Bolivia,* ed. C. Hastorf, pp. 9–16. Contributions of the University of California Archaeological Research Facility, Berkeley. University of California, Berkeley.

Baudin, Louis. 1928. *L'Empire Socialiste des Inka.* Institut d'Ethnologie, Paris.

Bauer, Brian. 1992a. *The Development of the Inca State.* University of Texas Press, Austin.

———. 1992b. "Ritual Pathways of the Inca: An Analysis of the Collasuyu Ceques in Cuzco, Peru." *Latin American Antiquity* 3 (3): 183–205.

———. 1996. "Legitimization of the State in Inca Myth and Ritual." *American Anthropologist* 98 (2): 327–337.

———. 1999. *The Early Ceramics of the Inca Heartland.* Fieldiana Anthropology, new series 31, Field Museum of Natural History, Chicago.

Bauer, Brian, and Charles Stanish. 2001. *Ritual and Pilgrimage in the Ancient Andes.* University of Texas Press, Austin.

Bennett, Wendell C. 1933. "Archaeological Hikes in the Andes." *Natural History* 33 (2): 163–174.

———. 1934. "Excavations at Tiahuanaco." *Anthropological Papers of the American Museum of Natural History* 34 (3): 359–494.

———. 1936. "Excavations in Bolivia." *Anthropological Papers of the American Museum of Natural History* 35 (4).

———. 1946a. "The Andean Highlands: An Introduction." In *Handbook of South American Indians,* vol. 2, *The Andean Civilizations,* ed. Julian Steward, pp. 1–60. Smithsonian Institution Press, Washington, D.C.

———. 1946b. "The Archaeology of the Central Andes." In *Handbook of South American Indians,* vol. 2, *The Andean Civilizations,* ed. Julian Steward, pp. 61–147. Smithsonian Institution Press, Washington, D.C.

———. 1948a. "A Revised Sequence for the South Titicaca Basin." In *A Reappraisal of Peruvian Archaeology.* Memoirs of the Society for American Archaeology, vol. 13, no. 4 (2), ed. W. C. Bennett, pp. 90–93.

———. 1948b. "The Peruvian Co-Tradition." In *A Reappraisal of Peruvian Archaeology.* Memoirs of the Society for American Archaeology, vol. 13, no. 4 (2), ed. W. C. Bennett, pp. 1–7.

———. 1950. "Cultural Unity and Disunity in the Titicaca Basin." *American Antiquity* 16 (2): 89–98.

Berenguer [R.], José. 1978. "La problemática Tiwanaku en Chile: Visión retrospectiva." *Revista Chilena de Anthropología* 1: 17–40.

———. 1985. "Evidencias de inhalación de alucíogenos en esculturas Tiwanaku." *Chungara* 14: 61–69.

Berenguer R., José, Victoria Castro R., and Osvaldo Silva G. 1980. "Reflexiones acerca de la presencia de Tiwanaku en el norte de Chile." *Estudios Arqueológicos* 5: 81–94. Universidad de Chile, Antofagasta.

Berenguer [R.], José, and Percy Dauelsberg. 1988. "El norte grande en la órbita de Tiwanaku (400 a 1200 d.c.)." In *Cultura de Chile: Prehistoria desde sus orígenes hasta los albores de la conquista,* ed. Jorge Hidalgo, pp. 129–180. Editorial Andrés Bello, Santiago, Chile.

Bermann, Marc. 1990. "Prehispanic Household and Empire at Lukurmata, Bolivia." Ph.D. diss., Department of Anthropology, University of Michigan.

———. 1994. *Lukurmata: Household Archaeology in Prehispanic Bolivia.* Princeton University Press, Princeton, N.J.

Bermann, Marc, Paul Goldstein, Charles Stanish, and Luis Watanabe M. 1989. "The Collapse of the Tiwanaku State: A View from the Osmore Drainage." In *Ecology, Settlement, and History in the Osmore Drainage,* British Archaeological Reports International Series, ed. D. Rice, C. Stanish, and P. Scarr, pp. 269–286.

Berthelet, Jean. 1986. "The Extraction of Precious Metals at the Time of the Inka." In *Anthropological History of Andean Polities,* ed. J. Murra, N. Wachtel, and J. Revel, pp. 69–88. Cambridge University Press, Cambridge.

Bertonio, Ludovico. 1956 [1612]. *Vocabulario de la lengua Aymará.* Facsimile edition, La Paz, Bolivia.

Betanzos, Juan de. 1996 [1557]. *Narrative of the Incas.* Trans. and ed. Roland Hamilton and Dana Buchanan. University of Texas Press, Austin.

Bettinger, Robert L. 1991. *Hunter-Gatherers: Archaeological and Evolutionary Theory.* Plenum, New York.

Bills, B. G., S. L. de Silva, D. R. Currey, R. S. Emenger, K. D. Lillquist, A. Donnellan, and B. Worden. 1994. "Hydro-Isostatic Deflections and Tectonic Tilting in the Central Andes: Initial Results of a GPS Survey of Lake Minchin Shorelines." *Geophysical Research Letters* 21 (4): 293–296.

Binford, Michael, and Mark Brenner. 1989. "Resultados de estudios de limnología en los ecosistemas de Tiwanaku." In *Arqueología de Lukurmata,* ed. A. Kolata, pp. 213–236. Producciones Pumapunku, La Paz, Bolivia.

Binford, Michael, Mark Brenner, and D. Engstrom. 1992. "Patrones de sedimentación temporal en la zona litoral del Huiñaimarca." In *El Lago Titicaca: Síntesis del Conocimiento,* ed. C. DeJoux and A. Iltis, pp. 47–58. ORSTROM/HISBOL, La Paz, Bolivia.

Binford, Michael, Mark Brenner, and Barbara Leyden. 1996. "Paleoecology and Tiwanaku Ecosystems." In *Tiwanaku and Its Hinterland: Archaeology and Paleoecology of an Andean Civilization,* ed. Alan Kolata, pp. 90–108. Smithsonian Institution Press, Washington, D.C.

Binford, Michael, and Alan Kolata. 1996. "The Natural and Human Setting." In *Tiwanaku and Its Hinterland: Archaeology and Paleoecology of an Andean Civilization,* ed. A. Kolata, pp. 23–56. Smithsonian Institution Press, Washington, D.C.

Binford, Michael, A. Kolata, M. Brenner, J. Janusek, M. Seddon, M. Abbott, and J. Curtis. 1997. "Climate Variation and the Rise and Fall of an Andean Civilization." *Quaternary Research* 47: 235–248.

Bird, Mc. K., David L. Browman, and Marshall E. Durbin. 1988. "Quechua and Maize: Mirrors of Central Andean History." *Journal of the Steward Anthropological Society* 15 (1–2).

Bittman, B. 1979. "Cobija y alrededores en la época colonial." *Actas del VII Congreso de Arqueología de Chile* 2: 327–256.

Boas, Franz. 1966. *Kwakiutl Ethnography,* ed. Helen Codere. University of Chicago Press, Chicago.

Boulange, Bruno, and Jaen E. Aquize. 1981. "Morphologie, hydrographie et climatologie du lac Titicaca et de son bassin versant." *Rev. Hydrobiol. Trop* 14 (4): 269–287.

Bourdieu, Pierre. 1977. *Outline of a Theory of Practice.* Cambridge University Press, Cambridge.

Bouysse-Cassagne, Thérèse. 1975. "Pertenencia étnica, status económico y lenguas en Charcas a fines del siglo XVI." In *Tasa de la Visita General de Francisco de Toledo,* ed. David Noble Cook, pp. 312–328. Universidad Nacional Mayor de San Marcos, Lima, Peru.

———. 1976. "Tributo y etnias en Charcas en la epoca del Virrey Toledo." *Historia y Cultura* 2: 97–114. Casa de la Cultura, La Paz, Bolivia.

———. 1986. "Urco and Uma: Aymara Concepts of Space." In *Anthropological History of Andean Polities,* ed. J. Murra, N. Wachtel, and J. Revel, pp. 201–227. Cambridge University Press, Cambridge.

———. 1987a. Comments on "Lenguas y pueblos altiplánicos en torno al siglo XVI" by A. Torero. In *Revista Andina* 5 (2): 377–379.

———. 1987b. *La Identidad Aymara.* HISBOL, La Paz, Bolivia.

———. 1991. "Poblaciones humanas antiquas y actuales." In *El Lago Titicaca: Sintesis del Conocimiento Limnológico Actual,* ed. C. DeJoux and A. Iltis, pp. 481–498. ORSTOM/HISBOL, La Paz, Bolivia.

———. 1992. "Le lac Titicaca: Histoire perdue d'une mer intérieure." *Bulletin de Institut Francais d'Etudes Andines* 21 (1): 89–159.

Brinton, Daniel Garrison. 1901. *The American Race: A Linguistic Classification and Ethnographic Description of the Native Tribes of North and South America.* D. McKay, Philadelphia.

Browman, David. 1978a. "Toward the Development of the Tiahuanaco (Tiwanaku) State." In *Advances in Andean Archaeology,* ed. D. L. Browman, pp. 327–349. Mouton Publishers, The Hague, Paris.

———. 1978b. "The Temple of Chiripa (Lake Titicaca, Bolivia)." In *III Congreso Peruano del Hombre y la Cultura Andina,* vol. 2, ed. R. Matos M., pp. 807–813. Lima, Peru.

———. 1980. "Tiwanaku Expansion and Altiplano Economic Patterns." Homenaje al II Congreso de Arqueología Chilena. *Estudios Arqueológicos* 5: 107–120.

———. 1981. "New Light on Andean Tiwanaku." *American Scientist* 69 (4): 408–419.

———. 1984. "Tiwanaku: Development of Interzonal Trade and Economic Expansion in the Altiplano." In *Social and Economic Organization in the Prehispanic Andes,* ed. D. L. Browman, R. L. Burger, and M. A. Rivera, pp. 117–142. British Archaeological Reports, International Series 194.

———. 1986. "Management of Agricultural Risk in the Titicaca Basin." Paper presented at the 51st annual meeting of the Society for American Archaeology, New Orleans, La.

———. 1994. "Titicaca Basin Archaeolinguistics: Uru, Pukina and Aymara A.D. 750–1450." *World Archaeology* 26 (2): 235–251.

Brown, James A. 1985. "Long-Term Trends to Sedentism and the Emergence of Complexity in the American Midwest." In *Prehistoric Hunter-Gatherers,* ed. T. D. Price and J. A. Brown, pp. 201–231. Academic Press, New York.

Brumfiel, Elizabeth M. 1994. "Factional Competition and Political Development in the New World: An Introduction." In *Factional Competition and Political Development in the New World,* ed. E. Brumfiel and J. W. Fox, pp. 3–13. Cambridge University Press, Cambridge.

Brumfiel, Elizabeth M., and Timothy K. Earle. 1987a. "Specialization, Exchange, and Complex Societies: An Introduction." In *Specialization, Exchange, and Complex Societies,* ed. E. M. Brumfiel and T. K. Earle, pp. 1–9. Cambridge University Press, Cambridge.

———, eds. 1987b. *Specialization, Exchange, and Complex Societies.* Cambridge University Press, Cambridge.

Brumfiel, Elizabeth M., and John W. Fox, eds. 1994. *Factional Competition and Political Development in the New World.* Cambridge University Press, Cambridge.

Burger, Richard L. 1982. "Pójoc and Waman Wain: Two Early Horizon Villages in the Chavín Heartland." *Ñawpa Pacha* 20: 3–40.

Burger, Richard L., Frank Asaro, Fred Stross, and Guido Salas. 1998. "The Chivay Obsidian Source and the Geological Origin of Titicaca Basin Type Obsidian Artifacts." *Andean Past* 5: 203–224.

Burger, Richard L., Karen L. Mohr Chávez, and Sergio J. Chávez. 2000. "Through the Glass Darkly: Prehispanic Obsidian Procurement and Exchange in Southern Peru and Northern Bolivia." *Journal of World Prehistory* 14 (3): 267–362.

Bürgi, Peter. 1993. "The Inka Empire's Expansion into the Coastal Sierra Region West of Lake Titicaca." Ph.D diss., Department of Anthropology, University of Chicago.

Caballero, Geraldine Byrne de. 1984. "El Tiwanaku en Cochabamba." *Arqueología Boliviana* 1: 67–72.

Calancha, A. de la. 1981 [1638]. *Corónica Moralizada del Orden de San Augustín en el Perú,* ed. I. Prado Pastor, Lima, Peru.

Camacho, J. 1943. "Urus, Changos y Atacamas." *Boletín de la Sociedad Geográfica de La Paz* 66: 9–35.

Carneiro, Robert L. 1998. "What Happened at the Flashpoint? Conjectures on Chiefdom Formation at the Very Moment of Conception." In *Chiefdoms and Chieftaincy in the Americas,* ed. Elsa Redmond, pp. 19–42. University Press of Florida, Gainesville.

Casanova, Eduardo. 1942. "Dos yacimientos arqueológicos en la Península de Copacabana (Bolivia)." *Antropología, Etnografía y Arqueología,* publication no. 82: 333–407.

Castro, Victoria, José Berenguer, and Osvaldo Silva. 1980. "Reflexiones acerca de la presencia de Tiwanaku en el norte de Chile." *Estudios Arqueológicos* 5. Universidad de Chile, Antofagasta.

Chávez, Karen L. Mohr. 1977. "Marcavalle: The Ceramics form an Early Horizon Site in the Valley of Cusco, Peru, and Implications for South Highland Socio-Economic Interaction." Ph.D. diss., Department of Anthropology, University of Pennsylvania. Philadelphia.

———. 1985. "Early Tiahuanaco-Related Ceremonial Burners from Cuzco, Peru." *Dialogo Andino* 4: 137–178.

———. 1988. "The Significance of Chiripa in Lake Titicaca Basin Developments." *Expedition* 30 (3): 17–26.

Chávez, Sergio. 1984. "La piedra del rayo y la estela de Arapa: Un caso de identidad estilística, Pucara-Tiahuanaco." *Arte y Arqueología* 8–9: 1–27.

———. 1988. "Archaeological Reconnaissance in the Province of Chumbivilcas, South Highland Peru." *Expedition* 30 (3): 27–38.

———. 1992. "The Conventionalized Rules in Pucara Pottery Technology and Iconography: Implications for Socio-Political Developments in the Northern Lake Titicaca Basin." Ph.D. diss., Department of Anthropology, Michigan State University.

Chávez, Sergio J., and Karen L. Mohr Chávez. 1970. "Newly Discovered Monoliths from the Highlands of Puno, Peru." *Expedition* 12 (4): 25–39.

———. 1975. "A Carved Stela from Taraco, Puno, Peru, and the Definition of an Early Style of Stone Sculpture from the Altiplano of Peru and Bolivia." *Ñawpa Pacha* 13: 45–83.

Chayanov, Aleksandr V. 1966. *The Theory of Peasant Economy,* ed. D. Thorner, Basile Kerblay, and R. E. Smith. American Economic Association, Homewood, Ill.

Cherry, John F. 1986. "Polities and Palaces: Some Problems in Minoan State Formation." In *Peer Polity Interaction and Socio-Political Change,* ed. Colin Renfrew and John F. Cherry, pp. 19–45. Cambridge University Press, Cambridge.

Chibnik, Michael. 1984. "A Cross-Cultural Examination of Chayanov's Theory." *Current Anthropology* 25 (3): 335–340.

Cieza de León, Pedro de. 1553. "La crónica del Perú." In *Crónica de la Conquista del Perú.* Editorial Nueva España, S.A., México D.F.

———. 1959 [1553]. *Crónica del Perú.* Trans. Harriet de Onis; ed. and introduction Victor Wolfgang von Hagen. University of Oklahoma Press, Norman.

———. 1976. *The Incas of Pedro de Cieza de León.* Ed. Victor von Hagan. University of Oklahoma Press, Norman.

Clark, John E., and Michael Blake. 1994. "The Power of Prestige: Competitive Generosity and the Emergence of Rank Societies in Lowland Mesoamerica." In *Factional Competition and Political Development in the New World,* ed. E. Brumfiel and J. W. Fox, pp. 17–30. Cambridge University Press, Cambridge.

Cobo, Bernabé. 1983 [1653]. *History of the Inca Empire.* Trans. Roland Hamilton. University of Texas Press, Austin.

———. 1990 [1653]. *Inca Religion and Customs.* University of Texas Press, Austin.

Conklin, William J. 1991. "Tiahuanaco and Huari: Architectural Comparisons and Interpretations." In *Huari*

Administrative Structure: Prehistoric Monumental Architecture and State Government, ed. W. Isbell and G. McEwan, pp. 281–291. Dumbarton Oaks, Washington, D.C.

———. 1997. "Huari Tunics." In Andean Art at Dumbarton Oaks, ed. Elizabeth Hill Boone, pp. 375–398. Dumbarton Oaks, Washington, D.C.

Conklin, William J., and Michael E. Moseley. 1988. "The Patterns of Art and Power in the Early Intermediate Period." In Peruvian Prehistory, ed. R. Keatinge, pp. 145–163. Cambridge University Press, New York.

Conrad, Geoff, and Ann Webster. 1989. "Household Unit Patterning at San Antonio." In Ecology, Settlement, and History in the Osmore Drainage, ed. D. Rice, C. Stanish, and P. Starr, pp. 395–414. British Archaeological Reports International Series, Oxford.

Cook, Anita G. 1994. Wari y Tiwanaku: Entre el Estilo y la Imagen. Pontifica Universidad Católica del Perú, Lima.

Cook, David Noble, ed. 1975. Tasa de la Visita General de Francisco de Toledo. Universidad Nacional Mayor de San Marcos, Lima, Peru.

Cordell, Linda. 1984. Prehistory of the Southwest. Academic Press, New York.

Cordero Miranda, Gregorio. 1971. "Reconocimiento arqueológico de Pucarani y sitios adyacentes." Pumapunku 3: 7–27.

———. 1972. "Estudio preliminar en las islas de Intja and Suriki del Lago Titikaka." Pumapunku 5: 22–39.

Cuentas Ormachea, Enrique A. 1982. "La danza 'Choqela' y su contenido mágico-religioso." Boletín de Lima 19: 54–70.

Dalton, George. 1968. Introduction to Primitive, Archaic, and Modern Economies: Essays of Karl Polanyi, ed. G. Dalton, pp. ix–liv. Beacon Press, Boston.

D'Altroy, Terence. 1992. Provincial Power in the Inka Empire. Smithsonian Institution Press, Washington, D.C.

D'Altroy, Terence, and R. L. Bishop. 1990. "The Provincial Organization of Inka Ceramic Production." American Antiquity 55 (1): 120–138.

D'Altroy, Terence, and Timothy K. Earle. 1992. "Staple Finance, Wealth Finance, and Storage in the Inka Political Economy." In Inka Storage Systems, ed. T. Y. LeVine, pp. 31–61. University of Oklahoma Press, Norman.

Dejoux, Claude, and Andre Iltis. 1991. Introduction to El Lago Titicaca, ed. C. Dejoux and A. Iltis, pp. 11–16. ORSTOM/HISBOL, La Paz, Bolivia.

———, eds. 1992. Lake Titicaca: A Synthesis of Limnological Knowledge. Dordrecht; Kluwer Academic Publishers, Boston.

de la Grasserie, Raoul. 1894. Langues Américaines, Langue Puquina, Textes Puquina Contenues dans le Rituale seu Manuele Peruanum de Geronimo de Oré. Maisonneuve, Paris.

de la Vega, Abel Edmundo. 1990. "Estudio arqueológico de Pucaras o poblados amurallados de cumbre en territorio Lupaqa: El caso de Pucara-Juli." Tesis bachiller, Universidad Catolica Santa María, Arequipa, Peru.

———. 1997. "Característica de la re-ocupación Tiwanaku en el sitio de Sillumocco-Huaquina, Juli (Puno)." Tesis licenciatura, Universidad Catolica Santa María, Arequipa, Peru.

de la Vega, Abel Edmundo, Kirk L. Frye, Cecilia Chávez J., Mario Núñez M., Fernando Sosa A., David Antesana B., Jose Nuñés, Doris Maldonado A., Norfelinda Cornejo G., Amadeo Mamani M., and Javier Chalcha S. 1995. "Proyecto de rescate del sitio arqueológico de Molino-Chilacachi (Acora). Proyecto Lupaqa, Universidad Nacional del Altiplano, Instituto Nacional de Cultura-Puno." Unpublished manuscript in possession of authors.

de Lucca D., Manuel. 1987. Diccionario Practico Aymara-Castellano. Editorial Los Amigos del Libro, La Paz, Bolivia.

Denevan, William M., and Billie Lee Turner II. 1974. "Forms, Functions, and Associations of Raised Fields in the Old World Tropics." Journal of Tropical Geography 39: 24–33.

Diehl, Richard A. 1983. Tula: The Toltec Capital of Ancient Mexico. Thames and Hudson, London.

Dietler, Michael. 1990. "Driven by Drink: The Role of Drinking in the Political Economy and the Case of Early Iron Age France." Journal of Anthropological Archaeology 9: 352–406.

———. 1996. "Feasts and Commensal Politics in the Political Economy: Food, Power and Status in Prehistoric Europe." In Food and the Status Quest, ed. P. Wiesner and W. Schiefenhövel, pp. 87–125. Berghahn Books, Providence, R.I.

Diez de San Miguel, Garci. 1964 [1567]. *Visita Hecha a La Provincia de Chucuito.* Ediciones de la Casa de la Cultura de Perú, Lima.

Disselhoff, H. D. 1968. "Huari und Tiahuanaco." *Zeitschrift für Ethnologie* 93: (1–2).

Donnan, Christopher, and Donna McClelland. 1999. *Moche Fineline Painting: Its Evolution and Its Artists.* UCLA Fowler Museum of Cultural History, Los Angeles.

D'Orbigny, Alcide Dessalines. 1944. *El hombre americano, considerado en sus aspectos fisiológicos y morales,* 2nd ed. Trans. Alfredo Cepeda. Editorial Futuro, Buenos Aires.

Duviols, Pierre. 1973. "Huari y Llacuaz. Agricultores y pastores: Un dualismo prehispánico de opposicíon y complementaridad." *Revista del Museo Nacional* 39: 153–187.

Earle, Timothy. 1977. "A Reappraisal of Redistribution: Complex Hawaiian Chiefdoms." In *Exchange Systems in Prehistory,* ed. T. K. Earle and J. E. Ericson, pp. 213–232. Academic Press, New York.

———. 1987. "Specialization and the Production of Wealth: Hawaiian Chiefdoms and the Inka Empire." In *Specialization, Exchange, and Complex Societies,* pp. 64–75, ed. E. M. Brumfiel and T. K. Earle. University of Cambridge Press, Cambridge.

———. 1997. *How Chiefs Come to Power.* Stanford University Press, Stanford, Calif.

Eisenstadt, Shmuel Noah. 1963. *The Political Systems of Empires.* Free Press of Glencoe, New York.

Erickson, Clark. 1988. "An Archaeological Investigation of Raised Field Agriculture in the Lake Titicaca Basin of Peru." Ph.D. diss., Department of Anthropology, University of Illinois at Champaign-Urbana. University Microfilms, Inc., no. 8908674.

———. 1993. "The Social Organization of Prehispanic Raised Field Agriculture in the Lake Titicaca Basin." In *Prehispanic Water Management Systems,* Supplement no. 7, Research in Economic Anthropology, ed. V. Scarborough and B. Isaac. JAI Press, Greenwich, Conn.

———. 1994. "Methodological Considerations in the Study of Ancient Andean Field Systems." In *The Archaeology of Garden and Field,* ed. N. Miller and K. Gleason, pp. 111–152. University of Pennsylvania Press, Philadelphia.

Escalante Moscoso, Javier F. 1994. *Arquitectura Prehis-*

pánic en los Andes Bolivianos. Producción CIMA, La Paz, Bolivia.

Esteves Castillo, José, and Javier Escalante Moscoso. 1994. "Investigaciónes arqueológicas in la Isla Pako (a Suriqui)." Documentos Internos INAR, La Paz, Bolivia.

Faldín A., Juan D. 1990. "La provincia Larecaja y el sistema precolombino del Norte de La Paz." In *Larecaja, Ayer, Hoy y Mañana,* pp. 73–90. Comité de Cultura, La Paz, Bolivia.

———. 1991. "La cerámica de Chiripa en los valles de Larecaja." *Pumapunku* 1 (n.s.): 119–132.

Feinman, Gary, and Joyce Marcus, ed. 1998. *Archaic States.* School of American Research Press, Santa Fe, New Mexico.

Feinman, Gary, and Jill Neitzel. 1984. "Too Many Types: An Overview of Sedentary Prestate Societies in the Americas." *Advances in Archaeological Theory and Method* 7: 39–102.

Feldman, Robert. 1989. "The Early Ceramic Periods of Moquegua." In *Ecology, Settlement and History in the Osmore Drainage,* ed. D. Rice, C. Stanish, and P. Scarr, pp. 207–217. British Archaeological Reports International Series, Oxford.

———. 1996. "Variations in Interregional Connections in the Archaeology of Moquegua." Paper presented at the 61st meeting of the Society for American Archaeology, New Orleans.

Flannery, Kent V. 1995. "Prehistoric Social Evolution." In *Research Frontiers in Anthropology,* ed. C. Ember and M. Ember, pp. 1–26. Prentice-Hall, Englewood Cliffs, N.J.

———. 1998. "The Ground Plans of Archaic States." In *Archaic States,* ed. G. Feinman and J. Marcus, pp. 15–57. School of American Research Press, Santa Fe, N. Mex.

———. 1999. "Process and Agency in Early State Formation." *Cambridge Archaeological Journal* 9 (1): 3–21.

Flores Ochoa, Jorge A., and Magno Percy Paz Flores. 1983. "La agricultura en lagunas del altiplano." *Ñawpa Pacha* 21: 127–152.

Focacci A., Guillermo. 1969. "Arqueología de Arica, secuencia cultural del periodo agroalfarero-horizonte Tiahuanaco." *Actas del V Congreso Nacional de Arqueología* 21–26. La Serena, Chile.

———. 1982. "Nuevos fechados para la época del Tiahuanaco en la arqueología del norte de Chile." *Chungará* 8: 63–78.

———. 1983. "El Tiwankau clásico en el valle de Azapa." In *Asentamientos Aldeanos en los Valles Costeros de Arica.* Documento de Trabajo no. 3, Universidad de Tarapacá, ed. I. Muñoz O. and G. Focacci A., pp. 94–113.

Folan, William J., Joyce Marcus, Sophia Pincemin, María del Rosario Domínguez Carrasco, Laraine Fletcher, and Abel Morales López. 1995. "Calakmul: New Data from an Ancient Maya Capital in Campeche, Mexico." *Latin American Antiquity* 6 (4): 310–334.

Forbes, David. 1870. "On the Aymara Indians of Bolivia and Peru." *Journal of the Ethnological Society of London,* n.s., 2: 193–305.

Forman, Sylvia. 1978. "The Future Value of the 'Verticality' Concept: Implications and Possible Applications in the Andes." *Actes du XLIIᵉ Congrès International des Amèricanistes* 4: 233–256. Paris.

Fox, John W. 1987. *Maya Postclassic State Formation.* Cambridge University Press, Cambridge.

Franco Inojosa, José María. 1937. "Informe sobre los restos arqueológicos de las cabeceras del Paucartambo." *Revista del Museo Nacional* 6 (2): 255–277.

———. 1940. "Arqueología sudperuana: Informe sobre los trabajos arqueológicos de la Misión Kidder en Pukara, Puno (enero a julio de 1939)." *Revista del Museo Nacional* 9 (1): 128–142.

Franco Inojosa, José María, and Alejandro González. 1936. "Departmento de Puno." *Revista del Museo Nacional* 5 (2): 157–183. Lima, Peru.

Franquemont, Edward. 1986. "The Ancient Pottery from Pucara, Peru." *Ñawpa Pacha* 24: 1–30.

Frye, Kirk Lawrence. 1997. "Political Centralization in the Altiplano Period in the Southwestern Titicaca Basin." In *Archaeological Survey in the Juli-Desaguadero Region of Lake Titicaca Basin, Southern Peru,* ed. C. Stanish et al., pp. 129–141. *Fieldiana Anthropology,* Field Museum of Natural History, Chicago.

Garcilaso de la Vega. 1989. *The Royal Commentaries of the Inca.* Discus Books, New York.

Gasparini, Graziano, and Luise Margolies. 1980. *Inca Architecture.* Trans. Patricia J. Lyon. Indiana University Press, Bloomington.

Girault, Louis. 1966. "Classification vernaculaire des plantes médicinales chez les Callawaya, médecins empiriques (Bolivie)." *Journal, Société des Américanistes* LV-I: 156–200.

———. 1989. *Rituales en las regiones andinas de Bolivia y Peru.* Trans. Hans van den Berg. Escuela Profesional Don Bosco, El Alto La Paz, Bolivia.

Gisbert, Teresa. 1987. "Los cronistas y las migraciones aimaras." *Historia y Cultura* 12. Casa de la Cultura, La Paz, Bolivia.

———. 1994. "El señorío de los Carangas y los chullpares del Río Lauca." *Revista Andina* 2: 427–485.

Goldstein, Paul S. 1989a. "The Tiwanaku Occupation of Moquegua." In *Ecology, Settlement, and History in the Osmore Drainage,* ed. D. Rice, C. Stanish, and P. Scarr, pp. 219–255. British Archaeological Reports International Series 545 (1), Oxford.

———. 1989b. "Omo, a Tiwanaku Provincial Center in Moquegua, Peru." Ph.D. diss., Department of Anthropology, University of Chicago.

———. 1990. "La ocupación Tiwanaku en Moquegua." *Gaceta Arqueológica Andina* 5: 75–104.

———. 1993a. "Tiwanaku Temples and State Expansion: A Tiwanaku Sunken-Court Temple in Moquegua, Peru." *Latin American Antiquity* 4 (1): 22–47.

———. 1993b. "House, Community, and State in the Earliest Tiwanaku Colony: Domestic Patterns and State Integration at Omo M12, Moquegua." In *Domestic Architecture in South Central Andean Prehistory,* ed. Mark Aldenderfer, pp. 25–41. University of Iowa Press, Iowa City.

———. 1995–1996. "Tiwanaku Settlement Patterns of the Azapa Valley, Chile: New Data, and the Legacy of Percy Dauelsberg." *Diálogo Andino* 14/15: 57–73.

———. 2001. "Exotic Goods and Everyday Chiefs: Long-Distance Exchange and Indigenous Sociopolitical Development in the South Central Andes." *Latin American Antiquity* 11(4): 335–361.

Goodman, Edward J. 1992. *The Explorers of South America.* University of Oklahoma Press, Norman.

Goodrich, Samuel Griswald. 1846. *The Manners, Customs, and Antiquities of the Indians of North and South America.* Thomas, Cowperthwait & Co., Philadelphia.

Goody, Jack. 1972. "The Evolution of the Family." In *Household and Family in Past Time,* ed. P. Laslett. Cambridge University Press, Cambridge.

Graf, Kurt. 1981. "Palynological Investigations of Two Post-Glacial Peat Bogs near the Boundary of Bolivia and Peru." *Journal of Biogeography* 8: 353–368.

Graffam, Gray Clayton. 1990. "Raised Fields without Bureaucracy: An Archaeological Examination of Intensive Wetland Cultivation in the Pampa Koani Zone, Lake Titicaca, Bolivia." Ph.D. diss., Department of Anthropology, University of Toronto.

———. 1992. "Beyond State Collapse: Rural History, Raised Fields, and Pastoralism in the South Andes." *American Anthropologist* 94 (4): 882–904.

Graffam, Gray Clayton, Mario Rivera, and Alvaro Carevič. 1996. "Ancient Metallurgy in the Atacama: Evidence for Copper Smelting during Chile's Early Ceramic Period." *Latin American Antiquity* 7 (2): 101–113.

Guamán Poma de Ayala, Felipe. 1980 [1616]. *El Primer Nueva Corónica y Buen Gobierno.* Siglo Veintiuno, Mexico City.

Gutiérrez Noriega, Carlos. 1935. "Jatun Malka." *Revista del Museo Nacional* 4 (1): 105–110. Lima, Peru.

———. 1937. "Ciudadelas chullparias de los Wankas." *Revista del Museo Nacional* 6 (1): 43–51. Lima, Peru.

Hamilton, Roland. 1983. "A Scientific Outlook of the Seventeenth Century." In *Introduction to History of the Inca Empire by Father Bernabe Cobo,* trans. R. Hamilton, pp. xviii–xix. University of Texas Press, Austin.

Hardman-de-Bautista, M. J. 1978. "Jaqi: The Linguistic Family." *International Journal of American Linguistics* 44: 146–153.

———. 1988. "Jaqi aru: La lengua humana." In *Raíces de América: El Mundo Aymara,* ed. X. Albó, pp. 155–216. Alianza Editorial, Madrid.

Harris, Marvin. 1968. *The Rise of Anthropological Theory.* Harper and Row, New York.

Harrison, Mark. 1975. "Chayanov and the Economics of the Russian Peasantry." *Journal of Peasant Studies* 2 (4): 389–417.

Hassig, Ross. 1985. *Trade, Tribute, and Transportation: The Sixteenth-Century Political Economy of the Valley of Mexico.* University of Oklahoma Press, Norman.

Hastorf, Christine A. 1993. *Agriculture and the Onset of Political Inequality before the Inka.* Cambridge University Press, Cambridge.

———. 1999a. "Conclusions." In *Early Settlement at Chiripa, Bolivia,* ed. C. Hastorf, pp. 123–124. Contributions of the University of California Archaeological Research Facility, Berkeley. University of California, Berkeley.

———. 1999b. "An Introduction to Chiripa and the Site Area." In *Early Settlement at Chiripa, Bolivia,* ed. C. Hastorf, pp. 1–6. Contributions of the University of California Archaeological Research Facility, Berkeley. University of California, Berkeley.

Hastorf, Christine A., and Sissel Johannessen. 1993. "Pre-Hispanic Political Change and the Role of Maize in the Central Andes of Peru." *American Anthropologist* 95 (1): 115–138.

Hayden, Brian. 1996. "Feasting in Prehistoric and Traditional Societies." In *Food and the Status Quest,* ed. Polly Wiessner and Wulf Scheffehövel, pp. 127–147. Berghahn Books, Providence and Oxford.

Helms, Mary W. 1979. *Ancient Panama: Chiefs in Search of Power.* University of Texas Press, Austin.

———. 1994. "Chiefdom Rivalries, Control, and External Contacts in Lower Central America." In *Factional Competition and Political Development in the New World,* ed. E. M. Brumfiel and J. W. Fox, pp. 55–60. Cambridge University Press, Cambridge.

Hewett, Edgar Lee. 1969 [1939]. *Ancient Andean Life.* Biblo and Tannen, New York.

Higueras-Hare, Alvaro. 1996. "Prehispanic Settlement and Land Use in Cochabamba, Bolivia." Ph.D. diss., Department of Anthropology, University of Pittsburgh. UMI no. 9728693.

Hodges, Richard. 1988. *Primitive and Peasant Markets.* Blackwell, Cambridge.

Hoyt, Margaret Ann. 1975. "Two New Pucara Style Stela Fragments from Yapura, near Capachica, Puno, Peru." *Ñawpa Pacha* 13: 27–34.

Huidobro Bellido, José, Freddy Arce Helguero, and Pascual Quispe Condori. 1994. *La Verdadera Escritura Aymara.* Producciones CIMA, La Paz, Bolivia.

Hyslop, John, Jr. 1976. "An Archaeological Investigation

of the Lupaca Kingdom and Its Origins." Ph.D. diss., Department of Anthropology, Columbia University.

———. 1977. "Chulpas of the Lupaca Zone of the Peruvian High Plateau." *Journal of Field Archaeology* 4: 149–170.

———. 1979. "El área Lupaca bajo el dominio Incaico: Un reconocimiento arqueológico." *Histórica* 3 (1): 53–79.

———. 1984. *The Inka Road System.* Academic Press, New York.

———. 1990. *Inca Settlement Planning.* University of Texas Press, Austin.

Ibarra Grasso, Dick Edgar. 1956. *Tiahuanaco.* Editorial Atlantica, Cochabamba, Bolivia.

———. 1994. *Sudamérica Indigena.* Tipográfica Editora Argentina, Buenos Aires.

Iltis, Andre, Jean-Pierre Carmouze, and Jacques Lemoalle. 1991. "Características físico-químicas del agua." In *El Lago Titicaca,* ed. Claude Dejoux and André Iltis, pp. 107–113. HISBOL, La Paz, Bolivia.

Isbell, William H. 1988. "City and State in Middle Horizon Huari." In *Peruvian Prehistory,* ed. Richard Keatinge, pp. 164–189. Cambridge University Press, Cambridge.

———. 1995. "Constructing the Andean Past or 'As You Like It.'" *Journal of the Steward Anthropological Society* 25 (1–2): 1–12.

———. 1997. *Mummies and Mortuary Monuments.* University of Texas Press, Austin.

Isbell, William H., Christine Brewster-Wray, and Lynda Spickard. 1991. "Architecture and Spatial Organization at Huari." In *Huari Administrative Structure: Prehistoric Monumental Architecture and State Government,* ed. W. Isbell and G. McEwan, pp. 19–53. Dumbarton Oaks, Washington, D.C.

Isbell, William H., and Anita G. Cook. 1987. "Ideological Origins of an Andean Conquest State." *Archaeology* 40 (4): 27–33.

Isbell, William H., and Gordon McEwan. 1991. "A History of Huari Studies and Introduction to Current Interpretations." In *Huari Administrative Structure: Prehistoric Monumental Architecture and State Government,* ed. W. H. Isbell and G. McEwan, pp. 1–17. Dumbarton Oaks, Washington, D.C.

Janusek, John Wayne. 1993. "Nuevos datos sobre el significado de la producción y uso de instrumentos musicales en el estado de Tiwanaku." *Pumapunku,* n.s., 4: 9–47.

———. 1994. "State and Local Power in a Prehispanic Andean Polity: Changing Patterns of Urban Residence in Tiwanaku and Lukurmata, Bolivia." Ph.D. diss., Department of Anthropology, University of Chicago.

———. 1999. "Craft and Local Power: Embedded Specialization in Tiwanaku Cities." *Latin American Antiquity* 10 (2): 107–131.

Johnson, Allen W., and Timothy Earle. 1987. *The Evolution of Human Societies.* Stanford University Press, Stanford, Calif.

Julien, Catherine. 1981. "A Late Burial from Cerro Azoguini, Puno." *Ñawpa Pacha* 19: 129–154.

———. 1982. "Inca Decimal Administration in the Lake Titicaca Region." In *The Inca and Aztec States, 1400–1800,* ed. G. A. Collier, R. I. Rosaldo, and J. D. Wirth, pp. 119–151. Academic Press, New York.

———. 1983. *Hatunqolla: A View of Inca Rule from the Lake Titicaca Region.* Series Publications in Anthropology, vol. 15. University of California Press, Berkeley.

———. 1985. "Guano and Resource Control in Sixteenth-Century Arequipa." In *Andean Ecology and Civilization,* ed. S. Masuda, I. Shimada, and C. Morris, pp. 185–231. University of Tokyo Press, Tokyo.

———. 1988a. "How Inca Decimal Organization Worked." *Ethnohistory* 35 (3): 257–279.

———. 1988b. "The Squier Causeway at Lake Umayo." *Expedition* 30 (3): 46–55.

———. 1993. "Finding a Fit: Archaeology and Ethnohistory of the Incas." In *Provincial Inca,* ed. Michael Malpass, pp. 177–233. University of Iowa Press, Iowa City.

———. 1998. "Coca Production on the Inca Frontier: The Yungas of Chuquioma." *Andean Past* 5: 129–147.

Junker, Laura Lee. 1994. "Trade Competition, Conflict, and Political Transformations in Sixteenth-Century Philippine Chiefdoms." *Asian Perspectives* 33 (2): 229–260.

Kaufmann-Doig, Federico. 1983. *Manual de Arqueología Peruana.* Kom Pak Tos, Lima, Peru.

Keeley, Lawrence H. 1996. *War before Civilization.* Oxford University Press, New York.

Kendall, Anne. 1985. "Aspects of Inca Architecture: Description, Function, and Chronology." *British Archaeological Reports International Series* 242, Oxford.

Kidder, Alfred, II. 1943. "Some Early Sites in the Northern Lake Titicaca Basin." *Papers of the Peabody Museum* (Harvard University) I: xxvii.

———. 1967 [1956]. "Digging in the Titicaca Basin." In *Peruvian Archaeology,* ed. J. Rowe and D. Menzel, pp. 132–145. Peek Publications, Palo Alto, Calif. Originally published in the *University Museum Bulletin* (University of Pennsylvania) 20(3): 16–29.

Kirch, Patrick. 1984. *The Evolution of the Polynesian Chiefdoms.* Cambridge University Press, Cambridge.

Knobloch, Patricia J. 1991. "Stylistic Date of Ceramics from the Huari Centers." In *Huari Administrative Structure: Prehistoric Monumental Architecture and State Government,* ed. W. H. Isbell and G. McEwan, pp. 247–258. Dumbarton Oaks, Washington, D.C.

Kolata, Alan. 1983. "The South Andes." In *Ancient South Americans,* ed. J. Jennings, pp. 241–285. Freeman, San Francisco.

———. 1985. "El papel de la agricultura intensiva en la economía política del estado de Tiwanaku." *Diálogo Andino* 4: 11–38.

———. 1986. "The Agricultural Foundations of the Tiwanaku State: A View from the Heartland." *American Antiquity* 51 (4): 748–762.

———. 1992. "Economy, Ideology, and Imperialism in the South-Central Andes." In *Ideology and Pre-Columbian Civilizations,* ed. A. Demarest and G. Conrad, pp. 65–85. School of American Research, Santa Fe, N. Mex.

———. 1993. *The Tiwanaku.* Basil Blackwell, London.

Kolata, Alan, and Gray Graffam. 1987. "The Raised Fields of Lukurmata." In *The Technology and Organization of Agricultural Production in the Tiwanaku State,* ed. A. Kolata, C. Stanish, and O. Rivera, pp. 175–205. University of Illinois, Chicago.

Kolata, Alan, and Charles Ortloff. 1996a. "Tiwanaku Raised-Field Agriculture in the Lake Titicaca Basin of Bolivia." In *Tiwanaku and Its Hinterland: Archaeology and Paleoecology of an Andean Civilization,* ed. Alan Kolata, pp. 109–151. Smithsonian Institution Press, Washington, D.C.

———. 1996b. "Agroecological Perspectives on the Decline of the Tiwanaku State." In *Tiwanaku and Its Hinterland: Archaeology and Paleoecology of an Andean Civilization,* ed. Alan Kolata, pp. 181–201. Smithsonian Institution Press, Washington, D.C.

Kolata, Alan, and Carlos Ponce Sanginés. 1992. "Tiwanaku: The City at the Center." In *The Ancient Americas,* ed. Richard F. Townsend, pp. 317–333. Art Institute of Chicago, Chicago.

Kroeber, Alfred. 1939. "Sudamérica. Peru." *Revista del Museo Nacional* 8 (2): 320–325.

La Barre, Weston. 1941. "The Uru of the Rio Desaguadero." Part I. *American Anthropologist* 43 (4) : 493–522.

———. 1946. "The Uru-Chipaya." In *Handbook of South American Indians,* ed. J. Steward, pp. 575–586. Smithsonian Institution Press, Washington, D.C.

———. 1948. *The Aymara Indians of the Lake Titicaca Plateau, Bolivia.* Memoir no. 68, American Anthropological Association, Menasha, Wis.

La Lone, Darrell E. 1982. "The Inca as a Nonmarket Economy: Supply on Command versus Supply and Demand." In *Contexts for Prehistoric Exchange,* ed. J. Ericson and T. K. Earle, pp. 291–316. Academic Press, New York.

Leach, Jerry W. 1983. "Introduction." In *The Kula: New Perspectives on Massim Exchange,* ed. J. W. Leach and E. Leach, pp. 1–26. Cambridge University Press, Cambridge.

Le Blanc, Steve. 1999. *Prehistoric Warfare in the American Southwest.* University of Utah Press, Salt Lake City.

Lennon, Thomas J. 1983. "Pattern Analysis of Prehispanic Raised Fields of Lake Titicaca, Peru." In *Drained Fields of the Americas,* ed. J. P. Darch, pp. 183–200. International Series no. 189, British Archaeological Reports, Oxford.

Levieil, Dominique P., and Benjamin Orlove. 1990. "Local Control of Aquatic Resources: Community and Ecology in Lake Titicaca, Peru." *American Anthropologist* 92 (2): 362–382.

Leyden, Barbara. 1989. "Datos polínicos del periodo Holoceno tardío en el Lago Titicaca, Bolivia: Una posible inundación en la pampa Koani." In *Arqueología de Lukurmata,* ed. A. Kolata, pp. 263–274. Producciones Pumapunku, La Paz, Bolivia.

Linares Malaga, Eloy. 1982. "Principales centros arqueológicos que conservan nombres autóctonos en quechua,
aymara y puquina, del Departamento de Arequipa,
Peru." Universidad Nacional San Andrés. Arequipa,
Peru.

López Rivas, Eduardo. 1976. *Cultura y Religión en el Altiplano Andino*. Los Amigos del Libro, La Paz, Bolivia.

Loza Balsa, Gregorio. 1972. "Acerca de la agricultura Aymara." *Pumapunka* 4: 71–76.

Lumbreras, Luis Guillermo. 1974a. *The Peoples and Cultures of Ancient Peru*. Smithsonian Institution Press,
Washington, D.C.

———. 1974b. "Los reinos post-Tiwanaku en el área alti-
planica." *Revista del Museo Nacional* 40: 55–85.

———. 1981. *Arqueología de la América Andina*. Editorial Milla Batres, Lima, Peru.

Lumbreras, Luis G[uillermo], and Hernán Amat. 1968.
"Secuencia arqueológica del altiplano occidental del Titicaca." *XXXVII Congreso Internacional de Americanistas, Actas y Memorias* 2: 75–106. Buenos Aires.

Lumbreras, Luis G[uillermo], and Elias Mujica. 1982a.
"Kallamarca: Relaciónes con Pukara y Paracas." *Gaceta Arqueológica Andina* 3: 8.

———. 1982b. "Cincuenta años de investigación en Tiwanaku." *Gaceta Arqueológica Andina* 3: 6–7.

Lumbreras, Luis G[uillermo], Elias Mujica, and Rodolfo
Vera. 1982. "Cerro Baúl: Un enclave Wari en territorio
Tiwanaku." *Gaceta Arqueológica Andina* 2 (1): 4–5.

Luque López, Donato P., and Teobaldo Canahua Saga.
1997. "Inventario registro y catalogación de sitios arqueológicos en la peninsula de Capachica. Informe Final." Centro de Investigación Educación y Desarrollo
CIRD—Puno, Peru.

Luttwak, Edward N. 1976. *The Grand Strategy of the Roman Empire from the First Century A.D. to the Third*.
Johns Hopkins University Press, Baltimore.

Lynch, Thomas F. 1981. "Recent Research." *American Antiquity* 46 (1): 203–204.

———. 1983. "Camelid Pastoralism and the Emergence
of Tiwanaku Civilization in the South Central Andes."
World Archaeology 15 (1): 1–14.

McAndrews, Timothy. 1995. "Tiwanaku Core and Periphery Region: A Settlement Pattern Approach." Paper presented at the 60th meeting of the Society for
American Archaeology, Minneapolis, Minn. Manuscript on file, Department of Anthropology, University of Pittsburgh.

McEwan, Gordon. 1991. "Investigations at the Pikillacta
Site: A Provincial Huari Center in the Valley of Cuzco."
In *Huari Administrative Structures: Prehistoric Monumental Architecture and State Government*, ed. W. Isbell
and G. McEwan, pp. 93–119. Dumbarton Oaks, Washington, D.C.

Malinowski, Bronislaw. 1961 [1922]. *Argonauts of the Western Pacific*. E. P. Dutton, New York.

Manelis de Klein, Harriet E. 1973. "Los Urus: El extraño
pueblo del altiplano." *Estudios Andinos* 7, vol. III (1):
129–150.

Mannheim, Bruce. 1991. *The Language of the Inka since the
European Invasion*. University of Texas Press, Austin.

Manzanilla, Linda. 1992. *Akapana: Una Pirámide en el
Centro del Mundo*. UNAM, Mexico City.

Manzanilla, Linda, and Eric Woodward. 1990. "Restos hu-
manos asociados a la pirámide de Akapana (Tiwanaku,
Bolivia)." *Latin American Antiquity* 1 (2): 133–149.

Marcus, Joyce. 1987. "Prehistoric Fishermen in the Kingdom of Huarco." *American Scientist* 75: 393–401.

———. 1989. "Zapotec Chiefdoms and the Nature of Formative Religions." In *Regional Perspectives on the Olmec*,
ed. R. Sharer and D. Grove, pp. 148–197. Cambridge
University Press, Cambridge.

———. 1992a. "Dynamic Cycles of Mesoamerican States."
National Geographic Research & Exploration 8: 392–411.

———. 1992b. *Mesoamerican Writing Systems: Propaganda, Myth, and History in Four Ancient Civilizations*.
Princeton University Press, Princeton, N.J.

———. 1993. "Ancient Maya Political Organization." In
Lowland Maya Civilization in the Eighth Century A.D.,
ed. J. Sabloff and J. Henderson, pp. 111–183. Dumbarton Oaks, Washington, D.C.

Marcus, Joyce, and Gary Feinman. 1998. Introduction to
Archaic States, ed. G. Feinman and J. Marcus, pp. 3–13.
School of American Research Press, Santa Fe, N. Mex.

Marcus, Joyce, and Kent Flannery. 1994. "Ancient Zapotec
Ritual and Religion: An Application of the Direct Historical Approach." In *The Ancient Mind*, ed. C. Renfrew and E. Zubrow, pp. 55–74. Cambridge University
Press, Cambridge.

———. 1996. *Zapotec Civilization: How Urban Society Evolved in Mexico's Oaxaca Valley.* Thames and Hudson, London.

Marcus, Joyce, Jeffrey D. Sommer, and Christopher P. Glew. 1999. "Fish and Mammals in the Economy of an Ancient Peruvian Kingdom." *Proceedings of the National Academy of Sciences* 96: 6564–6570.

Marroquín, José. 1944. "Medicina aborigen Puneña." *Revista del Museo Nacional* 13 (1): 1–14.

Mathews, James Edward. 1993. "Prehispanic Settlement and Agriculture in the Middle Tiwanaku Valley, Bolivia." Ph.D. diss., Department of Anthropology, University of Chicago.

Matos Mendieta, Ramiro. 1960. "Informe sobre trabajos arqueológicos en Castrovirreyna, Huancavelica." In *Antiguo Perú: Espacio y Tiempo,* ed. Ramiros Matos M., pp. 313–324. Editorial Juan Mejía Baca, Lima, Peru.

———. 1990. "Arqueología peruana (1970–1990): Algunos comentarios." *Revista Andina* 8 (2): 507–553.

Means, Philip Ainsworth. 1931. *Ancient Civilizations of the Andes.* C. Scribner's Sons, New York, London.

Meiklejohn, Norman. 1988. *La Iglesia y Los Lupaqas durante la Colonia.* Bartolomé de las Casas, Cuzco.

Mercado de Peñaloza, Pedro. 1965 [1583]. "Relacíon de la provincia de los Pacajes." In *Relaciones Geográficas del Perú.* BAE, Madrid.

Métraux, Alfred. 1936. "Les indiens Uro-Cipaya de Carangas." *Journal de la Société des Américanistes de Paris* 28: 155–207, 337–394.

Millon, Rene. 1988. "The Last Years of Teotihuacan Dominance." In *The Collapse of Ancient States and Civilizations,* ed. N. Yoffee and G. Cowgill, pp. 102–164. University of Arizona Press, Tucson.

Miño Grijalva, Manuel. 1984. "Chucuito en 1782: Una descripción." *Revista Andina* 2: 629–636.

Mohr, Karen. 1966. "An Analysis of Pottery from Chiripa, Bolivia: A Problem in Archaeological Classification and Inference." M.A. thesis, Department of Anthropology, University of Pennsylvania.

Montesinos, Fernando. 1991 [1630]. *Memorias Antiguas Historiales del Perú.* Trans. P. Means. Kraus Reprint Limited, Liechtenstein.

Morris, Craig. 1971. "The Identification of Function in Provincial Inca Architecture and Ceramics." In *Actas y Memorias de XXXIX Congreso Internacional de Americanistas* 3: 135–144. Instituto de Estudios Peruanos, Lima, Peru.

———. 1979. "Maize Beer in the Economics, Politics, and Religion of the Inca Empire." In *Fermented Beverages in Nutrition,* ed. G. Gastineau, W. J. Darby, and T. E. Turner, pp. 21–34. Academic Press, New York.

———. 1982. "The Infrastructure of Inka Control in Peruvian Central Highlands." In *The Inca and Aztec States, 1400–1800,* ed. G. A. Collier, R. I. Rosaldo, and John Wirth, pp. 153–171. Academic Press, New York.

———. 1985. "From Principles of Ecological Complementarity to the Organization and Administration of Tawantinsuyu." In *Andean Ecology and Civilization,* ed. S. Masuda, I. Shimada, and C. Morris, pp. 477–490. University of Tokyo Press, Tokyo.

———. 1988. "Progress and Prospect in the Archaeology of the Inca." In *Peruvian Prehistory,* ed. R. Keatinge, C. Morris, D. Thompson, pp. 233–256. Cambridge University Press, New York.

Morris, Craig, and Don Thompson. 1985. *Huánuco Pampa: An Inca City and Its Hinterland.* Thames and Hudson, London.

Moseley, Michael E. 1975. *The Maritime Foundations of Andean Civilization.* Cummings, Menlo Park, Calif.

———. 1990a. "Fortificaciones prehispánicas y la evolución de tácticas militares en el Valle de Moquegua." In *Trabajos Arqueológicos en Moquegua, Perú,* vol. 1, ed. L. Watanabe, M. E. Moseley, and F. Cabieses, pp. 237–252. Southern Peru Copper Corp., Lima, Peru.

———. 1990b. "Structure and History in the Dynastic Lore of Chimor." In *The Northern Dynasties: Kingship and Statecraft in Chimor,* ed. M. Moseley and A. Cordy-Collins, pp. 1–41. Dumbarton Oaks, Washington, D.C.

———. 1992. *The Incas and Their Ancestors.* Thames and Hudson, London.

Moseley, Michael E., Robert Feldman, Paul Goldstein, and Luis Watanabe. 1991. "Colonies and Conquest: Tiahuanaco and Huari in Moquegua." In *Huari Administrative Structure: Prehistoric Monumental Architecture and State Government,* ed. W. Isbell and G. McEwan, pp. 121–140. Dumbarton Oaks, Washington, D.C.

Moseley, Michael E., and Carol J. Mackey. 1973. "Chan

Chan, Peru's Ancient City of Kings." *National Geographic* 143 (3): 319–344.

Mourguiart, P., T. Correge, D. Wirrmann, J. Argollo, M. E. Montenegro, M. Pourchet, and P. Carbonel. 1998. "Holocene Palaeohydrology of Lake Titicaca Estimated from an Ostracod-Based Transfer Function." *Palaeogeography, Palaeoclimatology, Palaeoecology* 143 (1–3): 51–72.

Mujica, Elias. 1978. "Nueva hipótesis sobre el desarrollo temprano del altiplano, del Titicaca y de sus áreas de interacción." *Arte y Arqueología* 5/6: 285–308. Academia Nacional de Ciencias de Bolivia, La Paz, Bolivia.

————. 1985. "Altiplano-Coast Relationships in the South-Central Andes: From Indirect to Direct Complementarity." In *Andean Ecology and Civilization,* ed. S. Masuda, I. Shimada, and C. Morris, pp. 103–140. University of Tokyo Press, Tokyo.

————. 1987. "Cusipata: Una fase pre-Pukara en la cuenca norte del Titicaca." *Gaceta Arqueologica Andina* 13: 22–28.

————. 1988. "Peculiaridades del proceso histórico temprano en la cuenca del norte del Titicaca: Una propuesta inicial." *Boletín del Laboratorio de Arqueología,* pp. 75–124. Escuela de Arqueología e Historia, Universidad Nacional San Cristobal de Huamanga, Ayacucho.

Mujica, Elias, Mario Rivera, and Thomas Lynch. 1983. "Proyecto de estudio sobre la complementariedad económica Tiwanaku en los valles occidentales del centro-sur Andino." *Chungará* 11: 85–109.

Muñoz Ovalle, Iván. 1983a. "La fase Alto Ramírez en los valles del extremo norte de Chile." In *Asentamientos Aldeanos en los Valles Costeros de Arica.* Documento de Trabajo no. 3, pp. 3–42. Universidad de Tarapacá, Arica, Chile.

————. 1983b. "El poblamiento aldeano en el valle de Azapa y su vinculación con Tiwanaku (Arica-Chile)." In *Asentamientos Aldeanos en los Valles Costeros de Arica.* Documento de Trabajo no. 3, pp. 43–93. Universidad de Tarapacá, Arica, Chile.

Murra, John V. 1964. "Una apreciación etnología de la Visita." In *Visita Hecha a la Provincia de Chucuito por Garci Diez de San Miguel en el Año 1567. Documentos Regionales para el Etnología y Etnohistoria Andinas* (Lima, Peru) 1: 419–444.

————. 1968. "An Aymara Kingdom in 1567." *Ethnohistory* 15: 115–151.

————. 1972. "El 'control vertical' de un máximo de pisos ecológicos en la economía de las sociedades Andinas." In *Visita de la Provincia de León de Huánuco en 1562.* Vol. 2: *Documentos por la Historia y Etnología de Huanuco y la Selva Central,* pp. 427–476. Universidad Nacional Hermilio Valdizán, Huánuco.

————. 1978. "Los olleros del Inka. . . ." In *Historia, Problema y Promesa: Homenaje a Jorge Basadre,* ed. F. Miro Quesada C., F. Pease G. Y., and D. Sobrevilla A., pp. 415–423. Pontificia Universidad Católica del Perú, Lima.

————. 1979. "El valle de Sama, isla periferica del reino de Lupaqa, y su uso dentro de la economía minera Colonial." In *Amerikanistiche Studien,* Festschrift für Hermann Trimborn, pp. 87–94. Hans Völker und Kulturen, Anthropos-Institut, St. Augustin.

————. 1980. *The Economic Organization of the Inka State.* Research in Economic Anthropology, supplement 1. JAI Press, Greenwich, Conn.

————. 1982. "The *Mit'a* Obligations of Ethnic Groups to the Inka State." In *The Inca and Aztec States: 1400–1800,* ed. G. Collier, R. Rosaldo, and J. Wirth, pp. 239–262. Academic Press, New York.

————. 1985a. "El Archipelago Vertical Revisited." In *Andean Ecology and Civilization,* ed. S. Masuda, I. Shimada, and C. Morris, pp. 3–14. University of Tokyo Press, Tokyo.

————. 1985b. "The Limits and Limitations of the 'Vertical Archipelago' in the Andes." In *Andean Ecology and Civilization,* ed. S. Masuda, I. Shimada, and C. Morris, pp. 15–20. University of Tokyo Press, Tokyo.

————. 1988. "El Aymara libre de ayer." In *Raices de América: El Mundo Aymara,* ed. X. Albó, pp. 51–73. Alianza Editorial, Madrid.

Murra, John V., Nathan Wachtel, and Jaques Revel, eds. 1986. *Anthropological History of Andean Polities.* Cambridge University Press, Cambridge.

Nadaillac, Jean Francois Albert du Pougetde, Marquis de. 1969 [1885]. *Pre-Historic America.* Anthropological Publications, Oosterhout N.B.

Nash, Daphne. 1987. "Imperial Expansion under the Roman Republic." In *Centre and Periphery in the Ancient World,* ed. M. Rowlands, M. Larsen, and K. Kristiansen, pp. 87–103. Cambridge University Press, Cambridge.

Neira Avendaño, Maximo. 1962. "Informe preliminar de la expedición arqueológica al altiplano." *Kontisuyo, Boletín del Museo de Arqueológia e Historia de la UNSA.*

———. 1967. "Informe preliminar de las investigaciones arqueológicas en el Departamento de Puno." *Anales del Instituto de Estudios Socio Económicos* I (I). Universidad Técnica del Altiplano, Puno, Peru.

Niles, Susan A. 1987. *Callachaca: Style and Status in an Inca Community.* University of Iowa Press, Iowa City.

———. 1988. "Pachamama, Pachatata: Gender and Sacred Space on Amantaní." In *The Role of Gender in Precolumbian Art and Architecture,* ed. V. Miller, pp. 135–151. University Press of America, Washington, D.C.

———. 1993. "The Provinces in the Heartland: Stylistic Variation and Architectural Innovation near Inca Cuzco." In *Provincial Inca: Archaeological and Ethnohistorical Asessment of the Impact of the Inca State,* ed. M. Malpass, pp. 145–176. University of Iowa Press, Iowa City.

Nordenskiöld, Erland. 1906. *Arkeologiska Undersökninear I Perus och Bolivias Gränstrakter.* Almquist and Wiksell, Uppsala, Sweden.

———. 1917. "Die östiche ausbreitung der Tiahuanacokultur in Bolivien und ihre verhältnis zur Araukkulture in Mojos." *Zeitschrift für Ethnologie* 49: 10–20.

———. 1924. "The Ethnography of South America Seen from Mojos in Bolivia." *Comparative Ethnographical Studies* 3.

Núñez Mendiguri, Mario. 1977. "Informe: Trabajos arqueológicos en la Isla Esteves." Instituto Nacional de Cultura, Puno, Peru. Mimeograph.

Núñez Mendiguri, Mario, and Rolando Paredes. 1978. "Estévez: Un sitio de ocupación Tiwanaku." *III Congreso Peruano del Hombre y la Cultura Andina,* vol. 2, ed. R. Matos M., pp. 757–764. Lima, Peru.

Núñez del Prado, Juan V. 1972. "Dos nuevas estatuas del estilo Pucara en Chumbivilcas, Perú." *Ñawpa Pacha* 9: 23–32.

Oakland Rodman, Amy. 1992. "Textiles and Ethnicity: Tiwanaku in San Pedro de Atacama, North Chile." *Latin American Antiquity* 3 (4): 316–340.

Onofre, Luperio. 1989. "Arquitectura y cerámica en

Pucara-Juli." *Boletín del Instituto de Estudios Aymaras* (series 2) 33: 26–80.

———. 1997. "Contemporary Aymara Agricultural Soil Categories." In *Archaeological Survey in the Juli-Desaguadero Area, Lake Titicaca Basin, Peru,* by C. Stanish, Edmundo de la Vega, Lee Hyde Steadman, Kirk Lawrence Frye, Cecília Chávez J., Luperio Onofre, and Matthew Seddon, pp. 125–127. Fieldiana Anthropology, Chicago.

Orellana Rodriguez, Mario. 1985. "Relaciones culturales entre Tiwanaku y San Pedro de Atacama." *Dialogo Andino* 4: 247–257.

Orlove, Benjamin S. 1986. "Barter and Cash Sale on Lake Titicaca: A Test of Competing Approaches." *Current Anthropology* 27: 85–106.

Ortloff, Charles R., and Alan L. Kolata. 1989. "Hydraulic Analysis of Tiwanaku Aqueduct Structures at Lukurmata and Pajchiri, Bolivia." *Journal of Archaeological Science* 16: 513–535.

———. 1993. "Climate and Collapse: Agro-Ecological Perspectives on the Decline of the Tiwanaku State." *Journal of Archaeological Science* 20: 195–221.

Owen, Bruce. 1993. "A Model of Multiethnicity: State Collapse, Competition, and Social Complexity from Tiwanaku to Chiribaya in the Osmore Valley, Perú." Ph.D. diss., Department of Anthropology, University of California, Los Angeles.

———. 1999. "Bows and Spearthrowers in Southern Peru and Northern Chile: Evidence, Dating, and Why It Matters." Paper delivered at the 64th annual meeting of the Society for American Archaeology, Chicago.

Palao Berastain, Juan. 1995. *Pukara: Primera Gran Cultura del Altiplano.* Proyecto Especial Pampa II-UE, Programa de micro proyectos rurales Lampa-Melgar. Producciones CIMA, La Paz, Bolivia.

Pardo, Luis A. 1942. "Sillustani, un metrópoli Incaica." *Revista del Museo Nacional* 11 (2): 203–215. Lima, Peru.

Paredes, Max Rigoberto. 1956. *El Kollasuyu: Estudios Prehistóricos y Tradicionales.* Biblioteca Paceña, La Paz, Bolivia.

Parenti, Lynne R. 1984. "A Taxonomic Revision of the Andean Killifish Genus *Orestias* (Cyprinodontiformes, Cyprinodontidae)." *Bulletin of the American Museum of Natural History* 178 (2).

Parsons, Jeffrey. 1968. "An Estimate of Size and Population for Middle Horizon Tiahuanaco, Bolivia." *American Antiquity* 33 (2): 243–245.

———. 1990. "Critical Reflections on a Decade of Full-Coverage Regional Survey in the Valley of Mexico." In *The Archaeology of Regions,* ed. S. Fish and S. Kowalewski, pp. 7–31. Washington, D.C.: Smithsonian Institution Press.

Pärssinen, Martti. 1992. *Tawantinsuyu: The Inca State and Its Political Organization. Studia Historica* 43. Societas Historica Finlandiae, Helsinki.

———. 1993. "Torres funerarias decoradas in Caquiaviri." *Pumapunku* (n.s.) 5–6: 9–32.

Pärssinen, Martti, and Ari Süriäinen. 1997. "Inka-Style Ceramics and Their Chronological Relationship to the Inka Expansion in the Southern Lake Titicaca Area (Bolivia)." *Latin American Antiquity* 8 (3): 255–271.

Patterson, Thomas C. 1986. "The Last Sixty Years: Toward a Social History of Americanist Archaeology in the United States." *American Anthropologist* 88 (1): 7–26.

———. 1991. *The Inca Empire: Formation and Disintegration of a Pre-Capitalist State.* Berg, London.

Paz Soría, José Luis. 1999. "Excavations in the Llusco Area." In *Early Settlement at Chiripa, Bolivia,* ed. C. Hastorf, pp. 31–35. Contributions of the University of California Archaeological Research Facility, Berkeley. University of California, Berkeley.

Pease G. Y., Franklin. 1973. "Cambios en el reino Lupaqa (1567–1661)." *Historia y Cultura* 7: 89–105. Lima, Peru.

———. 1982a. "Relaciónes entre los grupos étnicos de la Sierra sur y la Costa: Continuidades y cambios." In *El Hombre y su Ambiente en los Andes Centrales,* ed. Luis Millones and Hiroyasu Tomoeda, pp. 107–122. Senri Ethnological Series 10, University of Tokyo, Tokyo.

———. 1982b. "The Formation of Tawantinsuyu: Mechanisms of Colonization and Relationship with Ethnic Groups." In *The Inca and Aztec States 1400–1800,* ed. G. A. Collier, R. I. Rosaldo, and J. D. Wirth, pp. 173–198. Academic Press, New York.

Pentland, Joseph Barclay. 1827. "Report on the Bolivian Republic." Microfilm 2045. Lima, Great Britain Consulate General, Public Record Office, Foreign Office, file 61/12.

Perrín Pando, Alberto. 1957. "Las tumbas subterraneas de Wakuyo (Isla del Sol)." *Arqueología Boliviana,* pp. 173–205.

Plourde, Aimée M. 1999. "The Role of Inter-regional Exchange in Pucara and Tiwanaku State Formation and Expansion, Northeastern Titicaca Basin, Perú." Paper presented at the Annual Meeting of American Archaeologists, Chicago.

Polanyi, Karl. 1957. "The Economy as Instituted Process." In *Trade and Market in the Early Empires,* ed. K. Polanyi, C. Arensberg, and H. Pearson, pp. 243–270. Free Press, New York.

———. 1968. "Societies and Economic Systems." In *Primitive, Archaic, and Modern Economies: Essays of Karl Polanyi,* ed. George Dalton, pp. 3–25 (reprinted from *The Great Transformation*). Beacon Press, Boston.

Ponce Sanginés, Carlos. 1969a. "La ciudad de Tiwanaku." *Arte y Arqueología* 1: 1–32.

———. 1969b. *Tunupa y Ekako, Arqueología y Tradición.* Los Amigos del Libro, La Paz, Bolivia.

———. 1970. *Las Culturas Wankarani y Chiripa y Su Relación con Tiwanaku.* Academia Nacional de Ciencias de Bolivia. Publicación no. 25, La Paz, Bolivia.

———. 1972. *Tiwanaku: Espacio, Tiempo y Cultura: Ensayo de Síntesis Arqueológica.* Academia Nacional de Ciencias, La Paz, Bolivia.

———. 1976. *La Ceramica de la Epoca I de Tiwanaku.* Publication 18, Instituto Nacional de Arqueología, La Paz, Bolivia.

———. 1977. *Reflexiones Sobre la Ciudad Pre-Colombiana de Iskanwaya.* Publicación no. 24. Instituto Nacional de Arqueología, La Paz, Bolivia.

———. 1981. *Tiwanaku: Espacio, Tiempo y Cultura: Ensayo de Síntesis Arqueológica.* Amigos del Libro, La Paz, Bolivia.

———. 1991a. "El urbanismo de Tiwanaku." *Pumapunku* (n.s.) 1: 7–27.

———. 1991b. "El lago Titicaca en el marco de la investigación científica." *Pumapunku* (n.s.) 2: 67–118.

———. 1993. "Investigaciónes arqueológicas en Salla y Totora." *Pumapunku* (n.s.) 5–6: 89–166.

———. 1994. "Análisis espectrográfico y patrón de impurezas en el cobre de las grapas Tiwanacotas." *Pumapunku* 7 (n.s.): 9–64.

————. 1995. *Tiwanaku: 200 Años de Investigaciones Arqueológicas.* CIMA, La Paz, Bolivia.

Ponce Sanginés, Carlos, Johan Reinhard, Max Portugal, Eduardo Pareja, and Leocadio Ticlla. 1992. *Exploraciones Arqueológicas Subacuáticas en el Lago Titikaka.* Editorial La Palabra Producciones, La Paz, Bolivia.

Portugal Ortiz, Max. 1972. "Galerías mineras antiquas cerca del Rio Choqueyapu." *Pumapunku* 6: 54–58.

————. 1981. "Expansión del estilo esculctorico Pa-Ajanu." *Arte y Arqueología* 7: 149–159.

————. 1988a. "Excavaciones arqueológicos en Titimani (II)." *Arqueología Boliviana,* pp. 51–81. Instituto Nacional de Arqueología, La Paz, Bolivia.

————. 1988b. "Informe de la prospección a Pacajes (Etapa I)." *Arqueología Boliviana* 3: 109–117.

————. 1991. "La prospección efectuada en zonas de la provincia de Camacho del departamento de La Paz." *Textos Antropológicos* 2: 9–42.

————. 1992. "Trabajos arqueológicos de Tiwanaku (I. parte)." *Textos Antropológicos* 4: 9–50.

Portugal Zamora, Maks. 1957. "Sullkatata." In *Arqueología Boliviana,* ed. C. Ponce S., pp. 225–234. Biblioteca Paceña, La Paz, Bolivia.

————. 1988. "Aspectos generales sobre Tiwanaku del área circundante al lago Titicaca (sector Bolivia)." *Arqueología Boliviana* 15–25. INAR, La Paz, Bolivia.

Portugal Zamora, Maks, and Dick Edgar Ibarra Grasso. 1957. *Copacabana: El santuario y la arqueología de la peninsula e Islas del Sol y de la Luna.* Editorial "Atlantic," Cochabamba, Bolivia.

Portugal Zamora, Maks, and Max Portugal Ortíz. 1975. "Qallamarka, nuevo yacimiento arqueológico descubierto cerca a Tiwanaku." *Arte y Arqueología* 3–4: 195–216.

Posnansky, Arturo. 1912. *Guía General Ilustrada para la Investigación de los Monumentos Prehistóricos de Tihuanacu e Islas del Sol y la Luna (Titicaca y Koaty) con Breves Apuntes sobre los Chullpas, Urus y Escritura Antigua de los Aborígenes del Altiplano Andino.* H. Heitmann, La Paz, Bolivia.

————. 1914. *Eine Praehistorische Metropole in Sudamerika.* Reimer, Berlin.

————. 1937. *Antropología y Sociología de las Razas Interandinas y de las Regiones Adyacentes.* Instituto "Ti-huanacu" de Antropología, Etnografía, y Prehistoria, Editorial "Renacimiento," La Paz, Bolivia.

————. 1938. "Simillake o Ayakewiña." In *Antropología y Sociología de las Razas Interandinas y de las Regiones Adyacentes,* pp. 106–113. Editorial "Renacimiento," La Paz, Bolivia.

————. 1945. *Tihuanacu, the Cradle of American Man.* J. J. Agustin, New York.

Pulgar Vidal, Javier. n.d. *Historia y Geografía del Perú: Los Ochos Regiones Naturales del Perú.* Universidad Nacional Mayor de San Marcos, Lima, Peru.

Ramos Gavilán, Alonso. 1988 [1621]. *Historia del Santuario de Nuestra Señora de Copacabana.* Ignacio Prado P., Lima, Peru.

Redmond, Elsa M. 1994. "External Warfare and the Internal Politics of Northern South American Tribes and Chiefdoms." In *Factional Competition and Political Development in the New World,* ed. E. M. Brumfiel and J. W. Fox, pp. 44–54. Cambridge University Press, Cambridge.

Reinhard, Johan. 1983. "High Altitude Archaeology and Mountain Worship in the Andes." *American Alpine Journal* 25: 54–67.

————. 1985. "Sacred Mountains: An Ethno-Archaeological Study of High Andean Ruins." *Mountain Research and Development* 5 (4): 299–317.

————. 1991. "Tiwanaku: Ensayo sobre su cosmovisión." *Pumapunku* (n.s.) 2: 8–66.

————. 1992a. "Underwater Archaeological Research in Lake Titicaca, Bolivia." In *Contributions to New World Archaeology,* ed. Nicholas Saunders, pp. 117–143. Oxbow Books, Oxford.

————. 1992b. "Investigaciones arqueológicas subacuáticas en el lago Titikaka." In *Exploraciones Arqueológicas Subacuáticas en el Lago Titikaka,* ed. Ponce Sanginés, Johan Reinhard, Max Portugal, Eduardo Pareja, and Leocadio Ticlla, pp. 421–530. Editorial La Palabra Producciones, La Paz, Bolivia.

————. 1993. "Llullaillaco: An Investigation of the World's Highest Archaeological Site." *Latin American Indian Literatures Journal* 9 (1): 32–65.

Renfrew, Colin. 1986. "Introduction: Peer Polity Interaction and Socio-Politcal Change." In *Peer Polity Interaction and Socio-Political Change,* ed. C. Renfrew and

J. Cherry, pp. 1–26. Cambridge University Press, Cambridge.

Revilla Becerra, Rosanna Liliana, and Mauro Alberto Uriarte Paniagua. 1985. "Investigación arqueológica en la zona de Sillustani-Sector Wakakancha-Puno." Bachelor's thesis, Universidad Católica Santa María, Arequipa, Peru.

Rice, Don Stephen. 1993. "The Making of Latin American Horizons: An Introduction to the Volume." In *Latin American Horizons,* ed. D. S. Rice, pp. 1–13. Dumbarton Oaks, Washington, D.C.

Rice, Don Stephen, Charles Stanish, and Phillip Scarr, eds. 1989. *Ecology, Settlement, and History in the Osmore Drainage.* British Archaeological Reports International Series, Oxford.

Rice, Prudence. 1999. "On the Origins of Pottery." *Journal of Archaeological Method and Theory* 6(1): 1–54.

Rice, Prudence, Peter Bürgi, Mary Van Buren, and Geoff Conrad. 1989. "Torata Alta: An Inka-Spanish Settlement." Paper presented at the 54th meeting of the Society for American Archaeology, Atlanta.

Rivera, Mario. 1977. "Prehistoric Chronology of Northern Chile." Ph.D. diss., Department of Anthropology, University of Wisconsin, Madison.

———. 1984. "Altiplano and Tropical Lowland Contacts in Northern Chilean Prehistory: Chinchorro and Alto Ramírez Revisited." In *Social and Economic Organization in the Prehispanic Andes,* ed. D. Browman, R. Burger, and M. Rivera, pp. 143–160. British Archaeological Reports International Series 194.

———. 1991. "The Prehistory of Northern Chile: A Synthesis." *Journal of World Prehistory* 5: 1–47.

———, ed. 1985. *La Problemática Tiwanaku Huari en el Contexto Panandino del Desarrollo Cultural. Diálogo Andino* 4, Universidad de Tarapacá, Arica.

Rivera Casanovas, Claudia. 1989. "Las torres funerarias de Viscachani." *Textos Antropológicos* 1 (1): 79–92. Universidad Mayor de San Andrés, La Paz, Bolivia.

———. 1994. "Ch'iji Jawira: Evidencias sobre la producción de cerámica en Tiwanaku." Tesis de Licenciatura, Carrera de Antropología, Universidad Mayor de San Andrés, La Paz, Bolivia.

Rivera Sundt, Oswaldo. 1978. "Arqueología de la península de Copacabana." *Pumapunku* 12: 69–86.

———. 1984. "La horka del Inka." *Arqueología Boliviana* 1: 91–106.

———. 1989. "Resultados de la excavación en el centro ceremonial de Lukurmata." In *Arqueología de Lukurmata,* ed. A. Kolata, pp. 59–88. Editorial Sui Generis, La Paz, Bolivia.

Rivero y Ustariz, Mariano Eduardo de, and Johann Jakob von Tschudi. 1855. *Peruvian Antiquities.* G. P. Putnam, New York.

Roche, Michel A., Jacques Bourges, José Cortes, and Roger Matos. 1991. "Climatología e hidrología de la cuenca del lago Titicaca." In *El Lago Titicaca,* ed. C. Dejoux and A. Iltis, pp. 83–104. HISBOL, La Paz, Bolivia.

Romero, Emilio. 1928. *Monografía del Departamento de Puno.* Imprenta Torres Aguirre, Lima, Peru.

Rosenblat, Angel. 1967. *La Población de América en 1492: Viejos y Nuevos Cálculos.* Colegio de México, Mexico City.

Rostworowski de Diez Canseco, María. 1978–80. "Guarco y Lunaguaná: Dos señoríos prehispánicos de la costa sur central del Perú." *Revista del Museo Nacional* 44: 153–214.

———. 1988. *Historia del Tahuantinsuyu.* Instituto de Estudios Peruanos, Lima.

Rowe, John H. 1942. "Sitios históricos en la región de Pucara, Puno." *Revista del Instituto Arqueológico* 6 (10, 11): 66–75.

———. 1944. "An Introduction to the Archaeology of Cuzco." *Papers of the Peabody Museum of American Archaeology and Ethnology* 27 (2).

———. 1946. "Inca Culture at the Time of the Spanish Conquest." *Handbook of South American Indians,* vol. 2, ed. Julian H. Stewart, pp. 183–330. Smithsonian Institution Press, Washington, D.C.

———. 1956. "Archaeological Explorations in Southern Peru, 1954–1955." *American Antiquity* 22 (2): 135–150.

———. 1958. "The Adventures of Two Pucara Statues." *Archaeology* 11 (4): 255–261.

———. 1960. "Cultural Unity and Diversification in Peruvian Archaeology." In *Man and Cultures: Selected Papers of the Fifth International Congress of Anthropological and Ethnological Science,* pp. 627–631. Philadelphia.

———. 1962. "Stages and Periods in Archaeological Interpretation." *Southwestern Journal of Anthropology* 18 (1): 40–54.

———. 1963. "Urban Settlements in Ancient Peru." *Ñawpa Pacha* 1 (1): 1–27.

Rowe, John H., and Catherine Brandel. 1971. "Pucara Style Pottery Designs." *Ñawpa Pacha* 7–8 (1969–1970): 1–16.

Rowe, John H., and John M. Donahue. 1975. "The Donahue Discovery, an Ancient Stela Found Near Ilave, Puno." *Ñawpa Pacha* 13: 35–44.

Ruiz Estrada, Arturo. 1976. *Hallazgos de oro Sillustani (Puno).* Serie Metalurgia, no. 1, Publicaciones del Museo Nacional de Antropología y Arqueología, Lima.

———. 1978. "Exploraciones arqueológicos en Cabanillas: Puno." In *III Congreso Peruano del Hombre y la Cultura Andina,* vol. 2, ed. R. Matos M., pp. 791–806. Lima, Peru.

Rydén, Stig. 1947. *Archaeological Researches in the Highlands of Bolivia.* Elanders Boktryckeri Aktiebolag, Göteborg.

———. 1957. *Andean Excavations I.* Publication no. 4. The Ethnographical Museum of Sweden, Stockholm.

———. 1959. *Andean Excavations II: Tuparaya and Cayhuasi: Two Tiahuanaco Sites.* The Ethnographical Museum of Sweden, Stockholm, publication no. 6.

Sagárnaga Meneses, Jédu Antonio. 1991. Review of *Asentamientos Prehispánicos del Valle de Tiwanaku,* by Juan Albarracin-Jordán and James Mathews. *Pumapunku* (n.s.) 1 (1): 91–98.

———. 1993. "La chullpa de Viacha." *Pumapunku* (n.s.) 5–6: 33–56.

Sahlins, Marshall. 1972. *Stone Age Economics.* Aldine, New York.

Saignes, Thierry. 1983. "¿Quiénes son los Kallawaya? Nota sobre un enigma etnohistórico." *Revista Andina* 1 (2): 357–384.

———. 1986. "The Ethnic Groups in the Valleys of Larecaja: From Descent to Residence." In *Anthropological History of Andean Polities,* ed. J. Murra, N. Wachtel, and J. Revel, pp. 311–341. Cambridge Unviersity Press, Cambridge.

Sallnow, Michael J. 1987. *Pilgrims of the Andes: Regional Cults in Cusco.* Smithsonian Institution Press, Washington, D.C.

Sanders, William T., and David Webster. 1988. "The Mesoamerican Urban Tradition." *American Anthropologist* 90 (3): 521–546.

Sandweiss, Daniel H. 1992. *The Archaeology of Chincha Fishermen: Specialization and Status in Inka Peru.* Bulletin no. 29, Carnegie Museum of Natural History, Pittsburgh.

Santley, Robert, and Rani Alexander. 1992. "The Political Economy of Core-Periphery Systems." In *Resources, Power, and Interregional Interaction,* ed. E. Schortman and P. Urban, pp. 23–49. Plenum, New York.

Schreiber, Katharina. 1987. "Conquest and Consolidation: A Comparison of the Wari and Inka Occupations of a Highland Peruvian Valley." *American Antiquity* 52 (2): 266–284.

———. 1992. *Wari Imperialism in Middle Horizon Peru.* Anthropological Papers of the Museum of Anthropology, University of Michigan, Ann Arbor.

———. 1993. "The Inca Occupation of the Province of Andamarca Lucanas, Peru." In *Provincial Inca: Archaeological and Ethnohistorical Assessment of the Impact of the Inca State,* ed. Michael Malpass, pp. 77–116. University of Iowa Press, Iowa City.

Seddon, Mathew Thomas. 1994. "Excavations in the Raised Fields of the Rio Catari Sub-Basin, Bolivia." Master's thesis, Department of Anthropology, University of Chicago.

———. 1998. "Ritual, Power, and the Development of a Complex Society: The Island of the Sun and the Tiwanaku State." Ph.D. diss., Department of Anthropology, University of Chicago.

Service, Elman. 1972. *Origins of the State and Civilization.* W. W. Norton, New York.

Sever, Jacques. 1921. "Chullpas des environs de Pucará (Bolivie)." *Société des Américanistes* 13: 55–58.

Shady Solís, Ruth. 1987. Comments on "Lenguas y pueblos altiplánicos en torno al siglo XVI" by A. Torero. *Revista Andina* 5 (2): 387–392.

Shimada, Izumi, Crystal Barker Schaaf, Lonnie G. Thompson, and Ellen Mosley-Thompson. 1991. "Cultural Impacts of Severe Droughts in the Prehistoric Andes: Application of a 1,500-Year Ice Core Precipitation Record." *World Archaeology* 22 (3): 247–270.

Silverman, Helaine. 1990. "The Early Nasca Pilgrimage Center of Cahuachi and the Nazca Lines: Anthropological and Archaeological Perspectives." In *The Lines of Nazca,* ed. A. F. Aveni, pp. 207–244. American Philosophical Society, Philadelphia.

———. 1993. *Cahuachi in the Ancient Nasca World.* University of Iowa Press, Iowa City.

———. 1994. "The Archaeological Identification of an Ancient Peruvian Pilgrimage Center." *World Archaeology* 26 (1): 1–18.

———. 1996. "The Formative Period on the South Coast of Peru: A Critical Review." *Journal of World Prehistory* 10 (2): 95–146.

Sinclair, Joseph H. 1929. *The Conquest of Peru as Recorded by a Member of the Pizarro Expedition.* The New York Public Library, New York.

Smith, Adam. 1937 [1776]. *An Inquiry into the Nature and Causes of the Wealth of Nations.* The Modern Library, Random House, New York.

Smith, C., W. Denevan, and P. Hamilton. 1968. "Ancient Ridged Fields in the Region of Lake Titicaca." *Geographical Journal* 134 (3): 353–366.

Snead, James. 1992. "Imperial Infrastructure and the Inka State Storage System." In *Inka Storage Systems,* ed. Terry Y. LeVine, pp. 62–106. University of Oklahoma Press, Norman.

Solc, Václav. 1966. "Observaciones preliminares sobre investigaciones arqueológicas en la región de las islas en el lago Titicaca." *Abhandlungen und Berichte des Staatlichen Museum für Volkerkunde Dresden* 25. Berlin.

———. 1969. *Los Aymaras de las Islas del Titicaca.* Instituto Indigenista Interamericano, Serie Antropología Social 12, Mexico City.

Spencer, Charles S. 1993. "Human Agency, Biased Transmission, and the Cultural Evolution of Chiefly Authority." *Journal of Anthropological Archaeology* 12: 41–74.

———. 1998. "A Mathematical Model of Primary State Formation." In *Cultural Dynamics* 10 (1): 1–16.

Spurling, Geoffrey Eugene. 1992. "The Organization of Craft Production in the Inka State: The Potters and Weavers of Milliraya." Ph.D. diss., Department of Anthropology, Cornell University, Ithaca, N.Y.

Squier, Ephraim. 1877. *Peru: Incidents of Travel and Exploration in the Land of the Incas.* Harper and Brothers, New York.

Stanish, Charles. 1985. "Post-Tiwanaku Regional Economies in the Otora Valley, Southern Peru." Ph.D. diss., Department of Anthropology, University of Chicago.

———. 1989a. "An Archaeological Evaluation of an Ethnohistorical Model." In *Ecology, Settlement, and History in the Osmore Drainage,* ed. D. Rice, C. Stanish, and P. Starr, pp. 303–320. British Archaeological Reports International Series, Oxford.

———. 1989b. "Household Archaeology: Testing Models of Zonal Complementarity in the South Central Andes." *American Anthropologist* 91 (1): 7–24.

———. 1989c. "Tamaño y complejidad de los asentamientos nucleares de Tiwanaku." In *Arqueología de Lukurmata,* ed. A. Kolata, pp. 41–57. Instituto Nacional de Arqueología, La Paz, Bolivia.

———. 1991. "A Late Pre-Hispanic Ceramic Chronology for the Upper Moquegua Valley, Peru." *Fieldiana* (n.s.) no. 16.

———. 1992. *Ancient Andean Political Economy.* University of Texas Press, Austin.

———. 1994. "The Hydraulic Hypothesis Revisited: A Theoretical Perspective on Lake Titicaca Basin Raised Field Agriculture." *Latin American Antiquity* 5: 312–332.

———. 1997. "Nonmarket Imperialism in a Prehispanic Context: The Inca Occupation of the Titicaca Basin." *Latin American Antiquity* 8 (3): 1–18.

———. 1999. "Settlement Pattern Shifts and Political Ranking." In *Fifty Years After Viru,* ed. Brian R. Billman and Gary M. Feinman, pp. 116–128. Smithsonian Institution Press, Washington, D.C.

———. 2000. "Negotiating Rank in an Imperial State: Lake Titicaca Basin Elite under Inca and Spanish Control." In *Hierarchies in Action: Cui Bono?,* ed. M. Diehl, pp. 317–339. Southern Illinois University Center for Archaeological Investigations, Occasional Paper no. 27, Carbondale.

———. 2001a. "Recent Regional Research on the Inka." *Journal of Archaeological Research* 9(3): 213–241.

———. 2001b. "The Origins of the State in South America." *Annual Reviews in Anthropology* 30: 41–64.

Stanish, Charles, and Brian Bauer. Forthcoming. "Pilgrimage and the Geography of Power in the Inka State." In *Variability in the Expressions of Inka Power,* ed. C. Morris, R. Burger, and R. Matos. Dumbarton Oaks, Washington, D.C.

Stanish, Charles, Lisa Cipolla, Richard Burger, and Michael Glascock. 2002. "Early Settlement of the Island of the Sun, Lake Titicaca." Unpublished manuscript.

Stanish, Charles, Edmundo de la Vega M., Cecília Chávez, Amanda Cohen, Aimée Plourde, Carol Schultze, and Elizabeth Arkush. 2000. "Archaeological Reconnaissance in the Northern Titicaca Basin." Working Papers of the Programa Collasuyu, no. 1.

Stanish, Charles, Edmundo de la Vega M., and Kirk Lawrence Frye. 1993. "Domestic Architecture of Lupaqa Area Sites." In *Domestic Architecture in South Central Andean Prehistory*, ed. M. Aldenderfer, pp. 83–93. University of Iowa Press, Iowa City.

Stanish, Charles, Edmundo de la Vega M., Lee Hyde Steadman, Kirk Lawrence Frye, Cecília Chávez J., Luperio Onofre, and Matthew Seddon. 1997. *Archaeological Survey in the Juli-Desaguadero Area, Lake Titicaca Basin, Peru*. Fieldiana Anthropology, Chicago.

Stanish, Charles, and Aimée Plourde. 2000. "Archaeological Survey in the Huancané-Putina Valley, Peru." Final report submitted to the National Institute of Culture, Lima, Peru. Manuscript in possession of authors.

Stanish, Charles, and Irene Pritzker. 1983. "Archaeological Reconnaissance in Southern Peru." *Bulletin of the Field Museum of Natural History* 54 (6): 6–17.

Stanish, Charles, and Don Rice. 1989. "The Osmore Drainage, Peru: An Introduction to the Work of Programa Contisuyu." In *Ecology, Settlement, and History in the Osmore Drainage*, ed. D. Rice, C. Stanish, and P. Scarr, pp. 1–14. British Archaeological Reports International Series, Oxford.

Stanish, Charles, and Lee Steadman. 1994. "Archaeological Research at the Site of Tumatumani, Juli, Peru." *Fieldiana Anthropology* (n.s.) no. 23. Field Museum of Natural History, Chicago.

———. 2000. "Archaeological Survey in the Huancané-Putina River Valley." Working Papers of the Programa Collasuyu, no. 2.

Steadman, Lee. 1994. "Pottery Analysis." In *Archaeological Research at the Site of Tumatumani, Juli, Peru*, by Charles Stanish and Lee Hyde Steadman. *Fieldiana An-*

thropology (n.s.) no. 23. Field Museum of Natural History, Chicago.

———. 1995. "Excavations at Camata: An Early Ceramic Chronology for the Western Titicaca Basin, Peru." Ph.D. diss., Department of Anthropology, University of California, Berkeley.

———. 1997. "Ceramic Perspective on the Yaya-Mama Religious Tradition." Paper presented at the 62nd meeting of the Society for American Archaeology, Nashville, Tenn.

———. Forthcoming. "The Ceramics from Quelcatani." In *Quelcatani and Evolution of a Pastoral Lifeway*, ed. Mark Aldenderfer. Smithsonian Institution Press.

Stein, Gil. 1998. "World Systems Theory and Alternative Modes of Interaction in the Archaeology of Culture Contact." In *Studies in Culture Contact: Interaction, Culture Change, and Archaeology*, ed. J. Cusick, pp. 220–255. Center for Archaeological Investigations Occasional Papers no. 25, Southern Illinois University Press, Carbondale.

Stern, Steve J. 1982. *Peru's Indian Peoples and the Challenge of Spanish Conquest: Huamanga to 1640*. University of Wisconsin Press, Madison.

Talbi, A., A. Coudrain, P. Ribstein, and B. Pouyaud B. 1999. "Computation of the Rainfall on Lake Titicaca Catchment during the Holocene." *Comptes Rendus de la Academie des Sciences, Serie II Fascicule A—Sciences de la Terre et des Planetes* 329 (3): 197–203.

Tapia Pineda, Felix B. 1975. "Cerámica Tiwanakota en Puno." *Jornadas Peruano-Bolivianas de Estudio Científico del Altiplano Boliviano y del Sur del Perú* 2: 339–360.

———. 1978a. "Investigaciones arqueológicas en Kacsili." *Pumapunku* 12: 7–37.

———. 1978b. "Contribuciones al estudio de la cultura precolombina en el Altiplano Peruano." Publicación no. 16, Instituto Nacional de Arqueología, La Paz, Bolivia.

———. 1978c. "El fenómeno de la expansión Tiwanacota." Documentos Internos INAR no. 26/78, La Paz, Bolivia.

Thomason, Sarah Grey, and Terrence Kaufmann. 1988. *Language Contact, Creolization, and Genetic Linguistics*. University of California Press, Berkeley.

Thompson, L. G., and E. Mosely-Thompson. 1987. "Evidence of Abrupt Climatic Change During the Last 1500 Years Recorded in Ice Cores from the Tropical Quelccaya Ice Cap." In *Abrupt Climate Change: Evidence and Implications,* ed. W. Bergen and L. Labeyrie, pp. 99–110. D. Reidel, New York.

Thompson, L. G., E. Mosely-Thompson, J. F. Bolzan, and B. R. Koci. 1985. "A 1500-year Record of Tropical Precipitation in Ice Cores from the Quelccaya Ice Cap, Peru." *Science* 229: 971–973.

Thompson, L. G., E. Mosely-Thompson, W. Dansgaard, and P. M. Grootes. 1986. "The Little Ice Age as Recorded in the Stratigraphy of the Tropical Quelccaya Ice Cap." *Science* 234: 361–364.

Thompson, L. G., E. Mosely-Thompson, M. E. Davis, and K-B Liu. 1988. "Pre-Incan Agricultural Activity Recorded in Dust Layers in Two Tropical Ice Cores." *Nature* 336: 763–765.

Torero, Alfredo. 1987. "Lenguas y pueblos altiplánicos en torno al Siglo XVI." *Revista Andina* 5 (2): 329–405.

————. 1990. "Procesos lingüísticos e identificación de dioses en los Andes centrales." *Revista Andina* 8 (1): 237–263.

————. 1992. "Acerca de la familia lingüística uruquilla (Uru-Chipaya)." *Revista Andina* 10 (1): 171–191.

Torres, Constantino M. 1985. "Estilo e iconografía en las tabletas para inhalar substancias psicoactivas." *Dialogo Andino* 4: 223–245.

Torres, Constantino M., and William J. Conklin. 1995. "Exploring the San Pedro de Atacama/Tiwanaku Relationship." In *Andean Art: Visual Expression and Its Relation to Andean Beliefs and Values,* ed. Penny Dransart, pp. 78–108. Avebury, Aldershot, U.K.

Tosi, Joseph. 1960. *Zonas de Vida Natural en el Perú.* Technical Bulletin no. 5, Organization of American States, Washington, D.C.

Tourtellot, Gair, Jeremey A. Sabloff, and Michael P. Smyth. 1990. "Room Counts and Population Estimation for Terminal Classic Sayil in the Puuc Region, Yucatan, Mexico." In *Precolumbian Population History in the Maya Lowlands,* ed. T. P. Culbert and D. S. Rice, pp. 245–262. University of New Mexico Press, Albuquerque.

Trimborn, Hermann. 1993. "Las chullpas de Sicasica." *Pumapunku* (n.s.) 5–6: 193–208.

Troll, Carl. 1968. "The Cordilleras of the Tropical Americas: Aspects of Climate, Phytogeographical and Agrarian Ecology." In *Geo-Ecology of the Mountainous Regions of the Tropical Americas,* ed. C. Troll, pp. 15–65. Geographisches Institut der Universität, Bonn.

Tschopik, Harry. 1946. "The Aymara." In *Handbook of South American Indians,* vol. 2, ed. J. Steward, pp. 501–574. Smithsonian Institution Press, Washington, D.C.

————. 1947. *Highland Communities of Central Peru: A Regional Survey.* Institute of Social Anthropology, Smithsonian Institution, Washington, D.C.

————. 1951. "The Aymara of Chucuito, Peru." *Anthropological Papers of the American Museum of Natural History* 44 (pt. 2). New York.

Tschopik, Marion. 1946. "Some Notes on the Archaeology of the Department of Puno." *Papers of the Peabody Museum of American Archaeology and Ethnology* 27 (3).

Urton, Gregory. 1990. *The History of a Myth: Pacariqtambo and the Origin of the Inkas.* University of Texas Press, Austin.

Valcárcel, Luis Eduardo. 1925. "Informe sobre las exploraciones arqueológicas en Pukará." *Revista Universitaria del Cuzco* 48: 14–21.

————. 1938. "Los estudios peruanistas en 1937." *Revista del Museo Nacional* 7 (1): 6–20.

Van Buren, Mary. 1996. "Rethinking the Vertical Archipelago: Ethnicity, Exchange, and History in the South Central Andes." *American Anthropologist* 98 (2): 338–351.

Vásquez, Emilio. 1937a. "Las ruinas de Kachakacha." *Revista del Museo Nacional* 6 (1): 52–57.

————. 1937b. "Sillustani: Una metrópoli pre-Incaika." *Revista del Museo Nacional* 6 (2): 278–290.

————. 1939. "Ruinas arqueológico de Puno, Qutimpu." *Revista del Museo Nacional* 8 (1): 117–123.

————. 1940. "Itinerario arqueológico del Kollao." *Revista del Museo Nacional* 9 (1): 143–150.

Vásquez, Emilio, Alfredo Carpio, and Daniel E. Velazco. 1935. "Informe sobre las ruinas de Tankatanka." *Revista del Museo Nacional* 4 (2): 240–244.

Vela Velarde, Carlos. 1992. "Tiwanaku en el Valle de Caplina (Tacna)." *Pumapunku* (n.s.) 3: 30–45.

von Hagen, Victor F., ed. 1959. *The Incas of Pedro de Cieza de León.* University of Oklahoma Press, Norman.

Wachtel, Nathan. 1982. "The *Mitimaes* of the Cocha-bamba Valley: The Colonization Policy of Huayna Ca-pac." In *The Inca and Aztec States: 1400–1800,* ed. G. A. Collier, R. I. Rosaldo, and J. D. Wirth, pp. 199–229. Academic Press, New York.

———. 1986. "Men of the Water: The Uru Problem (Six-teenth and Seventeenth Centuries)." In *Anthropologi-cal History of Andean Polities,* ed. J. Murra, N. Wach-tel, and J. Revel, pp. 283–310. Cambridge University Press, Cambridge.

———. 1987. Comments on "Lenguas y pueblos alti-plánicos en torno al siglo XVI" by A. Torero. In *Re-vista Andina* 5 (2): 392–394.

Wallace, Dwight. 1957. *The Tiahuanaco Horizon Styles in the Peruvian and Bolivian Highlands.* Ph.D. diss., De-partment of Anthropology, University of California, Berkeley.

Walle, Paul. 1914. *Bolivia, Its People and Its Resources, Its Railways, Mines, and Rubber-Forests.* Trans. Bernard Miall. T. F. Unwin, London.

Wassen, Henry. 1972. *A Medicine-Man's Implements and Plants in a Tiahuacanoid Tomb in Highland Bolivia.* Goteborgs Etnografiska Museum, Goetborg, Sweden.

Wheeler, Jane, and Elías Mujica. 1981. "Prehistoric Pas-toralism in the Lake Titicaca Basin, Peru, 1979–1980 Field Season." Report submitted to the National Sci-ence Foundation, grant no. BNS 7015119.

Whitehead, William. 1999. "Radiocarbon Dating." In *Early Settlement at Chiripa, Bolivia,* ed. C. Hastorf, pp. 17–21. Contributions of the University of California Ar-chaeological Research Facility, Berkeley. University of California, Berkeley.

Wiener, Charles. 1880. *Pérou et Bolivie: Récit de voyage suivi d'études archéologiques et ethnographiques et de notes sur l'écriture et les langues des populations indiennes.* Ha-chette, Paris.

Willey, Gordon R. 1971. *An Introduction to American Ar-chaeology,* vol. 2, *South America.* Prentice-Hall, Engle-wood Cliffs, N.J.

———. 1974. "The Virú Valley Settlement Pattern Study." In *Archaeological Research in Retrospect,* ed. G. Willey, pp. 149–176. Winthrop, Cambridge.

Willey, Gordon R., and Jeremy Sabloff. 1980. *A History of American Archaeology.* W. H. Freeman, San Francisco.

Winter, Carlos Thomas, M. Antonia Benavente Aninat, and Claudio Massone Mezzano. 1985. "Algunos efec-tos de Tiwanaku en la culturea de San Pedro de Ata-cama." *Dialogo Andino* 4: 259–275.

Wirrmann, Denis, Philippe Mourguiart, and Luis Fernan-do de Oliveira Almeida. 1990. "Holocene Sedimentol-ogy and Ostracods Distribution in Lake Titicaca—Paleohydrological Interpretations." In *Quaternary of South America and Antarctic Peninsula,* ed. Jorge Ra-bassa, pp. 89–128. Backema, Rotterdam.

Wirrmann, Denis, Jean-Pierre Ybert, and Philippe Mour-guiart. 1991. "Una evaluación paleohidrológica de 20,000 años." In *El Lago Titicaca,* ed. C. Dejoux and A. Iltis, pp. 61–68. HISBOL, La Paz, Bolivia.

Wissler, Clark. 1922. *The American Indian,* 2nd ed. Ox-ford University Press, New York.

Ybert, Jean-Pierre. 1991. "Los paisajes lacustres antiguos según el análisis palinológico." In *El Lago Titicaca: Sín-tesis del conocimiento limnológico actual,* ed. C. Dejoux and A. Iltis, pp. 69–79. ORSTROM, La Paz, Bolivia.

Zuidema, R. Tom. 1983. "Hierarchy and Social Space in Incaic Social Organization." *Ethnohistory* 30 (2): 49–75.

Index

Page numbers in italics represent figures, maps, and tables.

Qellojani, 244

Qeñuani (Fortina Vinto), 152, 182

Qeya Kollu Chico, 118

Qeya period (Tiwanaku III): Chiripa stone-lined temple in, 179; chronology of, 138–39; Kalasasaya's relationship to, 197; at Lukurmata, 162; pottery of, 139, 147–48, 158; Tiwanaku Valley settlement patterns in, 146–47

qocha (small water-filled depressions), 35, 36, 38

qolcas (Inca storehouses), 83, 259; on Pallalla Island, 249, 276–77

Quechua language: in Aymara migration model, 59, 222; Aymara's distinction from, 51–52, 301–2n5; distribution of, ca. A.D. 500, *223;* distribution of, in sixteenth century, 51, 53, *53;* as fourth migrant wave, 59; geographic zone of, 31, *32,* 301n3; Kallawaya's ties to, 58; and Pukina syntax, 225

Quelcatani, 100, 102

Quelccaya glacial data, 12, 13, 41, 42

Quelima, Esteban, 102, 118, 152, 278

Quellamarka, 155, 179, 199

Quellenata, 213

Quequerana pottery, 228

Quiljata Island, 248–49

Quinoa, 35

Quispe Condori, Pascual, 61

racism, against Aymara people, 72–73, 76–77

raiding, 7, 15, 282

rainfall. *See* precipitation

rain-fed agriculture: in Altiplano period, 226; crops of, 62–63; in Inca period, 254; in Late Sillumocco period, 163; in Pasiri period, 109; seasons of, 62; terraces of, 65, 302n15; in Tiwanaku period, 194

raised fields, 9, 302n8; abandonment of, in Altiplano period, 226; abandonment of, in Inca period, 252, 258, 259; current unpopularity of, 63–64; defined, 63; in Early Sillumocco period, 123, 125; elite context of, 289–90; evidence of, in surveys, 85; first field research on, 63; geographic distribution of, *64;* at Inca-period Kona Bay area, 257–58; land use categories for, 36; in Late Sillumocco period, 123; in Middle Formative period, 109–10; in Middle Formative–period Juli-Pomata area, 134; at Middle

Formative–period Linquinchira, 122; in pampas, 36, 38, 258; after Pucara collapse, 159; Quechua and Aymara terms for, 302n8; and settlement patterns, 134–35; as site type, 98; and tectonic shifts, 40; in Tiwanaku period, 180; in Tiwanaku-period Juli Pomata area, 193–94; at Tiwanaku-period Kanamarca, 180–81; in Tiwanaku-period Paucarcolla-Santa Barbara, 189; in Tiwanaku-period Puno area, 188; in Upper Formative period, 281–82; in Upper Formative–period Challa area, 152–53; near Upper Formative–period Ckackachipata, 151

Ramis River area, 189

Ramis ware, 101

Ramos Gavilán, Alonso, 45, 205, 256, 261, 272–73, 275, 276, 305n8

ranked political economies: competitive feasting in, 26–28; evolutionary models of, 22, 23–25; labor specialization in, 25–26; mechanisms of exchange in, 20–21, 162–63; Middle Formative–period development of, 278–81; state political economies vs., 28, 301n7; trophy head practice of, 162; use of term, 301n4; wealth's centrality to, 19–20, 21–22

ranked societies: debated concept of, 18–19; status-validating art of, 128–29; use of term, 301n4; Yaya-Mama tradition of, 132–33, *133. See also* ranked political economies

rapé (snuff) tablets, 192, 196

reciprocity (mechanism of exchange): in Andean life, 67; definition/examples of, 20; evolutionary framework of, 21; by Lupaqa peoples, 71; in Middle Formative–period regional centers, 279–80

reconnaissances, 84–85

redistribution (mechanism of exchange): of chicha beer, 68; in competitive feasting, 26–28; defined, 20; evolutionary framework of, 21; in Lupaqa region, 71; Visita on, 67

Redmond, Elsa, 28

Reinhard, Johan, 172, 276, 277

relict fields: at Inca-period Kona Bay area, 257; at Middle Formative–period Titikala, 127; at Middle Formative–period Titinhuayani, 118; as site type, 98; at Tiwanaku-period Maravillas, 189

Renfrew, Colin, 283

Revilla Becerra, Rosanna Liliana, 188, 227, 269

Text: 10.5/14 Adobe Garamond
Display: Adobe Garamond and Gill Sans
Cartographer: Bill Nelson
Compositor: Integrated Composition Systems
Printer and Binder: Sheridan Books, Inc.